Carolina Cooking

Telephone Pioneers of America
ANSWERING THE CALL OF THOSE IN NEED

Telephone Pioneers of America
ANSWERING THE CALL OF THOSE IN NEED

This cookbook is a collection of our favorite recipes
which are not necessarily original recipes.

Published by: Favorite Recipes® Press
P.O. Box 305142
Nashville, TN 37230

Printed in the United States of America
First Printing: 1990, 30,000 copies

Copyright© North Carolina Telephone Pioneers of America
North Carolina Chapter No. 35
P.O. Box 30188
Charlotte, N.C. 28230

Library of Congress Number: 90-3757
ISBN: 0-87197-281-6

EXPRESSION OF APPRECIATION

Thank you Pioneers, Pioneer Partners, Life Members, and Future Pioneers for contributing your favorite recipes. This cookbook is more than just a cookbook; it will touch many lives. The sharing of recipes is a small part of touching, but the results from the funds raised with this cookbook, along with the energies of our Pioneering Families will certainly enhance the quality of life for many in our communites.

A special Thanks to the Life Members and Pioneer Partners who dedicated their time to alphabetize, reproduce, sort and type recipes. This project would not have been possible without you. Also many thanks to Lou Picard, Nancy Mercier, Tim Sechler and Lency Wilson for the artwork on the divider pages, and the hours they worked.

For the many hours of researching and writing the Telephone Pioneer History, which was used in the annual assembly program book at the 75th anniversary of Pioneering and updated for this publication, a special Thank You goes to George Harmon.

Last but not least, I want to express my sincere appreciation to Wilma Burleson, Phyllis Jones, Delores Sossamon, and Sally Vinton for handling telephone calls and answering all of the many questions.

THANK YOU!

Shirley C. Helms

Shirley C. Helms
Budget & Fund Raising Chairperson
1990/1991

North Carolina Telephone Pioneer History

The Telephone Pioneers of America was founded in 1911 by veteran telephone employees. Pioneers are an honor society of men and women, both active and retired, who have given lengthy years of service to the telephone industry in the United States and Canada. Alexander Graham Bell was placed on the membership roll as Pioneer No. 1.

The triangular shape of the Pioneer emblem symbolized the organization's three principle objectives: Fellowship, Loyalty, and Service.

The base of the triangle stands for Fellowship, the reason for the founding of the Pioneer organization and the foundation stone on which Loyalty and Service rest.

Loyalty, represented by the left side of the triangle, marks the relationship of telephone people to each other as well as to the industry they serve. It is the link between Fellowship and Service.

Service is the natural outgrowth of Fellowship and Loyalty and is signified by the right side of the triangle. Through Service, Pioneering contributes to the happiness and well-being of those it reaches within the organization, the industry and the community.

The motto of Fellowship, Loyalty, and Service, and triangular design by which it is symbolized express the lasting companionship of those who have spent an important part of their lives as co-workers and friends, allegiance to work and associates, and the ideal of ever-increasing usefulness.

The dates "1875" and "1911", which appear at the left and right of the traditional bell, respectively are commemorative of the experiment of June 2, 1875, when Bell verified his theory of the electrical transmission of speech, and the organization of the Telephone Pioneers of America on November 2, 1911.

The number "174465", appearing on the center of the bell design is the one assigned by the United States Patent Office to Alexander Graham Bell's patent on the fundamental principal of the electric-speaking telephone. Although officially issued on March 7, 1876, the patent came to Bell as a birthday present, as it were, for it was granted on March 3, 1876—the twenty-ninth anniversary of his birth in Edinburgh, Scotland. Since the patent occupied an important place in the development of the industry, it was natural that the organizers of the Telephone Pioneers should select this number as typifying the early days of the telephone history in which most of the charter members of the organization had leading parts.

Over 100 years ago, Alexander Graham Bell and his family started the philanthropic traditions of aiding the needy–the deaf, the blind and the infirm. Alexander's father, Melville Bell built a reputation in speech, both theatrical and therapeutic, which laid the foundation for his later profession as Professor of Elocution at the University of London. In 1871 Alexander substituted for his father in a series of lectures which had been contracted for by Boston's School for the Deaf. His success on the lecture circuit was just one of many associations with the deaf. His own mother was deaf. Gardiner Greene Hubbard, a prominent Boston lawyer who practiced before the Supreme Court in Washington and was the first president of the National Geographic Society sought out Bell to assist with his beloved, handicapped daughter Mabel, who was totally deaf from the age of five after a severe case of scarlet fever. Bell's work with Mabel led to their eventual marriage. Learning of Alec's plans for marriage, Melville Bell wrote to his prospective daughter-in-law: "Alec...will make an excellent husband. He is hot-headed but warm-hearted –sentimental, dreamy, and self-absorbed, but sensitive and unselfish. He is ambitious, to a fault, ...I have told you all the faults I know in him, and this catalog is wonderfully short." Among the most notable that Bell worked with was Helen Keller. Deaf and blind, she came to him at age seven and he supervised her education under Annie Sullivan (the "Miracle Worker") until she graduated *cum laude* from Radcliffe College. They remained lifelong friends.

Alexander G. Bell

Today, Pioneers are the dedicated heirs to this splendid tradition. Organized under the banner of "United to Serve Others," volunteers seek ways of meeting the special needs of the communities in which they live. Pioneers and their younger Associates tutor potential dropouts, repair "talking book" record players for the blind, transcribe many thousands of textbook pages into braille, teach skills to the retarded, make mechanical devices to aid motion and speech handicapped, and screen preschool children for evidences of sight or hearing handicaps. They also entertain at hospitals, conduct blood drives for the Red Cross and perform a multitude of services to benefit others. In 1989 more than 771,000 Pioneer members, Life Members, Partners, Future Pioneers, Affiliates and Associates reported 25 million hours of community service and $10 million in net profit raised for various charities.

Robert W. Devonshire was the first employee in the Bell System in the world, beginning his telephone career in Boston on August 10, 1877. Mr. Devonshire was hired as a book-keeper and when he retired he was a Vice President of AT&T.

Henry W. Pope originated the idea of Telephone Pioneers of America and was elected its first Secretary and Treasurer at the 1911 meeting. He began his career as a telegraph operator and manager of the American Telegraph Company in Great Barrington, Massachusetts. In 1877 he became active in the telephone business and two years later accepted the post of General Superintendent of the Bell interests in New York.

Robert W. Devonshire

On a trip to St. Louis, Thomas Watson, Bell's assistant, interviewed an acquaintance of Bell's father-in-law, Gardiner Hubbard. The acquaintance was Theodore N. Vail, Superintendent of the Post Office's Railway Mail Service. Vail agreed to abandon his secure $4,500 a year job for the position of General Manager of the Bell Company and a salary of $2,500 a year and a $1,000 bonus if performance was satisfactory.

Henry W. Pope

Theodore N. Vail was elected the first President of the Telephone Pioneers of America in 1911. He held this office until his death in 1920. When the AT&T Company was formed in 1885, Mr. Vail became its first President. Leaving the business in 1887 because of ill health, he was recalled to the system in 1907 and resumed the Presidency. He put into effect a practical system for financing the business and in later years introduced the Employee Benefit and Pension plan. Because of his faith in the long distance telephone as the salvation of the industry, he directed the stringing of double copper wire over 10,000 poles from New York to Boston. This marked the turning point in the life of the telephone industry.

Theodore N. Vail

It was only 5 years after Vail's death that North Carolina formed its Pioneer Chapter. On July 1, 1925, a charter was granted by Mr. Ben S. Read, President of the Telephone Pioneers of America, authorizing organization of the J. Epps Brown Chapter No. 35 (No. 35 because the chapter was the 35th to be organized in the Association).

Prior to the formation of Chapter No. 35, North Carolina and South Carolina Pioneers were members of Dixie Chapter No. 23. Members were employees of Southern Bell as well as employees of the independent telephone companies. The suggestion that such a chapter should be organized originated with John C. McManus. The organizational meeting, with 49 charter members, was held on July 24, 1925 in the Chamber of Commerce Hall in Charlotte. Officers elected were: President – Morgan B. Speir, Carolinas' Manager of Southern Bell; Vice President – Charles P. McCluer, General Manager of Carolina Telephone & Telegraph Company; and Secretary–Treasurer – S. D. Lucas. The Chapter was named in honor of J. Epps Brown, Southern Bell President and a native of Newberry, South Carolina.

J. Epps Brown

Charles McCluer was the first member to join the Pioneer organization. He entered the service of Southern Bell in Richmond, Virginia in 1885 as a collection and errand boy. In 1898 he transferred to Charlotte where he held several executive positions until his appointment as General Manager of Carolina Telephone & Telegraph Company in 1905.

As early as 1949 it became evident that there was a need to split the J. Epps Brown Chapter. Prior to 1949 Southern Bell was organized so that North Carolina and South Carolina were part of the Carolinas Division. Due to the rapid growth in telephone business following World War II, Southern Bell found it necessary to divide the Carolinas Division into two separate divisions. In October 1949, a petition signed by thirty-one members of the J. Epps Brown Chapter No. 35 residing in Columbia, South Carolina, requested that consideration be given to the establishment of a South Carolina Chapter. A charter was granted on January 31, 1950, but the official announcement was withheld until June 10, 1950, to coincide with the Silver Anniversary of the J. Epps Brown Chapter No. 35 which was being celebrated by Pioneers in Charleston, South Carolina. This was the last joint annual meeting of the North and South Carolina Pioneers. The charter for the new chapter was presented to Chapter President-Elect J. M. Wasson. The North Carolina Pioneers retained the original charter and the original chapter number 35, but adopted the new name " North Carolina Chapter No. 35." South Carolina retained the old name "J. Epps Brown", and adopted 61 as the chapter number to correspond with its position as the 61st chapter formed in the association.

The Independent Telephone Pioneers Association was formed in 1920 at the USITA Convention in Indiana. However, it was not until October 3, 1966 that the Tar Heel Chapter was chartered and the organization meeting held in Raleigh on January 14, 1967 with 149 charter members. W. Mason Curtis was elected President; Jeff Seabock, 1st Vice President; W. W. Lawrence, 2nd Vice President; and Archie Thomas, Secretary-Treasurer.

As the telephone industry continued to grow, so did Pioneering. Old North State, made up of Western Electric employees in the Winston-Salem area, became the 79th chapter formed in the association. With the formation of Century Chapter in Atlanta during 1986, the association had 100 chapters, a fitting milestone as Pioneering celebrated its 75th year.

The 104 chapters in the United States and Canada are organized into 13 Regions. Region 7 encompasses the territory of North Carolina, South Carolina, Georgia and Florida. The eight chapters that make up Region 7 are: Dixie No. 23, North Carolina No. 35, North Florida No. 39, South Carolina No. 61, Old North State No. 79, Florida Gold Coast No. 83, Dogwood No. 84, and Century No. 100.

The highest position that an employee can attain in the Association unless he is a Company President is Region Vice President. Region Vice Presidents must come from the ranks of past Chapter Presidents and they are elected to serve two-year terms. There have been three North Carolina Chapter No. 35 members who have served as Region 7 Vice Presidents. They are Margaret Jackson, Larry Morgan and Joe Clontz.

The first Council within North Carolina Chapter No. 35 was formed on July 16, 1943, as the Piedmont Council. It was followed later that same year by the Asheville and the Raleigh Councils. The year 1946 saw the addition of the Coastal Council followed by the Independence Council in 1952, the Foothills Council in 1967, the Salem Council in 1968, the Hornets Nest Council in 1973 and the Central and Blue Ridge Councils in 1976. Two Councils, the Goldsboro and the Cardinial, have come and gone over the years as centralization and reorganization have dictated the location and need for Pioneer Councils.

The Telephone Pioneers of America is the single largest voluntary association of industrial employees in the world. Chartering with 439 members in 1911, the Association reached the 100,000 member milestone in 1946. By 1968 the numbers had swelled to 300,000. In 1977 the Association recorded its 500,000th member and by 1990 membership had reached 800,000.

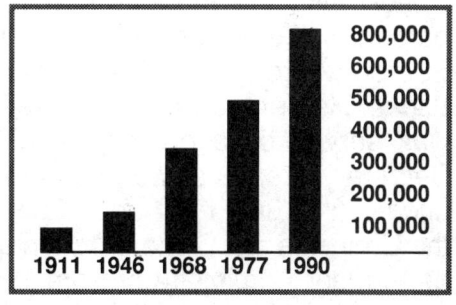

Pioneer Membership

North Carolina Chapter No. 35's growth has paralleled that of the Association. At the end of April, 1990, total chapter membership had reached 10,442, more than 213 times the 49 who originally chartered the chapter. The total is made up of 6,516 Active members, 3,441 Life members, 485 Affiliates and 226 Associates. Added to these numbers are untold numbers of Future Pioneers whose organization began in 1971. They are the future leaders of our organization and the custodians of the heritage we inherited from our predecessors in the telephone industry. In North Carolina an important ingredient in the preservation of that heritage has been the numbers and numbers of families who have encouraged other family members to join the company they were so proud of. It includes names like Anderson, Blythe, Clontz, Goodin, Graham, Groce, Guy, Gwyn, Huggins, Jackson, Knight, Lackey, Love, Lynch, McGraw, McNeal, Oehler, Oliver, Tisdale, Thomas, Warren, and Woodell to name only a few. Obviously there are many more but each has been driven by the Pioneer Statement of Purpose which states:

- *To promote and participate in activities that respond to community needs and problems;*
- *To provide a means of friendly association for eligible telecommunications employees and those retired;*
- *To foster among them a continuing fellowship and a spirit of mutual helpfulness;*
- *To contribute to the progress of the Association and promote the happiness, well-being and usefulness of the membership; and,*
- *To exemplify and perpetuate those principles which have come to be regarded as the ideals and traditions of the industry.*

Employees active in the Pioneer Chapter have always worked closely with the Pioneer Administrator. In the early years the person we know as the Pioneer Administrator was called the Secretary-Treasurer. The first Secretary-Treasurer was S. D. Lucas. He served from 1925-1926. Over the years the Chapter was served by a number of able men and women. The last Secretary-Treasurer was Blanche McManus. She served on two occasions: 1962-1964 and 1965-1969. Blanche was followed by the Chapter's first Pioneer Administrator, Nell Seegers. Nell served as Pioneer Administrator from 1969 until her retirement in 1986, a period of 17 years. Nell's tenure represents the longest period of service in the Secretary Treasurer/Pioneer Administrator position, making it easy to understand why she was often affectionately referred to as "Miss Pioneering". Shirley Burns served as Pioneer Administrator from 1986-1989 and brought a wealth of Pioneer experience, having previously served as Council and Chapter President. Wilma Burleson is the present Pioneer Administrator, serving since 1989.

North Carolina Chapter No. 35 has always been blessed with strong capable leaders. Since M. B. Speir was elected Chapter President in 1925 there have been 66 Chapter Presidents.

Evelyn Newman is the only person to have served more than one term as Chapter President serving from 1980-1981 and 1983-1984.

O. G. Bain, 1949-1950, was Chapter President when South Carolina splitoff to form their Chapter and Joe Chavis 1966-1967, was Chapter President when the Independent Telephone Companies formed their own Pioneer Chapter in 1967.

George Wray, who served from 1950-1951, ranks as the Chapter President living who served the longest time ago and is the oldest living past Chapter President.

There are 29 Past Chapter Presidents still living and most of them are still active in Pioneering although most are Life Members today. The Life Members are G. W. Wray, Ellen Heath, R. E. Evans, C. W. Toenes, E. L. George, J. T. Winn, J. H. Chavis, Margaret Jackson, L. L. Weltner, M. S. Grantt, O. A. Finlayson, W. H. Briggs, Ruth Smith, W. A. Stewart, G. K. McNeal, Joyce Gentry, J. H. Erwin, J. C. Griffis, J. N. Jordan, Murphy Hampton, R. E. Morris, Shirley Burns, Frank Joffrion, G. K. Livingston, and J. J. Swain. Only four Past Chapter Presidents are still active employees. They are: Evelyn Newman, George Harmon, Wilma Burleson and John Williams.

Southern Bell has also provided the top Association leadership on five occasions. The first was Ben S. Read who served as the Association President in 1925 when there were 10,128 Pioneers. Hal Dumas served 1951-52 when the membership was 167,943, Ben Gilmer 1963-64, when membership was 234,143 and Ed Rast served 1975-76 when membership was 455,265. Frank Skinner headed the Association from 1985-86 with membership of 631,737. Frank first became a Pioneer as a member of North Carolina Chapter 35 while serving as Vice President of Southern Bell's North Carolina operations.

The real "movers and shakers" of the Pioneer organization are the hundreds and hundreds who so graciously agree to take on leadership roles in the Councils. They devote untold personal hours to ensure that Pioneer programs in their Council territory carry out the Purpose of Pioneering.

THE CHAPTER OFFICERS FOR THE 1990-91 YEAR ARE:

Fred Hamff	Chapter President
Herman Baker	First Vice President
Randy Vinson	Second Vice President
Steve Market	Member at Large
Margie Moore	Member at Large
Peggy Pearce	Life Member Representative
Robert Morris	Life Member Representative

North Carolina Chapter 35 covers the mountains, foothills, piedmont and coastal area and is made up of ten Councils.

The ten Council Presidents are:

Asheville	C. E. (Chuck) Reiley
Blue Ridge	Sandra Weathers
Central	Ed Thomas
Coastal	Esther Ezzell
Foot Hills	Esther Nelson
Hornets Nest	Ray Lynch
Independence	Larry Helms
Piedmont	Mary Ann Shook
Raleigh	Wilma Brinson
Salem	Tim Mangum

Numerous honors have been received by North Carolina Chapter 35. During December, 1986, Chapter Environmental Chairman Dickie Hipps accepted a second-place honor from Keep America Beautiful, Inc. at its National Awards luncheon in Washington, D. C. for the Chapter's efforts in picking up tons of trash along Tar Heel highways and for educating the state's people about the devastating effects of litter.

Wilma Burleson, Chapter Community Services Chairperson, spearheaded the Chapter's Alzheimer's Disease project. Educating the public about this dreaded disease, about which little is known, earned the Chapter national recognition and won it the Association's most prestigious award—the coveted People Who Care award. In competition with the Association's other 99 Chapters, winning the honor marked a first for North Carolina Chapter No. 35. The award was presented at the General Assembly of Telephone Pioneers held in September, 1986, in Minneapolis, Minnesota.

During 1986, the National Kidney Foundation selected North Carolina Chapter No. 35 as a recipient of the National Kidney Foundation's 1986 Distinguished Service awards. The award is presented to organizations that have made a contribution to the Foundation's program of research, professional and patient education and community services. Chapter 35 provided for a network to be set up through Memorial Hospital in Chapel Hill, North Carolina to do research on Glomerular Kidney Diseases and won a second place People Who Care award at the General Assembly of Telephone Pioneers in New York City, in September, 1987, for this project.

In the fall of 1986, Dickie Hipps found a miniature house that taught children how to get out of a house should it be on fire. With the percentage of children in North Carolina that die from house fires being so high, Dickie wouldn't let go of the dream to have a house like this in North Carolina. With the hard work of the AT&T employees at the old Western Electric plant on North Tryon Street, the house became a reality. Under the very capable leadership of Claudia Spence and Clem McConnel and the many dedicated Pioneers from Asheville to Wilmington, this house has been taken from Cherokee, North Carolina to Currituck, North Carolina with over 300,000 children being trained about how to escape a house on fire. North Carolina Chapter 35 received a second place People Who Care award for the work they did educating children on fire safety at the General Assembly in Dallas, Texas, in September, 1988. Chapter 35 was awarded a Citation from President Reagan's The President's Voluntary Action Award, a C-Flag and a Citation from President Reagan's Program for Private Sector Initiative and a visit to the Rose Garden at the White House with President Reagan. Even more important are the two children who are alive today because of the training they received in that house when they had fires in their homes. This has been a very special project for all of the Pioneers in North Carolina Chapter No. 35.

Fire Safety continued to be a main project for North Carolina Chapter No. 35 during the 1988-89 year with a program to help educate adults on Fire Safety, placing smoke detectors in homes that had none and working with the Burn Center at Chapel Hill. Through the very capable leadership of Grace Phillips, North Carolina Chapter No. 35 was recognized with a C-Flag and a Citation was presented in Washington, D. C. from President Bush's program The President's Citation Program for Private Sector Initiative.

REDIMA, Restoring Dignity to Mature Adults, a program to provide transportation, counseling through the SHIIP program on medicare and insurance, and education of the agencies in North Carolina that offer services for the senior citizens was the major project for 1989-90. This very worthwhile project for the seniors of North Carolina was implemented under the leadership of Claudia Spence, Chapter Community Service Chairperson.

The year 1990-1991 holds for a historic year with a "Teens in Trouble" project under the leadership of Katherine Hord and Grace Phillips as they co-chair Community Service for North Carolina Chapter No. 35.

The list goes on and on, but these projects and the recognition they have brought to North Carolina Pioneering are only a sampling of what Pioneers have been doing for years, as well as what they will continue to do as long as there is a Telephone Pioneer left because **Answering the Call of those in Need is what Pioneering is all about.**

"The story of the telephone is more than the story of an invention and an industry. It is also the story of men and women who found in the telephone business, not only a livelihood, but a creed of service, a bond of comradeship." These are the words of Adrienne Yanekian as she compiled *The Telephone Pioneers of America 1911-1964.* The words are as true today as they were in 1964. Ever aware of the heritage the early Telephone Pioneers gave us, Pioneers have attempted to preserve a small portion of that heritage through a collection of memorabilia which is permanently displayed in the Telephone Pioneer Museum on the sixth floor of the Southern National Center in Charlotte, North Carolina. Pioneers, their families and friends are always welcome. Likewise, the North Carolina Chapter is always happy to add to this collection by way of gift or loan, either of which can be made through the Pioneer Administrator's office on the sixth floor of the Southern National Center.

Among the memorabilia you will see when visiting the museum is the first Vail Medal awarded to a Southern Bell employee in North Carolina. It was presented to Mrs. Janette C. Thredgill in 1922. Mrs. Thredgill was Chief Operator in Rockingham, North Carolina. The award reads "for coolness and courage during a fire under hazardous conditions".

The museum houses an interesting collection of ornate delegate badges worn by Pioneers at the 1911, 1912, 1913, 1915 and 1916 General Assemblies of Telephone Pioneers held in Boston, New York City, Chicago, San Francisco and Atlanta respectively.

Other interesting items include:

— *1930's wooden public telephone booth*
— *a copy of North Carolina Chapter 35's original charter*
— *the one millionth telephone installed in North Carolina*
— *a 1976 time capsule from the Hornets Nest Council to be opened in the year 2001*
— *early telephones including wall sets, the 1910 candlestick, and a replica of the original 1876 telephone*

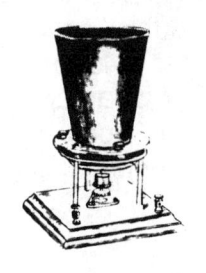

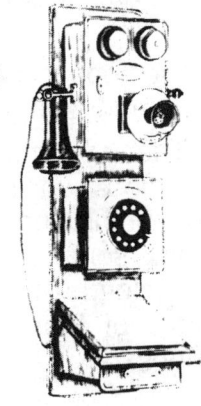

- *a 1915 license plate*
- *long golden curls of Catherine Neal cut in 1926 as a condition of employment in Southern Bell's Traffic Department*
- *a Number 3 Toll Switchboard used from the early 1930's until removed in 1980*
- *a section of a 50 pair lead cable placed in 1911*
- *a complete collection of old service emblems commemorating anniversaries beginning at 5 years and running through 50 years*
- *the 1984 Olympic Torch used by North Carolina Pioneers in the relay carrying the Olympic Torch across America*
- *an early 1900's typewriter used in the Independent Telephone Company Business Office in Oxford*
- *a special telephone made for John F. Kennedy's estate in Palm Beach, Florida, and used there for 26 years before its removal in 1973*
- *an early 1930's slide projector used for Public Relations programs*
- *a Western Electric "1919 Electrical Supply Year Book"*
- *a General Health Course for women of the Bell System dated 1925*
- *numerous citations to the Pioneers from mayors and governors*
- *tools, test sets, practices, telephone directories dating back to 1907, old photos, scrapbooks from throughout the years, and much, much more*

We hope this will whet your appetite for a visit to the Telephone Pioneer Museum.

Thank you for being the owner of one of these books as it will help the Councils to finance our "Teens in Trouble" project. As you leaf through this book you will see a number of logos representing some of the projects that North Carolina Chapter No. 35 has helped with. We hope you will treasure this book with the history of Pioneering in North Carolina and enjoy using the recipes.

The Spirit of Service

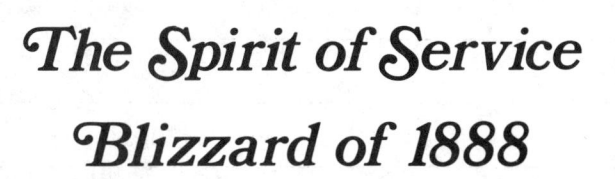

Blizzard of 1888

FAVORITE RECIPE FINDER

RECIPE TITLE	PAGE
☎	
☎	
☎	
☎	
☎	
☎	
☎	
☎	
☎	
☎	
☎	
☎	
☎	
☎	
☎	
☎	
☎	
☎	
☎	
☎	
☎	

Contents

Nutritional Analysis Guidelines 20
Appetizers, Dips and Beverages 21
Salads 53
Meats 97
Poultry & Seafood 161
Vegetables and Side Dishes 223
Bread 295
Cakes, Candy, Cookies & Pies 321
Desserts 503
Equivalent Chart 540
Substitution Chart 542
Refrigeration Chart 543
Herbs and Spices 544
No-Salt Seasoning 546
Bread Baking Guide 547
Cake Baking Guide 548
Glossary of Cooking Techniques 549
Index 554
Order Information 576

NUTRITIONAL ANALYSIS GUIDELINES

The editors have attempted to present these family recipes in a form that allows approximate nutritional values to be computed. Persons with dietary or health problems or whose diets require close monitoring should not rely solely on the nutritional information provided. They should consult their physician or a registered dietitian for specific information.

Abbreviations for Nutritional Analysis

Cal — Calories
Prot — Protein
Carbo — Carbohydrates
Fiber — Dietary Fiber
T Fat — Total Fat
Chol — Cholesterol
Sod — Sodium
g — gram
mg — milligram

Nutritional information for recipes is computed from values furnished by the United States Department of Agriculture Handbook. Many specialty items and new products now available on the market are not included in this handbook. However, producers of new products frequently publish nutritional information on each product's packaging and that information may be added, as applicable, for a more complete analysis. If the nutritional analysis notes the exclusion of a particular ingredient, check the package information.

Unless otherwise specified, the nutritional analysis of these recipes is based on all measurements being level.

- Artificial sweeteners vary in use and strength so should be used "to taste," using the recipe ingredients as a guideline.
- Artificial sweeteners using aspartame (NutraSweet and Equal) should not be used as a sweetener in recipes involving prolonged heating which reduces the sweet taste. For further information on the use of these sweeteners, refer to package information.
- Alcoholic ingredients have been analyzed for the basic ingredients, although cooking causes the evaporation of alcohol thus decreasing caloric content.
- Buttermilk, sour cream, and yogurt are commercial types.
- Cake mixes using package directions include 3 eggs and 1/2 cup oil.
- Chicken, cooked for boning and chopping, has been roasted; this method yields the lowest caloric values.
- Cottage cheese is cream-style with 4.2% creaming mixture. Dry-curd cottage cheese has no creaming mixture.
- Eggs are all large.
- Flour is unsifted all-purpose flour.
- Garnishes, serving suggestions and other optional additions and variations are not included in the analysis.
- Margarine and butter are regular, not whipped or presoftened.
- Milk is whole milk, 3.5% butterfat. Lowfat milk is 1% butterfat. Evaporated milk is whole milk with 60% of the water removed.
- Oil is any type of vegetable cooking oil. Shortening is hydrogenated vegetable shortening.
- Salt and other ingredients to taste as noted in the method have not been included in the nutritional analysis.

Appetizers, Dips and Beverages

Catch the Pioneer Spirit

— TELEPHONE PIONEERS —

APPETIZERS

BLEU CHEESE BALL

1 4-ounce jar bleu cheese
1 5-ounce jar Old English cheese
8 ounces cream cheese, softened
2 teaspoons mayonnaise
1 teaspoon minced onion
1/8 teaspoon Worcestershire sauce
Garlic salt to taste
1 cup chopped pecans

Combine bleu cheese, Old English cheese, cream cheese, mayonnaise, onion, Worcestershire sauce and garlic salt in bowl; mix well. Shape into ball; roll in pecans. Yield: 32 servings.

Approx Per Serving: Cal 79; Prot 2 g; Carbo 1 g; Fiber <1 g; T Fat 7 g; Chol 13 mg; Sod 125 mg.

Brenda Meachum, Independence

CHEESE RING

16 ounces sharp Cheddar cheese, shredded
1 cup chopped pecans
1 cup mayonnaise
1 small onion, grated
Black pepper and cayenne pepper to taste

Combine Cheddar cheese, pecans, mayonnaise, onion, black pepper and cayenne pepper in bowl; mix well. Shape into ring. Store, tightly covered, in refrigerator for 1 day or longer. May fill center with jelly. Serve with thin wheat crackers. Yield: 70 servings.

Approx Per Serving: Cal 61; Prot 2 g; Carbo 1 g; Fiber <1 g; T Fat 6 g; Chol 9 mg; Sod 58 mg.

Nell Seegers, Independence

CHIPPED BEEF CHEESE BALLS

24 ounces cream cheese, softened
4 ounces chopped chipped beef
1 tablespoon minced onion
2 tablespoons MSG
2 tablespoons Worcestershire sauce
1 1/2 cups chopped pecans

Combine cream cheese, chipped beef, onion, MSG and Worcestershire sauce in bowl; mix well. Shape into 2 balls on waxed paper. Chill for 3 hours or longer. Roll in pecans. Place on serving plates. Yield: 80 servings.

Approx Per Serving: Cal 47; Prot 1 g; Carbo 1 g; Fiber <1 g; T Fat 5 g; Chol 10 mg; Sod 371 mg.

Nelda Black, Hornets Nest

DEVILED HAM CHEESE LOG

1 4-ounce can deviled ham
1/4 cup finely chopped pecans
8 ounces cream cheese, softened
1/4 teaspoon garlic salt
1/2 teaspoon Worcestershire sauce
1/4 teaspoon Tabasco sauce
Paprika to taste

Combine deviled ham, pecans, cream cheese, garlic salt, Worcestershire sauce and Tabasco sauce in bowl; mix well. Shape into roll. Chill until firm. Shape into log on waxed paper sprinkled generously with paprika. Wrap in waxed paper. Chill overnight. Serve on crackers or party rye. Recipe from the Charlotte News, circa 1950. Yield: 24 servings.

Approx Per Serving: Cal 53; Prot 2 g; Carbo 1 g; Fiber <1 g; T Fat 5 g; Chol 13 mg; Sod 116 mg.

Helen Marie Woods, Hornets Nest

PIMENTO CHEESE SPREAD

8 ounces sharp Cheddar cheese, shredded
½ cup mayonnaise
1 4-ounce jar chopped pimento, drained

Combine cheese, mayonnaise and pimento in food processor container. Process until blended. Chill, tightly covered, until serving time. Yield: 24 servings.

Approx Per Serving: Cal 72; Prot 2 g; Carbo 1 g; Fiber <1 g; T Fat 7 g; Chol 13 mg; Sod 85 mg.

Wilhelmena Wallace, Independence

CREAMY PIMENTO CHEESE SPREAD

1 5-ounce can evaporated milk
8 ounces Cheddar cheese, shredded
1 tablespoon vinegar
1 2-ounce jar chopped pimento, mashed
¼ teaspoon salt
¼ teaspoon pepper

Heat evaporated milk and cheese in saucepan until cheese is melted, stirring frequently. Add vinegar, pimento, salt and pepper; mix well. Store, tightly covered, in refrigerator. Clipped from Charlotte News many years ago. Yield: 32 servings.

Approx Per Serving: Cal 35; Prot 2 g; Carbo 1 g; Fiber <1 g; T Fat 3 g; Chol 9 mg; Sod 65 mg.

Mrs. Hugh L. McAulay, Blue Ridge

☎ A tablespoon of any dry salad dressing mix in a cup of sour cream makes a quick dip.

CRAB SPREAD

8 ounces crab supreme
8 ounces cream cheese, softened
2 tablespoons mayonnaise
1 tablespoon minced onion
2 teaspoons white wine
1 teaspoon Worcestershire sauce

Combine crab meat, cream cheese, mayonnaise, onion, white wine and Worcestershire sauce in bowl; mix well. Chill, tightly covered, for 24 hours. Serve with crackers. Crab supreme is imitation crab meat, also called surimi, found in fresh seafood department. Yield: 32 servings.

Approx Per Serving: Cal 39; Prot 1 g; Carbo 1 g; Fiber <1 g; T Fat 3 g; Chol 10 mg; Sod 87 mg.

Jane Misle, Independence

PINEAPPLE CHEESE BALLS

16 ounces cream cheese, softened
1 8-ounce can crushed pineapple, drained
1 cup chopped pecans
1/4 cup minced green bell pepper
2 tablespoons minced onion
1 tablespoon seasoned salt
1 cup chopped pecans

Combine cream cheese, pineapple, 1 cup pecans, green pepper, onion and seasoned salt in bowl; mix well. Shape into 2 balls. Roll in remaining 1 cup pecans. Wrap in plastic wrap. Chill overnight. Serve with thin wheat crackers. Yield: 64 servings.

Approx Per Serving: Cal 52; Prot 1 g; Carbo 1 g; Fiber <1 g; T Fat 5 g; Chol 8 mg; Sod 121 mg.

Palma Lee Harris, Hornets Nest

SALMON PARTY BALL

2 cups flaked salmon
8 ounces cream cheese, softened
1 tablespoon lemon juice
2 teaspoons horseradish
1 teaspoon minced onion
1/4 teaspoon salt
1/4 teaspoon liquid smoke
3 tablespoons chopped parsley
1/2 cup chopped pecans

Combine salmon, cream cheese, lemon juice, horseradish, onion, salt and liquid smoke in bowl; mix well. Chill, tightly covered, for several hours. Shape into ball. Roll in mixture of parsley and pecans. Chill until serving time. Serve with crackers. Yield: 20 servings.

Approx Per Serving: Cal 92; Prot 6 g; Carbo 1 g; Fiber <1 g; T Fat 7 g; Chol 24 mg; Sod 187 mg.

Shirley T. Hinson, Hornets Nest

MOLDED SHRIMP SPREAD

8 ounces cream cheese, softened
1 cup mayonnaise
1 10-ounce can tomato soup, heated
2 envelopes unflavored gelatin
1/2 cup cold water
2 cups coarsely chopped cooked peeled shrimp
1 cup minced celery
1/3 cup minced onion
Salt to taste
Lemon juice to taste

Blend cream cheese and mayonnaise in bowl. Stir into hot soup. Soften gelatin in cold water. Add to soup mixture, stirring constantly until dissolved. Stir in shrimp, celery and onion. Season with salt and lemon juice. Spoon into mold. Chill, tightly covered, in refrigerator for 24 hours or more. Unmold onto serving plate. Serve with crackers or rye bread. Yield: 50 servings.

Approx Per Serving: Cal 60; Prot 2 g; Carbo 1 g; Fiber <1 g; T Fat 5 g; Chol 16 mg; Sod 89 mg.

Becky Adams, Coastal

FRESH MUSHROOM PÂTÉ

1 cup chopped fresh mushrooms
2 tablespoons butter
8 ounces cream cheese, softened
¾ teaspoon garlic salt

Sauté mushrooms in butter in skillet for 5 to 10 minutes or until mushrooms are tender and liquid evaporates. Combine mushroom mixture, cream cheese and garlic salt in food processor container. Process with steel blade until smooth. Spoon into bowl. Chill, covered, for 3 hours or longer. Garnish with chopped parsley. Yield: 32 servings.

Approx Per Serving: Cal 32; Prot 1 g; Carbo <1 g; Fiber <1 g; T Fat 3 g; Chol 10 mg; Sod 75 mg.

Barbara D. Scott, Independence

BEST HORS D'OEUVRES IN TEXAS

8 eggs, beaten
½ cup flour
1 teaspoon baking powder
¾ teaspoon salt
24 ounces Monterey Jack cheese, shredded
12 ounces cottage cheese
2 4-ounce cans chopped hot green chilies
Cayenne pepper to taste

Beat eggs in large bowl for 4 to 5 minutes. Combine flour, baking powder and salt in bowl. Add to eggs; mix well. Fold in Monterey Jack cheese, cottage cheese, chilies and cayenne pepper. Pour into greased 9x13-inch baking dish. Bake at 350 degrees for 40 minutes or until set and golden brown. Cut into 1-inch squares. Serve hot. Reheat to serving temperature if frozen. Yield: 117 servings.

Approx Per Serving: Cal 33; Prot 2 g; Carbo 1 g; Fiber <1 g; T Fat 2 g; Chol 20 mg; Sod 64 mg.

Gaynell Sherrill, Independence

JALAPEÑO CHEESE SQUARES

4 cups shredded Cheddar cheese
4 eggs, beaten
4 jalapeños, peeled, seeded, chopped
1 teaspoon minced onion

Combine cheese, beaten eggs, jalapeños and onion in bowl; mix well. Spread in ungreased 8-inch square baking dish. Bake at 350 degrees for 45 to 60 minutes or until knife inserted near center comes out clean. Let stand for 10 minutes. Cut into squares. Yield: 36 servings.

Approx Per Serving: Cal 61; Prot 4 g; Carbo 1 g; Fiber <1 g; T Fat 5 g; Chol 37 mg; Sod 86 mg.

Cheryl Griffin, Raleigh

CHILI QUICHE APPETIZERS

1/4 4-ounce jar jalapeños, sliced
8 ounces Monterey Jack cheese, shredded
8 ounces Cheddar cheese, shredded
1 cup baking mix
1 cup half and half
4 eggs
Hot sauce to taste

Sprinkle jalapeños, Monterey Jack cheese and Cheddar cheese in greased 9-inch square baking dish. Combine baking mix, half and half, eggs and hot sauce in blender container. Process at high speed for 15 seconds or until smooth. Pour into prepared baking dish. Bake at 375 degrees for 30 minutes or until golden brown and knife inserted near center comes out clean. Let stand for 10 minutes. Cut into 1 1/4-inch squares.
Yield: 36 servings.

Approx Per Serving: Cal 82; Prot 4 g; Carbo 3 g; Fiber <1 g; T Fat 6 g; Chol 39 mg; Sod 139 mg.

Debbie Wilkinson, Hornets Nest

CLAM QUICHE

1 unbaked 9-inch pie shell
1 15-ounce can clam chowder
1/2 cup bacon bits
1/2 cup sour cream
1/2 cup chopped onion
2 teaspoons chopped parsley
1/4 teaspoon pepper
4 ounces Cheddar cheese, shredded

Bake pie shell at 400 degrees for 7 minutes. Remove from oven; reduce temperature to 325 degrees. Combine clam chowder, bacon bits, sour cream, onion, parsley and pepper in bowl; mix well. Pour 2/3 of the mixture into pie shell. Top with Cheddar cheese. Pour remaining chowder mixture over cheese. Bake for 50 minutes at 325 degrees. Let stand for 20 minutes. Yield: 6 servings.

Approx Per Serving: Cal 335; Prot 9 g; Carbo 21 g; Fiber 3 g; T Fat 23 g; Chol 30 mg; Sod 797 mg.

Becky Adams, Coastal

SUNNY-SIDE GRAPEFRUIT

2 grapefruit halves
2 tablespoons brown sugar

Rinse grapefruit halves; sprinkle with brown sugar. Place on 10x15-inch baking sheet. Broil for 3 to 5 minutes or until bubbly. Yield: 2 servings.

Approx Per Serving: Cal 88; Prot 1 g; Carbo 23 g; Fiber 2 g; T Fat <1 g; Chol 0 mg; Sod 6 mg.

Helen Hunt, Independence

☎ Add raw cucumber and carrot strips, green beans and cauliflower to liquid left in pickle jar. Refrigerate for several days for easy cocktail snacks.

PICKLED HOT DOGS

20 hot dogs
1 6-ounce bottle of Texas Pete
2 cups vinegar
2 cups water
1 tablespoon salt
1 tablespoon sugar

Cut each hot dog into 3 pieces, trimming off tips. Heat hot sauce, vinegar, water, salt and sugar in saucepan, mixing well. Stir in hot dogs. Simmer for 30 minutes, stirring occasionally; do not boil. Store in airtight container for 24 hours. Drain well before serving. Yield: 60 servings.

Approx Per Serving: Cal 63; Prot 2 g; Carbo 1 g; Fiber 0 g;
   T Fat 6 g; Chol 10 mg; Sod 320 mg.

Neal Ballard, Independence

KABOB APPETIZERS

1 20-ounce can pineapple chunks, drained
35 bite-sized pieces fresh strawberries
35 bite-sized pieces Cheddar cheese
35 bite-sized pieces boiled ham
35 bite-sized pieces smoked turkey

Thread pineapple chunks, strawberries, cheese, ham and turkey onto 4-inch skewers. Yield: 35 servings.

Approx Per Serving: Cal 91; Prot 7 g; Carbo 3 g; Fiber <1 g;
   T Fat 5 g; Chol 24 mg; Sod 183 mg.

Wilma Burleson, Independence

☎ Freeze chicken livers and wings until you have enough for a party appetizer. Livers make excellent pâté and wings are delicious cooked in your favorite barbecue sauce.

COCKTAIL MEATBALLS

1 pound ground beef
1/2 cup bread crumbs
1/2 cup chopped onion
1/4 cup milk
1 egg
1 tablespoon chopped parsley
1 teaspoon salt
1/2 teaspoon Worcestershire sauce
1/8 teaspoon pepper
1/4 cup shortening
1 12-ounce bottle of hot sauce
1 10-ounce jar grape jelly

Combine ground beef, bread crumbs, onion, milk, egg, parsley, salt, Worcestershire sauce and pepper in bowl; mix well. Shape into 1-inch balls. Brown on all sides in shortening in 12-inch skillet. Remove from skillet; drain. Heat hot sauce and jelly in skillet until jelly is melted, stirring constantly. Stir in meatballs until coated. Simmer, uncovered, for 30 minutes. Serve in chafing dish or Crock•Pot. Yield: 60 servings.

Approx Per Serving: Cal 42; Prot 2 g; Carbo 4 g; Fiber <1 g; T Fat 2 g; Chol 9 mg; Sod 74 mg.

Brenda Ashe, Independence
Diane Grace, Raleigh

SAUSAGE MEATBALLS

1 pound pork sausage
Crumbs from 1 6-ounce package pork Stove Top stuffing mix
1 egg
1 cup minced celery
1 onion, minced

Combine sausage, bread crumbs, egg, celery and onion in bowl; mix well. Shape into 1-inch balls; place in baking dish. Bake at 350 degrees for 40 minutes. Serve with honey mustard. Yield: 48 servings.

Approx Per Serving: Cal 35; Prot 1 g; Carbo 3 g; Fiber <1 g; T Fat 2 g; Chol 7 mg; Sod 81 mg.

Bobby Kinney, Independence

GOURMET MEATBALLS

1 pound lean ground beef
1 pound hot pork sausage
1 egg
1 cup finely crushed bread crumbs
3/4 cup minced onion
1/2 cup minced green bell pepper
1/2 cup minced celery
1 teaspoon salt
1/2 teaspoon garlic powder
1/4 teaspoon basil
1/4 teaspoon chili powder
1/4 teaspoon thyme
1/4 teaspoon red peppercorns, crushed
Corn oil for frying
Red Wine Sauce

Combine ground beef, sausage, egg, bread crumbs, onion, green pepper, celery, salt, garlic, basil, chili powder, thyme and red pepper in bowl; mix well. Shape into 3/4-inch balls. Brown on all sides in oil in skillet; drain. Spoon meatballs into baking dish. Cover with Red Wine Sauce. Bake at 375 degrees for 45 minutes. May prepare ahead and freeze uncooked meatballs in sauce for up to 2 months. Yield: 96 servings.

Approx Per Serving: Cal 41; Prot 1 g; Carbo 3 g; Fiber <1 g; T Fat 3 g; Chol 9 mg; Sod 101 mg.
Nutritional information does not include corn oil for frying.

Red Wine Sauce

1/2 cup melted butter
1 15-ounce can tomato sauce
1/3 cup prepared mustard
2/3 cup sugar
1/3 cup Worcestershire sauce
1/2 cup red wine

Combine melted butter, tomato sauce, prepared mustard, sugar, Worcestershire sauce and red wine in bowl; mix well. May use additional can tomato sauce if desired.

Betty Hayes, Independence

☎ Process 1 pound ham, 1 tablespoon horseradish, 1/3 cup sour cream, 3/4 teaspoon onion and 3/4 teaspoon pepper until smooth. Serve on canapé breads, in miniature cream puffs or as dip.

OWENS' VEGETABLE MUNCH

1 bunch broccoli, chopped
1 head cauliflower, chopped
6 carrots, thinly sliced
3 stalks celery, thinly sliced
10 spring onions, chopped
2 cucumbers, peeled, chopped
1 cup oil
3/4 cup white cider vinegar
1 tablespoon sugar
1 tablespoon dillweed
1 tablespoon MSG
1 teaspoon salt
1 teaspoon pepper
1 teaspoon garlic salt

Place broccoli, cauliflower, carrots, celery, onions and cucumbers in large salad bowl. Combine oil, cider vinegar, sugar, dillweed, MSG, salt, pepper and garlic salt in bowl; mix well. Pour over vegetables. Marinate, covered, in refrigerator until chilled through. Yield: 8 servings.

Approx Per Serving: Cal 316; Prot 4 g; Carbo 17 g; Fiber 6 g; T Fat 28 g; Chol 0 mg; Sod 2183 mg.

Betty Owens, Hornets Nest

MEXICAN PINWHEELS

8 ounces Cheddar cheese, shredded
8 ounces cream cheese, softened
1 cup sour cream
1/2 cup chopped ripe olives
1/2 cup chopped green chilies
Seasoned salt to taste
10 flour tortillas

Combine Cheddar cheese, cream cheese, sour cream, olives, chilies and seasoned salt in bowl; mix well. Spread thinly on tortillas. Roll as for jelly rolls; chill thoroughly. Cut into 1-inch pieces. May substitute 1/4 cup chunky picante sauce for 1/4 cup sour cream. Add minced jalapeños or chopped green onions if desired. Yield: 64 servings.

Approx Per Serving: Cal 64; Prot 2 g; Carbo 5 g; Fiber <1 g; T Fat 4 g; Chol 9 mg; Sod 81 mg.

Daphne Beaty, Hornets Nest

SPINACH BALLS

2 10-ounce packages frozen chopped spinach
2 large onions, chopped
3/4 cup margarine
2 cups corn bread stuffing mix
5 eggs, beaten
1/2 cup Parmesan cheese
2 tablespoons garlic powder

Cook spinach using package directions; drain. Sauté onions in margarine in skillet until onions are transparent. Stir in stuffing mix, beaten eggs, Parmesan cheese and garlic powder. Roll into small balls. Place on baking sheet; freeze. Bake at 400 degrees for 15 to 20 minutes or until firm. Serve warm. May store frozen spinach balls in plastic bags in freezer and bake as needed. Yield: 112 servings.

Approx Per Serving: Cal 25; Prot 1 g; Carbo 2 g; Fiber <1 g; T Fat 2 g; Chol 10 mg; Sod 59 mg.

Jessie M. Godwin, Raleigh

PARTY STRAWBERRIES

1 14-ounce can sweetened condensed milk
1 teaspoon unflavored gelatin
2 6-ounce packages strawberry gelatin
1/4 ounce red food coloring
1 7-ounce can flaked coconut
2 cups finely chopped walnuts
1/4 cup green sugar
3/4 cup red sugar

Combine condensed milk, dry unflavored gelatin, dry strawberry gelatin and food coloring in bowl; mix well. Stir in coconut and chopped walnuts. Form into shape of strawberries; dip tops into green sugar. Roll in red sugar. Chill until serving time. Yield: 24 servings.

Approx Per Serving: Cal 241; Prot 5 g; Carbo 35 g; Fiber 2 g; T Fat 10 g; Chol 6 mg; Sod 69 mg.

Wilma Shellman, Foot Hills

MINIATURE HAM AND CHEESE ROLLS

2 18-count packages small tea rolls
8 ounces ham, sliced
6 ounces Swiss cheese, shredded
1/2 cup melted margarine
1 1/2 tablespoons poppy seed
1 1/2 tablespoons prepared mustard
1 tablespoon dried onion flakes
1/2 teaspoon Worcestershire sauce

Split each package of rolls into two layers. Do not separate into rolls. Place ham and cheese between layers of bread in foil trays. Combine melted margarine, poppy seed, mustard, onion flakes and Worcestershire sauce in bowl; mix well. Pour over bread. Let stand, uncovered, until margarine sets. Bake, covered, at 350 degrees for 15 minutes. May be chilled for 24 hours or frozen before baking. Yield: 36 servings.

Approx Per Serving: Cal 141; Prot 5 g; Carbo 14 g; Fiber 1 g; T Fat 7 g; Chol 8 mg; Sod 281 mg.

Marlene Dover, Independence
Edith McWhirter, Hornets Nest
Louise Bland, Central

CHEDDAR CHICKEN SALAD SANDWICHES

2 cups chopped cooked chicken
2 ounces sharp Cheddar cheese, shredded
1/2 cup light mayonnaise-type salad dressing
1/2 cup chopped ripe olives
1/4 cup chopped green bell pepper
1/4 cup chopped onion
6 croissants, split
6 lettuce leaves

Combine chicken, cheese, salad dressing, olives, green pepper and onion in bowl; mix lightly. Chill, covered, until serving time. Fill croissants with lettuce leaves and chicken mixture. Yield: 6 servings.

Approx Per Serving: Cal 439; Prot 20 g; Carbo 32 g; Fiber 2 g; T Fat 27 g; Chol 67 mg; Sod 788 mg.

Joyce Pruitt, Independence

BROILED CRAB SANDWICHES

8 ounces cream cheese, softened
1 tablespoon minced chives
1 tablespoon lemon juice
1 tablespoon Worcestershire sauce
1/2 teaspoon salt
1 7-ounce can king crab
6 English muffins, cut into halves
6 tomato slices
1/2 cup mayonnaise
4 ounces sharp Cheddar cheese, shredded

Blend cream cheese, chives, lemon juice, Worcestershire sauce and salt in bowl. Stir in crab meat. Spread mixture on muffin halves and place on baking sheet. Top each with tomato slice and mixture of mayonnaise and Cheddar cheese. Bake at 350 degrees for 15 minutes or until cheese is bubbly.
Yield: 12 servings.

Approx Per Serving: Cal 260; Prot 10 g; Carbo 15 g; Fiber 1 g;
  T Fat 17 g; Chol 51 mg; Sod 513 mg.

Mrs. W. C. McCaskill, Asheville

POOR MAN'S LUNCH SANDWICHES

4 slices white bread
4 1-ounce slices American cheese
1 16-ounce can pork and beans
4 slices crisp-fried bacon, crumbled

Place bread on baking sheet; top with cheese slices. Bake at 375 degrees until cheese is melted. Heat pork and beans in saucepan. Spoon heated pork and beans over cheese toast; top with crumbled bacon. Yield: 4 servings.

Approx Per Serving: Cal 344; Prot 17 g; Carbo 38 g; Fiber 7 g;
  T Fat 15 g; Chol 40 mg; Sod 1031 mg.

Nell Seegers, Independence

VEGETABLE SANDWICH SPREAD

2 carrots, chopped
1 green bell pepper, chopped
1 cucumber, chopped
1 stalk celery, chopped
1 small onion, chopped
8 ounces cream cheese, softened
1/2 cup mayonnaise
1/2 teaspoon salt

Combine carrots, green pepper, cucumber, celery and onion in bowl; mix well. Stir in cream cheese. Add enough mayonnaise to make of spreading consistency. Stir in salt. Add dash of horseradish if desired. Yield: 8 servings.

Approx Per Serving: Cal 219; Prot 3 g; Carbo 6 g; Fiber 2 g; T Fat 21 g; Chol 39 mg; Sod 307 mg.

Polly Mabrey, Hornets Nest

BANANA GRANOLA CRUNCH

2 1/4 cups uncooked oats
1/2 cup coarsely chopped pecans
1/2 cup honey
1 teaspoon dried orange rind
1/4 cup margarine
1 teaspoon vanilla extract
1 teaspoon cinnamon
1 cup dried banana chips
1/2 cup raisins

Combine uncooked oats, pecans, honey, orange rind, margarine, vanilla and cinnamon in large microwave-safe bowl; mix well. Microwave on High for 6 minutes, stirring 3 times. Stir in banana chips and raisins. Spread on foil-covered baking dish to cool. Store in airtight container. Yield: 10 servings.

Approx Per Serving: Cal 261; Prot 4 g; Carbo 43 g; Fiber 4 g; T Fat 10 g; Chol 0 mg; Sod 56 mg.

K. R. Rose, Piedmont

☎ Make miniature pizzas on party breads, English muffins, split pita rounds or bagels.

CHEESE PENNIES

2 cups shredded sharp
  Cheddar cheese
2 cups flour
1 cup melted butter
1 teaspoon salt
1/2 teaspoon red pepper
2 cups Rice Krispies

   Combine Cheddar cheese, flour, melted butter, salt and red pepper in large bowl; mix well. Stir in Rice Krispies. Shape into quarter-sized circles on lightly greased baking sheet. Bake at 375 degrees for 10 minutes or until slightly brown around edges. Yield: 60 servings.

Approx Per Serving: Cal 61; Prot 2 g; Carbo 4 g; Fiber <1 g;
  T Fat 4 g; Chol 12 mg; Sod 96 mg.

Shirley C. Helms, Independence

* *Kim Parker of Central* substitutes 1/2 cup margarine for half the butter and tops each with a pecan half.

OYSTER CRACKER SNACKS

1 large envelope ranch
  salad dressing mix
2/3 cup oil
2 teaspoons dillweed
2 11-ounce packages
  oyster crackers

   Combine salad dressing mix and oil in bowl; mix well. Stir in dillweed. Pour over crackers in large bowl. Mix by hand until all liquid is absorbed by crackers. Store in airtight container. Will keep for 1 week. Yield: 16 servings.

Approx Per Serving: Cal 244; Prot 4 g; Carbo 28 g; Fiber 1 g;
  T Fat 14 g; Chol 0 mg; Sod 489 mg.
  Nutritional information does not include salad dressing mix.

Priscilla Wise, Independence

SNACK CRACKERS

1 envelope ranch salad dressing mix
1 cup corn oil
1 teaspoon dillweed
1/2 teaspoon garlic powder
Lemon pepper to taste
1 10-ounce package oyster crackers
1/2 cup chopped pecans

Combine salad dressing mix, oil, dillweed, garlic powder and lemon pepper in large bowl with lid; mix well. Stir in crackers and pecans. Shake well 4 times at 15-minute intervals. Yield: 20 servings.

Approx Per Serving: Cal 176; Prot 2 g; Carbo 11 g; Fiber 1 g; T Fat 15 g; Chol 0 mg; Sod 178 mg.
Nutritional information does not include salad dressing mix.

Jo Ann Goins, Hornets Nest

SUGAR-COATED PEANUTS

1 cup sugar
1/2 cup water
2 cups shelled raw peanuts

Combine sugar and water in saucepan. Cook over medium heat until sugar is dissolved, stirring constantly. Add peanuts. Cook until peanuts are completely coated and no syrup remains, stirring frequently. Spread on ungreased baking sheet. Separate peanuts with fork. Bake at 300 degrees for 30 minutes, stirring every 10 minutes. Yield: 16 servings.

Approx Per Serving: Cal 153; Prot 5 g; Carbo 16 g; Fiber 2 g; T Fat 9 g; Chol 0 mg; Sod 2 mg.

Kim Parker, Central

ROASTED PECANS

1/2 cup melted margarine
3 tablespoons Worcestershire sauce
1 1/2 teaspoons garlic salt
1/2 teaspoon onion salt
4 cups chopped pecans

Combine melted margarine, Worcestershire sauce, garlic salt and onion salt in large bowl; mix well. Stir in pecans. Spread on lightly greased baking sheet. Bake at 350 degrees for 45 minutes, stirring frequently. Drain on paper towel.
Yield: 16 servings.

Approx Per Serving: Cal 252; Prot 2 g; Carbo 6 g; Fiber 2 g; T Fat 26 g; Chol 0 mg; Sod 287 mg.

Amanda Tucker, Independence

VONDA'S SPICED PECANS

2 cups pecan halves
1 cup sugar
2 teaspoons cinnamon
1 teaspoon ginger
1 teaspoon salt
1/2 teaspoon nutmeg
1/4 teaspoon cloves
2 egg whites, beaten
2 tablespoons water

Place pecans on ungreased baking sheet. Bake at 350 degrees for 5 minutes. Set aside. Combine sugar, cinnamon, ginger, salt, nutmeg, and cloves in large bowl; mix well. Dip pecans 1 at a time into mixture of egg whites and water; coat with spice mixture. Place on baking sheet. Bake at 275 degrees for 45 minutes, stirring occasionally. Yield: 10 servings.

Approx Per Serving: Cal 224; Prot 2 g; Carbo 24 g; Fiber 1 g; T Fat 15 g; Chol 0 mg; Sod 224 mg.

Laurie Hamff, Independence

SPECIAL TOASTED PECANS

1 egg white, beaten
1 tablespoon water
2 cups pecan halves
1/2 cup sugar
1 teaspoon cinnamon
3/4 teaspoon salt
1/4 teaspoon ground cloves
1/4 teaspoon nutmeg

Combine beaten egg white, water and pecans in bowl; mix well. Spread in lightly greased baking dish. Combine sugar, cinnamon, salt, cloves and nutmeg in bowl; mix well. Sprinkle over pecan mixture; stir until pecans are coated. Bake at 300 degrees for 30 minutes, stirring 3 times. Yield: 10 servings.

Approx Per Serving: Cal 184; Prot 2 g; Carbo 14 g; Fiber 1 g; T Fat 15 g; Chol 0 mg; Sod 165 mg.

Joanne Tallent, Independence

DIPS

ARTICHOKE DIP

1 14-ounce can
    artichokes, drained
1 cup mayonnaise
1 cup Parmesan cheese

Combine artichokes, mayonnaise and cheese in mixer bowl. Beat at medium speed until blended. Pour into baking dish. Bake at 350 degrees for 20 minutes. Serve with thin wheat crackers. Yield: 30 servings.

Approx Per Serving: Cal 71; Prot 2 g; Carbo 2 g; Fiber 0 g; T Fat 7 g; Chol 6 mg; Sod 101 mg.

Deni Dumford, Piedmont

HOT ARTICHOKE DIP

1 15-ounce can artichokes, drained, sliced
1 2-ounce jar chopped pimentos, drained
10 ripe olives, chopped
½ cup mayonnaise
½ cup Parmesan cheese
4 ounces mozzarella cheese, shredded
Garlic salt to taste

Combine artichokes, pimentos, olives, mayonnaise, Parmesan cheese, mozzarella cheese and garlic salt in bowl; mix well. Spread in lightly greased baking dish. Bake at 350 degrees for 30 minutes. Serve warm with tortilla chips. Yield: 60 servings.

Approx Per Serving: Cal 26; Prot 1 g; Carbo 1 g; Fiber <1 g; T Fat 2 g; Chol 3 mg; Sod 41 mg.

Sheri Camp, Independence

BELL PEPPER DIP

1 8-ounce can crushed pineapple
16 ounces cream cheese, softened
1 onion, chopped
1 green bell pepper, chopped
2 cups chopped pecans
1 tablespoon seasoned salt

Drain pineapple, reserving juice. Combine pineapple, cream cheese, onion, green pepper, pecans and seasoned salt in bowl; mix well. Add enough pineapple juice to make of desired consistency. Serve with chips or crackers. Yield: 96 servings.

Approx Per Serving: Cal 36; Prot 1 g; Carbo 1 g; Fiber <1 g; T Fat 3 g; Chol 5 mg; Sod 81 mg.

Gladys Hinson, Independence

HOT CHEESE DIP

16 ounces Velveeta cheese
1 can Cheddar cheese soup
1 8-ounce can jalapeño relish

Cut cheese into 1-inch pieces. Combine cheese, soup and relish in microwave-safe bowl; mix well. Microwave, loosely covered, on High for 5 to 6 minutes or until smooth, stirring twice. Serve with nachos. May substitute taco sauce for jalapeño relish. Yield: 48 servings.

Approx Per Serving: Cal 41; Prot 2 g; Carbo 1 g; Fiber <1 g; T Fat 3 g; Chol 9 mg; Sod 260 mg.

Ann Neeley, Independence

CHILI DIP

1 15-ounce can chili without beans

8 ounces cream cheese, softened

Heat chili and cream cheese in saucepan over low heat until cheese is melted, stirring frequently. Serve with corn chips or nachos. Yield: 32 servings.

Approx Per Serving: Cal 48; Prot 1 g; Carbo 1 g; Fiber 0 g; T Fat 4 g; Chol 8 mg; Sod 107 mg.

Martha Berrier, Hornets Nest

CHILI CON QUESO

1 pound ground beef
1 pound hot pork sausage
32 ounces Velveeta cheese
1 can cream of mushroom soup

3 jalapeños, seeded, chopped
1 small onion, chopped
1 tomato, chopped

Brown ground beef and sausage in skillet, stirring until crumbly; drain. Combine ground beef mixture, cheese, soup, jalapeños, onion, and tomato in Crock•Pot; mix well. Heat until cheese is melted. May add a small amount of milk if desired. Serve warm with tortilla chips. Yield: 128 servings.

Approx Per Serving: Cal 41; Prot 2 g; Carbo 1 g; Fiber <1 g; T Fat 3 g; Chol 10 mg; Sod 140 mg.

Susan M. Perry, Raleigh

CRAB MEAT DIP

8 ounces cream cheese, softened
2 tablespoons chopped onion
2 tablespoons catsup
2 tablespoons salad dressing
2 tablespoons half and half
1/2 teaspoon salt
1/4 teaspoon Worcestershire sauce
1 6-ounce can crab meat

Combine cream cheese, onion, catsup, salad dressing, half and half, salt and Worcestershire sauce in blender container. Process until blended. Fold in crab meat. Serve with crackers. Yield: 32 servings.

Approx Per Serving: Cal 36; Prot 2 g; Carbo 1 g; Fiber <1 g; T Fat 3 g; Chol 13 mg; Sod 90 mg.

Carolyn S. Starnes, Independence

HOT CRAB DIP

8 ounces cream cheese, softened
1 6-ounce can crab meat
2 tablespoons grated onion
2 tablespoons horseradish
1 tablespoon milk
1 tablespoon mayonnaise
1 teaspoon Worcestershire sauce
Salt and pepper to taste

Combine all ingredients in bowl; mix well. Spread in shallow baking dish. Bake at 375 degrees for 15 minutes or until crust forms on top. Serve with crackers. Yield: 10 servings.

Approx Per Serving: Cal 109; Prot 5 g; Carbo 1 g; Fiber <1 g; T Fat 9 g; Chol 43 mg; Sod 131 mg.

Shirley Burns, Independence

CURRY DIP FOR VEGETABLES

1 1/2 cups mayonnaise
2 teaspoons curry powder
1 teaspoon grated onion
1/2 teaspoon prepared mustard
1/2 teaspoon salt
1/8 teaspoon coarsely ground pepper
Tabasco sauce to taste

Combine mayonnaise, curry powder, onion, prepared mustard, salt, pepper and Tabasco sauce in bowl; mix well. Chill, tightly covered, for 2 hours. Yield: 32 servings.

Approx Per Serving: Cal 74; Prot <1 g; Carbo <1 g; Fiber <1 g; T Fat 8 g; Chol 6 mg; Sod 93 mg.

Irene M. Hooper, Asheville

DILL DIP

1 cup mayonnaise
1 cup sour cream
4 teaspoons dillweed
4 teaspoons Beau Monde seasoning
2 tablespoons chopped parsley
1/2 teaspoon grated onion

Combine mayonnaise, sour cream, dillweed, Beau Monde seasoning, parsley and onion in bowl; mix well. Chill until serving time. Yield: 32 servings.

Approx Per Serving: Cal 65; Prot <1 g; Carbo 1 g; Fiber <1 g; T Fat 7 g; Chol 7 mg; Sod 43 mg.

Virginia Bowie, Independence

NACHO DIP

8 ounces cream cheese, softened
1 cup sour cream
1 10-ounce can jalapeño bean dip
1 envelope chili seasoning mix
10 drops of Tabasco sauce
1/4 cup taco sauce
1 1/4 cups shredded Cheddar cheese
1 1/4 cups shredded Monterey Jack cheese

Blend cream cheese and sour cream in bowl. Stir in bean dip, seasoning mix, Tabasco sauce, taco sauce and half of each cheese. Spoon into 8x12-inch baking dish. Top with remaining cheeses. Bake at 325 degrees for 15 to 20 minutes or until cheese is melted. Serve with tortilla chips. Yield: 96 servings.

Approx Per Serving: Cal 31; Prot 1 g; Carbo 1 g; Fiber <1 g; T Fat 2 g; Chol 7 mg; Sod 80 mg.

Darlene Fulton, Hornets Nest

PEPPERONI PIZZA DIP

8 ounces cream cheese, softened
1/2 cup sour cream
1 teaspoon oregano
1/8 teaspoon garlic powder
Red pepper to taste
1/2 cup pizza sauce
1/2 cup chopped pepperoni
1/4 cup sliced green onion
1/4 cup chopped green bell pepper
1/2 cup shredded mozzarella cheese

Combine cream cheese, sour cream, oregano, garlic powder and red pepper in bowl; mix well. Spread in 9-inch pie plate. Top with pizza sauce. Sprinkle with pepperoni, green onion and green pepper. Bake at 350 degrees for 10 minutes. Sprinkle with cheese. Bake for 5 minutes longer or until cheese is melted. Serve hot with crackers or bite-sized fresh vegetables. May be prepared 24 hours ahead to allow flavors to blend; store in refrigerator. Reheat, covered with foil, for 25 minutes. Yield: 56 servings.

Approx Per Serving: Cal 34; Prot 1 g; Carbo 1 g; Fiber <1 g; T Fat 3 g; Chol 7 mg; Sod 69 mg.

Marie Bell, Raleigh

SHRIMP DIP

1 can cream of shrimp soup
8 ounces cream cheese, softened
1 teaspoon lemon juice
2 tablespoons chopped green onion
1/4 teaspoon curry powder
Garlic powder to taste
Hot sauce to taste

Combine soup, cream cheese, lemon juice, green onion, curry powder, garlic powder and hot sauce in mixer bowl. Beat at low speed until of serving consistency. Chill, covered, for several hours. Serve with fresh vegetables. Yield: 32 servings.

Approx Per Serving: Cal 32; Prot 1 g; Carbo 1 g; Fiber <1 g; T Fat 3 g; Chol 9 mg; Sod 95 mg.

Ernie Cole, Asheville

EASY SHRIMP DIP

1 envelope Italian salad dressing mix
16 ounces cream cheese, softened
1 cup sour cream
1 pound chopped cooked peeled shrimp

Combine salad dressing mix, cream cheese and sour cream in bowl; mix well. Stir in shrimp. Serve with crackers or vegetables. Yield: 80 servings.

Approx Per Serving: Cal 32; Prot 2 g; Carbo <1 g; Fiber 0 g; T Fat 3 g; Chol 19 mg; Sod 31 mg.
Nutritional information does not include salad dressing mix.

Lorene Gramlich, Independence

TACO DIP

1 16-ounce can refried beans
1 8-ounce package hot jalapeño cheese dip
1 envelope taco seasoning mix
1 cup sour cream
1/2 cup mayonnaise
8 ounces sharp Cheddar cheese, shredded
2 bunches green onions, chopped
3 tomatoes, chopped

Combine beans and cheese dip in bowl; mix well. Spread in 8x12- inch glass serving dish. Combine taco seasoning mix, sour cream and mayonnaise in bowl; mix well. Spoon over bean mixture. Top with shredded cheese. Sprinkle with green onions and tomatoes. Serve with tortilla chips. Yield: 96 servings.

Approx Per Serving: Cal 38; Prot 2 g; Carbo 2 g; Fiber 1 g; T Fat 3 g; Chol 6 mg; Sod 107 mg.

Peggy McGalliard, Hornets Nest

☎ Mix 1 can of drained minced clams with 1 package dry vegetable soup mix and 2 cups sour cream for an easy dip.

EASY TACO DIP

16 ounces cream cheese
1 16-ounce can chili without beans
1 cup shredded sharp Cheddar cheese

Slice cream cheese into small pieces. Place in microwave-safe baking dish. Pour chili over cream cheese. Microwave, loosely covered, on High for 5 minutes. Top with Cheddar cheese. Microwave, loosely covered, for 2 to 3 minutes longer or until cheese is melted. Serve with chips. Yield: 80 servings.

Approx Per Serving: Cal 32; Prot 1 g; Carbo 1 g; Fiber <1 g; T Fat 3 g; Chol 9 mg; Sod 55 mg.

Becky Adams, Coastal

MOCK SOUR CREAM

1 cup low-fat cottage cheese
2 tablespoons skim milk
1 tablespoon lemon juice

Combine cottage cheese, skim milk and lemon juice in blender container. Process at medium speed until smooth. Use as sour cream substitute. Yield: 16 servings.

Approx Per Serving: Cal 11; Prot 2 g; Carbo 1 g; Fiber <1 g; T Fat <1 g; Chol 1 mg; Sod 58 mg.

Addie F. Vance, Hornets Nest

BEVERAGES

BANANA PUNCH

4 cups sugar
6 cups water
Juice of 5 oranges
Juice of 2 lemons
5 bananas, mashed
1 46-ounce can pineapple juice
8 cups ginger ale

Combine sugar and water in saucepan. Boil over low heat for 3 minutes, stirring frequently. Let stand until cool. Combine with orange juice, lemon juice, mashed bananas and pineapple juice in 1-gallon jar. Freeze. Remove from freezer 2 hours before serving. Pour into punch bowl. Add ginger ale just before serving. Yield: 40 servings.

Approx Per Serving: Cal 130; Prot <1 g; Carbo 33 g; Fiber <1 g; T Fat <1 g; Chol 0 mg; Sod 4 mg.

Edith Lawson, Raleigh

FRUIT PUNCH

1 12-ounce can frozen orange juice concentrate
1 12-ounce can frozen lemonade concentrate
1 46-ounce can pineapple juice
4 cups strong sweetened tea
1 4-ounce jar maraschino cherries

Combine juice concentrates, pineapple juice, tea and maraschino cherries in large pitcher; mix well. Chill, tightly covered, until serving time. Pour into punch bowl. Yield: 20 servings.

Approx Per Serving: Cal 118; Prot 1 g; Carbo 30 g; Fiber 1 g; T Fat <1 g; Chol 0 mg; Sod 2 mg.

Madelon Haskin, Hornets Nest
Wilma Burleson, Independence

GRAPEFRUIT PUNCH

2 46-ounce cans grapefruit juice, chilled
2 cups vodka
1 ice ring
2 1-liter bottles of Champagne, chilled
1 lemon, sliced

Pour grapefruit juice and vodka over ice ring in punch bowl. Add Champagne. Float lemon slices on top of punch. Yield: 44 servings.

Approx Per Serving: Cal 78; Prot <1 g; Carbo 6 g; Fiber <1 g; T Fat <1 g; Chol 0 mg; Sod 3 mg.

Charlene Abel, Independence

HOLIDAY PUNCH

2 46-ounce cans unsweetened pineapple juice

3 2-liter bottles of Cheerwine soda

Combine pineapple juice and soda in pitcher; mix well. Chill until serving time. Pour into punch bowl. Yield: 72 servings.

Approx Per Serving: Cal 52; Prot <1 g; Carbo 13 g; Fiber <1 g; T Fat <1 g; Chol 0 mg; Sod 3 mg.

Bonnie Kramer, Independence

REQUEST PUNCH

2 24-ounce bottles of white grape juice

4 cups ginger ale

Combine grape juice and ginger ale in pitcher; mix well. Chill. Pour into chilled punch bowl. Add ice if desired. Yield: 20 servings.

Approx Per Serving: Cal 59; Prot <1 g; Carbo 14 g; Fiber <1 g; T Fat <1 g; Chol 0 mg; Sod 6 mg.

Wilma Burleson, Independence

VEGETABLE JUICE COCKTAIL

1 stalk celery
6 large onions, chopped
4 large green bell peppers, seeded, chopped,
1/4 cup salt
2 bay leaves
8 whole cloves
1 teaspoon cayenne pepper
25 tomatoes, cut into quarters
2 tablespoons lemon juice

Chop celery, reserving leaves. Combine celery, onions, green peppers and salt in bowl; mix well. Let stand, covered, for several hours. Place celery leaves, bay leaves, cloves and cayenne pepper in cheesecloth bag. Combine with tomatoes and onion mixture in saucepan; mix well. Cook over low heat until juice from tomatoes runs freely, stirring occasionally. Discard cheesecloth bag. Put mixture through food grinder; drain, reserving juice. Press out about half the pulp. Combine extracted juice and pulp with lemon juice in saucepan. Bring to a boil, stirring frequently. Ladle into 7 hot sterilized 1-quart jars, leaving 1/2-inch headspace; seal with 2-piece lids. Process in boiling water bath for 10 minutes. Serve cold. Yield: 28 servings.

Approx Per Serving: Cal 38; Prot 2 g; Carbo 8 g; Fiber 2 g; T Fat <1 g; Chol 0 mg; Sod 925 mg.

Gerri Evans, Hornets Nest

HOT CRANBERRY PUNCH

2 cups cranberry juice
1 3/4 cups pineapple juice
1 cup water
3 cinnamon sticks
1/2 cup packed brown sugar
1 tablespoon whole cloves
1 teaspoon allspice
1/4 teaspoon salt

Combine cranberry juice, pineapple juice and water in coffeepot. Place cinnamon sticks, brown sugar, cloves, allspice and salt in coffeepot basket. Percolate using manufacturer's directions. Strain into mugs. Yield: 8 servings.

Approx Per Serving: Cal 116; Prot <1 g; Carbo 29 g; Fiber <1 g; T Fat <1 g; Chol 0 mg; Sod 75 mg.

Virginia Bowie, Independence

HOT SPICED CRANBERRY TEA

6 cinnamon sticks
1 tablespoon whole cloves
1/2 teaspoon nutmeg
1 46-ounce can cranberry juice
8 cups apple cider
1/2 cup packed brown sugar
Juice of 1 lemon

Place cinnamon sticks, cloves and nutmeg in cheesecloth bag. Combine with cranberry juice, apple cider, brown sugar and lemon juice in saucepan; mix well. Bring to a boil, stirring frequently. Simmer for 10 minutes. Strain into cups.
Yield: 22 servings.

Approx Per Serving: Cal 95; Prot <1 g; Carbo 24 g; Fiber <1 g; T Fat <1 g; Chol 0 mg; Sod 6 mg.

Betty W. Hampton, Salem

HOT MULLED PUNCH

16 cups apple cider
1/2 cup packed brown sugar
1 1/2 teaspoons whole cloves
4 cinnamon sticks

Pour apple cider into coffeepot. Place brown sugar, cloves and cinnamon sticks in coffeepot basket. Percolate using manufacturer's directions. Strain into cups. Yield: 16 servings.

Approx Per Serving: Cal 142; Prot <1 g; Carbo 36 g; Fiber <1 g; T Fat <1 g; Chol 0 mg; Sod 10 mg.

Martha Berrier, Hornets Nest

CHRISTMAS WASSAIL

2 teaspoons ground cloves
2 teaspoons cinnamon
2 teaspoons allspice
1 teaspoon nutmeg
1 teaspoon salt
8 cups cranberry juice
8 cups pineapple juice
4 cups water

Place cloves, cinnamon, allspice, nutmeg and salt in cheesecloth bag. Combine with cranberry juice, pineapple juice and water in Crock•Pot; mix well. Heat to serving temperature. Serve in mugs garnished with cinnamon sticks. May substitute apple juice for pineapple juice. Yield: 24 servings.

Approx Per Serving: Cal 92; Prot <1 g; Carbo 23 g; Fiber 1 g; T Fat <1 g; Chol 0 mg; Sod 92 mg.

Betty W. Hampton, Salem

WASSAIL BOWL PUNCH

4 cups hot tea
4 cups cranberry juice
4 cups apple juice
2 cups orange juice
3/4 cup lemon juice
1 cup sugar
3 cinnamon sticks
12 whole cloves

Combine all ingredients in pitcher. Strain into cups garnished with orange or lemon slices. Yield: 20 servings.

Approx Per Serving: Cal 104; Prot <1 g; Carbo 27 g; Fiber <1 g; T Fat <1 g; Chol 0 mg; Sod 5 mg.

Wilma Brinson, Raleigh

Salads

TEENS IN TROUBLE

FRUIT SALADS

APPLESAUCE SALAD

1 16-ounce can applesauce
1 3-ounce package lime gelatin
1 12-ounce can 7-Up
1 16-ounce can crushed pineapple, drained

Heat applesauce to boiling point in saucepan. Stir in gelatin until dissolved. Add 7-Up; mix well. Chill until partially set. Add pineapple; mix well. Pour into 9x13-inch glass dish. Chill until set. Yield: 12 servings.

Approx Per Serving: Cal 86; Prot 1 g; Carbo 22 g; Fiber 1 g; T Fat <1 g; Chol 0 mg; Sod 27 mg.

Gladys Hinson, Independence

APRICOT DELIGHT

2 3-ounce packages apricot gelatin
2 cups boiling water
1 cup miniature marshmallows
1 20-ounce can crushed pineapple
2 cups cold water
2 bananas, finely chopped
1 cup chopped pecans
1 egg
2 tablespoons flour
1/2 cup sugar
2 tablespoons butter
3 ounces cream cheese, softened
1 envelope whipped topping mix

Dissolve gelatin in boiling water in bowl. Add marshmallows, stirring until almost melted. Drain pineapple, reserving 1/2 cup juice. Add pineapple, cold water, bananas and pecans to gelatin; mix well. Pour into 9x13-inch glass dish. Chill until set. Combine reserved juice, egg, flour and sugar in saucepan; mix well. Cook until thickened, stirring constantly. Stir in butter and cream cheese until melted. Chill completely. Prepare whipped topping using package directions. Fold into cream cheese mixture. Spread over gelatin. Chill for several hours. Yield: 12 servings.

Approx Per Serving: Cal 298; Prot 4 g; Carbo 44 g; Fiber 2 g; T Fat 13 g; Chol 32 mg; Sod 102 mg.

Beatrice Whicker, Salem

APRICOT GELATIN SALAD

2 3-ounce packages apricot gelatin
2 cups boiling water
2 cups apricot nectar
1 13-ounce can crushed pineapple, drained
2 bananas, sliced
2 cups miniature marshmallows
1 egg, beaten
2 tablespoons butter
¼ cup sugar
2 tablespoons flour
3 ounces cream cheese, softened
1 envelope whipped topping mix

Dissolve gelatin in boiling water in bowl. Stir in apricot nectar. Drain pineapple, reserving juice. Add pineapple, bananas and marshmallows to gelatin; mix well. Spoon into 9x13-inch dish. Chill until firm. Combine egg, butter, sugar, flour and reserved pineapple juice in saucepan. Cook until thickened, stirring constantly. Stir in cream cheese. Cool to room temperature. Prepare whipped topping using package directions. Add to cooked mixture. Spread over congealed layer. Chill until serving time. Yield: 12 servings.

Approx Per Serving: Cal 234; Prot 4 g; Carbo 42 g; Fiber 1 g; T Fat 7 g; Chol 32 mg; Sod 107 mg.

Mrs. Hugh L. McAulay, Blue Ridge

GOOD CHERRY SALAD

½ cup pineapple juice
1 4-ounce package vanilla instant pudding mix
1 banana, finely chopped
1 21-ounce can cherry pie filling
1 16-ounce can juice-pack pineapple tidbits

Combine pineapple juice and pudding mix in bowl; mix well. Add banana, pie filling and undrained pineapple; toss to mix. Pour into serving bowl. Chill until set. May substitute any fruit juice for pineapple juice. Yield: 10 servings.

Approx Per Serving: Cal 143; Prot 1 g; Carbo 37 g; Fiber 2 g; T Fat <1 g; Chol 0 mg; Sod 95 mg.

Daphne Beaty, Hornets Nest

CHERRY SALAD

1 16-ounce can pie cherries
1/2 cup (about) orange juice
1 3-ounce package cherry gelatin
1 cup sugar
1/2 cup chopped pecans
1/2 cup chopped celery

Drain cherries, reserving juice. Add enough orange juice to reserved juice to measure 1 cup. Bring juice to a boil in saucepan. Add gelatin, stirring until dissolved. Pour into bowl. Chill until partially set. Chop cherries. Combine cherries and sugar in saucepan. Cook for 2 minutes, stirring frequently. Cool. Add cooled cherries, pecans and celery to gelatin; mix well. Pour into large mold. Chill until set. Unmold onto lettuce-lined salad plate. Yield: 6 servings.

Approx Per Serving: Cal 320; Prot 3 g; Carbo 66 g; Fiber 1 g; T Fat 7 g; Chol 0 mg; Sod 57 mg.

Evelyn Clemmer, Hornets Nest

CRANBERRY SALAD

2 3-ounce packages cherry gelatin
3 cups boiling water
1 pound cranberries
2 apples
2 oranges
1 8-ounce can crushed pineapple
1 cup sugar

Dissolve gelatin in boiling water. Pour into serving dish. Chill until partially set. Process cranberries, apples, oranges, pineapple and sugar in blender until fresh fruit is chopped. Stir into partially congealed gelatin. Chill overnight.
Yield: 10 servings.

Approx Per Serving: Cal 199; Prot 2 g; Carbo 50 g; Fiber 3 g; T Fat <1 g; Chol 0 mg; Sod 55 mg.

Virginia Bowie, Independence

EASY CRANBERRY SALAD

1 1/2 cups cranberries
1 orange
1 8-ounce can crushed pineapple
1/2 cup (about) boiling water
1 3-ounce package cherry gelatin
1 1/2 cups sugar
1/2 cup chopped pecans

Chop cranberries and orange in food processor. Drain pineapple, reserving juice. Add enough boiling water to reserved juice to measure 1 cup. Combine with gelatin in bowl, stirring until gelatin is dissolved. Stir in cranberry mixture, sugar and pecans. Pour into mold. Chill until set. Unmold onto serving plate. Yield: 10 servings.

Approx Per Serving: Cal 218; Prot 1 g; Carbo 41 g; Fiber 2 g; T Fat 4 g; Chol 0 mg; Sod 1 mg.

Betty W. Hampton, Salem

HOLIDAY CRANBERRY SALAD

1 pound fresh cranberries
2 oranges
1 1/2 cups sugar
2 cups chopped pecans
1 8-ounce can crushed pineapple
1 envelope unflavored gelatin
1 cup cold water
2 3-ounce packages cherry gelatin
3 cups boiling water
1 cup cold water

Grind cranberries and oranges. Combine with sugar, pecans and pineapple in large bowl. Soften unflavored gelatin in 1 cup cold water. Dissolve cherry gelatin in boiling water in bowl. Stir in unflavored gelatin until dissolved. Add 1 cup cold water. Add to cranberry mixture; mix well. Spoon into serving dish. Chill until firm. Yield: 12 servings.

Approx Per Serving: Cal 326; Prot 4 g; Carbo 52 g; Fiber 4 g; T Fat 14 g; Chol 0 mg; Sod 47 mg.

Betty S. Bryant, Hornets Nest

CRANBERRY AND ORANGE SALAD

1 6-ounce package cherry gelatin
1 cup boiling water
1 16-ounce can crushed pineapple
1 16-ounce can cranberry-orange sauce
1 cup chopped celery
1/2 cup chopped pecans

Dissolve gelatin in boiling water in bowl. Drain pineapple, reserving juice. Add enough cold water to juice to measure 1 cup. Add juice, pineapple, cranberry-orange sauce, celery and pecans to gelatin; mix well. Pour into serving dish. Chill until set. Yield: 12 servings.

Approx Per Serving: Cal 117; Prot 2 g; Carbo 21 g; Fiber 1 g; T Fat 3 g; Chol 0 mg; Sod 54 mg.
Nutritional information does not include cranberry-orange sauce.

Carolyn Helms, Independence

THANKSGIVING CRANBERRY RELISH MOLD

1 medium orange
12 ounces fresh cranberries
1/2 cup sugar
1 3-ounce package black cherry gelatin

Cut orange into small sections; remove seeds. Process orange, cranberries and sugar in food processor until fruit is coarsely chopped. Prepare gelatin using package directions. Chill until partially set. Add chopped fruit; mix well. Pour into large mold. Chill until set. Unmold onto serving plate. Garnish with orange slices and parsley. Chill until serving time.
Yield: 8 servings.

Approx Per Serving: Cal 116; Prot 1 g; Carbo 29 g; Fiber 2 g; T Fat <1 g; Chol 0 mg; Sod 35 mg.

Wilhelmena Wallace, Independence

MIXED FRUIT SALAD

1 6-ounce package vanilla instant pudding mix
1⅓ cups buttermilk
2 16-ounce cans fruit cocktail, drained
2 11-ounce cans mandarin oranges, drained
1 cup miniature marshmallows
8 ounces whipped topping

Combine pudding mix and buttermilk in mixer bowl; beat until smooth. Fold in fruit cocktail, mandarin oranges, marshmallows and whipped topping. Chill completely. Yield: 12 servings.

Approx Per Serving: Cal 225; Prot 2 g; Carbo 46 g; Fiber 2 g; T Fat 5 g; Chol 1 mg; Sod 140 mg.

Marcie Burden, Hornets Nest

FROZEN FRUIT SALAD

1 8-ounce can crushed pineapple
3 bananas, sliced
½ cup maraschino cherries, chopped
1 cup chopped pecans
¼ cup mayonnaise
1 teaspoon lemon juice
1 cup sugar
8 ounces cream cheese, softened
1 cup whipping cream, whipped

Combine pineapple, bananas, maraschino cherries and pecans in bowl; mix well. Combine mayonnaise and lemon juice in mixer bowl; mix well. Add sugar; beat well. Blend in cream cheese. Fold in whipped cream. Add to fruit; toss to mix. Spoon into 9x13-inch dish. Freeze until firm. Yield: 10 servings.

Approx Per Serving: Cal 352; Prot 3 g; Carbo 38 g; Fiber 2 g; T Fat 22 g; Chol 28 mg; Sod 101 mg.

Becky Adams, Coastal

FIVE-CUP FRUIT SALAD

1 11-ounce can mandarin oranges, drained
1 16-ounce can pineapple chunks, drained
1 cup coconut
1 cup miniature marshmallows
8 ounces sour cream

Combine all ingredients in serving bowl; mix well. Chill for 2 hours before serving. Yield: 8 servings.

Approx Per Serving: Cal 209; Prot 2 g; Carbo 30 g; Fiber 2 g; T Fat 10 g; Chol 13 mg; Sod 55 mg.

Carolyn Jones, Independence

GRAPE-BLUEBERRY CONGEALED SALAD

2 3-ounce packages grape gelatin
2 cups boiling water
1 21-ounce can blueberry pie filling
1 8-ounce can crushed pineapple
8 ounces cream cheese, softened
1 cup sour cream
1/2 cup sugar
1/2 cup finely chopped pecans

Dissolve gelatin in boiling water in bowl. Add pie filling and pineapple; mix well. Pour into 9x13-inch glass dish. Chill until set. Combine cream cheese, sour cream and sugar in mixer bowl; beat until smooth. Spread over congealed gelatin. Sprinkle with pecans. Yield: 12 servings.

Approx Per Serving: Cal 286; Prot 4 g; Carbo 39 g; Fiber 1 g; T Fat 14 g; Chol 29 mg; Sod 126 mg.

Marjorie Harmon, Blue Ridge

* *Gladys Hinson of Independence* and *Diane Grace of Raleigh* add 1 teaspoon vanilla extract to topping and use 16-ounce cans of pineapple.

RUSSIAN SALAD

1 3-ounce package lime gelatin
2/3 cup boiling water
14 marshmallows
3 ounces cream cheese, softened
1/2 cup mayonnaise-type salad dressing
1/2 cup evaporated milk
1/2 cup pineapple juice
1 teaspoon lemon juice

Dissolve gelatin in boiling water in large saucepan. Add marshmallows and cream cheese. Cook over low heat until marshmallows and cream cheese are melted, stirring constantly. Cool. Add remaining ingredients; mix well. Pour into serving bowl. Chill until set. Yield: 6 servings.

Approx Per Serving: Cal 270; Prot 4 g; Carbo 36 g; Fiber <1 g; T Fat 13 g; Chol 27 mg; Sod 263 mg.

Jeanette M. Everett, Central

COOLING SUMMER SALAD

1 6-ounce package lime gelatin
1 envelope unflavored gelatin
2 cups boiling water
3/4 cup cold water
1 cup mayonnaise
1 cup cottage cheese
1 16-ounce can fruit cocktail, drained
1 8-ounce can crushed pineapple
1 cup chopped pecans

Mix lime gelatin and unflavored gelatin in bowl. Add boiling water, stirring until gelatins dissolve. Add cold water; mix well. Chill until partially congealed. Add mayonnaise; mix well. Stir in remaining ingredients. Pour into 9x13-inch shallow dish. Chill until set. Cut into squares. Yield: 12 servings.

Approx Per Serving: Cal 302; Prot 5 g; Carbo 23 g; Fiber 1 g; T Fat 22 g; Chol 13 mg; Sod 223 mg.

Sallie Greer, Hornets Nest

ORANGE FLUFF SALAD

2 3-ounce packages orange gelatin
2 cups boiling water
1 6-ounce can frozen orange juice concentrate
2 11-ounce cans mandarin oranges
1 20-ounce can pineapple
1 4-ounce package lemon instant pudding mix
1 envelope whipped topping mix, prepared

Dissolve orange gelatin in boiling water in bowl. Stir in orange juice concentrate. Combine oranges, pineapple and pudding mix in bowl; mix well. Fold pudding mixture and whipped topping into gelatin. Chill until firm. Yield: 8 servings.

Approx Per Serving: Cal 325; Prot 5 g; Carbo 72 g; Fiber 2 g; T Fat 4 g; Chol 6 mg; Sod 194 mg.

Lib Livingood, Hornets Nest

ORANGE GELATIN SALAD

2 3-ounce packages orange gelatin
2 cups boiling water
1 6-ounce can frozen orange juice concentrate
2 11-ounce cans mandarin oranges, drained
1 20-ounce can crushed pineapple, drained
1 4-ounce package lemon instant pudding mix
1 cup milk
1 cup whipping cream

Dissolve gelatin in boiling water in bowl. Add orange juice concentrate, stirring until thawed. Add mandarin oranges and crushed pineapple; mix well. Pour into 9x13-inch glass dish. Chill until set. Combine lemon pudding mix and milk in mixer bowl; mix well. Add whipping cream; beat well. Spread over gelatin. Chill until set. Yield: 10 servings.

Approx Per Serving: Cal 297; Prot 4 g; Carbo 52 g; Fiber 2 g; T Fat 10 g; Chol 36 mg; Sod 154 mg.

Faye Thomas, Central

CHEESY ORANGE SALAD

1 3-ounce package orange gelatin
12 ounces cottage cheese
1 11-ounce can mandarin oranges, drained
1 16-ounce can crushed pineapple, drained
8 ounces whipped topping

Combine dry orange gelatin and cottage cheese in bowl; mix well. Add mandarin oranges and pineapple; mix well. Fold in whipped topping. Spoon into serving dish. Yield: 12 servings.

Approx Per Serving: Cal 151; Prot 5 g; Carbo 21 g; Fiber 1 g; T Fat 6 g; Chol 4 mg; Sod 144 mg.

Joyce Waters, Salem

ORANGE-PINEAPPLE SALAD

1 3-ounce package lemon gelatin
1 3-ounce package orange gelatin
2 cups boiling water
1 1/2 cups cold water
1 cup finely chopped banana
1/2 cup chopped pecans
1 20-ounce can crushed pineapple
1 1/2 cups miniature marshmallows
3 tablespoons flour
1/2 cup sugar
1 egg, slightly beaten
Lemon juice to taste
2 teaspoons butter
2 cups whipped topping
1/2 cup shredded Cheddar cheese

Dissolve lemon and orange gelatins in boiling water in bowl. Stir in cold water. Chill until partially set. Add banana and pecans; mix well. Drain pineapple, reserving juice. Add pineapple to gelatin mixture; mix well. Pour into 9x13-inch glass dish. Sprinkle marshmallows over top, pushing under to coat. Chill until set. Combine flour, sugar and reserved pineapple juice in saucepan. Add egg and lemon juice; mix well. Cook until thickened, stirring constantly. Remove from heat. Stir in butter. Cool. Fold in whipped topping. Spread over congealed layer. Sprinkle cheese on top. Yield: 12 servings.

Approx Per Serving: Cal 267; Prot 4 g; Carbo 44 g; Fiber 1 g; T Fat 9 g; Chol 24 mg; Sod 96 mg.

Betty S. Bryant, Hornets Nest

PRETZEL SALAD

2 cups crushed pretzels
3/4 cup melted margarine
3 tablespoons sugar
8 ounces cream cheese, softened
1 cup sugar
10 ounces whipped topping
1 6-ounce package strawberry gelatin
1 1/2 cups boiling water
1 1/2 cups cold water
1 cup chopped apple
1 cup chopped pecans

Combine pretzels, margarine and 3 tablespoons sugar in bowl; mix well. Press into 9x13-inch baking dish. Bake at 400 degrees for 8 minutes. Cool. Combine cream cheese and 1 cup sugar in bowl; beat well. Fold in whipped topping. Spread over cooled crust. Chill until set. Dissolve gelatin in boiling water in bowl. Add cold water; mix well. Chill until partially set. Stir in apple and pecans. Spoon over cream cheese mixture. Chill overnight. Yield: 12 servings.

Approx Per Serving: Cal 482; Prot 5 g; Carbo 49 g; Fiber 1 g;
T Fat 31 g; Chol 21 mg; Sod 394 mg.

Reba P. Reece, Blue Ridge

PRETZEL STRAWBERRY SALAD

2 cups crushed pretzels
3/4 cup melted margarine
3 tablespoons sugar
8 ounces cream cheese, softened
1 cup sugar
2 cups whipped topping
1 6-ounce package strawberry gelatin
2 cups boiling water
2 10-ounce packages frozen strawberries

Combine first 3 ingredients in bowl; mix well. Press into 9x13-inch glass dish. Bake at 400 degrees for 6 minutes. Cool. Combine cream cheese and 1 cup sugar in bowl; mix well. Fold in whipped topping. Spread over cooled crust. Chill until set. Dissolve gelatin in boiling water in bowl. Add strawberries, stirring until thawed. Chill until partially set. Pour over cream cheese layer. Chill until set. Yield: 8 servings.

Approx Per Serving: Cal 587; Prot 6 g; Carbo 71 g; Fiber 2 g;
T Fat 32 g; Chol 31 mg; Sod 588 mg.

Mabel B. Mayes, Foot Hills
Bernice Griffin, Hornets Nest

STRAWBERRY AND PINEAPPLE SALAD

2 3-ounce packages wild strawberry gelatin
1¾ cups boiling water
2 10-ounce packages frozen strawberries
3 bananas, mashed
1 15-ounce can pineapple, drained
½ cup chopped pecans
1 package Jell-O cheesecake mix

Dissolve gelatin in boiling water in bowl. Stir in strawberries until thawed. Add bananas, pineapple and pecans; mix well. Pour half the mixture into 9x13-inch glass dish. Chill until set. Prepare cheesecake mix using package directions; beat until thick. Spread over congealed gelatin layer. Chill until set. Spread remaining liquid gelatin mixture over top. Chill until set.
Yield: 12 servings.

Approx Per Serving: Cal 425; Prot 7 g; Carbo 55 g; Fiber 4 g; T Fat 21 g; Chol 170 mg; Sod 251 mg.

Wilma Burleson, Independence

STRAWBERRY AND CREAM CHEESE SALAD

1⅔ cups graham cracker crumbs
¾ cup melted margarine
3 tablespoons sugar
8 ounces cream cheese, softened
1 cup sugar
8 ounces whipped topping
1 6-ounce package strawberry gelatin
2 cups boiling water
1 10-ounce package frozen strawberries

Combine graham cracker crumbs, margarine and 3 tablespoons sugar in bowl; mix well. Press into 9x13-inch baking dish. Bake at 350 degrees for 5 minutes. Cool. Combine cream cheese and 1 cup sugar in bowl; beat well. Fold in whipped topping. Spread over cooled crust. Chill for 1 hour. Dissolve gelatin in boiling water in bowl. Add frozen strawberries, stirring until thawed. Chill until partially congealed. Pour over cream cheese layer. Chill until firm. Yield: 12 servings.

Approx Per Serving: Cal 436; Prot 4 g; Carbo 52 g; Fiber 1 g; T Fat 25 g; Chol 21 mg; Sod 342 mg.

Ketha Sanders, Independence

SUNSET SALAD

1 3-ounce package orange gelatin
1 cup boiling water
3/4 cup cold water
1 cup shredded carrots
1 8-ounce can crushed pineapple
1 cup shredded Cheddar cheese

Dissolve gelatin in boiling water in bowl. Add cold water; mix well. Pour into serving bowl. Chill until partially set. Stir in carrots, pineapple and cheese. Chill until set. Yield: 6 servings.

Approx Per Serving: Cal 151; Prot 6 g; Carbo 18 g; Fiber 1 g;
T Fat 6 g; Chol 20 mg; Sod 168 mg.

Joyce Pruitt, Independence

FROZEN WALDORF SALAD

1 8-ounce can crushed pineapple
2 eggs, beaten
1/2 cup sugar
1/8 teaspoon salt
1/4 cup lemon juice
1/2 cup chopped celery
2 medium apples, chopped
1/2 cup chopped pecans
1 cup whipping cream, whipped

Drain pineapple, reserving juice. Add enough water to reserved juice to measure 1/2 cup. Combine with eggs, sugar, salt and lemon juice in saucepan; mix well. Cook until thickened, stirring constantly. Cool. Add pineapple, celery, apples and pecans; mix well. Fold in whipped cream. Spoon into 8-inch square glass dish. Freeze until firm. Let stand at room temperature for 20 to 30 minutes before serving. Yield: 8 servings.

Approx Per Serving: Cal 265; Prot 3 g; Carbo 27 g; Fiber 2 g;
T Fat 18 g; Chol 94 mg; Sod 69 mg.

Della Johnson, Hornets Nest

SARA'S WATERGATE SALAD

8 ounces whipped topping
1 4-ounce package pistachio instant pudding mix
1 20-ounce can crushed pineapple
1½ cups miniature marshmallows
1 cup chopped pecans

Combine whipped topping and pudding mix in bowl; mix well. Fold in undrained pineapple, marshmallows and pecans. Spoon into serving dish. Yield: 8 servings.

Approx Per Serving: Cal 331; Prot 2 g; Carbo 46 g; Fiber 2 g; T Fat 17 g; Chol 0 mg; Sod 112 mg.

Sara Duncan, Asheville

WATERGATE SALAD

1 16-ounce can crushed pineapple, drained
1 6-ounce package pistachio instant pudding mix
½ cup chopped pecans
1 cup miniature marshmallows
8 ounces whipped topping

Combine pineapple and pudding mix in bowl; mix well. Stir in pecans and marshmallows. Add whipped topping; mix well. Chill until serving time. Yield: 6 servings.

Approx Per Serving: Cal 380; Prot 2 g; Carbo 60 g; Fiber 2 g; T Fat 17 g; Chol 0 mg; Sod 209 mg.

Madelon Haskin, Hornets Nest

☎ Make a quick, easy Waldorf salad out of chopped unpeeled apples, raisins, walnuts and mayonnaise.

MAIN DISH SALADS

FRUITED CURRIED CHICKEN SALAD

2 cups chopped cooked chicken
1½ cups ½-inch cubes apple
¼ cup canned juice-pack crushed pineapple
Dressing

Combine chicken, apple and pineapple in large bowl; mix well. Add dressing; toss to mix. Yield: 4 servings.

Dressing for Fruited Curried Chicken Salad

2 tablespoons reduced-calorie mayonnaise
¼ cup plain nonfat yogurt
1 teaspoon curry powder
½ teaspoon sugar
¼ teaspoon salt
¼ teaspoon pepper
2 tablespoons finely chopped onion

Mix mayonnaise, yogurt, curry powder, sugar, salt, pepper and onion in small bowl.

Approx Per Serving: Cal 207; Prot 20 g; Carbo 13 g; Fiber 1 g; T Fat 8 g; Chol 63 mg; Sod 268 mg.

Phyllis Jones, Independence

☎ Serve chicken or seafood salad in avocado halves, tomato cups, melon rings or pineapple boats. This is an easy way to dress up leftovers.

GRAPE AND ALMOND CHICKEN SALAD

2 cups chopped cooked chicken
1 cup seedless grapes
1 cup chopped celery
1/2 cup toasted sliced almonds
Dressing

Combine chicken, grapes, celery and almonds in large bowl; toss to mix. Add dressing; mix well. Yield: 6 servings.

Dressing for Grape and Almond Chicken Salad

1/2 cup mayonnaise
1/4 cup sour cream
1 tablespoon sugar
1 tablespoon lemon juice
1 teaspoon grated lemon rind
1/2 teaspoon ginger
1/4 teaspoon salt

Combine mayonnaise, sour cream, sugar, lemon juice, lemon rind, ginger and salt in bowl; mix well.

Approx Per Serving: Cal 312; Prot 15 g; Carbo 10 g; Fiber 2 g; T Fat 24 g; Chol 54 mg; Sod 250 mg.

Phyllis Edwards, Hornets Nest

CHICKEN AND PINEAPPLE SALAD

2 cups chopped cooked chicken
1/2 cup chopped pecans
1/4 cup chopped green bell pepper
1/2 cup chopped celery
1 8-ounce can pineapple chunks, drained
1/3 cup mayonnaise

Combine chicken, pecans, green pepper, celery and pineapple in bowl; toss to mix. Add mayonnaise; mix well. Chill overnight. Yield: 8 servings.

Approx Per Serving: Cal 186; Prot 10 g; Carbo 4 g; Fiber 1 g; T Fat 15 g; Chol 34 mg; Sod 83 mg.

Palma Lee Harris, Hornets Nest

CHICKEN PASTA SALAD ORIENTAL

- 1 package Suddenly Salad pasta salad mix
- 1 teaspoon grated lemon rind
- 3 tablespoons lemon juice
- 2 tablespoons oil
- 2 tablespoons honey
- 1 8-ounce can sliced water chestnuts, drained
- 2 medium carrots, sliced
- 2 green onions, sliced
- 1/4 cup cashews
- 1 6-ounce can chunk chicken, drained, chopped

Prepare pasta salad pasta and vegetable envelope using package directions. Combine pasta salad seasoning mix, lemon rind, lemon juice, oil and honey in small bowl; mix well. Combine pasta and vegetable mixture, seasoning mixture, water chestnuts, carrots, green onions, cashews and pasta salad Parmesan cheese in bowl; mix well. Fold in chicken.
Yield: 4 servings.

Nutritional information for this recipe is not available.

Joyce Pruitt, Independence

SHRIMP AND PASTA SALAD

- 8 ounces rotini, cooked, drained
- 4 ounces snow peas, blanched
- 4 ounces fresh mushrooms, sliced
- 1 carrot, peeled, julienned
- 1/2 cup sliced green onions
- Dressing (See page 71)
- 8 ounces tiny shrimp, cooked

Combine rotini, snow peas, mushrooms, carrot and green onions in large bowl; mix well. Add Dressing; mix well. Chill for several hours. Stir in shrimp just before serving.
Yield: 10 servings.

Dressing for Shrimp and Pasta Salad

1/3 cup olive oil
1/3 cup lemon juice
3 tablespoons soy sauce
4 teaspoons sugar
1 teaspoon dry mustard
1 teaspoon sesame seed, toasted

Combine olive oil, lemon juice, soy sauce, sugar, mustard and sesame seed in jar. Shake, tightly covered, until well mixed.

Approx Per Serving: Cal 203; Prot 9 g; Carbo 23 g; Fiber 2 g; T Fat 8 g; Chol 39 mg; Sod 352 mg.

Sheri Camp, Independence

TACO SALAD STACK-UPS

2 pounds ground beef
2 packages chili seasoning mix
1/2 cup water
1 8-ounce can tomato sauce
1 16-ounce can kidney beans
Salt and pepper to taste
10 ounces Velveeta cheese, cubed
1 can Cheddar cheese soup
1/3 8-ounce jar mild taco sauce
1/2 head lettuce, chopped
2 tomatoes, chopped
10 flour tortillas

Brown ground beef in skillet, stirring until crumbly; drain. Combine with chili seasoning, water, tomato sauce, kidney beans, salt and pepper in Crock•Pot. Cook for 30 minutes. Combine cheese, soup and taco sauce in saucepan. Heat until cheese is melted, stirring constantly. Layer lettuce, tomatoes, ground beef mixture and cheese sauce on tortillas. Garnish with sour cream. Yield: 10 servings.

Approx Per Serving: Cal 580; Prot 32 g; Carbo 51 g; Fiber 6 g; T Fat 29 g; Chol 93 mg; Sod 1938 mg.

Jenny Givens, Independence

TACO SALAD

3 pounds ground beef
2 cups chopped onions
1 cup chopped celery
1 cup chopped green bell pepper
3 tablespoons cumin seed
3 cloves of garlic, minced
4 teaspoons chili powder
Salt and pepper to taste
8 ounces Velveeta cheese, shredded
1 10-ounce can Ro-Tel tomatoes
18 cups chopped lettuce
8 tomatoes, chopped
1 16-ounce package corn chips, crushed

Combine first 7 ingredients in Crock•Pot; mix well. Add salt and pepper. Cook on Low for 3 to 4 hours or until done to taste. Heat cheese and tomatoes in saucepan until cheese melts, stirring constantly. Layer lettuce, ground beef sauce, tomatoes, cheese sauce and crushed corn chips on individual plates. Yield: 12 servings.

Approx Per Serving: Cal 552; Prot 30 g; Carbo 31 g; Fiber 5 g; T Fat 34 g; Chol 92 mg; Sod 708 mg.

Barbara Morris, Salem

LINGUINE SALAD

16 ounces uncooked linguine
Flowerets of 1 head cauliflower
1 small onion, chopped
Flowerets of 1 bunch broccoli
1 4-ounce can sliced black olives
1 16-ounce bottle of zesty Italian salad dressing
1 jar Salad Supreme seasoning mix

Break linguine into 1-inch pieces. Cook using package directions; drain well. Combine cauliflower, onion, broccoli and olives in bowl; toss to mix. Add linguine, salad dressing and seasoning mix; mix well. Chill before serving. Yield: 24 servings.

Approx Per Serving: Cal 176; Prot 3 g; Carbo 18 g; Fiber 2 g; T Fat 13 g; Chol 0 mg; Sod 135 mg.
Nutritional information does not include Salad Supreme.

Jean Rushing, Hornets Nest

MACARONI SALAD

16 ounces uncooked macaroni
3 cups seedless grapes
1 cup chopped celery
1 2-ounce jar chopped pimento
1 green bell pepper, chopped
3/4 teaspoon celery seed
1 cup slivered almonds, toasted
1 3/4 cups mayonnaise
1/2 to 3/4 cup sugar
3 tablespoons lemon juice

Cook macaroni using package directions for 5 to 7 minutes or until just tender. Cool. Combine macaroni, grapes, celery, pimento, green pepper, celery seed and almonds in bowl; mix well. Combine mayonnaise, sugar and lemon juice in small bowl; mix until sugar is dissolved. Add to macaroni mixture; toss to mix. Chill overnight. Yield: 12 servings.

Approx Per Serving: Cal 494; Prot 8 g; Carbo 52 g; Fiber 4 g; T Fat 30 g; Chol 17 mg; Sod 176 mg.

Lyndia Calvert, Foot Hills

CURRIED CRAB MEAT RICE SALAD

8 ounces crab meat
2 cups cooked rice, chilled
1/4 cup chopped green bell pepper
1/2 cup sliced green onions
1 6-ounce jar marinated artichokes, drained
1/2 teaspoon curry powder
1/4 cup mayonnaise

Combine crab meat, rice, green pepper, green onions and artichokes in bowl; toss to mix. Blend curry powder and mayonnaise in small bowl. Add to crab mixture; mix well. Garnish with hard-boiled egg and tomato wedges. Serve with croissants and white wine. Yield: 6 servings.

Approx Per Serving: Cal 210; Prot 10 g; Carbo 20 g; Fiber 2 g; T Fat 10 g; Chol 43 mg; Sod 308 mg.

Cheryl Griffin, Raleigh

VEGETABLE SALADS

GREEN BEAN SALAD

1 16-ounce can French-style green beans, drained
1 16-ounce can corn, drained
1 16-ounce can kidney beans, drained
1 large green bell pepper, chopped
1 large onion, sliced into rings
Dressing

Combine green beans, corn, kidney beans, green pepper and onion rings in bowl; toss to mix. Add dressing; mix well. Marinate in refrigerator for several hours. Yield: 12 servings.

Dressing for Green Bean Salad

1/2 cup vinegar
1/2 cup oil
3/4 cup sugar
Salt and pepper to taste

Combine vinegar, oil, sugar, salt and pepper in small bowl; mix well.

Approx Per Serving: Cal 205; Prot 4 g; Carbo 29 g; Fiber 4 g; T Fat 10 g; Chol 0 mg; Sod 315 mg.

Bernice Griffin, Hornets Nest

COLD VEGETABLE SALAD

1 16-ounce can seasoned green beans, drained
1 16-ounce can whole kernel corn, drained
1 16-ounce can green peas, drained
1/2 cup chopped celery
1 onion, chopped
Dressing (See page 75)

Combine green beans, corn, green peas, celery and onion in large bowl; mix well. Add dressing; mix well. Marinate in refrigerator overnight. Drain before serving. Yield: 12 servings.

Dressing for Cold Vegetable Salad

1 cup sugar
¼ cup oil
1 cup vinegar
1¼ teaspoons salt
Pepper to taste

Combine sugar, oil, vinegar, salt and pepper in small bowl; mix well.

Approx Per Serving: Cal 176; Prot 3 g; Carbo 32 g; Fiber 3 g; T Fat 5 g; Chol 0 mg; Sod 493 mg.
Nutritional information includes entire amount of dressing.

Irene C. Black, Independence

THREE-BEAN SALAD

1 16-ounce can wax beans, drained
1 16-ounce can green beans, drained
1 16-ounce can pinto beans, drained
¼ cup chopped onion
¼ cup chopped green bell pepper
Dressing

Combine wax beans, green beans, pinto beans, onion and green pepper in large bowl; mix well. Add dressing; mix well. Marinate in refrigerator for 1 hour. Yield: 12 servings.

Dressing for Three-Bean Salad

¾ cup sugar
⅔ cup vinegar
½ cup oil
1 teaspoon salt
1 teaspoon pepper

Combine sugar, vinegar, oil, salt and pepper in small bowl; mix well.

Approx Per Serving: Cal 198; Prot 4 g; Carbo 27 g; Fiber 5 g; T Fat 9 g; Chol 0 mg; Sod 369 mg.

Wilma Brinson, Raleigh

BACON AND BROCCOLI SALAD

Flowerets of 1 bunch broccoli, chopped
4 ounces bacon, crisp-fried, crumbled
1/4 medium onion, chopped
1/3 cup raisins
1/2 cup chopped pecans
Dressing

Combine broccoli, bacon, onion, raisins and pecans in bowl; mix well. Add dressing; toss to mix. Chill for 2 hours. Yield: 8 servings.

Dressing for Bacon and Broccoli Salad

3/4 cup mayonnaise
1/3 cup sugar
1 1/2 tablespoons wine vinegar

Combine mayonnaise, sugar and vinegar in small bowl; mix until sugar dissolves.

Approx Per Serving: Cal 238; Prot 3 g; Carbo 17 g; Fiber 2 g; T Fat 19 g; Chol 16 mg; Sod 198 mg.

Karon Bishop, Independence

CHEESY BROCCOLI SALAD

Flowerets of 1 bunch broccoli, finely chopped
1 1/2 cups shredded Cheddar cheese
8 slices crisp-fried bacon, crumbled
1 onion, finely chopped
Dressing (See page 77)

Combine broccoli, cheese, bacon and onion in large bowl; mix well. Add dressing; mix well. Chill for 1 hour. Yield: 8 servings.

Dressing for Cheesy Broccoli Salad

½ cup mayonnaise-type salad dressing
¼ cup sugar
2 tablespoons red wine vinegar

Combine salad dressing, sugar and vinegar in small bowl; mix until sugar dissolves.

Approx Per Serving: Cal 222; Prot 9 g; Carbo 14 g; Fiber 2 g; T Fat 15 g; Chol 31 mg; Sod 349 mg.

Sandy Batson, Independence

CINDY'S BROCCOLI SALAD

4 cups broccoli flowerets
½ cup golden raisins
8 ounces bacon, crisp-fried crumbled
1 14-ounce can sweetened condensed milk
¾ cup vinegar
3 tablespoons Dijon mustard
1 egg
Salt and pepper to taste
1 red onion, sliced into rings

Combine broccoli, raisins and bacon in large bowl; mix well. Mix sweetened condensed milk, vinegar, mustard, egg, salt and pepper in bowl. Add desired amount of dressing to broccoli mixture; toss well. Top salad with onion rings. Chill for several hours to several days. May store dressing in refrigerator for several days. Yield: 10 servings.

Approx Per Serving: Cal 316; Prot 13 g; Carbo 34 g; Fiber 2 g; T Fat 16 g; Chol 54 mg; Sod 489 mg.
Nutritional information includes entire amount of dressing.

Billie P. Byrum, Independence

EASY BROCCOLI SALAD

Flowerets of 1 bunch broccoli
1 onion, chopped
8 slices crisp-fried bacon, crumbled
1/4 cup raisins
3/4 cup mayonnaise
1/4 cup sugar
2 tablespoons vinegar

Combine broccoli, onion, bacon and raisins in large bowl; mix well. Combine mayonnaise, sugar and vinegar in small bowl; mix until sugar dissolves. Chill both mixtures until 30 minutes before serving time. Pour dressing over broccoli mixture; mix well. Yield: 6 servings.

Approx Per Serving: Cal 324; Prot 5 g; Carbo 20 g; Fiber 3 g; T Fat 26 g; Chol 23 mg; Sod 308 mg.

Barbara Hutchins, Raleigh

GWEN'S BROCCOLI SALAD

Flowerets of 2 bunches broccoli, chopped
1 medium red onion, finely chopped
8 slices crisp-fried bacon, crumbled
1 cup golden raisins
1 cup reduced-calorie mayonnaise
1 tablespoon vinegar
1 tablespoon sugar

Combine broccoli, onion, bacon and raisins in large bowl. Mix mayonnaise, vinegar and sugar in small bowl. Chill both mixtures for 1 hour. Pour dressing over broccoli mixture; mix well. Chill for 2 or 3 days to improve flavor. Yield: 8 servings.

Approx Per Serving: Cal 205; Prot 5 g; Carbo 28 g; Fiber 4 g; T Fat 10 g; Chol 13 mg; Sod 278 mg.

Gwen Finlayson, Independence

OVERNIGHT BROCCOLI SALAD

Flowerets of 2 bunches broccoli
1 small onion, finely chopped
½ cup chopped pecans
3 ounces raisins
1 cup mayonnaise
2 tablespoons vinegar
⅓ cup sugar
8 slices crisp-fried bacon, crumbled

Combine broccoli, onion, pecans and raisins in large bowl; mix well. Mix mayonnaise, vinegar and sugar in small bowl until sugar dissolves. Add dressing to broccoli mixture; mix well. Chill overnight. Stir in bacon just before serving. Yield: 16 servings.

Approx Per Serving: Cal 188; Prot 3 g; Carbo 12 g; Fiber 2 g; T Fat 15 g; Chol 11 mg; Sod 142 mg.

Johnnie O. Baker, Independence

FAVORITE BROCCOLI SALAD

2 bunches broccoli, chopped
1 small onion, sliced into rings
½ cup golden raisins
½ cup chopped pecans
3 tablespoons vinegar
¾ cup mayonnaise
⅓ cup sugar

Combine broccoli, onion rings, raisins and pecans in bowl; mix well. Combine vinegar, mayonnaise and sugar in small bowl; mix well. Stir into broccoli mixture. Chill for 2 to 3 hours. May garnish with bacon bits if desired. Yield: 8 servings.

Approx Per Serving: Cal 290; Prot 4 g; Carbo 24 g; Fiber 4 g; T Fat 22 g; Chol 12 mg; Sod 143 mg.

Bertie Frye, Hornets Nest

SWEET MARINATED SLAW

1 head cabbage, chopped
1 green bell pepper, chopped
2 onions, chopped
1 cup sugar

¾ cup oil
1 cup vinegar
4 teaspoons sugar
1 teaspoon celery seed
1 teaspoon salt

Combine cabbage, green pepper and onions with 1 cup sugar in bowl; mix well. Combine oil, vinegar, 4 teaspoons sugar, celery seed and salt in saucepan. Bring to a boil, stirring to mix well. Pour over cabbage mixture; mix well. Spoon into airtight container. Chill for 4 hours or longer. Yield: 8 servings.

Approx Per Serving: Cal 313; Prot 1 g; Carbo 34 g; Fiber 2 g; T Fat 21 g; Chol 0 mg; Sod 275 mg.

Patricia L. Goodin, Independence

SHREDDED REFRIGERATOR SLAW

1 large head cabbage, shredded
1 large onion, thinly sliced into rings
⅓ cup oil
1 cup vinegar

¾ cup plus 2 tablespoons sugar
1 tablespoon dry mustard
1 tablespoon celery seed
1 tablespoon salt

Layer cabbage and onion in bowl. Combine oil, vinegar, sugar, dry mustard, celery seed and salt in saucepan. Bring to a boil. Pour over layers. Chill for up to 3 days. Yield: 10 servings.

Approx Per Serving: Cal 146; Prot 1 g; Carbo 22 g; Fiber 1 g; T Fat 7 g; Chol 0 mg; Sod 645 mg.

Evelyn Carson, Independence

REFRIGERATOR SLAW

1 large head cabbage, chopped
2 medium onions, chopped
1 green bell pepper, chopped
1 cup vinegar
1 cup oil
1 teaspoon dry mustard
1 teaspoon celery seed
1 tablespoon salt

Combine cabbage, onions and green pepper in bowl; mix well. Combine vinegar, oil, dry mustard, celery seed and salt in saucepan. Bring to a boil, stirring to mix well. Let stand until cool. Add to cabbage mixture. Store in refrigerator for up to 1 month. Yield: 10 servings.

Approx Per Serving: Cal 215; Prot 1 g; Carbo 6 g; Fiber 1 g; T Fat 22 g; Chol 0 mg; Sod 646 mg.

Madelon Haskin, Hornets Nest

MARINATED SLAW

2 small cabbages
1 green bell pepper
1 onion
4 carrots
Salt to taste
1 cup vinegar
1 cup water
1 cup sugar

Shred cabbages, green pepper, onion and carrots into colander, sprinkling layers with salt. Let drain at room temperature for 4 hours; press to remove remaining moisture. Combine vinegar, water and sugar in bowl; mix well. Combine with cabbage mixture in serving bowl; mix well. Marinate in refrigerator for 12 hours or longer. Yield: 16 servings.

Approx Per Serving: Cal 69; Prot 1 g; Carbo 18 g; Fiber 1 g; T Fat <1 g; Chol 0 mg; Sod 12 mg.

Wilma Brinson, Raleigh

CHEESY CABBAGE AND APPLE SLAW

1 1-pound head cabbage, thinly sliced
1 1/2 cups thinly sliced celery
1/2 cup sliced green onions
1 cup mayonnaise
1/2 cup sour cream
2 tablespoons lemon juice
1 teaspoon salt
1/4 teaspoon white pepper
1/2 teaspoon fennel seed, crushed
4 medium apples, coarsely chopped
4 ounces Cheddar cheese, cubed

Combine cabbage, celery and green onions in large bowl; mix well. Mix mayonnaise, sour cream, lemon juice, salt, white pepper and fennel seed in small bowl. Add to cabbage mixture; mix well. Chill, covered, for 2 to 3 hours. Add apples and cheese cubes; toss to mix. Yield: 12 servings.

Approx Per Serving: Cal 229; Prot 4 g; Carbo 11 g; Fiber 2 g; T Fat 20 g; Chol 25 mg; Sod 366 mg.

Doris Kelly, Hornets Nest

COLESLAW WITH APPLE

2 cups shredded cabbage
6 green onions, chopped
1 medium carrot, shredded
1 apple, chopped
1/2 green bell pepper, chopped
3 tablespoons plain yogurt
2 tablespoons sour cream
1 tablespoon mayonnaise
1 teaspoon lemon juice
1/4 teaspoon dillweed
1/2 teaspoon salt
Freshly ground pepper to taste

Combine cabbage, green onions, carrot, apple and green pepper in large bowl; mix well. Combine yogurt, sour cream, mayonnaise, lemon juice, dillweed, salt and pepper in bowl; mix well. Pour over cabbage mixture; mix well. Yield: 4 servings.

Approx Per Serving: Cal 92; Prot 2 g; Carbo 12 g; Fiber 3 g; T Fat 5 g; Chol 6 mg; Sod 311 mg.

John E. Miles, Independence

MARTY'S COLESLAW

1 8-ounce package chopped cabbage
1 small carrot, coarsely shredded
1 celery stalk, coarsely shredded
1/2 yellow onion, coarsely shredded

1/2 cup plain nonfat yogurt
1 tablespoon Durkees Famous Sauce
1 1/2 teaspoons sugar
1/4 teaspoon salt
1 teaspoon wine vinegar
1/4 teaspoon celery seed
4 slices dill pickle

Combine cabbage, carrot, celery and onion in large bowl; mix well. Process yogurt, Durkees Famous Sauce, sugar, salt, vinegar, celery seed and pickle in blender for 15 to 20 seconds or until well mixed. Pour over cabbage mixture; toss well. Chill for 2 to 4 hours. Yield: 4 servings.

Approx Per Serving: Cal 56; Prot 3 g; Carbo 11 g; Fiber 2 g; T Fat 1 g; Chol 2 mg; Sod 227 mg.

Martin J. Ambrose, Asheville

MARINATED COLESLAW

1 head cabbage, chopped
1 green bell pepper, chopped
1 medium onion, chopped
1 cup sugar

1 cup vinegar
3/4 cup oil
1 teaspoon mustard seed
1 teaspoon celery seed
1/8 teaspoon salt

Combine cabbage, green pepper and onion in large bowl; mix well. Combine sugar, vinegar, oil, mustard seed, celery seed and salt in saucepan; mix well. Bring to a boil. Pour over cabbage mixture; mix well. Chill; will keep in refrigerator for up to 10 days. Yield: 15 servings.

Approx Per Serving: Cal 162; Prot 1 g; Carbo 17 g; Fiber 1 g; T Fat 11 g; Chol 0 mg; Sod 24 mg.

Wanda Moffett, Independence

CONFETTI SLAW

3 pounds cabbage, shredded
1 4-ounce can chopped pimentos
1 16-ounce can tomatoes
1 medium green bell pepper, chopped
1 cup sugar
1 cup vinegar
1/8 teaspoon salt

Combine cabbage, pimentos, tomatoes and green pepper in large bowl. Mix sugar, vinegar and salt in small bowl. Add to cabbage mixture; toss well. Chill for 24 hours before serving. Yield: 24 servings.

Approx Per Serving: Cal 52; Prot 1 g; Carbo 13 g; Fiber 2 g; T Fat <1 g; Chol 0 mg; Sod 52 mg.

Karen Stallings, Independence

CAULIFLOWER AND GREEN PEA SALAD

1 10-ounce package frozen green peas
1 cup mayonnaise
1 small onion, grated
1/4 cup milk
1 1/2 teaspoons salt
1/2 teaspoon pepper
Flowerets of 1 medium head cauliflower
3 stalks celery, very thinly sliced

Cook green peas using package directions for 2 minutes or until just tender; drain. Cool. Combine mayonnaise, onion, milk, salt and pepper in large bowl; mix well. Add green peas, cauliflower and celery; toss lightly to mix. Chill for several hours to overnight. Yield: 12 servings.

Approx Per Serving: Cal 160; Prot 2 g; Carbo 5 g; Fiber 2 g; T Fat 15 g; Chol 12 mg; Sod 409 mg.

Carolyn B. Williams, Independence

CONGEALED VEGETABLE SALAD

2 envelopes unflavored gelatin
1 cup cold water
3/4 cup water
3/4 cup sugar
Salt and pepper to taste
1/3 cup vinegar
1 cup shredded cabbage
2 cups chopped celery
1 2-ounce jar chopped pimento
1 cup shredded carrot
1 8-ounce can green peas
1 cup chopped pecans

Soften gelatin in 1 cup cold water. Combine 3/4 cup water, sugar, salt, pepper and vinegar in saucepan. Bring to a boil. Stir in gelatin mixture until dissolved. Chill until partially set. Stir in cabbage, celery, pimento, carrot, green peas and pecans. Pour into greased individual molds or 9x13-inch glass dish. Chill until set. Unmold onto lettuce-lined salad plates. Garnish with mayonnaise thinned with cream. Yield: 10 servings.

Approx Per Serving: Cal 166; Prot 3 g; Carbo 22 g; Fiber 3 g; T Fat 8 g; Chol 0 mg; Sod 90 mg.

Betty Hovis, Hornets Nest

CUCUMBER SALAD

1 3-ounce package lemon gelatin
1/2 cup boiling water
1 large cucumber, chopped
1 small onion, chopped
1 green bell pepper, chopped
1 tablespoon vinegar
1/2 cup mayonnaise
12 ounces cottage cheese

Dissolve gelatin in boiling water in bowl. Add cucumber, onion, green pepper, vinegar, mayonnaise and cottage cheese; mix well. Pour into serving bowl. Chill until set. Yield: 6 servings.

Approx Per Serving: Cal 260; Prot 9 g; Carbo 19 g; Fiber 1 g; T Fat 17 g; Chol 19 mg; Sod 381 mg.

Ovid Smith, Hornets Nest

MOLDED CUCUMBER SALAD

1 3-ounce package lime gelatin
3/4 cup boiling water
6 ounces cream cheese, softened
1 teaspoon prepared horseradish
1 cup mayonnaise
1/2 teaspoon salt
2 tablespoons lemon juice
3/4 cup drained shredded cucumber
1 tablespoon finely chopped green onions

Dissolve gelatin in boiling water in mixer bowl. Add cream cheese, horseradish, mayonnaise and salt; beat until smooth. Add lemon juice; mix well. Chill until partially set. Add cucumber and onions; mix well. Pour into 4-cup mold. Chill until set. This is very pretty made in a fish-shaped mold. Use thinly sliced cucumber for scales and chives to outline the fins. Yield: 6 servings.

Approx Per Serving: Cal 420; Prot 4 g; Carbo 16 g; Fiber <1 g; T Fat 39 g; Chol 53 mg; Sod 516 mg.

Barbara D. Scott, Independence

VEGETABLE HEALTH SALAD

2 cups chopped cabbage
2 cups chopped celery
1 cup chopped carrots
1 cup chopped green pepper
1/2 cup chopped pecans
1/2 cup chopped onion
2 3-ounce packages lemon gelatin
2 cups boiling water
1/4 cup lemon juice
1 cup mayonnaise
3/4 teaspoon salt

Combine cabbage, celery, carrots, green pepper, pecans and onion in large bowl; mix well. Dissolve gelatin in boiling water in bowl. Add lemon juice, mayonnaise and salt; mix well. Pour over vegetables; mix well. Pour into serving dish. Chill until set. Yield: 12 servings.

Approx Per Serving: Cal 232; Prot 2 g; Carbo 18 g; Fiber 1 g; T Fat 18 g; Chol 11 mg; Sod 306 mg.

Julia S. Clark, Independence

LAYERED SALAD

1 head lettuce, broken into bite-sized pieces
1 16-ounce can Le Sueur green peas, drained
2 onions, thinly sliced
2 cups mayonnaise
1 1/2 tablespoons sugar
1 cup Parmesan cheese

Layer lettuce, green peas and onion slices into glass salad bowl. Spread mayonnaise over top, sealing to edge; sprinkle with sugar. Top with cheese. Chill, covered with plastic wrap, overnight. Yield: 12 servings.

Approx Per Serving: Cal 337; Prot 5 g; Carbo 10 g; Fiber 2 g; T Fat 31 g; Chol 27 mg; Sod 419 mg.

Betty W. Hampton, Salem

MARVELOUS MAKE-AHEAD SALAD

1 quart bite-sized lettuce
1 cup chopped green bell pepper
1 cup chopped celery
1 10-ounce package frozen peas, thawed
1/4 cup minced onion
10 hard-boiled eggs, sliced
1 cup shredded Cheddar cheese
1 16-ounce bottle of light buttermilk salad dressing

Layer lettuce, green pepper, celery, peas and onion in large salad bowl. Reserve center slices of egg for garnish. Layer remaining egg slices and half the cheese over vegetables. Spread dressing over salad, sealing to edge. Sprinkle with remaining cheese. Chill, covered, for 2 hours to overnight. Garnish with reserved egg slices and parsley. Yield: 12 servings.

Approx Per Serving: Cal 217; Prot 9 g; Carbo 11 g; Fiber 2 g; T Fat 15 g; Chol 197 mg; Sod 341 mg.

Shelia Chapman, Hornets Nest

☎ Place an inverted saucer in the bottom of the salad bowl for vegetable salads. Moisture will collect under saucer to keep salad crisp.

MARTHA'S LETTUCE SALAD

1 head lettuce, chopped
2 tablespoons poppy seed
1 medium onion, chopped
1/4 cup sliced almonds
1/4 cup sugar
1/4 cup vinegar
1/2 cup oil
2 teaspoons salt
1/2 teaspoon pepper
1 cup chow mein noodles

Combine lettuce, poppy seed, onion and almonds in bowl; mix well. Mix sugar, vinegar, oil, salt and pepper in small bowl. Place lettuce mixture on salad plates. Drizzle dressing over salads; top each with 2 tablespoons chow mein noodles.
Yield: 8 servings.

Approx Per Serving: Cal 212; Prot 2 g; Carbo 13 g; Fiber 1 g;
T Fat 18 g; Chol 1 mg; Sod 592 mg.

Martha Berrier, Hornets Nest

SEVEN-LAYER SALAD

1 medium head lettuce, shredded
1 cup coarsely chopped celery
1 cup chopped green bell pepper
1 1/2 cups chopped onion
1 8-ounce can green peas, drained
1 1/2 cups (about) mayonnaise
2 1/2 cups shredded Cheddar cheese

Layer lettuce, celery, green pepper, onion and green peas in large salad bowl. Spread mayonnaise over vegetables, sealing to edge. Sprinkle with cheese. Garnish with bacon bits if desired. Chill, covered, overnight. Yield: 12 servings.

Approx Per Serving: Cal 318; Prot 8 g; Carbo 6 g; Fiber 2 g;
T Fat 30 g; Chol 41 mg; Sod 354 mg.

Virginia Barnette, Hornets Nest

☎ Salt green salads at the table because salt tends to wilt and toughen salad greens.

PEGGY'S POTATO SALAD

6 medium potatoes
3 hard-boiled eggs, chopped
1/4 cup chopped green bell pepper
1/4 cup chopped onion
1/4 cup chopped sweet pickles
Dressing

Peel and coarsely chop potatoes. Cook in water to cover in saucepan until tender; drain. Cool. Combine potatoes, eggs, green pepper, onion and pickles in large bowl; toss to mix. Add dressing to potato mixture; mix well. Chill before serving. Yield: 12 servings.

Dressing for Peggy's Potato Salad

2 tablespoons mayonnaise
2 tablespoons Thousand Island salad dressing
1/2 teaspoon prepared mustard
Salt and pepper to taste

Combine mayonnaise, salad dressing, prepared mustard, salt and pepper in small bowl; mix well.

Approx Per Serving: Cal 164; Prot 4 g; Carbo 28 g; Fiber 2 g; T Fat 4 g; Chol 55 mg; Sod 95 mg.

Peggy Hall, Blue Ridge

POTATO SALAD

6 Idaho potatoes, chopped
Salt and pepper to taste
1/2 cup chopped green bell pepper
1/2 cup chopped onion
1/2 cup sweet pickle salad cubes
1/2 cup finely chopped celery
1 cup chopped hard-boiled eggs
1 cup mayonnaise-type salad dressing
1/4 cup prepared mustard

Cook potatoes in water to cover in saucepan until tender; drain. Add salt and pepper. Cool. Combine potatoes with remaining ingredients in large bowl; mix gently. Yield: 12 servings.

Approx Per Serving: Cal 226; Prot 4 g; Carbo 35 g; Fiber 3 g; T Fat 8 g; Chol 53 mg; Sod 303 mg.

Sandy Batson, Independence

SWEET PEA SALAD

1 8-ounce can green peas, drained
2 hard-boiled eggs, chopped
1 small onion, chopped
Salt and pepper to taste
2 tablespoons mayonnaise-type salad dressing

Combine green peas, eggs and onion in bowl; toss to mix. Add salt, pepper and salad dressing; mix well. Yield: 4 servings.

Approx Per Serving: Cal 138; Prot 6 g; Carbo 10 g; Fiber 3 g; T Fat 9 g; Chol 111 mg; Sod 196 mg.

Georgia Lee, Hornets Nest

CONFETTI SAUERKRAUT SALAD

1 16-ounce can sauerkraut
1 cup chopped onion
1 cup chopped green bell pepper
1 cup chopped celery
1 2-ounce jar chopped pimento
Dressing

Rinse sauerkraut; drain. Combine sauerkraut, onion, green pepper, celery and pimento in bowl; mix well. Add dressing; mix well. Chill, covered, overnight. May store in refrigerator for several days. Yield: 8 servings.

Dressing for Confetti Sauerkraut Salad

1½ cups sugar
¼ cup oil
¼ cup vinegar
Salt and pepper to taste

Combine sugar, oil, vinegar, salt and pepper in small bowl; mix well.

Approx Per Serving: Cal 230; Prot 1 g; Carbo 43 g; Fiber 2 g; T Fat 7 g; Chol 0 mg; Sod 390 mg.

Jewel Costner, Foot Hills

SAUERKRAUT SALAD

1 16-ounce can sauerkraut, drained, chopped
1 cup finely chopped celery
1 large onion, chopped
1 2-ounce jar chopped pimento
1 green bell pepper, chopped
Dressing

Combine sauerkraut, celery, onion, pimento and green pepper in bowl; toss to mix. Add dressing; mix well. Yield: 8 servings.

Dressing for Sauerkraut Salad

2 cups sugar
3/4 cup vinegar
1/2 cup oil
1 teaspoon celery seed

Combine sugar, vinegar, oil and celery seed in small bowl; mix well.

Approx Per Serving: Cal 341; Prot 1 g; Carbo 57 g; Fiber 2 g; T Fat 14 g; Chol 0 mg; Sod 391 mg.

Odelle McMullan, Independence

TANGY KRAUT SALAD

1 16-ounce can sauerkraut
1 cup sugar
1/2 cup vinegar
1/4 cup oil
1 cup finely chopped onion
1 cup finely chopped celery
1/2 cup finely chopped green bell pepper
1/4 cup chopped pimento

Rinse sauerkraut; drain well. Combine sugar, vinegar and oil in saucepan. Bring to a boil. Remove from heat. Combine sauerkraut, onion, celery, green pepper and pimento in large bowl; mix well. Pour hot dressing over mixture; mix well. Chill for 6 hours or longer. This recipe is from the kitchen of Jessie Fantroy who cooked for President Johnson for 16 years. Yield: 4 servings.

Approx Per Serving: Cal 363; Prot 2 g; Carbo 62 g; Fiber 4 g; T Fat 14 g; Chol 0 mg; Sod 779 mg.

Loretta Burgess, Independence

MANDARIN SALAD

1 pound fresh spinach
1 11-ounce can mandarin oranges, drained
1 cup sliced almonds
1 8-ounce bottle of oil and vinegar salad dressing

Wash spinach; drain. Layer spinach, mandarin oranges and almonds on individual salad plates. Top with desired amount of dressing. Yield: 6 servings.

Approx Per Serving: Cal 306; Prot 6 g; Carbo 14 g; Fiber 5 g; T Fat 27 g; Chol 0 mg; Sod 64 mg.
Nutritional information includes entire amount of dressing.

Jenny Givens, Independence

SCANDINAVIAN SALAD

1 16-ounce can green beans, drained
1 16-ounce can Le Sueur green peas, drained
1 2-ounce can chopped pimento
1 small onion, finely chopped
2 stalks celery, thinly sliced
1 cup sugar
1/4 cup oil
1 cup vinegar
1/2 teaspoon salt

Combine green beans, green peas, pimento, onion and celery in large bowl. Mix sugar, oil, vinegar and salt in small bowl. Pour over green bean mixture; toss to mix. Chill for 24 hours. Drain before serving. Yield: 10 servings.

Approx Per Serving: Cal 175; Prot 3 g; Carbo 31 g; Fiber 3 g; T Fat 6 g; Chol 0 mg; Sod 328 mg.
Nutritional information includes entire amount of marinade.

Kim Parker, Central

MARINATED SCANDINAVIAN SALAD

1 16-ounce can French-style green beans, drained
1 16-ounce can small green peas, drained
2 stalks celery, finely sliced
1 medium green bell pepper, chopped
1 medium onion, chopped
1 2-ounce jar chopped pimento
1 cup vinegar
1/2 cup oil
1 cup sugar
1/2 teaspoon paprika
Salt and pepper to taste

Combine green beans, green peas, celery, green pepper, onion, pimento, vinegar, oil, sugar, paprika, salt and pepper in bowl; mix well. Chill for 24 hours to several days. Drain before serving. Yield: 10 servings.

Approx Per Serving: Cal 227; Prot 3 g; Carbo 31 g; Fiber 3 g; T Fat 11 g; Chol 0 mg; Sod 222 mg.
Nutritional information includes entire amount of marinade.

Evelyn Carson, Independence

☎ For quick individual Salades Niçoise, place chunks of solid-pack tuna on lettuce-lined plates. Add drained green beans, sliced cooked potatoes, cherry tomatoes, hard-boiled egg quarters, black olives and a light vinaigrette.

☎ Make Thousand Island salad dressing by combining half a small bottle of catsup or chili sauce, 3 cups mayonnaise, 2 tablespoons prepared mustard, 1 cup sweet pickle relish and enough relish juice to make of desired consistency.

TEXAS CAVIAR

2 16-ounce cans black-eyed peas, drained
1 16-ounce can white hominy, drained
2 medium tomatoes, coarsely chopped
4 green onions, chopped
1 medium green bell pepper, chopped
2 cloves of garlic, minced
1 jalapeño pepper, chopped
1/2 cup fresh chopped parsley
1 8-ounce bottle of Italian salad dressing
2 tablespoons Texas Pete

Combine black-eyed peas, hominy, tomatoes, onions, green pepper, garlic, jalapeño pepper and parsley in large bowl; mix well. Add dressing and Texas Pete; mix well. Marinate in refrigerator overnight. Drain before serving. Yield: 12 servings.

Approx Per Serving: Cal 178; Prot 5 g; Carbo 19 g; Fiber 6 g; T Fat 12 g; Chol 0 mg; Sod 432 mg.
Nutritional information includes entire amount of marinade.

Julia S. Clark, Independence

TOMATO RING

2 envelopes unflavored gelatin
1/2 cup water
1 can tomato soup
1 teaspoon salt
1 tablespoon vinegar
1 cup mayonnaise
16 ounces small curd cottage cheese
1 small green bell pepper, chopped
1 small onion, chopped
1 stalk celery, chopped
1 small cucumber, chopped

Soften gelatin in water. Bring tomato soup to a boil in saucepan. Stir in gelatin until dissolved. Cool. Stir in salt, vinegar and mayonnaise. Add cottage cheese, green pepper, onion, celery and cucumber; mix well. Spoon into 12 individual molds sprayed with nonstick cooking spray. Chill until set. Unmold onto salad plates. Yield: 12 servings.

Approx Per Serving: Cal 200; Prot 6 g; Carbo 7 g; Fiber 1 g; T Fat 17 g; Chol 16 mg; Sod 616 mg.

Lib E. Linker, Piedmont

MARINATED MIXED VEGETABLES

- 1 16-ounce can French-style green beans, drained
- 1 16-ounce can sliced carrots, drained
- 1 16-ounce can bean sprouts, drained
- 1 8-ounce can sliced water chestnuts, drained
- 1 16-ounce can green peas, drained
- 1 16-ounce can whole kernel corn, drained
- 1 2-ounce jar chopped pimento, drained
- 1 2-ounce jar sliced green olives, drained
- 3 stalks celery, chopped
- 1 green bell pepper, chopped
- 1 onion, chopped
- Dressing

Combine green beans, carrots, bean sprouts, water chestnuts, peas, corn, pimento, olives, celery, green pepper and onion in large bowl; toss to mix. Add marinade to vegetable mixture; mix well. Marinate, covered, in refrigerator overnight. Yield: 20 servings.

Salad Dressing for Marinated Mixed Vegetables

- 1½ cups vinegar
- 1½ cups water
- 2 tablespoons oil
- ½ cup sugar
- 2 tablespoons (or less) salt
- 1 tablespoon pepper

Combine vinegar, water, oil, sugar, salt and pepper in small bowl; mix well.

Approx Per Serving: Cal 90; Prot 2 g; Carbo 18 g; Fiber 3 g; T Fat 2 g; Chol 0 mg; Sod 953 mg.

Mrs. Hugh L. McAulay, Blue Ridge

☎ Bottled salad dressings make a delicious marinade for salad vegetables.

SPINACH AND TOMATO SALAD

1 pound fresh spinach
1 cup oil
1/4 cup vinegar
1/2 cup sugar
1 small onion, finely chopped
1/3 cup catsup
1 teaspoon salt
1 tablespoon Worcestershire sauce
2 hard-boiled eggs, sliced
1 tomato, chopped
4 slices crisp-fried bacon, crumbled

Wash spinach; drain. Combine oil and vinegar in mixer bowl; beat for 3 to 5 minutes or until well blended. Add sugar, onion, catsup, salt and Worcestershire sauce; beat well. Combine spinach, eggs, tomato and bacon in large bowl. Add desired amount of dressing; toss to mix. Dressing will keep well in refrigerator. Yield: 6 servings.

Approx Per Serving: Cal 482; Prot 6 g; Carbo 27 g; Fiber 3 g; T Fat 41 g; Chol 75 mg; Sod 689 mg.
Nutritional information includes entire amount of dressing.

Jean W. Nance, Raleigh

SWEET AND SOUR DRESSING FOR SPINACH SALAD

1 medium onion, quartered
1 cup oil
1/2 cup sugar
1/4 cup vinegar
1 tablespoon Worcestershire sauce
1/3 cup catsup

Process onion in blender until minced. Add oil, sugar, vinegar, Worcestershire sauce and catsup. Process until well mixed. Yield: 12 servings.

Approx Per Serving: Cal 207; Prot <1 g; Carbo 12 g; Fiber <1 g; T Fat 18 g; Chol 0 mg; Sod 91 mg.

Cheryl Griffin, Raleigh

Meats

CHILDREN'S FIRE SAFETY HOUSE

BEEF

BARBECUED BRISKET

1 4-pound beef brisket
1½ cups catsup
¼ cup packed brown sugar
1½ cups water
1 medium onion, chopped
2 tablespoons liquid smoke
2 dashes of Tabasco sauce
1 teaspoon chili powder
1 teaspoon salt

Place brisket fat side up in roasting pan. Roast, uncovered, without liquid at 350 degrees for 2 hours. Combine catsup, brown sugar, water, onion, liquid smoke, Tabasco sauce, chili powder and salt in blender container; process until smooth. Pour over brisket. Reduce oven temperature to 300 degrees. Roast, covered, for 3 to 4 hours or until done to taste, basting every 30 minutes. Slice very thin. Yield: 6 servings.

Approx Per Serving: Cal 512; Prot 58 g; Carbo 28 g; Fiber 2 g; T Fat 18 g; Chol 170 mg; Sod 1166 mg.

Cheryl Griffin, Raleigh

BEEF BRISKET

1 6-pound brisket
1 12-ounce bottle of barbecue sauce
2 tablespoons Worcestershire sauce
Liquid smoke to taste
1 teaspoon garlic salt
1 teaspoon onion salt
2 teaspoons celery salt
1½ teaspoons salt
2 teaspoons pepper

Place brisket fat side up in 2-inch deep roasting pan. Roast, covered, at 250 degrees for 5 hours; do not drain pan drippings. Combine barbecue sauce, Worcestershire sauce, liquid smoke, garlic salt, onion salt, celery salt, salt and pepper in bowl; mix well. Pour over brisket. Bake for 1 hour longer. Yield: 15 servings.

Approx Per Serving: Cal 254; Prot 34 g; Carbo 3 g; Fiber <1 g; T Fat 11 g; Chol 102 mg; Sod 1036 mg.

Judy Smathers, Asheville

CROCK·POT ROAST

1 can cream of mushroom soup
1 can cream of celery soup
1 3-pound pot roast
Salt and pepper to taste
2 tablespoons shortening
1 envelope onion soup mix
1 soup can water

Combine mushroom soup and celery soup in Crock·Pot. Heat on Low. Sprinkle roast with salt and pepper. Brown on all sides in shortening in saucepan. Remove roast to plate. Stir onion soup mix into drippings in saucepan. Cook until brown. Add 1 soup can water; mix well. Add to soups in Crock·Pot; mix well. Add roast. Cook on Low for 8 hours. Yield: 6 servings.

Approx Per Serving: Cal 427; Prot 44 g; Carbo 8 g; Fiber <1 g; T Fat 23 g; Chol 134 mg; Sod 969 mg.

Peggy Stroupe, Foot Hills

CROCK·POT ROAST BEEF

1 3-pound sirloin tip roast
1/2 cup flour
1 envelope onion soup mix
1 envelope brown gravy mix
2 cups ginger ale

Coat roast with flour. Place in Crock·Pot. Combine soup mix, gravy mix, ginger ale and remaining flour in bowl; mix well. Add to Crock·Pot. Cook on Low for 8 to 10 hours or until roast is tender. Yield: 6 servings.

Approx Per Serving: Cal 381; Prot 44 g; Carbo 18 g; Fiber <1 g; T Fat 13 g; Chol 128 mg; Sod 382 mg.

Dee Wright, Foot Hills

☎ Make a delicious and easy Beef Burgundy with 3 pounds of stew beef, 3 cans of cream of mushroom soup and 1 envelope dry onion soup mix. Bake, covered, at 325 degrees for 3 hours, add canned mushrooms and serve over rice or noodles.

EYE-OF-ROUND ROAST WITH VEGETABLES

1 2-pound eye-of-round roast, trimmed
3 medium carrots, cut into 2-inch pieces
8 ounces new potatoes, peeled, cut into eighths
1 medium onion, coarsely chopped
2 stalks celery, cut into 4-inch pieces
1 tablespoon low-sodium soy sauce
1/2 cup dry red wine
1/2 cup beef stock
1/2 teaspoon freshly ground pepper
1 tablespoon cornstarch
1/4 cup cold water
1/2 cup chopped parsley

Place roast in oven-roasting bag. Add carrots, potatoes, onion, celery, soy sauce, wine, beef stock and pepper; secure bag. Place in baking pan; pierce several holes in top of bag. Roast at 325 degrees for 1 hour. Cool for 10 to 15 minutes. Remove roast to carving board; pour vegetables and drippings into saucepan. Remove vegetables to bowl with slotted spoon. Skim pan drippings. Spoon a small amount of drippings over roast; let roast stand for 10 minutes. Stir mixture of cornstarch and water into remaining drippings in saucepan. Cook until thickened, stirring constantly. Pour into gravy bowl. Slice roast cross grain; place on warm serving platter. Arrange vegetables around roast. Sprinkle with chopped parsley. Serve with gravy. Yield: 8 servings.

Approx Per Serving: Cal 218; Prot 23 g; Carbo 13 g; Fiber 2 g; T Fat 7 g; Chol 64 mg; Sod 267 mg.

Phyllis Jones, Independence

PEKING ROAST BEEF

1 5-pound beef roast
1 clove of garlic
1 small onion
1 cup vinegar
3 tablespoons oil
2 cups strong black coffee
2 cups water
Salt and pepper to taste

Cut slits completely through roast. Slice garlic and onion into slivers; insert into slits. Combine roast with vinegar in deep bowl. Marinate in refrigerator for 24 to 48 hours; drain. Cook roast in oil in heavy saucepan until dark brown on all sides. Add coffee and water. Simmer, covered, for 5 1/2 hours, adding water up to 1 cup at a time if necessary. Season with salt and pepper. Simmer for 20 minutes longer. May use cheaper cuts of beef for this recipe. Yield: 10 servings.

Approx Per Serving: Cal 341; Prot 43 g; Carbo 3 g; Fiber <1 g; T Fat 17 g; Chol 128 mg; Sod 71 mg.

Barbara Young, Asheville

BEEF AND BROCCOLI STIR-FRY

8 ounces boneless beef steak
1 tablespoon cornstarch
1 tablespoon soy sauce
1 teaspoon sugar
2 teaspoons minced fresh gingerroot
1 clove of garlic, minced
1 tablespoon cornstarch
3 tablespoons soy sauce
1 cup water
3 tablespoons peanut oil
Flowerets of 1 pound broccoli
1 onion, coarsely chopped
1 carrot, sliced

Cut beef cross grain into thin slices. Combine 1 tablespoon cornstarch, 1 tablespoon soy sauce, sugar, gingerroot and garlic in bowl. Add beef. Let stand for 15 minutes. Combine 1 tablespoon cornstarch and 3 tablespoons soy sauce with water in bowl; set aside. Heat 1 tablespoon oil in wok. Add beef. Stir-fry for 1 minute; remove beef. Heat remaining 2 tablespoons oil in wok. Add broccoli, onion and carrot. Stir-fry for 4 minutes or until tender-crisp. Add beef and reserved cornstarch mixture. Cook until sauce is thickened, stirring constantly. Serve immediately. Yield: 4 servings.

Approx Per Serving: Cal 245; Prot 16 g; Carbo 17 g; Fiber 5 g; T Fat 14 g; Chol 32 mg; Sod 1084 mg.

Patsy Prillaman, Independence

☎ Cooking frozen beef without pre-thawing not only saves time but the beef also retains more flavor, more juices and more nutritional value.

BEEF BOURGUIGNON

2 ounces salt pork
12 small white onions
2 pounds round steak, cut into 2-inch cubes
2 tablespoons flour
1/8 teaspoon marjoram
1/8 teaspoon thyme
1/8 teaspoon salt
1/8 teaspoon pepper
1 cup Burgundy
1 cup beef bouillon
8 ounces mushrooms, sliced

Render salt pork in saucepan. Add onions. Sauté until brown. Add beef. Cook until brown. Sprinkle with flour, marjoram, thyme, salt and pepper; mix well. Stir in wine and bouillon. Simmer for 4 to 5 hours. Add mushrooms. Cook for 45 minutes longer. May reserve sautéed onions and add with mushrooms. May bake in oven at 250 degrees until done to taste. Serve with hot noodles, rice or small potatoes. Yield: 6 servings.

Approx Per Serving: Cal 399; Prot 29 g; Carbo 20 g; Fiber 4 g; T Fat 20 g; Chol 79 mg; Sod 282 mg.

Connie S. Pfaff, Raleigh

BEEF BURGUNDY

2 pounds round steak, cut into cubes
1/4 cup flour
1 teaspoon salt
Pepper to taste
1/4 cup butter
1 cup Burgundy
1/2 cup chopped onion
1 6-ounce can mushrooms
1 tablespoon chopped parsley
1 clove of garlic, minced
1 bay leaf

Coat beef with mixture of flour, salt and pepper. Brown in butter in saucepan. Add wine, onion, mushrooms, parsley, garlic and bay leaf. Bring to a boil; reduce heat. Simmer, covered, for 1 hour or until tender. Remove bay leaf. Serve over rice. Yield: 6 servings.

Approx Per Serving: Cal 326; Prot 30 g; Carbo 7 g; Fiber 1 g; T Fat 17 g; Chol 106 mg; Sod 589 mg.

Patricia L. Goodin, Independence

BEEF STROGANOFF

2 pounds round steak
1/2 cup flour
Salt and pepper to taste
1/4 cup butter
4 medium onions, chopped
1/2 stalk celery, chopped
1 8-ounce can mushrooms, drained
1 clove of garlic, minced
1/4 cup butter
1 cup sour cream

1 can cream of mushroom soup
1/2 cup sweet red wine
3/4 cup catsup
1 tablespoon wine vinegar
Worcestershire sauce and Tabasco sauce to taste
1/2 teaspoon dry mustard
1 teaspoon thyme
1 bay leaf

Tenderize steak; cut into thin 1-inch strips. Shake with flour, salt and pepper in bag. Brown in 1/4 cup butter in saucepan. Sauté onions, celery, mushrooms and garlic in 1/4 cup butter in skillet. Add to steak. Add sour cream, soup, wine, catsup, vinegar, Worcestershire sauce, Tabasco sauce, dry mustard, thyme and bay leaf; mix well. Simmer for 30 minutes. Remove bay leaf. Serve over rice or Chinese noodles. Yield: 6 servings.

Approx Per Serving: Cal 603; Prot 34 g; Carbo 32 g; Fiber 3 g; T Fat 37 g; Chol 144 mg; Sod 1130 mg.

Woodfin Posey, Independence

SIMPLY ELEGANT STEAK AND RICE

1 1/2 pounds boneless round steak, thinly sliced
1 1/2 tablespoons oil
1 onion, sliced into rings
1 4-ounce can sliced mushrooms

1 can cream of mushroom soup
1/4 cup dry Sherry
1 1/2 teaspoons garlic salt

Brown steak in oil in skillet. Add onion rings. Sauté until tender-crisp. Drain mushrooms, reserving liquid. Combine reserved liquid with soup, Sherry and garlic salt in bowl; mix well. Stir into skillet. Add mushrooms. Simmer, covered, for 1 hour or until steak is tender. Serve over rice. Yield: 6 servings.

Approx Per Serving: Cal 257; Prot 23 g; Carbo 7 g; Fiber 1 g; T Fat 14 g; Chol 64 mg; Sod 1040 mg.

Louise Bland, Central

CHINESE BEEF

1½ pounds 1-inch thick round steak
½ cup cornstarch
¼ cup oil
4 green onions, cut into 1-inch pieces
1 clove of garlic, crushed
1 teaspoon ginger
½ teaspoon pepper
½ cup beef bouillon
¼ cup soy sauce
¼ cup vinegar
¼ cup cold water
3 tablespoons brown sugar
2 large onions, thinly sliced
1 cup sliced green bell pepper
2 cups diagonally sliced ½-inch pieces celery
1 carrot, thinly sliced

Freeze beef for 1 hour. Cut into ⅛-inch slices. Coat with cornstarch. Brown in hot oil in skillet for 2 minutes; remove to deep baking dish. Sauté green onions and garlic with ginger and pepper in drippings in skillet. Stir in beef bouillon, soy sauce, vinegar, water and brown sugar. Add to beef; liquid should cover beef. Place onion slices, green pepper, celery and carrot on top. Bake at 350 degrees for 1 hour. Serve over rice. May refrigerate, covered, overnight before baking. I bake rice at the same time in oven, allowing an additiional 15 minutes cooking time.
Yield: 6 servings.

Approx Per Serving: Cal 341; Prot 24 g; Carbo 26 g; Fiber 3 g; T Fat 16 g; Chol 64 mg; Sod 831 mg.

Doris G. Miller, Central

MARINATED SHISH KABOBS

½ cup oil
1 tablespoon cider vinegar
2 tablespoons fresh lemon juice
2 tablespoons finely chopped onion
1 small clove of garlic, minced
1 teaspoon chili powder
½ teaspoon poultry seasoning
½ teaspoon oregano
½ teaspoon ginger
2 teaspoons salt
¼ teaspoon pepper
2 pounds sirloin steak cubes
12 cherry tomatoes
12 small onions
2 green bell peppers, cut into 1-inch pieces

Combine oil, vinegar, lemon juice, chopped onion, garlic, chili powder, poultry seasoning, oregano, ginger, salt and pepper in bowl. Add steak cubes; mix well. Marinate in refrigerator overnight or at room temperature for 3 to 4 hours. Thread steak cubes on skewers alternately with cherry tomatoes, small onions and green pepper pieces. Grill for 15 to 20 minutes or until done to taste, turning frequently. Serve with rice or baked potatoes for a complete meal. Yield: 6 servings.

Approx Per Serving: Cal 432; Prot 31 g; Carbo 16 g; Fiber 4 g; T Fat 28 g; Chol 85 mg; Sod 765 mg.
Nutritional information includes entire amount of marinade.

Wilma Burleson, Independence

MAKE-A-MEAL SOUP

1 1/2 pounds boneless beef chuck, cut into cubes
3 cups water
1 small clove of garlic, minced
1 bay leaf
1 teaspoon salt
1/4 teaspoon pepper
2 stalks celery, sliced
2 carrots, sliced
1 onion, chopped
1/4 head cabbage, chopped
3 tablespoons uncooked rice
1 16-ounce can red beans, drained
1 15-ounce can tomato sauce

Combine beef with water, garlic, bay leaf, salt and pepper in large saucepan. Bring to a boil; reduce heat. Skim broth. Simmer, covered, for 1 1/2 hours or until beef is almost tender. Add celery, carrots, onion, cabbage, rice, beans and tomato sauce; mix well. Simmer for 30 minutes longer. Remove bay leaf. Yield: 6 servings.

Approx Per Serving: Cal 468; Prot 41 g; Carbo 61 g; Fiber 19 g; T Fat 7 g; Chol 64 mg; Sod 859 mg.

Wilma Burleson, Independence

☎ Wine and tomatoes as cooking liquid for cheaper cuts of meat act to break down tough fibers.

BEEF STEW

2 pounds beef chuck
2 tablespoons oil
3 carrots, chopped
3 potatoes, chopped
1 cup water
1 clove of garlic, minced
3 onions, cut into quarters
1 teaspoon Worcestershire sauce
1 teaspoon paprika
1 bay leaf
Salt to taste
1/2 teaspoon pepper

Cut beef into 1 1/2-inch cubes. Brown in oil in skillet. Combine with carrots, potatoes, water, garlic, onions, Worcestershire sauce, paprika, bay leaf, salt and pepper in Crock•Pot; mix well. Cook on Low for 10 to 12 hours or on High for 5 to 6 hours or until tender. Remove bay leaf. May precook carrots and potatoes partially to ensure tenderness. May add peas, celery and tomatoes if desired. Yield: 6 servings.

Approx Per Serving: Cal 392; Prot 32 g; Carbo 35 g; Fiber 5 g; T Fat 14 g; Chol 85 mg; Sod 77 mg.

Martha G. Bridges, Hornets Nest

HEARTY BEEF STEW

4 pounds boneless beef chuck, trimmed
1/2 cup flour
2 teaspoons salt
1/4 cup oil
5 cups beef broth
1 cup dry red wine
3 tablespoons tomato paste
2 teaspoons minced garlic
2 1 1/2-inch bay leaves
2 teaspoons thyme
2 teaspoons marjoram
1 1/2 pounds carrots, cut into 1-inch pieces
1 1/4 pounds small white turnips, cut into 1-inch wedges
2 large onions, cut into wedges
1 16-ounce package frozen cut green beans
1 pound fresh small mushrooms, cut into halves

Cut beef into 1 1/4-inch pieces. Coat with mixture of flour and salt, shaking to remove excess. Heat oil over medium-high heat in heavy 5 to 6-quart saucepan. Cook beef 1/3 at a time until brown on all sides, removing to bowl with slotted spoon. Drain saucepan. Return beef to saucepan. Add beef broth, wine, tomato paste, garlic, bay leaves, thyme and marjoram; mix well.

Bring to a boil; reduce heat. Simmer, covered, for 1 hour. Add carrots, turnips and onions. Simmer, covered, for 45 minutes or until carrots are almost tender. Add green beans and mushrooms. Simmer, covered, for 45 minutes or until vegetables and beef are tender, stirring occasionally. Remove bay leaves. Yield: 12 servings.

Approx Per Serving: Cal 348; Prot 33 g; Carbo 20 g; Fiber 5 g; T Fat 14 g; Chol 85 mg; Sod 790 mg.

Bobbie Finney, Hornets Nest

FIVE-HOUR STEW

2 pounds beef cubes
1 cup chopped celery
3 medium onions, sliced
6 carrots, chopped
3 cups chopped potatoes
3 tablespoons Minute tapioca
1 cup tomato juice
1 slice bread, torn
1 tablespoon sugar
3 bay leaves
1/2 teaspoon salt
Pepper to taste

Combine beef, celery, onions, carrots, potatoes, tapioca, tomato juice, bread, sugar, bay leaves, salt and pepper in 2-quart baking dish; mix well. Bake at 250 degrees for 5 hours. Remove bay leaves. Yield: 6 servings.

Approx Per Serving: Cal 414; Prot 33 g; Carbo 50 g; Fiber 7 g; T Fat 9 g; Chol 85 mg; Sod 447 mg.

Lillian Powers, Asheville

STEWED BEEF IN WINE SAUCE

1 pound stew beef
1 can cream of mushroom soup
1 envelope onion soup mix
1 cup red wine
1 4-ounce jar mushrooms

Combine beef, soup, soup mix, wine and mushrooms in baking dish; mix well. Bake at 325 degrees for 3 hours. Serve over rice or noodles. Yield: 3 servings.

Approx Per Serving: Cal 375; Prot 31 g; Carbo 12 g; Fiber 1 g; T Fat 17 g; Chol 86 mg; Sod 1243 mg.

Kim Parker, Central

VEAL PICCATA

8 2-ounce veal cutlets
½ cup flour
Salt and pepper to taste
¼ cup butter
Juice of 1 lemon
¼ cup dry white wine
2 tablespoons capers
2 tablespoons butter
1 lemon, sliced

Pound veal with meat mallet; coat with mixture of flour, salt and pepper, shaking off excess. Brown in ¼ cup butter in large skillet over medium heat for 2 minutes on each side. Remove to warm platter. Add lemon juice and wine to skillet, stirring with wooden spoon to deglaze. Add capers. Add 2 tablespoons butter, stirring just until butter is well mixed; remove from heat. Pour over veal. Garnish with lemon slices. Serve immediately. Yield: 4 servings.

Approx Per Serving: Cal 349; Prot 25 g; Carbo 14 g; Fiber 1 g; T Fat 21 g; Chol 140 mg; Sod 204 mg.

Murl F. Morris, Independence

BRUNSWICK STEW

1½ pounds lean stew beef
2½ pounds chicken pieces
1½ pounds lean pork
6 cups chopped tomatoes
4 cups chopped potatoes
2 cups butter beans
2 cups corn
1 cup finely chopped onion
¼ cup catsup
¼ cup vinegar
2 tablespoons Worcestershire sauce
1 tablespoon sugar
Salt and cayenne pepper to taste

Cook beef, chicken and pork in water to cover in saucepan until tender. Drain saucepan, reserving broth. Cool and shred meat. Cook tomatoes, potatoes, beans, corn and onion in reserved broth in saucepan until tender. Add meat, catsup, vinegar, Worcestershire sauce, sugar, salt and cayenne pepper. Simmer for 1½ hours or to desired consistency. Chill for several days and reheat for best flavor. May substitute canned vegetables for fresh if preferred. Yield: 16 servings.

Approx Per Serving: Cal 313; Prot 31 g; Carbo 29 g; Fiber 5 g; T Fat 8 g; Chol 82 mg; Sod 144 mg.

Joyce Pruitt, Independence

GROUND BEEF

DOTTIE'S BROCCOLI AND GROUND BEEF CASSEROLE

2 pounds lean ground beef
1 small onion, chopped
2 10-ounce packages frozen chopped broccoli
1 can cream of mushroom soup
1 soup can milk
Garlic powder, salt and pepper to taste
4 cups cooked rice
3 cups shredded Cheddar cheese

Brown ground beef with onion in skillet, stirring until ground beef is crumbly; drain. Cook broccoli using package directions; drain. Combine soup with milk, garlic powder, salt and pepper in bowl; mix well. Layer ground beef, rice, soup, broccoli and cheese 1/2 at a time in baking dish. Bake at 350 degrees for 30 to 40 minutes or until heated through. Serve with ambrosia, rolls and iced tea. Yield: 8 servings.

Approx Per Serving: Cal 518; Prot 38 g; Carbo 35 g; Fiber 3 g; T Fat 25 g; Chol 114 mg; Sod 639 mg.

Jenette M. Everett, Central

GROUND BEEF AND CABBAGE CASSEROLE

1 pound lean ground beef
1/2 cup uncooked rice
1 medium head cabbage, chopped
2 cans tomato soup
2 cups water
1 tablespoon salt

Brown ground beef in skillet, stirring until crumbly; drain. Layer ground beef, rice and cabbage in baking dish. Combine soup with water in bowl; mix well. Pour over layers; sprinkle with salt. Bake at 350 degrees for 30 minutes. Yield: 4 servings.

Approx Per Serving: Cal 352; Prot 26 g; Carbo 43 g; Fiber 3 g; T Fat 9 g; Chol 64 mg; Sod 2706 mg.

Gail Blevins, Blue Ridge

BEEFY CABBAGE WEDGE MEAL

1 small head cabbage
1 cup chopped onion
1/4 cup uncooked rice
1 pound ground beef
2 cups canned tomatoes
1 cup hot water
2 teaspoons salt
Pepper to taste

Remove outer leaves of cabbage; cut cabbage into 6 to 8 wedges. Place in buttered baking dish. Sprinkle onion and rice between wedges. Crumble ground beef between wedges. Combine tomatoes, water, salt and pepper in bowl; mix well. Pour over casserole. Bake, covered, at 350 degrees for 1 1/2 hours. Yield: 6 servings.

Approx Per Serving: Cal 162; Prot 16 g; Carbo 14 g; Fiber 2 g; T Fat 5 g; Chol 43 mg; Sod 873 mg.

Evelyn N. Goodman, Hornets Nest

CORN PONE CASSEROLE

1 pound ground chuck
1 medium onion, chopped
1 10-ounce can whole kernel corn, drained
1 16-ounce can tomatoes
1 16-ounce can chili hot beans
1 teaspoon chili powder
Salt and pepper to taste
Topping

Brown ground chuck with onion in large heavy skillet, stirring until ground beef is crumbly; drain. Add corn, tomatoes, beans, chili powder, salt and pepper; mix well. Simmer for 10 minutes. Spoon into 2-quart baking dish. Spread topping over casserole. Bake at 375 degrees for 40 minutes or until brown. Yield: 6 servings.

Topping for Corn Pone Casserole

1 cup self-rising cornmeal
1 egg
2/3 cup milk

Combine cornmeal, egg and milk in bowl; mix until smooth.

Approx Per Serving: Cal 433; Prot 26 g; Carbo 35 g; Fiber 12 g; T Fat 14 g; Chol 89 mg; Sod 284 mg.

Mrs. Frank Englebert, Independence

BEEFY MEXICAN CORN BREAD CASSEROLE

1 pound ground beef
1 cup self-rising cornmeal
2 eggs
1 cup milk
1 16-ounce can cream-style corn
1/4 cup oil
3/4 teaspoon salt
1 large onion, chopped
2 cups shredded Cheddar cheese

Brown ground beef in skillet, stirring until crumbly; drain. Combine cornmeal, eggs, milk, corn, oil and salt in bowl; mix well. Pour half the corn bread batter into greased large cast-iron skillet sprinkled with additional cornmeal. Layer ground beef, onion and cheese in prepared skillet. Top with remaining batter. Bake at 350 degrees for 45 minutes or until brown. Yield: 4 servings.

Approx Per Serving: Cal 876; Prot 45 g; Carbo 54 g; Fiber 6 g; T Fat 54 g; Chol 248 mg; Sod 1200 mg.

Martha G. Bridges, Hornets Nest

☎ Try these tips for hamburger magic:

- Shape patties around cubes of cheese.
- Sprinkle patties with shredded cheese and crumbled crisp-fried bacon.
- Top patties with horseradish and garlic salt.
- Simmer patties in spaghetti sauce.
- Spread hamburger buns with mixture of cream cheese and chives.
- Add catsup, green bell peppers and green onions to patties.
- Add pineapple juice, soy sauce, brown sugar and ginger to patties. Top with pineapple slices.
- Add wheat germ to patties for a nutty flavor.
- Top patties with Chinese sweet and sour sauce.

GROUND BEEF AND GREEN BEAN CASSEROLE

1 pound ground beef
4 potatoes, sliced
1 16-ounce can French-style green beans, drained
1 onion, sliced
Salt and pepper to taste
1 can tomato soup

Brown ground beef in skillet, stirring until crumbly; drain. Alternate layers of ground beef, potatoes, green beans and onion in baking dish until all ingredients are used, seasoning with salt and pepper to taste. Spoon tomato soup over top. Bake at 350 degrees for 1½ hours. Yield: 4 servings.

Approx Per Serving: Cal 537; Prot 29 g; Carbo 69 g; Fiber 7 g; T Fat 18 g; Chol 74 mg; Sod 896 mg.

Mrs. Larry Pridgen, Central

CHILI MACARONI AND CHEESE

1 pound ground beef
½ cup milk
1 cup soft bread crumbs
1 teaspoon salt
Pepper to taste
2 tablespoons shortening
1 clove of garlic, minced
¼ cup chopped onion
2 cans chili beef soup
1 soup can water
7 ounces uncooked mostaccioli
½ cup Parmesan cheese

Combine ground beef, milk, bread crumbs, salt and pepper in bowl; mix well. Shape into 5 oblong patties. Brown in shortening in electric skillet set at 350 degrees; remove to plate. Add garlic and onion to skillet. Sauté until tender but not brown. Stir in soup and water. Add beef patties. Bring to a boil; reduce heat. Simmer, covered, for 15 minutes. Cook pasta using package directions; drain. Place in serving dish. Arrange beef patties over pasta. Pour soup mixture over top; sprinkle with cheese. Yield: 5 servings.

Approx Per Serving: Cal 612; Prot 33 g; Carbo 56 g; Fiber 3 g; T Fat 28 g; Chol 81 mg; Sod 1647 mg.

J.A. Kelly, Raleigh

CHUCK WAGON SURPRISE

1 pound ground beef
1 large onion, chopped
1 green bell pepper, chopped
8 ounces elbow macaroni, cooked, drained
1 32-ounce jar chunky spaghetti sauce
2 cups shredded sharp Cheddar cheese

Brown ground beef with onion and green pepper in saucepan, stirring until ground beef is crumbly; drain. Add macaroni, spaghetti sauce and cheese; mix well. Simmer until heated through. Serve with salad and garlic bread. Yield: 8 servings.

Approx Per Serving: Cal 467; Prot 24 g; Carbo 42 g; Fiber 3 g; T Fat 23 g; Chol 67 mg; Sod 772 mg.

Sybil P. Peele, Hornets Nest

MACARONI PIZZA CASSEROLE

2 pounds lean ground beef
1 cup chopped onion
8 ounces small elbow macaroni, cooked, drained
1 16-ounce can tomato sauce
1/4 cup water
1/4 teaspoon oregano
1/2 teaspoon garlic salt
2 cups shredded mozzarella cheese
4 ounces pepperoni, sliced

Brown ground beef with onion in skillet, stirring until ground beef is crumbly; drain. Layer ground beef, macaroni and tomato sauce in 2-quart baking dish. Pour mixture of water, oregano and garlic salt over layers. Top with cheese and pepperoni. Bake at 375 degrees for 20 to 30 minutes or until heated through. Serve with salad and French bread. Yield: 8 servings.

Approx Per Serving: Cal 509; Prot 34 g; Carbo 28 g; Fiber 2 g; T Fat 29 g; Chol 101 mg; Sod 932 mg.

Shirley Hinson, Hornets Nest

PIZZA CASSEROLE

1 pound ground beef
1 1/2 cups chopped onions
1 1/2 cups macaroni, cooked, drained
1 15-ounce can tomato sauce with tomato bits
1/4 cup water
1/2 teaspoon basil
1/4 teaspoon oregano
1/2 teaspoon garlic salt
2 cups shredded mozzarella cheese

Brown ground beef with onions in skillet, stirring until ground beef is crumbly; drain. Add macaroni, tomato sauce, water, basil, oregano and garlic salt; mix well. Layer ground beef mixture and cheese 1/2 at a time in 2-quart baking dish. Bake at 375 degrees for 20 to 25 minutes or until heated through. Yield: 6 servings.

Approx Per Serving: Cal 337; Prot 27 g; Carbo 20 g; Fiber 2 g; T Fat 17 g; Chol 71 mg; Sod 819 mg.

Barbara Morris, Salem

GROUND BEEF CASSEROLE

8 ounces uncooked macaroni
1 large onion, chopped
1/4 cup margarine
1 pound ground beef
1 teaspoon salt
1/2 teaspoon pepper
1 cup shredded sharp Cheddar cheese
1 can tomato soup
1 cup milk
1/2 cup bread crumbs
2 tablespoons melted margarine

Cook macaroni using package directions; drain. Sauté onion in 1/4 cup margarine in skillet. Add ground beef, salt and pepper. Cook until ground beef is brown and crumbly, stirring frequently; drain. Layer macaroni, ground beef mixture and cheese in baking dish. Combine soup and milk in bowl; mix well. Pour over layers. Top with mixture of bread crumbs and 2 tablespoons margarine. Bake at 400 degrees for 30 minutes. Yield: 8 servings.

Approx Per Serving: Cal 453; Prot 20 g; Carbo 34 g; Fiber 2 g; T Fat 28 g; Chol 56 mg; Sod 778 mg.

Louise W. Hinson, Hornets Nest

SKILLET MACARONI AND GROUND BEEF

1 1/2 pounds ground beef
2 cups uncooked elbow macaroni
1/2 cup minced onion
1/2 cup chopped green bell pepper
1 cup water
2 8-ounce cans tomato sauce
1 1/2 tablespoons Worcestershire sauce
1 teaspoon salt
1/4 teaspoon pepper

Brown ground beef in large skillet, stirring until crumbly. Remove ground beef with slotted spoon; reserve drippings. Sauté macaroni, onion and green pepper in drippings in skillet. Add remaining ingredients. Simmer, covered, for 25 to 30 minutes or until macaroni is tender. Yield: 6 servings.

Approx Per Serving: Cal 402; Prot 27 g; Carbo 36 g; Fiber 3 g; T Fat 17 g; Chol 74 mg; Sod 915 mg.

Evelyn Clemmer, Hornets Nest

MEXICAN GROUND BEEF DELIGHT

1 1/2 pounds ground beef
1 onion, chopped
1 small green bell pepper, chopped
8 ounces uncooked narrow egg noodles
Salt to taste
1 16-ounce can tomatoes
1 16-ounce can whole kernel corn
1 can tomato soup
1 can cream of mushroom soup
1 8-ounce can tomato sauce
Garlic salt and pepper to taste
1/2 cup shredded Cheddar cheese

Brown ground beef with onion and green pepper in large electric skillet, stirring until ground beef is crumbly; drain. Cook noodles in salted water using package directions; drain. Add to ground beef. Stir in tomatoes, corn, soups, tomato sauce, garlic salt and pepper; mix well. Spoon into baking dish. Bake at 350 degrees for 25 minutes. Sprinkle with cheese. Bake for 5 minutes longer. Yield: 8 servings.

Approx Per Serving: Cal 450; Prot 25 g; Carbo 45 g; Fiber 3 g; T Fat 20 g; Chol 63 mg; Sod 1066 mg.

Phyllis Jones, Independence

ROMAN HOLIDAY

1 pound ground beef
1/4 cup chopped onion
1   15-ounce can spaghetti in tomato sauce with cheese
1/2 cup shredded Cheddar cheese

Brown ground beef with onion in skillet, stirring until ground beef is crumbly; drain. Add spaghetti. Spoon into 10x10-inch baking dish. Sprinkle with cheese. Bake at 350 degrees for 30 minutes. This recipe is from the 1930's Depression days. Serve with green vegetable or salad. Yield: 4 servings.

Approx Per Serving: Cal 371; Prot 27 g; Carbo 18 g; Fiber 1 g; T Fat 22 g; Chol 90 mg; Sod 559 mg.

Margaret B. Greene, Hornets Nest

QUICK PEPPERONI SPAGHETTI

1 pound ground beef
1 large onion, chopped
1 green bell pepper, chopped
3 ounces pepperoni, chopped
1   32-ounce jar spaghetti sauce with mushrooms
12 ounces uncooked spaghetti
1 cup shredded mozzarella cheese
1 tablespoon Parmesan cheese

Brown ground beef with onion, green pepper and pepperoni in large skillet, stirring until ground beef is crumbly; drain. Add spaghetti sauce. Bring to a boil; reduce heat. Simmer, covered, for 20 minutes, stirring occasionally. Cook spaghetti using package directions, omitting salt; drain. Place on ovenproof platter. Spoon ground beef mixture over top. Sprinkle with mozzarella cheese. Bake at 400 degrees for 3 to 5 minutes. Top with Parmesan cheese. Serve immediately. Yield: 6 servings.

Approx Per Serving: Cal 668; Prot 31 g; Carbo 70 g; Fiber 5 g; T Fat 29 g; Chol 70 mg; Sod 1172 mg.

Virginia Barnette, Hornets Nest

EASY SPAGHETTI

1 pound ground beef
1 32-ounce jar zesty Italian spaghetti sauce
16 ounces uncooked spaghetti
2 cups shredded mozzarella cheese

Brown ground beef in skillet, stirring until crumbly; drain. Stir in spaghetti sauce. Cook spaghetti using package directions; drain. Spoon into 9x13-inch baking dish. Pour sauce over top. Sprinkle with cheese. Bake at 350 degrees until cheese melts. Yield: 6 servings.

Approx Per Serving: Cal 704; Prot 34 g; Carbo 82 g; Fiber 5 g; T Fat 27 g; Chol 79 mg; Sod 936 mg.

Kitty Pennell, Hornets Nest

GROUND BEEF AND POTATO CASSEROLE

1 pound ground beef
1 tablespoon shortening
3/4 cup boiling water
1 small onion, finely chopped
1/2 teaspoon salt
1/4 teaspoon pepper
1 can cream of mushroom soup
6 medium potatoes, thinly sliced

Brown ground beef in shortening in skillet, stirring until crumbly; drain. Add boiling water, onion, salt and pepper. Simmer for 5 minutes. Mix soup and a small amount of boiling water in bowl. Layer potatoes, ground beef mixture and soup mixture 1/2 at a time in 1 1/2-quart casserole. Bake at 350 degrees for 1 hour. May add additional water for desired consistency.
Yield: 5 servings.

Approx Per Serving: Cal 541; Prot 24 g; Carbo 68 g; Fiber 6 g; T Fat 20 g; Chol 60 mg; Sod 778 mg.

Eva Peguese, Central

STUFFED PEPPERS

1 pound ground beef
1 medium onion, chopped
1 8-ounce can corn
2 cups cooked rice
1/2 teaspoon garlic salt
1/4 teaspoon salt
1/4 teaspoon pepper
1 15-ounce can tomato sauce
5 large green bell peppers
1 cup shredded Cheddar cheese

Brown ground beef in skillet, stirring until crumbly; drain. Add onion, corn, rice, garlic salt, salt, pepper and half the tomato sauce; mix well. Slice tops from peppers; discard seed. Spoon ground beef mixture into peppers. Place in baking dish. Top with cheese and remaining tomato sauce. Bake, covered, at 375 degrees for 50 minutes. Yield: 5 servings.

Approx Per Serving: Cal 461; Prot 28 g; Carbo 43 g; Fiber 4 g; T Fat 21 g; Chol 83 mg; Sod 1146 mg.

Donna M. King, Independence

POTATO AND GROUND BEEF MOUSSAKA

1 pound ground beef
1 large onion, sliced
1 teaspoon parsley flakes
1 teaspoon dried mint
Salt and pepper to taste
1 16-ounce can tomatoes
1 packet artificial sweetener
4 large potatoes, peeled, sliced 1/4 inch thick

Brown ground beef in saucepan, stirring until crumbly; drain. Add onion, parsley flakes, mint, salt and pepper; mix well. Sauté for 5 minutes or until onion is tender-crisp. Stir in tomatoes and artificial sweetener. Simmer for 5 to 10 minutes. Alternate layers of ground beef mixture and potatoes in large skillet, beginning and ending with ground beef; cover. Bring to the boiling point; reduce heat as low as possible. Simmer for 45 minutes to 1 hour or to desired consistency. Let stand for 15 minutes. Serve with tossed salad and garlic bread. May substitute yellow squash or zucchini for potatoes for a summer variation. May bake, covered, in casserole at 375 degrees for 1 hour if preferred. Yield: 6 servings.

Approx Per Serving: Cal 324; Prot 18 g; Carbo 39 g; Fiber 4 g; T Fat 11 g; Chol 49 mg; Sod 177 mg.

Shirley and Arky Arakelian, Foot Hills

SCALLOPED GROUND BEEF AND POTATOES

1 1/2 pounds ground beef
1 large onion, chopped
1/2 teaspoon garlic powder
1/2 teaspoon salt
Pepper to taste
4 large unpeeled potatoes, sliced
1 beef bouillon cube
1 cup boiling water
2 tablespoons margarine
1/2 cup shredded Cheddar cheese

Brown ground beef with onion, garlic powder, salt and pepper in skillet for 5 to 10 minutes, stirring frequently; drain. Arrange 1/3 of the potato slices in 2-quart baking dish. Layer ground beef mixture and remaining potato slices 1/2 at a time in dish. Dissolve bouillon cube in boiling water. Pour over layers. Dot with margarine. Bake at 425 degrees for 30 minutes. Sprinkle with cheese. Bake for 15 minutes longer. Yield: 6 servings.

Approx Per Serving: Cal 459; Prot 27 g; Carbo 36 g; Fiber 4 g; T Fat 23 g; Chol 84 mg; Sod 501 mg.

Sarah Barnes, Hornets Nest

TATER TOT AND GROUND BEEF CASSEROLE

2 pounds ground beef
1 medium onion, chopped
Salt and pepper to taste
1 can cream of mushroom soup
1/2 cup milk
1 16-ounce can French-style green beans, drained
1 3-ounce can French-fried onions
1 16-ounce package frozen Tater Tots

Brown ground beef with chopped onion in skillet, stirring until ground beef is crumbly; drain. Sprinkle with salt and pepper. Combine soup and milk in bowl; mix well. Fold in green beans. Stir in ground beef mixture. Spoon into 9x13-inch baking dish. Top with French-fried onions. Arrange single layer of Tater Tots over casserole. Bake at 350 degrees for 25 to 30 minutes or until heated through. Yield: 8 servings.

Approx Per Serving: Cal 457; Prot 25 g; Carbo 29 g; Fiber 2 g; T Fat 28 g; Chol 80 mg; Sod 963 mg.

Gladys Hinson, Independence

GROUND BEEF AND RICE CASSEROLE

1 pound lean ground beef
½ green bell pepper, chopped
3 onions, chopped
4 cups canned tomatoes
½ cup uncooked rice
2 teaspoons chili powder
Garlic to taste
Salt to taste

    Brown ground beef with green pepper and onions in skillet, stirring until ground beef is crumbly; drain. Add tomatoes, rice, chili powder, garlic and salt; mix well. Simmer for 5 minutes. Spoon into baking dish. Bake at 350 degrees for 1 hour. Garnish with sour cream. Yield: 5 servings.

Approx Per Serving: Cal 327; Prot 21 g; Carbo 31 g; Fiber 4 g;
   T Fat 14 g; Chol 59 mg; Sod 377 mg.

Pat Williams, Raleigh

EASY CHILI

1 pound ground round
1 teaspoon chili powder
Salt and pepper to taste
1 cup (about) catsup

    Brown ground round in skillet, stirring until crumbly; drain. Add chili powder, salt and pepper. Add enough catsup to make of desired consistency; mix well. May add a small amount of water if desired. Yield: 2 servings.

Approx Per Serving: Cal 609; Prot 45 g; Carbo 35 g; Fiber 3 g;
   T Fat 33 g; Chol 148 mg; Sod 1565 mg.

Wilma Sain, Foot Hills

☎ Spoon chili into parboiled green bell peppers and bake at 350 degrees for 20 minutes for Stuffed Green Peppers. Spoon into hollowed-out individual French loaves and bake until heated through for Stuffed French Loaves.

ALARM CHILI

- 1 pound extra-lean ground beef
- 1 medium onion, finely chopped
- 3 cloves of garlic, finely chopped
- 1 large green bell pepper, cut into 1/2-inch pieces
- 2 28-ounce cans tomatoes, crushed
- 1 tablespoon oil
- 2 teaspoons oregano
- 2 teaspoons cumin
- 3 tablespoons chili powder
- 2 tablespoons baking cocoa
- 2 teaspoons sugar
- 1 teaspoon crushed hot pepper
- 1 teaspoon Tabasco sauce
- 1 15-ounce can kidney beans, rinsed, drained

Cook ground beef in 2 1/2-quart saucepan over medium heat for 6 to 8 minutes or until well done, stirring until crumbly. Remove ground beef with slotted spoon to paper towels to drain. Drain and wipe saucepan. Sauté onion, garlic and green pepper with 1/2 cup tomatoes in oil in saucepan for 3 minutes. Add oregano, cumin, chili powder, cocoa, sugar, hot pepper and Tabasco sauce. Cook for 3 minutes. Add beans, ground beef and remaining tomatoes. Simmer for 25 minutes. Yield: 8 servings.

Approx Per Serving: Cal 255; Prot 18 g; Carbo 25 g; Fiber 8 g; T Fat 11 g; Chol 37 mg; Sod 360 mg.

Phyllis Jones, Independence

☎ Spoon chili over crushed taco chips and sprinkle with shredded lettuce, chopped tomatoes, green chilies and shredded cheese for Mexican Stack-Ups.

CHASEN'S FAMOUS CHILI

8 ounces dried pinto beans
2 16-ounce cans tomatoes
1 pound green bell peppers, coarsely chopped
1½ tablespoons oil
1½ pounds onions, coarsely chopped
2 cloves of garlic, crushed
½ cup chopped parsley
2½ pounds ground chuck
1 pound lean ground pork
¼ cup margarine
⅓ cup chili powder
1½ teaspoons cumin
2 tablespoons salt
1½ teaspoons pepper

Combine beans with enough water to cover by 2 inches in large saucepan. Soak overnight. Simmer, covered, in same water until tender. Add tomatoes. Simmer for 5 minutes. Sauté green peppers in oil in large skillet over low heat for 5 minutes. Add onions. Cook until tender, stirring frequently. Add garlic and parsley. Sauté ground chuck and pork in margarine in skillet for 15 minutes. Add to sautéed vegetables. Stir in chili powder. Cook for 10 minutes. Add to beans. Season with cumin, salt and pepper. Simmer, covered, for 1 hour. Simmer, uncovered, for 30 minutes longer; skim surface. Yield: 12 servings.

Approx Per Serving: Cal 413; Prot 32 g; Carbo 23 g; Fiber 8 g; T Fat 23 g; Chol 85 mg; Sod 1348 mg.

John E. Miles, Independence

RING OF FIRE CHILI

3 pounds ground chuck
2 cups coarsely chopped onions
2 tablespoons finely chopped garlic
¼ cup oil
1 teaspoon oregano
¼ cup chili powder
1 teaspoon cumin
1 teaspoon red pepper flakes
1 6-ounce can tomato paste
1 teaspoon salt
Pepper to taste
4 beef bouillon cubes
3½ cups water
½ 12-ounce can beer
3 16-ounce cans kidney beans, drained

Brown ground chuck in large skillet, stirring until crumbly; drain. Sauté onions and garlic in oil in skillet for 10 minutes. Add oregano, chili powder, cumin, red pepper, tomato paste, salt and pepper; mix well. Stir in bouillon cubes dissolved in water and beer. Add ground chuck; mix well. Simmer, covered, for 1½ hours. Add beans. Simmer for 30 minutes longer. May chill overnight and reheat for best flavor. Serve with plenty of bread and beer. Yield: 10 servings.

Approx Per Serving: Cal 533; Prot 39 g; Carbo 39 g; Fiber 14 g; T Fat 25 g; Chol 89 mg; Sod 683 mg.

Herb Poole, Hornets Nest

FAVORITE CHILI

1¼ pounds lean ground beef
1 large onion, finely chopped
¼ green bell pepper, finely chopped
1 8-ounce can tomato sauce
1 tomato sauce can water
1 envelope chili seasoning mix
2 tablespoons chili powder
1 tablespoon garlic powder
½ teaspoon cumin
¾ teaspoon oregano
½ teaspoon marjoram
1 16-ounce can tomatoes
3 16-ounce cans red kidney beans

Brown ground beef with onion and green pepper in heavy saucepan sprayed with nonstick cooking spray, stirring until ground beef is crumbly; drain. Combine tomato sauce, water, chili seasoning mix, chili powder, garlic powder, cumin, oregano and marjoram in bowl; mix well. Add to ground beef. Add tomatoes and beans; mix well. Simmer for 2½ to 3 hours or to desired consistency, stirring frequently. May add additional water if chili becomes too dry. Yield: 6 servings.

Approx Per Serving: Cal 452; Prot 32 g; Carbo 50 g; Fiber 20 g; T Fat 15 g; Chol 62 mg; Sod 1801 mg.

Agnes Williams, Independence

QUICK BEEFY CHILI BEANS

1 1/2 pounds ground beef
1 medium onion, chopped
1/2 cup chopped green bell pepper
1 can tomato soup
4 cups cooked pinto beans
1 16-ounce can whole tomatoes, chopped
1 tablespoon chili powder
1/2 teaspoon garlic powder
1 teaspoon salt
1/2 teaspoon pepper

Brown ground beef with onion and green pepper in heavy saucepan over medium heat, stirring until ground beef is crumbly; drain. Add soup, beans, undrained tomatoes, chili powder, garlic powder, salt and pepper; mix well. Reduce heat. Simmer, covered, for 1 hour, stirring occasionally. May sprinkle servings with cheese. Yield: 5 servings.

Approx Per Serving: Cal 542; Prot 39 g; Carbo 51 g; Fiber 18 g; T Fat 22 g; Chol 89 mg; Sod 1094 mg.

Jewel H. Ware, Piedmont

AUNT MARTHA'S CHINESE DISH

1 pound ground beef
1 small onion, chopped
4 sour pickles, sliced
1 16-ounce can mixed Chinese vegetables, drained
1 7-ounce can sliced water chestnuts, drained
2 tablespoons soy sauce
3 cups cooked rice
1 3-ounce can chow mein noodles

Brown ground beef with onion in saucepan, stirring until ground beef is crumbly; drain. Add pickles, mixed vegetables and water chestnuts; mix well. Stir in soy sauce. Simmer, covered, for 15 to 20 minutes or to desired consistency. Serve over rice and chow mein noodles. May add chopped cauliflower, broccoli and carrots if desired. Yield: 4 servings.

Approx Per Serving: Cal 599; Prot 32 g; Carbo 71 g; Fiber 8 g; T Fat 22 g; Chol 76 mg; Sod 1707 mg.

Linda Toms, Independence

GROUND BEEF AND VEGETABLE CHOW MEIN

1¼ pounds ground beef
1 small onion, chopped
1 can cream of mushroom soup
1 can chicken and rice soup
1 cup chopped celery
1 10-ounce package frozen mixed vegetables
1 3-ounce can chow mein noodles

Brown ground beef with onion in skillet, stirring until ground beef is crumbly; drain. Add soups, celery, mixed vegetables and half the noodles; mix well. Spoon into 2-quart baking dish. Bake at 350 degrees for 30 minutes or until bubbly. Serve with remaining noodles. Yield: 6 servings.

Approx Per Serving: Cal 363; Prot 23 g; Carbo 22 g; Fiber 3 g; T Fat 21 g; Chol 65 mg; Sod 814 mg.

Gerri Evans, Hornets Nest

CHINESE GROUND BEEF CASSEROLE

1 pound ground beef
1 10-ounce package frozen green peas and pearl onions, thawed
2 cups chopped celery
½ cup chopped onion
2 tablespoons milk
1 can cream of mushroom soup
1½ teaspoons salt
Pepper to taste
1 3-ounce can chow mein noodles

Brown ground beef in skillet, stirring until crumbly; drain. Layer ground beef and frozen peas and onions in 1½-quart baking dish. Sprinkle with celery and chopped onion. Combine milk, soup, salt and pepper in bowl; mix well. Pour over layers. Top with chow mein noodles. Bake at 375 degrees for 30 minutes. Yield: 5 servings.

Approx Per Serving: Cal 482; Prot 24 g; Carbo 42 g; Fiber 1 g; T Fat 18 g; Chol 61 mg; Sod 1417 mg.

Wilma Brinson, Raleigh

CHOW MEIN CASSEROLE

1 pound ground beef
1 medium onion, chopped
1/2 green bell pepper, chopped
1 can cream of mushroom soup
1 soup can water
1 1/2 tablespoons catsup
1 1/2 tablespoons Worcestershire sauce
Salt and pepper to taste
1 3-ounce can chow mein noodles

Brown ground beef in saucepan, stirring until crumbly; drain. Add onion and green pepper. Stir in soup, water, catsup, Worcestershire sauce, salt and pepper. Add noodles. Simmer until thickened to desired consistency. Yield: 4 servings.

Approx Per Serving: Cal 440; Prot 26 g; Carbo 24 g; Fiber 2 g; T Fat 27 g; Chol 77 mg; Sod 1018 mg.

Lib Livingood, Hornets Nest

JEAN'S GROUND BEEF SKILLET

1 pound lean ground beef
1 tart apple, peeled, finely chopped
1/4 cup finely chopped onion
1 1/2 teaspoons coriander
1 clove of garlic, minced
1 teaspoon turmeric
Salt to taste
1 cup frozen peas
1/4 cup water
1 cup sour cream

Brown ground beef with apple, onion, coriander, garlic, turmeric and salt in large skillet, stirring frequently; drain. Stir in peas and water. Cook, covered, for 5 minutes. Add sour cream. Cook just until heated through; do not boil. Serve over hot cooked rice. Yield: 4 servings.

Approx Per Serving: Cal 405; Prot 25 g; Carbo 14 g; Fiber 3 g; T Fat 28 g; Chol 100 mg; Sod 137 mg.

Barbara Clark, Independence

☎ Buy ground beef in quantities. Microwave in colander in bowl to catch drippings. Freeze in measured portions for later use.

TEXAS HASH

1 pound ground beef
1 medium onion, sliced into rings
1 16-ounce can tomatoes
Salt and pepper to taste
1 cup uncooked minute rice

Brown ground beef with onion in saucepan, stirring until ground beef is crumbly; drain. Add tomatoes, salt and pepper. Bring to a boil. Add rice; reduce heat. Simmer, covered, for 15 minutes. May substitute 1 can tomato soup and 1 soup can water for tomatoes if preferred. May add 1 can red kidney beans for Hungarian goulash. Yield: 4 servings.

Approx Per Serving: Cal 355; Prot 24 g; Carbo 27 g; Fiber 2 g; T Fat 16 g; Chol 74 mg; Sod 250 mg.

Gladys Hinson, Independence

MEATBALLS WITH SAUCE

1 pound ground beef
1/2 cup oats
1/2 cup evaporated milk
1/8 teaspoon salt
1/8 teaspoon pepper
Sauce

Combine ground beef, oats, evaporated milk, salt and pepper in bowl; mix well. Shape into balls. Pour sauce over meatballs in deep baking dish. Bake at 350 degrees for 1 hour. Yield: 6 servings.

Sauce for Meatballs

1/2 cup chopped green bell pepper
1/2 cup chopped onion
2 tablespoons steak sauce
1/2 cup catsup
1/2 cup water
1 1/2 tablespoons Worcestershire sauce
3 tablespoons sugar

Combine green pepper, onion, steak sauce, catsup, water, Worcestershire sauce and sugar in bowl; mix well.

Approx Per Serving: Cal 269; Prot 17 g; Carbo 22 g; Fiber 1 g; T Fat 13 g; Chol 56 mg; Sod 434 mg.

Patricia Triplett, Blue Ridge

ITALIAN MEATBALL SPAGHETTI SAUCE

- 2 16-ounce cans tomatoes
- 2 6-ounce cans tomato paste
- 1/4 cup chopped onion
- 2 tablespoons chopped parsley
- 1 clove of garlic, minced
- 2 teaspoons oregano
- 1/8 teaspoon fennel seed
- 1 teaspoon salt
- 1 cup water
- Meatballs

Combine tomatoes, tomato paste, onion, parsley, garlic, oregano, fennel seed and salt in deep saucepan. Rinse tomato paste cans with water; add to sauce. Add meatballs. Bring to a boil; reduce heat. Simmer, covered, for 1 1/2 hours or until thickened to desired consistency. Serve over hot cooked spaghetti with green salad and garlic bread. Yield: 8 servings.

Meatballs for Italian Meatball Spaghetti Sauce

- 1 egg
- 1/4 cup water
- 1/2 teaspoon basil
- 1 1/2 teaspoons salt
- 1/4 teaspoon pepper
- 1 1/2 pounds ground beef
- 1/2 cup fine dry bread crumbs
- 1/4 cup Parmesan cheese

Beat egg, water, basil, salt and pepper in bowl. Combine with crumbled ground beef, bread crumbs and cheese in large bowl; toss lightly with fork to mix. Shape into 1-inch balls. Brown on all sides in ungreased skillet over low heat; drain.

Approx Per Serving: Cal 279; Prot 21 g; Carbo 18 g; Fiber 3 g; T Fat 14 g; Chol 84 mg; Sod 782 mg.

Nancy T. Johnson, Salem

☎ Make up favorite meatball recipe and brown in skillet. Store meatballs in serving portions in plastic bags in refrigerator to be ready for busy-day meals.

PORCUPINE MEATBALLS WITH SAUCE

1 pound ground beef
1 pound ground pork
1 egg, beaten
1/2 cup milk
2/3 cup uncooked rice
1 teaspoon chili powder
2 teaspoons salt
Sauce

Combine ground beef, ground pork, egg, milk, rice, chili powder and salt in bowl; mix well. Shape into 1 1/2-inch balls. Brown on all sides in skillet. Add to sauce in saucepan; reduce heat. Simmer, covered, for 1 1/2 hours. Yield: 8 servings.

Sauce for Porcupine Meatballs

2 8-ounce cans tomato sauce
2 cups water
2 tablespoons chopped onion
1 teaspoon salt

Combine tomato sauce, water, onion and salt in saucepan. Bring to a boil.

Approx Per Serving: Cal 280; Prot 25 g; Carbo 15 g; Fiber 1 g; T Fat 13 g; Chol 100 mg; Sod 1317 mg.

Martha G. Bridges, Hornets Nest

GROUND BEEF PORCUPINES

1 pound ground beef
1/2 cup uncooked rice
2 tablespoons minced onion
1 teaspoon salt
1/4 teaspoon pepper
2 tablespoons shortening
1 can tomato soup
1 cup hot water

Combine ground beef, rice, onion, salt and pepper in bowl; mix well. Shape into 12 balls. Brown in shortening in heavy skillet; drain. Add soup and hot water. Simmer, covered, for 1 1/2 hours or until rice is tender. Yield: 6 servings.

Approx Per Serving: Cal 283; Prot 16 g; Carbo 19 g; Fiber <1 g; T Fat 16 g; Chol 49 mg; Sod 752 mg.

Joanne Tallent, Independence

MEATBALLS IN SWEET AND SOUR SAUCE

1 cup bread crumbs
1/2 cup milk
1 pound ground beef
1 1/2 tablespoons
  Worcestershire sauce
1 teaspoon salt
1 teaspoon pepper
Sauce

Mix bread crumbs with milk in bowl. Add ground beef, Worcestershire sauce, salt and pepper; mix well. Shape into 12 balls. Place in baking dish. Pour sauce over meatballs. Bake at 375 degrees for 45 minutes to 1 hour or until done to taste. Yield: 4 servings.

Sweet and Sour Sauce for Meatballs

1/4 cup vinegar
1/2 cup water
1 tablespoon brown sugar
1/2 cup catsup
1/2 cup chopped green bell pepper
1/2 cup chopped onion

Combine vinegar, water, brown sugar, catsup, green pepper and onion in bowl; mix well.

Approx Per Serving: Cal 412; Prot 26 g; Carbo 36 g; Fiber 2 g; T Fat 19 g; Chol 79 mg; Sod 1208 mg.

Gladys Hinson, Independence

SAUCY MEAT LOAF

2 slices bread
1 5-ounce can
  evaporated milk
1 pound ground chuck
1 small onion, chopped
1 egg
1 8-ounce can tomato
  sauce
Salt and pepper to taste
1 16-ounce can tomatoes

Soak bread in evaporated milk in bowl. Add ground chuck, onion, egg, tomato sauce, salt and pepper; mix well. Shape into loaf. Place in cast-iron baking pan. Pour tomatoes over top. Bake, covered, at 400 degrees for 1 hour. Yield: 5 servings.

Approx Per Serving: Cal 308; Prot 23 g; Carbo 17 g; Fiber 2 g; T Fat 17 g; Chol 110 mg; Sod 576 mg.

Gladys Smith, Hornets Nest

MINI MEAT LOAVES

2 pounds ground beef
1/4 cup dry bread crumbs
1 egg, slightly beaten
1/4 cup finely chopped onion
1 teaspoon salt
1/4 teaspoon pepper
1 can tomato soup
2 tablespoons shortening
2 tablespoons (or more) water

Combine ground beef, bread crumbs, egg, onion, salt, pepper and 1/4 cup soup in bowl; mix well. Shape into 6 miniature meat loaves. Brown in shortening in skillet; drain. Stir in remaining soup and water. Simmer, covered, for 20 minutes or until done to taste, stirring occasionally. Serve with potatoes and broccoli. Yield: 6 servings.

Approx Per Serving: Cal 411; Prot 31 g; Carbo 10 g; Fiber <1 g; T Fat 28 g; Chol 134 mg; Sod 837 mg.

Joanne Tallent, Independence

ORIENTAL MEAT LOAF

1 pound lean ground beef
1 egg, beaten
3/4 cup whole wheat bread crumbs
1/4 cup finely chopped onion
1/4 cup finely chopped green bell pepper
1/4 cup chopped water chestnuts
1/4 cup reduced-calorie catsup
1 1/2 tablespoons soy sauce
1/4 teaspoon pepper

Combine ground beef, egg, bread crumbs, onion, green pepper, water chestnuts, catsup, soy sauce and pepper in bowl; mix well. Shape into 5-inch round loaf. Place in microwave meat or bacon tray sprayed with nonstick cooking spray. Cover with heavy-duty plastic wrap. Microwave on High for 10 to 14 minutes or until done to taste, turning tray 1/2 turn after 5 minutes. Drain well; let stand for 5 minutes. Yield: 4 servings.

Approx Per Serving: Cal 303; Prot 25 g; Carbo 11 g; Fiber 1 g; T Fat 18 g; Chol 127 mg; Sod 663 mg.

Barbara Morris, Salem

BARBECUED HAMBURGERS

1 pound ground beef
1/2 cup milk
1 cup bread crumbs
Sauce

Combine ground beef, milk and bread crumbs in bowl; mix well. Shape into patties; place in baking dish. Pour sauce over patties. Bake, covered, at 350 degrees for 45 minutes. Yield: 4 servings.

Barbecue Sauce for Hamburgers

1/4 cup vinegar
1/2 cup catsup
1/2 cup water
1/2 cup chopped onion
1/2 cup chopped green bell pepper
1 1/2 teaspoons Worcestershire sauce
1 tablespoon sugar
1 teaspoon salt
1 teaspoon pepper

Combine vinegar, catsup, water, onion, green pepper, Worcestershire sauce, sugar, salt and pepper in bowl; mix well.

Approx Per Serving: Cal 421; Prot 27 g; Carbo 38 g; Fiber 3 g; T Fat 19 g; Chol 79 mg; Sod 1171 mg.

Betty S. Bryant, Hornets Nest

CREOLE BURGERS

1 pound ground beef
1/2 cup chopped onion
1 can chicken gumbo soup
1 tablespoon prepared mustard
2 tablespoons catsup
Salt and pepper to taste
6 hamburger buns
1/4 cup butter, softened

Brown ground beef with onion in skillet, stirring until ground beef is crumbly; drain. Add soup, prepared mustard, catsup, salt and pepper; mix well. Simmer for 5 to 10 minutes or until flavors are blended, stirring occasionally. Toast and butter buns. Serve ground beef mixture on buns. May top with lettuce if desired. Yield: 6 servings.

Approx Per Serving: Cal 384; Prot 19 g; Carbo 29 g; Fiber 2 g; T Fat 17 g; Chol 71 mg; Sod 793 mg.

Polly Mabrey, Hornets Nest

BURGER BUNDLES

1 cup herb-seasoned stuffing mix
1 pound ground beef
1/3 cup evaporated milk
1 tablespoon catsup
1 can cream of mushroom soup
2 teaspoons Worcestershire sauce

Prepare stuffing mix using package directions. Combine ground beef with evaporated milk in bowl; mix well. Shape into five 6-inch patties on waxed paper. Spoon 1/4 cup stuffing into center of each patty. Fold edges of patties over to enclose filling; seal edges. Place in 1 1/2-quart baking dish. Combine catsup, soup and Worcestershire sauce in saucepan. Heat to the boiling point. Pour over patties. Bake at 350 degrees for 45 to 50 minutes or until done to taste. Yield: 5 servings.

Approx Per Serving: Cal 445; Prot 25 g; Carbo 41 g; Fiber <1 g; T Fat 20 g; Chol 65 mg; Sod 1398 mg.

Nancy Riley, Independence

EASY PATTIES

1 pound ground beef
2 eggs
20 crackers, crushed
1 onion, chopped
1/2 cup catsup

Combine ground beef, eggs, cracker crumbs, onion and catsup in bowl; mix well. Shape into patties. Cook in skillet or on grill until done to taste. Yield: 6 servings.

Approx Per Serving: Cal 255; Prot 17 g; Carbo 15 g; Fiber 1 g; T Fat 14 g; Chol 124 mg; Sod 433 mg.

Deni Dumford, Piedmont

☎ Rinse and save flat styrofoam meat trays to place between layers of ground beef patties in the freezer. The desired number of frozen patties can be easily removed when needed.

SALISBURY STEAKS

1½ pounds lean ground beef
Garlic powder, onion powder, salt and pepper to taste
1 tablespoon oil
1 large onion, sliced into rings
2 tablespoons flour
1½ cups water

Shape ground beef into 8 patties; sprinkle with garlic powder, onion powder, salt and pepper. Brown lightly on both sides in oil in skillet; remove to 11x14-inch baking dish. Top with onion rings. Add flour and water to drippings in skillet, stirring to deglaze. Cook until thickened, stirring constantly. Pour over patties. Bake at 325 degrees for 45 minutes. Serve with mashed potatoes and green peas. Yield: 8 servings.

Approx Per Serving: Cal 202; Prot 16 g; Carbo 3 g; Fiber <1 g; T Fat 14 g; Chol 56 mg; Sod 49 mg.

Ann Corley, Central

EASY COMPANY LASAGNA

1 pound ground beef
1 32-ounce jar thick spaghetti sauce
1½ cups water
2 cups ricotta cheese
3 cups shredded mozzarella cheese
½ cup Parmesan cheese
2 eggs
¼ cup chopped parsley
1 teaspoon salt
¼ teaspoon pepper
8 ounces uncooked lasagna noodles

Brown ground beef in 3-quart saucepan, stirring until crumbly; drain. Add spaghetti sauce and water; mix well. Simmer for 10 minutes. Combine cheeses, eggs, parsley, salt and pepper in bowl; mix well. Spread 1 cup meat sauce in 9x13-inch baking dish. Layer 3 uncooked noodles, 1½ cups meat sauce and half the cheese mixture in prepared dish. Repeat layers. Top with layer of noodles and remaining meat sauce. Bake, covered with foil, at 350 degrees for 55 minutes to 1 hour. Bake, uncovered, for 10 minutes longer or until noodles are tender. Let stand for 10 minutes before cutting. Yield: 8 servings.

Approx Per Serving: Cal 567; Prot 33 g; Carbo 42 g; Fiber 1 g; T Fat 30 g; Chol 143 mg; Sod 1196 mg.

Kathy Spivey, Piedmont

LASAGNA DELUXE

- 12 ounces ground beef
- 2 cloves of garlic, finely chopped
- 1/2 cup chopped onion
- 1 6-ounce can tomato paste
- 1 8-ounce can Spanish-style tomato sauce
- 3/4 cup hot water
- 1 4-ounce can mushroom stems and pieces
- 1 tablespoon parsley flakes
- 1/2 teaspoon basil
- 3/4 teaspoon oregano
- 1/4 teaspoon red pepper flakes
- 1 1/2 teaspoons salt
- 6 uncooked lasagna noodles
- 1 egg, beaten
- 1 pound cottage cheese
- 8 ounces mozzarella cheese, thinly sliced
- 1/2 cup Parmesan cheese

Crumble ground beef into large skillet. Cook over medium heat until lightly browned, stirring occasionally; drain. Add garlic and onion. Sauté until onion is tender; drain. Stir in tomato paste, tomato sauce, water, undrained mushrooms, parsley flakes, basil, oregano, red pepper and salt. Simmer for 5 minutes. Cook noodles using package directions; drain. Mix egg with cottage cheese in bowl. Spread 1/4 of the meat sauce in 7x12-inch baking dish. Layer 3 noodles, 1/3 of the remaining meat sauce, half the cottage cheese mixture, half the mozzarella cheese and half the Parmesan cheese in prepared dish. Add layers of 1/2 of the remaining meat sauce, remaining cottage cheese mixture and mozzarella cheese. Top with remaining noodles, meat sauce and Parmesan cheese. Bake at 350 degrees for 30 minutes. May freeze before or after baking. Yield: 9 servings.

Approx Per Serving: Cal 330; Prot 25 g; Carbo 23 g; Fiber 2 g; T Fat 15 g; Chol 79 mg; Sod 986 mg.

Lowell Price, Salem

☎ When browning ground beef, invert a metal colander over the skillet. This will allow steam to escape but reduces spattering.

EASY LASAGNA

9 uncooked lasagna noodles
1 pound ground beef
1 32-ounce jar chunky mushroom and onion spaghetti sauce
1/2 cup Parmesan cheese
12 ounces cottage cheese
3 cups shredded mozzarella cheese

Cook noodles using package directions; drain. Brown ground beef in skillet, stirring until crumbly; drain. Stir in spaghetti sauce. Spread 3 spoonfuls in 9x13-inch baking dish. Layer noodles, remaining meat sauce, Parmesan cheese, cottage cheese and mozzarella cheese 1/3 at a time in prepared dish. Bake at 350 degrees for 45 minutes. Yield: 8 servings.

Approx Per Serving: Cal 545; Prot 33 g; Carbo 44 g; Fiber 1 g; T Fat 26 g; Chol 80 mg; Sod 1022 mg.

Jean Causby, Blue Ridge

LASAGNA

2 pounds ground beef
Salt and pepper to taste
2 32-ounce jars spaghetti sauce
1 pound cottage cheese
2 eggs, beaten
16 ounces uncooked lasagna noodles
1 pound mozzarella cheese, shredded
1/2 cup Parmesan cheese

Brown ground beef in skillet, stirring until crumbly; drain. Season with salt and pepper. Add spaghetti sauce; mix well. Cook until heated through. Stir in cottage cheese and eggs. Cook noodles using package directions; drain. Alternate layers of noodles, meat sauce and mozzarella cheese in baking dish. Top with Parmesan cheese. Bake at 350 degrees for 45 minutes or until cheeses melt. Yield: 8 servings.

Approx Per Serving: Cal 951; Prot 55 g; Carbo 81 g; Fiber 3 g; T Fat 45 g; Chol 184 mg; Sod 1747 mg.

Willie Collins, Independence

LASAGNA PIE

1 pound ground beef
1 6-ounce can tomato paste
1 1/2 teaspoons basil
1 teaspoon oregano
1/2 cup shredded mozzarella cheese
1/2 cup cream-style cottage cheese
1/4 cup Parmesan cheese
Topping
1/2 cup shredded mozzarella cheese

Brown ground beef in skillet, stirring until crumbly; drain. Add tomato paste, basil, oregano and 1/2 cup mozzarella cheese; mix well. Layer cottage cheese, Parmesan cheese and ground beef mixture in greased 10-inch pie plate. Pour topping over layers. Bake at 400 degrees for 30 to 35 minutes or until knife inserted between center and edge comes out clean. Sprinkle with 1/2 cup mozzarella cheese. Yield: 6 servings.

Topping for Lasagna Pie

2/3 cup baking mix
1 cup milk
2 eggs
1 teaspoon salt
1/4 teaspoon pepper

Combine baking mix, milk, eggs, salt and pepper in blender container or bowl. Process on high speed for 15 seconds or beat for 1 minute with rotary beater.

Approx Per Serving: Cal 383; Prot 27 g; Carbo 19 g; Fiber 1 g; T Fat 22 g; Chol 146 mg; Sod 860 mg.

Eddie Haskin, Hornets Nest

☎ Make an easy Mushroom Gravy for beef casserole from 1 can of cream of mushroom soup, 1/2 cup milk and 1 can of mushrooms.

CORN BREAD PIE

1 pound ground beef
1 large onion, chopped
1/2 cup chopped green bell
  pepper
1 can tomato soup
1 16-ounce can whole
  kernel corn, drained

2 cups water
1 tablespoon chili powder
1 teaspoon salt
3/4 teaspoon pepper
1 tablespoon bacon
  drippings
Topping

Brown ground beef with onion and green pepper in skillet, stirring until ground beef is crumbly; drain. Add soup, corn, water, chili powder, salt and pepper; mix well. Simmer for 15 minutes. Spoon into 9x13-inch baking dish greased with bacon drippings. Pour topping over ground beef mixture. Bake at 350 degrees for 30 minutes. Yield: 6 servings.

Topping for Corn Bread Pie

3/4 cup cornmeal
1 tablespoon flour
1 tablespoon sugar
1 1/2 teaspoons baking
  powder

1/8 teaspoon salt
1 egg
1/2 cup milk

Sift cornmeal, flour, sugar, baking powder and salt into bowl. Add mixture of egg and milk; mix well.

Approx Per Serving: Cal 383; Prot 20 g; Carbo 41 g; Fiber 3 g;
    T Fat 17 g; Chol 102 mg; Sod 1053 mg.

Kay L. Smith, Raleigh

☎ Serve Corn Bread Pie with salsa made by combining one 16-ounce can of tomatoes, 4 jalapeño peppers, 1 small onion, 1/2 green bell pepper and salt in food processor and pulsing until chunky.

HAMBURGER PIE

8 ounces ground beef
1/2 cup mayonnaise
1/2 cup milk
2 eggs
1 tablespoon cornstarch
1/2 teaspoon salt
1/4 teaspoon pepper
8 ounces Cheddar cheese, shredded
1 medium onion, chopped
1 unbaked 9-inch pie shell

Brown ground beef in skillet over medium heat, stirring until crumbly; drain. Combine mayonnaise, milk, eggs, cornstarch, salt and pepper in bowl; mix well. Stir in cheese, onion and ground beef. Pour into pie shell. Bake at 350 degrees for 30 to 40 minutes or until brown and set. Yield: 6 servings.

Approx Per Serving: Cal 563; Prot 21 g; Carbo 18 g; Fiber 1 g; T Fat 45 g; Chol 149 mg; Sod 753 mg.

Gladys Hinson, Independence

GROUND BEEF AND CORN PIE

1 egg
1 pound ground beef
1/4 cup milk
2 slices bread, crumbled
1 small onion, chopped
1 teaspoon Worcestershire sauce
1 teaspoon salt
Pepper to taste
1 12-ounce can whole kernel corn, drained
1 16-ounce can tomatoes, drained

Beat egg lightly in bowl. Add ground beef, milk, bread crumbs, onion, Worcestershire sauce, salt and pepper; mix well. Press into deep 9-inch pie plate to form shell. Press a second pie plate onto mixture to retain shape. Bake at 350 degrees for 5 minutes. Remove top pie plate. Combine corn and tomatoes in bowl. Pour into pie shell. Bake for 10 minutes. Reduce oven temperature to 300 degrees. Bake for 25 minutes longer. May top with green pepper strips 10 minutes before end of baking time if desired. Yield: 6 servings.

Approx Per Serving: Cal 266; Prot 19 g; Carbo 21 g; Fiber 2 g; T Fat 13 g; Chol 86 mg; Sod 725 mg.

Evelyn Furman, Hornets Nest

TAMALE PIE

1 pound ground beef
1 onion, chopped
1 cup catsup
2 cups water
1 16-ounce can whole kernel corn, drained
1 16-ounce can red kidney beans
½ green bell pepper, chopped
1 tablespoon chili powder
1 teaspoon salt
¼ teaspoon pepper
Cornmeal topping

Brown ground beef with onion in saucepan, stirring until ground beef is crumbly; drain. Add catsup, water, corn, beans, green pepper, chili powder, salt and pepper; mix well. Simmer for 15 minutes. Spoon into 2-quart baking dish. Spoon cornmeal topping over ground beef mixture. Bake at 425 degrees for 20 to 25 minutes or until brown. Yield: 6 servings.

Cornmeal Topping for Tamale Pie

¾ cup cornmeal
1 tablespoon flour
1 tablespoon baking powder
½ teaspoon salt
1 egg, beaten
⅓ cup milk
1 tablespoon melted shortening

Sift cornmeal, flour, baking powder and salt into bowl. Add egg and milk; mix well. Cut in shortening.

Approx Per Serving: Cal 440; Prot 24 g; Carbo 56 g; Fiber 10 g; T Fat 15 g; Chol 85 mg; Sod 1709 mg.

Joyce Sutton, Independence

☎ Make an easy Hamburger Pie by browning ground beef with onions and your favorite seasonings, spooning it into a frozen pie shell and topping with instant mashed potatoes. Bake until brown.

POTATO BURGER PIE

1 pound ground beef
1/4 cup chopped onion
2 eggs
1 medium potato, grated
1 8-ounce can tomato sauce
1 cup shredded Cheddar cheese
1 tablespoon Worcestershire sauce
1/2 teaspoon garlic salt
1/2 teaspoon salt
1/4 teaspoon pepper
1 partially baked 9-inch deep-dish pie shell

Brown ground beef with onion in skillet, stirring until ground beef is crumbly; drain. Add eggs, potato, tomato sauce, cheese, Worcestershire sauce, garlic salt, salt and pepper; mix well. Spoon into pie shell. Bake at 350 degrees for 45 minutes. Yield: 6 servings.

Approx Per Serving: Cal 458; Prot 24 g; Carbo 26 g; Fiber 2 g; T Fat 29 g; Chol 140 mg; Sod 971 mg.

Carolyn Austin, Independence

RAILROAD PIE

1 pound ground beef
1 large onion, chopped
1 12-ounce can whole kernel corn
1/2 cup chopped green bell pepper
1 can tomato soup
1 1/4 cups water
1 tablespoon chili powder
1 teaspoon salt
3/4 cup cornmeal mix
1 egg
1 tablespoon oil

Brown ground beef with onion in skillet, stirring until ground beef is crumbly; drain. Stir in corn, green pepper, soup, water, chili powder and salt. Simmer for 15 to 20 minutes. Pour into 2 1/2-quart baking dish. Combine cornmeal mix, egg and oil in bowl; mix well. Spoon over casserole. Bake at 350 degrees for 35 minutes or until topping is brown. Yield: 6 servings.

Approx Per Serving: Cal 344; Prot 18 g; Carbo 32 g; Fiber 2 g; T Fat 17 g; Chol 85 mg; Sod 1074 mg.

Carolyn Faulkenberry, Hornets Nest

CABBAGE AND BEEF SOUP

1 pound lean ground beef
Garlic salt, salt and pepper to taste
2 stalks celery, chopped
1 medium onion, chopped
1 16-ounce can kidney beans
1/2 head cabbage, chopped
1 29-ounce can tomatoes, crushed
2 cups water
4 beef bouillon cubes

Brown ground beef with garlic salt, salt and pepper in saucepan, stirring until crumbly; drain. Add celery, onion, beans, cabbage, tomatoes, water and bouillon cubes; mix well. Bring to a boil; reduce heat. Simmer for 1 hour. Yield: 4 servings.

Approx Per Serving: Cal 393; Prot 30 g; Carbo 32 g; Fiber 12 g; T Fat 17 g; Chol 74 mg; Sod 1681 mg.

Delores McNeeley, Independence

BEEFY NACHO CHEESE CHOWDER

8 ounces ground beef
1 green bell pepper, chopped
2 teaspoons oil
1 can nacho cheese soup
1 1/4 cups milk
1/2 cup whole kernel corn
1 medium tomato, chopped
1 teaspoon dried minced onion

Brown ground beef with green pepper in oil in large saucepan, stirring until ground beef is crumbly; drain. Stir in soup, milk, corn, tomato and onion. Simmer until heated through, stirring frequently. Yield: 4 servings.

Approx Per Serving: Cal 304; Prot 17 g; Carbo 17 g; Fiber 1 g; T Fat 19 g; Chol 65 mg; Sod 685 mg.

Gaynell Sherrill, Independence

☎ Add interest to your favorite soups with a different garnish. Try shredded cheese, grated hard-boiled egg, lemon slices, sunflower or sesame seed, a dollop of sour cream or yogurt, alfalfa sprouts or roasted nuts.

VEGETABLE BEEF SOUP

- 1½ pounds lean ground chuck
- 1 large onion, chopped
- ½ green bell pepper, chopped
- 6 potatoes, chopped, cooked
- 1 10-ounce package frozen whole kernel corn
- 3 16-ounce cans mixed corn, okra and tomatoes
- 1 32-ounce can tomato juice
- Worcestershire sauce to taste
- Garlic salt, salt and pepper to taste

Brown ground chuck with onion and green pepper in large saucepan, stirring until ground beef is crumbly; drain. Add remaining ingredients; mix well. Simmer for 2 hours or to desired consistency. Chill overnight and reheat to improve flavor. Serve with corn bread. Yield: 10 servings.

Approx Per Serving: Cal 375; Prot 20 g; Carbo 55 g; Fiber 7 g; T Fat 11 g; Chol 44 mg; Sod 559 mg.

Phyllis Jones, Independence

PORK

ROAST PORK BARBECUE

- ½ cup catsup
- 1½ cups water
- ½ cup Worcestershire sauce
- 1 medium onion, chopped
- 3 tablespoons sugar
- 3 tablespoons dry mustard
- 1 tablespoon salt
- ¼ teaspoon black pepper
- ¼ teaspoon cayenne pepper
- 1 4-pound Boston Butt pork roast

Mix catsup, water, Worcestershire sauce, onion, sugar, dry mustard, salt, black pepper and cayenne pepper in bowl. Pour over roast in roasting pan. Roast, covered, at 350 degrees for 4 hours. Let stand until cool; drain. Bone and pull roast apart; return to pan. Bake, uncovered, for 1 hour longer. Yield: 8 servings.

Approx Per Serving: Cal 379; Prot 46 g; Carbo 13 g; Fiber 1 g; T Fat 15 g; Chol 139 mg; Sod 1234 mg.

Marcie Burden, Hornets Nest

ITALIAN PORK PASTA SAUCE

1 2-pound pork loin roast
1 medium onion, finely chopped
2 cloves of garlic, crushed
2 tablespoons olive oil
2 6-ounce cans tomato paste
2 tomato paste cans water
1 28-ounce can Italian tomatoes
1 16-ounce can Italian tomatoes

Trim roast and cut into bite-sized pieces. Brown on all sides in skillet. Sauté onion and garlic in olive oil in large saucepan until onion is transparent; do not brown. Add tomato paste and water. Bring to a boil over medium heat. Add tomatoes. Bring to a boil. Add pork. Simmer for 1 1/2 to 2 hours or to desired consistency. Serve over shell macaroni with salad and garlic bread. Garnish with Parmesan cheese. May add hard-boiled eggs 30 minutes before end of cooking time if desired. Yield: 6 servings.

Approx Per Serving: Cal 355; Prot 34 g; Carbo 22 g; Fiber 5 g; T Fat 15 g; Chol 92 mg; Sod 448 mg.

Pat Pope, Hornets Nest

PORK CHOP CASSEROLE

6 boneless pork chops
6 tablespoons margarine
1 can beef consommé
1 cup uncooked rice
1 can beef consommé

Brown pork chops on both sides in skillet. Slice margarine into 8x8-inch baking dish. Add 1 can beef consommé. Sprinkle with rice. Arrange pork chops over top. Add remaining 1 can consommé. Bake, covered, at 350 degrees for 1 hour. Bake, uncovered, for 10 minutes longer. Yield: 6 servings.

Approx Per Serving: Cal 446; Prot 35 g; Carbo 25 g; Fiber <1 g; T Fat 22 g; Chol 98 mg; Sod 397 mg.

Doris Shillinglaw, Independence

HOPPING JOHN PORK CHOPS

2 slices bacon
6 4-ounce pork chops
1/2 cup chopped onion
1 clove of garlic, chopped
2 10-ounce cans mushroom gravy
1 10-ounce package frozen black-eyed peas
1/2 cup uncooked rice
1 green bell pepper, sliced into rings

Cook bacon in skillet until crisp; remove and crumble bacon. Add pork chops, onion and garlic to drippings in skillet. Cook until pork chops are brown and onion is tender. Stir in gravy and peas. Simmer, covered, for 20 minutes, stirring occasionally. Stir in rice. Cook for 25 minutes or until pork chops and rice are tender, stirring occasionally. Cook, uncovered, to desired consistency. Top with bacon and green pepper. Yield: 4 servings.

Approx Per Serving: Cal 526; Prot 45 g; Carbo 46 g; Fiber 7 g; T Fat 17 g; Chol 108 mg; Sod 948 mg.

Annie L. Feaster, Independence

PORK CHOPS AND POTATO DINNER

4 medium potatoes
2 medium onions, chopped
2 tablespoons butter
4 center-cut pork chops
Salt and pepper to taste
2 tablespoons vinegar
1/2 cup water

Peel potatoes and cut into quarters. Cook in boiling water to cover in saucepan for 1 1/2 minutes; drain. Sauté onions in butter in large skillet; remove with slotted spoon. Sprinkle pork chops on both sides with salt and pepper. Brown on both sides in drippings in skillet. Add onions. Arrange potatoes around pork chops. Add vinegar and water. Simmer, covered, for 20 to 30 minutes or until pork chops are tender, turning potatoes once to brown evenly. Serve with crisp salad. May substitute white wine for water if preferred. Yield: 4 servings.

Approx Per Serving: Cal 527; Prot 37 g; Carbo 57 g; Fiber 6 g; T Fat 17 g; Chol 113 mg; Sod 143 mg.

Peggy C. Tchecheff, Raleigh

QUICK PORK SUPPER DISH

1 pound zucchini, cut into cubes
1 clove of garlic, minced
1 large onion, chopped
8 ounces pork, cooked, chopped
1 can tomato soup
1 16-ounce can whole kernel corn, drained
1 tablespoon chili powder
1/2 cup shredded Cheddar cheese

Sauté zucchini, garlic and onion in skillet until tender. Add pork, soup, corn and chili powder; mix well. Spoon into buttered baking dish. Top with cheese. Bake at 350 degrees until brown. Serve with rice. May use leftover pork or substitute beef. Yield: 4 servings.

Approx Per Serving: Cal 317; Prot 21 g; Carbo 40 g; Fiber 4 g; T Fat 11 g; Chol 50 mg; Sod 976 mg.

Ila Mae Moses, Hornets Nest

PORK TENDERLOIN IN WINE SAUCE

10 ounces pork tenderloin
2 teaspoons flour
Garlic salt, salt and pepper to taste
1 large shallot, chopped
1/4 cup butter
1 2-ounce can sliced mushrooms, drained
1/8 teaspoon rosemary
1/4 cup dry white wine
1/4 cup chicken broth

Cut pork into 1-inch slices. Shake with mixture of flour, garlic salt, salt and pepper in plastic bag, coating well. Add pork and shallot to heated butter in skillet. Cook for 4 minutes or until brown on 1 side; turn pork. Add mushrooms and rosemary. Cook for 1 minute or until mushrooms are tender. Add mixture of wine and chicken broth. Cook for 3 minutes or until pork is tender. Yield: 3 servings.

Approx Per Serving: Cal 335; Prot 21 g; Carbo 11 g; Fiber 1 g; T Fat 22 g; Chol 99 mg; Sod 326 mg.

Gaynell Sherrill, Independence

MEXICAN PORK STEW

1 pound pork tenderloin, cut into 1-inch cubes
1 teaspoon oil
1 large onion, coarsely chopped
1 teaspoon minced garlic
1 16-ounce can tomatoes, chopped
1 green bell pepper, coarsely chopped
2 tablespoons chopped green olives
1 teaspoon capers
1 tablespoon chopped jalapeño pepper
2 tablespoons chopped parsley
1/2 teaspoon cumin
1/2 teaspoon oregano
1/4 teaspoon thyme
1/2 teaspoon salt
Freshly ground pepper to taste

Brown pork in oil in skillet over medium-high heat. Add onion and garlic. Cook for 2 minutes, stirring constantly. Add remaining ingredients; mix well. Bring to a boil; reduce heat. Simmer, covered, for 15 minutes. Yield: 4 servings.

Approx Per Serving: Cal 222; Prot 25 g; Carbo 10 g; Fiber 3 g; T Fat 10 g; Chol 70 mg; Sod 652 mg.

John E. Miles, Independence

BACON AND EGG CASSEROLE

6 slices bread
1 cup shredded Cheddar cheese
1 cup shredded Swiss cheese
12 ounces bacon, crisp-fried, crumbled
6 eggs
3 cups milk
1/2 teaspoon salt

Arrange bread in 9x13-inch baking dish. Layer Cheddar cheese, Swiss cheese and bacon over bread. Beat eggs with milk and salt in bowl. Pour over layers. Bake at 350 degrees for 35 to 40 minutes or until set. May chill overnight before baking. Yield: 8 servings.

Approx Per Serving: Cal 355; Prot 21 g; Carbo 16 g; Fiber <1 g; T Fat 23 g; Chol 211 mg; Sod 659 mg.

Deni Dumford, Piedmont

BRUNCH CASSEROLE

12 slices bread
1/2 cup butter
2 pounds bacon, crisp-fried, crumbled
2 cups shredded Cheddar cheese
8 eggs
1 quart milk
Salt and pepper to taste
1 cup crushed cornflakes

Toast bread; spread with butter. Cut toasted bread into cubes. Layer toast cubes, bacon and cheese 1/2 at a time in 9x13-inch baking dish. Beat eggs in large bowl. Add milk, salt and pepper; beat until smooth. Pour over layers. Chill overnight. Sprinkle with cornflakes. Bake at 375 degrees for 45 minutes to 1 hour or until brown and set. Yield: 12 servings.

Approx Per Serving: Cal 420; Prot 23 g; Carbo 23 g; Fiber 1 g; T Fat 36 g; Chol 344 mg; Sod 625 mg.

Irene M. Hooper, Asheville

QUICHE

1 unbaked 9-inch deep-dish pie shell
6 slices crisp-fried bacon, crumbled
1 cup shredded Swiss cheese
3 eggs, beaten
1 1/2 cups half and half
Nutmeg to taste
Salt and pepper to taste
2 tablespoons margarine

Bake pie shell at 375 degrees for 5 minutes. Sprinkle bacon into pie shell. Top with cheese. Combine eggs, half and half, nutmeg, salt and pepper in bowl; mix well. Pour over cheese. Dot with margarine. Bake at 375 degrees for 45 minutes. Yield: 8 servings.

Approx Per Serving: Cal 307; Prot 11 g; Carbo 13 g; Fiber <1 g; T Fat 24 g; Chol 114 mg; Sod 328 mg.

Nell Seegers, Independence

HUEVOS

1 medium onion, chopped
1/4 green bell pepper, chopped
2 cloves of garlic, minced
2 tablespoons chopped green olives
1 tablespoon chopped black olives
1 tablespoon oil
4 eggs
1/2 teaspoon turmeric
1 teaspoon cumin
Salt and pepper to taste
4 corn tortillas
2 cups oil
1 cup shredded Monterey Jack cheese

Sauté onion, green pepper, garlic and olives in 1 tablespoon oil in skillet over medium heat. Combine eggs, turmeric, cumin, salt and pepper in bowl; beat until smooth. Add to skillet. Cook until eggs are set, stirring constantly. Heat tortillas in 2 cups hot oil in skillet for 5 seconds on each side or until softened. Spoon egg mixture onto tortillas; fold to enclose filling. Place on ovenproof plate. Top with taco sauce and cheese. Broil until cheese melts; serve immediately. Yield: 2 servings.

Approx Per Serving: Cal 666; Prot 33 g; Carbo 46 g; Fiber 9 g; T Fat 41 g; Chol 479 mg; Sod 1346 mg.
Nutritional information does not include 2 cups oil for softening tortillas.

John E. Miles, Independence

QUICK AND EASY QUICHE

1 cup cubed ham
1/2 cup baking mix
1/2 cup melted butter
1 1/2 cups milk
3 eggs
1/4 teaspoon salt
Pepper to taste
1 cup shredded Swiss cheese

Sprinkle ham into 9-inch pie plate. Combine baking mix, butter, milk, eggs, salt and pepper in blender container; process until smooth. Pour over ham. Sprinkle with cheese. Bake at 300 degrees for 45 minutes. Let stand for several minutes.
Yield: 6 servings.

Approx Per Serving: Cal 386; Prot 16 g; Carbo 11 g; Fiber 0 g; T Fat 31 g; Chol 188 mg; Sod 736 mg.

Mrs. George W. Wray, Independence

HAMRONI

1½ tablespoons butter
1½ tablespoons flour
Salt to taste
1½ cups milk
8 ounces elbow macaroni, cooked
8 ounces ground cured ham
½ cup shredded mild Cheddar cheese
½ green bell pepper, finely chopped
½ cup milk

Blend butter, flour and salt in saucepan. Cook until bubbly. Stir in 1½ cups milk. Cook until thickened, stirring constantly. Layer macaroni, ham, cheese, green pepper and white sauce ½ at a time in greased 9x13-inch baking dish. Pour ½ cup milk over layers. Bake at 350 degrees for 30 minutes. Yield: 4 servings.

Approx Per Serving: Cal 531; Prot 27 g; Carbo 51 g; Fiber 3 g; T Fat 23 g; Chol 78 mg; Sod 849 mg.

Evelyn Clemmer, Hornets Nest

CHEESY HAM LOAF

6 slices bacon
6 eggs
¾ cup milk
1½ cups flour
2½ teaspoons baking powder
½ teaspoon salt
1 cup ½-inch cubes Monterey Jack cheese
1 cup ½-inch cubes mild Cheddar cheese
1 cup cubed cooked ham

Brown bacon lightly over medium heat in skillet; drain and crumble bacon. Beat eggs in bowl until foamy. Add milk, flour, baking powder and salt; beat until smooth. Stir in cheeses, ham and bacon. Spoon into greased and floured 5x9-inch loaf pan. Bake at 350 degrees for 50 minutes to 1 hour or until golden brown. Invert onto serving plate. Cut into slices; serve hot. Yield: 6 servings.

Approx Per Serving: Cal 453; Prot 27 g; Carbo 27 g; Fiber 1 g; T Fat 26 g; Chol 274 mg; Sod 993 mg.

Barbara Thrower, Independence

SOUTHERN BEAN AND HAM SOUP

1 1/2 cups dried Great
   Northern beans
3 1/2 quarts water
1 pound ham hocks
1 cup chopped onion
1 cup chopped celery
1 tablespoon salt
1/4 teaspoon pepper
2 cups cubed peeled
   potatoes
1 10-ounce package
   frozen chopped turnip
   greens
Red pepper sauce to taste

Bring beans and water to a boil in large saucepan. Boil for 2 minutes; remove from heat. Let stand, covered, for 1 hour. Add ham hocks, onion, celery, salt and pepper. Simmer, covered, for 1 1/2 hours. Add potatoes, turnip greens and pepper sauce. Simmer for 20 minutes or until vegetables are tender. Chop ham into small pieces; return to soup. Cook until heated through. Serve with corn bread. Yield: 8 servings.

Approx Per Serving: Cal 213; Prot 13 g; Carbo 37 g; Fiber 4 g;
   T Fat 2 g; Chol 5 mg; Sod 929 mg.

Carolyn Helms, Independence

GRILLED KIELBASA HAWAIIAN

1 pound kielbasa sausage
1 16-ounce can juice-
   pack pineapple chunks
2 tablespoons melted
   margarine

Cut sausage into bite-sized pieces. Drain pineapple, reserving juice. Alternate sausage and pineapple on skewers. Grill over medium coals until done to taste, basting with mixture of reserved pineapple juice and margarine. Yield: 4 servings.

Approx Per Serving: Cal 285; Prot 8 g; Carbo 19 g; Fiber 1 g;
   T Fat 20 g; Chol 35 mg; Sod 642 mg.

Chris and Betty Williams, Independence

☎ Chop leftover ham and add to scrambled eggs, macaroni and cheese, quiche or dried beans.

HACIENDA DINNER

1 pound pork sausage
1 cup chopped onion
1 cup chopped green bell pepper
1 16-ounce can tomatoes
½ cup barbecue sauce
1 14-ounce package deluxe macaroni and cheese dinner

Brown sausage with onion and green pepper in saucepan, stirring until sausage is crumbly; drain. Add tomatoes, barbecue sauce, uncooked macaroni and cheese sauce; mix well. Simmer, covered, for 20 minutes. Yield: 4 servings.

Approx Per Serving: Cal 650; Prot 26 g; Carbo 82 g; Fiber 2 g; T Fat 27 g; Chol 37 mg; Sod 1605 mg.

Kim Parker, Central

BREAKFAST SAUSAGE AND EGG SOUFFLÉ

1½ pounds hot pork sausage
9 eggs, slightly beaten
3 cups milk
1½ teaspoons dry mustard
1 teaspoon salt
3 slices bread, cut into ¼-inch cubes
1½ cups shredded sharp Cheddar cheese

Brown sausage in heavy skillet, stirring until crumbly; drain. Combine eggs, milk, dry mustard and salt in bowl. Stir in bread, sausage and cheese. Spoon into greased 9x13-inch baking pan. Chill, covered, overnight. Bake at 350 degrees for 1 hour. Yield: 10 servings.

Approx Per Serving: Cal 349; Prot 17 g; Carbo 9 g; Fiber <1 g; T Fat 27 g; Chol 243 mg; Sod 681 mg.

Neal Ballard, Independence

SAUSAGE AND EGG CASSEROLE

1¼ pounds pork sausage
12 eggs, beaten
4 slices bread, torn
1 cup shredded Cheddar cheese
2 cups milk
1 teaspoon dry mustard
1 teaspoon salt

Brown sausage in skillet, stirring until crumbly; drain. Combine with eggs, bread, cheese, milk, dry mustard and salt in bowl; mix well. Spoon into 2-quart baking dish. Chill overnight. Bake at 350 degrees for 45 minutes. Yield: 10 servings.

Approx Per Serving: Cal 312; Prot 16 g; Carbo 9 g; Fiber <1 g; T Fat 23 g; Chol 292 mg; Sod 629 mg.

Shirley Burns, Independence

SAUSAGE AND EGG BREAKFAST CASSEROLE

1 pound hot pork sausage
6 slices white bread, cut into cubes
6 eggs
2 cups milk
1 cup shredded sharp Cheddar cheese

Brown sausage in skillet, stirring until crumbly; drain. Layer bread cubes and sausage in 8x11-inch baking dish. Beat eggs with milk in bowl. Pour over layers. Top with cheese. Chill overnight. Bake at 350 degrees for 1 hour. Yield: 8 servings.

Approx Per Serving: Cal 321; Prot 15 g; Carbo 14 g; Fiber <1 g; T Fat 23 g; Chol 201 mg; Sod 451 mg.

Priscilla Wise, Independence

CAROLYN'S BREAKFAST SOUFFLÉ

1 pound pork sausage
4 slices bread, torn
1 cup shredded Cheddar cheese
6 eggs
2 cups milk
1 teaspoon dry mustard
1 teaspoon salt

Brown sausage in skillet, stirring until crumbly; drain. Layer bread, sausage and cheese in 9x13-inch baking dish. Combine eggs, milk, dry mustard and salt in bowl; mix well. Pour over layers. Chill, covered, overnight. Bake at 350 degrees for 35 to 40 minutes or until brown. Yield: 10 servings.

Approx Per Serving: Cal 242; Prot 12 g; Carbo 8 g; Fiber <1 g; T Fat 18 g; Chol 161 mg; Sod 545 mg.

Carolyn B. Williams, Independence

BREAKFAST CASSEROLE

6 slices bread
1 pound pork sausage
6 eggs
1½ cups milk
1 cup shredded sharp Cheddar cheese
1 teaspoon dry mustard
Salt and pepper to taste

Cut bread slices into quarters; place in greased 9x13-inch baking dish. Brown sausage in skillet, stirring until crumbly; drain. Layer over bread. Beat eggs with milk in bowl. Add cheese, dry mustard, salt and pepper; mix well. Pour over layers. Chill, covered, overnight. Place in cold oven; set oven temperature at 350 degrees. Bake for 35 minutes. Serve immediately. Yield: 8 servings.

Approx Per Serving: Cal 312; Prot 15 g; Carbo 13 g; Fiber <1 g; T Fat 22 g; Chol 199 mg; Sod 452 mg.

Carolyn Faulkenberry, Hornets Nest

BREAKFAST SAUSAGE AND CHEESE BAKE

1 8-count can crescent rolls
1 pound pork sausage
2 cups shredded mozzarella cheese
2 tablespoons chopped green bell pepper
4 eggs, beaten
3/4 cup milk
1/2 teaspoon oregano
1/8 teaspoon pepper

Line bottom and 1/2 inch up sides of 9x13-inch baking dish with roll dough; press seams to seal. Brown sausage in skillet, stirring until crumbly; drain. Sprinkle into prepared dish. Top with cheese and green pepper. Combine eggs, milk, oregano and pepper in bowl; beat until smooth. Pour over casserole. Bake at 400 degrees for 18 to 20 minutes or until set. Yield: 8 servings.

Approx Per Serving: Cal 337; Prot 15 g; Carbo 14 g; Fiber <1 g; T Fat 24 g; Chol 144 mg; Sod 584 mg.

Linda Griffin, Hornets Nest

SAUSAGE CASSEROLE

1 8-count can crescent rolls
1 pound pork sausage
3 cups shredded mozzarella cheese
4 eggs, beaten
3/4 cup milk
Salt and pepper to taste

Line 9x13-inch baking dish with roll dough; press seams to seal. Brown sausage in skillet, stirring until crumbly; drain. Layer sausage and cheese in prepared dish. Combine eggs, milk, salt and pepper in bowl; mix until smooth. Pour over layers. Bake at 375 degrees for 20 to 25 minutes or until set. Let stand for 5 minutes. Yield: 8 servings.

Approx Per Serving: Cal 385; Prot 17 g; Carbo 14 g; Fiber 0 g; T Fat 28 g; Chol 161 mg; Sod 610 mg.

Theresa Brhel, Hornets Nest

SAUSAGE AND EGG BAKE

1 pound pork sausage
3 slices bread, cut into cubes
1 cup shredded Cheddar cheese
6 eggs
1 cup milk
Salt and pepper to taste

Brown sausage in skillet, stirring until crumbly; drain. Layer bread cubes, sausage and cheese in baking dish. Combine eggs, milk, salt and pepper in bowl; beat until smooth. Pour over layers. Bake at 325 degrees for 30 to 45 minutes or until set. May place crescent roll dough in baking pan and on top of casserole and omit bread if preferred. Yield: 8 servings.

Approx Per Serving: Cal 265; Prot 13 g; Carbo 6 g; Fiber <1 g; T Fat 21 g; Chol 197 mg; Sod 366 mg.

Carolyn Buboltz, Independence

CHEESE AND SAUSAGE QUICHE

12 ounces pork sausage
1/2 cup thinly sliced onion
1/3 cup chopped green bell pepper
1 tablespoon flour
1 1/2 cups shredded sharp Cheddar cheese
1 unbaked 9-inch deep-dish pie shell
2 eggs, beaten
1 cup evaporated milk
1 tablespoon parsley flakes
1/4 teaspoon garlic salt
3/4 teaspoon seasoned salt
1/4 teaspoon pepper

Brown sausage in medium skillet, stirring until crumbly. Drain sausage on paper towel, reserving 2 tablespoons drippings. Sauté onion and green pepper in reserved drippings in skillet for 2 to 3 minutes. Mix flour and cheese in bowl. Stir in sausage and sautéed vegetables. Spoon into pie shell. Combine eggs, evaporated milk, parsley flakes, garlic salt, seasoned salt and pepper in bowl; mix until smooth. Pour over sausage mixture. Place on baking sheet. Bake at 375 degrees for 35 to 40 minutes or until brown and set. Yield: 6 servings.

Approx Per Serving: Cal 469; Prot 17 g; Carbo 21 g; Fiber 1 g; T Fat 35 g; Chol 131 mg; Sod 956 mg.

John E. Miles, Independence

SAUSAGE AND CHEDDAR QUICHE

1 unbaked 9-inch pie shell
1 pound pork sausage
1 4-ounce can sliced mushrooms, drained
1/2 cup chopped onion
1/4 cup chopped green bell pepper
1 teaspoon minced parsley
1/2 teaspoon basil leaves
Garlic to taste
1/8 teaspoon salt
1/2 cup shredded Cheddar cheese
1 cup milk
2 eggs
1 tablespoon cornstarch

Bake pie shell at 400 degrees for 10 minutes. Brown sausage in skillet, stirring until crumbly; drain. Add mushrooms, onion, green pepper, parsley, basil, garlic and salt; mix well. Spoon into pie shell. Top with cheese. Combine milk, eggs and cornstarch in bowl; beat until foamy. Pour evenly over cheese. Bake at 325 degrees for 50 minutes. Yield: 6 servings.

Approx Per Serving: Cal 403; Prot 12 g; Carbo 19 g; Fiber 1 g; T Fat 31 g; Chol 111 mg; Sod 644 mg.

Martha and Troy Hartley, Hornets Nest

CHRIS' SAUSAGE CASSEROLE

1 pound mild pork sausage
1/4 cup chopped onion
1/4 cup chopped green bell pepper
6 eggs
1/2 cup sour cream
Salt and pepper to taste

Brown sausage with onion and green pepper in heavy skillet, stirring until sausage is crumbly; drain. Press 3/4 of the mixture into baking dish. Combine eggs and sour cream in bowl; mix well. Season with salt and pepper. Pour over sausage mixture. Bake at 350 degrees until eggs are partially set; stir eggs. Top with remaining sausage mixture. Bake until eggs are set. Yield: 6 servings.

Approx Per Serving: Cal 272; Prot 11 g; Carbo 2 g; Fiber <1 g; T Fat 24 g; Chol 246 mg; Sod 316 mg.

Chris Roberts, Central

HOT DOG CASSEROLE

1 cup uncooked rice
1 pound hot dogs
1 small onion, chopped
1 small green bell pepper, chopped
1 tablespoon oil
1 envelope brown gravy mix
1 pound Cheddar cheese, shredded

Cook rice according to package directions. Cut hot dogs into bite-sized pieces. Cook with onion and green pepper in oil in skillet until brown. Prepare gravy mix using package directions. Add gravy and rice to hot dog mixture; mix well. Spoon into 9x13-inch baking dish. Top with cheese. Bake at 350 degrees for 30 minutes. Yield: 6 servings.

Approx Per Serving: Cal 704; Prot 30 g; Carbo 32 g; Fiber 1 g; T Fat 50 g; Chol 118 mg; Sod 1520 mg.

Happy Osborne, Independence

FUN IN THE BUN

1½ cups pancake mix
2 tablespoons sugar
½ cup cornmeal
1¼ cups milk
1 egg
1 pound hot dogs
Oil for deep frying

Combine pancake mix, sugar, cornmeal, milk and egg in bowl; mix well. Insert 1 popsicle stick into each hot dog. Dip into batter, coating well. Deep-fry until golden brown. Serve with mustard dip. Yield: 10 servings.

Approx Per Serving: Cal 268; Prot 9 g; Carbo 22 g; Fiber <1 g; T Fat 16 g; Chol 49 mg; Sod 785 mg.
Nutritional information does not include oil for deep frying.

Deni Dumford, Piedmont

ET CETERA

LEG OF LAMB WITH ARTICHOKES

1 5-pound leg of lamb, boned
1 clove of garlic
Juice of 1 lemon
1 clove of garlic, slivered
1 teaspoon oregano
2 teaspoons salt
1 teaspoon pepper
2 8-ounce cans tomato sauce
1 cup water
1 lemon, sliced
2 16-ounce cans artichoke hearts, drained

Rub cut edges of lamb with 1 clove of garlic; sprinkle with juice of 1/2 lemon. Roll lamb; tie at 1 1/2-inch intervals. Cut slits in lamb; insert slivers of 1 clove of garlic. Rub with remaining lemon juice, oregano, salt and pepper. Place in roasting pan. Roast at 400 degrees for 30 minutes. Reduce oven temperature to 350 degrees. Roast to 130 degrees on meat thermometer, basting frequently with pan drippings. Skim drippings. Add tomato sauce, water and lemon slices. Roast for 15 minutes. Add artichoke hearts. Roast for 15 minutes or to 150 to 160 degrees on meat thermometer for medium, basting frequently. Place lamb on heated platter. Arrange artichoke hearts around lamb. Strain sauce; serve with lamb. Yield: 10 servings.

Approx Per Serving: Cal 331; Prot 32 g; Carbo 14 g; Fiber 1 g; T Fat 18 g; Chol 104 mg; Sod 836 mg.

O. Douglas Smith, Central

☎ Make a Tenderizing Marinade for meat of 1 cup oil, 1/2 cup lemon juice or wine vinegar, 1/4 cup Worcestershire sauce, 3/4 cup soy sauce, 1/4 cup prepared mustard and 2 cloves of garlic.

VENISON CHILI

1½ pounds ground
  venison
1 medium onion, chopped
3 tablespoons
  Worcestershire sauce
3 tablespoons chili powder
½ cup catsup
1 16-ounce can pinto
  beans

Brown venison with onion and just enough water to prevent sticking in medium saucepan, stirring until venison is crumbly. Add Worcestershire sauce and chili powder. Simmer for 10 to 15 minutes. Stir in catsup and pinto beans. Simmer to desired consistency. Serve with buttermilk corn bread. Yield: 4 servings.

Approx Per Serving: Cal 382; Prot 41 g; Carbo 46 g; Fiber 16 g;
  T Fat 4 g; Chol 66 mg; Sod 597 mg.

Danny Navey, Foot Hills

ELEPHANT STEW

1 elephant
Seasoned brown gravy
2 rabbits (optional)

Cut elephant into bite-sized pieces. This should take about 2 months. Combine with brown gravy to cover in very large kettle. Cook on kerosene stove at 465 degrees for 4 weeks. Add rabbits only if more people are expected; most people do not like to find hare in their stew. Yield: 3800 servings.

Nutritional information for this recipe is not available.

Joe C. Deese, Jr., Hornets Nest

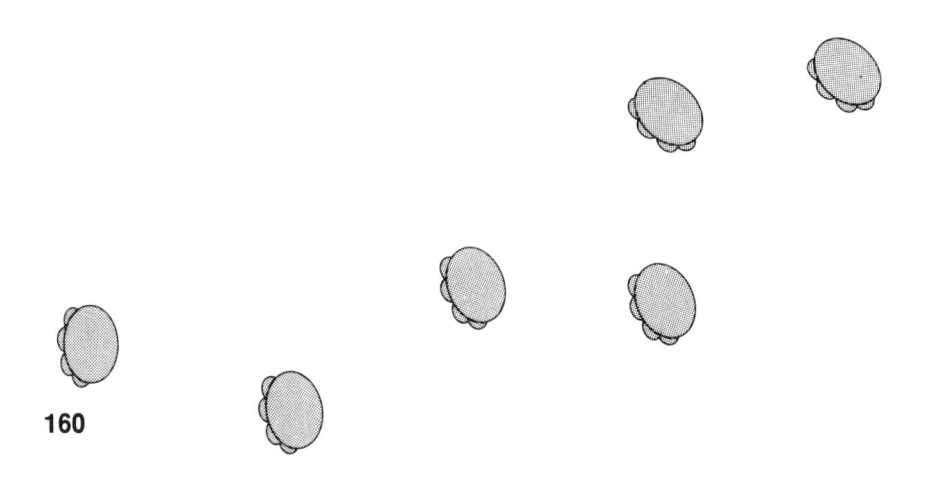

Poultry & Seafood

Jackies Guide to
Healthy Kidneys

How do we Keep our Kidneys healthy?

What are Kidneys?

What do Kidneys do?

What are kid's knees?

Animals have kidneys too.

— NC GLOMERULAR COLLABORATIVE NETWORK —

POULTRY

COUNTRY CHICKEN WITH ONION BISCUITS

2 1/2 cups chopped cooked chicken
4 slices crisp-fried bacon, crumbled
1 10-ounce package frozen mixed vegetables, cooked
2 medium tomatoes, chopped
1 cup shredded Cheddar cheese
1 can cream of chicken soup
3/4 cup milk
Onion Biscuit Dough
1/2 3-ounce can French-fried onions
1/2 cup shredded Cheddar cheese

Combine chicken, bacon, mixed vegetables, tomatoes and 1 cup cheese in 9x13-inch baking dish. Blend soup and milk in bowl. Pour over casserole. Bake, covered, at 400 degrees for 15 minutes. Drop Onion Biscuit Dough by spoonfuls into 12 biscuits on top of casserole. Bake, uncovered, for 15 to 20 minutes or until biscuits are golden brown. Top with French-fried onions and 1/2 cup cheese. Bake for 2 to 3 minutes or until cheese melts. Yield: 6 servings.

Onion Biscuit Dough

1 1/2 cups baking mix
2/3 cup milk
1/2 3-ounce can French-fried onions

Combine baking mix, milk and French-fried onions in bowl; mix well.

Approx Per Serving: Cal 550; Prot 33 g; Carbo 41 g; Fiber 3 g; T Fat 28 g; Chol 102 mg; Sod 1156 mg.

Martha Robertson, Hornets Nest

CRUSTY BROWN WHOLE BAKED CHICKEN

1 3½-pound chicken   Salt and pepper to taste

Rinse chicken and pat dry inside and out. Place breast side up in 2-quart baking pan sprayed with nonstick cooking spray. Bake at 350 degrees for 2 hours; do not open oven door during baking time. Sprinkle with salt and pepper. Let stand for 10 minutes before carving. Yield: 5 servings.

Approx Per Serving: Cal 284; Prot 43 g; Carbo 0 g; Fiber 0 g; T Fat 11 g; Chol 134 mg; Sod 128 mg.

Cheryl Griffin, Raleigh

BAKED CHICKEN IN WINE GRAVY

1 2½-pound chicken, cut up, skinned	1 soup can water
1 can cream of chicken soup	1 3-ounce can French-fried onions
	¾ cup Sauterne

Rinse chicken and pat dry. Place in 1½-quart baking dish. Add mixture of soup and water; top with French-fried onions. Bake, covered, at 350 degrees for 1 hour. Add wine. Bake for 1 hour longer. Serve chicken with gravy over rice or noodles. Yield: 4 servings.

Approx Per Serving: Cal 413; Prot 40 g; Carbo 14 g; Fiber <1 g; T Fat 18 g; Chol 127 mg; Sod 745 mg.

Frances Fitch, Raleigh

☎ Buy chicken in quantities and bake or stew. Store meal-sized portions of chopped chicken in plastic bags in freezer—ready for a busy-day meal.

LIGHT AND TASTY BAKED CHICKEN

2/3 cup dry milk powder
1 tablespoon poultry seasoning
1/4 teaspoon dry mustard
2 tablespoons parsley flakes
2 tablespoons paprika
2 tablespoons instant chicken bouillon
Salt and pepper to taste
4 chicken breasts, skinned

Combine dry milk powder, poultry seasoning, dry mustard, parsley flakes, paprika, instant bouillon, salt and pepper in bowl. Rinse chicken and pat dry. Roll in seasoning mixture, coating well. Place in baking pan. Bake at 400 degrees for 1 hour. Yield: 4 servings.

Approx Per Serving: Cal 149; Prot 25 g; Carbo 7 g; Fiber <1 g; T Fat 2 g; Chol 52 mg; Sod 986 mg.

Gladys Smith, Hornets Nest

CHICKEN BREAST STRIPS

6 chicken breast filets
1 1/2 eggs, beaten
1 cup seasoned bread crumbs
1 1/2 tablespoons oil
1 4-ounce can sliced mushrooms, drained
1 clove of garlic, minced
2 1/2 tablespoons wine
1 10-ounce can chicken broth
1 1/2 ounces mozzarella cheese, shredded

Rinse chicken and pat dry. Cut each filet into 4 long strips. Combine with eggs in bowl. Chill overnight. Roll in crumbs, coating well. Brown in oil in large skillet. Alternate layers of chicken, mushrooms and garlic in 9x13-inch baking dish until all ingredients are used. Pour mixture of wine and broth over top. Bake, covered, at 350 degrees for 30 minutes. Bake, uncovered, for 25 minutes. Sprinkle with cheese. Bake for 5 minutes longer. Yield: 8 servings.

Approx Per Serving: Cal 184; Prot 20 g; Carbo 10 g; Fiber 1 g; T Fat 6 g; Chol 82 mg; Sod 339 mg.

Jane Boyd, Independence

CHICKEN-IN-A-GARDEN

6 chicken breast filets
Marinade
2 tablespoons oil
3 green bell peppers, cut into 1-inch pieces
8 scallions, cut into 1/2-inch pieces
1 cup diagonally sliced 1-inch pieces celery
1 6-ounce package frozen snow peas, thawed, drained
1 teaspoon soy sauce
2 1/2 tablespoons cornstarch
3/4 cup water
3/4 teaspoon instant chicken bouillon
1/8 teaspoon ginger
3 medium tomatoes, peeled, chopped

Rinse chicken and pat dry. Cut into 1-inch pieces. Combine with marinade in bowl. Let stand for 20 minutes. Pour oil into preheated wok, coating well. Heat on medium-high (350 degrees) for 2 minutes. Add green peppers. Stir-fry for 4 minutes. Add scallions, celery and snow peas. Stir-fry for 2 minutes. Remove vegetables with slotted spoon. Add chicken. Stir-fry for 3 minutes. Combine soy sauce and cornstarch in bowl. Stir in water, instant bouillon and ginger. Add to wok with stir-fried vegetables and tomatoes. Cook over low heat (225 degrees) for 3 minutes or until thick and bubbly. Serve over hot cooked rice. Yield: 8 servings.

Marinade for Chicken-in-a-Garden

1 tablespoon oil
1 teaspoon soy sauce
1 1/2 tablespoons cornstarch
1/2 teaspoon garlic powder
1/4 teaspoon pepper

Combine with oil, soy sauce, cornstarch, garlic powder and pepper in bowl; mix well.

Approx Per Serving: Cal 172; Prot 17 g; Carbo 12 g; Fiber 3 g; T Fat 6 g; Chol 37 mg; Sod 365 mg.

Ann Neeley, Independence

CHICKEN AND WATER CHESTNUT SOUFFLÉ

4 1/2 slices white bread, crusts trimmed
2 cups chopped cooked chicken
1 4-ounce can sliced mushrooms, drained
1 7-ounce can sliced water chestnuts, drained
4 1/2 slices sharp Cheddar cheese
1/4 cup mayonnaise
1/4 cup melted margarine
2 eggs, beaten
1 cup milk
1/2 teaspoon salt
1 can cream of mushroom soup
1 2-ounce jar chopped pimento, drained
1 cup coarse bread crumbs
2 tablespoons melted butter

Arrange bread slices in buttered 8x8-inch baking dish. Layer chicken, mushrooms, water chestnuts and cheese in prepared dish. Combine mayonnaise, margarine, eggs, milk and salt in bowl; mix well. Pour over layers. Spoon mixture of soup and pimento over all. Chill, covered with foil, for 8 hours to overnight. Bake, uncovered, at 350 degrees for 30 minutes. Top with bread crumbs mixed with butter. Bake for 15 to 20 minutes longer or until set. Yield: 4 servings.

Approx Per Serving: Cal 884; Prot 42 g; Carbo 52 g; Fiber 4 g; T Fat 57 g; Chol 236 mg; Sod 1884 mg.

Mrs. Hugh L. McAulay, Blue Ridge

CURRIED CHICKEN

4 chicken breast filets
2 tablespoons margarine
3 tablespoons honey
2 tablespoons Dijon mustard
1 small clove of garlic, crushed
1 teaspoon lemon juice
1 teaspoon curry powder
1 tablespoon prepared mustard
1/2 teaspoon salt

Rinse chicken filets and pat dry. Arrange in buttered 9x13-inch baking dish. Melt margarine in saucepan over medium heat. Whisk in honey, Dijon mustard, garlic, lemon juice, curry powder, prepared mustard and salt. Pour over chicken. Bake, covered with foil, at 350 degrees for 10 minutes. Baste with sauce. Bake, uncovered, for 15 to 20 minutes or until done to taste, basting occasionally. Serve with hot rice. Yield: 4 servings.

Approx Per Serving: Cal 202; Prot 20 g; Carbo 14 g; Fiber <1 g; T Fat 7 g; Chol 49 mg; Sod 536 mg.

John E. Miles, Independence

CHICKEN DELUXE

4 chicken breasts, skinned, trimmed
1/8 teaspoon salt
1/8 teaspoon pepper
1 can cream of chicken soup
1/2 cup sour cream
1 teaspoon dried minced onion
1 teaspoon parsley flakes
1 6-ounce package sliced smoked ham
1 4-ounce jar sliced mushrooms, drained
1 cup coarse butter cracker crumbs

Rinse chicken and pat dry. Pierce with fork; sprinkle with salt and pepper. Arrange with thicker portions toward outside in 8x12-inch glass dish. Cover with vented plastic wrap. Microwave on High for 8 to 9 minutes or until thickest portion is no longer pink, rotating dish 1/4 turn after 4 minutes. Let stand, covered with foil, for 5 minutes; drain. Combine soup, sour cream, onion and parsley flakes in 4-cup glass measure. Microwave, uncovered, on High for 3 to 4 minutes or until mixture comes to a boil, stirring after 2 minutes. Layer ham and mushrooms over chicken. Pour sauce over layers. Sprinkle with cracker crumbs. Microwave, covered with waxed paper, on High for 5 to 6 minutes or until center bubbles, rotating dish 1/2 turn after 3 minutes. Yield: 4 servings.

Approx Per Serving: Cal 415; Prot 32 g; Carbo 25 g; Fiber 1 g; T Fat 23 g; Chol 92 mg; Sod 1626 mg.

Barbara Clark, Independence

CHICKEN DIVINE

4 chicken breasts, skinned
1 cup butter cracker crumbs
1 teaspoon mace
1 teaspoon tarragon
1/4 cup melted butter
1/2 cup minced onion
1 cup sliced mushrooms
1 cup chicken broth
1/2 cup white wine
1 cup seedless white grapes

Rinse chicken. Roll in mixture of cracker crumbs, mace and tarragon, coating well. Brown lightly in butter in skillet over medium heat. Remove chicken to drain. Add onion and mushrooms. Sauté until tender. Stir in chicken broth and wine. Bring to a boil; reduce heat. Simmer for 10 minutes. Arrange chicken in shallow baking dish. Pour sauce over chicken. Bake at 300 degrees for 15 minutes. Add grapes. Bake for 10 minutes longer. Yield: 4 servings.

Approx Per Serving: Cal 369; Prot 23 g; Carbo 25 g; Fiber 1 g; T Fat 20 g; Chol 80 mg; Sod 559 mg.

Kay M. Blackburn, Coastal

HAWAIIAN CHICKEN

6 chicken breasts
1/4 cup melted butter
1 8-ounce can crushed pineapple
1 13-ounce can pineapple tidbits, drained
1/2 cup light corn syrup
1/4 cup lemon juice
1 tablespoon soy sauce
1 teaspoon ginger
1 teaspoon salt
1/2 teaspoon pepper

Rinse chicken and pat dry. Arrange skin side up in baking dish. Combine butter, pineapple, corn syrup, lemon juice, soy sauce, ginger, salt and pepper in bowl; mix well. Spoon over chicken. Bake at 350 degrees for 1 hour, basting frequently with sauce. Arrange chicken on serving platter. Spoon sauce over top. Serve with rice and pineapple slices. Yield: 6 servings.

Approx Per Serving: Cal 302; Prot 20 g; Carbo 38 g; Fiber 1 g; T Fat 9 g; Chol 70 mg; Sod 660 mg.

Carolyn Austin, Independence

MARINATED CHICKEN BREASTS

12 chicken breasts
Marinade
1 1/2 cups butter cracker crumbs
1 1/2 cups saltine cracker crumbs
1/2 cup melted margarine

Rinse chicken and pat dry. Combine with marinade in bowl. Marinate in refrigerator overnight. Roll chicken in mixture of cracker crumbs, coating well. Place in baking dish. Drizzle with half the margarine. Bake at 300 degrees for 1 hour. Drizzle with remaining margarine. Bake for 45 minutes longer. Yield: 12 servings.

Marinade for Chicken Breasts

2 cups sour cream
1/4 cup lemon juice
4 teaspoons Worcestershire sauce
2 teaspoons paprika
2 teaspoons celery salt
1/2 teaspoon garlic salt
1 teaspoon pepper

Combine all ingredients in bowl; mix well.

Approx Per Serving: Cal 342; Prot 22 g; Carbo 18 g; Fiber <1 g; T Fat 21 g; Chol 70 mg; Sod 862 mg.

Delores Sossamon, Independence

CHICKEN-IN-THE-LIMELIGHT

3 pounds chicken pieces
Juice of 1 lime
1/3 cup flour
1/2 teaspoon paprika
1 teaspoon salt
3 tablespoons oil
Grated rind of 1 lime
2 tablespoons brown sugar
1/2 cup chicken broth
1/2 cup white wine

Rinse chicken and pat dry. Drizzle with lime juice. Shake with mixture of flour, paprika and salt in bag, coating well. Brown on all sides in hot oil in skillet over medium-high heat. Arrange in single layer in 9x13-inch baking dish. Sprinkle with mixture of lime rind and brown sugar. Add chicken broth and wine. Bake, covered, at 375 degrees for 45 minutes. Yield: 6 servings.

Approx Per Serving: Cal 337; Prot 34 g; Carbo 11 g; Fiber <1 g; T Fat 15 g; Chol 101 mg; Sod 520 mg.

John E. Miles, Independence

OVEN-FRIED CHICKEN

1 cup flour
1/2 teaspoon paprika
1/2 teaspoon salt
1/8 teaspoon pepper
1/4 cup margarine
1 small fryer, cut up

Sift flour, paprika, salt and pepper into plastic bag. Melt margarine in ovenproof skillet in 400-degree oven. Rinse chicken and pat dry. Shake 1 piece at a time in flour mixture, coating well. Arrange in margarine in skillet. Bake at 400 degrees for 45 minutes to 1 hour or until crisp and brown, turning chicken halfway through baking time. Drain on paper towel.
Yield: 5 servings.

Approx Per Serving: Cal 345; Prot 29 g; Carbo 19 g; Fiber 1 g; T Fat 16 g; Chol 81 mg; Sod 398 mg.

Donna Lee, Hornets Nest

ROLLED CHICKEN BREASTS

8 chicken breast filets
1 2-ounce package thinly sliced dried beef
8 slices bacon
1 cup sour cream
1 can cream of mushroom soup
1 4-ounce can sliced mushrooms, drained

Rinse chicken and pat dry. Wrap beef slices around each chicken filet. Wrap 1 slice bacon around beef on each filet; secure with toothpick. Arrange in baking dish. Mix sour cream and soup in bowl. Spoon over chicken. Bake at 350 degrees for 40 to 45 minutes or until chicken is tender. Top with mushrooms.
Yield: 8 servings.

Approx Per Serving: Cal 245; Prot 25 g; Carbo 5 g; Fiber <1 g; T Fat 13 g; Chol 79 mg; Sod 785 mg.

Martha Bridges, Hornets Nest

CHICKEN AND BEEF CASSEROLE

1 2-ounce package chipped dried beef
6 chicken breasts
3 slices bacon, cut into halves
1 cup sour cream
1 can cream of mushroom soup
Paprika to taste

Place dried beef in large baking dish. Rinse chicken and pat dry. Arrange in prepared baking dish. Top each chicken breast with 1/2 slice bacon. Combine sour cream and soup in bowl; mix well. Spoon over chicken. Sprinkle with paprika. Bake, uncovered, at 300 degrees for 1 1/2 hours. Bake, covered, for 1 hour longer. Yield: 6 servings.

Approx Per Serving: Cal 261; Prot 25 g; Carbo 6 g; Fiber <1 g; T Fat 15 g; Chol 85 mg; Sod 864 mg.

Katie Grist, Independence

GLENN'S BIRTHDAY CHICKEN

1 4-ounce jar dried beef
12 chicken breast filets
12 slices bacon
1 cup sour cream
1 can cream of mushroom soup
Paprika to taste

Chop dried beef; spread in large shallow baking dish. Rinse chicken and pat dry. Wrap each with 1 slice bacon; arrange in prepared dish. Broil until bacon begins to brown. Combine sour cream and soup in bowl; mix well. Spoon over chicken. Sprinkle with paprika. Bake at 275 degrees for 3 hours. Yield: 12 servings.

Approx Per Serving: Cal 212; Prot 25 g; Carbo 3 g; Fiber <1 g; T Fat 11 g; Chol 79 mg; Sod 699 mg.

Joyce Pruitt, Independence

BEEFY CHICKEN BREASTS

1 2-ounce jar chipped dried beef
8 chicken breasts
8 slices bacon
1 cup sour cream
1 can cream of mushroom soup

Place dried beef in baking dish. Rinse chicken breasts and pat dry. Wrap each with 1 slice of bacon. Place in prepared dish. Combine sour cream and soup in bowl; mix well. Pour over chicken. Bake at 275 degrees for 4 hours. Yield: 8 servings.

Approx Per Serving: Cal 242; Prot 25 g; Carbo 4 g; Fiber <1 g; T Fat 13 g; Chol 79 mg; Sod 725 mg.

Nell Seegers, Independence

CHICKEN SUPREME

1 2-ounce jar dried beef
6 chicken breast filets
6 slices bacon
1 cup sour cream
1 can cream of mushroom soup

Line 9x13-inch baking dish with beef. Rinse chicken and pat dry. Arrange in prepared dish. Top with bacon. Combine sour cream and soup in bowl. Pour over chicken. Bake, covered, at 275 degrees for 2½ hours. Yield: 6 servings.

Approx Per Serving: Cal 279; Prot 26 g; Carbo 6 g; Fiber <1 g; T Fat 16 g; Chol 87 mg; Sod 915 mg.

Doris Shillinglaw, Independence

☎ For quick chicken and dumplings, tear flour tortillas into simmering canned chicken broth and cook until tender. Add canned chunk chicken.

CHICKEN-BROCCOLI CASSEROLE

- 2 10-ounce packages frozen chopped broccoli
- 4 cups chopped cooked chicken breasts
- 1 can cream of mushroom soup
- 1 small onion, chopped
- 2 eggs
- 1 cup mayonnaise
- 1 cup shredded sharp Cheddar cheese
- 1 cup butter cracker crumbs
- 2 tablespoons margarine

Cook broccoli using package directions; drain. Combine with chicken, soup, onion, eggs, mayonnaise and cheese in bowl; mix well. Spoon into baking dish. Sprinkle with cracker crumbs; dot with margarine. Bake at 350 degrees for 35 to 40 minutes or until bubbly. Yield: 8 servings.

Approx Per Serving: Cal 550; Prot 29 g; Carbo 17 g; Fiber 3 g; T Fat 42 g; Chol 147 mg; Sod 785 mg.

Evelyn B. Jones, Foot Hills

CHICKEN AND BROCCOLI CASSEROLE

- 1 10-ounce package frozen broccoli
- 1 1/2 cups chopped cooked chicken
- 1 can cream of chicken with mushrooms soup
- 1/4 cup mayonnaise
- 2 tablespoons fresh lemon juice
- 1/2 teaspoon curry powder
- 1/4 cup shredded Cheddar cheese
- 1 cup stuffing mix

Cook broccoli in a small amount of water in saucepan for 5 minutes; drain. Layer broccoli and chicken in greased baking dish. Mix soup, mayonnaise, lemon juice and curry powder in bowl. Spoon over layers. Top with cheese and stuffing mix. Bake at 300 degrees for 30 minutes. Yield: 4 servings.

Approx Per Serving: Cal 430; Prot 25 g; Carbo 31 g; Fiber 2 g; T Fat 24 g; Chol 66 mg; Sod 1279 mg.

Robin M. May, Raleigh

BROCCOLI AND CHICKEN CASSEROLE

1 chicken, cooked
1 envelope onion soup mix
1 cup sour cream
1 can cream of mushroom soup
2 10-ounce packages frozen broccoli, cooked
1/4 cup Parmesan cheese

Bone chicken and shred into small pieces. Combine soup mix, sour cream and mushroom soup in bowl; mix well. Layer broccoli, half the soup mixture, chicken, remaining soup mixture and cheese in baking dish. Bake at 350 degrees for 20 to 30 minutes or until brown. Yield: 8 servings.

Approx Per Serving: Cal 296; Prot 30 g; Carbo 8 g; Fiber 2 g; T Fat 16 g; Chol 91 mg; Sod 539 mg.

Eddie Haskin, Hornets Nest

CHEESY BROCCOLI AND CHICKEN BAKE

1 10-ounce package frozen broccoli
1 can cream of chicken soup
1/2 cup sour cream
1 cup cooked rice
1 5-ounce can boned chicken
1 1/2 cups shredded sharp Cheddar cheese
1 8-ounce can sliced water chestnuts, drained
24 butter crackers, crushed
1/4 cup melted butter

Cook broccoli using package directions. Combine soup and sour cream in bowl; mix well. Layer broccoli, soup mixture, rice, chicken, cheese and water chestnuts in medium baking dish. Toss cracker crumbs with butter in bowl. Sprinkle over casserole. Bake at 350 degrees for 20 minutes. Yield: 8 servings.

Approx Per Serving: Cal 381; Prot 15 g; Carbo 33 g; Fiber 2 g; T Fat 22 g; Chol 62 mg; Sod 600 mg.

Nelda Black, Hornets Nest

BROCCOLI-RICE CHICKEN CASSEROLE

- 1/2 cup chopped onion
- 1/2 cup chopped celery
- 2 tablespoons oil
- 3/4 cup rice, cooked
- 2 10-ounce packages frozen chopped broccoli, thawed, drained
- 3 pounds chicken, cooked, chopped
- Lemon pepper and salt to taste
- 1 pound Velveeta cheese, shredded
- 1 can cream of mushroom soup
- 1/2 cup shredded Cheddar cheese
- 1/2 cup slivered almonds

Sauté onion and celery in oil in heavy skillet until transparent. Combine with next 5 ingredients in bowl; mix well. Melt Velveeta cheese with soup in saucepan over low heat, stirring constantly. Add to broccoli and rice mixture; mix well. Spoon into buttered baking dish. Top with Cheddar cheese and almonds. Bake at 350 degrees for 40 minutes. Yield: 10 servings.

Approx Per Serving: Cal 582; Prot 55 g; Carbo 12 g; Fiber 3 g; T Fat 35 g; Chol 171 mg; Sod 1067 mg.

Kay Joffrion, Independence

CHICKEN DIVAN

- 2 10-ounce packages frozen broccoli, thawed
- 2 cups sliced cooked chicken breasts
- 2 cans cream of chicken soup
- 3/4 cup mayonnaise
- 1 teaspoon lemon juice
- 1/2 teaspoon curry powder (optional)
- 1 cup shredded sharp Cheddar cheese
- 1/2 cup soft bread crumbs
- 1 teaspoon melted butter

Layer broccoli and chicken in greased 9x13-inch baking dish. Combine soup, mayonnaise, lemon juice and curry powder in bowl; mix well. Spoon over chicken. Sprinkle with cheese. Toss bread crumbs with butter in bowl. Sprinkle over casserole. Bake at 350 degrees for 30 minutes. Yield: 8 servings.

Approx Per Serving: Cal 388; Prot 19 g; Carbo 15 g; Fiber 2 g; T Fat 29 g; Chol 64 mg; Sod 902 mg.

Frankie Maxwell, Asheville

FAVORITE CHICKEN DIVAN

2 cans cream of chicken soup
1/2 cup mayonnaise
1/2 cup sour cream
1/2 teaspoon curry powder
2 teaspoons lemon juice
6 chicken breasts, cooked
2 10-ounce packages frozen broccoli
3/4 cup bread crumbs
1 1/2 cups shredded Cheddar cheese
1 tablespoon melted butter
Paprika to taste

Combine soup, mayonnaise, sour cream, curry powder and lemon juice in bowl; mix well. Bone chicken breasts; cut each into 2 strips. Layer broccoli and chicken in 9x11-inch baking dish. Spread soup mixture over top. Sprinkle with bread crumbs and cheese. Drizzle with butter. Sprinkle with paprika. Bake at 350 degrees for 30 to 45 minutes or until bubbly. Serve over rice. Yield: 6 servings.

Approx Per Serving: Cal 566; Prot 35 g; Carbo 24 g; Fiber 3 g; T Fat 38 g; Chol 112 mg; Sod 1274 mg.

Ruth Tucker, Hornets Nest

COMPANY CHICKEN DIVAN

1 chicken, broiled
2 10-ounce packages frozen broccoli spears
1 cup mayonnaise
2 cans cream of chicken soup
1 tablespoon lemon juice
1/4 teaspoon curry powder
2 slices bread, crumbled
2 tablespoons melted butter

Bone and shred chicken. Cook broccoli using package directions. Layer broccoli and chicken in greased 6x10-inch baking dish. Combine mayonnaise, soup, lemon juice and curry powder in bowl; mix well. Spread evenly over chicken. Combine bread crumbs and butter in bowl; mix well. Sprinkle over chicken. Bake at 350 degrees for 30 minutes. Yield: 8 servings.

Approx Per Serving: Cal 494; Prot 30 g; Carbo 14 g; Fiber 2 g; T Fat 36 g; Chol 106 mg; Sod 905 mg.

Madelon Haskin, Hornets Nest

CHICKEN AND BROCCOLI ROLL

2　8-count cans crescent rolls
1　10-ounce package frozen chopped broccoli, cooked
3 large chicken breasts, cooked, chopped
8 ounces mozzarella cheese, sliced

Unroll dough on baking sheet; press to seal perforations. Layer broccoli, chicken and cheese slices on dough. Roll as for jelly roll. Bake at 350 degrees for 18 to 20 minutes or until brown. Yield: 6 servings.

Approx Per Serving: Cal 479; Prot 32 g; Carbo 33 g; Fiber 1 g; T Fat 23 g; Chol 78 mg; Sod 820 mg.

Evelyn C. Goodman, Hornets Nest

CHICKEN WITH CAULIFLOWER AND PEAS

8 pieces chicken, skinned
1 clove of garlic, finely chopped
1/2 teaspoon basil
1/4 teaspoon paprika
1 teaspoon salt
1 medium onion, chopped
3 cups 1-inch cauliflowerets
1　10-ounce package frozen green peas
1/2 teaspoon salt
1/8 teaspoon pepper

Wash chicken and pat dry. Arrange with thicker portions toward outside in 7x12-inch glass dish. Sprinkle with garlic, basil, paprika and 1 teaspoon salt. Add onion. Cover tightly with plastic wrap. Microwave on High for 10 minutes. Add cauliflower and peas; sprinkle with 1/2 teaspoon salt and pepper. Microwave, covered, on High for 10 to 15 minutes or until chicken and vegetables are tender. Let stand, uncovered, for 3 minutes. Yield: 8 servings.

Approx Per Serving: Cal 113; Prot 18 g; Carbo 8 g; Fiber 3 g; T Fat 1 g; Chol 37 mg; Sod 386 mg.

Connie Mangum, Raleigh

CHICKEN DIJON

2 8-ounce chicken breasts, skinned, trimmed
2 tablespoons lemon juice
2 teaspoons Dijon mustard
1/2 teaspoon basil
Paprika to taste
1/4 teaspoon garlic salt
1/8 teaspoon pepper

Wash chicken and pat dry; pierce with fork. Place in 9x9-inch glass dish. Sprinkle on both sides with lemon juice. Let stand for 20 to 30 minutes, turning once. Arrange chicken with thicker portions toward outside of dish. Spread with mustard; sprinkle with basil, paprika, garlic salt and pepper. Microwave, covered with waxed paper, on High for 3 minutes. Rotate dish 1/2 turn. Microwave on Medium for 6 to 7 minutes or until done to taste, rotating dish 1/2 turn after 3 minutes. Let stand, covered with foil, for 5 minutes. Garnish with celery leaves and tomato rose. Serve with peas. Yield: 2 servings.

Approx Per Serving: Cal 194; Prot 40 g; Carbo 2 g; Fiber <1 g; T Fat 2 g; Chol 98 mg; Sod 431 mg.

Barbara Clark, Independence

CHICKEN ENCHILADAS

1 can cream of mushroom soup
1 can cream of chicken soup
1 12-ounce can chili salsa
4 chicken breasts, baked, chopped
1 12-count package flour tortillas
1 cup shredded Monterey Jack cheese
1 cup shredded sharp Cheddar cheese
Paprika to taste

Combine soups and salsa in bowl; mix well. Reserve 1/3 of the mixture. Add chicken to remaining soup mixture; mix well. Spoon onto tortillas. Roll to enclose filling; place in 9x13-inch baking dish. Spoon reserved soup mixture over enchiladas. Top with cheeses and paprika. Bake at 325 degrees for 30 minutes. Yield: 6 servings.

Approx Per Serving: Cal 668; Prot 33 g; Carbo 73 g; Fiber 4 g; T Fat 30 g; Chol 75 mg; Sod 1554 mg.

Mrs. William F. Cote, Blue Ridge

FOUR-CAN CHICKEN CASSEROLE

3 chicken breasts, cooked, chopped
1 can cream of mushroom soup
1 can cream of chicken soup
1 soup can milk
1 3-ounce can chow mein noodles

Combine chicken, soups, milk and chow mein noodles in bowl; mix well. Spoon into buttered 1-quart baking dish. Bake at 350 degrees for 25 minutes. Yield: 4 servings.

Approx Per Serving: Cal 369; Prot 23 g; Carbo 27 g; Fiber 1 g; T Fat 19 g; Chol 56 mg; Sod 1501 mg.

Cyndi Mabrey, Hornets Nest

GOLDEN CHICKEN CHEDDAR BAKE

3 cups chopped cooked chicken
1 1/2 cups sliced celery
1/4 cup chopped onion
1/4 cup slivered almonds
1 cup cubed sharp Cheddar cheese
3/4 cup mayonnaise-type salad dressing
2 tablespoons lemon juice
1/2 teaspoon salt
1/2 cup cornflake crumbs

Combine chicken, celery, onion, almonds and cheese in bowl; mix well. Add salad dressing, lemon juice and salt; mix well. Spoon into greased 6x10-inch baking dish. Top with cornflake crumbs. Bake at 325 degrees for 35 minutes. Yield: 6 servings.

Approx Per Serving: Cal 378; Prot 26 g; Carbo 15 g; Fiber 1 g; T Fat 24 g; Chol 85 mg; Sod 650 mg.

Bobbie A. Hege, Salem

☎ Baked or roasted chicken has fewer calories than stewed chicken. Remove skin to further reduce the number of calories.

I CAN DO IT

16 chicken breast filets
2 7-ounce cans mandarin oranges, drained
1 16-ounce can whole cranberry sauce
1 envelope onion soup mix
1 16-ounce bottle of Russian salad dressing

Rinse chicken and pat dry. Arrange in 9x13-inch baking dish. Combine oranges, cranberry sauce, soup mix and salad dressing in bowl; mix well. Spoon over chicken. Bake at 350 degrees for 1 hour. Yield: 8 servings.

Approx Per Serving: Cal 613; Prot 42 g; Carbo 42 g; Fiber 2 g; T Fat 32 g; Chol 135 mg; Sod 1573 mg.

Karen Breakfield, Independence

COMPANY CHICKEN

6 chicken breast filets
1 7-ounce can sliced water chestnuts, drained
1 16-ounce bottle of Russian salad dressing
1 envelope onion soup mix
1 12-ounce jar apricot preserves

Rinse chicken and pat dry. Arrange in 9x13-inch baking dish. Sprinkle with water chestnuts. Mix salad dressing and soup mix in bowl. Pour over chicken. Spoon preserves over top. Bake at 350 degrees for 1½ hours. Yield: 6 servings.

Approx Per Serving: Cal 639; Prot 22 g; Carbo 53 g; Fiber 2 g; T Fat 40 g; Chol 98 mg; Sod 824 mg.

Irene M. Hooper, Asheville

CHICKEN CASSEROLE

2 1/2 cups chopped cooked chicken
1 can cream of chicken soup
1 cup milk
1/2 teaspoon salt
3 cups crushed potato chips
1/2 cup shredded Cheddar cheese
Paprika to taste

Combine chicken, soup, milk and salt in saucepan. Bring to the boiling point, stirring constantly. Sprinkle half the potato chips in 2-quart baking dish. Layer chicken mixture and cheese 1/2 at a time in prepared dish. Top with remaining potato chips and paprika. Bake at 350 degrees for 25 to 30 minutes or until bubbly. Yield: 6 servings.

Approx Per Serving: Cal 369; Prot 24 g; Carbo 20 g; Fiber 1 g; T Fat 22 g; Chol 72 mg; Sod 835 mg.

Iceyphenolia S. Abernathy, Independence

CONFETTI CHICKEN CASSEROLE

1 can cream of mushroom soup
1 can cream of chicken soup
2/3 cup milk
1 tablespoon chopped onion
2 tablespoons chopped pimento
2 tablespoons chopped green bell pepper
1/4 cup shredded sharp Cheddar cheese
1 1/2 cups chopped cooked chicken
1 cup macaroni, cooked
1/4 cup margarine

Heat soups, milk, onion, pimento and green pepper in saucepan over low heat. Stir in cheese until melted. Add chicken, macaroni and margarine; mix well. Spoon into buttered baking dish. Bake at 350 degrees for 30 to 45 minutes or until bubbly. Yield: 10 servings.

Approx Per Serving: Cal 182; Prot 9 g; Carbo 10 g; Fiber <1 g; T Fat 12 g; Chol 27 mg; Sod 582 mg.

Virginia Bowie, Independence

LEMON PARMESAN CHICKEN

1/4 cup bread crumbs
3 tablespoons Parmesan cheese
1 tablespoon parsley flakes
6 4-ounce chicken breasts
1/2 cup melted margarine
1 tablespoon lemon juice

Combine bread crumbs, cheese and parsley in bowl. Rinse chicken. Roll in crumb mixture, coating well. Place in shallow 8-inch baking dish. Drizzle with mixture of margarine and lemon juice. Bake at 350 degrees for 1 hour. Yield: 6 servings.

Approx Per Serving: Cal 257; Prot 21 g; Carbo 4 g; Fiber <1 g; T Fat 17 g; Chol 51 mg; Sod 311 mg.

Anne Godwin, Independence

COMPANY CHICKEN CASSEROLE

1 cup chopped cooked chicken
1 cup chopped celery
1 cup cooked rice
1 can cream of chicken soup
2 tablespoons grated onion
3/4 cup mayonnaise
1 cup sliced water chestnuts
1/2 cup sliced almonds
1 cup crushed cornflakes
2 tablespoons melted margarine

Combine chicken, celery, rice, soup, onion, mayonnaise, water chestnuts and almonds in bowl; mix well. Spoon into 2-quart baking dish. Top with cornflake crumbs and margarine. Bake at 350 degrees for 45 minutes. Yield: 6 servings.

Approx Per Serving: Cal 466; Prot 12 g; Carbo 28 g; Fiber 2 g; T Fat 35 g; Chol 41 mg; Sod 781 mg.

Carolyn J. Irvin, Hornets Nest

CHICKEN CONTINENTAL

1½ cups uncooked rice
1 can cream of mushroom soup
1 can cream of chicken soup
1 can cream of celery soup
1 cup water
8 chicken breasts
½ cup butter
1½ tablespoons Parmesan cheese
1 teaspoon paprika

Sprinkle rice in greased 9x13-inch baking dish. Mix soups and water in bowl. Add ¾ of the soup mixture to rice; mix well. Rinse chicken and pat dry. Arrange on top of rice. Dot with butter. Top with remaining soup mixture, cheese and paprika. Bake, covered, at 275 degrees for 2½ to 3 hours or until chicken and rice are tender. Yield: 8 servings.

Approx Per Serving: Cal 403; Prot 20 g; Carbo 36 g; Fiber 1 g; T Fat 20 g; Chol 76 mg; Sod 1053 mg.

Nancy Riley, Independence

CHICKEN CASSEROLE WITH RICE

½ cup slivered almonds
2 tablespoons margarine
2 cups chopped cooked chicken
1 can cream of mushroom soup
2 cups cooked rice
1 cup milk
¼ cup white wine
½ teaspoon salt
1 cup bread crumbs
2 tablespoons melted butter

Sauté almonds in margarine in skillet until brown. Add chicken, soup, rice, milk, wine and salt; mix well. Spoon into 1½-quart baking dish. Top with bread crumbs mixed with butter. Bake at 350 degrees for 45 minutes. May substitute turkey or tuna for chicken if preferred. Yield: 6 servings.

Approx Per Serving: Cal 480; Prot 22 g; Carbo 37 g; Fiber 2 g; T Fat 28 g; Chol 71 mg; Sod 815 mg.

Esther Sossamon, Independence

EASY CHICKEN CASSEROLE

1 can cream of mushroom soup
1 envelope onion soup mix
1 1/2 soup cans water
1 fryer, cut up
1 cup uncooked rice
Salt and pepper to taste

Combine soup, soup mix and water in bowl; mix well. Rinse chicken and pat dry. Layer rice, soup mixture and chicken in buttered 2-quart glass baking dish. Sprinkle lightly with salt and pepper. Bake at 350 degrees for 1 1/4 hours. May microwave on High for 35 minutes if preferred. Yield: 5 servings.

Approx Per Serving: Cal 417; Prot 32 g; Carbo 44 g; Fiber 1 g; T Fat 13 g; Chol 82 mg; Sod 2097 mg.

Eva Peguese, Central

HOT CHICKEN AND RICE CASSEROLE

1 cup chopped cooked chicken
1 cup cooked rice
1 small onion, chopped
1/4 cup chopped celery
2 hard-boiled eggs, chopped
1 can cream of mushroom soup
1 tablespoon lemon juice
1/4 cup chopped sweet pickles
1/2 cup mayonnaise
1 cup crushed potato chips

Combine chicken, rice, onion, celery, eggs, soup, lemon juice, pickles and mayonnaise in bowl; mix well. Spoon into baking dish. Chill overnight. Let stand at room temperature for 30 minutes. Top with potato chips. Bake at 350 degrees for 45 minutes. Yield: 8 servings.

Approx Per Serving: Cal 271; Prot 9 g; Carbo 17 g; Fiber 1 g; T Fat 19 g; Chol 78 mg; Sod 506 mg.

Kim Parker, Central

CHICKEN AND RICE

1 4-pound chicken, cut up
4 cups water
1 large onion, chopped
3 stalks celery, chopped
1 tablespoon salt
1 teaspoon pepper
1 1/2 cups uncooked long grain rice

Rinse chicken. Combine with water, onion, celery, salt and pepper in 3-quart saucepan. Cook over medium heat for 40 minutes or until chicken is tender. Remove and bone chicken. Add rice to broth in saucepan. Cook over medium heat for 25 minutes, adding water if necessary. Stir in chicken. Heat to serving temperature. Yield: 6 servings.

Approx Per Serving: Cal 359; Prot 46 g; Carbo 15 g; Fiber 1 g; T Fat 11 g; Chol 135 mg; Sod 1479 mg.

Mary Ann Turnage, Hornets Nest

CHICKEN AND RICE CASSEROLE

1 cup uncooked rice
1 can cream of celery soup
1 can cream of chicken soup
1 cup water
6 chicken breasts
1/4 cup melted margarine

Sprinkle rice into 2-quart baking dish. Spoon mixture of soups and water over rice. Rinse chicken and pat dry. Dip in margarine; arrange over soup. Bake at 350 degrees for 1 hour or until chicken is tender. May cover with foil if necessary to prevent overbrowning. Yield: 6 servings.

Approx Per Serving: Cal 356; Prot 24 g; Carbo 32 g; Fiber 1 g; T Fat 14 g; Chol 59 mg; Sod 929 mg.

Jean Rushing, Hornets Nest

BAKED CHICKEN AND RICE

1 fryer, cut up
1 cup uncooked rice
1 can cream of mushroom soup
1 can cream of celery soup
1 soup can milk
1/2 teaspoon flour
1/2 envelope onion soup mix

Rinse chicken and pat dry. Sprinkle rice into greased 9x13-inch baking dish. Combine mushroom and celery soups, milk and flour in bowl; mix well. Spoon over rice. Sprinkle with soup mix. Arrange chicken over top. Bake, covered with foil, at 350 degrees for 1 1/4 hours. Bake, uncovered, for 15 minutes longer or until chicken is brown. Yield: 6 servings.

Approx Per Serving: Cal 377; Prot 27 g; Carbo 35 g; Fiber 1 g; T Fat 14 g; Chol 81 mg; Sod 935 mg.

Joanne Tallent, Independence

CHICKEN AND RICE DINNER

1/2 cup butter
1 1/2 cups uncooked rice
1 can cream of mushroom soup
6 pieces chicken, skinned
1 cup water
1 envelope onion soup mix

Melt butter in 9x13-inch baking dish. Stir in rice and soup. Rinse chicken and pat dry. Arrange over rice mixture. Pour water over top; sprinkle with soup mix. Bake at 350 degrees for 1 1/2 hours. Yield: 6 servings.

Approx Per Serving: Cal 451; Prot 24 g; Carbo 42 g; Fiber 1 g; T Fat 21 g; Chol 91 mg; Sod 702 mg.

Carolyn Jones, Independence

☎ Layer 1 cup uncooked rice, chicken pieces and 1 envelope dry onion soup mix in baking dish and pour 4 cups chicken broth over top. Bake at 375 degrees for 1 hour.

CHICKEN AND RICE SUPREME

1 7-ounce package long grain and wild rice mix
1 16-ounce can French-style green beans, drained
3 cups chopped cooked chicken
1 4-ounce jar chopped pimentos, drained
1 7-ounce can sliced water chestnuts, drained
1 can cream of celery soup
1 cup mayonnaise
Salt and pepper to taste
2 cups shredded Cheddar cheese

Cook rice using package directions. Combine with green beans, chicken, pimentos, water chestnuts, soup, mayonnaise, salt and pepper in bowl; mix well. Spoon into baking dish. Top with cheese. Bake at 300 to 350 degrees until cheese melts and casserole is heated through. Yield: 15 servings.

Approx Per Serving: Cal 296; Prot 14 g; Carbo 5 g; Fiber 1 g; T Fat 20 g; Chol 52 mg; Sod 432 mg.

Audrey Brock, Hornets Nest

CHICKEN AND SAUSAGE CASSEROLE

1 7-ounce package long grain and wild rice mix
2 pounds turkey sausage
1/2 to 1 teaspoon hot pepper flakes
1 large onion, chopped
1 large green bell pepper, chopped
5 stalks celery, chopped
2 tablespoons oil
3 cups chopped cooked chicken breasts
1 7-ounce can chopped water chestnuts, drained
4 chicken bouillon cubes
1 cup water
1/2 cup blanched almonds

Cook rice using package directions. Brown sausage with hot pepper flakes in skillet, stirring until crumbly. Combine rice and sausage in bowl; mix well. Sauté onion, green pepper and celery in oil in skillet. Add sautéed vegetables, chicken, water chestnuts and mixture of bouillon cubes and water to sausage and rice mixture; mix well. Spoon into baking dish. Top with almonds. Bake at 350 degrees for 1 hour. Yield: 10 servings.

Approx Per Serving: Cal 333; Prot 26 g; Carbo 7 g; Fiber 2 g; T Fat 15 g; Chol 70 mg; Sod 801 mg.

Betty W. Hampton, Salem

CHICKEN BREAST BAKE

6 chicken breast filets
6 thin slices provolone cheese
1 can cream of chicken soup
½ soup can water
½ cup white wine
Salt and pepper to taste
1 cup herb-seasoned stuffing mix
½ cup melted margarine

Rinse chicken and pat dry. Arrange in 9x13-inch baking dish sprayed with nonstick cooking spray. Top each filet with slice of cheese. Combine soup, water, wine, salt and pepper in bowl; mix well. Pour over chicken. Toss stuffing mix with margarine in bowl. Sprinkle over casserole. Bake, covered with foil, at 350 degrees for 45 minutes. Yield: 6 servings.

Approx Per Serving: Cal 531; Prot 33 g; Carbo 32 g; Fiber <1 g; T Fat 28 g; Chol 73 mg; Sod 1530 mg.

Elsie Allred, Central

CHICKEN DESIRÉE

6 chicken breast filets
Garlic powder and pepper to taste
6 slices Swiss cheese
1 can cream of chicken soup
¼ cup white wine
1 cup herb-seasoned stuffing mix
¼ cup melted margarine

Rinse chicken and pat dry. Arrange in lightly greased 9x13-inch baking dish. Sprinkle with garlic powder and pepper. Top with cheese slices. Spoon mixture of soup and wine over chicken. Sprinkle with stuffing mix; drizzle with margarine. Bake at 350 degrees for 55 minutes. Serve with rice or Rice-A-Roni. Yield: 6 servings.

Approx Per Serving: Cal 464; Prot 34 g; Carbo 32 g; Fiber <1 g; T Fat 21 g; Chol 79 mg; Sod 1267 mg.

Mattie Swaringen, Piedmont

CHICKEN AND STUFFING CASSEROLE

1 can cream of mushroom soup
1 can cream of chicken soup
1 cup milk
2 cups chicken broth
1 8-ounce package stuffing mix
5 chicken breasts, cooked, chopped

Combine soups and milk in bowl; mix well. Mix chicken broth with stuffing mix in bowl. Layer chicken, soup mixture and stuffing 1/2 at a time in 9x13-inch baking dish. Bake at 350 degrees for 45 minutes. Yield: 8 servings.

Approx Per Serving: Cal 266; Prot 20 g; Carbo 28 g; Fiber <1 g; T Fat 8 g; Chol 39 mg; Sod 1226 mg.

Tootsie Chapman, Independence

CHICKEN AND DRESSING CASSEROLE

4 large chicken breasts
1/2 cup melted margarine
1 8-ounce package corn bread stuffing mix
1 can cream of celery soup
1 can cream of chicken soup

Rinse chicken. Cook in water to cover in saucepan until tender. Bone and chop chicken, reserving broth. Combine margarine and stuffing mix in bowl; mix well. Mix each can soup with 1 soup can reserved broth. Layer 1/3 of the stuffing mix, half the chicken and all the celery soup in greased 9x13-inch baking dish. Repeat layers with chicken soup. Top with remaining stuffing mix. Bake at 350 degrees for 45 minutes to 1 hour or until heated through and top is brown. Yield: 6 servings.

Approx Per Serving: Cal 427; Prot 31 g; Carbo 23 g; Fiber 1 g; T Fat 23 g; Chol 75 mg; Sod 1405 mg.

Linda S. Griffin, Independence

EASY CHICKEN AND DRESSING CASSEROLE

1 2½-pound chicken
1 can cream of celery soup
1 can cream of chicken soup
½ cup milk
¼ cup melted margarine
1 8-ounce package herb-seasoned stuffing mix

Rinse chicken. Cook in water to cover in saucepan until tender. Remove chicken, reserving 1½ cups broth. Bone chicken and cut into pieces. Place in 9x13-inch baking dish. Spread soups over chicken. Pour milk over soups. Combine margarine, stuffing mix and reserved chicken broth in bowl; mix well. Spoon over casserole. Bake at 350 degrees for 30 minutes. Serve with tossed salad. Yield: 8 servings.

Approx Per Serving: Cal 364; Prot 26 g; Carbo 27 g; Fiber <1 g; T Fat 16 g; Chol 73 mg; Sod 1209 mg.

Sadie Hood, Hornets Nest

CHICKEN AND VEGETABLE CASSEROLE

¼ cup margarine
1 8-ounce package stuffing mix
4 whole chicken breasts, cooked, shredded
1 can cream of chicken soup
1 can cream of celery soup
1 soup can milk
1 16-ounce can mixed vegetables, drained
1 14-ounce can chicken broth

Melt margarine in large baking dish. Add half the stuffing mix; mix well. Layer chicken over stuffing. Combine soups, milk and mixed vegetables in bowl; mix well. Spread over chicken. Top with remaining stuffing mix. Pour broth over all. Bake at 350 to 375 degrees for 30 minutes or until bubbly. Yield: 6 servings.

Approx Per Serving: Cal 433; Prot 25 g; Carbo 45 g; Fiber 3 g; T Fat 17 g; Chol 50 mg; Sod 1903 mg.

Faye Southard, Independence

CHICKEN ROYAL

2 cups chopped cooked chicken
2 cups herb-seasoned stuffing mix
1/2 cup mayonnaise
2 cups chicken broth
2 tablespoons chopped onion
4 hard-boiled eggs, finely chopped
1 cup bread crumbs

Combine chicken, stuffing mix, mayonnaise, chicken broth, onion and eggs in bowl; mix well. Spoon into 9x13-inch baking dish. Top with bread crumbs. Bake at 350 degrees for 30 minutes. Yield: 6 servings.

Approx Per Serving: Cal 439; Prot 25 g; Carbo 31 g; Fiber 1 g; T Fat 24 g; Chol 196 mg; Sod 882 mg.

Edith McWhirter, Hornets Nest

CHICKEN PARMIGIANA

4 chicken breast filets
2 eggs, beaten
1 cup Italian bread crumbs
1/4 cup olive oil
1 32-ounce jar meat-flavored spaghetti sauce
1/2 cup Parmesan cheese
1 cup shredded mozzarella cheese

Rinse chicken and pat dry. Dip into eggs; coat well with bread crumbs. Cook in olive oil in skillet until tender and browned on both sides. Pour spaghetti sauce into 7x11-inch baking dish. Arrange chicken in sauce. Top with cheeses. Bake at 400 degrees for 15 minutes or until cheeses are melted and lightly browned. Yield: 4 servings.

Approx Per Serving: Cal 723; Prot 40 g; Carbo 56 g; Fiber 4 g; T Fat 38 g; Chol 187 mg; Sod 1693 mg.

Sheri Camp, Independence

EASY CHICKEN PIE

1 unbaked 9-inch pie shell
1 16-ounce can mixed vegetables, drained
3/4 cup chopped cooked chicken
1 can cream of chicken soup
1 1/4 cups butter cracker crumbs
1/2 cup melted butter

Bake pie shell at 350 degrees just until light brown. Combine mixed vegetables, chicken and soup in bowl; mix well. Spoon into pie shell. Toss cracker crumbs with butter in bowl. Sprinkle over pie. Bake at 350 degrees for 40 minutes. Yield: 4 servings.

Approx Per Serving: Cal 741; Prot 18 g; Carbo 55 g; Fiber 6 g; T Fat 54 g; Chol 93 mg; Sod 1523 mg.

Kim Parker, Central

BUSY-DAY CHICKEN PIE

1 3-pound chicken
3 hard-boiled eggs, chopped
1/8 teaspoon pepper
1 cup self-rising flour
1 cup milk
2 tablespoons butter

Rinse chicken. Cook in water to cover in saucepan until tender. Bone and chop chicken; reserve 1 1/2 cups chicken broth. Combine chicken, reserved broth, eggs and pepper in bowl; mix well. Combine flour and milk in small bowl; mix to form dough. Roll on floured surface to fit 3-quart baking dish. Place in dish. Dot with butter. Spoon chicken mixture into pastry. Bake at 350 degrees for 45 minutes. Yield: 6 servings.

Approx Per Serving: Cal 387; Prot 39 g; Carbo 18 g; Fiber 1 g; T Fat 17 g; Chol 224 mg; Sod 406 mg.

Jean Henderson, Hornets Nest

CHICKEN PIE

- 1 2½-pound chicken
- 1 16-ounce can green peas, drained
- 1 can cream of chicken soup
- 1 cup flour
- ½ cup melted butter
- 1 cup buttermilk

Rinse chicken. Cook in water to cover until tender. Bone and chop chicken; reserve 1½ cups chicken broth. Place chicken in 9x13-inch baking dish. Combine reserved broth, peas and soup in bowl; mix well. Pour over chicken. Stir flour into butter in bowl. Add buttermilk; mix well. Spoon over casserole. Bake at 425 degrees for 20 to 30 minutes or until brown. Yield: 6 servings.

Approx Per Serving: Cal 742; Prot 66 g; Carbo 34 g; Fiber 4 g; T Fat 36 g; Chol 224 mg; Sod 908 mg.

Frances G. Farmer, Central

QUICK CHICKEN PIE

- 2 cups chopped cooked chicken
- 1 14-ounce can chicken broth
- 2 cans cream of chicken soup
- 1 10-ounce package frozen mixed vegetables
- 1 cup flour
- ½ cup melted margarine
- 1 cup milk

Combine chicken, broth, soup and mixed vegetables in bowl; mix well. Spoon into 9x13-inch baking dish. Combine flour, margarine and milk in bowl; mix well. Spoon over chicken mixture. Bake at 400 degrees for 1 hour. Yield: 6 servings.

Approx Per Serving: Cal 472; Prot 23 g; Carbo 33 g; Fiber 3 g; T Fat 27 g; Chol 58 mg; Sod 1264 mg.

Daphine Scarborough, Independence

TWO-CRUST CHICKEN PIE

1 10-ounce package frozen peas and carrots
3 tablespoons butter
1/4 cup flour
1 1/4 cups chicken broth
1 cup milk
1/4 teaspoon poultry seasoning
1 1/2 teaspoons salt
1/8 teaspoon pepper
2 cups chopped cooked chicken
1 2-crust package refrigerator pie pastry

Microwave peas and carrots using package directions. Melt butter in saucepan. Blend in flour. Add chicken broth, milk, poultry seasoning, salt and pepper. Cook until thickened, stirring constantly. Add chicken and peas and carrots. Cook until heated through. Spoon into pastry-lined pie plate. Top with remaining pastry. Trim and seal edge; cut vents. Bake at 400 degrees for 30 minutes or until brown. Yield: 6 servings.

Approx Per Serving: Cal 478; Prot 22 g; Carbo 36 g; Fiber 3 g; T Fat 28 g; Chol 65 mg; Sod 1273 mg.

Debby Edgerton, Independence

CHICKEN BREAST POTPIE

1 can cream of potato soup
2 cups chicken broth
3 small carrots, sliced
4 chicken breasts, cooked, chopped
1 8-ounce can green peas, drained
Topping (See page 195)

Bring soup, chicken broth and carrots to a boil in saucepan. Stir in chicken and peas. Spoon into 9x9-inch baking dish. Drop topping by spoonfuls evenly over chicken mixture. Bake at 375 degrees for 40 minutes or until topping is golden brown. Yield: 8 servings.

Topping for Chicken Breast Potpie

1 cup self-rising flour
½ cup melted butter
1 cup buttermilk

Combine flour, butter and buttermilk in bowl; mix to form soft dough.

Approx Per Serving: Cal 276; Prot 16 g; Carbo 22 g; Fiber 3 g; T Fat 14 g; Chol 59 mg; Sod 892 mg.

Billie Mills, Independence

CHICKEN AND VEGETABLES POTPIE

1 3-pound chicken, cooked, chopped
1 10-ounce package frozen mixed vegetables, thawed
1 can cream of celery soup
1 can cream of chicken soup
Topping

Combine chicken, mixed vegetables and soups in bowl; mix well. Spoon into greased 9x13-inch baking dish. Spread topping evenly over chicken mixture. Bake at 350 degrees for 45 minutes to 1 hour or until brown. Yield: 8 servings.

Topping for Chicken and Vegetables Potpie

1 cup baking mix
1 cup milk
½ cup melted butter

Combine baking mix, milk and butter in bowl; mix well.

Approx Per Serving: Cal 434; Prot 29 g; Carbo 22 g; Fiber 2 g; T Fat 25 g; Chol 118 mg; Sod 981 mg.

Bonnie Kramer, Independence

CHICKEN AND BISCUITS POTPIE

1 3-pound chicken
1 can cream of chicken soup
1/2 teaspoon tarragon
1 16-ounce can peas and carrots, drained
Biscuit Topping

Rinse chicken. Cook in water to cover in saucepan until tender. Bone and chop chicken; reserve broth. Place chicken in 9x13-inch baking dish. Bring soup, 1 soup can reserved broth and tarragon to a boil in saucepan, stirring to mix well. Pour over chicken. Sprinkle peas and carrots over soup mixture. Spread Biscuit Topping evenly over casserole. Bake at 350 degrees for 1 hour or until brown. Yield: 6 servings.

Biscuit Topping

1 1/2 cups flour
2 teaspoons baking powder
1 1/2 cups buttermilk
1/2 cup melted butter

Combine flour, baking powder, buttermilk and butter in bowl; mix well.

Approx Per Serving: Cal 574; Prot 42 g; Carbo 38 g; Fiber 4 g; T Fat 28 g; Chol 149 mg; Sod 852 mg.

Jewel H. Ware, Piedmont

EASY CHICKEN POTPIE

4 chicken breasts
1 16-ounce can mixed vegetables, drained
1 can cream of celery soup
1 can cream of chicken soup
Topping (See page 197)

Rinse chicken. Cook in water to cover in saucepan until tender. Bone and chop chicken; reserve broth. Combine mixed vegetables, soups and 1 1/2 soup cans reserved broth in bowl; mix well. Layer chicken and vegetable mixture in 9x13-inch baking dish. Spread topping over casserole. Bake at 325 degrees for 45 minutes or until golden brown. Yield: 8 servings.

Topping for Easy Chicken Potpie

1 1/2 cups self-rising flour 1/2 cup melted margarine
1 cup milk 1/4 teaspoon pepper

Combine flour, milk, margarine and pepper in small bowl; mix well.

Approx Per Serving: Cal 348; Prot 17 g; Carbo 30 g; Fiber 3 g; T Fat 18 g; Chol 36 mg; Sod 1280 mg.

Joyce Waters, Salem

QUICK CHICKEN POTPIE

1 1/2 cups chicken broth 1 8-ounce can mixed
2 cups chopped cooked   vegetables, drained
   chicken Topping
1 can cream of celery soup

Combine chicken broth, chicken, soup and mixed vegetables in bowl; mix well. Spread in rectangular baking dish. Spread topping evenly over top. Bake at 400 degrees for 45 minutes or until topping is golden brown. Yield: 8 servings.

Topping for Quick Chicken Potpie

1 cup self-rising flour 1 cup milk
1/2 cup melted butter

Combine flour, butter and milk in bowl; mix well.

Approx Per Serving: Cal 285; Prot 14 g; Carbo 19 g; Fiber 2 g; T Fat 17 g; Chol 69 mg; Sod 779 mg.

Evelyn Allen, Independence

☎ Freeze leftover chicken stock in 1-cup freezer containers to use in aspics, as a base for clear soups or for dressing.

LINDA'S CHICKEN POTPIE

- 1 10-ounce package frozen mixed vegetables
- 2 cups chopped cooked chicken
- 1 can creamy chicken-mushroom soup
- 1¼ cups chicken broth
- 1 teaspoon thyme
- 1 cup baking mix
- 1 cup milk
- ½ cup melted butter

Cook mixed vegetables in a small amount of water in saucepan for 5 to 6 minutes; drain well. Combine chicken with soup, broth and thyme in bowl; mix well. Layer chicken mixture and vegetables in 9x13-inch baking dish. Combine baking mix, milk and butter in bowl; mix well. Spoon over casserole. Bake at 400 degrees for 30 to 40 minutes or until topping is golden brown and filling is bubbly. Yield: 6 servings.

Approx Per Serving: Cal 439; Prot 21 g; Carbo 27 g; Fiber 2 g; T Fat 28 g; Chol 93 mg; Sod 1035 mg.

Linda S Griffin, Hornets Nest

SUNDAY CHICKEN PIE

- 1 2½-pound fryer
- 1 can cream of mushroom soup
- 1 cup self-rising flour
- 1 cup buttermilk
- ½ cup melted margarine
- ½ teaspoon salt
- ½ teaspoon pepper

Rinse chicken. Cook in water to cover in large saucepan until tender. Remove chicken, reserving broth. Bone and chop chicken. Place in 9x13-inch baking dish. Bring soup and 2 cups reserved broth to a boil in saucepan, stirring constantly. Pour over chicken. Combine flour, buttermilk, margarine, salt and pepper in bowl; mix well. Spoon evenly over casserole. Bake at 425 degrees for 25 to 30 minutes or until brown. Yield: 6 servings.

Approx Per Serving: Cal 424; Prot 22 g; Carbo 40 g; Fiber 5 g; T Fat 21 g; Chol 44 mg; Sod 984 mg.

Louise M. Morton, Salem

CHICKEN POTPIE LIKE GRANDMA'S

1 3-pound fryer
1 can cream of mushroom soup
1 cup self-rising flour
1 teaspoon salt
1/2 teaspoon pepper
1/2 cup melted margarine
1 cup buttermilk

Rinse chicken. Cook in water to cover in saucepan until tender. Bone and chop chicken; reserve 2 cups broth. Place chicken in 9x13-inch baking dish. Combine reserved broth and soup in saucepan. Bring to a boil. Pour over chicken. Combine flour, salt, pepper, margarine and buttermilk in bowl; mix well. Spoon over casserole. Bake at 425 degrees for 30 minutes. Yield: 6 servings.

Approx Per Serving: Cal 394; Prot 28 g; Carbo 22 g; Fiber 1 g; T Fat 21 g; Chol 57 mg; Sod 1354 mg.

Nelda Black, Hornets Nest

MELT-IN-YOUR-MOUTH CHICKEN POTPIE

4 chicken breasts
1 can cream of chicken soup
1/2 teaspoon pepper
1 cup self-rising flour
1/2 cup melted margarine
1 cup buttermilk

Rinse chicken. Cook in water to cover in saucepan until tender. Bone and chop chicken; reserve 2 cups broth. Place chicken in 9x13-inch baking dish. Combine reserved broth, soup and pepper in bowl; mix well. Pour over chicken. Combine flour, margarine and buttermilk in bowl; mix well. Spoon over casserole. Bake at 425 degrees for 35 minutes or until brown. Yield: 8 servings.

Approx Per Serving: Cal 261; Prot 15 g; Carbo 16 g; Fiber <1 g; T Fat 15 g; Chol 29 mg; Sod 855 mg.

Frances Cook, Blue Ridge

OLD-FASHIONED CHICKEN PIE

1 3-pound fryer
1 can cream of chicken soup
1/2 cup melted margarine
1 cup self-rising flour
1 cup buttermilk
1 teaspoon salt
1/2 teaspoon pepper

Rinse chicken. Cook in water to cover in saucepan until tender. Bone and chop chicken; reserve 2 cups chicken broth. Place chicken in 9x13-inch baking dish. Bring reserved broth and soup to a boil in saucepan, stirring constantly. Pour over chicken. Combine margarine, flour, buttermilk, salt and pepper in bowl; mix well. Spoon over chicken. Bake at 425 degrees for 25 to 30 minutes or until brown. Yield: 8 servings.

Approx Per Serving: Cal 394; Prot 28 g; Carbo 22 g; Fiber 1 g; T Fat 21 g; Chol 57 mg; Sod 1887 mg.

Doris D. Keever, Hornets Nest

JOANNE'S CHICKEN PIE

1 3-pound fryer
1 can cream of chicken soup
1 cup self-rising flour
1/2 cup melted margarine
1 cup buttermilk

Rinse chicken. Cook in water to cover in saucepan until tender. Bone and chop chicken; reserve 2 1/2 cups broth. Place chicken in 9x13-inch baking dish. Bring reserved broth and soup to a boil in saucepan, stirring constantly. Pour over chicken. Mix flour, margarine and buttermilk in bowl. Spoon over chicken. Bake at 425 degrees for 25 to 30 minutes or until brown. Yield: 8 servings.

Approx Per Serving: Cal 394; Prot 28 g; Carbo 22 g; Fiber 1 g; T Fat 21 g; Chol 57 mg; Sod 1220 mg.

Joanne Tallent, Independence

SUNDAY CHICKEN POTPIE

4 chicken breasts, broiled, chopped
1 can cream of celery soup
1 16-ounce can peas and carrots, drained
1 16-ounce can new potatoes, drained
1¼ cups chicken broth
1 cup flour
1 cup milk
Pinch of baking powder
½ cup melted margarine

Combine chicken, soup, peas and carrots, potatoes and chicken broth in bowl; mix well. Spoon into baking dish. Combine flour, milk, baking powder and margarine in bowl; mix well. Spoon evenly over chicken mixture. Bake at 450 degrees for 30 minutes. Yield: 6 servings.

Approx Per Serving: Cal 462; Prot 22 g; Carbo 47 g; Fiber 4 g; T Fat 20 g; Chol 44 mg; Sod 1106 mg.

Willie Collins, Independence

VEG-ALL CHICKEN POTPIE

2 cups chopped cooked chicken
1 can cream of potato soup
1 can cream of celery soup
½ cup milk
½ teaspoon thyme
½ teaspoon pepper
1 16-ounce can mixed vegetables, drained
1 unbaked 9-inch deep-dish pie shell
1 unbaked 9-inch pie shell

Combine chicken, soups, milk, thyme and pepper in bowl; mix well. Stir in mixed vegetables. Add ¼ cup water if needed for desired consistency. Spoon into deep-dish pie shell. Top with remaining pie shell. Seal edge; cut vents. Bake at 375 degrees for 40 minutes. May substitute cream of chicken or mushroom soup for celery soup or substitute turkey for chicken if preferred. Yield: 6 servings.

Approx Per Serving: Cal 517; Prot 22 g; Carbo 43 g; Fiber 4 g; T Fat 28 g; Chol 55 mg; Sod 1319 mg.

Peggy D. Reid, Hornets Nest

VEGETABLE CHICKEN POTPIE

1   2½-pound fryer
1 teaspoon salt
½ teaspoon pepper
4 medium potatoes
5 stalks celery
8 ounces carrots
1   17-ounce can green peas, drained
½ cup butter
⅔ cup flour
1 cup milk
1 chicken bouillon cube
2 teaspoons salt
½ teaspoon pepper
1 recipe 2-crust pie pastry

Rinse chicken. Bring to a boil in water to cover with 1 teaspoon salt and ½ teaspoon pepper in heavy saucepan; reduce heat. Simmer, covered, for 1 hour or until tender. Remove and cool chicken, reserving broth. Bone and chop chicken. Chop potatoes, celery and carrots into 1-inch pieces. Combine with reserved broth in saucepan. Simmer until tender. Drain, reserving 3 cups broth. Combine chicken, cooked vegetables and peas in bowl; mix well. Spoon into 9x13-inch baking dish. Melt butter in saucepan over low heat. Blend in flour. Cook for 1 minute, stirring constantly. Stir in milk, reserved broth and bouillon cube gradually. Cook over medium heat until thickened, stirring constantly. Stir in 2 teaspoons salt and ½ teaspoon pepper. Pour over chicken mixture. Top with pastry; cut vents. Bake at 400 degrees for 45 to 55 minutes or until brown. Yield: 8 servings.

Approx Per Serving: Cal 712; Prot 31 g; Carbo 64 g; Fiber 8 g;
    T Fat 32 g; Chol 99 mg; Sod 1561 mg.

Ramona Dobbins, Raleigh

☎ Serve the filling for chicken potpie in toast cups, on English muffins or on corn bread. Top with canned biscuits for a quick crust.

CHICKEN PIE CASSEROLE

1 2½-pound chicken
1 16-ounce can peas, drained
1 16-ounce can carrots, drained
1 can cream of mushroom soup
1 8-ounce package stuffing mix
1 egg
¼ cup melted butter

Rinse chicken. Cook in water to cover in saucepan until tender. Bone and chop chicken; reserve broth. Place chicken in baking dish. Combine peas, carrots and soup in bowl; mix well. Spoon over chicken. Combine stuffing mix, egg and reserved broth in bowl; mix well. Spread over casserole. Drizzle with butter. Bake at 300 degrees for 35 minutes. Yield: 6 servings.

Approx Per Serving: Cal 523; Prot 38 g; Carbo 45 g; Fiber 5 g; T Fat 21 g; Chol 141 mg; Sod 1419 mg.

Barbara Thrower, Independence

MICROWAVE ELEGANT CHICKEN

1 medium onion, sliced into rings
1 cup sliced fresh mushrooms
1 clove of garlic, minced
Salt to taste
3 tablespoons olive oil
1 2½-pound fryer, cut up
2 tablespoons olive oil
1 tablespoon Kitchen Bouquet
½ cup dry white wine

Combine onion rings, mushrooms, garlic and salt with 3 tablespoons olive oil in 8x12-inch glass dish. Microwave, covered with waxed paper, on High for 3 to 6 minutes or until onion is tender. Rinse chicken and pat dry. Brush with mixture of 2 tablespoons olive oil and Kitchen Bouquet. Arrange skin side down over vegetables in dish. Microwave, covered, on High for 10 minutes. Rearrange chicken and rotate dish; baste with pan juices and wine. Microwave, covered, for 5 to 8 minutes longer or until chicken is tender. Serve with wild rice. Yield: 5 servings.

Approx Per Serving: Cal 366; Prot 34 g; Carbo 3 g; Fiber 1 g; T Fat 22 g; Chol 101 mg; Sod 100 mg.

Ila Mae Moses, Hornets Nest

BAKED CHICKEN SALAD

4 cups chopped cooked chicken
2 cups chopped celery
1 teaspoon minced onion
1 2-ounce jar chopped pimento, drained
4 hard-boiled eggs, sliced
3/4 cup mayonnaise
3/4 cup undiluted chicken soup
2 tablespoons lemon juice
1 teaspoon salt
Topping

Combine chicken, celery, onion, pimento, eggs, mayonnaise, soup, lemon juice and salt in bowl; mix well. Spoon into 1 1/2-quart baking dish. Sprinkle topping over casserole. Chill for several hours to overnight. Bake at 400 degrees for 25 minutes. Yield: 8 servings.

Crumb Topping for Baked Chicken Salad

1 cup crushed potato chips
1/3 cup slivered almonds
2/3 cup shredded sharp Cheddar cheese

Combine potato chips, almonds and Cheddar cheese in bowl; mix well.

Approx Per Serving: Cal 457; Prot 28 g; Carbo 9 g; Fiber 2 g; T Fat 34 g; Chol 193 mg; Sod 781 mg.

Blanche L. Drake, Coastal

☎ Bake frozen puff pastry patty shells using package directions. Fill with creamed chicken.

CHICKEN SALAD CASSEROLE

3 cups chopped cooked chicken
1 can chicken soup
2 tablespoons chopped onion
2 tablespoons chopped pimento
1 cup chopped celery
1/2 cup chopped almonds
1 7-ounce can sliced water chestnuts, drained
3/4 cup mayonnaise
1 cup crushed potato chips

Combine chicken, soup, onion, pimento, celery, almonds, water chestnuts and mayonnaise in bowl; mix well. Spoon into baking dish. Top with potato chips. Bake at 450 degrees until brown. Yield: 8 servings.

Approx Per Serving: Cal 384; Prot 19 g; Carbo 13 g; Fiber 2 g; T Fat 29 g; Chol 62 mg; Sod 511 mg.

Jessie M. Godwin, Raleigh

CHICKEN SALAD BAKE

2 2-ounce packages potato chips
2 cups chopped cooked chicken
2 hard-boiled eggs, chopped
1 cup chopped celery
1/2 cup slivered almonds
2 tablespoons chopped onion
1 2-ounce jar chopped pimento, drained
1 tablespoon lemon juice
1 can cream of mushroom soup
3/4 cup mayonnaise

Sprinkle 1 package potato chips into greased baking dish. Combine chicken, eggs, celery, almonds, onion, pimento, lemon juice, soup and mayonnaise in bowl; mix well. Spoon into prepared dish. Top with remaining package potato chips. Bake at 450 degrees for 15 minutes or until bubbly. Yield: 6 servings.

Approx Per Serving: Cal 536; Prot 20 g; Carbo 19 g; Fiber 3 g; T Fat 44 g; Chol 130 mg; Sod 738 mg.

Nell Seegers, Independence

HOT CHICKEN SALAD

4 cups chopped cooked chicken breasts
2 cups chopped celery
1/2 cup chopped green bell pepper
2 tablespoons chopped pimento
2 6-ounce cans sliced water chestnuts, drained
2 cups cooked minute rice
2 cans cream of chicken soup
1 1/2 cups mayonnaise
2 tablespoons minced onion
2 tablespoons lemon juice
1 tablespoon Worcestershire sauce

Combine chicken, celery, green pepper, pimento, water chestnuts and rice in bowl; toss lightly to mix. Spoon into buttered 3-quart baking dish. Combine soup, mayonnaise, onion, lemon juice and Worcestershire sauce in bowl; mix well. Add 1/3 of the soup mixture to chicken mixture; mix well. Spoon remaining soup mixture over top. Bake at 350 degrees for 45 minutes or until bubbly. Yield: 12 servings.

Approx Per Serving: Cal 376; Prot 17 g; Carbo 16 g; Fiber 1 g; T Fat 27 g; Chol 60 mg; Sod 624 mg.

Sallie R. Freeman, Salem

CHICKEN AND RICE SOUP

1 3 1/2-pound chicken
2 quarts water
1 onion, chopped
2 stalks celery, thinly sliced
1 bay leaf
1 1/2 teaspoons salt
1 teaspoon pepper
3/4 cup uncooked long grain rice
1 carrot, chopped

Rinse chicken. Combine with water, onion, celery, bay leaf, salt and pepper in heavy saucepan. Bring to a boil; reduce heat. Simmer, covered, for 45 minutes. Remove and cool chicken; discard bay leaf. Cut chicken into bite-sized pieces. Add rice and carrot to broth in saucepan. Bring to a boil; reduce heat. Simmer, covered, for 20 minutes or until rice is tender. Add chicken. Heat to serving temperature. Yield: 6 servings.

Approx Per Serving: Cal 298; Prot 40 g; Carbo 10 g; Fiber 1 g; T Fat 10 g; Chol 118 mg; Sod 795 mg.

Carolyn Helms, Independence

CHICKEN STEW

12 pounds chicken
4 16-ounce cans whole kernel corn
3 pounds Irish potatoes, chopped
¾ cup chopped onion
3 16-ounce cans tomatoes
6 ounces evaporated milk
2 cans tomato soup
Salt and pepper to taste

Rinse chicken. Combine with water to cover in 12-quart stockpot. Cook until tender; cool. Bone and chop chicken. Chill chicken and broth in separate containers. Skim broth. Combine broth, chicken, corn, potatoes, onion, tomatoes, evaporated milk, soup, salt and pepper in 12-quart stockpot; mix well. Simmer for 2 hours or to desired consistency. Yield: 12 servings.

Approx Per Serving: Cal 825; Prot 86 g; Carbo 72 g; Fiber 6 g; T Fat 23 g; Chol 240 mg; Sod 1200 mg.

Ed Thomas, Central

EASY CHICKEN TETRAZZINI

1 cup sliced fresh mushrooms
2 teaspoons margarine
4 cups cooked spaghetti
8 ounces chicken, cooked, chopped
½ cup Parmesan cheese
¼ teaspoon nutmeg
Salt to taste
2 teaspoons margarine
3 tablespoons flour
1 cup chicken broth
⅓ cup milk

Sauté mushrooms in 2 teaspoons margarine in saucepan. Combine with spaghetti in large bowl. Add chicken, cheese, nutmeg and salt; mix well. Melt 2 teaspoons margarine in small saucepan. Blend in flour. Add chicken broth and milk. Cook for 2 minutes or until thickened, stirring constantly. Add to spaghetti; mix well. Spoon into 8x8-inch baking dish. Bake at 400 degrees for 30 minutes. Yield: 4 servings.

Approx Per Serving: Cal 364; Prot 23 g; Carbo 46 g; Fiber 3 g; T Fat 9 g; Chol 35 mg; Sod 465 mg.

Diane Grace, Raleigh

CHICKEN TETRAZZINI

- 1   3-pound hen
- 8 ounces uncooked spaghetti
- 1/2 small green bell pepper, chopped
- 1   4-ounce jar chopped pimentos, drained
- 2 cans cream of mushroom soup
- 1 cup shredded mild Cheddar cheese

Rinse chicken. Cook in water to cover in saucepan until very tender. Bone and chop chicken; reserve broth. Cook spaghetti and green pepper in reserved broth in saucepan for 15 minutes; drain. Combine with chicken, pimentos and soup in bowl; mix well. Spoon into 9x13-inch baking dish. Top with cheese. Bake at 350 degrees for 30 minutes or until bubbly. Yield: 6 servings.

Approx Per Serving: Cal 542; Prot 44 g; Carbo 38 g; Fiber 3 g; T Fat 23 g; Chol 122 mg; Sod 1038 mg.

Evelyn Clemmer, Hornets Nest

STIR-FRY VEGETABLES AND CHICKEN

- 2 tablespoons oil
- 1   10-ounce package frozen oriental vegetables
- 1   7-ounce can sliced water chestnuts, drained
- 1 tablespoon soy sauce
- Garlic salt to taste
- 1 tablespoon cornstarch
- 1   7-ounce can chicken

Heat oil in skillet. Add oriental vegetables and water chestnuts. Stir-fry until tender. Add soy sauce and garlic salt. Stir in mixture of cornstarch and enough water to cover vegetables. Cook until thickened. Stir in chicken. Yield: 4 servings.

Approx Per Serving: Cal 224; Prot 16 g; Carbo 18 g; Fiber 4 g; T Fat 10 g; Chol 41 mg; Sod 321 mg.

Dinky Eckard, Foot Hills

ROLLED CHICKEN WASHINGTON

6 whole chicken breasts, boned, skinned
Salt to taste
Cheddar Filling
1/2 cup flour
2 eggs, slightly beaten
3/4 cup fine dry bread crumbs
Oil for deep frying

Rinse chicken and pat dry. Pound 1/4 inch thick with meat mallet. Sprinkle with salt. Spoon Cheddar Filling onto chicken; roll to enclose filling. Sprinkle chicken rolls with flour. Dip in egg; coat with bread crumbs. Chill, covered, for 1 hour. Deep-fry rolls in 375-degree oil for 5 minutes or until crisp and golden brown; drain. Place in baking dish. Bake at 325 degrees for 30 minutes. Yield: 6 servings.

Cheddar Filling

1/2 cup finely chopped mushrooms
2 tablespoons butter
2 tablespoons flour
1/2 cup light cream
1/4 teaspoon salt
Cayenne pepper to taste
1 1/4 cups shredded sharp Cheddar cheese

Sauté mushrooms in butter in skillet for 5 minutes. Stir in flour. Add cream, salt and cayenne pepper. Cook until thickened, stirring constantly. Add cheese. Cook over low heat until cheese melts, stirring constantly. Spoon into shallow dish. Chill for 1 hour.

Approx Per Serving: Cal 404; Prot 31 g; Carbo 20 g; Fiber 1 g; T Fat 22 g; Chol 178 mg; Sod 444 mg.
Nutritional information does not include oil for deep frying.

Wilma Shellman, Foot Hills

☎ Substitute crumbled bleu cheese or shredded Swiss cheese for Cheddar cheese to add variety to Rolled Chicken Washington.

WINE AND CHEESE CHICKEN

1 cup uncooked white or brown rice
1 can cream of chicken soup
1 can cream of mushroom soup
1 can cream of celery soup
1 4-ounce can sliced mushrooms, drained
1/2 cup dry white wine
1 10-ounce package frozen peas and carrots
1/2 cup sliced almonds
1/2 cup Parmesan cheese
8 chicken breast filets
Salt and paprika to taste

Combine rice, soups, mushrooms, wine and peas and carrots in bowl; mix well. Spoon into 9x13-inch baking dish. Sprinkle with half the almonds and half the cheese. Rinse chicken and pat dry. Sprinkle with salt. Arrange over casserole. Top with remaining almonds and cheese. Sprinkle with paprika. Bake at 325 degrees for 45 minutes to 1 hour or until chicken and rice are tender. Yield: 8 servings.

Approx Per Serving: Cal 376; Prot 29 g; Carbo 34 g; Fiber 3 g; T Fat 13 g; Chol 61 mg; Sod 1148 mg.

Mary Lou Wunderle, Central

SAUTÉED DOVE

12 dove
3/4 cup flour
Salt and pepper to taste
2 tablespoons butter
1/2 cup dry white wine

Rinse dove and pat dry. Coat with mixture of flour, salt and pepper. Brown in butter in heavy skillet. Reduce heat; add wine. Simmer, covered, for 45 minutes, adding water if necessary. Yield: 4 servings.

Approx Per Serving: Cal 408; Prot 42 g; Carbo 18 g; Fiber 1 g; T Fat 9 g; Chol 179 mg; Sod 50 mg.

Steve Dumford, Piedmont

ROAST TURKEY BREAST

1 8-pound turkey breast
1 medium onion, cut into quarters
2 carrots, sliced
1 stalk celery, sliced
3 cups white wine
Salt and pepper to taste

Rinse turkey and pat dry. Combine with onion, carrots and celery in roasting pan. Pour wine over turkey. Sprinkle with salt and pepper. Roast at 325 degrees for 2 to 2 1/2 hours or until done to taste. Let stand for 15 minutes before carving. Use Gallo or Almaden wine; do not use cooking wine. May process cooked vegetables in blender to use in gravy if desired.
Yield: 16 servings.

Approx Per Serving: Cal 230; Prot 34 g; Carbo 2 g; Fiber <1 g; T Fat 6 g; Chol 87 mg; Sod 88 mg.

Barbara D. Scott, Independence

TURKEY CHILI

1 pound ground fresh turkey
2 tablespoons light olive oil
1 large onion, chopped
2 cloves of garlic, finely chopped
1 tablespoon chili powder
1/2 teaspoon cumin
1/2 teaspoon salt
1 28-ounce can tomatoes packed in purée
2 16-ounce cans kidney beans, drained, rinsed

Brown turkey in olive oil in 6-quart saucepan over high heat, stirring until crumbly. Add onion and garlic. Cook over medium heat for 5 minutes; drain. Stir in chili powder, cumin and salt. Add tomatoes, stirring to break up. Bring to the boiling point, stirring occasionally. Stir in beans; reduce heat. Simmer for 15 minutes. Yield: 4 servings.

Approx Per Serving: Cal 496; Prot 37 g; Carbo 47 g; Fiber 20 g; T Fat 19 g; Chol 71 mg; Sod 1494 mg.

Paulene Gibson, Independence

MARINATED TURKEY

2 cups Sauterne
1 cup oil
1 cup soy sauce
1 clove of garlic, chopped
8 turkey breast filets

Combine wine, oil, soy sauce and garlic in bowl; mix well. Rinse turkey and pat dry. Add to marinade. Marinate, covered, for 24 to 26 hours. Place turkey on grill over low coals. Grill, with cover closed, for 45 minutes, turning occasionally.
Yield: 8 servings.

Approx Per Serving: Cal 432; Prot 27 g; Carbo 4 g; Fiber <1 g; T Fat 30 g; Chol 59 mg; Sod 2115 mg.

Margaret L. Fenner, Hornets Nest

TURKEY AND HOMINY SCRAMBLE

3 tablespoons margarine
1 pound ground fresh turkey
1 tablespoon flour
1/2 cup sliced green onions
1/2 teaspoon thyme
1/4 teaspoon pepper
1 16-ounce can hominy
1 cup chicken broth
2 tablespoons soy sauce
1 large carrot, coarsely shredded

Heat margarine in large skillet over medium heat until lightly browned. Add turkey. Cook until brown, stirring until crumbly. Stir in flour, green onions, thyme and pepper. Cook for 2 minutes. Add hominy, chicken broth and soy sauce. Cook until slightly thickened, stirring constantly. Simmer, covered, for 5 minutes. Stir in carrot. Ladle into bowls to serve. May use low-salt soy sauce, corn oil margarine and no-salt chicken broth if desired.
Yield: 4 servings.

Approx Per Serving: Cal 360; Prot 26 g; Carbo 18 g; Fiber 1 g; T Fat 20 g; Chol 72 mg; Sod 1242 mg.

Louis M. Cole, Foot Hills

SEAFOOD

BEER-BATTERED BASS

¾ cup pancake mix
¼ cup flour
½ teaspoon baking powder
½ teaspoon salt
1 egg
¾ cup warm beer
6 fish filets
Oil for deep frying

Combine pancake mix, flour, baking powder and salt in bowl. Add egg and beer; mix until smooth. Dip fish in batter, coating well. Deep-fry in hot oil until golden brown; drain. Yield: 6 servings.

Approx Per Serving: Cal 381; Prot 48 g; Carbo 18 g; Fiber <1 g; T Fat 10 g; Chol 143 mg; Sod 564 mg.
Nutritional information does not include oil for deep frying.

Steve Dumford, Piedmont

BAKED FLOUNDER

1 16-ounce package frozen flounder filets
Juice of 1 lemon
Seasoned salt to taste
1 can cream of celery soup
¼ cup milk
¾ cup herb-seasoned stuffing mix
¼ cup Parmesan cheese
2 tablespoons butter

Thaw fish filets enough to separate. Arrange in baking dish; sprinkle with lemon juice and seasoned salt. Combine soup and milk in bowl; mix well. Spread over fish. Sprinkle with stuffing mix and cheese; dot with butter. Bake at 350 degrees for 20 to 30 minutes or until fish flakes easily. Yield: 4 servings.

Approx Per Serving: Cal 293; Prot 27 g; Carbo 17 g; Fiber <1 g; T Fat 13 g; Chol 85 mg; Sod 992 mg.

Mrs. Hugh L. McAulay, Blue Ridge

BROILED MACKEREL

1 1/2 pounds mackerel
1/4 cup olive oil
1/4 cup lemon juice
1 tablespoon chopped parsley
1 tablespoon basil
1/2 cup Parmesan cheese
1/2 teaspoon chopped garlic

Cut fish into serving pieces; arrange in shallow ovenproof dish. Combine olive oil, lemon juice, parsley, basil, cheese and garlic in bowl; mix well. Pour over fish. Marinate for 1 hour, turning several times; drain. Broil for 5 to 7 minutes or until fish flakes easily. May grill 4 to 6 inches from coals for 5 to 7 minutes on each side if preferred. Yield: 6 servings.

Approx Per Serving: Cal 410; Prot 30 g; Carbo 1 g; Fiber <1 g; T Fat 31 g; Chol 90 mg; Sod 220 mg.

Betty W. Hampton, Salem

QUICK AND EASY BARBECUED TUNA

4 ounces drained tuna
1/4 teaspoon chili powder
1 tablespoon Worcestershire sauce
1 tablespoon dry mustard
1 tablespoon dried onion flakes
1/2 cup tomato juice

Combine tuna, chili powder, Worcestershire sauce, dry mustard, onion flakes and tomato juice in saucepan. Bring to a boil; reduce heat. Simmer for 5 minutes. Yield: 1 serving.

Approx Per Serving: Cal 269; Prot 35 g; Carbo 11 g; Fiber 1 g; T Fat 9 g; Chol 20 mg; Sod 990 mg.

Nancy Stirewalt, Hornets Nest

RED SALMON LOAF

1 16-ounce can red salmon, drained
1 cup crushed low-salt thin wheat crackers
1 egg white
1 small onion, chopped
1/3 cup chopped green bell pepper
3/4 cup milk
1/4 cup margarine

Flake salmon into bowl. Add cracker crumbs, egg white, onion, green pepper and milk; mix well. Pack into 5x9-inch loaf pan. Dot with margarine. Bake at 350 degrees for 1 hour. Yield: 6 servings.

Approx Per Serving: Cal 254; Prot 18 g; Carbo 9 g; Fiber 1 g; T Fat 16 g; Chol 37 mg; Sod 598 mg.

Kay Joffrion, Independence

SEAFOOD CASSEROLE

1 7-ounce package long grain and wild rice mix
1 cup chopped celery
1 medium onion, chopped
1 green bell pepper, chopped
1/4 cup margarine
1 4-ounce can mushrooms, drained
1 8-ounce package frozen crab meat, thawed
1 1/2 pounds peeled shrimp
1 4-ounce can chopped pimentos, drained
2 cans cream of mushroom soup
1/4 cup milk

Cook rice using package directions. Sauté celery, onion and green pepper in margarine in skillet. Add rice, mushrooms, crab meat, shrimp, pimentos, soup and milk; mix well. Spoon into greased 9x13-inch baking dish. Bake at 350 degrees for 45 minutes. Yield: 10 servings.

Approx Per Serving: Cal 284; Prot 22 g; Carbo 8 g; Fiber 2 g; T Fat 11 g; Chol 157 mg; Sod 825 mg.

Frances Cook, Blue Ridge

SCALLOPS À LA DOROTHY

1/4 cup chopped onion
1/2 cup sliced mushrooms
2 cloves of garlic, minced
2 tablespoons margarine
1/2 cup vermouth
Lemon pepper to taste
1/4 teaspoon thyme
1 1/2 teaspoons parsley
1/4 teaspoon salt
8 ounces bay scallops
2 tablespoons Parmesan cheese

Sauté onion, mushrooms and garlic in margarine in skillet over medium heat for 3 minutes or until onion is tender. Add wine, lemon pepper, thyme, parsley and salt; mix well. Bring to a simmer. Add scallops. Cook for 5 minutes, stirring frequently; do not overcook. Sprinkle with cheese. Serve over hot cooked rice. Yield: 2 servings.

Approx Per Serving: Cal 313; Prot 22 g; Carbo 10 g; Fiber 1 g; T Fat 14 g; Chol 41 mg; Sod 689 mg.

John E. Miles, Independence

BARBECUED SHRIMP

2 pounds shrimp, peeled
1 pound margarine
2 tablespoons Creole mustard
1 1/2 teaspoons chili powder
1/4 teaspoon basil
1/4 teaspoon thyme
2 teaspoons coarsely ground pepper
1/2 teaspoon oregano
1 teaspoon garlic powder
1 teaspoon onion powder
1/4 cup crab boil seasoning
1/2 teaspoon Tabasco sauce
1 teaspoon liquid smoke

Place shrimp in baking dish. Melt margarine in saucepan. Add mustard, chili powder, basil, thyme, pepper, oregano, garlic powder, onion powder, crab boil seasoning, Tabasco sauce and liquid smoke; mix well. Simmer for 5 minutes. Pour over shrimp. Bake at 375 degrees for 20 minutes, stirring occasionally. Serve immediately. Yield: 4 servings.

Approx Per Serving: Cal 1051; Prot 49 g; Carbo 3 g; Fiber <1 g; T Fat 94 g; Chol 442 mg; Sod 1689 mg.

John E. Miles, Independence

SHRIMP CAPRI

1 pound shrimp
1 clove of garlic, minced
1/2 cup butter
Salt and freshly ground
 pepper to taste

Peel shrimp, leaving tail portion; devein. Rinse and pat dry. Place in large ovenproof pan. Sauté garlic in butter in skillet for 3 minutes. Pour over shrimp. Sprinkle with salt and pepper. Broil 3 inches from heat source for 5 to 7 minutes or until done to taste. Yield: 3 servings.

Approx Per Serving: Cal 422; Prot 32 g; Carbo <1 g; Fiber <1 g; T Fat 32 g; Chol 378 mg; Sod 597 mg.

Janet Batrouny, Independence

CURRIED SHRIMP

3 pounds medium shrimp
9 cups water
1/4 cup butter
1 1/2 teaspoons curry powder
1/4 cup chopped fresh parsley
1/2 cup chopped green bell pepper
1/2 cup chopped celery
5 tablespoons flour
1/2 teaspoon garlic salt
3/4 teaspoon salt
3 cups milk
1 1/2 cups shredded Cheddar cheese
1/4 cup chopped pimento

Drop shrimp into boiling water in saucepan. Return to a boil; reduce heat. Simmer for 3 to 5 minutes or until done to taste; drain and rinse with cold water. Chill in refrigerator. Peel and devein shrimp. Melt butter in heavy saucepan over medium heat. Stir in curry powder, parsley, green pepper and celery. Cook for 2 minutes, stirring occasionally. Add flour, garlic salt and salt; mix well. Cook for 1 minute, stirring constantly; reduce heat. Stir in milk gradually. Cook until thickened, stirring constantly. Stir in cheese until melted. Add shrimp and pimento. Heat to serving temperature, stirring constantly. Yield: 10 servings.

Approx Per Serving: Cal 306; Prot 36 g; Carbo 7 g; Fiber <1 g; T Fat 14 g; Chol 306 mg; Sod 748 mg.

Kim Parker, Central

SHRIMP CASSEROLE

1 cup chopped celery
1/2 cup chopped green bell pepper
1 tablespoon grated onion
2 tablespoons oil
1/4 cup flour
1/2 teaspoon curry powder
2 teaspoons Worcestershire sauce
2 drops of Tabasco sauce
3/4 teaspoon salt
3 ounces cream cheese, softened
1 2/3 cups milk
4 cups cooked shrimp
1/3 cup soft bread crumbs
1 tablespoon melted butter
1/4 cup Parmesan cheese

Sauté celery, green pepper and onion in oil in saucepan until tender. Sprinkle with flour, curry powder, Worcestershire sauce, Tabasco sauce and salt. Cook for 2 minutes, stirring constantly. Stir in cream cheese until melted. Add milk gradually. Cook until thickened, stirring constantly; remove from heat. Stir in shrimp. Spoon into shallow 9x9-inch baking dish. Top with mixture of crumbs, butter and Parmesan cheese. Bake at 375 degrees for 35 to 45 minutes or until bubbly and light brown. Yield: 6 servings.

Approx Per Serving: Cal 297; Prot 26 g; Carbo 14 g; Fiber 1 g; T Fat 15 g; Chol 175 mg; Sod 618 mg.

Mildred Deese, Hornets Nest

PASTA IN SHRIMP AND WINE SAUCE

1 cup chopped onion
2 cloves of garlic, chopped
2 tablespoons butter
3 tablespoons olive oil
1 cup dry white wine
1 tablespoon instant chicken bouillon
1 teaspoon basil, crushed
1/2 teaspoon salt
1/8 teaspoon pepper
1 pound small shrimp, peeled
1 cup chopped, seeded peeled tomatoes
10 ounces pasta, cooked
1/4 cup melted butter
1/2 cup Parmesan cheese
1/2 cup chopped fresh parsley

Sauté onion and garlic in 2 tablespoons butter and olive oil in 2-quart saucepan until tender but not brown. Add wine, instant bouillon, basil, salt and pepper. Bring to a boil; reduce heat. Simmer for 12 to 15 minutes or until reduced by 2/3. Add shrimp.

Simmer, covered, for 5 minutes or until done to taste. Stir in tomatoes. Add pasta and 1/4 cup melted butter; toss to mix well. Add cheese and parsley; toss to mix well. May substitute 1 cup scallops for shrimp. Yield: 6 servings.

Approx Per Serving: Cal 488; Prot 26 g; Carbo 40 g; Fiber 3 g; T Fat 22 g; Chol 184 mg; Sod 866 mg.

Gaynell Sherrill, Independence

CLAM CHOWDER

6 slices bacon, chopped
1 cup chopped onion
1 cup chopped celery
1/2 cup chopped green bell pepper
1 21-ounce can minced clams
1 28-ounce can tomatoes
3 cups water
1/2 teaspoon thyme
1 bay leaf
1 teaspoon salt
1/4 teaspoon pepper
3 cups chopped potatoes
1 16-ounce can Shoe Peg corn
2 tablespoons margarine

Cook bacon in heavy saucepan until nearly crisp. Add onion, celery and green pepper. Cook over low heat for 10 minutes or until tender, stirring occasionally; drain. Drain clams, reserving liquid. Add clam liquid, tomatoes, water, thyme, bay leaf, salt and pepper to saucepan. Bring to a boil; reduce heat. Simmer, covered, for 1 hour. Add potatoes. Cook for 30 minutes or until potatoes are tender. Add clams and corn. Simmer for 15 minutes. Stir in margarine; discard bay leaf. Yield: 8 servings.

Approx Per Serving: Cal 249; Prot 12 g; Carbo 39 g; Fiber 4 g; T Fat 11 g; Chol 51 mg; Sod 743 mg.

Kathy E. Beam, Foot Hills

☎ Barbecue shrimp in a sauce of melted margarine, lemon juice, Italian salad dressing and pepper. Bake at 350 degrees for 30 minutes and then chill until serving time.

FISH CHOWDER

2 large carrots, grated
2 1/2 stalks celery, chopped
2 bay leaves
1/2 teaspoon salt
1 1/2 cups water
1 pound halibut, flaked
2 cups mashed cooked potatoes

Combine carrots, celery, bay leaves, salt and water in saucepan. Simmer until vegetables are tender. Add fish. Simmer until done to taste. Add potatoes; mix well. Discard bay leaves. Yield: 6 servings.

Approx Per Serving: Cal 150; Prot 17 g; Carbo 15 g; Fiber 2 g; T Fat 2 g; Chol 26 mg; Sod 453 mg.

Linda Davidson, Blue Ridge

SALMON CHOWDER

1 1/2 cups thinly sliced carrots
3 tablespoons olive oil
2 cups chopped potatoes
1/2 cup chopped green bell pepper
1 onion, chopped
1 16-ounce can stewed tomatoes
1/4 teaspoon thyme
Dash of hot pepper sauce
1 can cream of celery soup
4 cups skim milk
1 16-ounce can salmon, drained, flaked

Sauté carrots in olive oil in 6-quart saucepan. Add potatoes, green pepper and onion. Sauté for 10 minutes or until almost tender, stirring frequently. Add tomatoes, thyme and pepper sauce. Simmer, covered, for 6 to 8 minutes or until vegetables are tender. Stir in soup, milk and salmon. Heat to serving temperature over low heat. Yield: 6 servings.

Approx Per Serving: Cal 381; Prot 25 g; Carbo 37 g; Fiber 4 g; T Fat 15 g; Chol 41 mg; Sod 1014 mg.

Mildred Smith, Hornets Nest

SEAFOOD CHOWDER

4 ounces bacon, chopped
1 large bunch green onions with tops, chopped
2 28-ounce cans tomatoes
1 pound shrimp, chopped
6 medium potatoes, chopped
3 pounds fish filets, chopped
8 ounces crab meat
Salt and pepper to taste

Cook bacon in large saucepan over medium heat. Add green onions. Sauté until tender. Add tomatoes. Bring to a boil. Stir in shrimp, potatoes, fish, crab meat and enough water to make of desired consistency. Cook until potatoes are tender. Season to taste. Yield: 10 servings.

Approx Per Serving: Cal 515; Prot 58 g; Carbo 38 g; Fiber 5 g; T Fat 14 g; Chol 206 mg; Sod 718 mg.

Carrie Medlin, Piedmont

SHRIMP CHOWDER

2 large potatoes, chopped
1 14-ounce can chicken broth
1 1/2 broth cans water
3 bay leaves
1 onion, chopped
1/4 cup oil
1/2 10-ounce package frozen corn
3 tablespoons flour
2 cups half and half
1 12-ounce package frozen cooked shrimp, thawed

Combine potatoes with chicken broth, water and bay leaves in saucepan. Cook until potatoes are tender; discard bay leaves. Sauté onion in oil in skillet. Add onion and corn to potatoes in saucepan; reserve drippings in skillet. Stir flour into drippings in skillet. Stir into soup. Add half and half and shrimp. Cook over medium heat for 1 minute or until thickened to desired consistency. Yield: 4 servings.

Approx Per Serving: Cal 558; Prot 27 g; Carbo 47 g; Fiber 5 g; T Fat 30 g; Chol 174 mg; Sod 501 mg.

Linda Rutt, Raleigh

☎ Tips for seafood lovers:

- Be sure that the fish you buy is fresh. It will smell fishy, but it should smell clean and fresh as well. Gills should be pink to red, eyes should be firm and bulging, and flesh firm and elastic.
- Fresh shrimp will have a mild odor and firm meat.
- Purchase only live crab and lobsters. Tails of live lobsters will curl under when picked up.
- Fresh scallops should have a sweet odor and firm white flesh. They should be free of liquid when bought in packages.
- Shells of live clams, mussels and oysters should be tightly closed or, if slightly open, should close immediately when lightly tapped. Open shells indicate that the shellfish is dead and should not be eaten.
- Shucked oysters should be plump and naturally creamy in color.
- Store seafood in the coldest part of the refrigerator for up to 2 days. To keep it from flavoring other food in the refrigerator, wrap it in foil and store in a container with a tight-fitting cover.
- Rinse seafood before using and pat dry.
- As a general rule, cook seafood for 10 minutes for each inch of thickness, whatever the cooking method chosen. For example, poach a 4-inch piece of salmon for 40 minutes; sauté a 1/2-inch filet for 5 minutes; and broil a 1 1/2-inch steak for 7 1/2 minutes on each side.
- You should never microwave frozen fish without defrosting it first; it will be tasteless, dry and unevenly cooked. Do not even thaw seafood in the microwave.

Vegetables
and Side Dishes

CAMP CAREFREE

VEGETABLES

ASPARAGUS CASSEROLE

1/4 cup butter, softened
1/4 cup flour
1/2 teaspoon salt
2 cups milk
1/2 cup shredded Cheddar cheese
1 16-ounce can asparagus, drained
3 hard-boiled eggs, sliced
1/4 cup blanched slivered almonds, toasted
1/4 cup cracker crumbs
2 tablespoons butter

Melt 1/4 cup butter in saucepan. Blend in flour and salt. Add milk gradually. Cook until thickened, stirring constantly. Add cheese. Cook until cheese melts, stirring constantly; remove from heat. Cut asparagus into bite-sized pieces with scissors. Layer asparagus, eggs, almonds and sauce 1/2 at a time in 2-quart casserole. Sprinkle with cracker crumbs; dot with 2 tablespoons butter. Bake at 375 degrees until hot and bubbly. Serve immediately. Cool sauce and eggs before assembling casserole if not serving immediately. Yield: 8 servings.

Approx Per Serving: Cal 259; Prot 7 g; Carbo 11 g; Fiber 1 g; T Fat 21 g; Chol 130 mg; Sod 498 mg.

Mrs. Hugh L. McAulay, Blue Ridge

ASPARAGUS CASSEROLE AU GRATIN

1 16-ounce can asparagus
1 4-ounce can chopped pimentos, drained
3 eggs
1 cup shredded Cheddar cheese
1 1/4 cups cracker crumbs
1 1/2 cups milk
1/4 cup melted butter

Drain asparagus, reserving liquid. Cut asparagus into 1-inch pieces. Combine asparagus and reserved liquid with next 5 ingredients in 2-quart casserole; mix well. Drizzle with melted butter. Bake at 350 degrees for 20 to 30 minutes. Yield: 6 servings.

Approx Per Serving: Cal 309; Prot 12 g; Carbo 19 g; Fiber 2 g; T Fat 21 g; Chol 161 mg; Sod 657 mg.

Evelyn N. Goodman, Hornets Nest

ASPARAGUS CASSEROLE SUPREME

1 32-ounce can asparagus
20 saltine crackers, crumbled
4 hard-boiled eggs, chopped
10 ounces sharp Cheddar cheese, shredded
1 8-ounce can mushrooms, drained
2 1/2 ounces almonds, toasted
2 cans cream of mushroom soup
6 tablespoons butter, sliced
Pepper to taste
1 cup milk

Drain asparagus, reserving 3 tablespoons liquid. Cut asparagus into pieces. Place 1/4 of the cracker crumbs in 2-quart casserole. Layer asparagus, eggs, cheese, mushrooms, almonds, soup, butter, pepper and remaining cracker crumbs 1/3 at a time in prepared casserole. Mix milk with reserved asparagus liquid. Pour over casserole. Bake at 350 degrees for 30 to 40 minutes or until hot and bubbly. Yield: 6 servings.

Approx Per Serving: Cal 809; Prot 31 g; Carbo 31 g; Fiber 8 g; T Fat 66 g; Chol 243 mg; Sod 1967 mg.

Cheryl Griffin, Raleigh

BAKED BEANS

2 1/2 cups dried beans
1/2 cup catsup
8 ounces salt pork
1 1/4 teaspoons salt
3/4 teaspoon dry mustard
1 medium onion, sliced
3 tablespoons brown sugar

Wash beans. Let stand in water to cover in large saucepan overnight. Cook beans until tender, stirring occasionally; drain, reserving liquid. Combine beans with next 4 ingredients in 3-quart casserole; mix well. Top with onion slices. Sprinkle onions with brown sugar. Add enough reserved liquid to cover bean mixture. Bake, covered, at 300 degrees for 6 to 8 hours or until tender. Do not allow beans to cook dry. Remove cover during last 30 minutes of baking time to brown top. Yield: 12 servings.

Approx Per Serving: Cal 270; Prot 15 g; Carbo 31 g; Fiber 9 g; T Fat 10 g; Chol 16 mg; Sod 653 mg.

Ila Mae Moses, Hornets Nest

BAKED BEAN CASSEROLE

1 large onion, chopped
1/4 cup bacon drippings
1 teaspoon salt
1/2 teaspoon pepper
Garlic salt to taste
1 teaspoon mustard
1 16-ounce can pork and beans
1 16-ounce can kidney beans
1 16-ounce can butter beans
3/4 cup packed brown sugar
1/4 teaspoon vinegar
1/2 cup catsup
6 slices crisp-fried bacon, crumbled

Sauté onion in bacon drippings in large skillet. Add salt, pepper, garlic salt, mustard, pork and beans, kidney beans, butter beans, brown sugar, vinegar and catsup in 2-quart casserole; mix well. Bake at 350 degrees for 45 minutes to 1 hour or until brown and bubbly. Sprinkle with bacon. Yield: 12 servings.

Approx Per Serving: Cal 229; Prot 7 g; Carbo 36 g; Fiber 8 g; T Fat 7 g; Chol 33 mg; Sod 782 mg.

James Phillips, Independence

BAKED LIMA BEANS

1 pound dried lima beans
1/2 teaspoon garlic salt
1 pound bacon
3 cans tomato soup
1 cup packed brown sugar
1 large onion, chopped
Salt and pepper to taste

Combine beans with garlic salt in large saucepan. Add enough water to cover. Let stand overnight; drain. Fry bacon in skillet until crisp. Remove bacon to paper towels to drain. Crumble. Add soup and brown sugar to bacon drippings in saucepan; mix well. Stir in onion, salt and pepper. Combine soup mixture and bacon with lima beans in baking dish. Bake at 300 degrees for 3 to 4 hours or until beans are tender, stirring occasionally. May simmer on stove-top if preferred. Yield: 10 servings.

Approx Per Serving: Cal 551; Prot 27 g; Carbo 56 g; Fiber 15 g; T Fat 26 g; Chol 39 mg; Sod 2201 mg.

Irene M. Hooper, Asheville

LIMA BEAN CASSEROLE

1 10-ounce package frozen baby lima beans
1 10-ounce can cream of mushroom soup
1 4-ounce jar chopped pimentos, drained
1 teaspoon melted butter
1/2 cup cracker crumbs

Cook lima beans using package directions; drain. Combine lima beans, soup, pimentos and melted butter in 2-quart casserole; mix well. Sprinkle with cracker crumbs. Bake at 350 degrees for 35 minutes. Yield: 6 servings.

Approx Per Serving: Cal 141; Prot 4 g; Carbo 19 g; Fiber 5 g; T Fat 5 g; Chol 5 mg; Sod 521 mg.

Deni Dumford, Piedmont

GRAN'S BAKED LIMA BEANS

1 pound dried large lima beans
4 ounces bacon, cut into bite-sized pieces
1/2 cup chopped onion
1 cup coarsely chopped carrot
Salt and pepper to taste
1/2 cup maple syrup

Soak lima beans in water to cover in large saucepan overnight. Parboil; drain, reserving liquid. Sauté bacon in large skillet for 5 minutes. Add onion and carrot. Sauté until vegetables are brown. Add to beans; mix well. Add enough water to reserved liquid to measure 2 cups. Stir into bean mixture. Add salt, pepper and maple syrup; mix well. Pour into greased 9x13-inch baking pan. Bake, covered, at 325 degrees for 2 to 2 1/2 hours or until beans are tender. Yield: 12 servings.

Approx Per Serving: Cal 222; Prot 11 g; Carbo 34 g; Fiber 12 g; T Fat 5 g; Chol 8 mg; Sod 163 mg.

Edith G. Jack, Raleigh

BAKED BEANS WITH MOLASSES

1 20-ounce can pork and beans
2 tablespoons molasses
2 tablespoons brown sugar
1/4 cup catsup
3 drops of Tabasco sauce
1/4 cup chopped onion
1/4 cup chopped green bell pepper
1/4 cup chopped celery
6 slices bacon

Combine pork and beans, molasses, brown sugar, catsup, Tabasco sauce, onion, green pepper and celery in baking dish; mix well. Arrange bacon slices over top. Bake at 375 degrees for 30 minutes. Yield: 8 servings.

Approx Per Serving: Cal 142; Prot 5 g; Carbo 24 g; Fiber 4 g; T Fat 3 g; Chol 9 mg; Sod 410 mg.

Neal Ballard, Independence

THREE-BEAN BAKE

1 medium onion, chopped
1 medium green bell pepper, chopped
2 tablespoons bacon drippings
3 slices crisp-fried bacon, crumbled
2 16-ounce cans baked beans
1 16-ounce cans lima beans, drained
1 16-ounce can kidney beans
1/2 cup chili sauce
2 tablespoons brown sugar
3 tablespoons vinegar
1/2 teaspoon dry mustard
1/4 teaspoon pepper

Sauté onion and green pepper in bacon drippings in large skillet. Add bacon, baked beans, lima beans, kidney beans, chili sauce, brown sugar, vinegar, dry mustard and pepper; mix well. Pour into greased 2 1/2-quart casserole. Bake at 350 degrees for 1 hour. Yield: 8 servings.

Approx Per Serving: Cal 303; Prot 13 g; Carbo 51 g; Fiber 15 g; T Fat 7 g; Chol 31 mg; Sod 1071 mg.

John E. Miles, Independence

JOYCE'S BAKED BEANS

3/4 cup packed brown sugar
1 teaspoon dry mustard
2 16-ounce cans pork and beans
3 slices bacon, cut into pieces
1/2 cup catsup

Combine brown sugar and dry mustard in small bowl; mix well. Layer beans and brown sugar mixture 1/2 at a time in greased baking dish or bean pot. Sprinkle with bacon. Pour catsup over top. Bake at 325 degrees for 2 1/2 hours. Make ahead and chill overnight before baking to improve flavor.
Yield: 8 servings.

Approx Per Serving: Cal 235; Prot 7 g; Carbo 48 g; Fiber 7 g; T Fat 3 g; Chol 10 mg; Sod 605 mg.

Joyce Pruitt, Independence

CHUCK WAGON BEANS

1/2 cup chopped onion
2 tablespoons bacon drippings
2 cups cooked dried beans
1 pound ground beef
1/2 cup water
2 8-ounce cans tomato sauce
2 teaspoons chili powder
3/4 teaspoon salt
1 tablespoon brown sugar
1 tablespoon molasses

Sauté onion in bacon drippings in large saucepan until tender. Add beans, ground beef, water, tomato sauce, chili powder, salt, brown sugar and molasses; mix well. Simmer, covered, for 40 minutes. Yield: 4 servings.

Approx Per Serving: Cal 759; Prot 50 g; Carbo 70 g; Fiber 22 g; T Fat 32 g; Chol 143 mg; Sod 1234 mg.

Martha A. Rhyne, Foot Hills

☎ A few drops of liquid smoke give a "cook-out" flavor to bean dishes.

BROCCOLI BAKE

2 10-ounce packages frozen broccoli
1 can cream of mushroom soup
1/4 cup milk
1/2 cup shredded Cheddar cheese
1 cup baking mix
1/4 cup butter, softened

Cook broccoli using package directions; drain. Place in 2-quart casserole. Combine soup and milk in mixer bowl; beat until smooth. Pour over broccoli; sprinkle with cheese. Mix baking mix and butter in small bowl until crumbly. Sprinkle over cheese layer. Bake at 400 degrees for 20 to 25 minutes or until light brown. Yield: 8 servings.

Approx Per Serving: Cal 239; Prot 8 g; Carbo 18 g; Fiber 2 g; T Fat 16 g; Chol 32 mg; Sod 663 mg.

Joanne Williams, Independence

JULIA'S BROCCOLI CASSEROLE

2 10-ounce packages frozen chopped broccoli
2 eggs, beaten
1 cup mayonnaise
1 can cream of mushroom soup
1 medium onion, chopped
Salt and pepper to taste
1/2 cup shredded sharp Cheddar cheese
1/4 cup melted margarine
1/2 8-ounce package stuffing mix
1/2 cup shredded sharp Cheddar cheese

Cook broccoli using package directions boiling for 5 minutes. Drain and cool. Add eggs, mayonnaise, soup, onion, salt, pepper and 1/2 cup cheese; mix well. Mix margarine with stuffing mix in bowl. Add to broccoli mixture; mix well. Pour into buttered 9-inch square baking dish. Top with remaining 1/2 cup cheese. Bake at 325 degrees for 35 minutes or until bubbly. Yield: 8 servings.

Approx Per Serving: Cal 423; Prot 10 g; Carbo 16 g; Fiber 2 g; T Fat 37 g; Chol 85 mg; Sod 770 mg.

Julia S. Clark, Independence

BROCCOLI AND CHEESE CASSEROLE

1 5-ounce package dirty rice mix
2 10-ounce packages frozen broccoli
1 16-ounce jar Cheez Whiz
2 8-ounce cans sliced water chestnuts, drained

Cook rice using package directions. Cook broccoli using package directions; drain. Mix rice and broccoli in 3-quart glass casserole. Stir in Cheez Whiz and water chestnuts. Microwave on High for 5 minutes or bake at 350 degrees for 20 minutes. Yield: 12 servings.

Approx Per Serving: Cal 199; Prot 10 g; Carbo 20 g; Fiber 2 g; T Fat 9 g; Chol 24 mg; Sod 464 mg.

Wanda Alexander, Hornets Nest

CHEESY BROCCOLI CASSEROLE

2 10-ounce packages frozen chopped broccoli
1/2 cup margarine
8 ounces Velveeta cheese, cut into cubes
4 ounces butter crackers, crumbled
1/2 cup melted butter

Cook broccoli using package directions; drain. Place in greased baking dish. Melt 1/2 cup margarine and cheese in saucepan over low heat, stirring occasionally. Pour over broccoli. Mix crackers with 1/2 cup melted butter in small bowl. Sprinkle over broccoli. Bake at 350 degrees for 30 minutes. Yield: 8 servings.

Approx Per Serving: Cal 298; Prot 10 g; Carbo 14 g; Fiber 2 g; T Fat 25 g; Chol 43 mg; Sod 679 mg.

Virginia Bowie, Independence
Burline P. Thompson, Raleigh

☎ Substitute crushed wheat germ for buttered crumbs for a delicious, nutritious and easy casserole topping.

COMPANY BROCCOLI CASSEROLE

3 slices bread
2 10-ounce packages frozen chopped broccoli
2 eggs
1 can cream of chicken soup
2 tablespoons grated onion
¾ cup mayonnaise
½ cup shredded sharp Cheddar cheese
Salt and pepper to taste
½ cup shredded sharp Cheddar cheese
½ cup melted margarine

Toast bread slices. Trim crusts; crumble. Cook broccoli using package directions; drain. Beat eggs in large mixer bowl until frothy. Add soup, onion, mayonnaise, ½ cup cheese, salt and pepper; mix well. Stir in broccoli. Pour into 9x13-inch baking dish sprayed with nonstick cooking spray. Sprinkle with remaining ½ cup cheese. Sprinkle over casserole; drizzle with margarine. Bake at 300 degrees for 25 minutes. May substitute cream of mushroom soup for cream of chicken soup. May be frozen before baking, adding bread crumbs and margarine just before baking. Yield: 8 servings.

Approx Per Serving: Cal 360; Prot 9 g; Carbo 13 g; Fiber 2 g; T Fat 31 g; Chol 83 mg; Sod 659 mg.

Kathryn Henderson, Hornets Nest

CREAMY BROCCOLI CASSEROLE

2 10-ounce packages frozen chopped broccoli
3 ounces cream cheese, chopped
¼ cup butter, chopped
1 6-ounce roll garlic cheese, chopped
1 can cream of mushroom soup

Cook broccoli using package directions; drain. Combine cream cheese, butter and garlic cheese in bowl; mix well. Add soup; mix well. Layer broccoli and cheese sauce ½ at a time in 2-quart baking dish. Bake at 350 degrees for 30 minutes. May add one 4-ounce can mushrooms. May substitute fresh broccoli for frozen. Yield: 8 servings.

Approx Per Serving: Cal 216; Prot 7 g; Carbo 5 g; Fiber 1 g; T Fat 19 g; Chol 48 mg; Sod 701 mg.

Becky Adams, Coastal

EASY BROCCOLI CASSEROLE

2 10-ounce packages frozen chopped broccoli
1 can cream of mushroom soup
1 cup shredded Cheddar cheese
1 cup mayonnaise
1 small onion, finely chopped
2 eggs, slightly beaten

Cook broccoli using package directions; drain. Add soup, cheese, mayonnaise, onion and eggs; mix well. Pour into 2-quart casserole. Bake at 350 degrees for 45 minutes. Yield: 8 servings.

Approx Per Serving: Cal 338; Prot 8 g; Carbo 9 g; Fiber 2 g; T Fat 31 g; Chol 85 mg; Sod 587 mg.

Sheila Leach, Hornets Nest

FAVORITE BROCCOLI CASSEROLE

2 10-ounce packages frozen chopped broccoli
2 eggs, well beaten
1 can cream of mushroom soup
1/2 cup mayonnaise
1 cup shredded sharp Cheddar cheese
1 small onion, chopped
1 cup cheese-flavored butter cracker crumbs

Cook broccoli using package directions; drain. Combine eggs, soup, mayonnaise, cheese and onion in bowl; mix well. Fold in broccoli. Pour into 2-quart casserole. Sprinkle with crumbs. Bake at 350 degrees for 30 minutes. May substitute fresh broccoli for frozen broccoli increasing cream of mushroom soup to 2 cans. May add one 2-ounce jar chopped pimento or omit mayonnaise if desired. Yield: 8 servings.

Approx Per Serving: Cal 306; Prot 11 g; Carbo 22 g; Fiber 2 g; T Fat 21 g; Chol 77 mg; Sod 742 mg.

Mary K. Harmon, Blue Ridge

☎ Cook vegetables with the least amount of water possible to preserve both nutrients and flavor.

BROCCOLI AND PECAN CASSEROLE

- 2 10-ounce packages frozen chopped broccoli
- 2 eggs, slightly beaten
- 1 can cream of mushroom soup
- 1 cup mayonnaise
- 1 cup shredded sharp Cheddar cheese
- 1 medium onion, grated
- 1/2 cup chopped pecans
- 2 tablespoons butter, softened
- 1 cup cheese-flavored butter crackers, crumbled

Cook broccoli using package directions; drain. Combine eggs, soup, mayonnaise, cheese, onion and pecans in bowl; mix well. Fold in broccoli. Pour into buttered casserole. Dot with butter; sprinkle with cracker crumbs. Bake at 350 degrees for 20 to 30 minutes or until hot and bubbly. Yield: 6 servings.

Approx Per Serving: Cal 647; Prot 14 g; Carbo 22 g; Fiber 3 g; T Fat 59 g; Chol 133 mg; Sod 1002 mg.

Jenny Givens, Independence

BROCCOLI AND STUFFING CASSEROLE

- 2 10-ounce packages frozen chopped broccoli
- 1 egg, beaten
- 1 cup mayonnaise
- 2 onions, chopped
- 1 can cream of mushroom soup
- 2 cups herb-seasoned stuffing mix
- 3/4 cup milk

Cook broccoli using package directions; drain. Add egg, mayonnaise, onions, soup, stuffing mix and milk; mix well. Pour into greased 3-quart casserole. Bake at 350 degrees for 1 hour. To Microwave, sauté onions and broccoli in saucepan until tender. Add remaining ingredients; mix well. Pour into 3-quart glass casserole. Microwave on High for 15 minutes, turning dish twice. Yield: 8 servings.

Approx Per Serving: Cal 358; Prot 7 g; Carbo 24 g; Fiber 3 g; T Fat 27 g; Chol 46 mg; Sod 734 mg.

Mildred Smith, Hornets Nest

BROCCOLI AND RICE CASSEROLE

1 cup uncooked minute rice
1 10-ounce package frozen broccoli
1 small onion, chopped
2 tablespoons butter
1 cup cream of chicken soup
1/2 cup Cheez Whiz
1/2 cup milk
1 cup bread crumbs
1 tablespoon melted butter
1 cup shredded Cheddar cheese

Cook rice using package directions. Cook broccoli using package directions; drain. Sauté onion in 2 tablespoons butter in large saucepan until tender. Add soup, Cheez Whiz and milk; mix well. Cook until cheese melts, stirring constantly. Add onion, broccoli and rice; mix well. Pour into 3-quart casserole. Sprinkle with mixture of bread crumbs, 1 tablespoon melted butter and cheese. Bake at 350 degrees for 30 minutes. Yield: 8 servings.

Approx Per Serving: Cal 245; Prot 9 g; Carbo 22 g; Fiber 2 g; T Fat 14 g; Chol 37 mg; Sod 559 mg.

Debra Swilling, Asheville

BROCCOLI PUFF

2 10-ounce packages frozen chopped broccoli
1 can cream of mushroom soup
1 egg, beaten
1/4 cup milk
1/4 cup mayonnaise
1/2 cup shredded sharp Cheddar cheese
1/2 cup cracker crumbs
1 tablespoon melted butter

Cook broccoli using package directions; drain. Place in 2-quart casserole. Combine soup, egg, milk and mayonnaise in bowl; mix well. Add cheese; mix well. Pour over broccoli; mix lightly. Sprinkle with mixture of cracker crumbs and melted butter. Bake at 350 degrees for 45 minutes or until top is golden brown. Yield: 6 servings.

Approx Per Serving: Cal 247; Prot 8 g; Carbo 15 g; Fiber 3 g; T Fat 18 g; Chol 60 mg; Sod 667 mg.

Ruth Demos, Independence

BROCCOLI MEDLEY CASSEROLE

1 16-ounce package frozen mixed broccoli, carrots, red pepper and water chestnuts, thawed
1 can cream of chicken soup
1/2 cup cooked rice
4 ounces Cheddar cheese, cut into cubes
1/4 cup melted butter

Combine mixed vegetables, soup, rice and cheese in bowl; mix well. Pour into 2-quart baking dish. Pour butter over top. Bake at 425 degrees for 20 minutes or until bubbly and cheese melts. May substitute any flavor cream soup. May microwave on High for 3 to 5 minutes or until bubbly. Yield: 4 servings.

Approx Per Serving: Cal 346; Prot 13 g; Carbo 18 g; Fiber 3 g; T Fat 26 g; Chol 67 mg; Sod 899 mg.

Sallie Greer, Hornets Nest

BROCCOLI AND CORN BAKE

2 10-ounce packages frozen chopped broccoli
2 tablespoons chopped onion
2 tablespoons butter
1 tablespoon flour
1 1/4 cups milk
2 cups shredded Cheddar cheese
1 12-ounce can whole kernel corn, drained
1/2 cup cracker crumbs

Cook broccoli using package directions; drain. Place in 7x11-inch casserole. Sauté onion in butter in large skillet until tender. Stir in flour gradually. Add milk. Cook until thickened, stirring constantly. Add cheese. Cook until cheese melts, stirring constantly. Stir in corn and 1/4 cup crumbs. Pour over broccoli; sprinkle with remaining crumbs. Bake at 350 degrees for 30 minutes. May prepare casserole ahead and chill, covered, overnight. Increase baking time to 45 minutes. Yield: 8 servings.

Approx Per Serving: Cal 254; Prot 12 g; Carbo 22 g; Fiber 3 g; T Fat 14 g; Chol 45 mg; Sod 455 mg.

Deni Dumford, Piedmont

BROCCOLI CASSEROLE DELUXE

2 10-ounce packages frozen broccoli
1 can cream of mushroom soup
1 cup mayonnaise
2 eggs
1 onion, chopped
1 cup shredded Cheddar cheese
1/2 8-ounce package stuffing mix
1/2 cup melted butter

Cook broccoli using package directions; drain. Place in 2-quart casserole. Combine soup, mayonnaise, eggs and onion in bowl; mix well. Pour over broccoli. Sprinkle with cheese and mixture of stuffing mix and melted butter. Bake at 350 degrees for 30 minutes. Yield: 8 servings.

Approx Per Serving: Cal 406; Prot 15 g; Carbo 29 g; Fiber 2 g; T Fat 26 g; Chol 115 mg; Sod 993 mg.

Ruth B. Bumgardner, Hornets Nest

BROCCOLI CASSEROLE

2 10-ounce packages frozen chopped broccoli
2 eggs, beaten
1 can cream of chicken soup
1 cup mayonnaise
1 cup shredded Cheddar cheese
2 cups butter cracker crumbs
3 tablespoons margarine

Cook broccoli using package directions for 5 minutes or until tender; drain. Combine eggs, soup, mayonnaise and cheese in large bowl; mix well. Fold in broccoli. Pour into greased 2-quart casserole. Sprinkle with crumbs; dot with margarine. Bake at 350 degrees for 30 minutes. Yield: 6 servings.

Approx Per Serving: Cal 603; Prot 13 g; Carbo 30 g; Fiber 3 g; T Fat 52 g; Chol 117 mg; Sod 1118 mg.

Carolyn Irvin, Hornets Nest

CABBAGE AU GRATIN

1 medium cabbage, chopped
1 cup water
6 tablespoons margarine
1/4 cup flour
1 2/3 cups milk
Salt and pepper to taste
1 1/2 cups shredded Cheddar cheese

Cook cabbage in water in saucepan for 10 minutes; drain. Pour into casserole. Melt margarine in saucepan. Stir in flour. Add milk; mix well. Cook until thickened, stirring constantly. Pour over cabbage. Season with salt and pepper. Top with shredded cheese. Bake at 350 degrees for 30 minutes or until cheese is melted and light brown. May cook small onion with cabbage if desired. Yield: 6 servings.

Approx Per Serving: Cal 287; Prot 11 g; Carbo 10 g; Fiber 1 g; T Fat 23 g; Chol 39 mg; Sod 345 mg.

Doris Strider, Independence

CABBAGE CASSEROLE

1 medium cabbage, chopped
1/2 teaspoon salt
1 8-ounce can water chestnuts, drained
1 can cream of chicken soup
1/2 cup mayonnaise-type salad dressing
3/4 cup shredded Cheddar cheese
1 8-ounce package seasoned stuffing mix

Cook cabbage in a small amount of salted water in saucepan for 5 minutes; drain. Place in greased 9x13-inch casserole. Chop water chestnuts. Add to cabbage; mix well. Add soup; mix well. Spread salad dressing over mixture. Sprinkle with cheese and stuffing mix. Bake, covered with foil, at 350 degrees until mixture is hot and bubbly. Yield: 6 servings.

Approx Per Serving: Cal 350; Prot 11 g; Carbo 43 g; Fiber 2 g; T Fat 16 g; Chol 24 mg; Sod 1141 mg.

Linda S. Green, Independence

MARINATED CARROTS

2 pounds carrots, peeled, sliced
Salt to taste
1 onion, sliced
1 medium green bell pepper, chopped
1/2 cup oil
3/4 cup sugar
3/4 cup vinegar
1 teaspoon Worcestershire sauce
1 teaspoon prepared mustard
Pepper to taste

Cook carrots in salted water to cover in saucepan just until tender; drain. Layer carrots, onion and green pepper in shallow dish. Mix oil, sugar, vinegar, Worcestershire sauce, mustard, salt and pepper in small bowl. Pour over vegetables. Marinate in refrigerator for several hours to 2 weeks. Yield: 8 servings.

Approx Per Serving: Cal 257; Prot 2 g; Carbo 34 g; Fiber 4 g; T Fat 14 g; Chol 0 mg; Sod 67 mg.

Kim Parker, Central

COPPER PENNIES

2 pounds carrots, sliced
1 medium green bell pepper, thinly sliced
3 medium onions, sliced into rings
1 can tomato soup
3/4 cup sugar
1/2 cup oil
1 teaspoon prepared mustard
1 teaspoon Worcestershire sauce
3/4 cup vinegar

Cook carrots in water to cover in saucepan just until tender; drain. Layer carrots, green pepper and onion in shallow dish. Mix soup, sugar, oil, mustard, Worcestershire sauce and vinegar in bowl. Pour over vegetables. Marinate, tightly covered, for 12 hours or longer. Drain partially to serve. Serve as vegetable or salad with ham or chicken. Yield: 8 servings.

Approx Per Serving: Cal 294; Prot 3 g; Carbo 42 g; Fiber 5 g; T Fat 15 g; Chol 0 mg; Sod 321 mg.

Gloria W. Sadler, Hornets Nest

CARROTS DELIGHT

8 medium carrots, cut into strips
1 small onion, sliced
1 tablespoon butter
1 teaspoon dried parsley flakes
1/2 teaspoon grated lemon rind
1/4 teaspoon salt
1/4 teaspoon sugar
Dash of pepper
1 tablespoon butter

Combine carrots, onion and 1 tablespoon butter in glass dish. Microwave, covered, on High for 12 minutes or until carrots are tender. Mix parsley flakes, lemon rind, salt, sugar and pepper in small bowl. Add to carrots. Add remaining 1 tablespoon butter; mix well. Microwave, covered, on High for 2 minutes longer. Yield: 6 servings.

Approx Per Serving: Cal 65; Prot 1 g; Carbo 11 g; Fiber 3 g; T Fat 2 g; Chol 5 mg; Sod 139 mg.

Peggy W. Pearce, Independence

GINGERED CARROTS

1 pound carrots, cut into julienned strips
3 tablespoons butter
2 teaspoons ginger
3 tablespoons dark brown sugar
Salt and pepper to taste

Cook carrots in water to cover in saucepan for 5 to 6 minutes or until tender. Drain on paper towels; pat dry. Melt butter in saucepan. Add ginger, brown sugar, salt and pepper; mix well. Add carrots. Cook over low heat for 3 to 4 minutes, stirring gently. Serve hot with veal piccata. Yield: 4 servings.

Approx Per Serving: Cal 163; Prot 1 g; Carbo 21 g; Fiber 4 g; T Fat 9 g; Chol 23 mg; Sod 116 mg.

Murl Morris, Independence

TANGY MUSTARD CAULIFLOWER

1 medium head cauliflower
1/2 cup mayonnaise
1/2 teaspoon dried minced onion
1 teaspoon prepared mustard
1/4 teaspoon salt
1/2 cup shredded Cheddar cheese
Paprika to taste

Remove outer leaves from cauliflower; wash. Place in 1 1/2-quart glass bowl. Microwave, covered, on High for 9 minutes. Combine mayonnaise, onion, mustard and salt in small bowl. Spoon over cauliflower; sprinkle with cheese and paprika. Microwave, covered, on Medium-High for 1 1/2 to 2 minutes or until cheese melts. Let stand for 2 minutes before serving.
Yield: 6 servings.

Approx Per Serving: Cal 186; Prot 4 g; Carbo 4 g; Fiber 2 g; T Fat 18 g; Chol 21 mg; Sod 272 mg.

Phyllis Edwards, Hornets Nest

COUNTRY COLLARDS

3 slices salt pork
2 pounds collard greens, finely chopped
1 tablespoon salt

Render salt pork in skillet. Wash collard greens. Add greens and salt to pan drippings. Steam, covered, over low heat until tender, stirring frequently. Yield: 6 servings.

Approx Per Serving: Cal 43; Prot 4 g; Carbo 6 g; Fiber 3 g; T Fat 1 g; Chol 2 mg; Sod 866 mg.

Doris Everett, Central

FRESH CORN PUDDING

2 cups fresh corn
2 tablespoons melted
  butter
1 cup milk
2 tablespoons flour
1 teaspoon salt
1 tablespoon sugar
Pepper to taste
3 eggs, beaten

Combine corn with butter, milk, flour, salt and sugar in bowl. Add eggs; mix well. Pour into greased 1-quart baking dish. Place dish in baking pan half filled with boiling water. Bake at 350 degrees for 1¼ hours or until pudding is set. Yield: 6 servings.

Approx Per Serving: Cal 152; Prot 6 g; Carbo 14 g; Fiber 2 g; T Fat 9 g; Chol 122 mg; Sod 1513 mg.

Barbara D. Scott, Independence

CORN PUDDING

¼ cup sugar
3 tablespoons cornstarch
¼ teaspoon salt
3 eggs, beaten
⅓ cup milk
¼ teaspoon vanilla extract
1 tablespoon melted butter
1 16-ounce can cream-
  style corn

Combine sugar, cornstarch and salt in bowl; mix well. Add eggs, milk, vanilla and butter; mix well. Stir in corn. Pour into greased casserole. Bake at 350 degrees for 45 minutes to 1 hour or until pudding is set. Yield: 8 servings.

Approx Per Serving: Cal 93; Prot 1 g; Carbo 20 g; Fiber 1 g; T Fat 2 g; Chol 4 mg; Sod 251 mg.

Sallie Greer, Hornets Nest

EGGPLANT SOUFFLÉ

1 large eggplant, peeled,
  sliced
Salt to taste
1 egg, beaten
2 tablespoons chopped
  green bell pepper
1 teaspoon minced onion
8 ounces cream cheese,
  softened
1 tablespoon butter
2 cups shredded mild
  Cheddar cheese

Cook eggplant, covered, in salted water in saucepan; drain. Mash eggplant. Add egg, green pepper and onion; mix well. Melt cream cheese with butter in saucepan. Alternate eggplant, cream cheese sauce and Cheddar cheese 1/3 at a time in greased baking dish. Bake at 350 degrees for 30 minutes or until brown. Yield: 6 servings.

Approx Per Serving: Cal 332; Prot 14 g; Carbo 6 g; Fiber 2 g; T Fat 29 g; Chol 122 mg; Sod 554 mg.

Evelyn Clemmer, Hornets Nest

MUSHROOM BUSINESS

1 1/2 pounds fresh mushrooms, coarsely sliced
1 tablespoon butter
3/4 cup chopped onion
3/4 cup chopped celery
3/4 cup chopped green bell pepper
5 slices bread, cut into 1-inch cubes
1/4 cup melted butter
1 teaspoon salt
1/2 teaspoon pepper
3 eggs, slightly beaten
2 1/4 cups milk
2 cans cream of mushroom soup
2 cups shredded Swiss cheese

Sauté mushrooms in 1 tablespoon butter in skillet for 5 minutes. Remove with slotted spoon; drain. Sauté onion, celery and green pepper in skillet until tender; remove from heat. Toss bread with 1/4 cup melted butter in bowl. Place 1/3 of the bread cubes in greased 9x13-inch baking pan. Top with mushrooms and onion mixture; sprinkle with salt and pepper. Top with half the remaining bread cubes. Mix eggs with milk in bowl. Pour over casserole. Chill overnight. Spread evenly with soup. Sprinkle with remaining bread cubes. Top with cheese. Bake at 300 degrees for 1 hour or until cheese is brown and bubbly. May add cooked chicken or turkey if desired. Yield: 12 servings.

Approx Per Serving: Cal 265; Prot 12 g; Carbo 16 g; Fiber 2 g; T Fat 18 g; Chol 90 mg; Sod 784 mg.

Mrs. Hugh L. McAulay, Blue Ridge

ONION CASSEROLE

3½ cups sliced onions
½ cup sliced almonds
1 can cream of mushroom soup
1½ cups crushed cornflakes
½ cup melted margarine

Combine onions, almonds and soup in bowl; mix well. Pour into casserole. Top with mixture of cornflakes and melted margarine. Bake at 325 degrees for 45 minutes. Yield: 6 servings.

Approx Per Serving: Cal 332; Prot 5 g; Carbo 27 g; Fiber 3 g;
  T Fat 23 g; Chol 1 mg; Sod 803 mg.

Betty W. Hampton, Salem

CRUNCHY ONION CASSEROLE

4 cups sliced onions
Salt to taste
1 can cream of mushroom soup
1 cup crushed cornflakes
2 tablespoons melted margarine

Cook onions in salted water in saucepan until partially tender; drain. Place in casserole. Top with soup, cornflakes and margarine. Bake at 350 degrees for 20 minutes. Yield: 8 servings.

Approx Per Serving: Cal 117; Prot 2 g; Carbo 14 g; Fiber 1 g;
  T Fat 6 g; Chol <1 mg; Sod 448 mg.

Virginia Bowie, Independence

SWISS ONION CASSEROLE

2 large onions, sliced
3 tablespoons butter
2 cups shredded Swiss cheese
1 can cream of chicken soup
½ cup milk
1 teaspoon soy sauce
Pepper to taste
5 slices French bread
5 teaspoons butter, softened

Sauté onions in 3 tablespoons butter in skillet until tender. Place in 8x11-inch baking dish. Combine cheese, soup, milk, soy sauce and pepper in bowl; mix well. Pour over onions. Spread 1 side of French bread slices with remaining 5 teaspoons butter.

Arrange buttered side up over onions. Bake at 350 degrees for 40 minutes. Yield: 5 servings.

Approx Per Serving: Cal 538; Prot 21 g; Carbo 36 g; Fiber 2 g; T Fat 35 g; Chol 93 mg; Sod 1057 mg.

Betty Hovis, Hornets Nest

HEARTY FRENCH ONION SOUP

¼ **cup butter**	**1 bay leaf**
5 medium yellow onions, thinly sliced	¼ **teaspoon pepper**
	8 ½-inch slices French bread, toasted
⅛ **teaspoon sugar**	
2 tablespoons flour	**1 cup shredded Swiss cheese**
5 cups low-sodium beef broth	
	¼ **cup Parmesan cheese**
½ **teaspoon thyme, crumbled**	

Melt butter in large saucepan over medium heat. Add onions. Cook for 10 to 15 minutes or until golden, stirring gently. Stir in sugar and flour. Cook for 3 minutes longer, stirring constantly. Add broth, thyme, bay leaf and pepper; mix well. Bring to a boil over medium-high heat, stirring constantly. Boil for 6 minutes, stirring constantly; reduce heat. Simmer, loosely covered, for 30 minutes. Remove and discard bay leaf. Ladle into ovenproof bowls. Top with French bread; sprinkle with Swiss and Parmesan cheese. Broil 4 to 6 inches from heat source for 2 minutes or until golden. Yield: 4 servings.

Approx Per Serving: Cal 375; Prot 18 g; Carbo 26 g; Fiber 4 g; T Fat 23 g; Chol 62 mg; Sod 1328 mg.

Phyllis Jones, Independence

☎ Store onions in a bag or basket that provides good air circulation, in a cool, dark, dry, well-ventilated place. Don't refrigerate until onion is cut.

GARDEN PEA CASSEROLE

1 16-ounce can peas, drained
1 can cream of mushroom soup
1/2 cup shredded Cheddar cheese
1/2 cup bread crumbs
1/4 cup margarine

Combine peas with soup in 1 1/2-quart casserole. Sprinkle with cheese and crumbs; dot with margarine. Bake at 400 degrees until top is brown and cheese melts. Yield: 4 servings.

Approx Per Serving: Cal 364; Prot 12 g; Carbo 29 g; Fiber 6 g; T Fat 23 g; Chol 48 mg; Sod 1141 mg.

Polly Mabrey, Hornets Nest

STUFFED PEPPERS

4 medium red bell peppers
1/3 cup chopped red bell pepper
1/2 cup chopped onion
4 large mushrooms, sliced
2 tablespoons dry white wine
2 tablespoons wheat germ
1 10-ounce can whole kernel corn, drained
3/4 cup cooked brown rice
1/2 cup shredded sharp Cheddar cheese
1 teaspoon garlic powder
1 1/2 teaspoons dried rosemary
1 1/2 teaspoons parsley flakes
2 teaspoons wheat germ

Slice tops from whole red peppers; remove seeds. Sauté chopped red pepper, onion, mushrooms and wine in saucepan until tender. Remove from heat. Add 2 tablespoons wheat germ, corn, rice, cheese, garlic powder, rosemary and parsley; mix well. Spoon vegetable mixture into whole peppers. Place in baking pan; top each with 1/2 teaspoon wheat germ. Bake at 350 degrees for 30 minutes. Yield: 4 servings.

Approx Per Serving: Cal 207; Prot 9 g; Carbo 31 g; Fiber 4 g; T Fat 6 g; Chol 15 mg; Sod 256 mg.

Kim Parker, Central

TWICE-BAKED POTATOES

4 large baked potatoes
1 teaspoon salt
1/8 teaspoon pepper
1/4 cup butter, softened
1/2 cup milk

3 slices crisp-fried bacon, crumbled
1 cup shredded Cheddar cheese

Slice potatoes into halves. Scoop potato from skins, leaving 1/8-inch shell. Mash potato in large bowl. Add salt, pepper, butter, milk and crumbled bacon; mix well. Spoon into shells. Bake at 350 degrees for 20 minutes or until heated through. Yield: 8 servings.

Approx Per Serving: Cal 241; Prot 7 g; Carbo 26 g; Fiber 2 g; T Fat 12 g; Chol 35 mg; Sod 455 mg.

Carolyn Austin, Independence

RED'S POTATO CASSEROLE

1/4 cup margarine
5 cups cooked diced potatoes
1 cup sour cream
1/2 cup chopped onion
1 can cream of chicken soup

1/2 teaspoon (or more) salt
1/4 teaspoon pepper
1/4 cup margarine
2 cups crushed cornflakes

Melt 1/4 cup margarine in 9x13-inch baking dish. Layer potatoes in margarine. Mix sour cream, onion, soup, salt and pepper in bowl. Pour over potatoes. Mix remaining 1/4 cup margarine with cornflakes in bowl. Sprinkle over potatoes. Bake at 350 degrees for 30 minutes or until brown. Yield: 12 servings.

Approx Per Serving: Cal 263; Prot 4 g; Carbo 34 g; Fiber 2 g; T Fat 13 g; Chol 8 mg; Sod 533 mg.

Mrs. W. B. "Red" Rogers, Asheville

HASHED BROWN CASSEROLE

- 1 2-pound package frozen hashed brown potatoes
- 2 cans potato soup
- 8 ounces sharp Cheddar cheese, shredded
- 1 cup sour cream
- 1/2 teaspoon garlic salt
- 2 tablespoons butter
- 1/2 cup Parmesan cheese

Combine potatoes, soup, Cheddar cheese, sour cream, and garlic salt in large bowl; mix well. Spoon into greased 2 1/2-quart casserole. Dot with butter. Sprinkle with Parmesan cheese. Bake at 350 degrees for 1 hour. Yield: 12 servings.

Approx Per Serving: Cal 344; Prot 10 g; Carbo 27 g; Fiber 2 g; T Fat 23 g; Chol 39 mg; Sod 722 mg.

Linda Buchanan, Foot Hills

EASY HASHED BROWN CASSEROLE

- 1 16-ounce package frozen hashed brown potatoes
- 2 tablespoons melted margarine
- 1 cup sour cream
- 1 can cream of mushroom soup
- 1 onion, minced
- 4 ounces Cheddar cheese, shredded

Combine potatoes, margarine, sour cream, soup and onion in bowl; mix well. Spoon into baking dish. Sprinkle with cheese. Bake at 400 degrees for 30 minutes. Yield: 6 servings.

Approx Per Serving: Cal 417; Prot 9 g; Carbo 29 g; Fiber 2 g; T Fat 31 g; Chol 37 mg; Sod 619 mg.

Betty Storie, Blue Ridge

SHIRLEY'S POTATO CASSEROLE

1/2 cup melted butter
1 teaspoon salt
1/2 cup chopped onion
1 can cream of mushroom soup
2 cups sour cream
10 ounces Cheddar cheese, shredded
1 2-pound package frozen hashed brown potatoes, thawed
2 cups crushed cornflakes

Combine butter, salt, onion, soup, sour cream and cheese in large bowl; mix well. Add potatoes; mix well. Spoon into 9x13-inch casserole. Sprinkle cornflakes on top. Bake at 350 degrees for 45 minutes. Yield: 12 servings.

Approx Per Serving: Cal 482; Prot 11 g; Carbo 35 g; Fiber 2 g; T Fat 34 g; Chol 63 mg; Sod 781 mg.

Shirley C. Helms, Independence

POP'S POTATO POTLUCK

1 2-pound package frozen hashed brown potatoes, thawed
1/2 cup chopped onion
1/2 cup melted margarine
2 cups sour cream
1 can cream of chicken soup
2 cups shredded Cheddar cheese
1 teaspoon salt
Pepper to taste
2 cups cornflake crumbs
1/4 cup melted margarine

Combine potatoes, onion, 1/2 cup margarine, sour cream, soup, cheese, salt and pepper in bowl; mix well. Spoon into 9x13-inch baking dish. Top with mixture of cornflake crumbs and 1/4 cup margarine. Bake at 350 degrees for 45 minutes. Yield: 8 servings.

Approx Per Serving: Cal 773; Prot 16 g; Carbo 57 g; Fiber 3 g; T Fat 56 g; Chol 58 mg; Sod 1227 mg.

Mrs. Hugh L. McAulay, Blue Ridge

FAVORITE POTATO CASSEROLE

- 1/2 cup melted margarine
- 1 2-pound package frozen hashed brown potatoes, thawed
- 1 cup sour cream
- 1 can cream of chicken soup
- 1/2 cup chopped onion
- 2 cups shredded Cheddar cheese
- 1 teaspoon salt
- 1/2 teaspoon pepper
- 2 cups crushed cornflakes
- 1/2 cup melted margarine

Combine 1/2 cup margarine, potatoes, sour cream, soup, onion, cheese, salt and pepper in large bowl; mix well. Spoon into greased shallow 9x13-inch casserole. Mix cornflakes with remaining 1/2 cup margarine in bowl. Sprinkle over potato mixture. Bake at 350 degrees for 40 to 45 minutes or until brown. Yield: 12 servings.

Approx Per Serving: Cal 487; Prot 10 g; Carbo 35 g; Fiber 2 g; T Fat 36 g; Chol 30 mg; Sod 849 mg.

Lee Davis, Asheville

SPECIAL POTATO CASSEROLE

- 1 2-pound package frozen hashed brown potatoes, thawed
- 2 cups shredded sharp Cheddar cheese
- 1 cup sour cream
- 1 can cream of chicken soup
- 1/2 cup chopped onion
- 1 teaspoon salt
- 3 cups crushed cornflakes
- 1/2 cup melted margarine

Combine potatoes, cheese, sour cream, soup, onion and salt in bowl; mix well. Spoon into 9x13-inch baking dish sprayed with nonstick cooking spray. Top with cornflake crumbs; drizzle with margarine. Bake at 350 degrees for 1 hour. Yield: 15 servings.

Approx Per Serving: Cal 355; Prot 8 g; Carbo 32 g; Fiber 2 g; T Fat 23 g; Chol 23 mg; Sod 669 mg.

Jewel H. Ware, Piedmont

POTATO AND CHEESE CASSEROLE

1 2-pound package frozen hashed brown potatoes, thawed
1 can cream of mushroom soup
½ cup milk
½ cup melted margarine
½ teaspoon pepper
2 tablespoons dried onion flakes
½ teaspoon salt
1 cup sour cream
10 ounces mild Cheddar cheese, shredded

Place potatoes in large bowl. Mix soup, milk, margarine, pepper, onion flakes, salt and sour cream in saucepan. Heat thoroughly, stirring constantly. Pour over potatoes. Add half the cheese; mix well. Spoon into greased 9x13-inch baking dish. Sprinkle with remaining cheese. Bake at 350 degrees for 45 minutes. Yield: 12 servings.

Approx Per Serving: Cal 402; Prot 10 g; Carbo 25 g; Fiber 2 g; T Fat 30 g; Chol 35 mg; Sod 570 mg.

Juanita White, Raleigh

POTATO DELIGHT

½ cup butter
1 2-pound package frozen hashed brown potatoes, thawed
2 cans cream of mushroom soup
1 cup sour cream
8 ounces Cheddar cheese, shredded
1 small onion, finely chopped
1 cup crushed potato chips

Melt butter in 4-quart baking dish. Combine potatoes, soup, sour cream, cheese, onion and half the crushed potato chips in large bowl; mix well. Spoon into prepared baking dish. Sprinkle with remaining crushed potato chips. Bake at 350 degrees for 1 hour and 10 minutes. Yield: 20 servings.

Approx Per Serving: Cal 257; Prot 5 g; Carbo 18 g; Fiber 1 g; T Fat 19 g; Chol 30 mg; Sod 391 mg.

Mary Crews, Salem

ONION SOUP POTATOES

4 medium potatoes
1 envelope onion soup mix
½ cup margarine

Scrub potatoes; cut into ½-inch slices. Place in 1½-quart glass casserole. Sprinkle with onion soup mix; stir lightly. Dot with margarine. Microwave, covered, on High for 9 to 11 minutes or until potatoes are just tender, stirring once. Let stand, covered, for 5 minutes before serving. Yield: 6 servings.

Approx Per Serving: Cal 286; Prot 3 g; Carbo 35 g; Fiber 3 g; T Fat 15 g; Chol 0 mg; Sod 293 mg.

Ann Sharman, Foot Hills

PORTUGUESE POTATOES

8 potatoes
1 pound Velveeta cheese, cut into cubes
1 onion, chopped
1 2-ounce jar chopped pimento, drained
1 tablespoon parsley flakes
Paprika and garlic salt to taste
2 slices bread, cut into small cubes
1 cup melted margarine

Cut potatoes into cubes. Cook in water to cover in saucepan until just tender; drain. Layer potatoes and next 7 ingredients in 9x13-inch casserole. Pour margarine over top. Bake at 350 degrees for 15 minutes or until brown and bubbly. Yield: 8 servings.

Approx Per Serving: Cal 663; Prot 18 g; Carbo 58 g; Fiber 5 g; T Fat 41 g; Chol 54 mg; Sod 1131 mg.

Marty Ursery, Piedmont

SUPREME POTATO CASSEROLE

6 medium potatoes, boiled
2 cups cottage cheese
1 cup sour cream
2 tablespoons chopped green onions
1 teaspoon salt
1 teaspoon sugar
⅛ teaspoon garlic powder
1 cup shredded Cheddar cheese

Peel potatoes; cut into cubes. Combine potatoes with next 6 ingredients in bowl; mix well. Pour into lightly greased 1½-quart baking dish. Top with cheese. Bake at 350 degrees for 45 minutes. Yield: 12 servings.

Approx Per Serving: Cal 227; Prot 10 g; Carbo 28 g; Fiber 2 g; T Fat 9 g; Chol 24 mg; Sod 396 mg.

Betty W. Hampton, Salem

GRUYÈRE POTATOES

- 3 medium potatoes, thinly sliced
- 1½ cups milk
- 2 tablespoons melted butter
- 1 teaspoon salt
- ¼ teaspoon pepper
- 1 tablespoon minced garlic
- ½ cup shredded Gruyère cheese

Layer potatoes in 8-inch square baking dish. Mix milk, butter, salt, pepper and garlic in bowl. Pour over potatoes. Bake at 400 degrees for 40 minutes. Sprinkle with cheese. Bake for 5 minutes longer or until cheese is melted. Yield: 6 servings.

Approx Per Serving: Cal 260; Prot 10 g; Carbo 29 g; Fiber 2 g; T Fat 12 g; Chol 39 mg; Sod 484 mg.

John E. Miles, Independence

PARTY POTATOES

- 8 medium potatoes, cut into cubes
- 8 ounces cream cheese, softened
- 1 cup sour cream
- 5 tablespoons margarine
- ⅓ cup chopped chives
- Salt and pepper to taste
- 1 tablespoon margarine
- Paprika to taste

Cook potatoes in water to cover in saucepan until tender; drain. Combine cream cheese and sour cream in mixer bowl; beat until well mixed. Add hot potatoes; beat until smooth. Add 5 tablespoons margarine, chives, salt and pepper; mix well. Spoon into greased 2-quart casserole. Dot with remaining 1 tablespoon margarine; sprinkle with paprika. Bake at 350 degrees for 30 minutes or until brown. Yield: 10 servings.

Approx Per Serving: Cal 365; Prot 6 g; Carbo 43 g; Fiber 4 g; T Fat 20 g; Chol 35 mg; Sod 172 mg.

Mary Anne Long, Independence

HOT GERMAN POTATO SALAD

4 cups water
1 6-ounce package sour cream and chive dried potatoes
4 slices bacon
1 small onion, chopped
1 stalk celery, chopped
2 tablespoons sugar
1 1/2 cups water
1/3 cup cider vinegar

Bring 4 cups water to a boil in 2-quart saucepan. Stir in potatoes. Cook over medium heat for 15 minutes or until tender; drain. Cook bacon in skillet until crisp. Remove to paper towels to drain; crumble. Sauté onion and celery in bacon drippings until tender. Combine sour cream seasoning mix, sugar, 1 1/2 cups water and vinegar in saucepan. Cook until thickened, stirring constantly. Stir in potatoes, bacon, onion and celery. Simmer until of desired consistency. Yield: 6 servings.

Nutritional information for this recipe is not available.

Carrie Ledbetter, Foot Hills

GERMAN POTATO SALAD

4 ounces bacon
1 medium onion, chopped
2 cups plus 4 teaspoons water
2 tablespoons flour
3/4 cup vinegar
14 tablespoons plus 2 teaspoons sugar
Salt and pepper to taste
10 small potatoes, cooked, peeled, sliced

Cook bacon in skillet until brown and crisp. Remove to paper towels to drain. Drain skillet, reserving 5 tablespoons drippings. Sauté onion in bacon drippings until tender. Add water and flour, stirring until well mixed. Add vinegar, sugar, salt and pepper; mix well. Add potatoes. Simmer for 30 minutes or until flavors blend, stirring frequently. Yield: 8 servings.

Approx Per Serving: Cal 392; Prot 9 g; Carbo 75 g; Fiber 5 g; T Fat 7 g; Chol 12 mg; Sod 242 mg.

Kim Parker, Central

POTATO WEDGES

4 large potatoes
1/2 cup self-rising flour
1/2 cup Parmesan cheese
1 teaspoon salt
1 teaspoon pepper
1/2 teaspoon chili powder
1/2 teaspoon onion salt
1 tablespoon parsley flakes
1/2 cup melted butter

Scrub potatoes; do not peel. Cut each into 4 wedges. Soak in cold water to cover for several minutes; dry. Mix flour, cheese, salt, pepper, chili powder, onion salt and parsley flakes in shallow bowl. Dip potato wedges in melted butter; coat with flour mixture. Place in 9x13-inch baking dish. Bake at 350 degrees for 45 minutes or until tender and brown. May microwave, covered, for 7 minutes, stirring once. Yield: 8 servings.

Approx Per Serving: Cal 286; Prot 6 g; Carbo 36 g; Fiber 5 g; T Fat 15 g; Chol 35 mg; Sod 759 mg.

Joyce Campbell, Blue Ridge

SPINACH CASSEROLE

1/4 cup flour
1 pound cottage cheese
2 eggs, beaten
1 teaspoon salt
1/4 cup butter, chopped
2 cups Cheddar cheese cubes
2 10-ounce packages frozen spinach, thawed, drained

Combine flour, cottage cheese, eggs and salt in bowl; mix well. Add butter, cheese and spinach; mix well. Pour into greased Crock•Pot. Cook on Low for 3 to 4 hours, stirring occasionally. Yield: 6 servings.

Approx Per Serving: Cal 369; Prot 24 g; Carbo 12 g; Fiber 3 g; T Fat 26 g; Chol 143 mg; Sod 1064 mg.

Barbara Shuping Ray, Salem

SUPER SPINACH CASSEROLE

2 10-ounce packages frozen chopped spinach
1/4 cup melted margarine
8 ounces French onion dip
1/2 teaspoon salt
1/4 teaspoon pepper
1 cup (about) herb-seasoned stuffing mix

Cook spinach using package directions; drain well. Combine spinach, margarine, onion dip, salt and pepper in bowl; mix well. Spoon into 1-quart baking dish. Top with stuffing mix. Bake at 350 degrees for 20 minutes or until hot and bubbly. Yield: 6 servings.

Approx Per Serving: Cal 219; Prot 6 g; Carbo 15 g; Fiber 2 g; T Fat 16 g; Chol 17 mg; Sod 523 mg.

Essie Phillips, Hornets Nest

SQUASH CASSEROLE

7 yellow squash
1 medium onion, chopped
1 egg
1 can cream of mushroom soup
1/2 teaspoon salt
1/4 teaspoon pepper
10 saltine crackers, crushed
1 cup shredded Cheddar cheese
2 tablespoons melted margarine

Cook squash in small amount of water in saucepan until tender; drain. Cut into small cubes. Combine squash, onion, egg, soup, salt and pepper in bowl; mix well. Reserve 1/4 cup cracker crumbs and 1/4 cup cheese. Add remaining cracker crumbs and cheese to squash; mix well. Spoon into greased baking dish. Top with reserved cracker crumbs and cheese. Drizzle with margarine. Bake at 350 degrees for 45 minutes. Yield: 6 servings.

Approx Per Serving: Cal 247; Prot 9 g; Carbo 19 g; Fiber 4 g; T Fat 16 g; Chol 58 mg; Sod 829 mg.

Linda S. Griffin, Hornets Nest

CHEESY SQUASH CASSEROLE

2 cups cooked squash
1/4 cup butter, softened
2 eggs, beaten
1 teaspoon salt
1/2 teaspoon pepper
1 small onion, chopped
1 cup shredded Cheddar cheese
1 cup milk
2 cups bread crumbs

Mash squash in bowl. Add butter, eggs, salt, pepper, onion, cheese, milk and bread crumbs; mix well. Spoon into casserole. Bake at 375 degrees for 40 minutes or until hot and bubbly. Yield: 4 servings.

Approx Per Serving: Cal 510; Prot 20 g; Carbo 45 g; Fiber 3 g; T Fat 28 g; Chol 178 mg; Sod 1235 mg.

Kim Parker, Central

EASY SQUASH CASSEROLE

2 1/2 cups cooked squash
2 tablespoons parsley flakes
2 tablespoons bread crumbs
1/2 cup shredded sharp Cheddar cheese
1 egg, beaten
Salt and pepper to taste
1/2 cup Parmesan cheese

Combine squash, parsley flakes, bread crumbs, Cheddar cheese, egg, salt and pepper in bowl; mix well. Spoon into casserole. Sprinkle with Parmesan cheese. Bake at 375 degrees until light brown. Yield: 6 servings.

Approx Per Serving: Cal 101; Prot 7 g; Carbo 4 g; Fiber <1 g; T Fat 6 g; Chol 51 mg; Sod 212 mg.

Mildred Epps, Independence

☎ Make a delicious lemon butter for vegetables of 1/2 cup softened butter, 1 tablespoon lemon juice and 1 teaspoon salt.

SQUASH GARDEN CASSEROLE

7 small squash, coarsely chopped
2 small onions, chopped
1/8 teaspoon garlic salt
1/8 teaspoon pepper
3 tablespoons brown sugar
Salt to taste
3 canned tomatoes, chopped
1/2 cup shredded Cheddar cheese
1/4 cup melted margarine
1/4 cup bread crumbs

Cook squash, onions, garlic salt, pepper and brown sugar in small amount of salted water in saucepan until squash is tender; drain. Add tomatoes; mix well. Spoon into casserole. Sprinkle with cheese and mixture of margarine and bread crumbs. Bake at 350 degrees for 1 hour. Yield: 6 servings.

Approx Per Serving: Cal 188; Prot 5 g; Carbo 19 g; Fiber 3 g; T Fat 11 g; Chol 10 mg; Sod 260 mg.

Chris Roberts, Central

SPECIAL SQUASH CASSEROLE

2 cups mashed cooked yellow squash
1 can cream of mushroom soup
1 can cream of chicken soup
1 medium onion, chopped
1 carrot, shredded
1 cup sour cream
1 6-ounce package corn bread stuffing mix
1/2 cup melted butter

Combine squash, mushroom soup, chicken soup, onion, carrot and sour cream in bowl; mix well. Layer half the stuffing mix, squash mixture and remaining stuffing mix in 9x13-inch casserole. Drizzle with butter. Bake at 350 degrees for 30 to 40 minutes or until brown. Yield: 10 servings.

Approx Per Serving: Cal 267; Prot 5 g; Carbo 21 g; Fiber 1 g; T Fat 19 g; Chol 38 mg; Sod 806 mg.

Gladys Hinson, Independence

SQUASH AND STUFFING CASSEROLE

3 pounds summer squash, coarsely chopped
1 medium onion, chopped
Salt to taste
1 can cream of chicken soup
2 carrots, shredded
1 cup milk
2 eggs, beaten
1 cup sour cream
1/2 cup melted butter
2 cups herb-seasoned stuffing mix

Cook squash and onion in small amount of lightly salted water in saucepan until squash is tender; drain. Add soup, carrots, milk, eggs and sour cream; mix well. Mix butter and stuffing mix in small bowl; reserve 1/2 cup mixture. Add remaining stuffing mixture to squash; mix well. Spoon into greased 9x13-inch casserole. Sprinkle with reserved stuffing mixture. Bake at 350 degrees for 45 minutes or until golden brown.
Yield: 10 servings.

Approx Per Serving: Cal 280; Prot 7 g; Carbo 23 g; Fiber 3 g; T Fat 19 g; Chol 83 mg; Sod 548 mg.

Madelon Haskin, Hornets Nest

SQUASH AND BROCCOLI CASSEROLE

2 1/2 pounds squash, sliced
1 10-ounce package frozen broccoli
1 medium onion, chopped
1 large carrot, shredded
Salt to taste
1/2 cup water
1/2 cup margarine
1 cup sour cream
1 can cream of chicken soup
1 1/4 cups herb-seasoned stuffing mix
1 1/4 cups shredded medium sharp Cheddar cheese

Combine squash, broccoli, onion, carrot, salt and water in saucepan. Cook, covered, until vegetables are tender; drain. Add margarine, sour cream and soup; mix well. Stir in 1 cup stuffing mix and 1 cup cheese. Spoon into greased 2 1/2-quart casserole. Top with remaining stuffing mix and cheese. Bake at 350 degrees for 25 minutes or until hot and bubbly. Yield: 8 servings.

Approx Per Serving: Cal 359; Prot 11 g; Carbo 23 g; Fiber 4 g; T Fat 26 g; Chol 34 mg; Sod 719 mg.

Evelyn Allen, Independence

GLAZED SQUASH WITH ONIONS

3 medium acorn squash, cut into halves
2/3 cup water
2 cups drained cooked onions
1/2 cup chopped California walnuts
1/2 cup melted butter
1/2 cup dark corn syrup

Preheat electric skillet to 225 degrees. Cook squash cut side down in water in hot skillet for 20 minutes or until just tender. Turn squash over. Fill each half with portion of onions and walnuts. Mix butter and corn syrup in small bowl. Spoon over squash. Cook, covered, for 15 minutes or until tender. Yield: 6 servings.

Approx Per Serving: Cal 431; Prot 5 g; Carbo 61 g; Fiber 8 g; T Fat 22 g; Chol 41 mg; Sod 164 mg.

Wilma Brinson, Raleigh

SUMMER SQUASH CASSEROLE

2 pounds fresh zucchini
1/2 cup chopped onions
Salt to taste
1 can cream of chicken soup
1 cup sour cream
1 cup shredded carrots
1 6-ounce package herb-seasoned stuffing mix
1/2 cup margarine

Cook zucchini and onions in small amount of salted water in saucepan for 5 minutes; drain. Add soup, sour cream and carrots; mix well. Mix stuffing mix and margarine in bowl. Layer half the stuffing mixture, zucchini mixture and remaining stuffing mixture in 2-quart casserole. Bake at 350 degrees for 20 to 30 minutes or until hot and bubbly. Yield: 8 servings.

Approx Per Serving: Cal 304; Prot 6 g; Carbo 25 g; Fiber 2 g; T Fat 21 g; Chol 16 mg; Sod 739 mg.

Debra Swilling, Asheville

SQUASH CROQUETTES

2 cups grated squash
1 cup finely chopped onion
1 egg, beaten
1 teaspoon salt
1 teaspoon pepper
1 1/2 tablespoons flour
Oil for deep frying

Combine squash, onion, egg, salt, pepper and flour in bowl; mix well. Drop by teaspoonfuls into hot oil. Deep-fry until brown; drain. Serve hot. Yield: 32 servings.

Approx Per Serving: Cal 7; Prot <1 g; Carbo 1 g; Fiber <1 g; T Fat <1 g; Chol 7 mg; Sod 69 mg.
Nutritional information does not include oil for deep frying.

Carolyn Hord, Hornets Nest

SQUASH FRITTERS

4 small squash, finely chopped
1 onion, finely chopped
Salt, pepper, garlic salt and parsley flakes to taste
1 egg, beaten
1 teaspoon baking powder
2 tablespoons sugar
Flour
Oil for deep-frying
Confectioners' sugar

Cook squash and onion in small amount of water in saucepan until tender; drain. Add salt, pepper, garlic salt and parsley flakes; mix well. Add egg, baking powder and sugar; mix well. Add enough flour to mixture to form stiff dough. Roll 1 teaspoonful at a time in flour to coat. Deep-fry in hot oil until brown; drain. Roll in confectioners' sugar. Yield: 36 servings.

Nutritional information for this recipe is not available.

Terry B. Covell, Blue Ridge

☎ Add your favorite dry salad dressing mix to white sauce to give a different flavor to vegetables.

BOURBON SWEET POTATOES

6 medium sweet potatoes
1/2 cup melted butter
1/2 cup packed brown sugar
1/3 cup orange juice
1/4 cup Bourbon
1/2 teaspoon salt
1/2 teaspoon pumpkin pie spice
1/2 cup chopped pecans

Cook sweet potatoes in water to cover in saucepan for 20 to 25 minutes or until tender; drain. Cool. Peel potatoes. Mash potatoes in bowl. Add butter, brown sugar, orange juice, Bourbon, salt and pumpkin pie spice; mix well. Spoon into greased 1 1/2-quart casserole; sprinkle pecans around edge. Bake at 375 degrees for 45 minutes. Yield: 8 servings.

Approx Per Serving: Cal 311; Prot 2 g; Carbo 37 g; Fiber 3 g; T Fat 17 g; Chol 31 mg; Sod 245 mg.

John E. Miles, Independence

BUSY-DAY SWEET POTATO CASSEROLE

2 29-ounce cans yams, drained
1 cup sugar
2 eggs, beaten
1/2 cup melted butter
1 tablespoon vanilla extract
1/2 cup melted butter
1 cup packed brown sugar
1/3 cup flour
1 cup chopped pecans

Combine yams, sugar, egg, 1/2 cup butter and vanilla in bowl; mix well. Spoon into 2 1/2-quart casserole. Mix remaining 1/2 cup butter, brown sugar, flour and pecans in bowl. Spread over yams. Bake at 350 degrees for 30 minutes. Yield: 8 servings.

Approx Per Serving: Cal 752; Prot 8 g; Carbo 106 g; Fiber 6 g; T Fat 35 g; Chol 115 mg; Sod 376 mg.

Madelon Haskin, Hornets Nest

☎ Pick up chopped vegetables at the supermarket fresh produce section or salad bar for quick stir-fries and salads.

SWEET POTATO CASSEROLE

3 cups mashed cooked sweet potatoes
1/2 cup sugar
2 eggs, beaten
1/2 cup evaporated milk
1/2 teaspoon salt
1/4 cup melted margarine
1 teaspoon vanilla extract
1 cup packed brown sugar
1/3 cup melted margarine
1/3 cup flour
1 cup chopped walnuts
1/2 cup shredded coconut

Combine sweet potatoes, sugar, eggs, evaporated milk, salt and 1/4 cup margarine in bowl; mix well. Spoon into casserole. Mix brown sugar, remaining 1/3 cup margarine, flour, walnuts and coconut in bowl. Spread over sweet potatoes. Bake at 350 degrees for 30 minutes. Yield: 6 servings.

Approx Per Serving: Cal 726; Prot 10 g; Carbo 96 g; Fiber 5 g; T Fat 36 g; Chol 77 mg; Sod 545 mg.

Lib Livingood, Hornets Nest

SWEET POTATO SOUFFLÉ

2 cups mashed cooked sweet potatoes
2 eggs, beaten
6 tablespoons melted margarine
1 cup milk
1/2 teaspoon nutmeg
1/2 teaspoon cinnamon
1/2 cup sugar
3/4 cup crushed cornflakes
1/2 cup chopped pecans
1/2 cup packed brown sugar
6 tablespoons melted margarine

Combine sweet potatoes, eggs, 6 tablespoons margarine, milk, nutmeg, cinnamon and sugar in bowl; mix well. Spoon into casserole. Bake at 400 degrees for 20 minutes. Mix cornflakes, pecans, brown sugar and remaining melted margarine in bowl. Spread over sweet potatoes. Bake for 10 minutes longer. Yield: 6 servings.

Approx Per Serving: Cal 573; Prot 7 g; Carbo 66 g; Fiber 3 g; T Fat 33 g; Chol 77 mg; Sod 485 mg.

Carolyn Hord, Hornets Nest

ORANGE-CANDIED SWEET POTATOES

6 medium sweet potatoes
2 tablespoons margarine
2 cups orange marmalade
2 tablespoons orange juice
1 tablespoon lemon juice
1/8 teaspoon salt
1 tablespoon flaked
  coconut, toasted

Scrub potatoes. Cook in water to cover in saucepan for 25 to 30 minutes or until tender; drain. Cool. Peel potatoes; cut lengthwise into 1/2-inch slices. Melt margarine in large skillet. Stir in marmalade, orange juice, lemon juice and salt. Bring to a boil. Add potatoes. Cook over medium heat for 15 minutes, turning potatoes occasionally. Spoon onto serving dish; sprinkle with coconut. Yield: 8 servings.

Approx Per Serving: Cal 327; Prot 2 g; Carbo 77 g; Fiber 3 g; T Fat 3 g; Chol 0 mg; Sod 92 mg.

Carroll Baxley, Coastal

ORANGE-GLAZED SWEET POTATOES

1 16-ounce can sliced
   pineapple
1 3-ounce package
   orange gelatin
1/4 cup packed brown sugar
1/8 teaspoon salt
1/4 cup butter
6 medium sweet potatoes,
  cooked

Drain pineapple, reserving juice. Add enough water to juice to measure 1 cup. Bring to a boil in saucepan. Stir in gelatin until dissolved. Add brown sugar, salt and butter. Bring to a boil. Peel potatoes; cut crosswise into thick slices. Add potatoes and pineapple slices to boiling liquid. Simmer for 15 minutes or until glazed and syrup thickens, stirring frequently. Yield: 8 servings.

Approx Per Serving: Cal 249; Prot 3 g; Carbo 48 g; Fiber 3 g; T Fat 6 g; Chol 16 mg; Sod 128 mg.

Minnie B. Price, Central

FAVORITE SWEET POTATO SOUFFLÉ

3 cups mashed cooked
  sweet potatoes
1 cup sugar
2 tablespoons plus 2
  teaspoons melted butter
1/2 teaspoon salt
1/2 cup milk
2 eggs, slightly beaten
1 cup packed brown sugar
1 cup chopped pecans
1/3 cup flour
2 tablespoons plus 2
  teaspoons melted butter

Combine sweet potatoes, sugar, 2 tablespoons plus 2 teaspoons butter, salt, milk and eggs in bowl; mix well. Spoon into 2-quart casserole. Mix brown sugar, pecans, flour and remaining butter in bowl. Sprinkle over potatoes. Bake at 350 degrees for 30 minutes. May add 1 teaspoon vanilla extract to sweet potatoes if desired. Yield: 8 servings.

Approx Per Serving: Cal 510; Prot 6 g; Carbo 81 g; Fiber 3 g;
  T Fat 20 g; Chol 76 mg; Sod 306 mg.

Shelia Pendleton, Independence
Mrs. Larry Pridgen, Central
Odelle McMullan, Independence

CRUNCHY TOP SWEET POTATO CASSEROLE

3 cups mashed cooked
  sweet potatoes
1 cup sugar
1/2 cup melted butter
2 eggs
1/2 cup milk
1 cup packed brown sugar
1/3 cup flour
1/3 cup melted butter
1 cup chopped pecans

Combine sweet potatoes, sugar, 1/2 cup butter, eggs and milk in bowl; mix well. Spoon into baking dish. Combine brown sugar, flour, 1/3 cup butter and pecans in bowl; mix well. Sprinkle over casserole. Bake at 350 degrees for 30 minutes.
Yield: 8 servings.

Approx Per Serving: Cal 611; Prot 6 g; Carbo 81 g; Fiber 3 g;
  T Fat 31 g; Chol 107 mg; Sod 268 mg.

Gladys Hinson, Independence

SOUFFLÉED SWEET POTATOES

3 cups mashed cooked
  sweet potatoes
1 1/2 cups sugar
2 eggs
1/2 cup milk
1/2 cup butter
1 teaspoon vanilla extract
1 cup packed brown sugar
1/3 cup flour
1/3 cup butter
1 cup chopped pecans

Combine sweet potatoes, sugar, eggs, milk, 1/2 cup butter and vanilla in bowl; mix well. Spoon into buttered baking dish. Combine brown sugar, flour, 1/3 cup butter and pecans in bowl; mix until crumbly. Sprinkle over casserole. Bake at 350 degrees for 30 minutes. Yield: 8 servings.

Approx Per Serving: Cal 659; Prot 6 g; Carbo 94 g; Fiber 3 g;
  T Fat 31 g; Chol 107 mg; Sod 269 mg.

Willie Collins, Independence

HOLIDAY SWEET POTATO CASSEROLE

6 cups cooked sweet
  potatoes
1 cup sugar
3/4 cup milk
1/2 cup margarine
3 eggs
2 teaspoons vanilla extract
1 teaspoon salt
1 cup packed light brown
  sugar
2/3 cup flour
1/3 cup margarine
1 1/2 cups chopped pecans

Combine sweet potatoes, sugar, milk, 1/2 cup margarine, eggs, vanilla and salt in mixer bowl. Beat at high speed until smooth; do not scrape beaters. Spoon into buttered baking dish. Combine brown sugar, flour, 1/3 cup margarine and pecans in bowl; mix until crumbly. Sprinkle over casserole. Bake at 350 degrees for 30 minutes or until brown. Yield: 12 servings.

Approx Per Serving: Cal 528; Prot 7 g; Carbo 73 g; Fiber 4 g;
  T Fat 25 g; Chol 55 mg; Sod 453 mg.

Mildred Smith, Hornets Nest

COMPANY SWEET POTATO CASSEROLE

3 cups mashed cooked sweet potatoes
1 cup sugar
2 eggs, slightly beaten
1 teaspoon vanilla extract
Salt to taste

1/2 cup packed brown sugar
1/4 cup melted margarine
1 cup crushed cornflakes
1/2 cup chopped pecans

Combine sweet potatoes, sugar, eggs, vanilla and salt in bowl; mix until smooth. Spoon into 9x13-inch baking dish. Mix brown sugar, margarine, cornflake crumbs and pecans in bowl. Sprinkle over casserole. Bake at 350 degrees for 30 minutes. Serve hot or cold. Yield: 12 servings.

Approx Per Serving: Cal 266; Prot 3 g; Carbo 46 g; Fiber 2 g; T Fat 8 g; Chol 36 mg; Sod 178 mg.

Jo Ann Goins, Hornets Nest

COCONUT-TOPPED SWEET POTATO CASSEROLE

3 cups cooked sweet potatoes
1 cup sugar
1/4 cup margarine
1/2 cup evaporated milk
2 eggs

1/2 teaspoon butter flavoring
1 cup packed brown sugar
1/3 cup flour
1/4 cup margarine
1 cup coconut
1 cup chopped pecans

Mash potatoes in mixer bowl. Add sugar, 1/4 cup margarine, evaporated milk, eggs and butter flavoring; mix well. Spoon into baking dish. Combine brown sugar, flour, 1/4 cup margarine, coconut and pecans in bowl; mix until crumbly. Sprinkle over casserole. Bake at 350 degrees for 35 minutes. Yield: 8 servings.

Approx Per Serving: Cal 599; Prot 7 g; Carbo 86 g; Fiber 4 g; T Fat 27 g; Chol 58 mg; Sod 254 mg.

Shirley Carmichael, Hornets Nest

NEW PERRY HOTEL'S SHREDDED YAMS

2 pounds sweet potatoes
1 gallon water
1 tablespoon salt
1 cup pineapple juice
1 cup sugar
1/2 cup dark corn syrup
1/2 cup water
1/4 cup margarine

Peel and shred potatoes. Soak for several minutes in mixture of 1 gallon water and salt. Drain and rinse. Place in shallow baking dish. Pour pineapple juice over potatoes. Mix sugar, syrup and 1/2 cup water in saucepan. Cook until thickened, stirring constantly. Stir in margarine. Add to potatoes. Bake at 350 degrees for 35 minutes. Yield: 8 servings.

Approx Per Serving: Cal 341; Prot 2 g; Carbo 72 g; Fiber 4 g; T Fat 6 g; Chol 0 mg; Sod 893 mg.

Mrs. Hugh L. McAulay, Blue Ridge

CANDIED YAMS

1 29-ounce can yams, drained
1 egg, slightly beaten
1/2 cup sugar
1/2 cup milk
1/4 cup melted margarine
1 teaspoon vanilla extract
1 cup crushed pecans
2 cups miniature marshmallows

Combine yams, egg, sugar, milk, margarine, vanilla and 1/2 cup pecans in bowl; mix well. Spoon into 9-inch square casserole. Sprinkle with remaining 1/2 cup pecans and marshmallows. Bake at 350 degrees for 25 minutes or until brown. Yield: 8 servings.

Approx Per Serving: Cal 371; Prot 4 g; Carbo 53 g; Fiber 4 g; T Fat 17 g; Chol 29 mg; Sod 108 mg.

Peggy Morrow, Independence

TOMATO CASSEROLE

1 20-ounce can tomatoes
1 medium onion, grated
1 tablespoon melted butter
1 tablespoon bacon drippings
2 tablespoons sugar
½ teaspoon seasoned salt
½ teaspoon garlic salt
1 cup herb-seasoned stuffing mix
¾ cup shredded Cheddar cheese
¼ teaspoon oregano

Combine tomatoes, onion, butter, bacon drippings, sugar, seasoned salt and garlic salt in bowl; mix well. Layer half the stuffing mix, tomato mixture, cheese, oregano and remaining stuffing mix in greased baking dish. Bake at 350 degrees for 30 minutes. May substitute oil for bacon drippings. Yield: 6 servings.

Approx Per Serving: Cal 178; Prot 6 g; Carbo 18 g; Fiber 1 g; T Fat 10 g; Chol 34 mg; Sod 754 mg.

Evelyn Carson, Independence

TOMATO DELIGHT

4 teaspoons mayonnaise-type salad dressing
4 slices white bread
1 large tomato, sliced
¼ teaspoon salt
¼ teaspoon pepper
1 cup milk, ice cold

Spread salad dressing on 1 side of each slice bread. Layer tomato slices, salt and pepper on 2 slices bread. Top with remaining bread. Let stand for 15 minutes. Place on serving plate. Pour milk into glass and serve. This is especially good with German Johnson tomatoes. Yield: 1 serving.

Approx Per Serving: Cal 550; Prot 19 g; Carbo 76 g; Fiber 4 g; T Fat 19 g; Chol 38 mg; Sod 1360 mg.

Chris Wood, Piedmont

CALICO CASSEROLE

1 16-ounce package frozen mixed vegetables
1 cup finely chopped celery
1 cup finely chopped onion
2½ cups shredded Cheddar cheese
1 cup mayonnaise
8 ounces saltine crackers, crushed
½ cup melted margarine

Cook mixed vegetables without salt using package directions; drain. Add celery, onion, cheese and mayonnaise; mix well. Spoon into greased 2-quart casserole. Mix cracker crumbs and margarine. Sprinkle over vegetables. Bake at 350 degrees for 30 to 40 minutes or until brown and bubbly. Yield: 12 servings.

Approx Per Serving: Cal 401; Prot 8 g; Carbo 21 g; Fiber 2 g; T Fat 32 g; Chol 42 mg; Sod 606 mg.

Shirley Burns, Independence

SWISS VEGETABLE MEDLEY

1 16-ounce package frozen broccoli, carrots and cauliflower
1 can cream of mushroom soup
½ cup shredded Swiss cheese
⅓ cup sour cream
¼ teaspoon pepper
1 4-ounce jar chopped pimentos, drained
1 3-ounce can French-fried onions
½ cup shredded Swiss cheese

Thaw frozen vegetables; drain. Combine vegetables, soup, ½ cup cheese, sour cream, pepper, pimentos and half the French-fried onions in bowl; mix well. Spoon into 1-quart casserole. Bake, covered, at 350 degrees for 30 minutes. Top with remaining cheese and onions. Bake for 5 minutes longer. May microwave, covered, on High for 8 minutes, turning after 4 minutes. Top with remaining cheese and onions. Microwave, uncovered, for 1 minute or until cheese melts. Yield: 6 servings.

Approx Per Serving: Cal 223; Prot 9 g; Carbo 16 g; Fiber 3 g; T Fat 15 g; Chol 29 mg; Sod 517 mg.

Joanne Tallent, Independence

VEGETABLE CASSEROLE

4 potatoes, thinly sliced
1/2 teaspoon salt
1 8-ounce can green peas, drained
1 tablespoon margarine
Pepper to taste
2 hard-boiled eggs, sliced
1 can cream of mushroom soup
3 slices Old English sharp cheese, chopped
1 3-ounce can French-fried onions

Cook potatoes with salt in water to cover in saucepan until tender; drain. Layer peas in casserole; dot with margarine. Sprinkle with pepper. Add layers of potatoes, egg slices and soup; sprinkle with cheese. Bake at 350 degrees for 30 minutes. Sprinkle with French-fried onions. Yield: 4 servings.

Approx Per Serving: Cal 552; Prot 17 g; Carbo 72 g; Fiber 8 g; T Fat 22 g; Chol 135 mg; Sod 1430 mg.

Martha G. Bridges, Hornets Nest

CHEESY VEGETABLE CASSEROLE

1 16-ounce can white Shoe Peg corn, drained
1 16-ounce can French-style green beans, drained
1/2 cup chopped onion
1/2 cup chopped celery
1/2 cup chopped green bell pepper
1 can cream of celery soup
1 cup shredded Cheddar cheese
1 cup sour cream
1/2 cup melted butter
1 1/2 cups crushed butter crackers
1 2-ounce package sliced almonds

Combine corn, green beans, onion, celery, green pepper, soup, cheese, sour cream and butter in bowl; toss to mix. Spoon into 9x13-inch baking dish. Sprinkle cracker crumbs and almonds over top. Bake at 350 degrees for 30 to 45 minutes or until brown and bubbly. Yield: 16 servings.

Approx Per Serving: Cal 215; Prot 5 g; Carbo 16 g; Fiber 2 g; T Fat 17 g; Chol 32 mg; Sod 464 mg.

Janey C. Norman, Asheville

VEG-ALL CASSEROLE

- 2 16-ounce cans Veg-All, drained
- 1 cup chopped water chestnuts
- 1 cup chopped onion
- 1 cup chopped celery
- 3/4 cup mayonnaise
- 1 can cream of chicken soup
- 1 cup shredded Cheddar cheese
- 1 cup saltine cracker crumbs
- 1/2 cup melted margarine

Combine first 6 ingredients in bowl; mix well. Spoon into casserole. Sprinkle with cheese. Mix cracker crumbs and margarine in bowl. Spread over top. Bake at 350 degrees for 30 to 35 minutes or until brown and bubbly. Yield: 8 servings.

Approx Per Serving: Cal 457; Prot 9 g; Carbo 26 g; Fiber 6 g; T Fat 36 g; Chol 34 mg; Sod 958 mg.

Correen W. Strickland, Raleigh

DR. ANDERSON'S NINE-BEAN SOUP

- 2 cups mixed black beans, black-eyed peas, garbanzo beans, kidney beans, lentils, lima beans, mung beans, pinto beans, soybeans, split peas and/or white beans
- 2 quarts water
- 1 1-pound ham bone, skin and fat removed
- 1 large onion, chopped
- 1 clove of garlic, minced
- 2 bay leaves
- 1 16-ounce can tomatoes, coarsely chopped
- 1/2 teaspoon basil
- 1/2 teaspoon oregano
- 1 15-ounce can seasoned tomato sauce

Rinse beans. Place in large stockpot with enough water to cover by 2 inches. Let soak overnight. Drain. Add 2 quarts water, ham bone, onion, garlic and bay leaves. Bring to a boil. Reduce heat. Simmer for 1 1/2 to 2 hours or until beans are tender, stirring occasionally. Add tomatoes, basil, oregano and tomato sauce. Simmer for 30 minutes longer. Remove ham bone and bay leaves. Serve hot. Yield: 6 servings.

Approx Per Serving: Cal 248; Prot 16 g; Carbo 48 g; Fiber 18 g; T Fat 1 g; Chol 0 mg; Sod 564 mg.
Nutritional information does not include ham bone.

Paulene Gibson, Independence

BROCCOLI CHEESE SOUP

½ cup margarine
¾ cup flour
2 quarts milk
5 chicken bouillon cubes

1 20-ounce package
 frozen chopped broccoli
11 ounces Velveeta
 cheese, cut into cubes

Melt margarine in large saucepan. Stir in flour until well mixed. Add milk and bouillon cubes. Cook until smooth and thickened, stirring constantly. Cook broccoli using package directions. Add broccoli and cheese to soup. Add water if too thick. Cook until heated through, stirring frequently. Yield: 4 servings.

Approx Per Serving: Cal 899; Prot 38 g; Carbo 47 g; Fiber 3 g; T Fat 63 g; Chol 137 mg; Sod 2999 mg.

Delores McNeeley, Independence

THICK TOMATO-VEGETABLE-BEEF SOUP

⅓ cup uncooked macaroni
1 cup water
1 can vegetable-beef soup
1 soup can water
⅓ cup uncooked minute
 rice

1 can tomato soup
1 soup can water
Salt to taste

Cook macaroni in 1 cup water in saucepan until tender and water is evaporated, stirring frequently. Add vegetable-beef soup and 1 soup can water; mix well. Bring to a boil. Add rice, tomato soup, remaining soup can water and salt; mix well. Simmer until rice is tender. Yield: 4 servings.

Approx Per Serving: Cal 161; Prot 4 g; Carbo 31 g; Fiber 2 g; T Fat 3 g; Chol 0 mg; Sod 1041 mg.

Naomi H. Cox, Raleigh

☎ Store leftover vegetables in airtight container in freezer. Use for quick vegetable soup.

SIDE DISHES

FRUIT CASSEROLE

1 pound pitted prunes
6 ounces dried apricots
1 16-ounce can pineapple chunks
1 21-ounce can cherry pie filling
1 cup water

Combine prunes, apricots, pineapple, cherry pie filling and water in 1½-quart casserole; mix well. Bake, covered, at 350 degrees for 1½ hours. Yield: 10 servings.

Approx Per Serving: Cal 241; Prot 2 g; Carbo 63 g; Fiber 7 g; T Fat <1 g; Chol 0 mg; Sod 21 mg.

Mrs. Keith McNeal, Piedmont

SPECIAL FRUIT CASSEROLE

1 16-ounce can pineapple chunks
3 tablespoons flour
¼ cup sugar
1 cup shredded Cheddar cheese
1 16-ounce can sliced pears, drained
1 16-ounce can sliced peaches, drained
¼ cup melted butter
½ cup butter cracker crumbs

Drain pineapple, reserving ½ cup juice. Combine reserved juice, flour and sugar in bowl; mix well. Add cheese; mix well. Stir in pineapple, pears and peaches. Spoon into greased 9x13-inch baking dish. Mix butter and cracker crumbs in bowl. Spread over fruit. Bake at 325 degrees for 20 to 30 minutes or until brown and bubbly. Yield: 10 servings.

Approx Per Serving: Cal 217; Prot 4 g; Carbo 33 g; Fiber 2 g; T Fat 9 g; Chol 26 mg; Sod 169 mg.

Elizabeth Stirewalt, Salem

PINEAPPLE-CHEESE BAKE

1   20-ounce can
    pineapple chunks
1/2 cup sugar
3 tablespoons flour
1 cup shredded Cheddar
    cheese
1/4 cup melted margarine
1/2 cup butter cracker
    crumbs

Drain pineapple, reserving 3 tablespoons juice. Combine reserved juice, sugar and flour in bowl; mix well. Stir in cheese. Add pineapple; mix well. Spoon into greased 1-quart casserole. Mix margarine and cracker crumbs in small bowl. Sprinkle over pineapple. Bake at 350 degrees for 20 to 30 minutes or until brown. Yield: 6 servings.

Approx Per Serving: Cal 331; Prot 6 g; Carbo 44 g; Fiber 1 g;
    T Fat 16 g; Chol 20 mg; Sod 278 mg.

Frances Reynolds, Independence

PINEAPPLE CASSEROLE

2   20-ounce cans
    pineapple chunks,
    drained
1 cup sugar
6 tablespoons flour
2 cups shredded Cheddar
    cheese
1 cup crushed saltine
    crackers
1/2 cup melted margarine

Combine pineapple, sugar, flour and cheese in bowl; mix well. Spoon into 8x12-inch baking dish. Sprinkle with cracker crumbs; drizzle with margarine. Bake at 425 degrees for 30 minutes. Serve warm as side dish or dessert. Yield: 8 servings.

Approx Per Serving: Cal 451; Prot 9 g; Carbo 57 g; Fiber 2 g;
    T Fat 22 g; Chol 33 mg; Sod 447 mg.

Carolyn S. Starnes, Independence

RITZY PINEAPPLE CASSEROLE

2   15-ounce cans pineapple chunks
6 tablespoons flour
1 cup sugar
2 cups finely shredded sharp Cheddar cheese
4 ounces Ritz crackers, crushed
1/2 cup melted margarine

Drain pineapple, reserving 1/2 cup juice. Place pineapple in baking dish. Sprinkle with mixture of flour and sugar. Pour reserved juice over top. Sprinkle with cheese and cracker crumbs. Drizzle with margarine. Bake at 350 degrees for 30 minutes. Serve with ham. Yield: 8 servings.

Approx Per Serving: Cal 487; Prot 9 g; Carbo 61 g; Fiber 1 g; T Fat 26 g; Chol 30 mg; Sod 453 mg.

Mary Reeves, Independence

BAKED PINEAPPLE CASSEROLE

2   16-ounce cans pineapple tidbits, drained
2/3 cup sugar
5 tablespoons flour
1 1/2 cups shredded sharp Cheddar cheese
1 cup butter cracker crumbs
1/2 cup melted margarine

Place pineapple in baking dish sprayed with nonstick cooking spray. Sprinkle with mixture of sugar and flour. Top with cheese and cracker crumbs. Drizzle with margarine. Bake at 350 degrees for 30 to 35 minutes or until brown and bubbly. Yield: 8 servings.

Approx Per Serving: Cal 380; Prot 7 g; Carbo 43 g; Fiber 1 g; T Fat 22 g; Chol 22 mg; Sod 372 mg.

Evelyn Carson, Independence

CHEESY PINEAPPLE CASSEROLE

1 cup coarsely chopped carrots
1 16-ounce can juice-pack pineapple chunks
1 20-ounce can juice-pack crushed pineapple
1 cup sugar
6 tablespoons flour
2 cups shredded Cheddar cheese
1 cup butter cracker crumbs
1/2 cup melted butter

Cook carrots in water to cover in saucepan for 6 minutes or until just tender; drain. Drain pineapple, reserving 3 tablespoons juice. Combine reserved juice, sugar and flour in bowl; mix well. Add carrots, cheese and pineapple; mix well. Spoon into 2-quart casserole. Sprinkle with cracker crumbs. Top with butter. Bake at 350 degrees for 20 to 30 minutes or until brown. Yield: 12 servings.

Approx Per Serving: Cal 312; Prot 6 g; Carbo 39 g; Fiber 1 g; T Fat 16 g; Chol 41 mg; Sod 256 mg.

Jo Ann Husband, Hornets Nest

EASY PINEAPPLE AND CHEESE CASSEROLE

2 16-ounce cans pineapple chunks, drained
6 tablespoons self-rising flour
3/4 cup sugar
1 1/2 cups shredded sharp Cheddar cheese
4 ounces butter crackers, crushed
1/2 cup melted margarine

Combine pineapple, flour, sugar and cheese in bowl; mix well. Spoon into casserole. Sprinkle with crackers. Top with margarine. Bake at 325 degrees for 20 minutes.
Yield: 12 servings.

Approx Per Serving: Cal 273; Prot 5 g; Carbo 33 g; Fiber 1 g; T Fat 15 g; Chol 15 mg; Sod 315 mg.

Brenda Meachum, Independence

PINEAPPLE STRATA

1 cup melted margarine
2 cups sugar
3 eggs, beaten
3/4 cup milk
2 20-ounce cans crushed pineapple, drained
8 slices white bread, crusts trimmed
Cinnamon to taste

Combine margarine, sugar, eggs and milk in bowl; mix well. Stir in pineapple. Cut bread into cubes. Layer half the bread and half the pineapple mixture in greased 2-quart casserole. Repeat layers. Sprinkle with cinnamon. Chill, covered, for 12 hours to overnight. Bake at 350 degrees for 1 hour or until brown and bubbly. Yield: 12 servings.

Approx Per Serving: Cal 392; Prot 4 g; Carbo 56 g; Fiber 1 g; T Fat 18 g; Chol 55 mg; Sod 300 mg.

Elsie M. Mills, Independence

WINE FRUIT

1 cup water
1 cup red wine
1 cup sugar
1 16-ounce can sliced peaches, drained
1 16-ounce can sliced pears, drained
2 sticks cinnamon
1/2 teaspoon grated lemon rind

Combine water, wine and sugar in saucepan. Bring to a boil, stirring constantly until sugar dissolves. Combine peaches and pears in bowl. Add cinnamon sticks and lemon rind. Pour hot mixture over fruit. May store, covered, in refrigerator for several weeks. May also use apricots and pineapple. Yield: 6 servings.

Approx Per Serving: Cal 241; Prot 1 g; Carbo 56 g; Fiber 2 g; T Fat <1 g; Chol 0 mg; Sod 11 mg.

Shirley Burns, Independence

☎ Substitute bulgur wheat, hominy grits or kasha for rice as a side dish to spice up meals.

OLD-FASHIONED CORN BREAD DRESSING

2 cups cornmeal
2 teaspoons baking powder
1 teaspoon soda
1 teaspoon salt
2 eggs, beaten
2 cups buttermilk
2 tablespoons melted bacon drippings
3 stalks celery, chopped
1 medium onion, chopped
2 tablespoons melted butter
12 slices day-old bread, crumbled
2 1/2 cups chicken broth
1 cup milk
2 eggs, beaten
1 teaspoon salt
1 teaspoon poultry seasoning
1/4 teaspoon pepper

Mix cornmeal, baking powder, soda and 1 teaspoon salt in large mixer bowl. Add 2 eggs, buttermilk and bacon drippings; mix well. Pour into hot greased 10-inch baking pan. Bake at 450 degrees for 35 minutes or until light brown. Cool. Crumble corn bread into large bowl. Sauté celery and onion in butter in skillet until tender. Add to crumbled corn bread. Add crumbled bread slices, chicken broth, milk, 2 eggs, 1 teaspoon salt, poultry seasoning and pepper; mix well. Spoon into greased 9x13-inch baking dish. Bake at 450 degrees for 25 to 30 minutes or until brown. Yield: 12 servings.

Approx Per Serving: Cal 267; Prot 9 g; Carbo 37 g; Fiber 3 g; T Fat 9 g; Chol 95 mg; Sod 875 mg.

Linda Toms, Independence

MOM'S CORN BREAD STUFFING

2 cups self-rising corn bread mix
2 slices white bread, cubed
2 cups turkey broth
1/4 cup melted butter
1 1/2 cups chopped celery
1 1/2 cups chopped onion
4 eggs, beaten
Salt and pepper to taste

Prepare corn bread using package directions. Cool. Crumble into bowl. Add cubed bread, broth, butter, celery, onion, eggs, salt and pepper; mix well. Spoon into 9x13-inch casserole. Bake at 350 degrees for 1 hour or until brown. Yield: 12 servings.

Approx Per Serving: Cal 172; Prot 4 g; Carbo 20 g; Fiber 1 g; T Fat 8 g; Chol 82 mg; Sod 413 mg.

Ila Mae Moses, Hornets Nest

BARLEY CASSEROLE

1 6-ounce can sliced mushrooms
1 cup pearl barley
1 medium onion, chopped
1/2 cup margarine
1/2 cup slivered almonds
2 cups chicken broth
1 envelope onion soup mix
1 8-ounce can sliced water chestnuts

Drain mushrooms, reserving liquid. Sauté barley, onion and mushrooms in margarine in skillet until onion is golden brown. Add almonds, chicken broth, soup mix, water chestnuts and reserved mushroom liquid; mix well. Spoon into casserole. Bake, covered at 350 degrees for 1 hour, adding additional liquid if too dry. Yield: 6 servings.

Approx Per Serving: Cal 393; Prot 10 g; Carbo 42 g; Fiber 9 g; T Fat 23 g; Chol <1 mg; Sod 1410 mg.

Betty W. Hampton, Salem

FETTUCINI ALFREDO

8 ounces uncooked linguine
6 tablespoons butter
1 1/2 cups whipping cream
1 cup Parmesan cheese
Salt, pepper and nutmeg to taste

Cook linguine using package directions until just tender; drain. Brown butter in large skillet over high heat, stirring frequently. Add 1/2 cup whipping cream. Boil rapidly until slightly thickened, stirring constantly. Reduce heat to medium. Add linguine; mix gently. Add 1/2 cup cream and 1/2 cup Parmesan cheese; toss gently. Add remaining cream and Parmesan cheese; mix gently. Season with salt, pepper and nutmeg. Serve immediately. Yield: 4 servings.

Approx Per Serving: Cal 762; Prot 18 g; Carbo 46 g; Fiber 2 g; T Fat 57 g; Chol 185 mg; Sod 557 mg.

Diane Grace, Raleigh

MACARONI AND CHEESE

1 cup uncooked macaroni
1 cup milk, scalded
1 cup soft bread cubes
1/4 cup butter
1 pimento, chopped
1 tablespoon chopped chives
1 1/2 cups cubed Cheddar cheese
3/8 teaspoon salt
1/8 teaspoon pepper
1/8 teaspoon paprika
3 eggs, beaten

Cook macaroni using package directions until just tender; drain. Pour hot milk over bread cubes in bowl. Add butter, pimento, chives, cheese, salt, pepper, paprika and eggs; mix well. Place macaroni in casserole. Pour mixture over macaroni. Bake at 325 degrees for 50 minutes or until hot and bubbly. May be served with mushroom sauce. Yield: 6 servings.

Approx Per Serving: Cal 287; Prot 13 g; Carbo 11 g; Fiber <1 g; T Fat 22 g; Chol 162 mg; Sod 463 mg.

Marjory West, Raleigh

MACARONI-CHEESE CASSEROLE

8 ounces uncooked elbow macaroni
1 can cream of chicken soup
1 cup milk
1 1/2 cups shredded Cheddar cheese
1/8 teaspoon Tabasco sauce
Paprika to taste

Cook macaroni using package directions; drain. Combine macaroni, soup, milk, cheese and Tabasco in bowl; mix well. Spoon into buttered casserole. Sprinkle with paprika. Bake at 350 degrees for 25 to 30 minutes or until hot and bubbly. Yield: 6 servings.

Approx Per Serving: Cal 325; Prot 15 g; Carbo 34 g; Fiber 2 g; T Fat 14 g; Chol 39 mg; Sod 595 mg.

Roe Ann Hill, Independence

BUSY-DAY MACARONI AND CHEESE CASSEROLE

2 16-ounce cans cheese and macaroni
8 ounces sharp Cheddar cheese, shredded
3 eggs, beaten

Heat cheese and macaroni in saucepan. Reserve 1/2 cup shredded cheese for topping. Add remaining cheese to saucepan, stirring until melted. Add a small amount of hot mixture to beaten eggs; stir eggs into hot mixture. Spoon into 1 1/2-quart casserole. Sprinkle with reserved cheese. Bake at 400 degrees for 40 to 45 minutes or until light brown. This recipe was given to me by my 90-year-old mother-in-law. Yield: 8 servings.

Approx Per Serving: Cal 252; Prot 14 g; Carbo 13 g; Fiber 1 g; T Fat 16 g; Chol 121 mg; Sod 547 mg.

Agnes Bost, Hornets Nest

PASTA AND FRESH VEGETABLES

3 cloves of garlic, minced
3 tablespoons margarine
2 tablespoons flour
1/8 teaspoon hot pepper sauce
1 1/2 cups chicken broth
2 tablespoons lemon juice
8 ounces uncooked broad noodles
Flowerets of 1 bunch broccoli
3 medium carrots, sliced

Sauté garlic in margarine in large skillet for 3 minutes. Stir in flour until well mixed. Add hot pepper sauce, broth and lemon juice gradually, stirring well after each addition. Cook until sauce thickens, stirring constantly. Cook noodles using package directions; drain. Combine noodles, broccoli and carrots in serving dish. Pour sauce over vegetables. Yield: 6 servings.

Approx Per Serving: Cal 245; Prot 9 g; Carbo 38 g; Fiber 5 g; T Fat 7 g; Chol <1 mg; Sod 293 mg.

Sally Vinton, Independence

BROWN RICE

1 cup uncooked rice
2 cans beef bouillon

6 tablespoons melted margarine

Combine rice, bouillon and margarine in 2-quart casserole; mix well. Bake at 350 degrees for 1 hour. Yield: 6 servings.

Approx Per Serving: Cal 229; Prot 5 g; Carbo 25 g; Fiber <1 g; T Fat 12 g; Chol <1 mg; Sod 903 mg.

Doris Pope, Independence

CHRISTMAS RICE

1 cup uncooked rice
2 cans chicken with rice soup
1 2-ounce jar chopped pimento, drained

1 cup water
1 medium green bell pepper, chopped
1 medium onion, chopped
1/2 cup margarine

Combine rice, soup, pimento, water, green pepper and onion in casserole; mix well. Dot with margarine. Bake at 350 degrees for 45 minutes to 1 hour or until rice is tender. Yield: 6 servings.

Approx Per Serving: Cal 288; Prot 4 g; Carbo 31 g; Fiber 2 g; T Fat 16 g; Chol 3 mg; Sod 525 mg.

Glenna Hawkins, Asheville

DIRTY RICE

1 6-ounce package rice Florentine
2 tablespoons butter

2 1/3 cups water
8 ounces sausage

Combine contents of both packets from rice Florentine package, butter and water in saucepan; mix well. Bring to a boil. Simmer, tightly covered, for 20 minutes. Remove from heat. Let stand, covered, for 5 minutes. Shape sausage into thin patties. Fry in skillet until brown and crisp; drain on paper towels. Crumble sausage into cooked rice mixture; mix well. Yield: 8 servings.

Nutritional information for this recipe is not available.

Dolores S. Howell, Hornets Nest

FRENCH RICE

1 can French onion soup
1/2 cup melted butter
1 4-ounce jar sliced mushrooms
1 8-ounce can sliced water chestnuts
1 cup uncooked rice

Combine soup and butter in bowl; mix well. Drain mushrooms and water chestnuts, reserving liquid. Add enough water to liquid to measure 1 1/3 cups. Add to soup mixture. Stir in mushrooms, water chestnuts and rice. Pour into greased casserole. Bake, covered, at 350 degrees for 1 hour. Yield: 8 servings.

Approx Per Serving: Cal 212; Prot 3 g; Carbo 24 g; Fiber 1 g; T Fat 12 g; Chol 31 mg; Sod 327 mg.

Chris Roberts, Central

WILD RICE PILAF

1 cup uncooked wild rice
1/2 cup butter
1/2 cup slivered almonds
1 8-ounce jar mushrooms, drained
2 tablespoons chopped green onions
3 cups chicken broth

Rinse and drain wild rice. Melt butter in skillet. Add rice, almonds, mushrooms and green onions. Sauté for 20 minutes or until almonds are brown. Pour into 1 1/2-quart casserole. Bring chicken broth to a boil in skillet. Pour over rice mixture; mix well. Bake, covered, at 350 degrees for 1 1/2 hours or until all liquid is absorbed. Yield: 8 servings.

Approx Per Serving: Cal 255; Prot 6 g; Carbo 22 g; Fiber 2 g; T Fat 17 g; Chol 31 mg; Sod 480 mg.

Robert Kinney, Independence

PAULA'S APPLE BUTTER

4 cups cooked apple purée
3 cups sugar
2 tablespoons vinegar
1 teaspoon cinnamon
2 tablespoons lemon juice
1/4 teaspoon cloves

Combine apple purée, sugar, vinegar, cinnamon, lemon juice and cloves in saucepan. Cook until smooth and thick, stirring frequently. Ladle into hot sterilized jars, leaving 1/2-inch headspace; seal with 2-piece lids. Process in boiling water bath for 10 minutes. Yield: 60 servings.

Approx Per Serving: Cal 54; Prot <1 g; Carbo 14 g; Fiber 1 g; T Fat <1 g; Chol 0 mg; Sod 4 mg.

Paula Mills, Foot Hills

APPLE-ORANGE MARMALADE

5 cups sugar
1 1/2 cups water
1 orange, cut into strips
2 tablespoons lemon juice
8 cups thinly sliced tart apples

Heat sugar and water in saucepan until sugar dissolves, stirring frequently. Add orange, lemon juice and apples. Boil rapidly for 12 to 15 minutes or until mixture thickens, stirring constantly. Ladle into hot sterilized jars, leaving 1/2-inch headspace; seal with 2-piece lids. Process in boiling water bath for 10 minutes. Cool for 30 minutes. Shake jars gently to distribute fruit. Store in cool, dry, dark place. Yield: 50 servings.

Approx Per Serving: Cal 89; Prot <1 g; Carbo 23 g; Fiber 1 g; T Fat <1 g; Chol 0 mg; Sod 1 mg.

Barbara Morris, Salem

CRANBERRY RELISH

1/2 orange
1 1/2 cups fresh cranberries
1 medium red Delicious apple, cut into quarters
1 8-ounce can pineapple tidbits, drained

Process orange in food processor fitted with knife blade until finely chopped. Add cranberries, apple and pineapple. Pulse 4 times. Chill, covered, until serving time. Yield: 12 servings.

Approx Per Serving: Cal 25; Prot <1 g; Carbo 6 g; Fiber 1 g; T Fat <1 g; Chol 0 mg; Sod <1 mg.

Cheryl Griffin, Raleigh

JALAPEÑO JELLY

4 large green bell peppers, chopped
12 jalapeño peppers, chopped
1 1/2 cups cider vinegar
6 1/2 cups sugar
Several drops of green food coloring
1 bottle of Certo

Combine green peppers, jalapeño peppers, vinegar and sugar in saucepan. Boil for 10 minutes, stirring frequently. Strain through cheesecloth. Add food coloring. Bring to a boil. Add Certo. Boil for 1 minute. Remove from heat. Skim. Pour into hot sterilized jars, leaving 1/2-inch headspace; seal with 2-piece lids. Process in boiling water bath for 10 minutes. May substitute red food coloring for green. Yield: 36 servings.

Approx Per Serving: Cal 149; Prot <1 g; Carbo 39 g; Fiber <1 g; T Fat <1 g; Chol 0 mg; Sod 2 mg.
Nutritional information does not include Certo.

Irene M. Hooper, Asheville

SPICED PEACHES

2 29-ounce cans cling peach halves
1⅓ cups sugar
1 cup cider vinegar
4 sticks cinnamon
3 teaspoons whole cloves

Drain peaches, reserving juice. Combine juice, sugar, vinegar, cinnamon and cloves in saucepan. Bring to a boil. Simmer for 10 minutes, stirring frequently. Pour hot syrup over peaches. Store in refrigerator. Yield: 10 servings.

Approx Per Serving: Cal 229; Prot 1 g; Carbo 61 g; Fiber 1 g; T Fat <1 g; Chol 0 mg; Sod 11 mg.

Becky Adams, Coastal

FROZEN STRAWBERRY PRESERVES

2 cups mashed strawberries
4 cups sugar
1 box Sure-Jel
¾ cup water

Mix strawberries and sugar in bowl. Boil Sure-Jel and water for 1 minute in saucepan. Pour over strawberries. Stir for 3 minutes. Pour into sterilized jars, leaving ½-inch headspace; add lids. Let stand at room temperature for 24 hours. Freeze until firm. May substitute peaches, blueberries or other fruit for strawberries. Yield: 16 servings.

Approx Per Serving: Cal 201; Prot <1 g; Carbo 52 g; Fiber 1 g; T Fat <1 g; Chol 0 mg; Sod 2 mg.
Nutritional information does not include Sure-Jel.

Karen Stallings, Independence

☎ To eliminate extra cleanup when using the food processor for several steps, start with dryer ingredients and work through to moister ones.

SWEET DILL PICKLES

1 cup white vinegar
2 cups sugar
1 46-ounce jar dill
  pickles, drained
¼ teaspoon celery seed

Bring vinegar and sugar to a boil in saucepan; remove from heat. Cool. Slice dill pickles very thin. Place celery seed in pickle jar. Return sliced pickles to jar. Pour cooled vinegar mixture over pickles. Chill in refrigerator for 3 days before serving, inverting jar several times. Store in refrigerator. Yield: 30 servings.

Approx Per Serving: Cal 56; Prot <1 g; Carbo 15 g; Fiber 1 g; T Fat 0 g; Chol 0 mg; Sod 496 mg.

Nell Seegers, Independence

MINNESOTA CUCUMBERS

7 cups thinly sliced
  cucumbers
1 cup thinly sliced green
  bell pepper
1 cup thinly sliced onion
1 tablespoon celery seed
2 tablespoons salt
2 cups sugar
1 cup vinegar

Combine cucumbers, green pepper, onion, celery seed and salt in bowl; mix well. Stir sugar into vinegar in small bowl until dissolved. Pour over vegetables. Chill, covered, in refrigerator overnight. May store in refrigerator for 2 weeks. Yield: 36 servings.

Approx Per Serving: Cal 46; Prot <1 g; Carbo 12 g; Fiber <1 g; T Fat <1 g; Chol 0 mg; Sod 356 mg.

Julia S. Clark, Independence

REFRIGERATOR SWEET PICKLES

4 cups sugar
4 cups cider vinegar
1/2 cup salt
1 1/4 teaspoons turmeric
1 1/4 teaspoons celery seed
1 1/2 teaspoons mustard seed
4 pounds small cucumbers, thinly sliced
6 small onions, thinly sliced

Combine sugar, vinegar, salt, turmeric, celery seed and mustard seed in large jar. Shake, covered, until sugar and salt are dissolved. Pack cucumber slices and onion slices into sterilized jars. Add vinegar mixture. Chill in refrigerator for 5 days before serving. Store in refrigerator. Yield: 20 servings.

Approx Per Serving: Cal 184; Prot 1 g; Carbo 48 g; Fiber 2 g; T Fat <1 g; Chol 0 mg; Sod 2562 mg.

Nell Seegers, Independence

PICKLED EGGS

2 tablespoons mustard
2 cups vinegar
1/2 cup water
1 cup sugar
1 tablespoon salt
1 tablespoon celery seed
1 tablespoon mustard seed
6 whole cloves
12 hard-boiled eggs
2 small onions, thinly sliced

Blend mustard and a small amount of vinegar in saucepan. Add remaining vinegar, water, sugar, salt, celery seed, mustard seed and cloves; mix well. Bring to a boil. Simmer for 10 minutes, stirring frequently. Cool. Combine whole eggs and onion slices in bowl. Add cooled vinegar mixture. Chill, covered, overnight. Yield: 12 servings.

Approx Per Serving: Cal 157; Prot 6 g; Carbo 21 g; Fiber <1 g; T Fat 6 g; Chol 213 mg; Sod 636 mg.

Evelyn Carson, Independence

PICKLED OKRA

1 quart vinegar
2 cups water
1/2 cup salt
6 cloves of garlic
1 teaspoon dill
1 teaspoon dry mustard
1 teaspoon celery seed
3 hot red peppers, cut into halves
2 teaspoons ground red pepper
12 cups okra pods

Combine vinegar, water, salt, garlic, dill, mustard, celery seed, red peppers and ground red pepper in saucepan. Bring to a boil, stirring frequently. Combine okra and water to cover in saucepan. Bring to a boil; drain. Pack okra pods tightly into 6 hot sterilized pint jars. Place 1/2 red pepper from vinegar mixture in each jar. Pour vinegar mixture over okra, leaving 1/2-inch headspace; seal with 2-piece lids. Process in boiling water bath for 10 minutes. Yield: 24 servings.

Approx Per Serving: Cal 43; Prot 2 g; Carbo 11 g; Fiber 2 g; T Fat <1 g; Chol 0 mg; Sod 2136 mg.

Evelyn Carson, Independence

ED'S PICKLED OKRA

4 pounds okra, rinsed, trimmed
10 hot peppers
10 cloves of garlic
3/4 cup pickling salt
8 cups vinegar
1 cup water

Pack okra in 10 sterilized pint jars. Place 1 hot pepper and 1 garlic clove in each jar. Combine salt, vinegar and water in saucepan. Bring to a boil, stirring frequently. Pour over okra, leaving 1/2-inch headspace; seal with 2-piece lids. Process in boiling water bath for 10 minutes. Let stand for several weeks before serving. May add addition hot peppers for spicier flavor. Yield: 50 servings.

Approx Per Serving: Cal 20; Prot 1 g; Carbo 6 g; Fiber 1 g; T Fat <1 g; Chol 0 mg; Sod 1538 mg.

Ed Thomas, Central

CANNED SWEET PEPPERS

2 quarts green bell pepper quarters
1 quart red bell pepper quarters
1 quart yellow bell pepper quarters
1/4 cup oil
4 teaspoons salt
1 quart water
1 quart vinegar
3 cups sugar

Combine green, red and yellow pepper quarters with water to cover in saucepan. Bring to a boil, stirring occasionally. Cook for 4 minutes; drain. Pack in 4 hot sterilized quart jars. Add 1 tablespoon oil and 1 teaspoon salt to each jar. Combine 1 quart water, vinegar and sugar in saucepan. Bring to a boil, stirring frequently. Pour over peppers, leaving 1/2-inch headspace; seal with 2-piece lids. Process in boiling water bath for 10 minutes. Yield: 64 servings.

Approx Per Serving: Cal 51; Prot <1 g; Carbo 12 g; Fiber <1 g; T Fat 1 g; Chol 0 mg; Sod 135 mg.

Gerri Evans, Hornets Nest

PEPPER RELISH BY MRS. GLENN

16 green tomatoes, finely chopped
12 ripe tomatoes, finely chopped
12 green bell peppers, finely chopped
9 red bell peppers, finely chopped
3 cups sugar
5 cups vinegar

Combine green tomatoes, ripe tomatoes, green peppers, red peppers, sugar and vinegar in large saucepan; mix well. Simmer for 45 minutes, stirring frequently. Ladle into hot sterilized jars, leaving 1/2-inch headspace; seal with 2-piece lids. Process in boiling water bath for 10 minutes. May add chopped onion if desired. Yield: 48 servings.

Approx Per Serving: Cal 69; Prot 1 g; Carbo 18 g; Fiber 1 g; T Fat <1 g; Chol 0 mg; Sod 7 mg.

Kathryn Woolum, Central

SQUASH RELISH

8 large squash, chopped
5 medium onions, chopped
2 cups chopped red bell peppers
2 cups chopped green bell peppers
2 tablespoons salt
2 cups sugar
2 teaspoons celery seed
2 teaspoons mustard seed
1/2 teaspoon turmeric
2 cups cider vinegar

Combine squash, onions, red peppers and green peppers in large bowl. Add salt; mix well. Let stand for 1 hour. Drain and rinse. Combine sugar, celery seed, mustard seed, turmeric and vinegar in large saucepan. Bring to a boil. Add vegetable mixture; mix well. Bring to a boil. Cook for 1 minute, stirring frequently. Ladle into hot sterilized jars, leaving 1/2-inch headspace; seal with 2-piece lids. Process in boiling water bath for 10 minutes. Yield: 60 servings.

Approx Per Serving: Cal 35; Prot <1 g; Carbo 9 g; Fiber 1 g; T Fat <1 g; Chol 0 mg; Sod 214 mg.

Shirley Carmichael, Hornets Nest

BARBECUE SAUCE FOR PORK

8 cups vinegar
2 cups margarine
1/4 cup Worcestershire sauce
1/4 cup Tabasco sauce
1/4 cup chili powder
1/2 cup paprika
3/4 cup black pepper
3/4 cup salt
3 teaspoons dry mustard
1 quart catsup
1/2 cup red pepper
2 cups water

Combine vinegar, margarine, Worcestershire sauce, Tabasco sauce, chili powder, paprika, black pepper, salt, mustard, catsup, red pepper and water in 6-quart saucepan; mix well. Bring to a boil. Cook for 15 minutes, stirring constantly. Store in airtight container in refrigerator. Will keep for several months. Yield: 128 servings.

Approx Per Serving: Cal 41; Prot <1 g; Carbo 4 g; Fiber 1 g; T Fat 3 g; Chol 0 mg; Sod 732 mg.

Ed Thomas, Central

MAYBERRY'S BARBECUE SAUCE

1 cup thick catsup
1/2 cup oil
2 tablespoons sugar
2 tablespoons Worcestershire sauce
2 tablespoons vinegar
1 teaspoon salt
1/2 teaspoon pepper
Hot pepper sauce to taste

Combine catsup, oil, sugar, Worcestershire sauce, vinegar, salt, pepper and hot pepper sauce in bowl; mix well. Baste chicken, pork or shrimp when cooking on grill. Yield: 16 servings.

Approx Per Serving: Cal 86; Prot <1 g; Carbo 6 g; Fiber <1 g; T Fat 7 g; Chol 0 mg; Sod 330 mg.

Mary Mayberry, Raleigh

BARBECUE SAUCE

1 cup catsup
1/8 teaspoon dry mustard
2 tablespoons brown sugar
1/8 teaspoon pepper
2 teaspoons chili powder
2 tablespoons vinegar
1 tablespoon paprika
1/8 teaspoon garlic salt

Combine all ingredients in bowl; mix well. Use over poultry or meat. Yield: 10 servings.

Approx Per Serving: Cal 43; Prot 1 g; Carbo 10 g; Fiber 1 g; T Fat <1 g; Chol 0 mg; Sod 317 mg.

Evelyn Carson, Independence

QUICK BARBECUE SAUCE

1 can tomato soup
4 teaspoons sweet pickle relish
1/2 cup chopped onion
1 teaspoon brown sugar
1 teaspoon vinegar
1 teaspoon Worcestershire sauce

Combine soup, relish, onion, brown sugar, vinegar and Worcestershire sauce in saucepan; mix well. Simmer, covered, for 10 minutes, stirring occasionally. Yield: 16 servings.

Approx Per Serving: Cal 18; Prot <1 g; Carbo 4 g; Fiber <1 g; T Fat <1 g; Chol 0 mg; Sod 145 mg.

Deni Dumford, Piedmont

HOMEMADE BARBECUE SAUCE

2 tablespoons vinegar
1/4 cup lemon juice
3 tablespoons Worcestershire sauce
1 medium onion, chopped
2 tablespoons brown sugar
1 cup catsup
1 cup water
Salt and pepper to taste
1/2 cup finely chopped celery

Combine vinegar, lemon juice, Worcestershire sauce, onion, brown sugar, catsup, water, salt, pepper and celery in bowl; mix well. Let stand in refrigerator overnight. Delicious on chicken or pork chops. Yield: 25 servings.

Approx Per Serving: Cal 20; Prot <1 g; Carbo 5 g; Fiber <1 g; T Fat <1 g; Chol 0 mg; Sod 134 mg.

Phyllis Jones, Independence

GRAVY

2 tablespoons flour
2 tablespoons pan drippings
1 cup water
1 tablespoon soy sauce
1 teaspoon Worcestershire sauce
1 tablespoon catsup
Salt and pepper to taste

Blend flour into drippings in skillet. Add water, soy sauce and Worcestershire sauce; mix well. Cook until smooth and thickened, stirring constantly. Add catsup, salt and pepper; mix well. Add additional water if too thick. May make ahead and reheat in microwave. Yield: 2 servings.

Approx Per Serving: Cal 170; Prot 1 g; Carbo 9 g; Fiber <1 g; T Fat 14 g; Chol 84 mg; Sod 768 mg.

Barbara Morris, Salem

Bread

LIGHT THE DARKNESS

ALZHEIMER'S

1+800 621-0379

— ALZHEIMER'S DISEASE —

BREADS

EASY BISCUITS

1 cup flour
½ cup milk
2 tablespoons mayonnaise

Combine flour, milk and mayonnaise in bowl; mix well. Fill greased muffin cups. Bake at 450 degrees for 15 minutes or until golden brown. Yield: 6 servings.

Approx Per Serving: Cal 121; Prot 3 g; Carbo 17 g; Fiber 1 g; T Fat 5 g; Chol 5 mg; Sod 35 mg.

Shirley C. Helms, Independence

CHEESE BISCUITS

2 cups margarine, softened
1 pound sharp Cheddar cheese, shredded
5 cups flour
½ teaspoon cayenne pepper
Sesame seed to taste

Cream margarine and cheese in large bowl until smooth. Mix flour and cayenne pepper together. Add to cheese mixture gradually, mixing well after each addition. Knead on floured surface until elastic. Shape into 1-inch balls. Place 1 inch apart on baking sheet. Sprinkle with sesame seed. Bake at 400 degrees for 9 to 12 minutes or until brown. May be frozen before baking. Yield: 250 servings.

Approx Per Serving: Cal 30; Prot 1 g; Carbo 2 g; Fiber <1 g; T Fat 2 g; Chol 2 mg; Sod 28 mg.

Wilma Burleson, Independence

HOMEMADE BISCUITS

4 cups self-rising flour
1 tablespoon baking powder
2 teaspoons sugar
7 tablespoons shortening
2 cups buttermilk

Sift first 3 ingredients into medium bowl. Cut in shortening until crumbly. Add buttermilk; mix well. Roll 1½ inches thick on floured surface. Cut with biscuit cutter. Place on greased baking sheet. Bake at 400 degrees for 15 to 20 minutes.
Yield: 24 servings.

Approx Per Serving: Cal 117; Prot 3 g; Carbo 17 g; Fiber 1 g; T Fat 4 g; Chol 1 mg; Sod 287 mg.

Polly Mabrey, Hornets Nest

QUICK LOW-CHOLESTEROL BISCUITS

2 cups self-rising flour
⅔ cup buttermilk
¼ cup corn oil

Combine flour, buttermilk and oil in medium bowl; stir just until moistened. Knead on floured surface 3 or 4 times. Roll dough ½ inch thick. Cut with 2-inch biscuit cutter. Arrange on baking sheet. Bake at 425 degrees for 10 to 12 minutes or until brown. Yield: 12 servings.

Approx Per Serving: Cal 119; Prot 3 g; Carbo 16 g; Fiber 1 g; T Fat 5 g; Chol 1 mg; Sod 239 mg.

Gerri Evans, Hornets Nest

SOUR CREAM BISCUITS

1 cup self-rising flour
¼ teaspoon soda
¾ cup sour cream

Combine flour, soda and sour cream in bowl; mix until smooth. Knead several times on lightly floured surface. Pat dough to ½-inch thickness. Cut with 2-inch biscuit cutter. Place on lightly greased baking sheet. Bake at 450 degrees for 10 to 12 minutes or until golden brown. Yield: 6 servings.

Approx Per Serving: Cal 135; Prot 3 g; Carbo 17 g; Fiber 1 g; T Fat 6 g; Chol 13 mg; Sod 1030 mg.

Virginia Bowie, Independence

V-8 BISCUITS

3 cups self-rising flour
⅛ teaspoon soda
⅛ teaspoon salt
1 tablespoon sugar
½ cup shortening
2 4-ounce cans vegetable juice cocktail

Combine flour, soda, salt and sugar in medium bowl; mix well. Cut in shortening until crumbly. Add enough juice to form soft dough. Knead on floured surface until smooth and elastic. Roll ½ inch thick. Cut with biscuit cutter. Place on greased baking sheet. Bake at 400 degrees for 8 to 10 minutes or until brown. Yield: 18 servings.

Approx Per Serving: Cal 129; Prot 2 g; Carbo 17 g; Fiber 1 g; T Fat 6 g; Chol 0 mg; Sod 291 mg.

Margaret L. Fenner, Hornets Nest

☎ Hot rolls or biscuits will stay hot longer if you place aluminum foil under the napkin in the basket.

CHEESE BREAD

2 cups baking mix
3/4 cup milk
2 eggs, beaten
2 teaspoons dry mustard
1 1/2 cups shredded sharp
   Cheddar cheese

Combine baking mix, milk, eggs and mustard in medium bowl; mix well. Stir in cheese. Spoon into greased 5x9-inch loaf pan. Bake at 350 degrees for 40 to 45 minutes or until loaf tests done. May brush top with melted butter if desired.
Yield: 12 servings.

Approx Per Serving: Cal 170; Prot 7 g; Carbo 15 g; Fiber 0 g;
   T Fat 9 g; Chol 52 mg; Sod 370 mg.

Peggy W. Pearce, Independence

FRESH BERRY COFFEE CAKE

1 1/2 cups sifted flour
1 teaspoon baking powder
1/4 teaspoon salt
1/2 cup unsalted
   margarine, softened
1 cup sugar
2 eggs
1 teaspoon vanilla extract
3 tablespoons sour cream
1/3 cup milk
1 1/2 cups blueberries
1/3 cup sugar
1/4 cup flour
1/2 teaspoon cinnamon
3 tablespoons butter,
   softened

Sift 1 1/2 cups flour, baking powder and salt into bowl. Cream 1/2 cup margarine and 1 cup sugar in mixer bowl until smooth. Add eggs 1 at a time, mixing well after each addition. Add vanilla and sour cream; mix well. Add flour mixture alternately with milk, mixing well after each addition and beginning and ending with flour mixture. Spoon half the batter into greased 9-inch baking pan. Top with blueberries then remaining batter. Combine remaining 1/3 cup sugar, 1/4 cup flour and cinnamon in small bowl; mix well. Cut in butter until crumbly. Sprinkle over batter. Bake at 350 degrees for 30 to 35 minutes or until golden brown. Cool on wire rack for 5 minutes. Serve warm.
Yield: 9 servings.

Approx Per Serving: Cal 368; Prot 4 g; Carbo 51 g; Fiber 1 g;
   T Fat 17 g; Chol 61 mg; Sod 152 mg.

Phyllis Jones, Independence

BUTTERQUICK COFFEE CAKE

1/3 cup margarine, softened
1 cup sugar
1 egg
2 cups sifted self-rising flour
1 cup milk
2 tablespoons margarine, softened
2 tablespoons flour
1/4 cup packed brown sugar
1/2 cup chopped walnuts

Cream 1/3 cup margarine and sugar in mixer bowl until light and fluffy. Add egg; mix well. Add flour alternately with milk, mixing well after each addition. Beat for 2 minutes. Spoon into greased 9-inch baking pan. Combine remaining 2 tablespoons margarine, 2 tablespoons flour, brown sugar and walnuts in small bowl; mix well. Sprinkle over batter. Bake at 350 degrees for 30 to 45 minute or until golden brown. Yield: 9 servings.

Approx Per Serving: Cal 363; Prot 5 g; Carbo 53 g; Fiber 1 g; T Fat 15 g; Chol 27 mg; Sod 431 mg.

Delores Sossamon, Independence

BROCCOLI CORN BREAD

1 large onion, chopped
1 10-ounce package chopped broccoli, thawed
4 eggs, beaten
1/2 cup melted margarine
3/4 cup cottage cheese
1 teaspoon salt
1 7-ounce package corn muffin mix

Combine onion, broccoli, eggs, margarine, cottage cheese and salt in bowl; mix well. Stir in muffin mix just until moistened. Spoon into greased 9x13-inch baking dish. Bake at 400 degrees for 20 minutes or until golden brown. Freezes well. Yield: 12 servings.

Approx Per Serving: Cal 151; Prot 5 g; Carbo 9 g; Fiber 1 g; T Fat 11 g; Chol 73 mg; Sod 423 mg.

Gerri Evans, Hornets Nest

JERRY'S FAVORITE CORN BREAD

1/2 cup margarine, softened
2 eggs
1 8-ounce can cream-style corn
8 ounces sour cream
1 7-ounce package corn bread mix

Combine margarine, eggs, corn and sour cream in medium bowl; mix well. Add corn bread mix, stirring just until moistened. Pour into greased 9x13-inch baking pan. Bake at 400 degrees for 30 minutes or until bread tests done. Yield: 12 servings.

Approx Per Serving: Cal 168; Prot 2 g; Carbo 10 g; Fiber 1 g; T Fat 13 g; Chol 44 mg; Sod 238 mg.

Brenda Lathan, Independence

MISSISSIPPI CORN BREAD

2 cups self-rising cornmeal
2 eggs
1/2 cup oil
1 cup sour cream
1 8-ounce can cream-style corn
1 small onion, grated

Combine cornmeal, eggs, oil, sour cream, corn and onion in bowl; mix well. Pour into greased cast-iron skillet. Bake at 350 degrees for 30 to 35 minutes or until bread tests done. Yield: 8 servings.

Approx Per Serving: Cal 354; Prot 6 g; Carbo 35 g; Fiber 3 g; T Fat 22 g; Chol 66 mg; Sod 196 mg.

Gail Blevins, Blue Ridge

☎ Add crumbled crisp-fried bacon, cheese, green chilies or whole kernel corn to your favorite corn bread recipe.

NEVER-FAIL CORN BREAD

1 cup self-rising flour
1 cup self-rising cornmeal
2 eggs
2 tablespoons sugar
1 cup milk
3 tablespoons melted shortening

　　Combine flour, cornmeal, eggs, sugar, milk, and shortening in bowl; mix well. Pour into greased 9-inch cast-iron skillet. Bake at 450 degrees for 15 to 20 minutes or until brown. Yield: 8 servings.

Approx Per Serving: Cal 211; Prot 5 g; Carbo 30 g; Fiber 2 g;
　　T Fat 8 g; Chol 57 mg; Sod 199 mg.

Frances Cook, Blue Ridge

OLD SOUTHERN CORN BREAD

2 cups self-rising cornmeal
1 cup self-rising flour
½ cup sugar
3 tablespoons bacon drippings
2 eggs, beaten
2 cups buttermilk
2 tablespoons bacon drippings

　　Combine cornmeal, flour and sugar in medium bowl; mix well. Add 3 tablespoons bacon drippings, eggs and buttermilk; mix well. Heat remaining 2 tablespoons bacon drippings in 10-inch cast-iron skillet until sizzling hot. Pour batter into skillet. Cook over medium heat until batter is bubbly. Bake at 400 degrees for 35 to 45 minutes or until brown. Yield: 10 servings.

Approx Per Serving: Cal 281; Prot 6 g; Carbo 43 g; Fiber 2 g;
　　T Fat 9 g; Chol 86 mg; Sod 271 mg.

Audrey Brock, Hornets Nest

SKILLET CORN BREAD

1 1/2 cups self-rising
  cornmeal
1/2 cup self-rising flour
1 tablespoon brown sugar
2 eggs, beaten
1/4 cup oil
1 1/2 cups buttermilk

Combine cornmeal, flour and brown sugar in bowl; mix well. Stir in eggs, oil and buttermilk. Pour into greased 9-inch baking dish. Bake at 425 degrees for 25 minutes or until brown. Yield: 9 servings.

Approx Per Serving: Cal 202; Prot 5 g; Carbo 27 g; Fiber 2 g; T Fat 8 g; Chol 49 mg; Sod 189 mg.

Elsie M. Mills, Independence

SPOON BREAD

3/4 cup self-rising cornmeal
1 tablespoon sugar
3 tablespoons melted
  butter
1 cup boiling water
1 cup buttermilk
2 eggs, beaten

Combine cornmeal and sugar in bowl; mix well. Stir in butter. Add water gradually, beating constantly until smooth. Stir in buttermilk and eggs; mix well. Pour into 9x13-inch baking dish. Bake at 350 degrees for 30 to 40 minutes or until golden brown. Yield: 12 servings.

Approx Per Serving: Cal 82; Prot 2 g; Carbo 9 g; Fiber 1 g; T Fat 4 g; Chol 44 mg; Sod 57 mg.

Daisy Dills, Central

HUSH PUPPIES

½ cup flour
1 cup cornmeal
½ teaspoon salt
½ green bell pepper, finely chopped
½ medium onion, finely chopped
1 egg, beaten
½ cup (about) water
1¼ teaspoons baking powder
Oil for deep frying

Combine flour, cornmeal and salt in bowl; mix well. Add green pepper, onion, egg and water; mix well. Chill, covered, in refrigerator for 12 hours or longer. Stir in baking powder. Drop by tablespoonfuls into hot oil in skillet. Deep-fry until golden brown. Drain on paper towel. Yield: 24 servings.

Approx Per Serving: Cal 36; Prot 1 g; Carbo 7 g; Fiber 1 g; T Fat <1 g; Chol 9 mg; Sod 65 mg.
Nutritional information does not include oil for deep frying.

Lee Beall, Independence

CRÊPES

1 cup flour
1½ cups milk
½ teaspoon salt
3 eggs
1 tablespoon melted butter

Combine flour, milk, salt, eggs and melted butter in blender container. Process until smooth. Pour scant ¼ cup batter into hot lightly greased crêpe pan. Tilt pan to spread batter evenly. Bake until light brown on both sides; stack between waxed paper. May sprinkle with sugar or confectioners' sugar or fill with jam, fresh fruit or preserves. Yield: 12 servings.

Approx Per Serving: Cal 85; Prot 4 g; Carbo 10 g; Fiber <1 g; T Fat 3 g; Chol 60 mg; Sod 127 mg.

Candace W. Joehrendt, Raleigh

FUNNEL CAKES

2 eggs, beaten
1½ cups milk
2 6-ounce envelopes Martha White Flapjax mix
1 tablespoon sugar
½ teaspoon vanilla extract
Oil for deep frying
Confectioners' sugar to taste

Combine eggs, milk, Flapjax mix, sugar and vanilla in medium bowl; mix until smooth. Heat oil to 375 degrees in heavy skillet. Spoon ¼ cup batter into funnel, holding finger over funnel opening. Release batter into hot oil in spiral, starting from center. Fry until golden brown on both sides; drain on paper towel. Repeat with remaining batter. Sprinkle generously with confectioners' sugar. Serve warm. Yield: 10 servings.

Approx Per Serving: Cal 170; Prot 6 g; Carbo 28 g; Fiber 0 g; T Fat 4 g; Chol 48 mg; Sod 440 mg.
Nutritional information does not include oil for deep frying.

Cyndi Mabrey, Hornets Nest

ITALIAN SAUSAGE BREAD

2 loaves frozen bread dough
1 pound ground beef
1 pound Italian sausage, skinned, crumbled
1 onion, chopped
1 green bell pepper, chopped
3 cups shredded Cheddar cheese

Place frozen bread dough on well-greased baking sheets. Grease top of each loaf. Let stand, covered, for 2 hours or until thawed. Do not let rise. Brown ground beef and sausage with onion and green pepper in skillet, stirring frequently; drain. Cool. Press dough with greased hands over surface of baking sheets. Layer with ground beef mixture and cheese. Roll as for jelly roll. Place seamside down on baking sheets. Bake at 350 degrees for 20 minutes or until golden brown. Yield: 24 servings.

Approx Per Serving: Cal 275; Prot 15 g; Carbo 19 g; Fiber 1 g; T Fat 15 g; Chol 46 mg; Sod 469 mg.

Lee Davis, Asheville

APPLE BREAD

2 cups flour
2 teaspoons baking powder
1 teaspoon cinnamon
1/4 teaspoon nutmeg
1 teaspoon salt
1/2 cup butter, softened
1 1/2 cups sugar
2 eggs
2 cups finely shredded apples
1/2 cup chopped walnuts

Sift first 5 ingredients into medium bowl. Cream butter and sugar in large bowl until light and fluffy. Add eggs 1 at a time, mixing well after each addition. Add flour mixture and apples 1/2 at a time, mixing well after each addition. Stir in walnuts. Spoon into well-greased 5x9-inch loaf pan. Bake at 350 degrees for 1 hour or until loaf tests done. Cool in pan for 10 minutes. Remove to wire rack to cool completely. Yield: 12 servings.

Approx Per Serving: Cal 292; Prot 4 g; Carbo 45 g; Fiber 1 g; T Fat 12 g; Chol 56 mg; Sod 488 mg.

Betty Quick, Central

SPICED APPLESAUCE BREAD

1 1/4 cups applesauce
1 cup sugar
1/2 cup oil
2 eggs
3 tablespoons milk
2 cups sifted flour
1 teaspoon soda
1/2 teaspoon baking powder
1/2 teaspoon cinnamon
1/4 teaspoon salt
1/4 teaspoon nutmeg
1/4 teaspoon allspice
1/2 cup chopped pecans
1/4 cup packed brown sugar
1/2 teaspoon cinnamon
1/4 cup chopped pecans

Combine first 5 ingredients in mixer bowl; beat until well blended. Sift flour, soda, baking powder, 1/2 teaspoon cinnamon, salt, nutmeg and allspice into medium bowl. Add to applesauce mixture; mix well. Fold in 1/2 cup pecans. Spoon into well-greased 5x9-inch loaf pan. Combine brown sugar, remaining 1/2 teaspoon cinnamon and 1/4 cup pecans in bowl. Sprinkle over batter. Bake at 350 degrees for 1 hour or until loaf tests done. Remove to wire rack to cool. Yield: 12 servings.

Approx Per Serving: Cal 317; Prot 4 g; Carbo 43 g; Fiber 1 g; T Fat 15 g; Chol 36 mg; Sod 143 mg.

Sally Vinton, Independence

BANANA BREAD

1/2 cup margarine
1 cup sugar
2 eggs, beaten
1 1/2 cups flour
1 teaspoon soda
1/2 teaspoon salt
3 large ripe bananas, mashed
1/2 cup chopped walnuts

Cream margarine and sugar in bowl until light and fluffy. Add eggs; mix well. Sift flour, soda and salt into margarine mixture; mix until well blended. Stir in bananas and walnuts. Spoon into greased 5x9-inch loaf pan. Bake at 350 degrees for 25 to 30 minutes or until loaf tests done. Cool in pan for 10 minutes. Remove to wire rack to cool completely.
Yield: 12 servings.

Approx Per Serving: Cal 260; Prot 4 g; Carbo 36 g; Fiber 1 g; T Fat 12 g; Chol 36 mg; Sod 260 mg.

Bobby Kinney, Independence

BANANA BRAN LOAF

1 cup mashed ripe bananas
1/2 cup sugar
1/3 cup oil
2 egg whites
1/3 cup skim milk
1 1/4 cups flour
1 cup oat bran
2 teaspoons baking powder
1/2 teaspoon soda

Combine bananas, sugar, oil, egg whites and milk in bowl; mix well. Stir in flour, oat bran, baking powder and soda just until moistened. Spoon into 5x9-inch loaf pan sprayed with nonstick cooking spray. Bake at 350 degrees for 55 minutes to 1 hour or until loaf tests done. Cool in pan for 10 minutes. Remove to wire rack to cool completely. Freezes well. Yield: 16 servings.

Approx Per Serving: Cal 130; Prot 3 g; Carbo 21 g; Fiber 2 g; T Fat 5 g; Chol <1 mg; Sod 78 mg.

Mrs. Hugh L. McAulay, Blue Ridge

MORAVIAN PUMPKIN BREAD

3 cups sugar
1 cup oil
4 eggs
2/3 cup water
2 cups pumpkin
1 teaspoon vanilla extract
3 1/2 cups flour

1/2 teaspoon baking powder
2 teaspoons soda
1 tablespoon cinnamon
1 teaspoon nutmeg
1 1/2 teaspoons salt
1 cup chopped pecans

Combine sugar, oil, eggs, water, pumpkin and vanilla in medium bowl; mix well. Sift flour, baking powder, soda, cinnamon, nutmeg and salt into small bowl. Add pecans. Stir into pumpkin mixture. Spoon into 2 greased 4x8-inch loaf pans. Bake at 350 degrees for 60 minutes or until loaves test done. Cool in pans for 10 minutes. Remove to wire rack to cool completely. Yield: 16 servings.

Approx Per Serving: Cal 445; Prot 5 g; Carbo 62 g; Fiber 2 g; T Fat 20 g; Chol 53 mg; Sod 333 mg.

Hallene L. Brindle, Salem

PUMPKIN BREAD

3 cups sugar
3 1/2 cups flour
4 eggs
1 cup oil
2/3 cup water
2 cups canned pumpkin

2 teaspoons baking powder
1 1/2 teaspoons salt
1 teaspoon cinnamon
1 teaspoon nutmeg

Combine sugar, flour, eggs, oil, water, pumpkin, baking powder, salt, cinnamon and nutmeg in bowl; beat until smooth. Spoon into 2 greased and floured loaf pans. Bake at 350 degrees for 1 hour. Remove to wire rack to cool. May add nuts if desired. Yield: 24 servings.

Approx Per Serving: Cal 263; Prot 3 g; Carbo 41 g; Fiber 1 g; T Fat 10 g; Chol 36 mg; Sod 174 mg.

Sheryl Taylor, Raleigh

PUMPKIN AND DATE BREAD

3½ cups flour
2 teaspoons baking soda
2 teaspoons cinnamon
2 teaspoons cloves
1½ teaspoons salt
3 cups sugar
4 eggs
1½ teaspoons vanilla extract
⅔ cup water
1 cup oil
2 cups pumpkin
1 cup chopped dates
¾ cup chopped pecans

Sift flour, soda, cinnamon, cloves, salt and sugar into bowl. Combine eggs, vanilla, water, oil and pumpkin in mixer bowl; mix well. Add flour mixture gradually, beating constantly until well mixed. Stir in dates and pecans. Pour into 2 greased 5x9-inch loaf pans. Bake at 350 degrees for 1 hour and 10 minutes or until loaves test done. Cool in pans for 10 minutes. Remove to wire rack to cool completely. Yield: 24 servings.

Approx Per Serving: Cal 309; Prot 4 g; Carbo 47 g; Fiber 2 g; T Fat 13 g; Chol 36 mg; Sod 215 mg.

Brenda Ashe, Independence

WALNUT PUMPKIN BREAD

4 eggs
3 cups sugar
1 cup oil
⅓ cup water
2 cups pumpkin
3½ cups sifted flour
2 teaspoons soda
1 teaspoon cinnamon
1½ teaspoons salt
1½ cups chopped dates
1½ cups chopped walnuts

Beat eggs with sugar in bowl. Add oil, water and pumpkin; mix well. Mix in flour, soda, cinnamon and salt. Stir in dates and walnuts. Spoon into 3 greased and floured loaf pans. Bake at 350 degrees for 1 hour. Remove to wire rack to cool. Yield: 30 servings.

Approx Per Serving: Cal 269; Prot 3 g; Carbo 39 g; Fiber 2 g; T Fat 12 g; Chol 28 mg; Sod 173 mg.

Karen Stallings, Independence

HARVEST PUMPKIN BREAD

2 2/3 cups shortening
2 2/3 cups sugar
4 eggs, beaten
2/3 cup water
2 cups pumpkin
3 1/2 cups flour
1/2 teaspoon baking powder
2 teaspoons soda
1 teaspoon cinnamon
1/2 teaspoon cloves
1 1/2 teaspoons salt
2/3 cup chopped pecans
2/3 cup raisins
2/3 cup chopped dates

Cream shortening and sugar in mixer bowl until light. Add eggs, water and pumpkin; mix well. Add sifted mixture of flour, baking powder, soda, cinnamon, cloves and salt; mix well. Mix in pecans, raisins and dates. Spoon into 2 greased and floured loaf pans. Bake at 350 degrees for 1 hour. Remove to wire rack to cool. Yield: 20 servings.

Approx Per Serving: Cal 506; Prot 4 g; Carbo 55 g; Fiber 2 g; T Fat 31 g; Chol 43 mg; Sod 267 mg.

Deni Dumford, Piedmont

ZUCCHINI BREAD

3 eggs
1 cup oil
2 cups sugar
1 teaspoon vanilla extract
2 cups peeled, shredded zucchini
3 cups flour
1/4 teaspoon baking powder
1 teaspoon soda
1 tablespoon cinnamon
1 teaspoon salt
1/2 cup walnuts

Beat eggs, oil, sugar and vanilla in mixer bowl until well blended. Squeeze zucchini dry. Add to egg mixture; mix well. Stir in mixture of dry ingredients until moistened. Fold in walnuts. Spoon into 2 greased 5x9-inch loaf pans. Bake at 325 degrees for 1 hour to 1 hour and 10 minutes or until loaves test done. Cool in pans for 10 minutes. Remove to wire rack to cool completely. Yield: 24 servings.

Approx Per Serving: Cal 229; Prot 3 g; Carbo 29 g; Fiber 1 g; T Fat 12 g; Chol 27 mg; Sod 136 mg.

Mary Ann Shook, Piedmont
Madelon Haskin, Hornets Nest

SPICY PINEAPPLE ZUCCHINI BREAD

3 eggs
1 cup oil
2 cups sugar
2 teaspoons vanilla extract
2 cups shredded zucchini
1 8-ounce can crushed pineapple, drained
3 cups flour
2 teaspoons soda
1/2 teaspoon baking powder
1 1/2 teaspoons cinnamon
3/4 teaspoons nutmeg
1 teaspoon salt
1 cup chopped walnuts
1 cup raisins

Combine eggs, oil, sugar and vanilla in mixer bowl; beat until foamy. Stir in zucchini and pineapple. Combine flour, soda, baking powder, cinnamon, nutmeg and salt in medium bowl; mix well. Add to zucchini mixture; mix well. Fold in walnuts and raisins gently. Spoon into 2 greased and floured 5x9-inch loaf pans. Bake at 350 degrees for 1 hour and 10 minutes or until loaves test done. Cool in pans for 10 minutes. Remove to wire rack to cool completely. Yield: 24 servings.

Approx Per Serving: Cal 272; Prot 3 g; Carbo 37 g; Fiber 1 g; T Fat 13 g; Chol 27 mg; Sod 175 mg.

Irene M. Hooper, Asheville

BANANA-APPLE OAT MUFFINS

1 ripe banana, mashed
1 2/3 cups skim milk
1 teaspoon safflower oil
1/3 cup honey
1 teaspoon vanilla extract
1/2 cup peeled, chopped apple
1/4 cup raisins
2 1/2 cups oat bran
1 tablespoon baking powder
3/4 teaspoon soda
1 teaspoon cinnamon

Grease muffin cups; dust with small amount of oat bran. Combine first 7 ingredients in bowl; mix well. Combine oat bran, baking powder, soda and cinnamon in small bowl. Add to banana mixture; stir just until moistened. Fill prepared muffin cups 2/3 full. Bake at 400 degrees for 25 minutes or until lightly browned. Cool for 5 minutes. Remove to wire rack. Yield: 12 servings.

Approx Per Serving: Cal 112; Prot 5 g; Carbo 29 g; Fiber 4 g; T Fat 1 g; Chol 1 mg; Sod 157 mg.

Ovid Smith, Hornets Nest

BANANA-NUT MUFFINS

2¼ cups oat bran
¼ cup packed brown sugar
¼ cup chopped walnuts
1 tablespoon baking powder
⅓ cup (about) milk
2 ripe bananas, mashed
2 egg whites
2 tablespoons oil

Combine oat bran, brown sugar, walnuts and baking powder in bowl; mix well. Combine milk, bananas, egg whites and oil in small bowl; mix well. Stir into oat bran mixture just until moistened. Fill paper-lined muffin cups ⅔ full. Bake at 425 degrees for 17 minutes or until brown. Yield: 12 servings.

Approx Per Serving: Cal 115; Prot 4 g; Carbo 22 g; Fiber 3 g; T Fat 5 g; Chol 0 mg; Sod 97 mg.

Mildred Deese, Hornets Nest

BRAN MUFFINS

1 cup bran
¾ cup flour
1 tablespoon baking powder
½ teaspoon salt
3 tablespoons sugar
1 egg, beaten
¾ cup milk
¼ cup oil

Combine bran, flour, baking powder, salt and sugar in bowl; mix well. Stir in egg, milk and oil. Fill muffin cups sprayed with nonstick cooking spray. Bake at 400 degrees for 20 minutes or until brown. Yield: 12 servings.

Approx Per Serving: Cal 104; Prot 2 g; Carbo 12 g; Fiber 1 g; T Fat 6 g; Chol 20 mg; Sod 184 mg.

Mrs. Hugh L. McAulay, Blue Ridge

☎ Substitute ½ cup maple syrup for ½ cup milk in your favorite muffin recipe for Maple Syrup Muffins.

SIX-WEEK BRAN MUFFINS

1 15-ounce box Raisin Bran cereal
5 cups flour
3 cups sugar
5 teaspoons soda
2 tablespoons salt
1 cup raisins
4 eggs
1 cup oil
1 quart buttermilk
1 1/2 cups chopped pecans

Combine cereal, flour, sugar, soda, salt and raisins in large bowl; mix well. Combine eggs, oil and buttermilk in bowl. Stir into cereal mixture. Fold in pecans gently. Store, covered, in refrigerator for up to 6 weeks. Fill greased muffin cups 2/3 full. Bake at 400 degrees for 15 to 20 minutes or until brown. Freezes well. Yield: 60 servings.

Approx Per Serving: Cal 172; Prot 3 g; Carbo 27 g; Fiber 1 g; T Fat 6 g; Chol 15 mg; Sod 347 mg.

Dorothy McKnight, Independence

CHEDDAR-PIMENTO MUFFINS

2 cups flour
3 1/2 teaspoons baking powder
1/2 teaspoon salt
1 teaspoon paprika
1 cup shredded Cheddar cheese
1 4-ounce jar chopped pimentos
1 egg, beaten
1 cup milk
1/4 cup melted margarine
Dash of Tabasco sauce

Combine flour, baking powder, salt, paprika, cheese and pimentos in bowl; mix well. Make a well in center. Combine egg, milk, margarine and Tabasco sauce. Pour into well; stir just until moistened. Fill greased muffin cups 2/3 full. Bake at 425 degrees for 20 minutes or until brown. Remove to wire rack to cool. Yield: 12 servings.

Approx Per Serving: Cal 171; Prot 6 g; Carbo 18 g; Fiber 1 g; T Fat 8 g; Chol 30 mg; Sod 302 mg.

Peggy George, Independence

LEMON-RASPBERRY MUFFINS

2 cups self-rising flour
1 cup sugar
1 cup half and half
1/2 cup oil
1 teaspoon lemon extract
2 eggs
1 cup raspberries

Combine flour and sugar in large bowl; mix well. Combine half and half, oil, lemon extract and eggs in bowl; mix well. Add to flour mixture; stir just until moistened. Fold in raspberries gently. Fill paper-lined muffin cups 3/4 full. Bake at 425 degrees for 18 to 22 minutes or until brown. Cool for 5 minutes. Remove to wire rack. Yield: 12 servings.

Approx Per Serving: Cal 262; Prot 4 g; Carbo 34 g; Fiber 1 g; T Fat 13 g; Chol 43 mg; Sod 245 mg.

Essie Phillips, Hornets Nest

OAT BRAN AND RAISIN MUFFINS

2 cups 100% bran cereal
2 teaspoons baking powder
1 teaspoon cinnamon
1/2 teaspoon nutmeg
1 cup skim milk
1/3 cup honey
1/4 cup oil
2 egg whites
1 cup raisins

Combine cereal, baking powder, cinnamon and nutmeg in bowl; mix well. Combine milk, honey, oil and egg whites in small bowl; mix well. Add to cereal mixture; stir just until moistened. Fold in raisins gently. Fill greased muffin cups 2/3 full. Bake at 425 degrees for 20 minutes or until brown. Yield: 12 servings.

Approx Per Serving: Cal 150; Prot 3 g; Carbo 28 g; Fiber 4 g; T Fat 5 g; Chol <1 mg; Sod 152 mg.

Martha A. Rhyne, Foot Hills

SWEET POTATO MUFFINS

2 cups sugar
1 1/2 cups oil
4 eggs
1 teaspoon cinnamon
3 cups self-rising flour
1 cup mashed sweet potatoes
1 cup chopped walnuts
1 cup raisins

Combine sugar and oil in bowl until light. Stir in eggs until well blended. Add cinnamon, flour, sweet potatoes, walnuts and raisins; stir just until moistened. Fill greased muffin cups 1/2 full. Bake at 350 degrees for 15 to 20 minutes or until brown. Cool for 5 minutes. Remove to wire rack to cool completely. Yield: 36 servings.

Approx Per Serving: Cal 211; Prot 2 g; Carbo 25 g; Fiber 1 g; T Fat 12 g; Chol 24 mg; Sod 126 mg.

Lib Sandlin, Central

BANANA STACK PANCAKES

2 cups baking mix
2 eggs
1 cup skim milk
1/2 cup plain yogurt
2 bananas, sliced

Combine baking mix, eggs, milk and yogurt in bowl; mix well. Pour batter into 4-inch rounds on hot greased griddle. Bake until pancakes just begin to set. Place banana slices on pancakes. Dot each banana slice with additional batter. Bake until golden brown on bottom and bubbles form on top. Turn carefully. Bake until brown on both sides. Serve hot with favorite toppings. Yield: 8 servings.

Approx Per Serving: Cal 202; Prot 6 g; Carbo 30 g; Fiber 1 g; T Fat 6 g; Chol 55 mg; Sod 440 mg.

Ovid Smith, Hornets Nest

CHEESE-WINE BREAD

1/2 cup dry white wine
1/2 cup margarine
2 teaspoons sugar
1 teaspoon salt
1 package dry yeast
3 cups (about) flour
3 eggs
1 cup shredded Monterey Jack cheese

Combine wine, margarine, sugar and salt in small saucepan. Cook over low heat until margarine is melted and mixture is very warm. Cool slightly. Combine yeast and 1 1/2 cups flour in large mixer bowl. Add wine mixture and eggs. Beat at medium speed for 2 minutes. Add cheese and remaining 1 1/2 cups flour gradually, beating constantly to form soft dough. Knead on floured surface for 8 to 10 minutes or until smooth and elastic. Place in greased bowl, turning to coat surface. Let rise, covered, in warm place for 1 1/2 hours or until doubled in bulk. Punch dough down. Let rest for 10 minutes. Shape into loaf; place in greased 1-quart soufflé dish. Let rise, covered, in warm place for 40 minutes or until doubled in bulk. Bake at 375 degrees for 20 minutes. Cover loosely with foil. Bake for 20 minutes longer or until loaf tests done. Yield: 12 servings.

Approx Per Serving: Cal 248; Prot 7 g; Carbo 25 g; Fiber 1 g; T Fat 12 g; Chol 62 mg; Sod 336 mg.

Kim Parker, Central

PIZZA DOUGH

1 cup milk
1 cup water
1/4 cup oil
1 tablespoon sugar
1 teaspoon salt
2 packages dry yeast
5 cups flour

Heat milk, water, oil, sugar and salt in saucepan until warm. Combine yeast and 2 cups flour in large bowl. Add milk mixture; mix until smooth. Stir in remaining 3 cups flour until soft dough forms. Knead on floured board until smooth and elastic. Place in greased bowl, turning to coat surface. Let rise, covered, in warm place for 3 hours. Shape as desired. Yield: 24 servings.

Approx Per Serving: Cal 125; Prot 3 g; Carbo 21 g; Fiber 1 g; T Fat 3 g; Chol 1 mg; Sod 94 mg.

Kim Parker, Central

CINNAMON ROLLS

1 cup milk
1 package dry yeast
1/4 cup sugar
3 cups flour
1 teaspoon salt
2 eggs, beaten
1/4 cup oil

3 tablespoons butter, softened
1 teaspoon cinnamon
1/2 cup packed brown sugar
1 tablespoon melted butter
1/4 cup packed brown sugar
1/4 cup water

Scald milk. Cool to lukewarm in bowl. Add yeast, sugar and 1 1/2 cups flour; mix well. Let stand until bubbly. Stir in salt, eggs, oil and remaining 1 1/2 cups flour to form soft dough. Knead on floured surface until smooth and elastic. Place in greased bowl, turning to coat surface. Let rise, covered, in warm place until doubled in bulk. Roll 1/4 inch thick on floured surface. Spread with 3 tablespoons softened butter. Sprinkle with mixture of cinnamon and 1/2 cup brown sugar. Roll as for jelly roll. Slice 1 1/2 inches thick; place in greased baking dish. Combine 1 tablespoon butter, 1/4 cup brown sugar and water in bowl. Drizzle over rolls. Bake at 350 degrees for 35 minutes or until golden brown. Yield: 12 servings.

Approx Per Serving: Cal 282; Prot 5 g; Carbo 42 g; Fiber 1 g; T Fat 10 g; Chol 49 mg; Sod 237 mg.

Carolyn S. Starnes, Independence

PRIZE ROLLS

2 packages dry yeast
2 1/2 cups warm water
7 teaspoons sugar

4 teaspoons salt
7 1/2 cups sifted flour
1/2 cup melted shortening

Dissolve yeast in warm water in large bowl. Add sugar and salt; mix well. Combine flour and shortening in bowl; mix well. Add flour mixture to yeast mixture gradually to form soft dough. Place in greased bowl, turning to coat surface. Let rise, covered, until doubled in bulk. Punch dough down. Let stand for 5 minutes. Shape into rolls. Place on greased baking sheet. Let rise, covered, until doubled in bulk. Bake at 400 degrees for 12 to 15 minutes or until lightly browned. Yield: 40 servings.

Approx Per Serving: Cal 105; Prot 2 g; Carbo 17 g; Fiber 1 g; T Fat 3 g; Chol 0 mg; Sod 214 mg.

Wilhelmenia Cofield, Hornets Nest

FEATHER ROLLS

5 cups flour
1 package dry yeast
1/2 cup mashed potatoes
1 1/2 cups warm water
1/3 cup oil
1/4 cup sugar
1 teaspoon salt

Combine 2 cups flour and yeast in mixer bowl; mix well. Combine potatoes, warm water, oil, sugar and salt in small bowl; mix well. Add to flour mixture. Beat at low speed for 1/2 minute. Beat at high speed for 3 minutes. Stir in remaining 3 cups flour by hand form soft dough. Place on lightly floured surface. Let rest, covered, for 10 minutes. Knead for 10 minutes or until smooth and elastic. Place in greased bowl, turning to coat surface. Let rise, covered, in warm place until doubled in bulk. Shape into rolls. Place in greased baking dish. Let rise, covered, until doubled in bulk. Bake at 375 degrees for 15 to 20 minutes or until golden brown. Yield: 24 servings.

Approx Per Serving: Cal 134; Prot 3 g; Carbo 23 g; Fiber 1 g; T Fat 3 g; Chol <1 mg; Sod 103 mg.

Martha A. Rhyne, Foot Hills

BETTY'S HOMEMADE ROLLS

2 packages dry yeast
1 cup warm water
1 cup boiling water
1 cup shortening
2/3 cup sugar
2 teaspoons salt
2 eggs, beaten
6 cups (about) sifted flour

Dissolve yeast in 1 cup warm water. Pour 1 cup boiling water over shortening in large bowl; stir until shortening is melted. Add sugar and salt; mix well. Cool to lukewarm. Stir in yeast, eggs and flour to form soft dough. Let rise, covered, in warm place until doubled in bulk. Punch dough down. Chill, covered, in refrigerator for 1 1/2 to 2 hours or longer. Knead briefly on floured surface. Shape into rolls. Place in greased baking dishes. Bake at 425 degrees for 12 minutes or until golden brown. Yield: 36 servings.

Approx Per Serving: Cal 140; Prot 3 g; Carbo 18 g; Fiber 1 g; T Fat 6 g; Chol 12 mg; Sod 123 mg.

Betty W. Hampton, Salem

SOUR CREAM DINNER ROLLS

8 ounces sour cream, scalded
1/2 cup sugar
1 teaspoon salt
1/2 cup melted margarine
1/2 cup warm water
2 packages dry yeast
2 eggs
4 cups flour
1/4 cup melted margarine

Combine sour cream, sugar, salt and 1/2 cup melted margarine in bowl. Cool to lukewarm. Combine warm water and yeast in large bowl. Add sour cream mixture, eggs and flour; mix well. Chill, covered, in refrigerator overnight. Divide dough into 4 portions. Roll each portion into circle on floured board. Cut into 12 wedges; roll up from wide end. Place on greased baking sheets. Let rise, covered, in warm place until doubled in bulk. Bake at 375 degrees for 15 minutes or until golden brown. Brush with remaining 1/4 cup melted margarine. Yield: 48 servings.

Approx Per Serving: Cal 86; Prot 2 g; Carbo 10 g; Fiber <1 g; T Fat 4 g; Chol 11 mg; Sod 84 mg.

Mrs. George F. Cloninger, Foot Hills

SOUR CREAM YEAST ROLLS

1 package dry yeast
1/4 cup warm water
2 cups sour cream
2 tablespoons sugar
1/4 teaspoon soda
5 1/4 cups baking mix

Dissolve yeast in water. Combine sour cream, sugar and soda in large bowl; mix well. Add 2 cups baking mix and yeast; mix until well blended. Stir in 3 cups baking mix until soft dough forms. Knead on surface dusted with remaining 1/4 cup baking mix until smooth and elastic. Shape into walnut-sized rolls. Place in buttered 9x13-inch baking dish. Let rise, covered, until doubled in bulk. Bake at 375 degrees for 15 minutes or until brown. Yield: 72 servings.

Approx Per Serving: Cal 55; Prot 1 g; Carbo 7 g; Fiber <1 g; T Fat 3 g; Chol 3 mg; Sod 122 mg.

Daphne Beaty, Hornets Nest

☎ Expand your bread-baking repertoire with your favorite recipes and a change of flour for all or just a portion of the original flour measure.

- **All-purpose Flour** is the backbone of most baked goods. It is a blend of hard and soft wheats that have been milled, processed and bleached.
- **Unbleached Flour** is all-purpose flour without the bleaching step. Use it interchangeably with all-purpose flour for a slightly heavier texture and heartier flavor.
- **Buckwheat Flour** is a dark flour made from the seeds of the buckwheat plant. Substitute 1 cup buckwheat flour for about 1 1/3 to 1 1/2 cups all-purpose flour in recipes. Pancakes and waffles are especially good with this flour added.
- **Oat Flour** can be purchased or make your own by processing old-fashioned oats in the blender or food processor until of coarse flour consistency. Substitute 1 cup oat flour for about 1 1/4 cups all-purpose flour.
- **Rye Flour** is the dark distinctive tasting flour made from rye grains. Most breads use rye flour for 1/3 to 1/2 the total amount of flour.
- **Self-rising Flour** is a white flour containing leavening and salt. Do not use this for yeast breads and when using it in recipes calling for all-purpose flour; omit salt and baking powder.
- **Whole Wheat or Graham Flour** is milled but unrefined wheat flour. It is rich in vitamins and fiber because it retains most of the bran. Substitute about 1 cup whole wheat flour for 1 1/3 cups all-purpose flour.

Cakes, Candy, Cookies & Pies

REDIMA

CAKES

SAUCY APPLE SWIRL CAKE

1/4 cup sugar
2 teaspoons cinnamon
1 2/3 cups applesauce
1 2-layer package yellow cake mix
3 eggs

Mix sugar and cinnamon in small bowl. Grease 10-inch bundt pan. Sprinkle with 1 tablespoon sugar mixture. Combine applesauce, cake mix and eggs in mixer bowl. Mix using package directions. Pour 1/2 of the batter into prepared pan. Sprinkle with remaining sugar mixture. Top with remaining batter. Bake at 350 degrees for 35 to 45 minutes or until cake tests done. Cool in pan for 15 minutes. Invert onto serving plate. Yield: 16 servings.

Approx Per Serving: Cal 184; Prot 3 g; Carbo 35 g; Fiber <1 g; T Fat 4 g; Chol 40 mg; Sod 210 mg.

Theresa Brhel, Hornets Nest

APPLE CAKE

1 1/4 cups oil
2 cups sugar
3 eggs
1 1/2 teaspoons vanilla extract
2 tablespoons cinnamon
1/2 teaspoon ginger
1 teaspoon nutmeg
2 cups self-rising flour
3 cups chopped peeled apples
3/4 cup chopped dates
1/2 cup chopped pecans
1/2 cup raisins

Combine oil, sugar, eggs, vanilla, cinnamon, ginger and nutmeg in mixer bowl; mix well. Beat for 3 1/2 minutes. Add flour gradually, beating until smooth. Fold in apples, dates, pecans and raisins. Pour into greased and floured bundt pan. Bake at 350 degrees for 55 minutes to 1 hour or until cake tests done. Yield: 16 servings.

Approx Per Serving: Cal 395; Prot 3 g; Carbo 51 g; Fiber 2 g; T Fat 21 g; Chol 40 mg; Sod 183 mg.

Jean Redding, Salem

DUTCH APPLE CAKE

1 egg
¾ cup sugar
1 cup chopped apples
½ cup chopped pecans
2 tablespoons flour
2 teaspoons baking powder
1 teaspoon vanilla extract

Beat egg in mixer bowl until foamy. Add sugar; beat well. Add apples, pecans, flour, baking powder and vanilla; mix well. Pour into greased and floured 4x8-inch loaf pan. Bake at 300 degrees for 35 minutes. Remove to wire rack to cool. Serve warm with whipped cream. Cake will rise to top of pan and fall, leaving a crusty top. Yield: 12 servings.

Approx Per Serving: Cal 99; Prot 1 g; Carbo 16 g; Fiber 1 g; T Fat 4 g; Chol 18 mg; Sod 69 mg.

Evelyn Furman, Hornets Nest

FRESH APPLE NUT CAKE

3 cups self-rising flour
1 teaspoon cinnamon
¾ cup oil
4 cups chopped peeled apples
1 teaspoon vanilla extract
2 eggs
2 cups sugar
1 cup chopped pecans

Sift flour and cinnamon into large bowl. Add oil, apples and vanilla; beat for 2 minutes. Beat eggs in medium mixer bowl until light. Add sugar gradually, beating until fluffy. Stir into apple mixture; fold in pecans. Pour into greased and floured tube pan. Bake at 350 degrees for 1 hour and 10 minutes. Cool in pan for several minutes. Invert onto serving plate. Yield: 16 servings.

Approx Per Serving: Cal 346; Prot 4 g; Carbo 48 g; Fiber 2 g; T Fat 16 g; Chol 27 mg; Sod 262 mg.

Katherine Hord, Hornets Nest
Delores Sossamon, Independence

GLAZED FRESH APPLE CAKE

2 cups sugar
1½ cups oil
2 eggs
2 teaspoons vanilla extract
3 cups flour
1½ teaspoons soda
1 teaspoon salt
½ teaspoon cinnamon
½ teaspoon nutmeg
½ teaspoon cloves
3 cups finely chopped unpeeled apples
1 cup chopped pecans
Glaze

Beat sugar, oil, eggs and vanilla in large mixer bowl until light. Sift flour, soda, salt, cinnamon, nutmeg and cloves together. Add to egg mixture; mix well. Fold in apples and pecans. Pour into greased and floured 9x13-inch cake pan. Bake at 325 degrees for 55 minutes. Pierce cake with fork. Drizzle glaze over warm cake. Yield: 15 servings.

Glaze for Fresh Apple Cake

1 cup sugar
½ cup buttermilk
½ teaspoon soda
1 tablespoon corn syrup
½ cup margarine
½ teaspoon vanilla extract

Combine sugar, buttermilk, soda, corn syrup, margarine, and vanilla in small saucepan; mix well. Bring mixture to a boil, stirring constantly. Boil for 2 to 3 minutes or just until thickened, stirring constantly.

Approx Per Serving: Cal 578; Prot 4 g; Carbo 65 g; Fiber 2 g; T Fat 34 g; Chol 29 mg; Sod 343 mg.

Marcie Burden, Hornets Nest

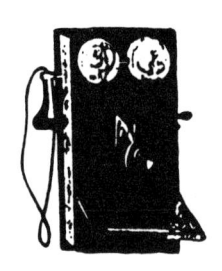

APPLE CAKE WITH WALNUTS

3 cups flour
1 teaspoon salt
1 teaspoon soda
2 cups sugar
2 teaspoons cinnamon
2 teaspoons vanilla extract
1 cup oil
3 eggs, beaten
3 cups chopped peeled apples
2 cups chopped black walnuts
Cream Cheese Frosting

Combine flour, salt, soda, sugar and cinnamon in large bowl; mix well. Beat vanilla, oil and eggs in small mixer bowl until foamy. Add to flour mixture; mix well. Stir in apples and walnuts. Pour into greased and floured 9x13-inch cake pan. Bake at 325 degrees for 1 hour. Cool. Spread with Cream Cheese Frosting. Yield: 15 servings.

Cream Cheese Frosting

1/4 cup butter, softened
8 ounces cream cheese, softened
1 teaspoon vanilla extract
3 cups confectioners' sugar

Cream butter and cream cheese in mixer bowl until light and fluffy. Stir in vanilla. Add confectioners' sugar; beat until of spreading consistency.

Approx Per Serving: Cal 640; Prot 9 g; Carbo 79 g; Fiber 2 g; T Fat 34 g; Chol 67 mg; Sod 283 mg.

Linda S. Griffin, Independence

FRESH APPLE CAKE

1½ cups oil
2 cups sugar
3 eggs
2½ cups sifted flour
1 teaspoon salt
1 teaspoon soda
2 teaspoons baking powder
1 teaspoon vanilla extract
3 cups chopped peeled apples
1½ cups confectioners' sugar
2 teaspoons vanilla extract
1 cup chopped black walnuts

Combine oil, sugar and eggs in large mixer bowl; beat well. Sift flour, salt, soda and baking powder. Add to egg mixture; beat well. Stir in 1 teaspoon vanilla. Fold in apples. Pour into greased and waxed paper-lined 10-inch tube pan. Bake at 350 degrees for 1 hour. Cool in pan for several minutes. Invert onto serving plate. Combine confectioners' sugar with enough water to make thin glaze. Stir in remaining 2 teaspoons vanilla. Drizzle over cooled cake. Sprinkle with walnuts. Yield: 16 servings.

Approx Per Serving: Cal 463; Prot 5 g; Carbo 54 g; Fiber 1 g; T Fat 26 g; Chol 40 mg; Sod 240 mg.

Evelyn N. Goodman, Hornets Nest

APPLE AND BUTTERSCOTCH CHIP CAKE

2½ cups flour
1 teaspoon soda
1 teaspoon cinnamon
2 teaspoons baking powder
1 teaspoon salt
2 cups sugar
1 cup oil
2 eggs
2 teaspoons vanilla extract
3 cups chopped apples
1 cup chopped walnuts
2 cups butterscotch chips

Sift flour, soda, cinnamon, baking powder and salt together. Combine sugar and oil in large mixer bowl; mix well. Add eggs; beat well. Stir in vanilla. Add flour mixture, beating until smooth. Fold in apples and walnuts. Pour into oiled 9x13-inch cake pan. Sprinkle with butterscotch chips. Bake at 350 degrees for 1 hour. Yield: 15 servings.

Approx Per Serving: Cal 499; Prot 5 g; Carbo 61 g; Fiber 2 g; T Fat 29 g; Chol 28 mg; Sod 255 mg.

Willie Collins, Independence

APPLESAUCE CAKE

3 cups flour
1 tablespoon soda
1 tablespoon baking cocoa
1 teaspoon cinnamon
1 teaspoon cloves
1 teaspoon allspice

2 cups sugar
3 cups applesauce
1/4 cup butter, softened
1 cup chopped pecans
1 cup raisins
Frosting

Combine flour, soda, baking cocoa, cinnamon, cloves and allspice in large bowl; mix well. Mix sugar with applesauce in bowl; mix well. Add to flour mixture; mix well. Stir in butter, pecans and raisins. Pour into 3 greased and floured 9-inch round cake pans. Bake at 350 degrees for 25 to 30 minutes or until layers test done. Remove to wire racks to cool. Spread frosting between layers and over top and side of cake. Yield: 12 servings.

Frosting for Applesauce Cake

1 1/2 cups sugar
1 20-ounce can crushed pineapple

1 7-ounce can coconut
1 tablespoon flour

Combine sugar, pineapple, coconut and flour in saucepan. Cook until thickened, stirring constantly.

Approx Per Serving: Cal 642; Prot 6 g; Carbo 124 g; Fiber 6 g; T Fat 16 g; Chol 10 mg; Sod 247 mg.

Sarah Bame, Salem

☎ To prevent a soggy or heavy cake, be sure that layers, filling and frosting are completely cool before assembling cake.

POTATO AND CARAMEL CAKE

2/3 cup margarine, softened
2 cups sugar
2 cups self-rising flour
1/2 cup milk
4 eggs
1 cup mashed cooked potatoes
1 teaspoon cinnamon
1 teaspoon cloves
1 teaspoon nutmeg
3 tablespoons baking cocoa
1 15-ounce package raisins
1 cup chopped English walnuts
Frosting

Cream margarine and sugar in mixer bowl until light and fluffy. Add flour, milk, eggs and potatoes; beat well. Stir in cinnamon, cloves, nutmeg and baking cocoa. Fold in raisins and walnuts. Pour into 2 greased and floured 9-inch round cake pans. Bake at 350 degrees for 30 to 35 minutes or until layers test done. Remove to wire racks to cool. Spread frosting between layers and over top and side of cake. Yield: 12 servings.

Frosting for Potato and Caramel Cake

1/2 cup margarine
5 tablespoons evaporated milk
2 cups packed brown sugar
1 teaspoon vanilla extract

Melt margarine in saucepan. Stir in evaporated milk and brown sugar. Bring to a boil, stirring constantly. Boil for 2 minutes, stirring constantly; remove from heat. Add vanilla; beat until smooth.

Approx Per Serving: Cal 709; Prot 8 g; Carbo 119 g; Fiber 4 g; T Fat 26 g; Chol 74 mg; Sod 537 mg.

Polly Mabrey, Hornets Nest

☎ An apple cut in half and placed in the cake container will keep the cake fresh for several days longer.

CARAMEL NUT CAKE

1 cup margarine, softened
1/2 cup shortening
1 1-pound package light brown sugar
1 cup sugar
5 eggs
3 cups flour
1/2 teaspoon salt
1/2 teaspoon baking powder
1 cup plus 1 tablespoon milk
2 tablespoons vanilla extract
1 8-ounce package black walnut-flavored peanuts

Cream margarine, shortening, brown sugar and sugar in mixer bowl until light and fluffy. Add eggs 1 at a time, beating well after each addition. Mix flour, salt and baking powder in bowl. Add to creamed mixture alternately with milk, beating well after each addition. Stir in vanilla. Fold in peanuts. Pour into greased and floured tube pan. Bake at 325 degrees for 1 1/4 hours or until cake tests done. Cool in pan for several minutes. Invert onto serving plate. Frost with favorite caramel icing. Yield: 16 servings.

Approx Per Serving: Cal 518; Prot 9 g; Carbo 62 g; Fiber 2 g; T Fat 27 g; Chol 69 mg; Sod 253 mg.

Katie Grist, Independence

FRUITED CARROT CAKE

2 cups sugar
1 1/2 cups oil
4 eggs
3 cups self-rising flour
1 1/2 teaspoons cinnamon
2 cups shredded carrots
1 10-ounce bottle of maraschino cherries, chopped
1 6-ounce can black walnuts, chopped
1 3-ounce can coconut

Beat sugar and oil in mixer bowl until smooth. Add eggs 1 at a time, beating well after each addition. Add mixture of flour and cinnamon gradually, beating until smooth. Stir in carrots, cherries, walnuts and coconut. Pour into greased and floured bundt pan. Bake at 350 degrees for 1 1/4 hours. Yield: 16 servings.

Approx Per Serving: Cal 494; Prot 7 g; Carbo 53 g; Fiber 2 g; T Fat 30 g; Chol 53 mg; Sod 277 mg.

Regina Phillips, Independence

CARROT CAKE

2 cups flour
1 teaspoon salt
1 tablespoon soda
2 teaspoons cinnamon
2 cups sugar
4 eggs
1 cup oil
3 cups shredded carrots
1 8-ounce can crushed pineapple
Frosting

Sift flour, salt, soda and cinnamon together 3 times. Beat sugar and eggs in large mixer bowl until smooth. Add flour mixture alternately with oil, beating well after each addition. Stir in carrots and pineapple. Pour into greased and floured tube pan. Bake at 350 degrees for 45 minutes. Cool in pan for several minutes. Invert onto serving plate. Spread frosting over top and side of cake. Yield: 16 servings.

Frosting for Carrot Cake

1/2 cup margarine, softened
8 ounces cream cheese, softened
1 1/2 pounds confectioners' sugar
1 cup chopped pecans

Cream margarine and cream cheese in mixer bowl until light and fluffy. Add confectioners' sugar; beat until smooth. Stir in pecans.

Approx Per Serving: Cal 663; Prot 5 g; Carbo 95 g; Fiber 2 g; T Fat 31 g; Chol 69 mg; Sod 422 mg.

Margie Wylie, Independence

CARROT AND PECAN CAKE

2 cups sugar
1 1/2 cups oil
4 eggs
2 cups flour
1/2 teaspoon salt
2 teaspoons cinnamon
2 teaspoons soda
2 teaspoons baking powder
3 cups shredded carrots
1/2 cup white raisins
1 cup chopped pecans
Frosting

Beat sugar and oil in mixer bowl until smooth. Add eggs 1 at a time, beating well after each addition. Mix flour, salt, cinnamon, soda and baking powder in bowl. Add to egg mixture; beat well. Add carrots gradually, mixing well. Stir in raisins and pecans. Pour into 3 greased and floured 9-inch round cake pans. Bake at 325 degrees for 25 minutes. Remove to wire racks to cool. Spread frosting between layers and over top and side of cake. Garnish with additional pecans. Yield: 12 servings.

Frosting for Carrot and Pecan Cake

1/4 cup margarine, softened
8 ounces cream cheese, softened
1 1-pound package confectioners' sugar
1 tablespoon lemon juice
2 teaspoons vanilla extract

Cream margarine and cream cheese in mixer bowl until light and fluffy. Add confectioners' sugar; beat well. Stir in lemon juice and vanilla.

Approx Per Serving: Cal 848; Prot 7 g; Carbo 105 g; Fiber 3 g; T Fat 47 g; Chol 92 mg; Sod 416 mg.

Evelyn N. Goodman, Hornets Nest

SUPREME CARROT CAKE

2 cups sugar
4 eggs
1/2 teaspoon soda
2 teaspoons cinnamon
1 teaspoon vanilla extract
3 cups shredded carrots
1 1/4 cups oil
2 cups self-rising flour
Frosting

Combine sugar, eggs, soda, cinnamon, vanilla, carrots and oil in large mixer bowl. Beat at medium speed for 5 minutes. Add flour; mix well. Pour into 3 greased and floured 9-inch round cake pans. Bake at 350 degrees for 30 minutes. Remove to wire racks to cool. Spread frosting between layers and over top and side of cooled cake. Yield: 12 servings.

Frosting for Supreme Carrot Cake

1 1-pound package confectioners' sugar
8 ounces cream cheese, softened
1/2 cup margarine, softened
1 teaspoon vanilla extract
1 cup chopped pecans
1 7-ounce can coconut

Cream confectioners' sugar and cream cheese in mixer bowl until light and fluffy. Beat in margarine and vanilla. Stir in pecans and coconut.

Approx Per Serving: Cal 887; Prot 7 g; Carbo 105 g; Fiber 3 g; T Fat 51 g; Chol 92 mg; Sod 500 mg.

Sybil P. Peele, Hornets Nest

EASY CARROT CAKE

2¼ cups cake flour
2 teaspoons soda
1 teaspoon salt
2 teaspoons cinnamon
2 cups sugar
1½ cups oil
4 eggs
1 cup chopped pecans
2   8-ounce jars baby food carrots
Frosting

Sift cake flour, soda, salt and cinnamon together. Beat sugar, oil and eggs in mixer bowl until smooth. Add flour mixture; beat well. Stir in pecans and carrots. Pour into greased and floured 9x13-inch cake pan. Bake at 325 degrees for 40 minutes or until cake tests done. Cool. Spread frosting over cooled cake. Yield: 15 servings.

Frosting for Easy Carrot Cake

¼ cup margarine, softened
8 ounces cream cheese, softened
1   1-pound package confectioners' sugar
1 teaspoon vanilla extract

Cream margarine and cream cheese in mixer bowl until light and fluffy. Add confectioners' sugar; beat until smooth. Stir in vanilla.

Approx Per Serving: Cal 663; Prot 5 g; Carbo 81 g; Fiber 2 g; T Fat 37 g; Chol 73 mg; Sod 372 mg.

Annie Hall, Hornets Nest

CHOCOLATE CAKE

1 1/2 cups flour
1 cup sugar
3 tablespoons baking
  cocoa
1 teaspoon soda

1/2 teaspoon salt
6 tablespoons oil
1 tablespoon vinegar
1 teaspoon vanilla extract
1 cup cold water

Sift flour, sugar, cocoa, soda and salt into large bowl; mix well. Make 3 wells in dry ingredients. Pour oil into first well, vinegar into second well and vanilla into third well. Pour water over top; mix well. Pour into greased 9x13-inch cake pan. Bake at 350 degrees for 25 to 35 minutes or until cake tests done. Cool. Yield: 15 servings.

Approx Per Serving: Cal 149; Prot 2 g; Carbo 24 g; Fiber 1 g; T Fat 6 g; Chol 0 mg; Sod 127 mg.

Bobby Kinney, Independence

FLOURLESS CHOCOLATE CAKE

3 1/3 ounces unsalted butter
10 ounces semisweet
  chocolate

8 extra-large egg yolks
8 extra-large egg whites
3/4 cup sugar

Melt butter and chocolate in top of double boiler over hot water, stirring constantly; remove from heat. Beat in egg yolks. Beat egg whites in large mixer bowl until soft peaks form. Add sugar gradually, beating until stiff peaks form. Fold in chocolate mixture. Pour into greased and lightly floured 9-inch springform pan. Bake at 325 degrees for 40 minutes or until firm but not cracked. Cool in pan for 1 minute. Remove to serving plate; let stand until cool. Yield: 12 servings.

Approx Per Serving: Cal 276; Prot 5 g; Carbo 27 g; Fiber 1 g; T Fat 19 g; Chol 159 mg; Sod 44 mg.

Carolyn Bales, Independence

OLD-FASHIONED CHOCOLATE CAKE

½ cup margarine
½ cup oil
¼ cup baking cocoa
1 cup milk
2 cups self-rising flour
2 cups sugar
½ cup buttermilk
2 eggs
1 teaspoon soda
¼ teaspoon salt
Frosting

Combine margarine, oil, baking cocoa and milk in saucepan. Bring to a boil, stirring constantly; remove from heat. Add flour and sugar; mix well. Add buttermilk, eggs, soda and salt; mix well. Pour into greased and floured 9x13-inch cake pan. Bake at 350 degrees for 30 minutes. Spread frosting over cake. Yield: 15 servings.

Frosting for Old-Fashioned Chocolate Cake

½ cup margarine, softened
¼ cup baking cocoa
6 tablespoons evaporated milk
1 1-pound package confectioners' sugar
1 teaspoon vanilla extract

Combine margarine, baking cocoa and evaporated milk in saucepan. Bring to a boil, stirring constantly; remove from heat. Add confectioners' sugar; mix until smooth. Stir in vanilla.

Approx Per Serving: Cal 514; Prot 4 g; Carbo 78 g; Fiber 1 g; T Fat 22 g; Chol 33 mg; Sod 446 mg.

Doris D. Keever, Hornets Nest

☎ Sprinkle flour in greased cake pans with a new powder puff.

QUICK CHOCOLATE FUDGE CAKE

2 cups flour
1 teaspoon soda
2 cups sugar
1 cup water
3 tablespoons baking cocoa

1 cup margarine, softened
1/2 teaspoon cinnamon
2 eggs
1/2 cup buttermilk
1 teaspoon vanilla extract
Frosting

Sift flour, soda and sugar into large bowl. Combine water, cocoa and margarine in saucepan; mix well. Bring to a boil, stirring constantly. Pour over flour mixture; mix well. Add cinnamon, eggs, buttermilk and vanilla; beat until smooth. Pour into greased 11x16-inch pan. Bake at 400 degrees for 20 to 25 minutes or until cake tests done. Cool for 5 minutes. Spread frosting over cake. Yield: 24 servings.

Frosting for Quick Chocolate Fudge Cake

1/2 cup margarine, softened
6 to 8 tablespoons milk
3 tablespoons baking cocoa

1 1-pound package confectioners' sugar
1 teaspoon vanilla extract
1 cup chopped pecans

Combine margarine, milk and cocoa in saucepan; mix well. Bring to a boil, stirring constantly; remove from heat. Add confectioners' sugar; beat well. Stir in vanilla and pecans.

Approx Per Serving: Cal 341; Prot 3 g; Carbo 49 g; Fiber 1 g; T Fat 16 g; Chol 19 mg; Sod 182 mg.

Dianne Lee, Hornets Nest

KERR SCOTT'S $10,000.00 CHOCOLATE CAKE

2 cups flour
2 teaspoons baking powder
1/2 cup baking cocoa
2 cups sugar
1/2 cup butter, softened
2 eggs
1 1/2 cups milk
2 teaspoons vanilla extract
Frosting

Mix flour, baking powder and cocoa in bowl. Cream sugar and butter in mixer bowl until light and fluffy. Add eggs 1 at a time, beating well after each addition. Add flour mixture and half the milk; mix well. Add remaining milk and vanilla. Beat for 2 minutes. Pour into 3 greased and floured 8-inch round cake pans. Bake at 350 degrees for 25 to 30 minutes or until layers test done. Remove to wire racks to cool. Spread frosting between layers and over top and side of cake. Yield: 12 servings.

Frosting for $10,000.00 Chocolate Cake

1/2 cup butter, softened
1 1-pound package confectioners' sugar
1/2 cup baking cocoa
1/4 to 1/2 cup boiling water
1 teaspoon vanilla extract

Cream butter, confectioners' sugar and cocoa in mixer bowl until light and fluffy. Add enough boiling water to make of desired consistency. Stir in vanilla.

Approx Per Serving: Cal 569; Prot 6 g; Carbo 100 g; Fiber 3 g; T Fat 19 g; Chol 81 mg; Sod 211 mg.

Janie B. Summers, Foot Hills

CHOCOLATE SHEATH CAKE

2 cups self-rising flour
2 cups sugar
1 teaspoon cinnamon
1/2 cup margarine, softened
1/2 cup oil
1/4 cup baking cocoa

1 cup water
1/2 cup buttermilk
2 eggs
1 teaspoon vanilla extract
Frosting

Mix flour, sugar and cinnamon in bowl. Combine margarine, oil, baking cocoa and water in saucepan; mix well. Bring to a rapid boil, stirring constantly. Combine buttermilk, eggs and vanilla in large mixer bowl; beat well. Add cocoa mixture alternately with flour mixture, mixing well after each addition. Pour into greased and floured 9x13-inch cake pan. Bake at 400 degrees for 20 minutes. Cool in pan. Pour frosting over hot cake. May omit frosting if preferred. Yield: 15 servings.

Frosting for Chocolate Sheath Cake

1/2 cup margarine, softened
6 tablespoons milk
1 teaspoon vanilla extract
1/4 cup baking cocoa

1/2 cup chopped pecans
1 1-pound package
  confectioners' sugar

Combine margarine, milk, vanilla, cocoa and pecans in saucepan; mix well. Bring to a boil, stirring constantly; remove from heat. Pour over confectioners' sugar in bowl; mix well.

Approx Per Serving: Cal 527; Prot 4 g; Carbo 78 g; Fiber 2 g; T Fat 24 g; Chol 30 mg; Sod 344 mg.

Katherine Hord, Hornets Nest
Irene C. Black, Independence

☎ Add 1/2 cup mayonnaise to any 2-layer cake mix for moistness.

CHOCOLATE FUDGE SHEET CAKE

2 cups flour
2 cups sugar
1/2 teaspoon salt
1/2 cup margarine, softened
3 1/2 tablespoons baking cocoa
1/2 cup shortening
1 cup water
2 eggs, slightly beaten
1 teaspoon vanilla extract
1 teaspoon soda
1/2 cup buttermilk
Frosting

Sift flour, sugar and salt into large bowl. Combine margarine, baking cocoa, shortening and water in saucepan. Bring to a boil, stirring constantly. Add to flour mixture; mix well. Add eggs, vanilla, soda and buttermilk; mix well. Pour into greased and floured 11x18-inch cake pan. Bake at 350 degrees for 30 minutes. Pour frosting over hot cake. Yield: 15 servings.

Frosting for Chocolate Fudge Sheet Cake

1/2 cup margarine
3 1/2 tablespoons baking cocoa
1/2 cup milk
1 1-pound package confectioners' sugar
1 cup chopped pecans
1/8 teaspoon salt
1 teaspoon vanilla extract

Combine margarine, baking cocoa and milk in saucepan. Bring to a boil, stirring constantly; remove from heat. Add confectioners' sugar, beating until smooth. Stir in pecans, salt and vanilla.

Approx Per Serving: Cal 551; Prot 4 g; Carbo 79 g; Fiber 2 g; T Fat 26 g; Chol 30 mg; Sod 309 mg.

Ella Mae Sutphin, Piedmont

* *Shirley Carmichael of Hornets Nest* substitutes 7 tablespoons evaporated milk for 1/2 cup milk in frosting.

CHOCOLATE SOUR CREAM CAKE

3 cups sifted flour
1/2 teaspoon baking powder
1/2 cup baking cocoa
1 cup margarine, softened
1/2 cup shortening
3 cups sugar
5 eggs
1 cup sour cream
1/2 cup milk
2 teaspoons vanilla extract

Mix flour, baking powder and baking cocoa in bowl. Cream margarine, shortening and sugar in large mixer bowl until light and fluffy. Add eggs 1 at a time, beating well after each addition. Add flour mixture alternately with sour cream and milk, beating well after each addition. Stir in vanilla. Pour into greased and floured 10-inch tube pan. Bake at 325 degrees for 1 1/2 hours. Cool in pan for several minutes. Invert onto serving plate. Yield: 16 servings.

Approx Per Serving: Cal 449; Prot 5 g; Carbo 56 g; Fiber 1 g; T Fat 24 g; Chol 74 mg; Sod 178 mg.

Phyllis E. Jones, Independence

DOUBLE CHOCOLATE CAKE

3/4 cup margarine, softened
1 3/4 cups sugar
2 eggs
1 teaspoon vanilla extract
2 cups flour
3/4 cup baking cocoa
1 1/4 teaspoons soda
1/2 teaspoon salt
1 1/3 cups water
Frosting (See page 341)

Cream margarine and sugar in mixer bowl until light and fluffy. Add eggs and vanilla. Beat for 1 minute. Mix flour, baking cocoa, soda and salt in bowl. Add to creamed mixture alternately with water, beating well after each addition. Pour into 2 greased and floured 8-inch round cake pans. Bake at 350 degrees for 35 to 40 minutes or until layers test done. Remove to wire racks to cool completely. Spread frosting between layers and over top and side of cake. Yield: 12 servings.

Frosting for Double Chocolate Cake

6 tablespoons margarine, softened
2 2/3 cups confectioners' sugar
1/2 cup baking cocoa
1/3 cup milk
1 teaspoon vanilla extract

Beat margarine in mixer bowl until light. Add confectioners' sugar and baking cocoa alternately with milk, beating well after each addition. Stir in vanilla.

Approx Per Serving: Cal 485; Prot 5 g; Carbo 76 g; Fiber 3 g; T Fat 20 g; Chol 36 mg; Sod 392 mg.

Cathy Douglas, Central

CHOCOLATE DELIGHT CAKE

1 1/2 cups margarine, softened
8 ounces cream cheese, softened
2 1-pound packages confectioners' sugar
4 ounces German's sweet chocolate
1/4 cup hot water
1 teaspoon vanilla extract
1/4 cup oil
3 eggs
2 1/4 cups flour
1 teaspoon salt
1 teaspoon soda
1 cup buttermilk

Cream margarine, cream cheese and confectioners' sugar in mixer bowl until light and fluffy. Combine chocolate, hot water and vanilla in saucepan. Heat until chocolate melts, stirring constantly. Stir into creamed mixture. Remove and reserve 3 cups chocolate mixture. Add oil, eggs, flour, salt, soda and buttermilk to remaining chocolate mixture; mix well. Pour into 3 greased and floured 9-inch round cake pans. Bake at 350 degrees for 30 to 35 minutes or until layers test done. Remove to wire racks to cool. Spread reserved chocolate mixture between layers and over top and side of cake. Yield: 12 servings.

Approx Per Serving: Cal 823; Prot 7 g; Carbo 115 g; Fiber 1 g; T Fat 39 g; Chol 75 mg; Sod 611 mg.

Marlene Fesperman, Hornets Nest

GERMAN CHOCOLATE CAKE

4 ounces German's sweet chocolate
1/2 cup boiling water
1 cup butter, softened
2 cups sugar
4 egg yolks
1 teaspoon vanilla extract
2 cups flour
1 teaspoon soda
1/2 teaspoon salt
1 cup buttermilk
4 egg whites, stiffly beaten
Frosting

Melt chocolate in boiling water. Cream butter and sugar in large mixer bowl until light and fluffy. Add egg yolks; beat well. Stir in vanilla and melted chocolate. Mix flour, soda and salt in bowl. Add to creamed mixture alternately with buttermilk, beating well after each addition. Fold in egg whites gently. Pour into 3 greased and floured 9-inch round cake pans. Bake at 350 degrees for 30 minutes. Cool in pans for 15 minutes. Remove to wire racks to cool completely. Spread frosting between layers and over top and side of cake. Yield: 12 servings.

Frosting for German Chocolate Cake

1 cup evaporated milk
1 cup sugar
3 egg yolks, slightly beaten
1/2 cup butter, softened
1 teaspoon vanilla extract
1 1/3 cups coconut
1 cup chopped pecans

Combine evaporated milk, sugar, egg yolks, butter and vanilla in saucepan; mix well. Cook over medium heat until thickened, stirring constantly; remove from heat. Stir in coconut and pecans. Cool to desired spreading consistency.

Approx Per Serving: Cal 708; Prot 9 g; Carbo 80 g; Fiber 3 g; T Fat 41 g; Chol 193 mg; Sod 440 mg.

Betty C. Hayes, Independence

☎ Split 2 chocolate cake layers and fill with mixture of 16 ounces whipped topping, 8 ounces softened cream cheese, 4 cups confectioners' sugar, 2 cups miniature chocolate chips and 1/2 cup nuts.

GERMAN CHOCOLATE UPSIDE-DOWN CAKE

1 cup chopped pecans
1 cup coconut
1 2-layer package German chocolate cake mix
1/2 cup margarine, softened
8 ounces cream cheese, softened
1 1-pound package confectioners' sugar

Combine pecans and coconut in small bowl. Sprinkle in greased 9x13-inch cake pan. Prepare cake mix using package directions. Pour into prepared pan. Cream margarine and cream cheese in mixer bowl until light and fluffy. Add confectioners' sugar; beat until smooth. Spread over batter. Bake at 325 degrees for 1 hour. Cool. Yield: 15 servings.

Approx Per Serving: Cal 570; Prot 5 g; Carbo 82 g; Fiber 1 g; T Fat 27 g; Chol 17 mg; Sod 285 mg.

Molly Alexander, Independence

HOT FUDGE PUDDING CAKE

1/2 gallon vanilla ice cream
1 cup flour
3/4 cup sugar
2 tablespoons baking cocoa
2 teaspoons baking powder
1/4 teaspoon salt
1/2 cup milk
2 tablespoons oil
1 teaspoon vanilla extract
1 cup chopped pecans
1 cup packed brown sugar
1/4 cup baking cocoa
1 3/4 cups very hot water

Scoop ice cream into 8 portions on chilled tray. Freeze, uncovered, for 24 hours. Combine flour, sugar, 2 tablespoons cocoa, baking powder and salt in ungreased 9x9-inch cake pan. Stir in milk, oil and vanilla with fork until smooth. Stir in pecans. Spread evenly. Sprinkle with brown sugar and remaining 1/4 cup cocoa. Pour hot water over top. Bake at 350 degrees for 40 minutes. Let stand for 15 minutes. Spoon into serving dishes, reserving sauce in pan. Top pudding cake with ice cream portions. Drizzle with reserved sauce. Yield: 8 servings.

Approx Per Serving: Cal 653; Prot 9 g; Carbo 95 g; Fiber 3 g; T Fat 29 g; Chol 61 mg; Sod 285 mg.

Carolyn Faulkenberry, Hornets Nest

COCA-COLA CAKE

2 cups flour
2 cups sugar
1 cup Coca-Cola
1/2 cup oil
1/2 cup margarine, softened
1/4 cup baking cocoa
1 1/2 cups miniature marshmallows
1/2 cup buttermilk
1 teaspoon soda
2 eggs
1 teaspoon vanilla extract
Frosting

Mix flour and sugar in large bowl. Combine Coca-Cola, oil, margarine and baking cocoa in medium saucepan; mix well. Bring to a boil, stirring constantly; remove from heat. Stir in marshmallows. Add buttermilk, soda, eggs and vanilla; mix well. Add to flour mixture, stirring to mix well. Pour into greased and floured 9x13-inch cake pan. Bake at 325 degrees for 45 to 50 minutes or until cake tests done. Pour frosting over warm cake. Yield: 15 servings.

Frosting for Coca-Cola Cake

3 tablespoons baking cocoa
6 tablespoons Coca-Cola
1/2 cup margarine, softened
1 teaspoon vanilla extract
1 1-pound package confectioners' sugar
1 cup chopped pecans

Combine baking cocoa, Coca-Cola, margarine and vanilla in saucepan; mix well. Bring to a boil, stirring constantly; remove from heat. Stir in confectioners' sugar and pecans.

Approx Per Serving: Cal 578; Prot 4 g; Carbo 86 g; Fiber 2 g; T Fat 26 g; Chol 29 mg; Sod 223 mg.

Rosa P. Miller, Blue Ridge

PEPSI CAKE

1 1/2 cups miniature marshmallows
3/4 cup plus 1 tablespoon Pepsi Cola
1 cup melted margarine
3 tablespoons baking cocoa
2 cups self-rising flour
2 cups sugar
2 eggs
1/2 cup buttermilk
1 teaspoon soda
1 teaspoon vanilla extract
Frosting

Combine marshmallows, Pepsi Cola, margarine and baking cocoa in saucepan. Cook over medium heat until marshmallows melt, stirring constantly. Combine flour, sugar, eggs, buttermilk, soda and vanilla in large mixer bowl; mix well. Add marshmallow mixture; beat well. Pour into greased 9x13-inch cake pan. Bake at 350 degrees for 30 to 35 minutes or until cake tests done. Do not overbake. Spread frosting over hot cake. Yield: 15 servings.

Frosting for Pepsi Cake

1/2 cup margarine, softened
1 1-pound package confectioners' sugar
1 tablespoon baking cocoa
6 tablespoons Pepsi Cola
1 teaspoon vanilla extract

Cream margarine and confectioners' sugar in mixer bowl until light and fluffy. Stir in baking cocoa, Pepsi Cola and vanilla; beat well.

Approx Per Serving: Cal 509; Prot 3 g; Carbo 83 g; Fiber 1 g; T Fat 20 g; Chol 29 mg; Sod 473 mg.

Joanne Tallent, Independence

☎ Cut a hot cake with a thread or dental floss instead of a knife.

COCONUT DEVIL'S FOOD CAKE

¾ cup plus 1 tablespoon baking cocoa
⅔ cup boiling water
1¾ cups flour
1½ teaspoons soda
¼ teaspoon salt
¾ cup butter, softened
2 cups sugar
1 teaspoon vanilla extract
2 eggs, at room temperature
¾ cup buttermilk
Frosting
1 3-ounce can coconut

Mix baking cocoa with boiling water in small bowl until smooth. Mix flour, soda and salt together. Cream butter, sugar and vanilla in large mixer bowl until light and fluffy. Add eggs 1 at a time, beating well after each addition. Add flour mixture alternately with buttermilk, beating well after each addition. Stir in cocoa mixture. Pour into 2 greased and floured 9-inch round cake pans. Bake at 350 degrees for 35 minutes. Cool in pans for 10 minutes. Remove to wire racks to cool completely. Spread frosting between layers and over top and side of cake. Sprinkle with coconut; press lightly into frosting. Yield: 12 servings.

Frosting for Coconut Devil's Food Cake

2 egg whites
1½ cups sugar
⅓ cup water
⅛ teaspoon salt
¼ teaspoon vanilla extract

Combine egg whites, sugar, water and salt in double boiler over boiling water. Beat with electric mixer for 7 minutes or until stiff peaks form; remove from heat. Beat in vanilla.

Approx Per Serving: Cal 463; Prot 5 g; Carbo 79 g; Fiber 3 g; T Fat 16 g; Chol 67 mg; Sod 306 mg.

Carroll Baxley, Coastal

MOUND CAKE

- 1 2-layer package chocolate cake mix
- 1 14-ounce can sweetened condensed milk
- 1/2 12-ounce can cream of coconut
- 8 ounces whipped topping
- 1 7-ounce package coconut

Prepare and bake cake mix using package directions for a 9x13-inch cake pan. Pierce holes in top of cake with fork. Combine sweetened condensed milk and cream of coconut in bowl; mix well. Pour over cake. Cool completely. Spread with whipped topping; sprinkle with coconut. Chill overnight. Yield: 15 servings.

Approx Per Serving: Cal 444; Prot 6 g; Carbo 67 g; Fiber 2 g; T Fat 19 g; Chol 9 mg; Sod 238 mg.
Nutritional information does not include cream of coconut.

Debbie Wilkinson, Hornets Nest

SUPER DELIGHT CAKE

- 1 2-layer package butter-recipe fudge cake mix
- 1 6-ounce package vanilla instant pudding mix
- 12 ounces whipped topping

Prepare and bake cake mix using package directions for a 9x13-inch cake pan. Cool completely. Prepare pudding mix using package directions. Spread over cooled cake. Top with whipped topping. Chill until serving time. Yield: 15 servings.

Approx Per Serving: Cal 325; Prot 4 g; Carbo 49 g; Fiber 0 g; T Fat 14 g; Chol 1 mg; Sod 200 mg.

Barbara G. Russell, Piedmont

RED VELVET CAKE

- 3/4 cup shortening
- 1 1/2 cups sugar
- 2 eggs
- 2 tablespoons baking cocoa
- 1 1-ounce bottle of red food coloring
- 1 tablespoon water
- 2 1/4 cups cake flour
- 1/8 teaspoon salt
- 1 teaspoon vanilla extract
- 1 cup buttermilk
- 1 teaspoon soda
- 1 tablespoon vinegar
- Frosting

Cream shortening in large mixer bowl until light. Add sugar; beat until fluffy. Add eggs 1 at a time, beating well after each addition. Mix baking cocoa, food coloring and water in small bowl to make paste. Stir into creamed mixture. Mix flour and salt together. Add to creamed mixture alternately with mixture of vanilla and buttermilk, beating well after each addition. Sprinkle with soda; drizzle with vinegar. Stir gently until mixed; do not beat. Pour into 3 greased and floured 9-inch round cake pans. Bake at 325 degrees for 25 minutes. Remove to wire racks to cool. Spread frosting between layers and over top and side of cake. Garnish with coconut. This is a beautiful Valentine or Christmas treat. Yield: 12 servings.

Frosting for Red Velvet Cake

- 1 cup water
- 2 tablespoons cornstarch
- 1 cup margarine, softened
- 1 cup sugar
- 1 teaspoon vanilla extract
- 1/2 cup chopped pecans

Combine water and cornstarch in saucepan. Cook until thickened, stirring constantly; remove from heat. Cool. Beat until fluffy. Cream margarine and sugar in mixer bowl until light and fluffy. Stir in vanilla. Add cornstarch mixture; beat until soft peaks form. Fold in pecans.

Approx Per Serving: Cal 547; Prot 4 g; Carbo 62 g; Fiber 1 g; T Fat 33 g; Chol 36 mg; Sod 305 mg.

Evangeline Presler Reynolds, Coastal

VELVET ALMOND FUDGE CAKE

1 cup blanched slivered almonds
1 2-layer package chocolate fudge cake mix
1 4-ounce package chocolate instant pudding mix
4 eggs
1 cup sour cream
1/2 cup water
1/4 cup oil
1/2 teaspoon vanilla extract
1/2 teaspoon almond extract
2 cups chocolate chips

Chop almonds; place on baking sheet. Bake at 350 degrees for 3 to 5 minutes or until toasted. Sprinkle 1/2 cup toasted almonds in well-greased 10-inch tube pan. Combine cake mix, pudding mix, eggs, sour cream, water, oil and flavorings in large mixer bowl; mix well. Beat at medium speed for 4 minutes. Fold in remaining almonds and chocolate chips. Spoon into prepared pan. Bake at 350 degrees for 1 hour and 10 minutes or until cake pulls away from side of pan. Do not underbake. Cool in pan for 15 minutes. Invert onto wire rack to cool completely. Place on serving plate. Garnish with whipped topping. Yield: 16 servings.

Approx Per Serving: Cal 401; Prot 6 g; Carbo 48 g; Fiber 2 g; T Fat 23 g; Chol 60 mg; Sod 273 mg.

Mrs. Charles A. Anderson, Asheville

CHERRY AND CHOCOLATE CAKE

1 2-layer package devil's food cake mix
1/2 cup chopped maraschino cherries
2 cups whipped topping
1 2-layer package chocolate frosting mix

Prepare and bake cake mix using package directions for two 9-inch round cake pans. Remove to wire racks to cool completely. Fold maraschino cherries into whipped topping. Spread between layers. Prepare frosting mix using package directions. Spread over top and side of cake. Chill until serving time. Store in refrigerator. Yield: 12 servings.

Approx Per Serving: Cal 539; Prot 4 g; Carbo 89 g; Fiber <1 g; T Fat 20 g; Chol 0 mg; Sod 309 mg.

Mary Reeves, Independence

CHOCOLATE AND CHERRY BUNDT CAKE

1 tablespoon sugar
1 2-layer package pudding-recipe chocolate cake mix
1 21-ounce can cherry pie filling
3 eggs
¾ cup water
¼ cup oil
1 teaspoon almond extract
Glaze

Sprinkle greased 12-cup microwave-safe bundt pan with sugar, shaking to coat well. Combine cake mix, 1 cup pie filling, eggs, water, oil and almond extract in large bowl; mix well. Mix using cake package directions. Pour into prepared pan. Microwave on Defrost for 28 to 29 minutes or until cake tests done, rotating pan every 5 minutes. Cool in pan for 10 minutes. Invert onto serving plate. Cool completely. Drizzle glaze over cake. Let stand for several minutes or until glaze sets. Garnish with cherries from remaining pie filling. Yield: 16 servings.

Glaze for Chocolate and Cherry Bundt Cake

3 ounces cream cheese
3 to 4 teaspoons milk
¾ cup confectioners' sugar

Place cream cheese in 1-quart glass mixer bowl. Microwave on Defrost for 30 seconds or until softened. Beat in enough milk and confectioners' sugar to make glaze.

Approx Per Serving: Cal 261; Prot 3 g; Carbo 43 g; Fiber 1 g; T Fat 9 g; Chol 46 mg; Sod 237 mg.

Priscilla S. Moraida, Central

☎ For a quick confectioners' sugar frosting, blend 2 tablespoons softened margarine, 2 cups confectioners' sugar and enough milk to make of spreading consistency. Flavor and tint as desired.

SOUR CREAM AND CINNAMON CAKE

2/3 cup margarine, softened
1/4 cup flour
1/4 cup packed brown sugar
2 teaspoons cinnamon
1 cup chopped pecans

1 2-layer package butter-recipe yellow cake mix
3/4 cup oil
1/2 cup sugar
1 cup sour cream
4 eggs, beaten

Mix margarine, flour, brown sugar and cinnamon in bowl until crumbly. Stir in pecans. Combine cake mix, oil, sugar, sour cream and eggs in mixer bowl. Beat at medium speed for 2 to 3 minutes or until smooth. Pour 1/3 of the batter into greased tube pan. Sprinkle with half the pecan mixture. Top with remaining batter; sprinkle with remaining pecan mixture. Bake at 325 degrees for 1 hour. Cool in pan for 1 hour. Invert onto serving plate. May bake for several minutes longer for crispy side. Yield: 16 servings.

Approx Per Serving: Cal 423; Prot 4 g; Carbo 40 g; Fiber 1 g; T Fat 28 g; Chol 56 mg; Sod 308 mg.

Louise W. Hinson, Hornets Nest

COCONUT CAKE

1 2-layer package pudding-recipe white cake mix
1 12-ounce can cream of coconut

16 ounces whipped topping
1 8-ounce package frozen coconut

Prepare and bake cake mix using package directions for a 9x13-inch cake pan. Pierce holes in top of cake with fork. Pour cream of coconut over top of hot cake. Cool completely. Spread with whipped topping; sprinkle with frozen coconut. Chill until serving time. Store in refrigerator. Yield: 15 servings.

Approx Per Serving: Cal 461; Prot 4 g; Carbo 57 g; Fiber 2 g; T Fat 26 g; Chol 0 mg; Sod 216 mg.

Wilma Burleson, Independence

SOUR CREAM AND COCONUT CAKE

2 cups sour cream
2 cups sugar
2 teaspoons vanilla extract
1 8-ounce package frozen coconut, thawed
1 2-layer package yellow cake mix
1 8-ounce package frozen coconut, thawed

Combine sour cream, sugar, vanilla and 1 package coconut in bowl; mix well. Chill overnight. Prepare and bake cake mix using package directions for two 9-inch round cake pans. Split cooled layers to make 4 layers. Spread sour cream mixture between layers and over top and side of cake. Sprinkle with remaining 1 package coconut. Chill for 2 days before serving. Chilling for 2 days makes cake moister. Yield: 12 servings.

Approx Per Serving: Cal 702; Prot 6 g; Carbo 106 g; Fiber 5 g; T Fat 31 g; Chol 17 mg; Sod 327 mg.

Lois Goodrum, Independence

THREE-DAY COCONUT CAKE

1 2-layer package white cake mix
2 8-ounce packages frozen coconut
2 cups sour cream
2 cups sugar
16 ounces whipped topping

Prepare and bake cake mix using package directions for two 9-inch round cake pans. Remove to wire racks to cool completely. Split layers into halves horizontally. Mix coconut, sour cream and sugar in bowl. Measure and reserve 1/2 cup coconut mixture. Spread remaining coconut mixture between layers. Mix reserved coconut mixture with whipped topping. Spread over top and side of cake. Chill, covered, for 3 days before serving. Yield: 12 servings.

Approx Per Serving: Cal 820; Prot 7 g; Carbo 115 g; Fiber 5 g; T Fat 40 g; Chol 17 mg; Sod 336 mg.

Evelyn N. Goodman, Hornets Nest

MINIATURE BOURBON FRUITCAKES

1/2 cup margarine, softened
2/3 cup sugar
1/2 cup packed brown sugar
2 eggs
1 1/2 cups flour
1 teaspoon soda
1 teaspoon cinnamon
1 teaspoon nutmeg
1/2 cup Bourbon
1 pound candied cherries
1 pound candied pineapple
3 cups golden raisins
3 cups chopped pecans

Cream margarine, sugar and brown sugar in large mixer bowl until light and fluffy. Add eggs 1 at a time, beating well after each addition. Mix flour, soda, cinnamon and nutmeg in bowl. Add to creamed mixture alternately with Bourbon, beating well after each addition. Add cherries, pineapple, raisins and pecans; mix well. Fill paper-lined miniature muffin cups 2/3 full. Bake at 325 degrees for 20 minutes or until light brown.
Yield: 60 servings.

Approx Per Serving: Cal 160; Prot 1 g; Carbo 26 g; Fiber 1 g; T Fat 6 g; Chol 7 mg; Sod 36 mg.

Elizabeth Stirewalt, Salem

REFRIGERATOR FRUITCAKE

1 16-ounce package marshmallows
1 cup whipping cream
1 16-ounce package graham crackers, crushed
1 15-ounce package golden raisins
1 pound pecans, chopped
1 pound English walnuts, chopped
1 cup chopped maraschino cherries

Melt marshmallows in cream in large saucepan, stirring constantly; remove from heat. Add remaining ingredients; mix well. Press into greased and waxed paper-lined 9x13-inch glass dish. Chill until firm. Yield: 24 servings.

Approx Per Serving: Cal 485; Prot 7 g; Carbo 54 g; Fiber 4 g; T Fat 30 g; Chol 14 mg; Sod 141 mg.

Irene C. Black, Independence

CANDIED FRUITCAKE

- 2 cups flour
- 2 teaspoons baking powder
- 1/2 teaspoon salt
- 1 pound whole candied cherries
- 8 cups pecan halves
- 1 pound candied pineapple, coarsely chopped
- 1 1/2 pounds pitted dates, coarsely chopped
- 4 eggs
- 1 cup sugar
- 1/4 cup light corn syrup

Sift flour, baking powder and salt into large bowl. Reserve several cherries and pecan halves for tops of loaves. Add pineapple, remaining cherries and dates to flour mixture; stir to coat well. Beat eggs in mixer bowl until frothy. Add sugar gradually, beating until well mixed. Stir into fruit mixture. Fold in remaining pecan halves. Press into 2 greased and waxed paper-lined 5x9-inch loaf pans. Arrange reserved cherries and pecan halves over tops of loaves. Bake at 275 degrees for 1 1/2 hours. Cool in pans for 5 minutes. Remove waxed paper. Place on wire racks to cool completely. Brush tops with corn syrup. Store, tightly wrapped, in cool place. Yield: 24 servings.

Approx Per Serving: Cal 557; Prot 6 g; Carbo 78 g; Fiber 5 g; T Fat 28 g; Chol 36 mg; Sod 87 mg.

Barbara Thrower, Independence

LIGHT FRUITCAKE

- 2 cups butter, softened
- 2 cups sugar
- 6 eggs
- 1 2-ounce bottle of lemon extract
- 3 cups sifted flour
- 1 pound white raisins
- 1 1/2 pounds candied cherries, cut into halves
- 1 pound candied pineapple, chopped
- 1 pound pecans, chopped

Cream butter and sugar in mixer bowl until light and fluffy. Add eggs 1 at a time, beating well after each addition. Add flour; mix well. Stir in lemon extract. Fold in raisins, cherries, pineapple and pecans. Pour into waxed paper-lined tube pan. Place on rack in center of oven. Place shallow pan half filled with water on lower

rack of oven. Bake at 275 degrees for 2 1/2 to 3 hours or until cake tests done. Do not substitute margarine for butter.
Yield: 16 servings.

Approx Per Serving: Cal 910; Prot 8 g; Carbo 127 g; Fiber 4 g; T Fat 45 g; Chol 142 mg; Sod 224 mg.

Shirley Carmichael, Hornets Nest

LEMON EXTRACT FRUITCAKE

- 2 cups butter, softened
- 2 1/2 cups sugar
- 6 eggs
- 3 tablespoons lemon extract
- 3 1/2 cups sifted flour
- 1 1/2 teaspoons baking powder
- 1/2 teaspoon salt
- 8 ounces candied cherries
- 4 ounces candied pineapple
- 4 ounces white raisins
- 4 cups chopped pecans
- 1/2 cup flour

Cream butter and sugar in large mixer bowl until light and fluffy. Add eggs and lemon extract; beat well. Sift 3 1/2 cups flour, baking powder and salt together. Add to creamed mixture; beat well. Mix cherries, pineapple, raisins, pecans and remaining 1/2 cup flour in bowl until coated. Stir into batter. Pour into greased and floured 10-inch tube pan. Bake at 300 degrees for 2 1/2 to 3 hours or until cake tests done. May bake in 2 greased and floured 5x9-inch loaf pans for 1 1/2 to 2 hours or until loaves test done.
Yield: 16 servings.

Approx Per Serving: Cal 749; Prot 8 g; Carbo 82 g; Fiber 3 g; T Fat 46 g; Chol 142 mg; Sod 488 mg.

Barbara Thrower, Independence

☎ Holiday fruitcakes can be stored indefinitely. Wrap them in Brandy or wine-soaked cloths and then in foil. Store in an airtight container in a cool place.

ICEBOX FRUITCAKE

- 1 16-ounce package graham crackers, crushed
- 1 14-ounce can sweetened condensed milk
- 1 15-ounce package raisins
- 1 8-ounce package dates, chopped
- 1 10-ounce jar maraschino cherries, cut into halves
- 1 3-ounce can coconut
- 1 pound walnuts, chopped
- 2 pounds pecans, chopped

Cut large side of empty graham cracker box to make large flap opening. Line with waxed paper. Seal original opening with masking tape. Place graham cracker crumbs in large bowl. Add sweetened condensed milk, raisins, dates, cherries and juice, coconut, walnuts and pecans; mix well. Press firmly into prepared graham cracker box. Seal with masking tape; wrap in foil. Freeze for 24 hours or longer. Yield: 24 servings.

Approx Per Serving: Cal 616; Prot 9 g; Carbo 60 g; Fiber 6 g; T Fat 42 g; Chol 6 mg; Sod 142 mg.

Agnes Williams, Independence

FRUITED PECAN CAKE

- 2 cups butter, softened
- 2 cups packed brown sugar
- 6 egg yolks
- 2 cups flour
- 1 teaspoon baking powder
- 3 tablespoons lemon extract
- 8 ounces candied cherries, chopped
- 8 ounces candied pineapple, chopped
- 2 cups flour
- 2 cups pecan halves
- 6 egg whites, stiffly beaten

Grease and flour 10-inch tube pan. Line bottom with waxed paper. Cream butter and brown sugar in mixer bowl until light and fluffy. Add egg yolks; beat well. Mix 2 cups flour and baking powder in bowl. Add to egg mixture alternately with lemon extract, beating well after each addition. Combine cherries, pineapple and remaining 2 cups flour in bowl; toss to coat. Stir into batter. Add pecans; mix well. Fold in egg whites. Spoon into prepared tube pan. Let stand, covered with clean cloth, at room temperature overnight. Bake at 250 degrees for 3½ hours. Cool in pan for 10 minutes. Remove to wire rack to cool completely. May brush cake with honey and press additional cherries and pineapple gently into top of cake during last 10 minutes of baking time. Yield: 16 servings.

Approx Per Serving: Cal 622; Prot 7 g; Carbo 76 g; Fiber 2 g; T Fat 34 g; Chol 62 mg; Sod 264 mg.

Martha A. Rhyne, Foot Hills

PECAN FRUITCAKE

½ cup butter, softened
1 cup sugar
5 eggs
1 cup flour
½ teaspoon baking powder
4 teaspoons vanilla extract
4 teaspoons lemon extract
1 pound chopped candied pineapple
1 pound chopped candied red cherries
1 pound chopped candied green cherries
1 pound chopped pecans
1 cup flour

Cream butter and sugar in mixer bowl until light and fluffy. Add eggs; beat well. Combine 1 cup flour and baking powder in bowl; mix well. Add to creamed mixture alternately with flavorings, beating well after each addition. Combine pineapple, cherries, pecans and remaining 1 cup flour in bowl; toss to coat. Pour batter over fruit mixture; mix well. Pour into foil-lined tube pan. Bake at 250 degrees for 3 hours. Cool in pan for several minutes. Invert onto serving plate. Yield: 16 servings.

Approx Per Serving: Cal 647; Prot 6 g; Carbo 99 g; Fiber 2 g; T Fat 27 g; Chol 82 mg; Sod 81 mg.

Julia S. Clark, Independence

☎ Raisins and fruit coated with flour will not sink to the bottom when added to cake batter.

FRIENDSHIP CAKE

- 1 2-layer package white cake mix
- 1 1/2 cups Friendship Cake Starter
- 2/3 cup oil
- 4 eggs
- 1 cup chopped pecans

Combine cake mix, Friendship Cake Starter, oil and eggs in bowl; mix well. Stir in pecans. Pour into greased and floured bundt pan. Bake at 325 degrees for 1 hour. Cool in pan for several minutes. Invert onto serving plate. Yield: 12 servings.

Approx Per Serving: Cal 551; Prot 5 g; Carbo 82 g; Fiber 1 g; T Fat 24 g; Chol 71 mg; Sod 286 mg.

Friendship Cake Starter

- 1 16-ounce can fruit cocktail
- 1 16-ounce can peaches
- 2 1/2 cups sugar
- 1 20-ounce can pineapple tidbits
- 2 1/2 cups sugar
- 1 8-ounce jar maraschino cherries
- 2 1/2 cups sugar

Combine fruit cocktail with juice, peaches with juice and 2 1/2 cups sugar in large glass jar; stir with wooden spoon until sugar is dissolved. Cover. Let stand at room temperature. Stir each day for 10 days. Add pineapple with juice and 2 1/2 cups sugar; mix well. Stir each day for 10 days. Add cherries with juice and remaining 2 1/2 cups sugar; mix well. Stir each day for 10 days. Store in refrigerator. May store in refrigerator indefinitely.
Yield: enough for 7 cakes.

Approx Per Serving: Cal 1021; Prot 1 g; Carbo 264 g; Fiber 2 g; T Fat <1 g; Chol 0 mg; Sod 15 mg.

Edna M. Barham, Raleigh

FRUIT COCKTAIL CAKE

2 cups self-rising flour
2 cups sugar
2 eggs
1 16-ounce can fruit cocktail
1/2 teaspoon cinnamon
1/2 teaspoon salt
1 teaspoon vanilla extract
Frosting

Combine flour, sugar, eggs, fruit cocktail, cinnamon, salt and vanilla in bowl; mix well. Pour into greased and floured 9x13-inch cake pan. Bake at 350 degrees for 30 to 35 minutes or until cake tests done. Pour frosting over hot cake.
Yield: 15 servings.

Frosting for Fruit Cocktail Cake

1 cup sugar
1 cup evaporated milk
1/2 cup margarine
1 cup chopped pecans
1 cup coconut

Mix sugar, evaporated milk and margarine in saucepan. Bring to a boil, stirring constantly. Boil for 10 minutes or until thickened, stirring constantly; remove from heat. Stir in pecans and coconut.

Approx Per Serving: Cal 399; Prot 5 g; Carbo 63 g; Fiber 2 g; T Fat 15 g; Chol 33 mg; Sod 353 mg.

Polly Mabrey, Hornets Nest

☎ When baking cakes, place pans in center of oven, making sure they don't touch each other or sides of oven. Also, be sure they are not placed directly under each other as this will cut down heat circulation.

MRS. GIBSON'S FRUIT COCKTAIL CAKE

2 eggs
1 1/2 cups sugar
2 cups self-rising flour
1 teaspoon vanilla extract
1 20-ounce can fruit cocktail
Topping

Combine eggs, sugar, flour, vanilla and fruit cocktail in bowl; mix well. Pour into greased 12x18-inch cake pan. Bake at 350 degrees for 30 to 35 minutes or until cake tests done. Pour topping over hot cake. Yield: 20 servings.

Topping for Mrs. Gibson's Fruit Cocktail Cake

1/2 cup butter
1 cup sugar
1 cup evaporated milk
1/2 cup chopped pecans
1/2 cup coconut

Combine butter, sugar and evaporated milk in saucepan. Cook over medium heat for 10 minutes, stirring frequently. Stir in pecans and coconut.

Approx Per Serving: Cal 255; Prot 3 g; Carbo 42 g; Fiber 1 g; T Fat 9 g; Chol 37 mg; Sod 197 mg.

Phyllis Cox, Central

FAVORITE FRUIT COCKTAIL CAKE

2 cups flour
2 cups sugar
1 teaspoon salt
1 teaspoon soda
2 eggs, beaten
1 16-ounce can fruit cocktail
Topping (See page 361)

Sift flour, sugar, salt and soda into large bowl. Add eggs; mix well. Stir in fruit cocktail with juice. Pour into greased 9x13-inch cake pan. Bake at 350 degrees for 35 minutes. Pour topping over hot cake. Yield: 15 servings.

Topping for Favorite Fruit Cocktail Cake

1 cup sugar
1 cup evaporated milk
½ cup margarine
1 cup coconut
½ cup chopped pecans

Combine sugar, evaporated milk and margarine in saucepan. Bring to a boil, stirring constantly. Boil for 3 minutes; remove from heat. Stir in coconut and pecans.

Approx Per Serving: Cal 373; Prot 4 g; Carbo 63 g; Fiber 2 g; T Fat 13 g; Chol 33 mg; Sod 299 mg.

Irene C. Black, Independence

BONNIE'S FRUIT COCKTAIL CAKE

1½ cups sugar
2 eggs
2 cups flour
2 teaspoons soda
¼ teaspoon salt
1 teaspoon vanilla extract
1 16-ounce can fruit cocktail
Frosting

Beat sugar and eggs in mixer bowl until thick and lemon-colored. Add flour, soda, salt and vanilla; mix well. Add fruit cocktail; mix lightly. Spoon into greased and floured 9x13-inch cake pan. Bake at 350 degrees for 35 minutes. Spread frosting over cake. Yield: 12 servings.

Frosting For Bonnie's Fruit Cocktail Cake

½ cup butter
1 13-ounce can evaporated milk
1 cup sugar
½ cup chopped pecans
½ cup coconut

Combine butter, evaporated milk and sugar in saucepan. Cook over low heat until thickened to consistency of syrup. Add pecans and coconut; mix well.

Approx Per Serving: Cal 434; Prot 6 g; Carbo 70 g; Fiber 2 g; T Fat 16 g; Chol 65 mg; Sod 339 mg.

Bonnie Krammer, Independence

LIGHT-AS-A-FEATHER GINGERBREAD

2 cups flour
3/4 teaspoon salt
1/2 teaspoon soda
1 1/4 teaspoons baking powder
1 1/4 teaspoons ginger
1 1/4 teaspoons cinnamon
1/2 teaspoon cloves
1/2 to 2/3 cup oil
2 eggs
1 1/3 cups molasses
1/2 cup boiling water
Lemon Sauce

Sift flour, salt, soda, baking powder, ginger, cinnamon and cloves into large bowl. Stir in enough oil to make mixture crumbly. Add eggs; beat well. Combine molasses and boiling water in bowl; mix well. Add 3/4 cup molasses mixture to flour mixture; beat until smooth. Add remaining molasses mixture, stirring just until well-mixed. Pour into greased 8-inch square baking pan. Bake at 325 degrees for 1 hour or until gingerbread tests done. Serve warm with Lemon Sauce. Yield: 16 servings.

Lemon Sauce

2/3 cup sugar
1 1/4 tablespoons flour
1/8 teaspoon salt
1 1/4 cups boiling water
1 1/2 tablespoons butter, softened
1 1/2 tablespoons lemon juice

Combine sugar, flour and salt in saucepan; mix well. Stir in boiling water and butter. Bring to a boil, stirring constantly. Boil for 5 minutes. Stir in lemon juice.

Approx Per Serving: Cal 247; Prot 2 g; Carbo 36 g; Fiber <1 g; T Fat 11 g; Chol 30 mg; Sod 211 mg.

Sybil P. Peele, Hornets Nest

JIM ADAMS' GREAT-GRANDMOTHER'S GINGERBREAD

2 1/2 cups sifted flour
1/2 teaspoon salt
1 1/2 teaspoons soda
1 teaspoon cinnamon
1 teaspoon ginger
1/2 teaspoon cloves

1/2 cup sugar
1/2 cup butter, softened
1 cup molasses
1 egg, beaten
1 cup hot water

Sift flour, salt, soda, cinnamon, ginger and cloves together. Cream sugar and butter in mixer bowl until light and fluffy. Add molasses and egg; beat well. Add flour mixture; mix well. Pour in hot water; beat until smooth. Pour into greased and floured 9-inch square baking pan. Bake at 350 degrees for 35 minutes. Yield: 9 servings.

Approx Per Serving: Cal 334; Prot 4 g; Carbo 55 g; Fiber 1 g; T Fat 11 g; Chol 51 mg; Sod 384 mg.

Cheryl Griffin, Raleigh

GRANDMA'S HOT MILK CAKE

4 eggs, well beaten
2 cups sugar
2 cups flour
1 cup milk

1/2 cup butter, softened
1 teaspoon baking powder
1 teaspoon vanilla extract
1/8 teaspoon salt

Beat eggs, sugar and flour in large mixer bowl until smooth. Combine milk and butter in saucepan. Bring to a boil, stirring constantly; remove from heat. Pour over flour mixture. Stir in baking powder, vanilla and salt. Pour into greased and floured tube pan. Bake at 325 degrees for 1 hour. Yield: 16 servings.

Approx Per Serving: Cal 234; Prot 4 g; Carbo 38 g; Fiber <1 g; T Fat 8 g; Chol 71 mg; Sod 110 mg.

Evelyn Furman, Hornets Nest

HONEY BUN CAKE

1 2-layer package yellow cake mix
1/2 cup sugar
1 cup oil
1 cup sour cream
4 eggs
1 cup packed brown sugar
1 cup raisins
2 tablespoons cinnamon
1 cup chopped pecans
2 cups confectioners' sugar
1/4 cup milk
1 teaspoon vanilla extract

Combine cake mix, sugar, oil, sour cream and eggs in mixer bowl; mix well. Combine brown sugar, raisins, cinnamon and pecans in bowl; mix well. Add to egg mixture; mix well. Pour into greased and floured 10x15-inch cake pan. Bake at 300 degrees for 35 to 40 minutes or until cake tests done. Combine confectioners' sugar, milk and vanilla in small bowl; mix well. Drizzle over hot cake. Yield: 24 servings.

Approx Per Serving: Cal 351; Prot 3 g; Carbo 48 g; Fiber 1 g; T Fat 17 g; Chol 40 mg; Sod 154 mg.

Phyllis E. Jones, Independence

HONEY GRAHAM CRACKER CAKE

1 cup butter, softened
2 cups sugar
4 eggs
1 cup milk
1 teaspoon vanilla extract
1 teaspoon baking powder
1 3-ounce can coconut
1 cup chopped pecans
1 16-ounce package honey graham crackers, crushed
Pineapple Frosting (See page 365)

Cream butter and sugar in mixer bowl until light and fluffy. Add eggs, milk, vanilla and baking powder; beat well. Stir in coconut, pecans and crumbs. Pour into 4 greased and floured 8-inch round cake pans. Bake at 375 degrees for 30 to 35 minutes or until layers test done. Remove to wire racks to cool. Spread Pineapple Frosting between layers and over top and side of cake. Yield: 12 servings.

Pineapple Frosting

2 tablespoons flour
1¼ cups sugar
1 20-ounce can crushed pineapple

Dissolve flour in a small amount of water in saucepan. Stir in sugar and pineapple. Cook until thickened, stirring constantly.

Approx Per Serving: Cal 686; Prot 7 g; Carbo 100 g; Fiber 3 g; T Fat 31 g; Chol 115 mg; Sod 424 mg.

Joyce T. Smith, Central

ITALIAN CRÈME CAKE

½ cup shortening
½ cup margarine, softened
2 cups sugar
5 egg yolks
2 cups self-rising flour
1 teaspoon soda
1 cup buttermilk
1 teaspoon vanilla extract
1 6-ounce package frozen coconut
1 cup chopped pecans
5 egg whites, stiffly beaten
Frosting
½ cup chopped pecans

Cream shortening and margarine in mixer bowl until light and fluffy. Add sugar gradually, beating well. Beat in egg yolks. Mix flour and soda in bowl. Add to creamed mixture alternately with buttermilk. Stir in vanilla, coconut and pecans. Fold in egg whites. Pour into 3 greased and floured 9-inch round cake pans. Bake at 350 degrees for 25 minutes or until layers test done. Remove to wire racks to cool. Spread frosting between layers, sprinkling with pecans. Spread remaining frosting over top and side of cake. Yield: 12 servings.

Frosting for Italian Crème Cake

8 ounces cream cheese, softened
¼ cup margarine, softened
1 1-pound package confectioners' sugar
1 teaspoon vanilla extract

Beat cream cheese and margarine in mixer bowl until smooth. Add sugar; beat well. Stir in vanilla.

Approx Per Serving: Cal 830; Prot 8 g; Carbo 105 g; Fiber 3 g; T Fat 44 g; Chol 110 mg; Sod 566 mg.

Becky Rabon, Salem

CHOLESTEROL-FREE LEMON CHIFFON CAKE

5 egg whites, at room temperature
2 tablespoons sifted confectioners' sugar
1 1/2 cups sifted cake flour
1 cup sugar
2 teaspoons baking powder
1/4 teaspoon salt
1/2 cup oil
Grated zest of 2 lemons
1/2 cup fresh lemon juice

Beat egg whites with confectioners' sugar in large mixer bowl just until stiff peaks form. Sift flour, sugar, baking powder and salt into medium mixer bowl. Make well in center. Pour oil into well. Add lemon zest and juice. Beat on medium-low speed until smooth. Fold into egg whites gently. Spoon into greased and floured 9-inch tube pan. Bake at 350 degrees for 35 minutes or until top of cake is golden brown. Cool in pan for 5 minutes. Invert onto wire rack to cool completely. Glaze with lemon icing or lemon sorbet. Yield: 16 servings.

Approx Per Serving: Cal 152; Prot 2 g; Carbo 21 g; Fiber <1 g; T Fat 7 g; Chol 0 mg; Sod 91 mg.

Phyllis Jones, Independence

EASY LEMON DELIGHT CAKE

1 angel food cake
1 21-ounce can lemon pie filling
1 cup lemon yogurt
16 ounces whipped topping

Slice angel food cake into 4 layers. Mix pie filling and yogurt in bowl. Spread between layers. Spread whipped topping over top and side of cake. Chill until serving time. Yield: 16 servings.

Approx Per Serving: Cal 234; Prot 3 g; Carbo 40 g; Fiber 1 g; T Fat 7 g; Chol 1 mg; Sod 228 mg.

Faye Swisher, Hornets Nest

LEMON GEM MINIATURE CAKES

1 2-layer package lemon cake mix
1 1-pound package confectioners' sugar
Juice and grated rind of 3 lemons

Prepare cake batter using package directions. Spoon by teaspoonfuls into greased and floured miniature muffin cups. Bake at 350 degrees for 10 minutes or until light brown. Combine confectioners' sugar, lemon juice and rind in small bowl; stir until sugar dissolves. Place wire racks over waxed paper. Dip hot miniature cakes in glaze. Place on wire racks to cool completely. Yield: 96 servings.

Approx Per Serving: Cal 61; Prot <1 g; Carbo 12 g; Fiber <1 g; T Fat 1 g; Chol 0 mg; Sod 26 mg.

Nell Seegers, Independence

NUT CAKE

2 cups butter, softened
2 cups sugar
6 eggs
2 1/2 cups self-rising flour
1 teaspoon vanilla extract
3 cups chopped pecans
1 cup chopped black walnuts
1 1/2 cups all-purpose flour
1 large apple, peeled, chopped

Cream butter and sugar in mixer bowl until light and fluffy. Add eggs 2 at a time, beating well after each addition. Add self-rising flour; mix well. Stir in vanilla. Combine pecans, walnuts and all-purpose flour in bowl; toss to coat. Fold into batter. Stir in apples. Pour into ungreased tube pan. Bake at 300 degrees for 1 1/4 hours. Cool in pan for several minutes. Invert onto serving plate. Yield: 16 servings.

Approx Per Serving: Cal 643; Prot 9 g; Carbo 55 g; Fiber 3 g; T Fat 45 g; Chol 142 mg; Sod 431 mg.

Mary Reeves, Independence

LAZY DAISY OATMEAL CAKE

1¼ cups boiling water
1 cup oats
½ cup butter, softened
1 cup sugar
1 cup packed brown sugar
1 teaspoon vanilla extract

2 eggs
1½ cups flour
½ teaspoon salt
1 teaspoon soda
¾ teaspoon cinnamon
Frosting

Pour boiling water over oats in small bowl. Let stand, covered, for 20 minutes. Beat butter in large mixer bowl until light. Add sugar and brown sugar gradually, beating until fluffy. Add vanilla and eggs; beat well. Stir in oats. Sift flour, salt, soda and cinnamon together. Stir into oats mixture. Pour into greased and floured 9x13-inch cake pan. Bake at 350 degrees for 50 to 55 minutes or until cake tests done. Spread frosting over top of cake. Bake until bubbly. Yield: 15 servings.

Frosting for Lazy Daisy Oatmeal Cake

½ cup melted butter
½ cup packed brown sugar

½ cup chopped pecans
¾ cup coconut
5 tablespoons milk

Combine butter and brown sugar in bowl; mix well. Stir in pecans, coconut and milk.

Approx Per Serving: Cal 366; Prot 4 g; Carbo 50 g; Fiber 2 g; T Fat 18 g; Chol 62 mg; Sod 252 mg.

Bonnie Kramer, Independence

MANDARIN ORANGE CAKE

1 2-layer package yellow cake mix
4 eggs
½ cup oil
1 11-ounce can mandarin oranges
Frosting

Combine cake mix, eggs and oil in mixer bowl; beat well. Add 1 can mandarin oranges with juice. Beat just until oranges are slightly chopped and mixture is smooth. Pour into greased and floured 9x13-inch cake pan. Bake at 350 degrees for 20 to 25 minutes or until cake tests done. Do not overbake. Cool completely. Spread frosting over cake. Chill. Best when served the second day. Yield: 15 servings.

Frosting for Mandarin Orange Cake

1 8-ounce can crushed pineapple
1 4-ounce package vanilla instant pudding mix
12 ounces whipped topping
1 11-ounce can mandarin oranges, drained

Drain pineapple, reserving ¼ cup juice. Pierce top of cake with fork. Pour reserved juice over cake. Blend pudding mix and whipped topping in bowl. Stir in pineapple and mandarin oranges.

Approx Per Serving: Cal 369; Prot 4 g; Carbo 51 g; Fiber 1 g; T Fat 17 g; Chol 57 mg; Sod 287 mg.

Madelon Haskin, Hornets Nest

IRENE'S MANDARIN ORANGE CAKE

- 1 2-layer package butter cake mix
- 1 11-ounce can mandarin oranges
- 4 eggs
- 1/2 cup oil
- Frosting

Combine cake mix, undrained oranges, eggs and oil in mixer bowl. Beat for 4 to 5 minutes or until well mixed. Spoon into greased and floured 9x13-inch cake pan. Bake at 350 degrees for 35 minutes. Spread frosting over cake. Yield: 12 servings.

Frosting for Irene's Mandarin Orange Cake

- 1 6-ounce package vanilla instant pudding mix
- 1 16-ounce can crushed pineapple
- 16 ounces whipped topping

Prepare pudding mix using package directions. Add pineapple and whipped topping; mix well.

Approx Per Serving: Cal 508; Prot 5 g; Carbo 70 g; Fiber 1 g; T Fat 24 g; Chol 71 mg; Sod 391 mg.

Irene Black, Independence

MANDARIN ORANGE CAKE DELUXE

- 1 2-layer package yellow cake mix
- 1 11-ounce can mandarin oranges
- 4 eggs
- 1/2 cup oil
- Frosting (See page 371)

Combine cake mix, oranges, eggs and oil in mixer bowl. Beat for 2 to 3 minutes or until well mixed. Pour into 3 greased and floured 9-inch cake pans. Bake at 350 degrees for 25 to 30 minutes or until layers test done. Remove to wire rack to cool. Spread frosting between layers and over top and side of cake. Yield: 12 servings.

Frosting for Mandarin Orange Cake Deluxe

- 1   16-ounce can crushed pineapple
- 1   4-ounce package vanilla instant pudding mix
- 9 ounces whipped topping
- 1 cup coconut
- 1/2 cup chopped pecans
- 1/2 cup chopped cherries

Combine pineapple, pudding mix and whipped topping in bowl; mix well. Stir in coconut, pecans and cherries.

Approx Per Serving: Cal 499; Prot 5 g; Carbo 65 g; Fiber 2 g; T Fat 25 g; Chol 71 mg; Sod 341 mg.

Shirley Hinson, Hornets Nest

TINY ORANGE CUPCAKES

- 1/2 cup shortening
- 1 cup sugar
- 2 eggs, at room temperature
- 2 cups flour
- 1 teaspoon soda
- 1/2 teaspoon salt
- 2/3 cup buttermilk
- 1/2 teaspoon vanilla extract
- 2/3 cup chopped pecans
- Juice and rind of 3 oranges
- 1 1/2 cups sugar

Cream shortening and 1 cup sugar in mixer bowl until light and fluffy. Add eggs; beat well. Sift flour, soda and salt together. Add to creamed mixture alternately with mixture of buttermilk and vanilla, beating well after each addition. Stir in pecans. Fill ungreased miniature muffin cups 1/3 full. Do not overfill muffin cups. Bake at 375 degrees for 10 to 12 minutes or until tops spring back when touched. Combine orange juice and rind with remaining 1 1/2 cups sugar in saucepan. Cook until sugar dissolves, stirring constantly. Spoon hot glaze over hot cupcakes in muffin cups to fill cups. Cool in pans. Loosen edges with knife; remove to serving plate. May be frozen between layers of waxed paper. Yield: 84 servings.

Approx Per Serving: Cal 56; Prot 1 g; Carbo 9 g; Fiber <1 g; T Fat 2 g; Chol 5 mg; Sod 26 mg.

Ovid Smith, Hornets Nest

ORANGE SHERBET CAKE

2 cups sour cream
2 cups sugar
2 tablespoons orange juice
2 9-ounce packages frozen coconut
12 ounces whipped topping
1 2-layer package orange cake mix
1 3-ounce package orange gelatin
2 eggs
1/2 cup oil
1 cup water

Mix sour cream, sugar and orange juice in large bowl. Stir in coconut. Reserve 1 cup whipped topping. Fold remaining whipped topping into sour cream mixture. Chill for 24 hours. Combine cake mix, gelatin, eggs, oil and water in mixer bowl; beat well. Pour into 2 greased and floured 9-inch round cake pans. Bake at 350 degrees for 20 to 25 minutes or until layers test done. Remove to wire racks to cool. Split layers into halves horizontally. Reserve 1 cup icing. Spread remaining icing between layers. Mix reserved whipped topping and reserved icing in bowl. Spread over top of cake. Chill in airtight container in refrigerator for 1 to 2 days. Yield: 12 servings.

Approx Per Serving: Cal 793; Prot 7 g; Carbo 101 g; Fiber 5 g; T Fat 42 g; Chol 53 mg; Sod 333 mg.

Martha Berrier, Hornets Nest

ORANGE FRUITCAKE

1/2 cup butter, softened
1 cup sugar
Grated rind of 1 orange
2 eggs
2 cups flour
1 teaspoon soda
1/8 teaspoon salt
2/3 cup buttermilk
1 cup chopped dates
1/2 cup chopped pecans
1/2 cup orange juice
1 cup sugar

Cream butter and 1 cup sugar in mixer bowl until light and fluffy. Beat in 1 tablespoon orange rind. Add eggs 1 at a time, beating well after each addition. Mix flour, soda and salt in bowl. Add to creamed mixture alternately with buttermilk, beating well after each addition. Stir in dates and pecans. Pour into greased and floured 9x13-inch cake pan. Bake at 300 degrees for 35 to 40 minutes or until cake tests done. Mix remaining orange rind, orange juice and remaining 1 cup sugar in small bowl until sugar dissolves. Pour over warm cake. Cool. Cut into squares. Yield: 15 servings.

Approx Per Serving: Cal 296; Prot 4 g; Carbo 50 g; Fiber 2 g; T Fat 10 g; Chol 45 mg; Sod 146 mg.

Evelyn Clemmer, Hornets Nest

HUMMINGBIRD CAKE

3 cups flour
2 cups sugar
1 teaspoon salt
1 teaspoon soda
1 teaspoon cinnamon
3 eggs, beaten
1 1/2 cups oil
1 1/2 teaspoons vanilla extract
1 8-ounce can crushed pineapple
2 cups chopped pecans
2 cups chopped bananas

Combine flour, sugar, salt, soda and cinnamon in large bowl; mix well. Add eggs and oil, stirring just until moistened. Stir in vanilla, pineapple, pecans and bananas. Spoon into 3 well-greased 9-inch round cake pans. Bake at 325 degrees for 30 minutes. Cool in pans for 10 minutes. Remove to wire racks to cool completely. Spread favorite frosting between layers and over top and side of cake. Yield: 12 servings.

Approx Per Serving: Cal 675; Prot 7 g; Carbo 71 g; Fiber 3 g; T Fat 43 g; Chol 53 mg; Sod 265 mg.
Nutritional information does not include frosting.

Betty Quick, Central

☎ The top layer of a layer cake won't slip as you ice it if you hold it in place with a wire cake-tester or thin skewers inserted through all layers. Remove the tester just before completing the job.

HUMMINGBIRD CAKE DELUXE

3 cups flour
2 cups sugar
1 teaspoon soda
1 teaspoon salt
3 eggs, beaten
¾ cup oil
1½ teaspoons vanilla extract
1 8-ounce can crushed pineapple
1 cup chopped pecans
2 cups chopped bananas
1 cup raisins
Frosting
½ cup chopped pecans

Combine flour, sugar, soda and salt in large bowl; mix well. Add eggs and oil, stirring just until moistened. Stir in vanilla, pineapple, 1 cup pecans, bananas and raisins. Spoon into 3 greased and floured 9-inch cake pans. Bake at 350 degrees for 20 to 30 minutes. Cool in pans for 10 minutes. Remove to wire racks to cool completely. Spread frosting between layers and over top and side of cake. Sprinkle with remaining ½ cup pecans. Yield: 12 servings.

Frosting for Hummingbird Cake Deluxe

½ cup margarine, softened
12 ounces cream cheese, softened
1 teaspoon vanilla extract
1 teaspoon lemon extract
1 1-pound package confectioners' sugar

Cream margarine and cream cheese in mixer bowl until light and fluffy. Add vanilla, lemon extract and confectioners' sugar; beat well.

Approx Per Serving: Cal 905; Prot 9 g; Carbo 126 g; Fiber 3 g; T Fat 43 g; Chol 84 mg; Sod 440 mg.

Ruby Brown, Raleigh

NEVA'S HUMMINGBIRD CAKE

3 cups flour
2 cups sugar
1 teaspoon soda
1 teaspoon cinnamon
1 teaspoon salt
1½ cups oil
3 eggs, beaten
2 cups chopped bananas
1 8-ounce can crushed pineapple
2 cups chopped pecans
2 teaspoons vanilla extract
Frosting

Combine flour, sugar, soda, cinnamon and salt in bowl. Add oil and eggs; stir until ingredients are moistened; do not beat. Stir in bananas, undrained pineapple, pecans and vanilla. Spoon into 3 greased and floured 8-inch cake pans. Bake at 350 degrees for 25 to 30 minutes or until layers test done. Remove to wire rack to cool. Spread frosting between layers and over top and side of cake. Yield: 12 servings.

Frosting for Neva's Hummingbird Cake

¼ cup butter, softened
8 ounces cream cheese, softened
1 1-pound package confectioners' sugar
1 cup chopped pecans

Cream butter and cream cheese in mixer bowl until light and fluffy. Add confectioners' sugar and pecans; mix well.

Approx Per Serving: Cal 1016; Prot 9 g; Carbo 119 g; Fiber 3 g; T Fat 60 g; Chol 84 mg; Sod 354 mg.

Neva Schneider, Hornets Nest

☎ Freeze a frosted cake, then wrap it. The wrapping won't stick to the frosting. Remove the wrapping before thawing the cake.

DO-NOTHING CAKE

2 cups flour
2 cups sugar
1 teaspoon soda
1/2 teaspoon salt
2 eggs
1 tablespoon vanilla extract
1   20-ounce can unsweetened crushed pineapple
Frosting

Combine flour, sugar, soda, salt, eggs and vanilla in mixer bowl; mix well. Stir in pineapple. Pour into greased and floured 9x13-inch cake pan. Bake at 350 degrees for 45 minutes. Pour frosting over hot cake. Yield: 15 servings.

Frosting for Do-Nothing Cake

1/2 cup margarine
1 cup sugar
2/3 cup evaporated milk
1 cup chopped pecans
1 cup coconut

Combine margarine, sugar and evaporated milk in small saucepan. Bring to a boil, stirring constantly. Boil for 5 minutes, stirring constantly; remove from heat. Stir in pecans and coconut.

Approx Per Serving: Cal 396; Prot 4 g; Carbo 64 g; Fiber 2 g; T Fat 15 g; Chol 32 mg; Sod 233 mg.

Virginia Bowie, Independence

CALIFORNIA CAKE

1/4 teaspoon salt
1 cup sugar
1 teaspoon lemon extract
1/2 cup butter, softened
1 cup chopped pecans
1   17-ounce package pound cake mix
2 eggs
1 cup sour cream
1   15-ounce can pineapple tidbits, drained

Combine salt, sugar and lemon extract in bowl; mix well. Cut in butter until crumbly and moist. Stir in pecans. Prepare pound cake mix according to package directions using 2 eggs and substituting sour cream for milk. Pour into greased and floured

9x13-inch cake pan. Top with pineapple; sprinkle with crumb mixture. Bake at 325 degrees for 45 minutes or until light brown and cake tests done. Cool. Cut into squares. Yield: 15 servings.

Approx Per Serving: Cal 454; Prot 5 g; Carbo 60 g; Fiber 1 g; T Fat 23 g; Chol 52 mg; Sod 265 mg.

Elizabeth Stirewalt, Salem

PINEAPPLE FLUFF CAKE

1 2-layer package butter-recipe yellow cake mix	1 11-ounce can mandarin oranges
4 eggs	Frosting
1/2 cup oil	

Combine cake mix, eggs, oil and undrained mandarin oranges in bowl; mix well. Pour into 3 greased and floured 9-inch round cake pans. Bake at 350 degrees for 20 to 25 minutes or until layers test done. Remove to wire racks to cool. Spread frosting between layers and over top and side of cake. Yield: 12 servings.

Frosting for Pineapple Fluff Cake

1 4-ounce package vanilla instant pudding mix	12 ounces whipped topping
1 8-ounce can crushed pineapple, drained	

Combine pudding mix, pineapple and whipped topping in bowl; mix well.

Approx Per Serving: Cal 445; Prot 4 g; Carbo 59 g; Fiber 1 g; T Fat 22 g; Chol 71 mg; Sod 357 mg.

Ruth Tucker, Hornets Nest

☎ Cake flour is specially milled from selected winter wheats to make delicate, fine-textured cakes.

BASIC POUND CAKE

3 2/3 cups flour
1 teaspoon baking powder
1/4 teaspoon salt
1 cup butter, softened
1/2 cup shortening
3 cups sugar
6 eggs
1 cup milk
1 teaspoon vanilla extract
1 teaspoon lemon extract

Sift flour, baking powder and salt together 3 times. Cream butter, shortening and sugar in large mixer bowl until light and fluffy. Add eggs 1 at a time, beating well after each addition. Stir in milk and flavorings. Add flour mixture; mix well. Pour into greased and floured tube pan. Place in cold oven. Set oven temperature at 325 degrees. Bake for 1 1/2 hours. Cool in pan for several minutes. Invert onto serving plate. Yield: 16 servings.

Approx Per Serving: Cal 447; Prot 6 g; Carbo 60 g; Fiber 1 g; T Fat 21 g; Chol 113 mg; Sod 184 mg.

Ruby H. Webb, Piedmont

JEAN'S POUND CAKE

1 1/2 cups shortening
3 cups sugar
6 eggs
3 1/2 cups sifted flour
1 teaspoon salt
1 cup milk
1/2 teaspoon lemon extract
1/2 teaspoon vanilla extract

Line bottom of 10-inch tube pan with waxed paper. Grease and lightly flour side of pan. Cream shortening and sugar in mixer bowl until light and fluffy. Beat in eggs 2 at a time. Sift flour and salt together. Add to batter alternately with milk, mixing well after each addition and beginning and ending with flour. Add flavorings. Spoon into prepared cake pan. Bake at 325 degrees for 1 hour and 25 minutes or until cake tests done. Remove to wire rack. Wipe crumbs and grease from pan. Invert pan over cake to cool. Yield: 25 servings.

Approx Per Serving: Cal 285; Prot 3 g; Carbo 37 g; Fiber <1 g; T Fat 14 g; Chol 52 mg; Sod 107 mg.

Jean Rushing, Hornets Nest

JEWEL'S POUND CAKE

1 cup margarine, softened
1 cup shortening
3 cups sugar
6 eggs, beaten
1 tablespoon lemon extract
1 teaspoon vanilla extract
4 or 5 drops of yellow food coloring
3 cups flour
1/2 teaspoon baking powder
1/4 teaspoon salt
1 cup milk

Cream margarine, shortening and sugar in mixer bowl until light and fluffy. Beat in eggs. Mix in flavorings and food coloring. Sift flour, baking powder and salt together. Add to batter alternately with milk, adding 1/2 at a time and mixing well after each addition. Spoon into greased and floured tube pan. Bake at 325 degrees for 1 hour. Reduce oven temperature to 300 degrees. Bake for 25 minutes longer or until cake tests done. Remove to wire rack to cool. Yield: 16 servings.

Approx Per Serving: Cal 485; Prot 5 g; Carbo 56 g; Fiber 1 g; T Fat 27 g; Chol 82 mg; Sod 211 mg.

Jewel H. Ware, Piedmont

ANNA RENA BLAKE'S POUND CAKE

1 cup butter, softened
1 2/3 cups sugar
1 tablespoon almond extract
2 teaspoons vanilla extract
5 eggs
2 cups sifted flour

Cream butter and sugar in mixer bowl until light and fluffy. Add flavorings; mix well. Add eggs 1 at a time, beating well after each addition. Add flour; mix well. Pour into greased and floured 9-inch tube pan. Bake at 300 degrees for 15 minutes. Increase oven temperature to 325 degrees. Bake for 45 minutes longer. Cool in pan for several minutes. Invert onto wire rack; cover with clean towel. Cool completely. Yield: 16 servings.

Approx Per Serving: Cal 260; Prot 4 g; Carbo 32 g; Fiber <1 g; T Fat 13 g; Chol 98 mg; Sod 119 mg.

Mrs. Hugh L. McAulay, Blue Ridge

BUTTER POUND CAKE

1 cup butter, softened
1/2 cup shortening
3 cups sugar
5 eggs
3 1/2 cups flour
1 1/2 cups milk
1 teaspoon vanilla extract
1/2 teaspoon salt
1/2 teaspoon baking powder

Cream butter, shortening and sugar in mixer bowl until light and fluffy. Add eggs 1 at a time, mixing well after each addition. Add flour alternately with milk, beating well after each addition. Mix vanilla, salt and baking powder in small bowl. Stir into batter. Pour into greased tube pan. Bake at 350 degrees for 1 hour and 25 minutes. Cool in pan for several minutes. Invert onto serving plate. For chocolate pound cake, add 4 teaspoons baking cocoa and decrease flour to 3 cups. Yield: 16 servings.

Approx Per Serving: Cal 442; Prot 6 g; Carbo 60 g; Fiber 1 g; T Fat 21 g; Chol 101 mg; Sod 206 mg.

Cheryl Griffin, Raleigh

COMPANY POUND CAKE

3 cups sugar
1 cup butter-flavored shortening
1/2 cup oil
6 eggs, at room temperature
3 cups sifted flour
1/2 teaspoon salt
1/2 teaspoon baking powder
1 cup evaporated milk
1 teaspoon vanilla extract
1 teaspoon lemon extract

Cream sugar and shortening in large mixer bowl until light and fluffy. Beat in oil. Add eggs 1 at a time, beating well after each addition. Mix flour, salt and baking powder in bowl. Add to creamed mixture alternately with evaporated milk, beating well after each addition. Stir in flavorings. Pour into greased and floured 10-inch tube pan. Bake at 300 degrees for 1 1/2 hours or until cake tests done. Do not open oven door until last 5 minutes of baking time. Yield: 16 servings.

Approx Per Serving: Cal 448; Prot 6 g; Carbo 56 g; Fiber 1 g; T Fat 23 g; Chol 85 mg; Sod 121 mg.

Kathryn Henderson, Hornets Nest

CRUSTY POUND CAKE

2 cups plus 2 tablespoons flour
1 cup shortening
2 cups sugar
6 eggs, at room temperature
½ teaspoon salt
1½ teaspoons vanilla extract

Preheat oven to 250 degrees. Sift flour 3 times; measure 2 cups plus 2 tablespoons. Cream shortening and sugar in mixer bowl until light and fluffy. Add eggs alternately with flour, beating well after each addition. Add salt and vanilla; beat well. Pour into greased and floured 10-inch tube pan. Increase oven temperature to 325 degrees. Bake for 1 hour and 10 minutes. Do not open oven door during baking time. Cool in pan for 10 minutes. Invert onto serving plate. Yield: 16 servings.

Approx Per Serving: Cal 301; Prot 4 g; Carbo 38 g; Fiber <1 g; T Fat 15 g; Chol 80 mg; Sod 94 mg.

Gladys Hinson, Independence

EASY POUND CAKE

3 cups flour
3 cups sugar
9 eggs
1½ cups shortening
1 tablespoon (or less) lemon extract

Combine flour, sugar, eggs, shortening and lemon extract in large mixer bowl; mix well. Beat at medium speed for 10 to 15 minutes or until very fluffy. Spoon into greased 10-inch tube pan. Bake at 300 degrees for 1¼ hours or until cake tests done. Cake will be crispy. Yield: 16 servings.

Approx Per Serving: Cal 444; Prot 6 g; Carbo 56 g; Fiber 1 g; T Fat 23 g; Chol 120 mg; Sod 40 mg.

Edna Beach, Blue Ridge

☎ Grease baking pans with the wrapper from margarine or butter.

EASY MOIST POUND CAKE

- 1/2 cup shortening
- 1 cup margarine, softened
- 3 cups sugar
- 5 eggs, at room temperature, beaten
- 3 cups flour
- 1/4 teaspoon baking powder
- 1 cup milk, at room temperature
- 1 teaspoon lemon extract
- 1 teaspoon vanilla extract
- 1 teaspoon butter extract
- 1/4 teaspoon almond extract

Cream shortening and margarine until light. Add sugar gradually, beating until fluffy. Add eggs 1 at a time, beating well after each addition. Mix flour and baking powder in bowl. Add to creamed mixture alternately with milk, beating well after each addition. Stir in flavorings. Pour into greased and floured 10-inch tube pan. Place in cold oven. Set oven temperature at 325 degrees. Bake for 1 hour and 20 minutes. Cool in pan for several minutes. Invert onto serving plate. Yield: 16 servings.

Approx Per Serving: Cal 423; Prot 5 g; Carbo 56 g; Fiber 1 g; T Fat 20 g; Chol 69 mg; Sod 168 mg.

Sarah Barnes, Hornets Nest

FAVORITE POUND CAKE

- 2 cups butter, softened
- 3 cups all-purpose flour
- 1 cup self-rising flour
- 8 eggs
- 2 cups sugar
- 1 teaspoon vanilla extract

Cream butter in mixer bowl until light. Sift all-purpose flour and self-rising flour together 2 times. Add to creamed butter gradually, beating until smooth. Beat eggs in small mixer bowl until frothy. Add sugar gradually, beating until sugar dissolves. Add to flour mixture. Beat at medium speed for 5 minutes. Stir in vanilla. Pour into greased tube pan. Bake at 275 degrees for 1 1/2 hours. Cool in pan for several minutes. Invert onto serving plate. Yield: 16 servings.

Approx Per Serving: Cal 453; Prot 6 g; Carbo 49 g; Fiber 1 g; T Fat 26 g; Chol 169 mg; Sod 313 mg.

Ellen Martin, Raleigh

FIVE-FLAVOR POUND CAKE

1 cup butter, softened
1/2 cup shortening
3 cups sugar
1 teaspoon coconut extract
1 teaspoon rum extract
1 teaspoon vanilla extract
1 teaspoon butter extract
1 teaspoon lemon extract
5 eggs, well beaten
3 cups flour
1/2 teaspoon baking powder
1/4 teaspoon salt
1 cup evaporated milk

Cream butter, shortening and sugar in large mixer bowl until light and fluffy. Add flavorings; beat well. Beat in eggs. Sift flour, baking powder and salt together. Add to creamed mixture alternately with evaporated milk. Spoon into greased and floured 10-inch tube pan. Bake at 325 degrees for 1 1/2 hours. Cool in pan for 10 to 15 minutes. Invert onto serving plate. Yield: 16 servings.

Approx Per Serving: Cal 435; Prot 6 g; Carbo 57 g; Fiber 1 g; T Fat 21 g; Chol 102 mg; Sod 180 mg.

Mrs. F. H. Waldrop, Raleigh

HEAVENLY POUND CAKE

1 1/2 cups butter, softened
1 1-pound package confectioners' sugar
5 eggs
1 teaspoon vanilla extract
1 teaspoon lemon extract
2 cups sifted cake flour

Cream butter and confectioners' sugar in large mixer bowl until light and fluffy. Add eggs 1 at a time, beating well after each addition. Add flavorings alternately with flour, beating well after each addition. Pour into greased and floured tube pan. Bake at 350 degrees for 1 hour. Cool in pan for 10 minutes. Invert onto serving plate. May spread with cream cheese icing if desired. Yield: 16 servings.

Approx Per Serving: Cal 353; Prot 3 g; Carbo 44 g; Fiber <1 g; T Fat 19 g; Chol 113 mg; Sod 167 mg.

Mable Bullard, Central

PERFECT POUND CAKE

8 egg whites
2 2/3 cups sugar
2 cups butter, softened
8 egg yolks, well beaten
3 1/4 cups sifted flour
1 1/2 teaspoons vanilla extract
1/2 cup half and half

Beat egg whites in large mixer bowl until soft peaks form. Add 6 tablespoons sugar gradually, beating until stiff peaks form. Cream remaining sugar and butter in large mixer bowl until light and fluffy. Add egg yolks; beat well. Sift flour 3 times. Mix vanilla with half and half in small bowl. Add to creamed mixture alternately with flour, beating well after each addition. Beat at low speed for 10 minutes. Add egg whites by tablespoonfuls, stirring vigorously. Pour into lightly greased 10-inch tube pan. Bake at 300 degrees for 1 3/4 hours. Invert pan onto wire rack. Cool in pan for several minutes. Loosen edges. Remove to serving plate. Yield: 16 servings.

Approx Per Serving: Cal 467; Prot 6 g; Carbo 52 g; Fiber 1 g; T Fat 27 g; Chol 171 mg; Sod 227 mg.

Peggy Maynard, Piedmont

ALMOND POUND CAKE

1 1-pound package confectioners' sugar
1 1/2 cups margarine, softened
6 eggs, at room temperature
2 cups flour
1 tablespoon vanilla extract
1 tablespoon almond extract

Cream confectioners' sugar and margarine in mixer bowl until light and fluffy. Add eggs 1 at a time, beating well after each addition. Add flour, vanilla extract and almond extract. Beat at medium speed for 10 minutes. Do not underbeat. Pour into greased and floured tube pan. Bake at 300 degrees for 1 to 1 1/2 hours or until cake tests done. Remove to wire rack. Cool completely. Wrap in plastic wrap. May freeze for later use. Yield: 16 servings.

Approx Per Serving: Cal 373; Prot 4 g; Carbo 46 g; Fiber <1 g; T Fat 19 g; Chol 80 mg; Sod 227 mg.

Cindi Hoffner, Hornets Nest

BANANA AND PECAN POUND CAKE

3 eggs
1½ cups oil
2½ cups sugar
1½ cups mashed ripe bananas
½ cup buttermilk
1 tablespoon vanilla extract

3 cups flour
1 teaspoon soda
¾ tablespoon salt
1 cup chopped pecans
1 cup coconut
Frosting

Beat eggs in large mixer bowl until light. Add oil and sugar; beat until fluffy. Combine bananas, buttermilk and vanilla in bowl; mix well. Sift flour, soda and salt together. Add to egg mixture alternately with banana mixture, beating well after each addition. Stir in pecans and coconut. Pour into greased and floured tube pan. Bake at 325 degrees for 1 hour and 20 minutes. Cool in pan for several minutes. Invert onto serving plate. Spread frosting over cooled cake. Yield: 16 servings.

Frosting for Banana and Pecan Pound Cake

½ cup margarine, softened
8 ounces cream cheese, softened

1 1-pound package confectioners' sugar, sifted

Cream margarine and cream cheese in medium mixer bowl until light and fluffy. Add confectioners' sugar gradually, beating until smooth.

Approx Per Serving: Cal 729; Prot 6 g; Carbo 92 g; Fiber 2 g; T Fat 39 g; Chol 56 mg; Sod 494 mg.

Virginia Barnette, Hornets Nest

☎ The most convenient way to measure ½ cup shortening is to place small dollops of shortening in ½ cup water. When water level reaches 1 cup, the shortening measurement below the water level is ½ cup.

BLACK WALNUT POUND CAKE

1 cup butter, softened
3/4 cup shortening
3 cups sugar
6 eggs
4 cups sifted cake flour
1/4 teaspoon salt
1/2 teaspoon baking powder
1 cup milk
1 teaspoon vanilla extract
1 teaspoon black walnut extract
2 tablespoons oil, warmed
2 cups chopped black walnuts

Cream butter, shortening and sugar in large mixer bowl until light and fluffy. Add eggs 1 at a time, beating well after each addition. Sift flour, salt and baking powder together. Reserve 1/4 cup flour mixture. Add remaining flour mixture alternately with milk to creamed mixture, beating well after each addition. Stir in flavorings. Drizzle warm oil over walnuts in bowl. Add reserved flour mixture; toss to coat. Stir into batter. Spoon into greased and floured 10-inch tube pan. Bake at 300 degrees for 1 1/4 hours or until cake tests done. Yield: 16 servings.

Approx Per Serving: Cal 569; Prot 9 g; Carbo 81 g; Fiber 2 g; T Fat 35 g; Chol 115 mg; Sod 213 mg.

Katherine Bailes, Hornets Nest

BROWN SUGAR POUND CAKE

1/2 cup butter, softened
1 cup shortening
1 cup sugar
1 1-pound package light brown sugar
1 1/2 teaspoons vanilla extract
5 eggs
3 1/2 cups sifted cake flour
1/2 teaspoon baking powder
1 teaspoon salt
1 cup evaporated milk
1 cup coconut
1 cup chopped pecans
Glaze (See page 387)

Cream butter and shortening in large mixer bowl until light. Add sugar and brown sugar gradually; beat until fluffy. Add vanilla; mix well. Add eggs 1 at a time, beating well after each addition. Sift flour, baking powder and salt together. Add to creamed mixture alternately with evaporated milk, beating well after each addition. Stir in coconut and pecans. Pour into well-greased and floured 10-inch tube pan. Bake at 325 degrees for

1 hour and 40 minutes. Cool in pan for several minutes. Invert onto serving plate. Spread glaze over cake. Yield: 16 servings.

Glaze for Brown Sugar Pound Cake

1/3 cup butter
1 cup packed brown sugar
1/4 cup evaporated milk
1 teaspoon vanilla extract

Melt butter in small saucepan. Add brown sugar; stir until dissolved. Stir in evaporated milk. Bring to a rolling boil, stirring constantly. Boil for 2 minutes, stirring constantly; remove from heat. Cool. Stir in vanilla. Beat until smooth.

Approx Per Serving: Cal 604; Prot 6 g; Carbo 75 g; Fiber 2 g; T Fat 32 g; Chol 87 mg; Sod 286 mg.

Brenda Brown, Foot Hills

CHERRY AND PECAN POUND CAKE

1 1/2 cups shortening
3 cups sugar
6 eggs
3 3/4 cups flour
3/4 cup milk
1/2 teaspoon vanilla extract
1 cup chopped pecans
1 4-ounce jar maraschino cherries, chopped
3 ounces cream cheese, softened
1/4 cup margarine, softened
1 1-pound package confectioners' sugar
1 teaspoon vanilla extract
1/2 4-ounce jar maraschino cherries, chopped
1/2 cup chopped pecans

Cream shortening and sugar in large mixer bowl until light and fluffy. Add eggs 1 at a time, beating well after each addition. Add flour alternately with milk, beating well after each addition. Stir in 1/2 teaspoon vanilla and 1 cup pecans. Fold in 4 ounces cherries. Pour into greased and floured tube pan. Bake at 300 degrees for 2 hours. Cool in pan for several minutes. Invert onto serving plate. Beat cream cheese and margarine in mixer bowl until light. Add confectioners' sugar and remaining 1 teaspoon vanilla; beat until fluffy. Fold in remaining cherries and 1/2 cup pecans. Spread over cake. Yield: 16 servings.

Approx Per Serving: Cal 721; Prot 7 g; Carbo 100 g; Fiber 2 g; T Fat 34 g; Chol 87 mg; Sod 82 mg.

Evelyn N. Goodman, Hornets Nest

BLACK WALNUT AND CHOCOLATE POUND CAKE

1 cup butter, softened
1/2 cup shortening
3 cups sugar
5 eggs
3 cups flour
1/2 teaspoon baking powder
5 tablespoons baking cocoa
1/2 teaspoon salt
1 cup milk
1 teaspoon black walnut extract
1 ounce unsweetened chocolate, melted
1/2 cup chopped black walnuts

Cream butter, shortening and sugar in mixer bowl until light and fluffy. Add eggs 1 at a time, beating well after each addition. Sift flour, baking powder, cocoa and salt together 3 times. Add to creamed mixture alternately with milk, beating well after each addition. Stir in black walnut extract and chocolate. Fold in walnuts. Pour into well-greased tube pan. Bake at 275 degrees for 1 hour and 55 minutes. Do not open oven door during baking time. Cool in pan for several minutes. Invert onto serving plate. Yield: 16 servings.

Approx Per Serving: Cal 459; Prot 6 g; Carbo 58 g; Fiber 2 g; T Fat 24 g; Chol 100 mg; Sod 203 mg.

Mary Anne Long, Independence

CHOCOLATE POUND CAKE

1 cup butter, softened
1/2 cup shortening
3 cups sugar
5 eggs
3 cups cake flour
1/2 teaspoon baking powder
5 tablespoons (heaping) baking cocoa
1 cup milk
2 teaspoons vanilla extract
Frosting (See page 389)

Cream butter, shortening and sugar in large mixer bowl until light and fluffy. Add eggs 1 at a time, beating well after each addition. Sift flour, baking powder and cocoa together. Add to creamed mixture alternately with milk. Stir in vanilla. Pour into greased and floured 10-inch tube pan. Bake at 350 degrees for 1 hour and 20 minutes. Cool in pan for several minutes. Invert onto serving plate. Spread frosting over cake. May omit frosting if preferred. Yield: 16 servings.

Frosting for Chocolate Pound Cake

3 ounces unsweetened chocolate
1/2 cup margarine, softened
3 tablespoons milk
1 egg, beaten
1 1-pound package confectioners' sugar
1 teaspoon vanilla extract

Bring chocolate, margarine and milk to a boil in medium saucepan, stirring constantly; remove from heat. Stir a small amount of hot mixture into beaten egg; stir egg into hot mixture. Add confectioners' sugar and vanilla. Beat until smooth and of spreading consistency.

Approx Per Serving: Cal 634; Prot 6 g; Carbo 91 g; Fiber 2 g; T Fat 30 g; Chol 113 mg; Sod 210 mg.

Callie W. Whitener, Foot Hills

BASIC CHOCOLATE POUND CAKE

1 cup margarine, softened
1/2 cup shortening
3 cups sugar
5 eggs
3 cups flour
1/2 cup baking cocoa
1/2 teaspoon baking powder
1/2 teaspoon salt
1 cup milk
1 tablespoon vanilla extract

Cream margarine, shortening and sugar in mixer bowl until light and fluffy. Beat in eggs 1 at a time. Sift flour, cocoa, baking powder and salt together. Add to creamed mixture alternately with milk, mixing well after each addition. Mix in vanilla. Spoon into greased and floured 10-inch tube pan. Bake at 325 degrees for 1 1/4 hours. Remove to wire rack to cool. Yield: 16 servings.

Approx Per Serving: Cal 432; Prot 5 g; Carbo 58 g; Fiber 1 g; T Fat 21 g; Chol 69 mg; Sod 241 mg.

Patricia Goodman, Hornets Nest

☎ Store flour in airtight container. Whole wheat flour should be stored in refrigerator because it contains natural oils.

FAVORITE CHOCOLATE POUND CAKE

1/2 cup shortening
1 cup margarine, softened
2 1/2 cups sugar
5 eggs
3 cups cake flour
1/2 cup baking cocoa
1/2 teaspoon baking powder
1/4 teaspoon salt
1 cup milk
1 teaspoon vanilla extract
1 cup chopped walnuts

Cream shortening, margarine and sugar in mixer bowl until light and fluffy. Add eggs 1 at a time, mixing well after each addition. Sift flour, cocoa, baking powder and salt together. Add to creamed mixture alternately with milk, mixing well after each addition. Mix in vanilla and walnuts. Spoon into greased and floured tube pan. Bake at 325 degrees for 1 1/2 hours. Remove to wire rack to cool. Yield: 16 servings.

Approx Per Serving: Cal 435; Prot 5 g; Carbo 51 g; Fiber 2 g; T Fat 25 g; Chol 69 mg; Sod 208 mg.

Faye Thomas, Central

OLD-FASHIONED CHOCOLATE POUND CAKE

1 cup margarine, softened
1/2 cup shortening
3 cups sugar
5 eggs
3 cups sifted flour
1/2 teaspoon baking powder
1/2 cup baking cocoa
1/4 teaspoon salt
1 1/4 cups milk
1 teaspoon vanilla extract

Cream margarine, shortening and sugar in mixer bowl until fluffy. Add eggs 1 at a time, mixing well after each addition. Sift flour, baking powder, cocoa and salt together. Add to creamed mixture alternately with milk, mixing well after each addition. Mix in vanilla. Spoon into greased and floured tube pan. Bake at 325 degrees for 1 1/2 hours. Remove to wire rack to cool. May bake in 3 layers if preferred. Yield: 16 servings.

Approx Per Serving: Cal 425; Prot 5 g; Carbo 55 g; Fiber 1 g; T Fat 21 g; Chol 106 mg; Sod 208 mg.

Beatrice Whicker, Salem

DOUBLE CHOCOLATE POUND CAKE

1 1/2 cups butter, softened
1/3 cup shortening
3 cups sugar
5 eggs
3 cups flour
3/4 cup baking cocoa
1/2 teaspoon baking powder
1 teaspoon salt
1 cup milk
1 teaspoon vanilla extract
Frosting

Cream butter, shortening and sugar in large mixer bowl until light and fluffy. Add eggs 1 at a time, beating well after each addition. Mix flour, cocoa, baking powder and salt in bowl. Add to creamed mixture alternately with mixture of milk and vanilla, beating well after each addition. Pour into well-greased and floured 10-inch tube pan. Bake at 300 degrees for 1 1/4 hours. Cool in pan for several minutes. Invert onto serving plate. Spread frosting over cake. Yield: 16 servings.

Frosting for Double Chocolate Pound Cake

1 1-pound package confectioners' sugar
2 tablespoons (heaping) baking cocoa
1/8 teaspoon salt
1/2 cup melted butter
1 egg
1 teaspoon vanilla extract

Combine confectioners' sugar, baking cocoa, salt, melted butter and egg in mixer bowl; beat well. Stir in vanilla.

Approx Per Serving: Cal 654; Prot 6 g; Carbo 92 g; Fiber 2 g; T Fat 31 g; Chol 144 mg; Sod 389 mg.

Bertie Frye, Hornets Nest

☎ Allow for the variation in oven temperatures by setting the timer for the minimum time indicated in the recipe. Test by inserting a cake tester or toothpick into the center of the cake. If the tester comes out clean, the cake is done.

LOW-CHOLESTEROL CHOCOLATE POUND CAKE

6 egg whites, at room temperature
1¼ cups corn oil margarine, softened
3 cups sugar
3 cups sifted flour
1 teaspoon baking powder
½ teaspoon salt
½ cup baking cocoa
1¼ cups skim milk, at room temperature
1 teaspoon vanilla extract

Beat egg whites in medium mixer bowl until stiff peaks form. Cream margarine and sugar in large mixer bowl until light and fluffy. Sift flour, baking powder, salt and baking cocoa together 3 times. Add to creamed mixture alternately with mixture of milk and vanilla, beating well after each addition. Fold in egg whites gently. Pour into 10-inch tube pan sprayed with nonstick cooking spray. Bake at 300 degrees for 1 hour and 25 minutes. Cool in pan for several minutes. Invert onto serving plate. Yield: 16 servings.

Approx Per Serving: Cal 394; Prot 5 g; Carbo 56 g; Fiber 1 g; T Fat 18 g; Chol <1 mg; Sod 118 mg.

Faye Brantley, Hornets Nest

RED VELVET POUND CAKE

1 cup shortening
3 cups sugar
7 eggs
3 cups sifted flour
1 teaspoon baking powder
½ teaspoon salt
7 ounces milk
3 1-ounce bottles of red food coloring
2 teaspoons vanilla extract
Frosting (See page 393)

Cream shortening and sugar in mixer bowl until light and fluffy. Add eggs 1 at a time, beating well after each addition. Mix flour, baking powder and salt in bowl. Add to creamed mixture alternately with milk, beating well after each addition. Mix in food coloring and vanilla. Pour into well-greased and floured tube pan. Bake at 325 degrees for 1½ hours. Cool in pan for several minutes. Invert onto serving plate. Spread frosting over cake. Garnish with chopped pecans. Yield: 16 servings.

Frosting for Red Velvet Pound Cake

1 1-pound package confectioners' sugar
1/2 cup margarine
8 ounces cream cheese, softened
2 teaspoons vanilla extract

Cream confectioners' sugar, margarine and cream cheese in mixer bowl until light and fluffy. Stir in vanilla.

Approx Per Serving: Cal 591; Prot 6 g; Carbo 84 g; Fiber 1 g; T Fat 27 g; Chol 110 mg; Sod 234 mg.

Nora Freeman, Foot Hills

BASIC RED VELVET POUND CAKE

1 cup shortening
3 cups sugar
7 eggs
1 cup milk
3 cups flour
1/4 teaspoon salt
2 teaspoons vanilla extract
1 1-ounce bottle of red food coloring

Cream shortening and sugar in mixer bowl until light and fluffy. Beat in eggs 1 at a time. Add milk alternately with flour, salt and vanilla, mixing well after each addition. Mix in food coloring. Spoon into greased and floured tube pan. Bake at 325 degrees for 1 hour and 45 minutes. Remove to wire rack to cool. Yield: 16 servings.

Approx Per Serving: Cal 386; Prot 6 g; Carbo 56 g; Fiber 1 g; T Fat 16 g; Chol 95 mg; Sod 71 mg.

Virginia Barnette, Hornets Nest

☎ You can make an emergency substitute for confectioners' sugar by processing a small amount of granulated sugar at a time in the blender.

BERTIE'S RED VELVET POUND CAKE

1½ cups shortening
3 cups sugar
7 eggs
3 cups flour
½ teaspoon baking powder
½ teaspoon salt
1 cup milk
1 1-ounce bottle of red food coloring
2 teaspoons vanilla extract
Frosting

Cream shortening and sugar in mixer bowl until light and fluffy. Beat in eggs 1 at a time. Combine flour, baking powder and salt in small bowl. Add to creamed mixture alternately with milk, mixing well after each addition. Mix in food coloring and vanilla. Spoon into greased and floured 10-inch tube pan. Bake at 350 degrees for 1 hour. Remove to wire rack to cool. Spread with frosting. Yield: 16 servings.

Frosting for Bertie's Red Velvet Pound Cake

1 teaspoon vanilla extract
1 1-pound package confectioners' sugar
8 ounces cream cheese, softened

Combine vanilla, confectioners' sugar and cream cheese in mixer bowl; mix until smooth and creamy.

Approx Per Serving: Cal 605; Prot 7 g; Carbo 85 g; Fiber 1 g; T Fat 27 g; Chol 111 mg; Sod 158 mg.

Bertie Frye, Hornets Nest

JO ANN'S RED VELVET POUND CAKE

1 cup margarine, softened
1/2 cup shortening
3 cups sugar
5 eggs
3 cups flour
1/4 teaspoon baking powder
1/2 cup baking cocoa
1/8 teaspoon salt
1 cup milk
1 teaspoon vanilla extract
2 1-ounce bottles of red food coloring
Frosting

Cream margarine, shortening and sugar in mixer bowl until light and fluffy. Beat in eggs 1 at a time. Combine flour, baking powder, cocoa and salt in small bowl. Add to creamed mixture alternately with milk, mixing well after each addition. Mix in vanilla and food coloring. Spoon into greased and floured tube pan. Bake at 300 degrees for 1 1/2 hours. Remove to wire rack to cool. Spread with frosting. May bake in heart-shaped pan for a Valentine cake. Yield: 16 servings.

Frosting for Jo Ann's Red Velvet Pound Cake

1/2 cup margarine, softened
8 ounces cream cheese, softened
1 1-pound package confectioners' sugar
1 teaspoon vanilla extract

Cream margarine and cream cheese in mixer bowl until light. Add confectioners' sugar and vanilla; beat until smooth.

Approx Per Serving: Cal 641; Prot 7 g; Carbo 86 g; Fiber 1 g; T Fat 31 g; Chol 84 mg; Sod 278 mg.

Jo Ann Goins, Hornets Nest

RED VELVET COCOA POUND CAKE

1 cup margarine, softened
1/2 cup shortening
3 cups sugar
5 eggs
3 cups flour
1 teaspoon baking powder
1/2 teaspoon salt
1/2 cup baking cocoa
1 cup milk
1 1-ounce bottle of red food coloring
1 teaspoon vanilla extract

Cream margarine, shortening and sugar in mixer bowl until light and fluffy. Add eggs 1 at a time, beating well after each addition. Mix flour, baking powder, salt and baking cocoa together. Add to creamed mixture alternately with milk, beating well after each addition. Mix in food coloring and vanilla. Pour into greased and floured tube pan. Bake at 350 degrees for 1 hour or until cake tests done. Cool in pan. Invert onto serving plate. Yield: 16 servings.

Approx Per Serving: Cal 430; Prot 5 g; Carbo 58 g; Fiber 1 g; T Fat 21 g; Chol 69 mg; Sod 251 mg.

Bonnie Ayers, Salem

SOUR CREAM AND CHOCOLATE POUND CAKE

1 cup butter, softened
2 cups sugar
2 eggs, at room temperature
2 ounces unsweetened chocolate, melted
2 teaspoons vanilla extract
2 1/2 cups flour
2 teaspoons soda
1/4 teaspoon salt
1 cup sour cream, at room temperature
1 cup boiling water

Cream butter and sugar in mixer bowl until light and fluffy. Add eggs 1 at a time, beating well after each addition. Stir in melted chocolate and vanilla. Mix flour, soda and salt in bowl. Add to chocolate mixture alternately with sour cream, beating well after each addition. Stir in boiling water. Pour into greased and floured 10-inch tube pan. Bake at 325 degrees for 1 1/4 hours. Cool in pan. Invert onto serving plate. Yield: 16 servings.

Approx Per Serving: Cal 329; Prot 4 g; Carbo 42 g; Fiber 1 g; T Fat 17 g; Chol 64 mg; Sod 250 mg.

Anne Godwin, Independence
Katie Grist, Independence

COCONUT POUND CAKE

1/2 cup margarine, softened
1 cup shortening
3 cups sugar
5 eggs
3 cups flour
1/2 teaspoon baking powder
1 cup milk
1 cup coconut
1 teaspoon vanilla extract

Cream margarine and shortening in mixer bowl until light. Add sugar; beat until fluffy. Add eggs 1 at a time, beating well after each addition. Mix flour and baking powder in bowl. Add to creamed mixture alternately with milk, beating well after each addition. Stir in coconut and vanilla. Pour into greased and floured tube pan. Bake at 325 degrees for 1 1/4 hours. Cool in pan for several minutes. Invert onto serving plate. Yield: 16 servings.

Approx Per Serving: Cal 451; Prot 5 g; Carbo 58 g; Fiber 1 g; T Fat 23 g; Chol 69 mg; Sod 118 mg.

Martha G. Bridges, Hornets Nest

PRIZE-WINNING COCONUT POUND CAKE

2 1/2 cups sugar
1 1/2 cups shortening
5 eggs
3 cups flour
1 teaspoon baking powder
1 cup milk
1 teaspoon coconut extract
1 cup coconut

Cream sugar and shortening in mixer bowl until light and fluffy. Add eggs 1 at a time, beating well after each addition. Mix flour and baking powder in bowl. Add to creamed mixture alternately with milk, beating well after each addition. Stir in coconut extract and coconut. Pour into greased and floured tube pan. Place in cold oven. Set oven temperature at 325 degrees. Bake for 1 1/4 hours. Cool in pan for several minutes. Invert onto serving plate. Yield: 16 servings.

Approx Per Serving: Cal 432; Prot 5 g; Carbo 52 g; Fiber 1 g; T Fat 23 g; Chol 69 mg; Sod 62 mg.

Phyllis E. Jones, Independence

RICH COCONUT POUND CAKE

3 cups sugar
1 cup butter, softened
1 cup shortening
7 egg yolks
3 1/4 cups flour
1 teaspoon baking powder
1/8 teaspoon salt
1 cup milk
1 1-ounce bottle of coconut extract
7 egg whites, stiffly beaten
1 cup coconut
Glaze

Cream sugar, butter and shortening in large mixer bowl until light and fluffy. Add egg yolks; beat well. Sift flour, baking powder and salt together. Add to creamed mixture alternately with milk, beating well after each addition. Add coconut extract; mix well. Fold in egg whites and coconut. Pour into greased and floured 10-inch tube pan. Place in cold oven. Set oven temperature at 325 degrees. Bake for 1 1/2 hours. Cool in pan for several minutes. Invert onto serving plate. Drizzle glaze over top and side of cake. Yield: 24 servings.

Glaze for Rich Coconut Pound Cake

3 tablespoons shortening
5 tablespoons milk
2 cups confectioners' sugar
1/2 1-ounce bottle of coconut extract
1/2 cup coconut

Melt shortening in milk in saucepan, stirring constantly: remove from heat. Add confectioners' sugar, coconut extract and coconut; mix well.

Approx Per Serving: Cal 407; Prot 4 g; Carbo 50 g; Fiber 1 g; T Fat 22 g; Chol 85 mg; Sod 114 mg.

Betty Sigmon, Foot Hills

☎ Read recipes all the way through before you start to be sure you have all the required ingredients and plenty of time to complete it.

COLD OVEN POUND CAKE

1 cup margarine, softened
1/2 cup shortening
3 cups sugar
5 eggs
1 teaspoon vanilla extract
1 teaspoon lemon extract
3 cups cake flour
1 cup milk

Cream margarine and shortening in mixer bowl until light. Add sugar; beat until fluffy. Add eggs 1 at a time, beating well after each addition. Add flavorings. Add flour to creamed mixture alternately with milk, beating well after each addition. Beat until light and creamy. Pour into greased and floured 10-inch tube pan. Place in cold oven. Set oven temperature at 325 degrees. Bake for 1 hour. Increase temperature to 350 degrees. Bake for 30 minutes longer. Do not open oven door during baking time. Cool in pan on wire rack for 15 minutes; remove to wire rack to cool completely. Yield: 16 servings.

Approx Per Serving: Cal 412; Prot 4 g; Carbo 55 g; Fiber 1 g; T Fat 20 g; Chol 69 mg; Sod 163 mg.

Ada B. Lehardy, Raleigh

* *Betty Bryant of Hornets Nest* and *Patricia Goodman of Hornets Nest* add 1 teaspoon almond extract.

* *Anne Godwin of Independence* uses 2 teaspoons lemon extract and omits vanilla extract.

CREAM CHEESE POUND CAKE

1 cup margarine, softened
1/2 cup butter, softened
8 ounces cream cheese, softened
3 cups sugar
6 eggs
3 cups sifted cake flour
2 teaspoons vanilla extract

Cream first 3 ingredients in mixer bowl. Add sugar gradually, beating until light and fluffy. Add eggs 1 at a time, beating well after each addition. Add flour; mix well. Stir in vanilla. Pour into greased 10-inch tube pan. Bake at 325 degrees for 1 3/4 hours or until cake tests done. Cool in pan for 10 minutes. Yield: 16 servings.

Approx Per Serving: Cal 443; Prot 5 g; Carbo 53 g; Fiber 1 g; T Fat 24 g; Chol 111 mg; Sod 251 mg.

Phyllis E. Jones, Independence

CRUSTY CREAM CHEESE POUND CAKE

1 cup butter, softened
½ cup shortening
3 cups sugar
8 ounces cream cheese, softened
3 cups sifted cake flour
6 eggs
1 tablespoon vanilla extract

Cream butter and shortening in mixer bowl until light. Add sugar gradually, beating at medium speed until fluffy. Beat in cream cheese. Add flour alternately with eggs, beginning and ending with flour and mixing well after each addition. Stir in vanilla. Spoon into greased and floured 10-inch tube pan. Bake at 325 degrees for 1¼ hours or until wooden pick inserted near center comes out clean. Cool in pan for 10 minutes. Remove to wire rack to cool completely. Yield: 16 servings.

Approx Per Serving: Cal 450; Prot 5 g; Carbo 52 g; Fiber 1 g; T Fat 25 g; Chol 126 mg; Sod 166 mg.

Jo Litaker, Independence

BASIC CREAM CHEESE POUND CAKE

1½ cups butter, softened
8 ounces cream cheese, softened
3 cups sugar
6 eggs
3 cups sifted cake flour
Salt to taste
1½ teaspoons vanilla extract

Cream butter, cream cheese and sugar in mixer bowl until light and fluffy. Add eggs 1 at a time, mixing well after each addition. Stir in flour, salt and vanilla. Spoon into greased tube pan. Bake at 325 degrees for 1½ hours or until cake tests done. Yield: 16 servings.

Approx Per Serving: Cal 446; Prot 5 g; Carbo 52 g; Fiber 0 g; T Fat 25 g; Chol 124 mg; Sod 172 mg.

Joyce T. Smith, Central

CREAM CHEESE AND PECAN POUND CAKE

½ cup chopped pecans
1½ cups butter, softened
8 ounces cream cheese, softened
3 cups sugar
6 eggs
3 cups cake flour
⅛ teaspoon salt
1½ teaspoons vanilla extract
1 cup chopped pecans

Sprinkle ½ cup pecans in greased and floured 10-inch tube pan. Cream butter and cream cheese in mixer bowl until light. Add sugar; beat until fluffy. Add eggs 1 at a time, beating well after each addition. Add flour and salt; mix well. Stir in vanilla and remaining 1 cup pecans. Pour into prepared pan. Bake at 325 degrees for 1½ hours or until cake tests done. Cool in pan for 10 minutes. Invert onto serving plate. Yield: 16 servings.

Approx Per Serving: Cal 526; Prot 6 g; Carbo 56 g; Fiber 1 g; T Fat 32 g; Chol 142 mg; Sod 231 mg.

Marjorie Sapp, Independence

HEART-HEALTHY LEMON POUND CAKE

1 2-layer package Duncan Hines lemon supreme cake mix
1 4-ounce package lemon instant pudding mix
1 cup water
⅓ cup oil
1 cup egg substitute

Combine all ingredients in large mixer bowl; mix well. Beat at low speed until blended. Beat at medium speed for 2 minutes. Pour into greased and floured bundt pan. Bake at 350 degrees for 55 minutes. Cool in pan for 25 minutes. Invert onto serving plate. For chocolate pound cake, substitute Duncan Hines chocolate cake mix, one 4-ounce package chocolate instant pudding mix or one 4-ounce package vanilla instant pudding mix and 2 tablespoons baking cocoa, 1¼ cups water and ½ cup oil. This only works with Duncan Hines cake mixes. This is a heart-healthy modification of a standard recipe which is no-cholesterol, low-fat and tastes good. Yield: 16 servings.

Approx Per Serving: Cal 210; Prot 3 g; Carbo 34 g; Fiber <1 g; T Fat 7 g; Chol 0 mg; Sod 265 mg.

Winifred T. Nicholas, Independence

LEMON POUND CAKE

1 cup butter, softened
3 cups sugar
5 eggs
3 cups flour
1 cup milk
1 teaspoon vanilla extract
1 teaspoon lemon extract

Cream butter and sugar in mixer bowl until light and fluffy. Add eggs 1 at a time, beating well after each addition. Add flour alternately with milk, beating well after each addition. Stir in flavorings. Pour into greased tube pan. Bake at 350 degrees for 1 1/4 hours. Cool in pan for several minutes. Invert onto serving plate. Yield: 16 servings.

Approx Per Serving: Cal 366; Prot 5 g; Carbo 56 g; Fiber 1 g; T Fat 14 g; Chol 100 mg; Sod 126 mg.

Chris Roberts, Central

LEMON BUTTERMILK POUND CAKE

1 1/2 cups butter, softened
2 1/2 cups sugar
4 eggs
3 1/2 cups flour
1/2 teaspoon salt
1/2 teaspoon soda
1 cup buttermilk
2 tablespoons lemon extract

Cream butter and sugar in mixer bowl until light and fluffy. Add eggs 1 at a time, beating well after each addition. Sift flour, salt and soda together. Add to creamed mixture alternately with buttermilk, beating well after each addition. Stir in lemon extract. Pour into greased and floured tube pan. Bake at 325 degrees for 1 1/4 hours. Cool in pan. Invert onto serving plate. Yield: 16 servings.

Approx Per Serving: Cal 398; Prot 5 g; Carbo 53 g; Fiber 1 g; T Fat 19 g; Chol 100 mg; Sod 272 mg.

Wilhelmenia Cofield, Hornets Nest

LOW-CHOLESTEROL POUND CAKE

1 cup corn oil margarine, softened
1/2 cup shortening
2 3/4 cups sugar
1 egg white
1 cup egg substitute
3 3/4 cups sifted flour
1 cup skim milk
1/2 teaspoon butter extract
1 tablespoon vanilla extract

Cream margarine, shortening and sugar in mixer bowl until light and fluffy. Add egg white; beat well. Add egg substitute 1/4 cup at a time, beating well after each addition. Add flour alternately with milk, beating well after each addition. Add flavorings. Pour into greased and floured 10-inch tube pan. Bake at 350 degrees for 1 hour and 20 minutes. Cool in pan for several minutes. Invert onto serving plate. May use 2 greased and floured 9x13-inch cake pans in place of tube pan. Bake at 325 degrees for 25 minutes. Yield: 16 servings.

Approx Per Serving: Cal 405; Prot 5 g; Carbo 56 g; Fiber 1 g; T Fat 18 g; Chol <1 mg; Sod 168 mg.

Betty S. Bryant, Hornets Nest

PINEAPPLE POUND CAKE

1 1/2 **cups margarine, softened**
1/3 **cup shortening**
2 3/4 **cups sugar**
5 **eggs**
3 **cups flour**
1/2 **teaspoon baking powder**
1/4 **teaspoon salt**
1 **cup crushed pineapple**
1/2 **cup margarine, softened**
1 1-**pound package confectioners' sugar**
1/2 **cup crushed pineapple**

Cream 1 1/2 cups margarine, shortening and sugar in mixer bowl until light and fluffy. Add eggs 1 at a time, beating well after each addition. Combine flour, baking powder and salt in bowl. Add to creamed mixture alternately with 1 cup pineapple, mixing well after each addition. Pour into greased and floured tube pan. Bake at 300 degrees for 1 hour and 10 minutes. Cool in pan for several minutes. Invert onto serving plate. Cream remaining 1/2 cup margarine and confectioners' sugar in mixer bowl until light and fluffy. Fold in remaining 1/2 cup pineapple. Spoon over warm cake. Yield: 16 servings.

Approx Per Serving: Cal 633; Prot 5 g; Carbo 91 g; Fiber 1 g; T Fat 29 g; Chol 67 mg; Sod 335 mg.

Bertie Frye, Hornets Nest

SEVEN-UP POUND CAKE

1/2 cup margarine, softened
1/2 cup shortening
2 1/2 cups sugar
5 eggs
3 cups flour
1 cup 7-Up
1 teaspoon vanilla extract
1 teaspoon lemon extract
Frosting

Cream margarine and shortening in mixer bowl until light. Add sugar; beat until fluffy. Add eggs 1 at a time, beating well after each addition. Add flour alternately with 7-Up, beating well after each addition. Stir in flavorings. Pour into greased and floured tube pan. Bake at 325 degrees for 1 hour and 20 minutes. Cool in pan for several minutes. Invert onto serving plate. Spread frosting over cooled cake. Yield: 16 servings.

Frosting for Seven-Up Pound Cake

1/2 cup melted margarine, cooled
8 ounces cream cheese, softened
1 1-pound package confectioners' sugar
1 teaspoon vanilla extract

Cream margarine and cream cheese in mixer bowl until light. Add confectioners' sugar gradually, beating until fluffy. Stir in vanilla.

Approx Per Serving: Cal 577; Prot 6 g; Carbo 85 g; Fiber 1 g; T Fat 25 g; Chol 82 mg; Sod 200 mg.

Beatrice S. Whicker, Salem

☎ If a toothpick is too short to test a cake for doneness, use a piece of uncooked spaghetti.

UNFROSTED SEVEN-UP POUND CAKE

1 cup butter, softened
1/2 cup shortening
3 cups flour
3 cups sugar
5 eggs
1 cup 7-Up
1 teaspoon vanilla extract

Combine butter, shortening, flour, sugar, eggs, 7-Up and vanilla in mixer bowl. Beat for 20 minutes. Spoon into greased and floured tube pan. Bake at 325 degrees for 1 hour or until cake springs back when lightly pressed with finger. Do not underbake. Remove to wire rack to cool. Yield: 16 servings.

Approx Per Serving: Cal 420; Prot 4 g; Carbo 57 g; Fiber 1 g; T Fat 20 g; Chol 98 mg; Sod 121 mg.

Ruth B. Bumgardner, Hornets Nest

SPECIAL SEVEN-UP POUND CAKE

1/2 cup shortening
1 cup margarine, softened
3 cups sugar
5 eggs
3 1/2 cups flour
1 1/2 cups 7-Up
1 teaspoon vanilla extract
1 1/2 teaspoons lemon extract
Frosting

Cream shortening, margarine and sugar in mixer bowl until light and fluffy. Beat in eggs 1 at a time. Add flour alternately with 7-Up, mixing well after each addition. Stir in flavorings. Spoon into greased and floured tube pan. Bake at 325 degrees for 1 hour and 20 minutes. Remove to wire rack to cool. Spread with frosting. Yield: 16 servings.

Frosting for Special Seven-Up Pound Cake

1/4 cup margarine, softened
4 ounces cream cheese, softened
2 cups confectioners' sugar
1/2 teaspoon vanilla extract

Cream margarine and cream cheese in mixer bowl until light. Add confectioners' sugar and vanilla; beat until smooth.

Approx Per Serving: Cal 545; Prot 5 g; Carbo 76 g; Fiber 1 g; T Fat 25 g; Chol 74 mg; Sod 214 mg.

Martha G. Bridges, Hornets Nest

SOUR CREAM POUND CAKE

½ cup shortening
1 cup margarine, softened
3 cups sugar
5 eggs
3 cups flour
1 teaspoon baking powder
½ cup milk
1 cup sour cream
1 teaspoon lemon extract
1½ teaspoons vanilla extract
Frosting

Cream shortening, margarine and sugar in mixer bowl until light and fluffy. Add eggs 1 at a time, beating well after each addition. Sift flour and baking powder together. Add to creamed mixture alternately with milk and sour cream, beating well after each addition. Stir in flavorings. Pour into greased and floured tube pan. Bake at 325 degrees for 1½ hours. Cool in pan for several minutes. Invert onto serving plate. Spread frosting over cake. Yield: 16 servings.

Frosting for Sour Cream Pound Cake

½ cup margarine, softened
3 ounces cream cheese, softened
1 1-pound package confectioners' sugar
Juice of 1 lemon

Cream margarine and cream cheese in mixer bowl until light. Add confectioners' sugar gradually, beating until fluffy. Stir in lemon juice.

Approx Per Serving: Cal 651; Prot 6 g; Carbo 95 g; Fiber 1 g; T Fat 31 g; Chol 80 mg; Sod 271 mg.

Jo Ann Goins, Hornets Nest

WHIPPING CREAM POUND CAKE

3 cups cake flour
1/8 teaspoon salt
1 cup shortening
3 cups sugar
6 eggs
1 cup whipping cream
1 teaspoon vanilla extract
1 teaspoon orange extract
Frosting

Sift flour and salt together. Cream shortening and sugar in mixer bowl until light and fluffy. Add eggs 1 at a time, beating well after each addition. Add flour mixture alternately with whipping cream, beating well after each addition. Stir in flavorings. Pour into greased and floured 10-inch tube pan. Bake at 300 degrees for 1 1/2 hours. Cool in pan for several minutes. Invert onto serving plate. Spread frosting over cooled cake. Yield: 16 servings.

Frosting for Whipping Cream Pound Cake

1/4 cup margarine, softened
8 ounces cream cheese, softened
1 1-pound package confectioners' sugar
1 teaspoon vanilla extract

Cream margarine and cream cheese in mixer bowl until light. Add confectioners' sugar gradually, beating until fluffy. Add vanilla; beat until smooth.

Approx Per Serving: Cal 690; Prot 5 g; Carbo 93 g; Fiber 1 g; T Fat 28 g; Chol 116 mg; Sod 125 mg.

Faye Thomas, Central

PRUNE CAKE

2 cups flour
1 teaspoon soda
1 teaspoon nutmeg
1 teaspoon cinnamon
1 teaspoon allspice
1 1/2 cups sugar
1 cup oil

3 eggs
1 cup buttermilk
1 teaspoon vanilla extract
1 cup chopped pecans
1 cup chopped, seeded cooked prunes
Frosting

Mix flour, soda, nutmeg, cinnamon and allspice in bowl. Blend sugar and oil in large mixer bowl. Add eggs; beat well. Add flour mixture alternately with buttermilk, beating well after each addition. Stir in vanilla, pecans and prunes. Pour into buttered 9x13-inch cake pan. Bake at 300 degrees for 45 minutes or until brown. Pour frosting over hot cake. Yield: 15 servings.

Frosting for Prune Cake

1 cup sugar
1/2 teaspoon soda
1 tablespoon light corn syrup

1/4 cup butter, softened
1/2 cup buttermilk
1/2 teaspoon vanilla extract

Combine sugar, soda, corn syrup, butter, buttermilk and vanilla in small saucepan; mix well. Cook over medium heat to 234 to 240 degrees on candy thermometer, soft-ball stage.

Approx Per Serving: Cal 444; Prot 5 g; Carbo 54 g; Fiber 2 g; T Fat 25 g; Chol 52 mg; Sod 150 mg.

Willie Womble, Raleigh

SAUCY PRUNE CAKE

3 eggs
1 cup oil
2 cups sugar
1 cup buttermilk
1 teaspoon soda
2 cups flour
1 teaspoon baking powder
1 teaspoon nutmeg
1 teaspoon cinnamon
1/2 teaspoon cloves
1 cup chopped pecans
1 cup chopped cooked prunes
1/4 cup prune juice
1 teaspoon vanilla extract
Sauce

Combine eggs, oil and sugar in large mixer bowl; mix well. Mix buttermilk and soda in cup. Sift flour, baking powder, nutmeg, cinnamon and cloves into bowl. Stir in pecans. Add flour mixture to egg mixture alternately with buttermilk, mixing well after each addition. Mix in prunes, prune juice and vanilla. Spoon into greased tube pan. Bake at 325 degrees for 45 to 50 minutes or until toothpick inserted near center comes out clean. Invert onto serving plate. Pour sauce over cake immediately.
Yield: 16 servings.

Sauce for Saucy Prune Cake

1/2 cup buttermilk
2 teaspoons white corn syrup
1 cup sugar
1/2 cup butter
1/2 teaspoon soda
1/2 teaspoon vanilla extract

Combine buttermilk, corn syrup, sugar, butter, soda and vanilla in saucepan. Bring to a boil. Cook for 2 minutes.

Approx Per Serving: Cal 466; Prot 4 g; Carbo 57 g; Fiber 2 g; T Fat 26 g; Chol 56 mg; Sod 185 mg.

Ann T. Clifton, Central

EASY PRUNE CAKE

2 cups sifted self-rising flour
2 cups sugar
1 teaspoon cinnamon
1/2 teaspoon cloves
1 cup oil
3 eggs
2 4-ounce jars baby food prunes
1 cup chopped pecans

Combine flour, sugar, cinnamon and cloves in large mixer bowl; mix well. Add oil, eggs and prunes; beat well. Stir in pecans. Pour into greased and floured 9x13-inch cake pan. Bake at 325 degrees for 35 minutes or until toothpick inserted in center comes out clean. Cover with foil immediately. May drizzle with favorite glaze if desired. This cake freezes well. Cake will be moister if placed in freezer while still hot. Yield: 15 servings.

Approx Per Serving: Cal 375; Prot 4 g; Carbo 45 g; Fiber 2 g; T Fat 21 g; Chol 43 mg; Sod 195 mg.

Eleanor S. Perdue, Piedmont

PUMPKIN CAKE

2 cups flour
2 teaspoons soda
1/2 teaspoon salt
1 teaspoon baking powder
2 teaspoons cinnamon
2 cups sugar
1 cup oil
4 eggs
2 cups canned pumpkin
1 cup chopped pecans
1/2 cup butter, softened
8 ounces cream cheese, softened
1 1-pound package confectioners' sugar
2 teaspoons vanilla extract
1/4 cup chopped pecans

Sift flour, soda, salt, baking powder and cinnamon together. Beat sugar, oil and eggs in mixer bowl until frothy. Add flour mixture; beat well. Stir in pumpkin and 1 cup pecans. Pour into greased and floured 9x13-inch cake pan. Bake at 350 degrees for 45 minutes. Cool. Cream butter and cream cheese in mixer bowl until light. Add confectioners' sugar gradually, beating until fluffy. Stir in vanilla. Spread over cooled cake. Sprinkle with remaining 1/4 cup pecans. Yield: 15 servings.

Approx Per Serving: Cal 639; Prot 6 g; Carbo 81 g; Fiber 2 g; T Fat 34 g; Chol 90 mg; Sod 281 mg.

Yvonne S. Griffin, Raleigh

PUMPKIN AND RAISIN CAKE

2 cups sugar
2 cups canned pumpkin
3/4 cup oil
4 eggs
2 cups flour
1 teaspoon baking powder
2 teaspoons soda
1 teaspoon salt
1 teaspoon cinnamon
1 teaspoon nutmeg
1 8-ounce can crushed pineapple, drained
1 cup raisins
1 cup chopped pecans
2 teaspoons vanilla extract
Nutty Cream Cheese Frosting
1/4 cup chopped pecans

Beat sugar, pumpkin, oil and eggs in mixer bowl. Combine flour, baking powder, soda, salt, cinnamon and nutmeg in bowl; mix well. Add to egg mixture. Beat at medium speed for 1 minute. Stir in pineapple, raisins, 1 cup pecans and vanilla. Pour into greased 9x13-inch cake pan. Bake at 325 degrees for 50 to 55 minutes. Cool completely. Spread Nutty Cream Cheese Frosting over cooled cake. Sprinkle with remaining 1/4 cup pecans. Yield: 15 servings.

Nutty Cream Cheese Frosting

1/4 cup butter, softened
3 ounces cream cheese, softened
1 1/2 cups confectioners' sugar

Cream butter and cream cheese in mixer bowl until light. Add confectioners' sugar gradually, beating until fluffy.

Approx Per Serving: Cal 498; Prot 5 g; Carbo 68 g; Fiber 2 g; T Fat 25 g; Chol 71 mg; Sod 339 mg.

Elizabeth Stirewalt, Salem

☎ Every time the oven door is opened during baking, the temperature drops from 25 to 30 degrees.

ROCKY MOUNTAIN CAKE

1 cup butter, softened
2 cups sugar
8 egg whites
3 cups flour
2 teaspoons baking powder
¾ cup milk
Almond extract to taste
Frosting

Cream butter and sugar in large mixer bowl until light and fluffy. Add egg whites 1 at a time, beating well after each addition. Mix flour and baking powder in bowl; mix well. Add to egg white mixture alternately with milk, beating well after each addition. Stir in almond extract. Pour into 4 greased and floured 8-inch round cake pans. Bake at 350 degrees for 25 to 30 minutes or until cakes test done. Remove to wire racks to cool. Spread frosting between layers and over top and side of cake. Yield: 24 servings.

Frosting for Rocky Mountain Cake

1½ cup water
3 cups sugar
6 egg whites
12 ounces dates, chopped
12 ounces figs, chopped
12 ounces raisins
1 pound slivered almonds
8 ounces citron
1 14-ounce package coconut

Combine water and sugar in saucepan. Bring to a boil, stirring until sugar dissolves. Cook over high heat to 234 to 240 degrees on candy thermometer, soft-ball stage; do not stir. Beat egg whites in mixer bowl until stiff peaks form. Pour hot syrup over egg whites gradually, beating constantly until cool. Fold in dates, figs, raisins, almonds, citron and coconut.

Approx Per Serving: Cal 605; Prot 9 g; Carbo 97 g; Fiber 7 g; T Fat 24 g; Chol 27 mg; Sod 161 mg.

Lottie B. Canady, Coastal

RUM CAKE

1 cup chopped pecans
1 4-ounce package vanilla instant pudding mix
1 2-layer package yellow cake mix
1/2 cup cold water
4 eggs
1/2 cup oil
1/2 cup dark rum
Glaze

Sprinkle pecans in bundt pan. Combine pudding mix, cake mix, cold water, eggs, oil and rum in mixer bowl; beat until smooth. Pour into prepared pan. Bake at 325 degrees for 1 hour. Cool in pan for several minutes. Invert onto serving plate. Pierce top of cake with fork. Drizzle glaze slowly over top and side of cake, allowing cake to absorb glaze. Yield: 16 servings.

Glaze for Rum Cake

1/2 cup butter, softened
1/4 cup water
1 cup sugar
1/2 cup dark rum

Melt butter in small saucepan. Stir in water and sugar. Bring to a boil, stirring constantly. Boil for 5 minutes, stirring constantly; remove from heat. Stir in rum.

Approx Per Serving: Cal 408; Prot 4 g; Carbo 47 g; Fiber 1 g; T Fat 22 g; Chol 69 mg; Sod 310 mg.

Wilhelmenia Cofield, Hornets Nest

☎ When chopping nuts for cakes in a blender or food processor, add 2 teaspoons sugar to each 1/2 cup nuts to prevent forming a paste.

SAUERKRAUT CAKE

2½ cups self-rising flour
¼ cup baking cocoa
1½ cups sugar
⅔ cup shortening
3 eggs
1¼ teaspoons vanilla extract
1 cup water
½ cup chopped drained sauerkraut
Frosting

Combine flour, cocoa and sugar in large mixer bowl; mix well. Cut in shortening until crumbly. Add eggs, vanilla and water; beat well. Stir in sauerkraut. Pour into 3 greased and floured 8-inch round cake pans. Bake at 375 degrees for 35 minutes or until layers test done. Remove to wire racks to cool. Spread frosting between layers and over top and side of cake.
Yield: 12 servings.

Frosting for Sauerkraut Cake

¾ cup butter, softened
⅛ teaspoon salt
1 1-pound package confectioners' sugar
2 teaspoons vanilla extract
5 teaspoons baking cocoa
8 teaspoons milk

Cream butter, salt and confectioners' sugar in mixer bowl until light and fluffy. Stir in vanilla and baking cocoa. Add enough milk to make of spreading consistency.

Approx Per Serving: Cal 598; Prot 5 g; Carbo 92 g; Fiber 2 g; T Fat 25 g; Chol 85 mg; Sod 485 mg.

Irene C. Black, Independence

STRAWBERRY CAKE

- 1 2-layer package white cake mix
- 3 tablespoons flour
- 1 3-ounce package strawberry gelatin
- 1 cup oil
- ½ cup water
- 4 eggs
- ¾ to 1 cup mashed strawberries
- Frosting

Combine cake mix, flour and gelatin in large mixer bowl; mix well. Add oil, water, eggs and strawberries; beat well. Pour into 2 greased and floured 9-inch round cake pans. Bake at 350 degrees for 25 to 30 minutes or until layers test done. Remove to wire racks to cool. Spread frosting between layers and over top and side of cake. Chill until serving time. Yield: 12 servings.

Frosting for Strawberry Cake

- ½ cup margarine, softened
- 1 1-pound package confectioners' sugar
- ¼ to ⅓ cup mashed strawberries

Cream margarine and confectioners' sugar in medium mixer bowl until light and fluffy. Stir in strawberries.

Approx Per Serving: Cal 650; Prot 5 g; Carbo 90 g; Fiber <1 g; T Fat 31 g; Chol 71 mg; Sod 397 mg.

Joyce Pruitt, Independence
Amanda Tucker, Independence

STRAWBERRY AND PECAN CAKE

4 eggs
1 cup oil
1 3-ounce package strawberry gelatin
1 cup frozen strawberries, thawed
1/2 cup milk
1 2-layer package white cake mix
1 cup coconut
1 cup chopped pecans
Frosting

Beat eggs in mixer bowl until foamy. Add oil, gelatin, strawberries and milk; beat well. Add cake mix; beat well. Stir in coconut and pecans. Pour into 3 greased and floured 8-inch round cake pans. Bake at 350 degrees for 25 to 30 minutes or until layers test done. Remove to wire racks to cool. Spread frosting between layers and over top and side of cake.
Yield: 12 servings.

Frosting for Strawberry and Pecan Cake

1/2 cup margarine, softened
1 1-pound package confectioners' sugar
1/2 cup frozen strawberries, thawed
1/2 cup coconut
1/2 cup chopped pecans

Cream margarine and confectioners' sugar in medium mixer bowl until light and fluffy. Add strawberries, coconut and pecans; mix well.

Approx Per Serving: Cal 794; Prot 6 g; Carbo 96 g; Fiber 3 g; T Fat 45 g; Chol 72 mg; Sod 418 mg.

Evelyn N. Goodman, Hornets Nest

SUNDROP CAKE

3 cups sugar
1 cup margarine, softened
½ cup shortening
3 cups flour
5 eggs

1 teaspoon vanilla extract
1 teaspoon lemon extract
¾ cup Sundrop
Frosting

    Cream sugar, margarine and shortening in mixer bowl until light and fluffy. Add flour and eggs; beat well. Add flavorings; mix well. Stir in Sundrop. Pour into greased and floured tube pan. Bake at 325 degrees for 1¼ hours. Cool in pan for several minutes. Invert onto serving plate. Spread frosting over cake. Yield: 16 servings.

Frosting for Sundrop Cake

2 cups confectioners' sugar
¼ cup Sundrop

2 tablespoons melted margarine

    Mix confectioners' sugar, Sundrop and melted margarine in small bowl to make of glaze consistency.

Approx Per Serving: Cal 491; Prot 5 g; Carbo 72 g; Fiber 1 g; T Fat 21 g; Chol 67 mg; Sod 175 mg.

Irene C. Black, Independence

☎ You may substitute 1 cup all-purpose flour, 1 teaspoon baking powder and ½ teaspoon salt for 1 cup self-rising flour.

GLAZED SWEET POTATO CAKE

1 cup butter, softened
2 cups sugar
4 eggs
2 1/2 cups mashed cooked sweet potatoes
1 teaspoon vanilla extract
1 teaspoon cinnamon
1/2 teaspoon nutmeg
3 cups flour
2 teaspoons baking powder
1/2 teaspoon salt
1/2 teaspoon soda
1/2 cup coconut
1/2 cup chopped pecans
1/2 cup sugar
1/4 cup pineapple juice

Cream butter and 2 cups sugar in large mixer bowl until light and fluffy. Add eggs 1 at a time, beating well after each addition. Add potatoes, vanilla, cinnamon and nutmeg; beat well. Sift flour, baking powder, salt and soda together. Add to potato mixture; beat well. Stir in coconut and pecans. Pour into greased and lightly floured 10-inch tube pan. Bake at 325 degrees for 1 1/4 hours. Cool in pan for 10 minutes. Invert onto serving plate. Combine remaining 1/2 cup sugar and pineapple juice in small saucepan. Bring just to the boiling point, stirring constantly. Drizzle over cooled cake. May serve with whipped cream. May substitute orange juice for pineapple juice. Yield: 16 servings.

Approx Per Serving: Cal 407; Prot 5 g; Carbo 61 g; Fiber 2 g; T Fat 17 g; Chol 84 mg; Sod 284 mg.

Barbara Thrower, Independence

☎ To clean blender quickly, place 3 inches of hot water and squirt of dishwashing detergent in container. Process, covered, on high speed for 1 minute; rinse.

FROSTED SWEET POTATO CAKE

1½ cups oil
1½ cups sugar
4 egg yolks
¼ cup water
2 cups flour
1 teaspoon baking powder
¼ teaspoon salt
1 teaspoon cinnamon
1 teaspoon nutmeg
1½ cups mashed cooked sweet potatoes
1 teaspoon vanilla extract
1 cup chopped pecans
4 egg whites, stiffly beaten
Frosting

Combine oil and sugar in large mixer bowl; beat until sugar dissolves. Add egg yolks and water; beat well. Combine flour, baking powder, salt, cinnamon and nutmeg in bowl; mix well. Add to egg yolk mixture, beating until blended. Stir in potatoes, vanilla and pecans. Fold in egg whites gently. Pour into 3 greased and floured 9-inch round cake pans. Bake at 350 degrees for 25 to 30 minutes or until layers test done. Remove to wire racks to cool. Spread frosting between layers and over top and side of cake. Yield: 12 servings.

Frosting for Sweet Potato Cake

1   12-ounce can evaporated milk
1½ cups sugar
3 egg yolks
¼ cup margarine, softened
1 teaspoon vanilla extract
1½ cups coconut
1 cup chopped pecans

Combine evaporated milk, sugar, egg yolks, margarine and vanilla in saucepan. Cook over medium heat for 10 to 12 minutes or until thickened, stirring constantly. Stir in coconut and pecans. Beat until cooled.

Approx Per Serving: Cal 849; Prot 9 g; Carbo 86 g; Fiber 4 g; T Fat 54 g; Chol 133 mg; Sod 224 mg.

Evelyn N. Goodman, Hornets Nest

MARY CARTER'S TEN-LAYER CAKE

6 eggs
1½ cups sugar
3 cups self-rising flour
1 cup shortening
1 cup milk
1 teaspoon vanilla extract
Frosting

    Combine eggs, sugar, flour, shortening, milk and vanilla in large mixer bowl; beat well. Pour 3 tablespoons batter into each of 10 greased and floured 9-inch round cake pans. Bake at 400 degrees for 4 to 5 minutes or until light brown. Remove to wire racks to cool. Spread frosting between layers and over top of cake. Yield: 12 servings.

Frosting for Ten-Layer Cake

4 ounces unsweetened chocolate
½ cup cold water
5 cups sugar
1 12-ounce can evaporated milk
¾ cup margarine, softened

    Combine chocolate, cold water, sugar, evaporated milk and margarine in saucepan; mix well. Bring to a boil, stirring constantly. Boil for 10 minutes, stirring constantly.

Approx Per Serving: Cal 920; Prot 10 g; Carbo 138 g; Fiber 2 g; T Fat 39 g; Chol 118 mg; Sod 547 mg.

Mary Carter, Central

☎ Budget-conscious shoppers avoid impulse buying by taking a shopping list to the market—and sticking to it. Arrange it according to the layout of the store to save time and steps.

VANILLA WAFER CAKE

1 cup butter, softened
1½ cups sugar
6 eggs
½ cup milk
1 12-ounce package vanilla wafers, crushed
1 cup chopped pecans
1 7-ounce package extra-fine coconut

Cream butter and sugar in large mixer bowl until light and fluffy. Add eggs 1 at a time, beating well after each addition. Add milk alternately with vanilla wafer crumbs, beating well after each addition. Stir in pecans and coconut. Pour into well-greased and floured tube pan. Bake at 300 degrees for 1½ hours or until cake tests done. Cool in pan for several minutes. Invert onto serving plate. Yield: 16 servings.

Approx Per Serving: Cal 415; Prot 5 g; Carbo 42 g; Fiber 2 g; T Fat 27 g; Chol 125 mg; Sod 238 mg.

Helen Marie Woods, Hornets Nest

WHITE LAYER CAKE

1 cup margarine, softened
2 cups sugar
3 cups sifted cake flour
1 tablespoon baking powder
1 cup low-fat milk
½ teaspoon salt
1 teaspoon vanilla extract
1 teaspoon lemon extract
6 egg whites, stiffly beaten

Cream margarine and sugar in large mixer bowl until light and fluffy. Combine flour and baking powder in bowl; mix well. Add to creamed mixture alternately with milk, beating well after each addition. Add salt, vanilla and lemon extract; beat well. Fold in egg whites gently. Pour into 3 greased and floured 9-inch round cake pans. Bake at 375 degrees for 25 to 30 minutes or until layers test done. Remove to wire racks to cool completely. Top with favorite icing, fruit or strawberries. Yield: 12 servings.

Approx Per Serving: Cal 371; Prot 4 g; Carbo 54 g; Fiber 1 g; T Fat 16 g; Chol 1 mg; Sod 386 mg.

Evelyn M. Walker, Raleigh

CARAMEL ICING

1 cup margarine, softened
1 cup packed light brown sugar
1 cup sugar
1 cup evaporated milk
1 teaspoon vanilla extract

Combine margarine, brown sugar, sugar and evaporated milk in large saucepan; mix well. Bring to a rolling boil over medium heat, stirring constantly. Boil for 15 minutes or until mixture begins to thicken, stirring constantly; remove from heat. Stir in vanilla. Pour into large mixer bowl. Beat at high speed until smooth. Spread over cake layers. May prepare Caramel Fudge by cooking mixture to 250 to 268 degrees on candy thermometer, hard-ball stage. Remove from heat; stir in 1 cup chopped pecans. Pour into greased glass dish. Cool. Cut into squares.
Yield: enough for 1 cake, 12 servings, or 20 servings fudge.

Approx Per Serving: Cal 298; Prot 2 g; Carbo 37 g; Fiber 0 g; T Fat 17 g; Chol 6 mg; Sod 208 mg.
Nutritional information is for 12 cake servings.

Carolyn S. Starnes, Independence

CHOCOLATE ICING

1/2 cup margarine, softened
3 ounces cream cheese
1 1-pound package confectioners' sugar
1/4 cup evaporated milk
3 tablespoons baking cocoa
1 teaspoon vanilla extract

Cream margarine and softened cream cheese in mixer bowl until light and fluffy. Add confectioners' sugar, evaporated milk, baking cocoa and vanilla; beat well.
Yield: enough for 1 cake, 12 servings.

Approx Per Serving: Cal 279; Prot 1 g; Carbo 47 g; Fiber <1 g; T Fat 11 g; Chol 9 mg; Sod 116 mg.

Patricia Goodman, Hornets Nest

ORANGE AND LEMON GLAZE

Grated rind of 1 orange
Grated rind of 1/2 lemon
3 tablespoons orange juice
1 1/2 cups confectioners' sugar

Combine orange rind, lemon rind and orange juice in small bowl; mix well. Mix in confectioners' sugar. Pour over hot cake. Yield: enough for 1 pound cake, 12 servings.

Approx Per Serving: Cal 61; Prot <1 g; Carbo 16 g; Fiber <1 g; T Fat <1 g; Chol 0 mg; Sod <1 mg.

Patricia Goodman, Hornets Nest

FROSTING FOR MANY CAKES

2 cups sugar
1 cup water
4 egg whites, stiffly beaten

Combine sugar and water in saucepan. Cook over medium heat to 270 to 290 degrees on candy thermometer, soft-crack stage; remove from heat. Pour over egg whites. Beat well. May add mashed bananas for banana cake, drained crushed pineapple for pineapple cake, coconut for coconut cake and chopped pecans for pecan cake. Yield: enough for 3-layer cake, 12 servings.

Approx Per Serving: Cal 134; Prot 1 g; Carbo 33 g; Fiber 0 g; T Fat 0 g; Chol 0 mg; Sod 18 mg.

Margaret Sawyer, Raleigh

☎ For quick cupcake frosting, place 1 large marshmallow on each cupcake for 1 or 2 minutes before removing from oven.

CANDY

CHOCOLATE PEANUT CLUSTERS

2 tablespoons peanut butter
1 cup butterscotch chips
1 cup chocolate chips
2 cups salted peanuts

Melt peanut butter with butterscotch chips and chocolate chips with peanut butter in heavy saucepan, stirring constantly. Fold in peanuts until well coated. Drop by teaspoonfuls onto waxed paper-lined tray. Chill in refrigerator until firm. Store in airtight container in refrigerator. Yield: 36 servings.

Approx Per Serving: Cal 179; Prot 7 g; Carbo 9 g; Fiber 2 g; T Fat 15 g; Chol 0 mg; Sod 94 mg.

Norma C. Parrish, Central

CINNAMON GRAHAM CONFECTIONS

8 ounces cinnamon graham crackers
1 cup margarine
1/2 cup sugar
3/4 cup chopped pecans

Line foil-covered baking sheet with graham crackers. Combine margarine and sugar in saucepan. Bring to a boil. Cook for 2 to 3 minutes, stirring constantly. Pour mixture quickly over graham cracker layer. Sprinkle with pecans. Bake at 350 degrees for 3 to 5 minutes or until bubbly. Cool before removing from foil. Cut into squares. May omit pecans. May use plain graham crackers. Yield: 24 servings.

Approx Per Serving: Cal 149; Prot 1 g; Carbo 12 g; Fiber <1 g; T Fat 11 g; Chol 0 mg; Sod 147 mg.

Jo Litaker, Independence

COOKIE CONFECTIONS

8 ounces graham crackers
1 cup crushed pecans
1/2 cup margarine
1/2 cup butter
1/2 cup sugar

Break graham crackers into halves. Arrange in single layer on baking sheet. Sprinkle with pecans. Combine margarine, butter and sugar in saucepan. Bring to a boil. Boil for 3 minutes. Pour over crackers. Bake at 350 degrees for 10 minutes. Remove immediately to foil-lined tray to cool. Yield: 24 servings.

Approx Per Serving: Cal 157; Prot 1 g; Carbo 12 g; Fiber 1 g; T Fat 12 g; Chol 10 mg; Sod 135 mg.

Barbara P. Banister, Independence

CHRISTMAS DIVINITY

3 cups sugar
3/4 cup light corn syrup
3/4 cup water
2 egg whites
1 3-ounce package fruit-flavored gelatin
1 cup chopped pecans
1/2 cup coconut

Combine sugar, corn syrup and water in heavy saucepan. Bring to a boil, stirring constantly. Reduce heat. Cook to 252 degrees on candy thermometer, hard-ball stage, stirring frequently. Cool slightly. Beat egg whites in mixer bowl until foamy. Beat in dry gelatin until stiff peaks form. Add syrup gradually, beating at high speed until very stiff. Fold in pecans and coconut. Drop by spoonfuls onto waxed paper. Cool. Yield: 60 servings.

Approx Per Serving: Cal 72; Prot <1 g; Carbo 15 g; Fiber <1 g; T Fat 2 g; Chol 0 mg; Sod 10 mg.

Mrs. Hugh L. McAulay, Blue Ridge

PECAN DIVINITY

3 cups sugar
1/2 cup light corn syrup
1/2 cup water
2 egg whites, at room temperature
1/8 teaspoon cream of tartar
1 teaspoon vanilla extract
2 cups chopped pecans

Combine sugar, corn syrup and water in heavy saucepan. Cook over medium heat to 270 to 290 degrees on candy thermometer, soft-crack stage, stirring frequently. Beat egg whites with cream of tartar in mixer bowl until stiff peaks form. Add hot syrup 1/3 at a time to egg whites, beating constantly until stiff. Stir in vanilla and pecans. Drop by teaspoonfuls onto waxed paper. Yield: 36 servings.

Approx Per Serving: Cal 122; Prot 1 g; Carbo 21 g; Fiber <1 g; T Fat 4 g; Chol 0 mg; Sod 5 mg.

Agnes Williams, Independence

MARGARET TUCKER'S CHOCOLATE FUDGE

5 cups sugar
1 cup margarine
1 12-ounce can evaporated milk
3 cups semisweet chocolate chips
1 13-ounce jar marshmallow creme
1 1/2 cups chopped walnuts
1 teaspoon vanilla extract

Bring sugar, margarine and evaporated milk to a boil in saucepan, stirring constantly. Cook for 6 minutes. Remove from heat. Stir in chocolate chips, marshmallow creme, walnuts and vanilla. Pour into buttered 8x8-inch and 9x13-inch pans. Cool. Cut into small squares. Yield: 96 servings.

Approx Per Serving: Cal 113; Prot 1 g; Carbo 17 g; Fiber <1 g; T Fat 5 g; Chol 1 mg; Sod 30 mg.

Amanda Tucker, Independence

FUDGE

3 cups sugar
3 tablespoons baking
  cocoa
¼ cup margarine
1 12-ounce can
   evaporated milk
1 teaspoon vanilla extract
½ cup chopped walnuts

Combine sugar, baking cocoa, margarine and evaporated milk in heavy saucepan. Bring to a boil over medium heat, stirring constantly. Cook, uncovered, to 234 to 240 degrees on candy thermometer, soft-ball stage. Remove from heat. Stir in vanilla; beat until thickened. Fold in walnuts. Pour into buttered 8-inch square dish. Cool. Cut into squares. Yield: 48 servings.

Approx Per Serving: Cal 75; Prot 1 g; Carbo 14 g; Fiber <1 g; T Fat 2 g; Chol 2 mg; Sod 19 mg.

Jo Ann Goins, Hornets Nest

PEANUT FUDGE

4½ cups sugar
1 12-ounce can
   evaporated milk
4 cups semisweet
  chocolate chips
1 teaspoon vanilla extract
1 cup margarine
1 cup peanuts

Bring sugar and evaporated milk to a boil in saucepan. Boil for 6 minutes, stirring constantly. Remove from heat. Stir in chocolate chips, vanilla, margarine and peanuts. Beat until thickened and creamy. Pour into buttered 9x13-inch pan. Cool. Cut into squares. Store in airtight container in refrigerator. May substitute peanut butter chips for chocolate chips. Yield: 80 servings.

Approx Per Serving: Cal 123; Prot 1 g; Carbo 17 g; Fiber <1 g; T Fat 7 g; Chol 1 mg; Sod 33 mg.

Peggy Pearce, Raleigh

PEANUT BUTTER FUDGE

2 cups sugar
3/4 cup milk
4 teaspoons peanut butter
1 teaspoon vanilla extract
1/2 teaspoon salt

Combine sugar and milk in heavy saucepan. Bring to a boil. Cook over medium heat to 234 to 240 degrees on candy thermometer, soft-ball stage. Remove from heat. Add peanut butter, vanilla and salt; mix well. Beat until thickened and creamy. Pour into buttered dish. Cool. Cut into squares. Yield: 30 servings.

Approx Per Serving: Cal 68; Prot 1 g; Carbo 14 g; Fiber <1 g; T Fat 1 g; Chol 1 mg; Sod 47 mg.

Audrey Brock, Hornets Nest

PEANUT BRITTLE

1 1/2 cups sugar
1/2 cup light corn syrup
2 cups raw Spanish peanuts
1/8 teaspoon salt
2 tablespoons melted paraffin
1 teaspoon (heaping) soda

Combine sugar, corn syrup, peanuts, salt and paraffin in iron skillet. Cook over medium heat for 10 minutes or to 300 to 310 degrees on candy thermometer, hard-crack stage, stirring constantly. Remove from heat. Stir in soda quickly. Spread as thinly as possible on foil-lined tray. Cool. Remove foil. Break into pieces. Store in airtight container. Yield: 32 servings.

Approx Per Serving: Cal 103; Prot 2 g; Carbo 15 g; Fiber 1 g; T Fat 4 g; Chol 0 mg; Sod 76 mg.

Mrs. Hugh L. McAulay, Blue Ridge

MICROWAVE PEANUT BRITTLE

1 cup sugar
1/2 cup light corn syrup
1 cup salted peanuts
1 teaspoon margarine
1 teaspoon vanilla extract
1 teaspoon soda

Combine sugar and corn syrup in microwave-safe glass dish. Microwave on High for 8 minutes, stirring once with wooden spoon. Stir in peanuts, margarine and vanilla. Microwave for 2 minutes. Stir in soda until light and foamy. Spread as thinly as possible on buttered tray. Cool. Break into pieces. Store in airtight container. Yield: 20 servings.

Approx Per Serving: Cal 109; Prot 2 g; Carbo 18 g; Fiber 1 g; T Fat 4 g; Chol 0 mg; Sod 83 mg.

Esther Sossamon, Independence

PEANUT BUTTER BALLS

2 cups margarine
1 1/2 cups peanut butter
2 1-pound packages confectioners' sugar
3/4 to 1 block paraffin
1 1/2 cups semisweet chocolate chips

Cream margarine and peanut butter in medium bowl until light. Add confectioners' sugar gradually, mixing well after each addition. Shape into 1-inch balls. Place balls on waxed paper-lined tray. Melt paraffin and chocolate chips in heavy saucepan over low heat, stirring constantly. Insert toothpick into each peanut butter ball; dip into chocolate mixture. Place on waxed paper-lined tray. Let stand until set. Store in airtight container. Pariffin measurement assumes paraffin to have 4 blocks in box. May add chopped pecans to peanut butter mixture or place pecan over hole made by toothpick. Yield: 80 servings.

Approx Per Serving: Cal 138; Prot 2 g; Carbo 16 g; Fiber <1 g; T Fat 8 g; Chol 0 mg; Sod 74 mg.

Becky Adams, Coastal

REECE'S CUP SQUARES

3/4 cup melted margarine
1 cup peanut butter
1 1-pound package
   confectioners' sugar
1 8-ounce milk chocolate
   bar, melted

Combine margarine and peanut butter in medium bowl; mix well. Stir in confectioners' sugar. Spread into bottom of 9x13-inch dish. Pour chocolate over top. Let stand until firm. Cut into squares. Yield: 40 servings.

Approx Per Serving: Cal 150; Prot 2 g; Carbo 18 g; Fiber 1 g;
   T Fat 9 g; Chol 1 mg; Sod 71 mg.

Carolyn Buboltz, Independence

ROCKY ROAD SQUARES

2 cups semisweet
   chocolate chips
2 tablespoons butter
1 14-ounce can
   sweetened condensed
   milk
2 cups dry-roasted
   peanuts
1 10-ounce package
   miniature marshmallows

Melt chocolate chips and butter with sweetened condensed milk over low heat in saucepan, stirring constantly. Remove from heat. Cool slightly. Combine peanuts and marshmallows in large bowl. Fold in chocolate mixture until well coated. Spread in waxed paper-lined 9x13-inch dish. Chill in refrigerator for 2 hours or until firm. Remove waxed paper. Cut into squares. Store, covered, at room temperature.
Yield: 24 servings.

Approx Per Serving: Cal 240; Prot 5 g; Carbo 29 g; Fiber 2 g;
   T Fat 14 g; Chol 8 mg; Sod 43 mg.

Jane Misle, Independence

CONFECTIONS

BABY RUTH BARS

1 cup sugar
1 cup light corn syrup
1¾ cups peanut butter
5 cups Special-K cereal, crushed
1 cup chocolate chips
1 cup butterscotch chips

Combine sugar and corn syrup in saucepan. Bring to a boil over medium heat. Remove from heat. Stir in peanut butter. Pour over crushed cereal in 9x13-inch dish. Melt chocolate and butterscotch chips over low heat in small saucepan, stirring constantly. Spread over peanut butter mixture. Chill in refrigerator for 30 minutes or until firm. Cut into squares. Yield: 40 servings.

Approx Per Serving: Cal 162; Prot 4 g; Carbo 20 g; Fiber 1 g; T Fat 9 g; Chol 0 mg; Sod 75 mg.

Ella S. Richards, Raleigh

CHOCOLATE BOURBON BALLS

1 cup semisweet chocolate chips
½ cup Bourbon
3 tablespoons light corn syrup
2½ cups vanilla wafer crumbs
½ cup sifted confectioners' sugar
1 cup finely chopped pecans
Sugar

Melt chocolate chips in double boiler over hot water, stirring occasionally. Remove from heat. Stir in Bourbon and corn syrup. Combine next 3 ingredients in small bowl; mix well. Add to chocolate mixture; mix well. Let stand for 30 minutes. Shape into 1-inch balls. Roll in sugar to coat. Place on waxed paper. Let stand until firm. Store in airtight container in refrigerator. Yield: 60 servings.

Approx Per Serving: Cal 55; Prot <1 g; Carbo 6 g; Fiber <1 g; T Fat 3 g; Chol 2 mg; Sod 15 mg.
Nutritional information does not include sugar for coating Bourbon balls.

John E. Miles, Independence

CHOCOLATE OATMEAL NO-BAKE COOKIES

2 cups sugar
3 tablespoons baking cocoa
1/2 cup milk
1/2 cup butter

3 cups oats
2 tablespoons peanut butter
1/2 teaspoon vanilla extract

Combine sugar, baking cocoa, milk and butter in saucepan. Bring to a boil for 2 minutes, stirring constantly. Remove from heat. Add oats, peanut butter and vanilla; mix well. Drop by teaspoonfuls onto waxed paper-lined trays. Let stand until cool. Yield: 32 servings.

Approx Per Serving: Cal 113; Prot 2 g; Carbo 18 g; Fiber 1 g; T Fat 4 g; Chol 8 mg; Sod 30 mg.

Patricia L. Goodin, Independence

CHOCOLATE OATMEAL COOKIES

2 cups sugar
1/2 cup margarine
3 tablespoons baking cocoa
1/2 cup milk

2 1/2 cups oats
2 teaspoons vanilla extract
1 cup chopped walnuts
1 cup coconut

Combine sugar, margarine, baking cocoa and milk in saucepan. Bring to a boil for 1 1/2 minutes, stirring constantly. Remove from heat. Stir in oats, vanilla, walnuts and coconut. Drop by teaspoonfuls onto waxed paper-lined trays. Cool until firm. Yield: 32 servings.

Approx Per Serving: Cal 140; Prot 2 g; Carbo 18 g; Fiber 1 g; T Fat 6 g; Chol 1 mg; Sod 46 mg.

Irene C. Black, Independence

CHOCOLATE AND PEANUT BUTTER OATMEAL COOKIES

2 cups sugar
3 tablespoons baking cocoa
1/2 cup milk
1/2 cup margarine
1/2 cup peanut butter
3 cups quick-cooking oats
1 teaspoon vanilla extract

Combine sugar, baking cocoa, milk and margarine in saucepan. Bring just to the boiling point over low heat, stirring constantly. Add peanut butter, oats and vanilla; mix well. Drop by teaspoonfuls onto waxed paper-lined trays. Cool until firm. Yield: 32 servings.

Approx Per Serving: Cal 131; Prot 3 g; Carbo 19 g; Fiber 1 g; T Fat 6 g; Chol 1 mg; Sod 52 mg.

Gladys Hinson, Independence

DATE BALLS

1 8-ounce package whole pitted dates, chopped
1/2 cup margarine
3/4 cup sugar
1 egg
1 cup chopped pecans
2 1/2 cups crisp rice cereal
Confectioners' sugar

Combine dates, margarine, sugar and egg in heavy saucepan. Cook over low heat until thickened and creamy, stirring constantly. Remove from heat. Stir in pecans and cereal. Shape into balls. Roll in confectioners' sugar. Place on waxed paper. Let stand until cool. Store in airtight container. Yield: 32 servings.

Approx Per Serving: Cal 99; Prot 1 g; Carbo 13 g; Fiber 1 g; T Fat 6 g; Chol 7 mg; Sod 63 mg.
Nutritional information does not include confectioners' sugar.

Jo Ann Goins, Hornets Nest

DATE AND COCONUT BALLS

½ cup butter
1 cup packed brown sugar
1 8-ounce package
 chopped dates
2 cups crisp rice cereal
1 cup chopped walnuts
½ cup coconut
Confectioners' sugar

Combine butter, brown sugar and dates in saucepan. Cook over medium heat until sugar is dissolved and butter is melted, stirring constantly. Remove from heat. Stir in cereal, walnuts and coconut. Cool. Shape into balls. Roll in confectioners' sugar. Place on waxed paper. Let stand until cool. Recipe may be doubled. Yield: 48 servings.

Approx Per Serving: Cal 71; Prot 1 g; Carbo 10 g; Fiber 1 g;
 T Fat 4 g; Chol 5 mg; Sod 35 mg.
 Nutritional information does not include confectioners' sugar.

Evelyn N. Goodman, Hornets Nest

HOLIDAY DATE BALLS

1 cup margarine
2 8-ounce packages
 dates, chopped
1 3½-ounce can flaked
 coconut
2 cups packed light brown
 sugar
2 cups chopped pecans
4 cups crisp rice cereal
1½ cups confectioners'
 sugar

Combine margarine, dates, coconut and brown sugar in saucepan. Cook for 6 minutes, stirring constantly; remove from heat. Stir in pecans and cereal. Let stand until cool enough to handle. Shape into small balls. Roll in confectioners' sugar, coating well. Yield: 36 servings.

Approx Per Serving: Cal 215; Prot 1 g; Carbo 31 g; Fiber 2 g;
 T Fat 11 g; Chol 0 mg; Sod 110 mg.

Wilma Burleson, Independence

DATE NUT BALLS

½ cup butter
2 eggs
1 cup sugar
1 8-ounce package chopped dates
3 cups crisp rice cereal
¾ cup coconut
¾ cup finely chopped pecans
½ teaspoon vanilla extract

Combine butter, eggs, sugar and dates in saucepan. Cook over medium heat for 10 minutes, stirring constantly. Remove from heat. Stir in cereal, coconut, pecans and vanilla. Cool for 2 to 3 minutes. Shape into 1-inch balls. Place on waxed paper. Let stand until cool. Store in airtight container. Balls may be rolled in confectioners' sugar, finely chopped pecans or coconut. May be pressed into greased pan and cut into squares.
Yield: 48 servings.

Approx Per Serving: Cal 76; Prot 1 g; Carbo 10 g; Fiber 1 g; T Fat 4 g; Chol 14 mg; Sod 44 mg.

Gladys Hinson, Independence

GOLF BALLS

1 cup margarine, softened
1 1-pound package confectioners' sugar
1 cup peanut butter
2 cups graham cracker crumbs
1½ cups chopped pecans
1 cup coconut
2 cups semisweet chocolate chips
½ block paraffin

Cream margarine and confectioners's sugar in bowl until light and fluffy. Add peanut butter; mix well. Stir in graham cracker crumbs, pecans and coconut. Shape into 1-inch balls. Melt chocolate chips and paraffin in double boiler over hot water. Dip balls into chocolate mixture. Place on waxed paper. Let stand until firm. Yield: 72 servings.

Approx Per Serving: Cal 133; Prot 2 g; Carbo 14 g; Fiber 1 g; T Fat 8 g; Chol 0 mg; Sod 68 mg.

Vicki S. Soles, Hornets Nest

GOOF BALLS

1 cup melted margarine
1/2 cup chunky peanut butter
1 1-pound package confectioners' sugar
1 teaspoon vanilla extract
8 ounces graham crackers, crushed
1 cup chopped pecans
1 cup coconut
1 cup chocolate chips
1/2 bar paraffin

Combine margarine, peanut butter, confectioners' sugar and vanilla in bowl until light and fluffy. Stir in graham cracker crumbs, pecans and coconut. Roll into 1-inch balls. Melt chocolate chips and paraffin in double boiler over hot water. Dip balls into chocolate mixture. Place on waxed paper. Let stand until firm. Yield: 72 servings.

Approx Per Serving: Cal 104; Prot 1 g; Carbo 12 g; Fiber 1 g; T Fat 6 g; Chol 0 mg; Sod 59 mg.

Martha G. Bridges, Hornets Nest

GRAHAM CRACKER BARS

1 cup sugar
3/4 cup margarine
2 eggs
2 1/2 cups graham cracker crumbs
1 1/2 cups miniature marshmallows
1/2 cup chopped walnuts
1/2 cup coconut

Combine sugar, margarine and eggs in double boiler over boiling water. Cook for 20 to 30 minutes or until mixture thickens, stirring frequently. Remove from heat. Cool. Combine graham cracker crumbs, marshmallows, walnuts and coconut in large bowl; mix well. Add cooled sugar mixture, stirring until well coated. Press into 9-inch square pan. Chill in refrigerator. Cut into squares. Yield: 18 servings.

Approx Per Serving: Cal 237; Prot 3 g; Carbo 30 g; Fiber 1 g; T Fat 13 g; Chol 24 mg; Sod 209 mg.

Jo Litaker, Independence

HUMDINGERS

½ cup margarine
¾ cup sugar
1 cup chopped dates
1½ cups crisp rice cereal
1 cup chopped walnuts
1 teaspoon vanilla extract
2 tablespoons toasted
 sesame seed
Confectioners' sugar

Combine margarine, sugar and dates in saucepan. Cook over medium heat for 5 minutes. Remove from heat. Stir in cereal, walnuts, vanilla and sesame seed. Shape into 1-inch balls. Roll in confectioners' sugar. Let stand until cool. Store in airtight container. Yield: 36 servings.

Approx Per Serving: Cal 82; Prot 1 g; Carbo 10 g; Fiber 1 g;
 T Fat 5 g; Chol 0 mg; Sod 45 mg.
 Nutritional information does not include confectioners' sugar.

Jim and Barbara Brodmerkel, Independence

INCREDIBLES

¾ cup melted butter
2 cups graham cracker
 crumbs
1 12-ounce jar chunky
 peanut butter
2 cups confectioners'
 sugar
2 cups semisweet
 chocolate chips

Pour melted butter over graham cracker crumbs in large bowl; mix well. Add peanut butter and confectioners' sugar; mix well. Spread evenly in 9x13-inch dish. Melt chocolate chips in small saucepan. Pour over top. Chill in refrigerator for 1 hour or until firm. Yield: 36 servings.

Approx Per Serving: Cal 192; Prot 4 g; Carbo 19 g; Fiber 1 g;
 T Fat 13 g; Chol 10 mg; Sod 113 mg.

James and Paula Hays, Asheville

NUTTY GRAHAM SQUARES

12 ounces graham crackers
1 cup butter
1 cup sugar
1 egg
1/2 cup milk
1 cup coconut
1 cup chopped pecans
1 cup graham cracker crumbs
6 tablespoons butter, softened
1 tablespoon milk
2 cups confectioners' sugar
1 teaspoon vanilla extract

Line 9x13-inch pan with graham crackers. Combine 1 cup butter, sugar, egg and 1/2 cup milk in saucepan. Bring to a boil. Cook over medium heat for 2 minutes or until thickened, stirring constantly. Remove from heat. Stir in coconut, pecans and graham cracker crumbs. Spoon over graham crackers. Top with another layer of graham crackers. Cream remaining 6 tablespoons butter, remaining 1 tablespoon milk, confectioners' sugar and vanilla in small bowl until light and fluffy. Spread over top. Let stand until cool. Cut into squares. Yield: 24 servings.

Approx Per Serving: Cal 356; Prot 2 g; Carbo 41 g; Fiber 1 g; T Fat 17 g; Chol 38 mg; Sod 220 mg.

Shirley Carmichael, Hornets Nest

NUTTY CLUSTERS

2 cups butterscotch chips
1 3-ounce can chow mein noodles
1 cup (or more) peanuts

Melt butterscotch chips in double boiler over hot water. Remove from heat. Stir in chow mein noodles and peanuts. Drop by spoonfuls onto waxed paper. Chill until firm. Yield: 36 servings.

Approx Per Serving: Cal 83; Prot 2 g; Carbo 8 g; Fiber 1 g; T Fat 6 g; Chol <1 mg; Sod 42 mg.

Jo Ann Goins, Hornets Nest

PEANUT BUTTER COCONUT BALLS

1 cup melted margarine
1 1/2 cups graham cracker crumbs
1/2 cup peanut butter
1/2 cup chopped pecans
1 cup coconut
1 1-pound package confectioners' sugar
1 teaspoon vanilla extract
2 cups semisweet chocolate chips
3/4 block paraffin

Combine margarine, graham cracker crumbs, peanut butter, pecans, coconut, confectioners' sugar and vanilla in bowl; mix well. Shape into 1-inch balls. Melt chocolate chips and paraffin in double boiler over hot water. Dip peanut butter balls into chocolate mixture. Place on waxed paper. Let stand until firm. Yield: 48 servings.

Approx Per Serving: Cal 161; Prot 2 g; Carbo 20 g; Fiber 1 g; T Fat 9 g; Chol 0 mg; Sod 84 mg.

Gladys Hinson, Independence

BOILED PEANUT BUTTER COOKIES

2 cups sugar
1/2 cup margarine
1/4 cup baking cocoa
1/2 cup milk
2 1/2 cups quick-cooking oats
1/2 cup peanut butter
1/4 cup chopped walnuts
2 teaspoons vanilla extract

Combine sugar, margarine, baking cocoa and milk in saucepan. Bring to a rolling boil. Cook over medium heat for 1 1/2 minutes, stirring constantly. Remove from heat. Stir in oats, peanut butter, walnuts and vanilla. Drop by spoonfuls onto waxed paper. Let stand until firm. Yield: 24 servings.

Approx Per Serving: Cal 177; Prot 3 g; Carbo 24 g; Fiber 2 g; T Fat 8 g; Chol 1 mg; Sod 69 mg.

Sallie Greer, Hornets Nest
Audrey Brock, Hornets Nest

TOMMY'S NO-COOK PEANUT BUTTER CANDY

2 cups sugar
1/4 cup baking cocoa
1/2 cup margarine

1/2 cup milk
3/4 cup peanut butter
2 teaspoons vanilla extract

Combine sugar, baking cocoa, margarine and milk in saucepan. Bring to a boil. Cook for 1 1/2 minutes. Remove from heat. Stir in peanut butter and vanilla. Drop by spoonfuls onto waxed paper. Let stand until cool. May add raisins. May make cookies by adding 2 1/2 cups oats and reducing peanut butter to 1/2 cup. Yield: 48 servings.

Approx Per Serving: Cal 76; Prot 1 g; Carbo 9 g; Fiber <1 g; T Fat 4 g; Chol <1 mg; Sod 40 mg.

Patricia S. Hart, Raleigh

PRALINE CONFECTIONS

24 whole graham crackers
1 cup packed light brown sugar

1 cup butter
1 cup chopped pecans

Line 10x15-inch pan with graham crackers. Combine brown sugar and butter in heavy saucepan. Bring to a rolling boil. Boil for 2 minutes, stirring constantly. Remove from heat. Cool slightly. Stir in pecans. Spoon mixture over graham cracker layer. Bake at 350 degrees for 10 minutes. Cool slightly before cutting into small squares. Yield: 80 servings.

Approx Per Serving: Cal 50; Prot <1 g; Carbo 5 g; Fiber <1 g; T Fat 4 g; Chol 6 mg; Sod 34 mg.

Harry L. Beauchamp, Central

☎ It is usually more successful to make 2 recipes of candy than to double the recipe.

COOKIES

AMBROSIA COOKIES

1 cup butter, softened
3/4 cup packed brown sugar
3/4 cup sugar
2 eggs
2 1/2 cups flour
1 teaspoon baking powder
1/2 teaspoon soda
1/2 teaspoon salt
1 teaspoon vanilla extract
1 1/2 cups uncooked oats
1 cup coconut
1 cup chopped dates
1 cup raisins
1 cup chopped pecans
1 tablespoon grated orange rind
1 tablespoon grated lemon rind

Cream butter, brown sugar and sugar in bowl until light and fluffy. Add eggs; mix well. Combine flour, baking powder, soda and salt in bowl; mix well. Add to creamed mixture. Stir in vanilla, uncooked oats, coconut, dates, raisins, pecans, orange rind and lemon rind; mix well. Drop by teaspoonfuls 2 inches apart onto lightly greased cookie sheet. Bake at 325 degrees for 10 to 11 minutes or until firm. Cool on cookie sheet for 2 minutes. Remove to wire rack to cool completely. Yield: 132 servings.

Approx Per Serving: Cal 51; Prot 1 g; Carbo 7 g; Fiber <1 g; T Fat 2 g; Chol 7 mg; Sod 29 mg.

Elizabeth Stirewalt, Salem

ANGEL DROPS

2 egg whites
2/3 cup sugar
1/8 teaspoon salt
1 teaspoon vanilla extract
1 cup chopped pecans

Preheat oven to 350 degrees. Beat egg whites in bowl until frothy. Add sugar 1 tablespoon at a time, beating constantly. Add salt and vanilla; mix well. Fold in pecans. Drop by teaspoonfuls onto foil-lined cookie sheet. Place in preheated oven; turn off oven. Let stand in oven overnight. May substitute 1 cup chocolate, butterscotch or peanut butter chips for pecans. Yield: 36 servings.

Approx Per Serving: Cal 37; Prot <1 g; Carbo 4 g; Fiber <1 g; T Fat 2 g; Chol 0 mg; Sod 10 mg.

Zona Norwood, Raleigh

APRICOT-WALNUT BARS

2 1/2 cups sifted flour
1 1/2 teaspoons soda
1 teaspoon cinnamon
1/2 teaspoon salt
4 eggs, beaten
2 1/2 cups packed light brown sugar
1 2/3 cups evaporated milk
2 tablespoons lemon juice
1 cup chopped dried apricots
1 cup chopped walnuts
1 cup coconut
1/2 cup confectioners' sugar

Sift flour, soda, cinnamon and salt into bowl. Add beaten eggs, brown sugar, evaporated milk and lemon juice, stirring just until blended. Fold in apricots, walnuts and coconut. Pour into 2 well-greased 10x15-inch jelly roll pans. Bake at 350 degrees for 20 minutes. Cool in pans. Sprinkle with confectioners' sugar. Cut into bars. Store in airtight container. Yield: 60 servings.

Approx Per Serving: Cal 94; Prot 2 g; Carbo 17 g; Fiber 1 g; T Fat 3 g; Chol 16 mg; Sod 58 mg.

Mrs. Hugh L. McAulay, Blue Ridge

BISCOCHITOS

1 1/2 cups shortening
1 cup sugar
1 egg, beaten
1 tablespoon anise seed
3 cups flour
1 teaspoon baking powder
1/4 teaspoon salt
1/4 cup sugar
1 teaspoon cinnamon

Cream shortening in bowl until light and fluffy. Stir in 1 cup sugar gradually. Add egg; mix well. Stir in anise seed. Sift flour, baking powder and salt together. Add to creamed mixture; mix well. Roll 1/8 inch thick on lightly floured surface. Cut as desired. Place on ungreased cookie sheet. Sprinkle with mixture of remaining 1/4 cup sugar and cinnamon. Bake at 450 degrees for 10 minutes or until lightly browned. Cool on cookie sheet for 2 minutes. Remove to wire rack to cool completely.
Yield: 36 servings.

Approx Per Serving: Cal 143; Prot 1 g; Carbo 15 g; Fiber <1 g; T Fat 9 g; Chol 6 mg; Sod 26 mg.

Nina A. Valdez, Foot Hills

EASY BROWNIES

1½ cups flour
2 cups sugar
4 eggs
1 cup oil
¼ cup water
8 tablespoons baking cocoa
2 teaspoons vanilla extract
1 teaspoon salt
½ cup chopped pecans

Combine flour, sugar, eggs, oil, water, baking cocoa, vanilla and salt in bowl; mix well. Stir in pecans. Spread in greased 11x15-inch baking pan. Bake at 350 degrees for 40 minutes. Cool. Cut into squares. Yield: 48 servings.

Approx Per Serving: Cal 104; Prot 1 g; Carbo 12 g; Fiber 1 g; T Fat 6 g; Chol 18 mg; Sod 51 mg.

Shirley C. Helms, Independence

BLONDE BROWNIES

½ cup butter, softened
2¼ cups packed light brown sugar
2 eggs, beaten
1½ cups flour
1 teaspoon vanilla extract
2 cups chopped pecans

Cream butter and brown sugar in bowl until light and fluffy. Add beaten eggs; mix well. Stir in flour, vanilla and pecans. Spread in greased 10x15-inch baking pan. Bake at 350 degrees for 20 to 25 minutes or until brownies test done. Cool. Cut into squares. Yield: 48 servings.

Approx Per Serving: Cal 107; Prot 1 g; Carbo 14 g; Fiber 1 g; T Fat 6 g; Chol 14 mg; Sod 23 mg.

Vickie Brown, Central

☎ Cool cookies completely in a single layer on a wire rack before storing. Store soft and chewy cookies in an airtight container and crisp cookies in a jar with a loose-fitting lid.

CHOCOLATE BROWNIES

2 ounces unsweetened chocolate, melted
1/2 cup melted butter
2 eggs, beaten
1 cup sugar
3/4 cup self-rising flour
1 teaspoon vanilla extract
1/2 cup chopped pecans

Combine melted chocolate and melted butter in bowl; mix well. Stir in eggs and sugar. Add flour and vanilla; mix well. Dust pecans lightly with additional flour. Stir into batter. Spread in greased 8-inch square baking pan. Bake at 325 degrees for 25 to 30 minutes or until brownies test done. Cool. Cut into squares. Yield: 24 servings.

Approx Per Serving: Cal 115; Prot 1 g; Carbo 12 g; Fiber 1 g; T Fat 7 g; Chol 28 mg; Sod 81 mg.

Norma C. Parrish, Central

GRAHAM-CHOCOLATE BROWNIES

1 2/3 cups graham cracker crumbs
2 cups chocolate chips
1 cup chopped pecans
1 15-ounce can sweetened condensed milk

Combine graham cracker crumbs, chocolate chips, pecans and condensed milk in bowl; mix well. Spread in well-greased 8-inch square baking pan. Bake at 350 degrees for 30 minutes. Cut into squares while hot. Cool completely before removing from pan. Yield: 16 servings.

Approx Per Serving: Cal 296; Prot 4 g; Carbo 38 g; Fiber 1 g; T Fat 16 g; Chol 9 mg; Sod 113 mg.

Nelle Laetsch, Asheville

☎ For Double Chocolate Brownies, arrange milk chocolate candy bars, chocolate chips or chocolate-covered peppermint patties over hot baked brownies. Return to the oven for 1 minute or until softened. Spread or swirl with knife to cover completely. Cool and cut as desired.

BUTTER COOKIES

1 cup flour
1/2 cup sugar
1/2 cup butter, softened
1 egg yolk
1 teaspoon vanilla extract
1/8 teaspoon salt
1/2 cup raspberry jelly

Combine flour, sugar, butter, egg yolk, vanilla and salt in bowl; mix well. Shape into 1-inch balls. Place on lightly greased cookie sheet. Make indentation in each cookie with back of spoon. Fill indentations with jelly. Bake at 350 degrees for 20 to 30 minutes or until lightly browned. Cool on cookie sheet for 2 minutes. Remove to wire rack to cool completely. May substitute almond extract for vanilla. May substitute other jellies or nuts for raspberry jelly. Yield: 24 servings.

Approx Per Serving: Cal 88; Prot 1 g; Carbo 12 g; Fiber <1 g; T Fat 4 g; Chol 19 mg; Sod 45 mg.

Kim Parker, Central

GREEK BUTTER COOKIES

2 cups butter, softened
1/2 cup confectioners' sugar, sifted
2 egg yolks
1 teaspoon vanilla extract
4 1/2 cups flour, sifted
1 teaspoon baking powder
1/2 cup (or more) confectioners' sugar

Cream butter in bowl for 10 to 15 minutes or until very light. Add 1/2 cup confectioners' sugar, egg yolks and vanilla; mix well. Stir in flour and baking powder. Shape dough into small crescents. Place 1 inch apart on 2 ungreased cookie sheets. Bake at 375 degrees for 15 minutes or until lightly browned. Place cookies carefully on waxed paper sprinkled with 1/4 cup confectioners' sugar. Sprinkle with remaining confectioners' sugar. Cool thoroughly. Store in airtight container. Yield: 60 servings.

Approx Per Serving: Cal 98; Prot 1 g; Carbo 9 g; Fiber <1 g; T Fat 6 g; Chol 24 mg; Sod 58 mg.

Anne Beratis, Independence

BUTTERHORNS

1 cup margarine
2 cups flour
1 egg, separated
¾ cup sour cream
¾ cup sugar
¾ cup finely chopped pecans
½ cup confectioners' sugar

Cut margarine into flour in bowl with pastry blender until crumbly. Add mixture of egg yolk and sour cream; mix well. Chill, covered, overnight. Roll dough into 3 circles. Cut each into 16 wedges. Place on ungreased cookie sheet. Combine sugar, pecans and half the egg white in bowl; mix well. Spoon onto wedges. Roll up from wide end. Bake at 375 degrees for 15 to 20 minutes. Sprinkle with confectioners' sugar. Cool on cookie sheet for 2 minutes. Remove to wire rack to cool. Yield: 48 servings.

Approx Per Serving: Cal 92; Prot 1 g; Carbo 9 g; Fiber <1 g; T Fat 6 g; Chol 6 mg; Sod 48 mg.

Delores McNeeley, Independence

CHERRY WINKS

¾ cup shortening
1 cup sugar
2 eggs
2 tablespoons milk
1 teaspoon vanilla extract
2½ cups flour, sifted
1 teaspoon baking powder
½ teaspoon soda
½ teaspoon salt
1 cup chopped pecans
1 cup chopped dates
⅓ cup chopped maraschino cherries
2½ cups crushed cornflakes
36 maraschino cherry quarters

Combine shortening, sugar, eggs, milk and vanilla in bowl; mix well. Stir in flour, baking powder, soda and salt. Add pecans, dates and cherries; mix well. Shape into 36 balls. Roll in crushed cornflakes. Place on ungreased cookie sheet. Top with cherry slices. Bake at 350 degrees for 10 to 12 minutes. Cool on cookie sheet for 2 minutes. Remove to wire rack to cool completely. Store in airtight container. Yield: 36 servings.

Approx Per Serving: Cal 152; Prot 2 g; Carbo 21 g; Fiber 1 g; T Fat 7 g; Chol 12 mg; Sod 113 mg.

Madelon Haskin, Hornets Nest

CHOCOLATE CHERRY BARS

1 2-layer package fudge cake mix
2 eggs, beaten
1 teaspoon almond extract
1 21-ounce can cherry pie filling
1 cup sugar
5 tablespoons butter
⅓ cup milk
1 cup chocolate chips

Combine cake mix, eggs and almond extract in bowl; mix well. Stir in pie filling gradually. Pour into lightly greased and floured 9x13-inch baking pan. Bake at 350 degrees for 25 to 30 minutes or until cake tests done. Combine sugar, butter and milk in saucepan; mix well. Bring to a boil over medium heat, stirring frequently. Remove from heat. Stir in chocolate chips. Spread icing over hot cake. Yield: 30 servings.

Approx Per Serving: Cal 170; Prot 2 g; Carbo 29 g; Fiber 1 g; T Fat 6 g; Chol 20 mg; Sod 124 mg

Wilma Burleson, Independence

CHOCOLATE CHIP COOKIES

½ cup butter, softened
1 cup packed brown sugar
1 egg
½ teaspoon vanilla extract
1 cup flour
¼ teaspoon baking powder
¼ teaspoon salt
1 cup chopped pecans
1 cup semisweet chocolate chips

Cream butter and brown sugar in bowl until light and fluffy. Add egg and vanilla; mix well. Stir in flour, baking powder and salt. Add pecans and chocolate chips; mix well. Drop by tablespoonfuls 2 inches apart onto lightly greased cookie sheet. Bake at 375 degrees for 10 minutes or until cookies spring back when lightly touched. Cool on cookie sheet for 1 minute. Remove to wire rack to cool completely. May make giant cookies by using ice cream scoop and flattening with floured hand.
Yield: 36 servings.

Approx Per Serving: Cal 106; Prot 1 g; Carbo 12 g; Fiber <1 g; T Fat 7 g; Chol 13 mg; Sod 44 mg.

Carroll Baxley, Coastal

EASY CHOCOLATE CHIP COOKIES

1   2-layer package white cake mix
1 cup semisweet chocolate chips
¾ cup oil
1 egg

Combine cake mix, chocolate chips, oil and egg in bowl; mix well. Shape into small balls. Place on ungreased cookie sheet. Bake at 350 degrees for 6 to 8 minutes. Cookies will be soft and will not look done. Bake longer for crisper cookies. May add ½ cup chopped nuts and ¼ cup light brown sugar or use butterscotch chips and yellow cake mix. Yield: 36 servings.

Approx Per Serving: Cal 127; Prot 1 g; Carbo 15 g; Fiber <1 g; T Fat 8 g; Chol 6 mg; Sod 90 mg.

Theresa M. Brhel, Hornets Nest

ST. LOUIS CHOCOLATE CHIP COOKIES

1 cup butter, softened
1 cup sugar
1 cup packed brown sugar
2 eggs
1 teaspoon vanilla extract
2 cups flour
2½ cups oats
1 teaspoon baking powder
½ teaspoon salt
2 cups chocolate chips
1   4-ounce Hershey bar, melted
1½ cups chopped pecans

Cream butter, sugar and brown sugar in bowl until light and fluffy. Beat in eggs and vanilla. Stir in mixture of flour, oats, baking powder and salt. Add chocolate chips, melted chocolate and pecans; mix well. Shape into large balls. Place on ungreased cookie sheet. Bake at 375 degrees for 8 minutes. Cool on cookie sheet for 2 minutes. Remove to wire rack to cool completely. Yield: 60 servings.

Approx Per Serving: Cal 143; Prot 2 g; Carbo 17 g; Fiber 1 g; T Fat 8 g; Chol 16 mg; Sod 56 mg.

Nancy Luckey, Independence

COWBOY COOKIES

1 cup shortening
1 cup sugar
1 cup packed brown sugar
2 cups oats
2 cups flour
2 eggs
1 teaspoon soda
1/2 teaspoon baking powder
1/2 teaspoon salt
1 teaspoon vanilla extract
1 cup chocolate chips
1/2 cup chopped pecans

Cream shortening, sugar and brown sugar in bowl until light and fluffy. Stir in oats, flour, eggs, soda, baking powder, salt, vanilla, chocolate chips and pecans. Drop by teaspoonfuls 2 inches apart onto greased cookie sheet. Bake at 350 degrees for 10 to 12 minutes or until lightly browned. Cool on cookie sheet for 2 minutes. Remove to paper towel to cool completely. Yield: 36 servings.

Approx Per Serving: Cal 201; Prot 2 g; Carbo 26 g; Fiber 1 g; T Fat 11 g; Chol 12 mg; Sod 65 mg.

Iceyphenolia S. Abernathy, Independence

CHRISTMAS BALLS

3 cups chopped dates
2 3-ounce cans coconut
8 ounces candied red cherries
8 ounces candied green cherries
1 14-ounce can sweetened condensed milk
4 cups chopped pecans

Combine dates, coconut, cherries, condensed milk and pecans in bowl; mix well. Shape into 2-inch balls. Place on lightly greased cookie sheet. Bake at 300 degrees for 25 minutes. Cool for 2 minutes on cookie sheet. Remove to wire rack to cool completely. Yield: 36 servings.

Approx Per Serving: Cal 226; Prot 2 g; Carbo 32 g; Fiber 3 g; T Fat 12 g; Chol 4 mg; Sod 16 mg.

Betty S. Bryant, Hornets Nest

FRUIT BARS

2 cups pecan halves
1 cup self-rising flour
1 egg, beaten
1 cup packed light brown sugar
10 tablespoons melted butter
1 cup mixed candied fruit

Arrange pecan halves in greased 8-inch square baking pan. Combine flour, egg, brown sugar and melted butter in bowl; mix well. Pour into prepared baking pan. Press candied fruit lightly into batter. Bake at 350 degrees for 40 to 45 minutes or until lightly browned. Cool. Cut into squares. Yield: 25 servings.

Approx Per Serving: Cal 182; Prot 2 g; Carbo 21 g; Fiber 1 g; T Fat 11 g; Chol 21 mg; Sod 46 mg.

Roe Ann Hill, Independence

FRUITCAKE BARS

6 tablespoons margarine
1 cup graham cracker crumbs
1 cup chopped candied cherries
1 cup chopped pecans
1 cup chopped candied pineapple
1 14-ounce can sweetened condensed milk

Melt margarine in 9x13-inch baking pan. Sprinkle with graham cracker crumbs. Combine cherries, pecans, pineapple and condensed milk in bowl; mix well. Spread in prepared pan. Bake at 300 degrees for 35 minutes. Cool. Cut into bars. Yield: 15 servings.

Approx Per Serving: Cal 310; Prot 4 g; Carbo 47 g; Fiber 1 g; T Fat 13 g; Chol 9 mg; Sod 136 mg.

Lorene Gramlick, Independence

ICE CREAM COOKIES

½ cup butter, softened
½ cup margarine, softened
1 cup sugar
2 eggs

1½ cups flour
½ teaspoon salt
1 teaspoon vanilla extract
72 pecan halves

Cream butter, margarine and sugar in bowl until light and fluffy. Beat in eggs. Add flour and salt; mix well. Beat in vanilla. Chill, tightly covered, overnight. Shape into 1-inch balls. Top with pecans. Place 2 inches apart on foil-lined cookie sheet. Bake at 300 degrees for 20 minutes or until light brown around edges. Remove foil and cookies from cookie sheet immediately. Cool on foil. Store in airtight container. Yield: 72 servings.

Approx Per Serving: Cal 58; Prot 1 g; Carbo 5 g; Fiber <1 g; T Fat 4 g; Chol 9 mg; Sod 43 mg.

Anna B. Davenport, Central

LADYFINGERS

1 cup butter, softened
⅓ cup sugar
2 teaspoons water
2 teaspoons vanilla extract

2 cups sifted flour
1 cup chopped pecans
½ cup confectioners' sugar

Cream butter and sugar in bowl until light and fluffy. Add water and vanilla. Stir in flour and pecans. Chill, tightly covered, for 4 hours. Shape into ladyfingers. Place on ungreased cookie sheet. Bake at 325 minutes for 20 minutes. Remove from pan; cool slightly on wire rack. Roll in confectioners' sugar. Yield: 36 servings.

Approx Per Serving: Cal 105; Prot 1 g; Carbo 9 g; Fiber <1 g; T Fat 7 g; Chol 14 mg; Sod 43 mg.

Wilma Burleson, Independence

LEMON SQUARES

- 1 2-layer package lemon cake mix
- 1 egg, beaten
- 1/2 cup melted butter
- 8 ounces cream cheese, softened
- 2 eggs
- 2 tablespoons lemon juice
- 1 1-pound package confectioners' sugar

Combine cake mix, beaten egg and melted butter in bowl; mix well. Press into 9x13-inch baking pan sprayed with nonstick cooking spray. Combine cream cheese, remaining 2 eggs, lemon juice and confectioners' sugar in bowl; mix well. Spread into prepared pan. Bake at 350 degrees for 40 minutes. Cool. Cut into squares. Garnish with additional confectioners' sugar.
Yield: 15 servings.

Approx Per Serving: Cal 409; Prot 4 g; Carbo 65 g; Fiber <1 g; T Fat 15 g; Chol 76 mg; Sod 320 mg.

Katie Grist, Independence

LEMON-CREAM CHEESE BROWNIES

- 1 2-layer package yellow cake mix
- 1 egg
- 1/2 cup margarine, softened
- 1 1-pound package confectioners' sugar
- 2 eggs
- 8 ounces cream cheese, softened
- 1 tablespoon lemon extract

Combine cake mix, 1 egg and margarine in bowl; mix well. Press into 9x13-inch baking dish. Combine confectioners' sugar, 2 eggs, cream cheese and lemon extract in bowl; mix well. Spoon into prepared dish. Bake at 350 degrees for 40 minutes. Cool completely; cut into squares. Yield: 15 servings.

Approx Per Serving: Cal 409; Prot 4 g; Carbo 65 g; Fiber 0 g; T Fat 15 g; Chol 59 mg; Sod 340 mg.

Mrs. Clayton Murphy, Piedmont

NEIMAN MARCUS ALMOND SQUARES

1 2-layer package pudding-recipe yellow cake mix
2 eggs, beaten
1/2 cup melted butter
1 cup chopped almonds

8 ounces cream cheese, softened
1/2 cup melted butter
2 eggs, beaten
1 1-pound package confectioners' sugar

Combine cake mix, 2 eggs, 1/2 cup melted butter and almonds in bowl; mix well. Press into greased 9x13-inch baking pan. Combine cream cheese, remaining 1/2 cup melted butter, 2 eggs and confectioners' sugar in bowl; mix well. Pour into prepared pan. Bake at 325 degrees for 1 hour. May substitute pecans or coconut for almonds. Cool; cut into squares.
Yield: 15 servings.

Approx Per Serving: Cal 519; Prot 6 g; Carbo 67 g; Fiber 1 g; T Fat 26 g; Chol 106 mg; Sod 377 mg.

Loretta Burgess, Independence

NEIMAN MARCUS SQUARES

1 2-layer package white cake mix
10 tablespoons butter, softened
1 1/4 cups chopped pecans
1 egg
1 egg white

1 1-pound package confectioners' sugar
12 ounces cream cheese, softened
1 tablespoon vanilla extract
2 eggs
1 egg yolk

Combine cake mix, butter and chopped pecans in mixer bowl; mix well. Add 1 egg and egg white, beating just until moist. Spread in lightly greased and floured 9x13-inch baking pan. Cream confectioners' sugar, cream cheese and vanilla in bowl until light and fluffy. Beat in remaining 2 eggs and egg yolk 1 at a time, scraping bowl frequently. Pour into prepared pan. Bake at 350 degrees for 45 minutes or until top is lightly browned. Cool in pan. Chill, covered with foil, overnight. Yield: 32 servings.

Approx Per Serving: Cal 247; Prot 3 g; Carbo 32 g; Fiber <1 g; T Fat 13 g; Chol 55 mg; Sod 171 mg.

Candy Finley, Raleigh

OAT BRAN COOKIES

3/4 cup shortening
1 cup packed brown sugar
1/2 cup sugar
1 egg
1/4 cup water
1 teaspoon vanilla extract
1 teaspoon black walnut flavoring

1 1/2 cups oats
1 1/2 cups oat bran
1 cup flour
1 teaspoon salt
1/2 teaspoon soda
1 cup raisins
1/2 cup chopped walnuts

Cream first 3 ingredients in bowl until light and fluffy. Beat in egg, water and flavorings. Stir in oats, oat bran, flour, salt and soda. Add raisins and walnuts; mix well. Drop by teaspoonfuls 2 inches apart onto greased cookie sheet. Bake at 350 degrees for 12 minutes or until lightly browned. Cool on cookie sheet for 2 minutes. Remove to wire rack to cool. Yield: 48 servings.

Approx Per Serving: Cal 100; Prot 2 g; Carbo 15 g; Fiber 1 g; T Fat 4 g; Chol 4 mg; Sod 58 mg.

Dorothy Byrum, Independence

MOLASSES OATMEAL COOKIES

1/2 cup shortening
3/4 cup light molasses
1 egg
1 1/2 cups sifted flour
1/2 teaspoon salt
1/2 teaspoon soda
2 teaspoons cinnamon

1/2 teaspoon baking powder
1/2 teaspoon nutmeg
1 1/2 cups oats
1/2 cup chopped walnuts
1 cup seedless raisins
1/4 cup sugar

Cream shortening and molasses in bowl until light and fluffy. Beat in egg. Combine flour, salt, soda, cinnamon, baking powder and nutmeg in large bowl; mix well. Add to creamed mixture. Stir in oats, walnuts and raisins; mix well. Chill, covered, for several hours. Shape into balls. Roll in sugar. Place on greased cookie sheet. Bake at 375 degrees for 12 to 15 minutes or until lightly browned. Yield: 54 servings.

Approx Per Serving: Cal 69; Prot 1 g; Carbo 10 g; Fiber 1 g; T Fat 3 g; Chol 4 mg; Sod 33 mg.

Mrs. Hugh L. McAulay, Blue Ridge

CREAM-FILLED OATMEAL COOKIES

2 cups shortening
2 cups packed brown sugar
2 cups sugar
1 teaspoon vanilla extract
4 eggs
2 cups sifted flour
6 cups quick-cooking oats
1 1/2 cups coconut
2 teaspoons salt
2 teaspoons soda
Filling

Cream shortening, brown sugar and sugar in bowl until light and fluffy. Stir in vanilla. Beat in eggs 1 at a time, beating well after each addition. Stir in mixture of sifted flour, oats, coconut, salt and soda. Roll into balls. Place on greased cookie sheet. Bake at 350 degrees for 8 to 10 minutes or until lightly browned. Cool on cookie sheet for 2 minutes. Remove to wire rack to cool completely. Spread filling between cookies.
Yield: 36 servings.

Filling for Oatmeal Cookies

5 tablespoons flour
1 cup milk
1 cup butter, softened
1 cup sugar
1/4 teaspoon salt
1 teaspoon vanilla extract

Combine flour with enough milk to make paste in saucepan. Stir in remaining milk. Cook over low heat until thickened, stirring constantly. Cream butter, sugar, salt and vanilla in bowl until light and fluffy. Stir in flour mixture.

Approx Per Serving: Cal 363; Prot 4 g; Carbo 45 g; Fiber 2 g; T Fat 19 g; Chol 38 mg; Sod 239 mg.

Carolyn B. Williams, Independence

SOUR CREAM OATMEAL COOKIES

1 cup margarine, softened
1½ cups sugar
2 cups oats
1 teaspoon soda
1 cup sour cream
½ teaspoon baking powder
2 cups flour
2 teaspoons cinnamon
1 cup chopped pecans
1 cup raisins

Combine margarine, sugar, oats, soda, sour cream, baking powder, flour, cinnamon, pecans and raisins in bowl; mix well, adding more flour if necessary. Drop by teaspoonfuls onto greased cookie sheet. Bake at 350 degrees for 15 to 18 minutes or until lightly browned. Remove to wire rack to cool.
Yield: 36 servings.

Approx Per Serving: Cal 169; Prot 2 g; Carbo 21 g; Fiber 1 g; T Fat 9 g; Chol 3 mg; Sod 91 mg.

Brenda Kendrick, Independence

NUTTY FINGERS

1 cup butter, softened
¼ cup confectioners' sugar
2 cups flour
1 cup chopped pecans
¼ cup confectioners' sugar

Cream butter and ¼ cup confectioners' sugar in bowl until light and fluffy. Stir in flour. Add pecans; mix well. Shape by 2 tablespoonfuls into 3-inch fingers on lightly greased cookie sheet. Bake at 350 degrees for 20 minutes. Roll warm cookies in remaining ¼ cup confectioners' sugar. Cool on wire rack completely. Yield: 24 servings.

Approx Per Serving: Cal 148; Prot 2 g; Carbo 11 g; Fiber 1 g; T Fat 11 g; Chol 21 mg; Sod 65 mg.

Kim Parker, Central

ORANGE SLICE COOKIES

3 eggs, beaten
2 cups packed brown sugar
1 teaspoon vanilla extract
1 tablespoon water
2 cups flour
1 16-ounce package orange slice candy, chopped
1 cup coconut
1 cup chopped pecans

Combine beaten eggs, brown sugar, vanilla and water in bowl; mix well. Stir in flour and candy. Add coconut and pecans; mix well. Drop by tablespoonfuls 2 inches apart onto lightly greased cookie sheet. Bake at 350 degrees for 25 minutes or until lightly browned. Cool on cookie sheet for 2 minutes. Remove to wire rack to cool completely. Yield: 24 servings.

Approx Per Serving: Cal 231; Prot 2 g; Carbo 45 g; Fiber 1 g; T Fat 5 g; Chol 27 mg; Sod 32 mg.

Carolyn Austin, Independence

PEANUT BUTTER COOKIES

1 cup peanut butter
1 cup sugar
2 eggs, beaten

Combine peanut butter, sugar and beaten eggs in bowl; mix well. Drop by teaspoonfuls 2 inches apart onto ungreased cookie sheet. Flatten with fork. Bake at 325 degrees for 10 minutes or just until light brown. Cool on cookie sheet for 2 minutes. Remove to wire rack to cool completely. May add pecans or use chunky peanut butter. Yield: 24 servings.

Approx Per Serving: Cal 102; Prot 4 g; Carbo 10 g; Fiber 1 g; T Fat 6 g; Chol 18 mg; Sod 49 mg.

Elaine Furr, Independence

EASY PEANUT BUTTER COOKIES

1 cup sugar
1 cup peanut butter
1 egg, beaten

    Combine sugar and peanut butter in bowl; mix well with fork. Add egg; mix well. Drop by teaspoonfuls onto ungreased cookie sheet; press with tines of fork. Bake at 350 degrees for 18 minutes or until brown. Remove to wire rack to cool. Yield: 24 servings.

Approx Per Serving: Cal 99; Prot 3 g; Carbo 10 g; Fiber 1 g;
   T Fat 6 g; Chol 9 mg; Sod 46 mg.

Jean Henderson, Hornets Nest

CHRISTMAS PEANUT BUTTER COOKIES

1/2 cup butter, softened
1/2 cup peanut butter
1/2 cup sugar
1/2 cup packed brown sugar
1 egg
2 tablespoons milk
1 teaspoon vanilla extract
1 1/4 cups sifted flour
1 teaspoon soda
1/2 teaspoon salt
1/4 cup red sugar
1/4 cup green sugar
1 10-ounce package chocolate candy kisses

    Cream butter, peanut butter, sugar and brown sugar in bowl until light and fluffy. Beat in egg, milk and vanilla. Stir in mixture of flour, soda and salt. Shape into balls. Roll in colored sugars. Place 2 inches apart on ungreased cookie sheet. Make small hole in center of each ball. Bake at 375 degrees for 10 to 12 minutes or until lightly browned. Insert kisses, point side down, into each cookie. Cool on cookie sheet for 2 minutes. Remove to wire rack to cool completely. Yield: 42 servings.

Approx Per Serving: Cal 117; Prot 2 g; Carbo 14 g; Fiber 1 g;
   T Fat 6 g; Chol 11 mg; Sod 85 mg.

Kitty Pennell, Hornets Nest

CRUNCHY PEANUT BUTTER COOKIES

½ cup shortening
½ cup sugar
½ cup packed brown sugar
½ cup chunky peanut butter
1 egg
1¼ cups sifted flour
½ teaspoon baking powder
¾ teaspoon soda
¼ teaspoon salt

Cream shortening, sugar, brown sugar and peanut butter in bowl until light and fluffy. Add egg; mix well. Stir in mixture of flour, baking powder, soda and salt. Chill, covered, for several hours. Roll into large balls. Place 3 inches apart on lightly greased cookie sheet. Flatten in crisscross pattern with fork dipped in additional flour. Bake at 375 degrees for 10 to 12 minutes or until set but not hard. Remove to wire rack to cool. Yield: 36 servings.

Approx Per Serving: Cal 85; Prot 2 g; Carbo 9 g; Fiber <1 g; T Fat 5 g; Chol 6 mg; Sod 54 mg.

Kim Parker, Central

PECAN CHEWS

½ cup butter, softened
2¼ cups packed light brown sugar
3 eggs
1 teaspoon vanilla extract
2 cups self-rising flour
1 cup chopped pecans
¼ cup confectioners' sugar

Cream butter and brown sugar in bowl until light and fluffy. Beat in eggs and vanilla. Stir in flour and pecans. Spread in greased 9x13-inch baking pan. Bake at 350 degrees for 30 minutes. Sprinkle with confectioners' sugar. Cool. Cut into squares. Yield: 15 servings.

Approx Per Serving: Cal 313; Prot 3 g; Carbo 48 g; Fiber 1 g; T Fat 13 g; Chol 59 mg; Sod 260 mg.

Joyce Waters, Salem

PECAN CRISPIES

1 egg white, stiffly beaten
3/4 cup packed light brown sugar
2 cups pecan halves

Combine egg white and brown sugar in bowl; mix well. Stir in pecans. Drop by teaspoonfuls 2 inches apart onto cookie sheet sprayed with nonstick cooking spray. Bake at 275 degrees for 20 minutes. Turn off oven. Let stand in closed oven for 25 minutes longer. Yield: 18 servings.

Approx Per Serving: Cal 115; Prot 1 g; Carbo 11 g; Fiber 1 g; T Fat 8 g; Chol 0 mg; Sod 7 mg.

Cheryl Griffin, Raleigh

PECAN FINGERS

1 cup flour
2 tablespoons sugar
1/2 cup melted margarine
1 teaspoon vanilla extract
1/8 teaspoon salt
1 cup finely chopped pecans
1/4 cup confectioners' sugar

Combine flour, sugar, melted margarine, vanilla and salt in bowl; mix well. Stir in pecans. Shape into fingers on lightly greased cookie sheet. Bake at 325 degrees for 20 minutes. Cool on cookie sheet for 2 minutes. Remove to wire rack to cool completely. Roll in confectioners' sugar. Yield: 12 servings.

Approx Per Serving: Cal 191; Prot 2 g; Carbo 15 g; Fiber 1 g; T Fat 14 g; Chol 0 mg; Sod 112 mg.

Martha G. Bridges, Hornets Nest

☎ Be careful not to use too much flour when rolling cookies; excessive flour will make the cookies dry and tough. Make cookies a uniform size to assure even baking.

NUTTY FINGERS

½ cup butter, softened
2 tablespoons sugar
1 cup flour
1 cup pecan meal
1 teaspoon vanilla extract
½ cup sifted confectioners' sugar

Cream butter and sugar in mixer bowl until light and fluffy. Add flour, pecan meal and vanilla; mix well. Shape into fingers; place on cookie sheet. Bake at 325 degrees for 20 minutes. Roll warm cookies in confectioners' sugar, coating well.
Yield: 24 servings.

Approx Per Serving: Cal 98; Prot 1 g; Carbo 8 g; Fiber <1 g; T Fat 7 g; Chol 10 mg; Sod 33 mg.

Chris Roberts, Central

RANGER COOKIES

1 cup margarine, softened
1 cup sugar
1 cup packed brown sugar
2 eggs, beaten
2 cups cornflakes
2 cups oats
2 cups flour
1 teaspoon baking powder
½ teaspoon salt
2 teaspoons soda
1 cup chopped pecans
1 teaspoon vanilla extract
1 cup raisins

Combine margarine, sugar, brown sugar, beaten eggs, cornflakes, oats, flour, baking powder, salt, soda, pecans, vanilla and raisins in bowl; mix well. Mixture will be dry. Drop by teaspoonfuls ½ inch apart onto foil-lined cookie sheet. Bake at 350 degrees for 15 minutes. Cool on cookie sheet for 2 minutes. Remove to wire rack to cool completely. Store in airtight container. Yield: 60 servings.

Approx Per Serving: Cal 112; Prot 2 g; Carbo 16 g; Fiber 1 g; T Fat 5 g; Chol 7 mg; Sod 119 mg.

Betty R. Bye, Independence

SEVEN-LAYER COOKIES

1/2 cup melted butter
1 cup graham cracker crumbs
1 cup coconut
1 cup chocolate chips
1 cup butterscotch chips
1 14-ounce can sweetened condensed milk
1 cup chopped pecans

Pour melted butter into 9x13-inch baking pan. Layer graham cracker crumbs, coconut, chocolate chips, butterscotch chips and condensed milk in prepared pan. Sprinkle with pecans. Bake at 325 degrees for 30 minutes. Cool. Cut into squares. May use more pecans if desired. Yield: 15 servings.

Approx Per Serving: Cal 364; Prot 4 g; Carbo 37 g; Fiber 2 g; T Fat 24 g; Chol 26 mg; Sod 139 mg.

Wilma Burleson, Independence
Martha G. Bridges, Hornets Nest

SUGAR COOKIES

1 cup margarine, softened
2 cups sugar
2 eggs
1/2 teaspoon vanilla extract
3 cups flour
1 tablespoon cream of tartar
1 teaspoon soda

Cream margarine and sugar in bowl until light and fluffy. Beat in eggs and vanilla. Stir in mixture of flour, cream of tartar and soda. Chill, covered, for several hours. Shape into small balls. Place on lightly greased cookie sheet. Bake at 350 degrees for 10 minutes. Remove to wire rack to cool. Yield: 24 servings.

Approx Per Serving: Cal 196; Prot 2 g; Carbo 29 g; Fiber <1 g; T Fat 8 g; Chol 18 mg; Sod 130 mg.

Anne Godwin, Independence

☎ Use frosting to pipe names of guests on rectangular cookies for place cards at holiday dinners.

ICEBOX SUGAR COOKIES

1/2 cup margarine, softened
1/2 cup sugar
1/2 cup packed brown sugar
1 egg, beaten
1 1/2 cups self-rising flour
1 teaspoon vanilla extract

Cream first 3 ingredients in bowl until light and fluffy. Add egg; mix well. Stir in flour. Add vanilla; mix well. Shape into three 1-inch logs. Chill, covered, overnight. Cut into 1-inch slices. Place on greased cookie sheet. Bake at 350 degrees for 10 minutes or until lightly browned. Yield: 24 servings.

Approx Per Serving: Cal 99; Prot 1 g; Carbo 15 g; Fiber <1 g; T Fat 4 g; Chol 9 mg; Sod 134 mg.

Phyllis Cox, Central

OLD-TIME TEA CAKES

1 cup butter, softened
2 cups sugar
1 teaspoon salt
1 teaspoon vanilla extract
1 teaspoon lemon extract
3 eggs
5 cups sifted flour
1/2 cup buttermilk
1 teaspoon soda

Cream butter, sugar, salt, vanilla extract and lemon extract in bowl until light and fluffy. Beat in eggs 1 at a time, beating well after each addition. Add flour alternately with mixture of buttermilk and soda; mix well. Chill, covered, overnight. Roll 1/8 to 1/4 inch thick on floured surface. Cut with cookie cutter. Place 2 inches apart on cookie sheet sprayed with nonstick cooking spray. Bake at 350 degrees for 10 to 12 minutes or until lightly browned. Cool on cookie sheet for 2 minutes. Remove to wire rack to cool completely. Store in plastic bags in airtight containers.
Yield: 100 servings.

Approx Per Serving: Cal 56; Prot 1 g; Carbo 8 g; Fiber <1 g; T Fat 2 g; Chol 11 mg; Sod 49 mg.

Mrs. Hugh L. McAulay, Blue Ridge

GRANDMA'S TEA COOKIES

1/2 cup margarine, softened
1 1/4 cups sugar
4 eggs
1 tablespoon vanilla extract
4 1/2 to 5 cups self-rising flour

Cream margarine and sugar in bowl until light and fluffy. Beat in eggs and vanilla. Add enough flour gradually to make soft dough. Shape into 5 balls. Roll 1/8 inch thick on floured surface. Cut with cookie cutter. Place 2 inches apart on greased cookie sheet. Bake at 350 degrees for 8 minutes or until lightly browned. Cool on cookie sheet for 2 minutes. Remove to wire rack to cool completely. Store in airtight container. Yield: 144 servings.

Approx Per Serving: Cal 30; Prot 1 g; Carbo 5 g; Fiber <1 g; T Fat 1 g; Chol 6 mg; Sod 56 mg.

Hanna Dillard, Raleigh

THUMBPRINT COOKIES

1/4 cup shortening
1/4 cup butter, softened
1/4 cup packed brown sugar
1 egg yolk
1/4 teaspoon vanilla extract
1 cup flour
1/8 teaspoon salt
1 egg white
1 cup finely chopped pecans
1/2 cup butter, softened
1 1-pound package confectioners' sugar
1/8 teaspoon salt
1 teaspoon vanilla extract
3 to 4 tablespoons milk

Cream first 5 ingredients in bowl until light and fluffy. Stir in mixture of flour and salt. Chill, covered, for 1 hour. Roll into 1-inch balls. Dip into egg white. Roll in pecans. Place 1 inch apart on ungreased cookie sheet. Bake at 350 degrees for 5 minutes. Press with thumb. Bake for 6 to 8 minutes longer. Cookies will look doughy. Cool on cookie sheet for 2 minutes. Remove to wire rack to cool. Cream butter, 1/3 of the confectioners' sugar and salt in bowl until light and fluffy. Add vanilla, 2 tablespoons milk and remaining confectioners' sugar; mix well. Stir in enough remaining 1 to 2 tablespoons milk to make of spreading consistency. Spoon frosting onto center of cookies. Yield: 24 servings.

Approx Per Serving: Cal 223; Prot 1 g; Carbo 30 g; Fiber <1 g; T Fat 12 g; Chol 25 mg; Sod 75 mg.

Marjorie Sapp, Independence

PIES

APPLE PIE

1/2 cup melted margarine
1 cup sugar
2 eggs, beaten
1/2 teaspoon cinnamon
1/2 teaspoon nutmeg
1 teaspoon lemon juice
2 cups finely shredded apples
1 unbaked 9-inch pie shell

Combine margarine, sugar and eggs in bowl; mix well. Add cinnamon, nutmeg, lemon juice and apples. Spoon into pie shell. Bake at 350 degrees for 60 minutes or until brown. Pie will resemble pecan pie in color. Yield: 6 servings.

Approx Per Serving: Cal 462; Prot 4 g; Carbo 52 g; Fiber 1 g; T Fat 27 g; Chol 71 mg; Sod 386 mg.

Lib Livingood, Hornets Nest

SOUR CREAM APPLE PIE

2 tablespoons flour
3/4 cup sugar
1/8 teaspoon salt
1 egg
1 cup sour cream
1 teaspoon vanilla extract
1/4 teaspoon nutmeg
2 cups finely chopped apples
1 unbaked 9-inch pie shell
1/3 cup sugar
1/2 cup flour
1/4 cup butter
1 teaspoon cinnamon

Sift 2 tablespoons flour, sugar and salt into medium bowl. Stir in egg, sour cream, vanilla and nutmeg. Fold in apples. Spoon into pie shell. Bake at 400 degrees for 15 minutes. Reduce temperature to 350 degrees. Bake for 30 minutes longer. Combine remaining 1/3 cup sugar, 1/2 cup flour, butter and cinnamon in small bowl until crumbly. Sprinkle over top of pie. Bake for 10 minutes longer or until brown. Yield: 6 servings.

Approx Per Serving: Cal 523; Prot 6 g; Carbo 66 g; Fiber 2 g; T Fat 27 g; Chol 73 mg; Sod 326 mg.

Maxine T. Braswell, Blue Ridge

BUTTERMILK PIE

¼ cup flour
¼ cup cold water
¾ cup sugar
2 egg yolks
1 cup buttermilk
2 tablespoons butter
1 teaspoon vanilla extract
1   9-inch baked pie shell
2 egg whites
½ cup sugar

Combine flour, water, ¾ cup sugar and egg yolks in double boiler; mix well. Add buttermilk and butter. Cook over hot water until thickened, stirring constantly. Remove from heat. Stir in vanilla. Cool. Spoon into pie shell. Beat egg whites in mixer bowl until foamy. Add remaining ½ cup sugar gradually, beating until stiff peaks form. Spread meringue over filling, sealing to edge. Bake at 325 degrees for 15 minutes or until lightly browned. Yield: 6 servings.

Approx Per Serving: Cal 408; Prot 6 g; Carbo 61 g; Fiber 1 g;
    T Fat 16 g; Chol 83 mg; Sod 279 mg.

Ruby Norton, Raleigh

MAMA'S BUTTERSCOTCH PIE

3 tablespoons flour
1 tablespoon sugar
1 cup packed brown sugar
3 egg yolks
1 cup milk
3 tablespoons water
2 tablespoons butter
⅛ teaspoon salt
1 teaspoon vanilla extract
1 baked 9-inch pie shell
2 egg whites
¼ cup sugar

Combine flour, 1 tablespoon sugar, brown sugar and egg yolks in saucepan; mix well. Add milk, water, butter and salt. Cook over low heat until thickened, stirring constantly. Stir in vanilla. Spoon into pie shell. Beat egg whites in mixer bowl until soft peaks form. Add remaining ¼ cup sugar gradually, beating until stiff peaks form. Spread over top of pie, sealing to edge. Bake at 325 degrees for 15 minutes or until lightly browned.
Yield: 6 servings.

Approx Per Serving: Cal 438; Prot 6 g; Carbo 64 g; Fiber 1 g;
    T Fat 18 g; Chol 122 mg; Sod 314 mg.

Nell Seegers, Independence

IMPOSSIBLE CHERRY PIE

2 tablespoons margarine, softened
1/4 cup sugar
1/2 cup packed brown sugar
1/2 cup baking mix
1/2 teaspoon cinnamon
1 cup milk
2 eggs
1/4 teaspoon almond extract
1 21-ounce can cherry pie filling
1/2 cup margarine
1/2 cup baking mix
1/2 cup packed brown sugar
1/2 teaspoon cinnamon

Combine 2 tablespoons margarine, sugar, 1/2 cup brown sugar, 1/2 cup baking mix and 1/2 teaspoon cinnamon in mixer bowl. Add milk, eggs and almond extract; beat for 1 minute or until smooth. Pour into greased 10-inch pie plate. Spoon pie filling on top. Bake at 400 degrees for 25 minutes. Combine remaining 1/2 cup margarine, 1/2 cup baking mix, 1/2 cup brown sugar and 1/2 teaspoon cinnamon in small bowl until crumbly. Sprinkle over pie. Bake for 10 minutes or until topping is lightly browned.
Yield: 6 servings.

Approx Per Serving: Cal 575; Prot 5 g; Carbo 85 g; Fiber 1 g; T Fat 25 g; Chol 77 mg; Sod 574 mg.

Jennifer McKinley, Independence

CHESS PIE

1/4 cup melted margarine
1 cup sugar
2 eggs, beaten
1 5-ounce can evaporated milk
1 tablespoon vanilla extract
1 tablespoon cornmeal
1/8 teaspoon cinnamon
1 unbaked 9-inch pie shell

Combine margarine, sugar, eggs and evaporated milk in medium bowl; mix well. Add vanilla, cornmeal and cinnamon, stirring until well blended. Spoon into pie shell. Bake at 350 degrees for 30 to 45 minutes or until set. Cool for 20 minutes before serving. Yield: 6 servings.

Approx Per Serving: Cal 417; Prot 6 g; Carbo 51 g; Fiber 1 g; T Fat 21 g; Chol 78 mg; Sod 321 mg.

Rosemary Crabtree, Raleigh

CHOCOLATE PIE

1 cup sugar
1/4 cup cornstarch
1/4 cup baking cocoa
1 5-ounce can
   evaporated milk
2 eggs
1/4 cup butter
1 tablespoon vanilla
   extract
1/8 teaspoon salt
1 9-inch baked pie shell
8 ounces whipped topping

Combine sugar, cornstarch and baking cocoa in top of double boiler; mix well. Combine evaporated milk with enough water to measure 2 cups. Add to baking cocoa mixture; stir until well blended. Add eggs, butter, vanilla and salt. Cook over hot water until thickened, stirring constantly. Pour into pie shell. Chill in refrigerator until firm. Top with whipped topping just before serving. Yield: 6 servings.

Approx Per Serving: Cal 560; Prot 7 g; Carbo 65 g; Fiber 2 g;
   T Fat 32 g; Chol 99 mg; Sod 351 mg.

Willie Collins, Independence

FAVORITE CHOCOLATE PIE

1 cup sugar
3 tablespoons baking
   cocoa
2 tablespoons cornstarch
2 egg yolks
1 12-ounce can
   evaporated milk
1 teaspoon vanilla extract
1 baked 9-inch pie shell
2 egg whites
1/4 cup sugar

Combine 1 cup sugar, baking cocoa, cornstarch and egg yolks in heavy saucepan; mix well. Add a small amount evaporated milk; mix well. Stir in remaining evaporated milk. Cook over medium heat until thickened, stirring constantly. Add vanilla; mix well. Pour into pie shell. Beat egg whites in mixer bowl until soft peaks form. Add remaining 1/4 cup sugar gradually, beating until stiff peaks form. Spread over top of filling, sealing to edge. Bake at 350 degrees until lightly browned.
Yield: 6 servings.

Approx Per Serving: Cal 431; Prot 8 g; Carbo 64 g; Fiber 1 g;
   T Fat 17 g; Chol 88 mg; Sod 264 mg.

Jewel H. Ware, Piedmont

CHOCOLATE MERINGUE PIE

1/2 cup sugar
1/4 cup flour
2 tablespoons baking cocoa
2 egg yolks
2 cups milk
1 tablespoon margarine
1 teaspoon vanilla extract
1 baked 9-inch pie shell
2 egg whites
1/2 cup sugar

Combine 1/2 cup sugar, flour, baking cocoa, egg yolks, milk and margarine in double boiler; mix well. Cook over hot water until thickened, stirring constantly. Add vanilla; stir until well blended. Pour into pie shell. Beat egg whites in mixer bowl until soft peaks form. Add remaining 1/2 cup sugar gradually, beating until stiff peaks form. Spread meringue over filling, sealing to edge. Bake at 350 degrees until lightly browned.
Yield: 6 servings.

Approx Per Serving: Cal 398; Prot 7 g; Carbo 55 g; Fiber 1 g; T Fat 17 g; Chol 82 mg; Sod 260 mg.

Ruby Norton, Raleigh

RICH CHOCOLATE MERINGUE PIE

1 tablespoon (heaping) flour
2 tablespoons baking cocoa
1 cup sugar
3 egg yolks, beaten
1 12-ounce can evaporated milk
1/2 cup margarine
1 baked 9-inch pie shell
3 egg whites
1 tablespoon sugar

Combine flour, baking cocoa, 1 cup sugar, egg yolks, evaporated milk and margarine in double boiler. Cook over hot water until thickened, stirring constantly. Pour into pie shell. Beat egg whites in mixer bowl until soft peaks form. Add remaining 1 tablespoon sugar gradually, beating until stiff peaks form. Spread over filling, sealing to edge. Bake at 350 degrees for 10 to 12 minutes or until lightly browned. Yield: 6 servings.

Approx Per Serving: Cal 553; Prot 9 g; Carbo 58 g; Fiber 1 g; T Fat 33 g; Chol 123 mg; Sod 452 mg.

Carroll Baxley, Coastal

OLD-FASHIONED CHOCOLATE PIE

1/4 cup melted margarine
1 1/2 cups sugar
2 eggs
1 5-ounce can evaporated milk
2 1/2 tablespoons baking cocoa
1 teaspoon vanilla extract
1 unbaked 9-inch deep-dish pie shell

Combine margarine, sugar, eggs, evaporated milk, baking cocoa and vanilla in mixer bowl; mix until well blended. Pour into pie shell. Bake at 325 degrees for 40 to 45 minutes or until set. Yield: 6 servings.

Approx Per Serving: Cal 477; Prot 6 g; Carbo 67 g; Fiber 1 g; T Fat 22 g; Chol 78 mg; Sod 322 mg.

Kitty Pennell, Hornets Nest

CHOCOLATE BROWNIE PIE

1/2 cup margarine
3 tablespoons baking cocoa
1 cup sugar
1/4 cup flour
2 eggs, beaten
1 teaspoon vanilla extract
1 cup chopped pecans
1 unbaked 9-inch pie shell

Melt margarine with baking cocoa in saucepan; stir until well blended. Remove from heat. Stir in sugar, flour, eggs and vanilla. Add pecans; mix well. Pour into pie shell. Bake at 325 degrees for 30 to 35 minutes or until set. Do not store in refrigerator. Yield: 6 servings.

Approx Per Serving: Cal 601; Prot 7 g; Carbo 56 g; Fiber 3 g; T Fat 41 g; Chol 71 mg; Sod 386 mg.

Nell Seegers, Independence

CHOCOLATE NUT PIE

1/2 cup margarine
1 cup chocolate chips
1/2 cup sugar
1/2 cup packed brown sugar
1/2 cup flour
2 eggs
1 teaspoon vanilla extract
1 cup chopped pecans
1 9-inch graham cracker pie shell

Melt margarine in saucepan. Pour over chocolate chips in bowl; stir until chocolate chips are melted. Add sugar and brown sugar; mix well. Stir in flour, eggs, vanilla and pecans. Pour into pie shell. Bake at 350 degrees for 30 minutes. Yield: 6 servings.

Approx Per Serving: Cal 883; Prot 8 g; Carbo 97 g; Fiber 3 g; T Fat 55 g; Chol 71 mg; Sod 533 mg.

Evelyn N. Goodman, Hornets Nest

GERMAN CHOCOLATE PIES

3 cups sugar
1/4 cup baking cocoa
1/2 cup melted margarine
4 eggs
1 teaspoon vanilla extract
1 cup flaked coconut
1 cup evaporated milk
1 cup chopped walnuts
1/8 teaspoon salt
2 unbaked 9-inch pie shells

Combine sugar, baking cocoa, melted margarine, eggs and vanilla in medium bowl; mix well. Add coconut, evaporated milk, walnuts and salt; mix well. Pour into pie shells. Bake at 350 degrees for 50 minutes or until set. Yield: 12 servings.

Approx Per Serving: Cal 563; Prot 7 g; Carbo 71 g; Fiber 2 g; T Fat 30 g; Chol 77 mg; Sod 366 mg.

Jessie M. Godwin, Raleigh

GERMAN CHOCOLATE COCONUT PIE

1 cup sugar
3 tablespoons melted margarine
2 eggs
2/3 cup milk
1 teaspoon vanilla extract
2 tablespoons flour
2 tablespoons cornstarch
2 tablespoons baking cocoa
1/4 teaspoon salt
1/2 cup chopped walnuts
2/3 cup coconut
1 unbaked 9-inch pie shell

Combine sugar, margarine, eggs, milk and vanilla in medium bowl; mix well. Add flour, cornstarch, baking cocoa and salt; mix well. Stir in walnuts and coconut. Spoon into pie shell. Bake at 400 degrees for 30 minutes or until set. Yield: 6 servings.

Approx Per Serving: Cal 500; Prot 7 g; Carbo 59 g; Fiber 3 g; T Fat 28 g; Chol 75 mg; Sod 377 mg.

Shirley C. Helms, Independence

FAVORITE GERMAN CHOCOLATE PIES

3/4 cup coconut
2 unbaked 10-inch pie shells
3/4 cup chopped pecans
3 1/2 cups sugar
1 1/2 teaspoons cake flour
1 teaspoon cornstarch
2 eggs
1/2 cup melted margarine
2 ounces unsweetened chocolate, melted
2 cups evaporated milk
1 teaspoon vanilla extract
1/8 teaspoon salt

Sprinkle coconut over bottom of pie shells. Sprinkle pecans over coconut. Combine sugar, cake flour and cornstarch in mixer bowl. Add eggs, margarine and chocolate; beat until well blended. Add evaporated milk gradually, mixing constantly. Stir in vanilla and salt. Spoon into prepared pie shells. Bake at 350 degrees for 40 minutes or until set. Yield: 12 servings.

Approx Per Serving: Cal 605; Prot 7 g; Carbo 80 g; Fiber 2 g; T Fat 31 g; Chol 47 mg; Sod 349 mg.

Virginia S. Smith, Independence

MOTHER'S GERMAN CHOCOLATE PIE

1 cup sugar
1 tablespoon (heaping) baking cocoa
1 tablespoon (heaping) flour
1 egg, beaten
1 cup evaporated milk
1/3 tablespoon vanilla extract
1/3 cup chopped pecans
1/3 cup coconut
1 unbaked 8-inch pie shell

Combine sugar, baking cocoa and flour in bowl; mix well. Add beaten egg, evaporated milk and vanilla; mix well. Stir in pecans and coconut. Pour into pie shell. Bake at 350 degrees for 40 minutes or until set. Yield: 6 servings.

Approx Per Serving: Cal 421; Prot 7 g; Carbo 55 g; Fiber 2 g; T Fat 20 g; Chol 48 mg; Sod 251 mg.

Frances Simmons, Hornets Nest

CHOCOLATE FUDGE NUT PIES

1/2 cup melted margarine
2 1/2 cups sugar
6 tablespoons baking cocoa
4 eggs
1 12-ounce can evaporated milk
1 cup chopped pecans
1 cup coconut
2 teaspoons vanilla extract
2 unbaked 10-inch deep-dish pie shells

Combine margarine, sugar and baking cocoa in mixer bowl; mix well. Beat in eggs and evaporated milk at medium speed for 2 minutes or until well blended. Stir in pecans, coconut and vanilla. Pour into pie shells. Bake at 325 degrees for 40 to 50 minutes or until set. Yield: 12 servings.

Approx Per Serving: Cal 548; Prot 7 g; Carbo 64 g; Fiber 3 g; T Fat 31 g; Chol 79 mg; Sod 343 mg.

Ella S. Richards, Raleigh

FUDGE PIE

2 eggs
1 cup sugar
1/2 cup melted butter
2 ounces melted unsweetened chocolate
1 teaspoon vanilla extract
1/4 cup sifted flour
1/8 teaspoon salt

Combine eggs and sugar in bowl; mix well. Stir in cooled butter and chocolate. Add vanilla, flour and salt; mix well. Spoon into greased 8-inch pie plate. Bake at 350 degrees for 20 minutes or until set. Cool for 10 minutes. Serve warm with vanilla ice cream. Yield: 6 servings.

Approx Per Serving: Cal 358; Prot 4 g; Carbo 40 g; Fiber 2 g; T Fat 22 g; Chol 112 mg; Sod 198 mg.

Anna Faye Martin, Asheville

CHOCOLATE SWIRL CHEESE PIE

24 ounces cream cheese, softened
5 eggs
1 cup sugar
1 tablespoon vanilla extract
1 4-ounce package German's sweet chocolate, melted

Beat 8 ounces cream cheese and 1 egg in mixer bowl until light. Add remaining 16 ounces cream cheese and sugar; beat until well blended. Add remaining 4 eggs 1 at a time, beating well after each addition. Stir in vanilla. Fold cooled chocolate into 2 cups cream cheese mixture in small bowl. Spoon remaining cream cheese mixture into well-greased 10-inch pie plate. Top with spoonfuls of chocolate mixture. Swirl with knife. Bake at 350 degrees for 40 to 45 minutes or until set. Cool. Chill in refrigerator before serving. Yield: 6 servings.

Approx Per Serving: Cal 696; Prot 14 g; Carbo 48 g; Fiber 1 g; T Fat 51 g; Chol 301 mg; Sod 397 mg.

Patsy Prillaman, Independence

CREAM CHEESE PIES

1 cup chopped pecans
2 unbaked 9-inch pie shells
8 ounces cream cheese, softened
4 cups confectioners' sugar
16 ounces frozen whipped topping, thawed
1 21-ounce can fruit pie filling

Sprinkle pecans into bottom of pie shells. Bake at 350 degrees until lightly browned. Cool. Beat cream cheese and confectioners' sugar in mixer bowl until light. Fold in whipped topping. Spoon into pie shells. Top with pie filling. Chill in refrigerator until firm. May use cherry, blueberry or strawberry pie filling. Yield: 12 servings.

Approx Per Serving: Cal 604; Prot 5 g; Carbo 76 g; Fiber 2 g; T Fat 33 g; Chol 21 mg; Sod 264 mg.

Martha Bridges, Hornets Nest

COCONUT PIES

1¾ cups sugar
½ cup self-rising flour
4 eggs
¼ cup melted margarine
2 cups milk
1 teaspoon vanilla extract
2 cups coconut
2 unbaked 9-inch pie shells

Combine sugar, flour, eggs, margarine, milk and vanilla in bowl; mix well. Fold in coconut. Spoon into pie shells. Bake at 350 degrees for 30 to 35 minutes until set and lightly browned. Yield: 12 servings.

Approx Per Serving: Cal 426; Prot 6 g; Carbo 54 g; Fiber 2 g; T Fat 21 g; Chol 77 mg; Sod 356 mg.

Audrey Brock, Hornets Nest

☎ Pies with cream or custard filling should be cooked to room temperature and then stored in the refrigerator to prevent spoilage.

COCONUT CUSTARD PIE

1 1/2 cups sugar
1/4 cup melted butter
5 eggs
2 cups milk
1 teaspoon vanilla extract
1/2 cup self-rising flour
1 cup flaked coconut

Combine sugar, butter, eggs, milk, vanilla and flour in bowl; mix well. Stir in coconut. Spoon into greased 10-inch pie plate. Bake at 350 degrees for 40 minutes or just until set.
Yield: 6 servings.

Approx Per Serving: Cal 472; Prot 9 g; Carbo 67 g; Fiber 2 g; T Fat 19 g; Chol 209 mg; Sod 272 mg.

Annie Hall, Hornets Nest

COCONUT MERINGUE PIE

1 cup sugar
1/4 cup flour
2 cups milk
4 egg yolks, beaten
1 teaspoon vanilla extract
2 tablespoons butter
1 1/2 cups coconut
1 baked 10-inch deep-dish pie shell
4 egg whites, at room temperature
3 tablespoons sugar

Combine 1 cup sugar and flour in saucepan; mix well. Add milk gradually, stirring until well blended. Add egg yolks, vanilla and butter. Cook over low heat until thickened, stirring constantly. Stir in coconut. Pour into pie shell. Beat egg whites in mixer bowl until soft peaks form. Add remaining 3 tablespoons sugar gradually, beating until stiff peaks form. Spread meringue over filling, sealing to edge. Sprinkle with additional coconut, if desired. Bake at 350 degrees until lightly browned.
Yield: 6 servings.

Approx Per Serving: Cal 548; Prot 10 g; Carbo 70 g; Fiber 3 g; T Fat 26 g; Chol 163 mg; Sod 337 mg.

Nell Seegers, Independence

☎ Fruit, mince and chiffon pies freeze well. Custard and meringue pies do not freeze well.

CREAMY COCONUT PIES

1 cup sugar
3 tablespoons cornstarch
1 12-ounce can evaporated milk
1 evaporated milk can water
4 egg yolks, beaten

2 tablespoons butter
1 teaspoon vanilla extract
1 14-ounce package coconut
2 baked 9-inch pie shells
4 egg whites
1/2 cup sugar

Combine 1 cup sugar and cornstarch in double boiler. Add evaporated milk, water, egg yolks, butter and vanilla; mix well. Cook over hot water until thickened, stirring constantly. Remove from heat. Stir in coconut. Pour into pie shells. Beat egg whites in mixer bowl until soft peaks form. Add remaining 1/2 cup sugar gradually, beating until stiff peaks form. Spread meringue over filling, sealing to edge. Bake at 350 degrees until lightly browned. Yield: 12 servings.

Approx Per Serving: Cal 493; Prot 7 g; Carbo 59 g; Fiber 5 g; T Fat 27 g; Chol 85 mg; Sod 334 mg.

Vickie Brown, Central

AUNT LULA'S COCONUT PIES

1 1/4 cups sugar
5 tablespoons cornstarch
4 cups milk
5 egg yolks, beaten
1 teaspoon vanilla extract
2 tablespoons margarine

1 1/2 cups flaked coconut
2 baked 9-inch pie shells
5 egg whites
10 tablespoons sugar
1/4 teaspoon cream of tartar

Combine 1 1/4 cups sugar, cornstarch, milk, egg yolks, vanilla and margarine in double boiler. Cook over hot water until thickened, stirring constantly. Stir in coconut. Pour into pie shells. Beat egg whites in mixer bowl until soft peaks form. Add remaining 10 tablespoons sugar and cream of tartar gradually, beating until stiff peaks form. Spread over pie fillings, sealing to edges. Sprinkle with additional coconut if desired. Bake at 400 degrees until lightly browned. Yield: 12 servings.

Approx Per Serving: Cal 426; Prot 7 g; Carbo 55 g; Fiber 2 g; T Fat 20 g; Chol 100 mg; Sod 266 mg.

Ramona K. Hedgpeth, Raleigh

COCONUT CREAM PIES

1/2 cup sugar
1/3 cup flour
1/2 teaspoon salt
3 cups milk
3 egg yolks, beaten
1 cup coconut
1 teaspoon vanilla extract
2 9-inch graham cracker pie shells
3 egg whites
6 tablespoons sugar
1/2 cup coconut

Combine 1/2 cup sugar, flour and salt in saucepan. Add milk and egg yolks; mix well. Cook over medium heat until thickened, stirring constantly. Remove from heat. Stir in 1 cup coconut and vanilla. Spoon into pie shells. Beat egg whites in mixer bowl until soft peaks form. Add remaining 6 tablespoons sugar 2 tablespoons at a time, beating until stiff peaks form. Spread over fillings, sealing to edges. Sprinkle pies with remaining 1/2 cup coconut. Bake at 350 degrees for 15 minutes or until lightly browned. Yield: 12 servings.

Approx Per Serving: Cal 444; Prot 7 g; Carbo 59 g; Fiber 2 g; T Fat 21 g; Chol 62 mg; Sod 471 mg.

Phyllis Jones, Independence

IMPOSSIBLE COCONUT PIES

1 3/4 cup sugar
1/2 cup self-rising flour
4 eggs, beaten
1/4 cup melted butter
2 cups milk
1 teaspoon vanilla extract
1 7-ounce can coconut

Combine sugar and flour in bowl; mix well. Add eggs; mix until well blended. Stir in butter, milk, vanilla and coconut. Pour into 2 greased 9-inch pie plates. Bake at 350 degrees for 35 minutes or until brown. Yield: 12 servings.

Approx Per Serving: Cal 290; Prot 4 g; Carbo 42 g; Fiber 2 g; T Fat 12 g; Chol 87 mg; Sod 132 mg.

Joyce Waters, Salem

AMANDA'S COCONUT-PINEAPPLE PIES

½ cup melted margarine
2 cups sugar
4 eggs
1 15-ounce can pineapple
1 8-ounce package coconut
2 unbaked 9-inch pie shells

Combine margarine and sugar in bowl; mix well. Add eggs, pineapple and coconut; mix well. Pour into pie shells. Bake at 350 degrees for 30 minutes or until set. Yield: 12 servings.

Approx Per Serving: Cal 490; Prot 5 g; Carbo 63 g; Fiber 3 g; T Fat 26 g; Chol 71 mg; Sod 345 mg.

Amanda Tucker, Independence

COCONUT AND PINEAPPLE PIES

4 eggs, well beaten
2 cups sugar
½ cup melted margarine
1 3-ounce can coconut
1 8-ounce can crushed pineapple
2 unbaked 8-inch pie shells

Combine eggs and sugar in mixer bowl; mix well. Stir in margarine. Add coconut and pineapple. Spoon into pie shells. Bake at 350 degrees until light brown. Yield: 12 servings.

Approx Per Serving: Cal 419; Prot 4 g; Carbo 53 g; Fiber 2 g; T Fat 22 g; Chol 71 mg; Sod 298 mg.

Gladys Hinson, Independence

☎ Always prick the bottom and side of a pie shell which is baked before filling. This will prevent puffing. Brush the bottom with 1 egg white beaten with 1 teaspoon water just before shell is finished baking to keep shell from becoming soggy when filled.

NO-CRUST TOASTED COCONUT PIE

6 tablespoons margarine
1 cup (heaping) sugar
2 tablespoons cornstarch
1 12-ounce can evaporated milk
1 tablespoon vanilla extract
3 eggs
1 5-ounce can coconut

Cream margarine, sugar and cornstarch in bowl until light and fluffy. Add evaporated milk, vanilla and eggs; mix well. Stir in coconut. Spoon into well-greased and floured glass pie plate. Bake at 350 degrees for 35 to 40 minutes or until set and brown. Yield: 6 servings.

Approx Per Serving: Cal 475; Prot 8 g; Carbo 54 g; Fiber 3 g; T Fat 26 g; Chol 123 mg; Sod 289 mg.

Polly Mabrey, Hornets Nest
Evelyn N. Goodman, Hornets Nest

EGG CUSTARD PIE

¼ cup butter, softened
1½ cups sugar
¼ cup flour
⅛ teaspoon salt
2 eggs, beaten
1 cup milk, at room temperature
1 teaspoon vanilla extract
1 unbaked 9-inch pie shell

Combine butter, sugar, flour and salt in bowl; mix well. Add eggs, milk and vanilla; mix well. Pour into pie shell. Bake at 350 degrees for 30 to 40 minutes or until set. Yield: 6 servings.

Approx Per Serving: Cal 483; Prot 6 g; Carbo 69 g; Fiber 1 g; T Fat 21 g; Chol 97 mg; Sod 334 mg.

Karen Stallings, Independence

EGG CUSTARD MERINGUE PIE

2/3 cup sugar
1 tablespoon cornstarch
2 tablespoons flour
3 egg yolks
1 egg
1 tablespoon melted margarine
2 cups scalded milk
1 teaspoon vanilla extract
1 unbaked 9-inch pie shell
3 egg whites
2 tablespoons sugar
1/2 teaspoon vanilla extract

Combine 2/3 cup sugar, cornstarch and flour in mixer bowl. Add egg yolks and egg; mix well. Stir in margarine, milk and 1 teaspoon vanilla. Pour into pie shell. Place in cold oven. Bake at 350 degrees for 30 minutes. Beat egg whites in mixer bowl until soft peaks form. Add remaining 2 tablespoons sugar and remaining 1/2 teaspoon vanilla gradually, beating until stiff peaks form. Spread over filling, sealing to edge. Bake at 350 degrees for 15 minutes or until lightly browned. Yield: 6 servings.

Approx Per Serving: Cal 389; Prot 9 g; Carbo 47 g; Fiber 1 g; T Fat 18 g; Chol 153 mg; Sod 281 mg.

Amanda Tucker, Independence

TEXAS CUSTARD PIE

1/2 cup butter
2 cups sugar
3 eggs
1 cup milk
3 tablespoons flour
1 unbaked 9-inch pie shell

Cream butter and sugar in bowl until light and fluffy. Add eggs 1 at a time, mixing well after each addition. Stir in milk and flour until smooth. Pour into pie shell. Place in 425 degree oven. Reduce temperature immediately to 350 degrees. Bake for 40 minutes or until set. Yield: 6 servings.

Approx Per Serving: Cal 621; Prot 7 g; Carbo 85 g; Fiber 1 g; T Fat 30 g; Chol 153 mg; Sod 366 mg.

Barbara L. Goble, Raleigh

EGGNOG PIE

1 envelope unflavored gelatin
1/4 cup cold water
3/4 cup sugar
1 tablespoon cornstarch
1/8 teaspoon salt
2 egg yolks
1 1/2 cups milk
4 teaspoons vanilla extract
1 teaspoon nutmeg
2 egg whites, at room temperature
1/4 cup sugar
1 baked 9-inch pie shell
1 cup whipped cream

Soften gelatin in water; set aside. Combine 3/4 cup sugar, cornstarch and salt in saucepan; mix well. Add well-beaten mixture of egg yolks and milk. Bring to a boil over medium heat. Boil for 1 minute, stirring constantly. Remove from heat. Stir in gelatin, vanilla and nutmeg. Cool to lukewarm. Beat egg whites in mixer bowl until soft peaks form. Add remaining 1/4 cup sugar 1 tablespoon at a time, beating until stiff peaks form. Fold into filling. Spoon into pie shell. Chill in refrigerator for 8 hours or longer. Pipe ring of whipped cream around top edge. Garnish with finely chopped candied fruit and a sprinkle of nutmeg.
Yield: 6 servings.

Approx Per Serving: Cal 432; Prot 7 g; Carbo 63 g; Fiber 1 g; T Fat 17 g; Chol 79 mg; Sod 233 mg.

Kim Parker, Central

FRUIT PIE

1/4 cup butter
2/3 cup sugar
2/3 cup self-rising flour
2/3 cup milk
1 16-ounce can fruit

Melt butter in 350 degree oven in 1 1/2 quart baking dish. Combine sugar, flour and milk in small bowl; mix well. Pour into dish. Top with fruit. Bake at 350 degrees for 30 to 40 minutes.
Yield: 6 servings.

Approx Per Serving: Cal 312; Prot 3 g; Carbo 58 g; Fiber 2 g; T Fat 9 g; Chol 24 mg; Sod 254 mg.

Bonnie Kramer, Independence

HELEN'S JAPANESE FRUIT PIE

3/4 cup melted margarine
1 cup sugar
2 eggs, beaten
1/2 cup raisins
1/2 cup coconut
1/2 cup chopped pecans
1 teaspoon vinegar
1 unbaked 9-inch pie shell

Combine margarine and sugar in bowl; mix well. Add eggs; mix until smooth. Stir in raisins, coconut, pecans and vinegar. Pour into pie shell. Bake at 325 degrees for 40 to 45 minutes or until set. Yield: 6 servings.

Approx Per Serving: Cal 644; Prot 6 g; Carbo 62 g; Fiber 3 g; T Fat 43 g; Chol 71 mg; Sod 478 mg.

Helen M. Helms, Hornets Nest

JAPANESE FRUIT PIE

2 eggs
1/2 cup melted margarine
1 cup sugar
1/2 cup coconut
1/2 cup raisins
1/2 cup chopped pecans
1 unbaked 9-inch pie shell
1 teaspoon vanilla extract

Beat eggs in bowl with fork. Add margarine and sugar; mix well. Stir in coconut, raisins and pecans. Add vanilla; mix well. Spoon into pie shell. Bake at 325 degrees for 40 minutes. Cool completely before cutting. Yield: 6 servings.

Approx Per Serving: Cal 576; Prot 5 g; Carbo 62 g; Fiber 3 g; T Fat 36 g; Chol 71 mg; Sod 388 mg.

Agnes Williams, Independence

☎ To add variety to your pastry, add 1/2 cup finely chopped nuts, add 1/2 to 1 cup shredded cheese or substitute orange juice for water and add grated orange rind to taste.

HAWAIIAN PIES

1 15-ounce can crushed pineapple, drained
¾ cup sugar
2 tablespoons flour
3 bananas
2 baked 9-inch pie shells
1 cup coconut
1 cup chopped pecans
8 ounces frozen whipped topping, thawed

Combine pineapple, sugar and flour in saucepan. Cook over low heat until thickened, stirring occasionally. Slice bananas; place in pie shells. Pour filling over bananas. Sprinkle with coconut and pecans. Spoon whipped topping over top. Chill in refrigerator overnight. This tastes like a banana split.
Yield: 12 servings.

Approx Per Serving: Cal 402; Prot 4 g; Carbo 47 g; Fiber 3 g; T Fat 24 g; Chol 0 mg; Sod 190 mg.

Lorraine Raxton, Foot Hills

HEAVENLY PIES

1 14-ounce can sweetened condensed milk
1 tablespoon lemon juice
1 20-ounce can crushed pineapple, drained
1 cup chopped walnuts
16 ounces whipped topping
3 9-inch graham cracker pie shells

Combine condensed milk and lemon juice in bowl. Add pineapple and walnuts; mix well. Fold in whipped topping. Spoon into pie shells. Chill in refrigerator overnight. Yield: 18 servings.

Approx Per Serving: Cal 483; Prot 5 g; Carbo 58 g; Fiber 2 g; T Fat 27 g; Chol 7 mg; Sod 354 mg.

Gladys Hinson, Independence

☎ To cook a frozen unbaked pie, add 15 to 20 minutes to the time specified in the recipe.

ICE CREAM PIES

1 2-layer package devil's food cake mix
¾ cup water
¼ cup oil
1 16-ounce can chocolate-fudge frosting
6 cups ice cream

Combine cake mix, water, oil and ¾ cup frosting in mixer bowl. Beat at low speed just until moistened. Beat at high speed for 2 minutes longer or until smooth. Spread batter over bottoms and up sides of 2 well-greased 9-inch pie plates. Bake at 350 degrees for 25 to 30 minutes or just until shells test done. Do not overbake. Cakes will collapse to form shells. Cool completely. Beat ice cream in large mixer bowl until smooth. Spoon into pie shells, leaving a ½-inch rim. Heat remaining frosting in saucepan until soft. Swirl over top of ice cream. Freeze, tightly wrapped, for 2 hours or longer. Yield: 12 servings.

Approx Per Serving: Cal 512; Prot 8 g; Carbo 75 g; Fiber 0 g; T Fat 15 g; Chol 30 mg; Sod 402 mg.

Joanne Tallent, Independence

NUTTY BUDDY PIES

8 ounces cream cheese, softened
2 cups confectioners' sugar
1 cup milk
⅔ cup chunky peanut butter
16 ounces frozen whipped topping, thawed
3 9-inch chocolate wafer pie shells
½ cup chocolate syrup
½ cup chopped salted peanuts

Beat cream cheese, confectioners' sugar and milk in mixer bowl until light and fluffy. Add peanut butter; mix well. Fold in whipped topping. Spoon into pie shells. Drizzle with chocolate syrup. Sprinkle with peanuts. Yield: 18 servings.

Approx Per Serving: Cal 282; Prot 6 g; Carbo 27 g; Fiber 1 g; T Fat 18 g; Chol 16 mg; Sod 112 mg.
Nutritional information does not include chocolate pie shells.

Shirley T. Hinson, Hornets Nest

OATMEAL PIE

1/2 cup melted margarine
2 eggs
2/3 cup sugar
2/3 cup light corn syrup
2/3 cup oats
1/4 teaspoon salt
1 teaspoon vanilla extract
2/3 cup coconut
1/2 cup chopped pecans
1 9-inch deep-dish pie shell

Combine margarine, eggs, sugar, corn syrup, oats, salt and vanilla in bowl; mix well. Stir in coconut and pecans. Spoon into pie shell. Bake at 350 degrees for 30 minutes or until set. Yield: 6 servings.

Approx Per Serving: Cal 637; Prot 7 g; Carbo 74 g; Fiber 3 g; T Fat 37 g; Chol 71 mg; Sod 492 mg.

Mrs. Larry Harrington, Blue Ridge

PEANUT BUTTER PIES

8 ounces cream cheese, softened
1 cup chunky peanut butter
16 ounces frozen whipped topping, thawed
1 1/2 cups sifted confectioners' sugar
2 9-inch graham cracker pie shells

Beat cream cheese and peanut butter at medium speed in large mixer bowl until light and fluffy. Add whipped topping and confectioners' sugar gradually, beating until smooth. Spoon into pie shells. Freeze for 8 hours to overnight. Garnish with chocolate shavings just before serving, if desired. Yield: 12 servings.

Approx Per Serving: Cal 644; Prot 10 g; Carbo 62 g; Fiber 2 g; T Fat 42 g; Chol 21 mg; Sod 471 mg.

Kim Parker, Central

QUICK PEANUT BUTTER PIE

1/4 cup chunky peanut butter
3 ounces cream cheese, softened
1 cup confectioners' sugar
12 ounces whipped topping
1 9-inch graham cracker pie shell

Cream peanut butter, cream cheese and confectioners' sugar in mixer bowl until light and fluffy. Fold in whipped topping. Spoon into pie shell. Chill until serving time. Yield: 8 servings.

Approx Per Serving: Cal 482; Prot 5 g; Carbo 52 g; Fiber 1 g; T Fat 30 g; Chol 12 mg; Sod 314 mg.

Phyllis Edwards, Hornets Nest

SUGARLESS PEAR AND DATE PIE

6 cups sliced, peeled pears
1/4 cup raisins
3/4 cup chopped pitted whole dates
3/4 cup unsweetened pineapple juice
1 tablespoon cornstarch
1/2 teaspoon cinnamon
1/8 teaspoon nutmeg
1 recipe 2-crust pie pastry

Combine pears and raisins in large bowl. Combine dates, pineapple juice, cornstarch, cinnamon and nutmeg in saucepan; mix well. Cook over medium heat until thickened, stirring constantly. Pour into pear and raisin mixture; mix until well coated. Spoon into pastry-lined deep-dish pie plate. Top with remaining pastry, sealing edge and cutting vents. Brush with a small amount of milk. Cover edge of pastry with foil. Bake at 375 degrees for 25 minutes. Remove foil. Bake for 30 to 35 minutes longer. Do not use chopped sugar-coated pitted dates. May substitute favorite fruit for pears and unsweetened orange or apple juice for pineapple juice. Yield: 6 servings.

Approx Per Serving: Cal 535; Prot 5 g; Carbo 76 g; Fiber 8 g; T Fat 19 g; Chol 0 mg; Sod 370 mg.

Ovid Smith, Hornets Nest

PECAN PIES

1 1-pound package light brown sugar
4 eggs
3 tablespoons flour
1/2 cup milk
1/2 cup melted margarine
1 teaspoon vanilla extract
2 unbaked 9-inch pie shells
1 cup chopped pecans

Combine brown sugar, eggs, flour, milk, margarine and vanilla in bowl; mix well. Spoon into pie shells. Sprinkle with pecans. Bake at 350 degrees for 30 minutes or until set. Yield: 12 servings.

Approx Per Serving: Cal 466; Prot 5 g; Carbo 54 g; Fiber 1 g; T Fat 27 g; Chol 72 mg; Sod 317 mg.

Doris Keever, Hornets Nest

BEST PECAN PIE

1/2 cup butter
1 cup light corn syrup
3 eggs
1/2 teaspoon lemon juice
1 teaspoon vanilla extract
1/8 teaspoon salt
1 cup chopped pecans
1 unbaked 9-inch pie shell

Cook butter in saucepan until golden brown, stirring constantly. Cool. Combine corn syrup, eggs, lemon juice, vanilla, salt and pecans in medium bowl; mix well. Stir in browned butter. Pour into pie shell. Bake at 425 degrees for 10 minutes. Reduce temperature to 325 degrees. Bake for 40 minutes longer. Yield: 6 servings.

Approx Per Serving: Cal 612; Prot 7 g; Carbo 58 g; Fiber 2 g; T Fat 42 g; Chol 148 mg; Sod 416 mg.

Barbara D. Scott, Independence

DEEP-DISH PECAN PIE

1½ cups chopped pecans
1 10-inch deep-dish pie shell
½ cup melted margarine
3 eggs, beaten
1½ cups sugar
1 tablespoon flour
¼ cup buttermilk
1 teaspoon vanilla extract

Sprinkle pecans into bottom of pie shell. Combine margarine, eggs, sugar, flour, buttermilk and vanilla in bowl; mix well. Spoon into pie shell. Bake at 350 degrees for 50 minutes or until set. Yield: 6 servings.

Approx Per Serving: Cal 728; Prot 8 g; Carbo 71 g; Fiber 3 g; T Fat 48 g; Chol 107 mg; Sod 408 mg.

Minnie B. Price, Central

MYSTERY PECAN PIE

8 ounces cream cheese, softened
⅓ cup sugar
¼ teaspoon salt
1 teaspoon vanilla extract
1 egg
1 unbaked 9-inch pie shell
1¼ cups chopped pecans
1 cup light corn syrup
3 eggs
¼ cup sugar
1 teaspoon vanilla extract

Beat cream cheese, ⅓ cup sugar, salt, 1 teaspoon vanilla and 1 egg in mixer bowl until light and fluffy. Spoon into pie shell. Sprinkle with pecans. Combine corn syrup, remaining 3 eggs, remaining ¼ cup sugar and remaining 1 teaspoon vanilla in small bowl; mix well. Pour over pecan layer. Bake at 375 degrees for 35 to 40 minutes or until set. Yield: 6 servings.

Approx Per Serving: Cal 731; Prot 11 g; Carbo 80 g; Fiber 2 g; T Fat 44 g; Chol 183 mg; Sod 456 mg.

Virginia Barnette, Hornets Nest

OLD-FASHIONED PECAN PIES

½ cup melted margarine
4 eggs
1 1-pound package light brown sugar
2 tablespoons cornmeal
2 tablespoons water
1 tablespoon vanilla extract
1 teaspoon salt
2 cups chopped pecans
2 unbaked 9-inch pie shells

Combine margarine and eggs in medium bowl; mix well. Stir in brown sugar, cornmeal, water, vanilla, salt and pecans. Pour into pie shells. Bake at 325 degrees for 45 minutes or until set. Yield: 12 servings.

Approx Per Serving: Cal 526; Prot 6 g; Carbo 55 g; Fiber 2 g; T Fat 33 g; Chol 71 mg; Sod 490 mg.

Carolyn Paul, Central

QUICK PECAN PIES

½ cup melted margarine
1 1-pound package light brown sugar
3 eggs
½ cup evaporated milk
1 teaspoon vanilla extract
½ cup finely chopped pecans
2 unbaked 9-inch pie shells

Combine margarine and brown sugar in bowl; mix until smooth. Stir in eggs, evaporated milk, vanilla and pecans. Spoon into pie shells. Bake at 350 degrees for 45 minutes or until set. Yield: 12 servings.

Approx Per Serving: Cal 427; Prot 5 g; Carbo 52 g; Fiber 1 g; T Fat 36 g; Chol 57 mg; Sod 318 mg.

Anne Smith, Independence

SOUTHERN PECAN PIE

1/2 cup sugar
2 tablespoons melted butter
3 eggs, beaten
1 cup dark corn syrup
1 teaspoon vanilla extract
1/4 teaspoon salt
1 cup chopped pecans
1 unbaked 9-inch pie shell

Combine sugar, butter and eggs in medium bowl; mix well. Stir in corn syrup, vanilla, salt and pecans. Pour into pie shell. Bake at 350 degrees for 45 minutes or until set. Yield: 6 servings.

Approx Per Serving: Cal 580; Prot 6 g; Carbo 75 g; Fiber 2 g; T Fat 30 g; Chol 117 mg; Sod 377 mg.

Phyllis Cox, Central

PECAN TARTS

1/2 cup butter
1 cup dark corn syrup
1 cup sugar
3 eggs
1/2 teaspoon salt
1 1/2 teaspoons vanilla extract
2 cups chopped pecans
6 unbaked 3-inch tart shells

Melt butter in saucepan. Remove from heat. Stir in corn syrup, sugar, eggs, salt and vanilla. Add pecans; mix well. Spoon into tart shells. Bake at 350 degrees for 30 to 35 minutes. Yield: 6 servings.

Approx Per Serving: Cal 879; Prot 8 g; Carbo 95 g; Fiber 3 g; T Fat 55 g; Chol 148 mg; Sod 563 mg.

Martha Berrier, Hornets Nest

PEPPERMINT CANDY ICE CREAM PIE

1 1/2 cups chocolate wafer crumbs
6 tablespoons melted butter
1 pint peppermint ice cream, softened
8 ounces frozen whipped topping, partially thawed
3 tablespoons finely crushed peppermint candy

Combine chocolate wafer crumbs and butter in small bowl; mix well. Press over bottom and up side of 9-inch pie plate. Combine ice cream and whipped topping in bowl; mix until smooth. Spoon into pie shell. Sprinkle with crushed candy. Freeze until firm. Garnish with additional crushed peppermint candy, if desired. Yield: 6 servings.

Approx Per Serving: Cal 606; Prot 5 g; Carbo 65 g; Fiber 1 g; T Fat 37 g; Chol 51 mg; Sod 414 mg.

Kim Parker, Central

PINEAPPLE COOL WHIP PIES

1 14-ounce can sweetened condensed milk
Juice of 1 lemon
1 20-ounce can crushed pineapple, drained
8 ounces whipped topping
1 cup chopped walnuts
2 9-inch graham cracker pie shells

Combine sweetened condensed milk and lemon juice in bowl; mix well. Stir in pineapple. Fold in whipped topping and walnuts. Spoon into pie shells. Chill in refrigerator until serving time. Yield: 12 servings.

Approx Per Serving: Cal 529; Prot 7 g; Carbo 65 g; Fiber 2 g; T Fat 28 g; Chol 11 mg; Sod 367 mg.

Irene C. Black, Independence

PUMPKIN PIE

1½ cups evaporated milk
1½ cups canned pumpkin
1¼ cups sugar
2 eggs
1 teaspon cinnamon
½ teaspoon nutmeg
½ teaspoon ginger
1 partially baked 9-inch pie shell

Combine evaporated milk, pumpkin, sugar, eggs, cinnamon, nutmeg and ginger in medium bowl; mix well. Pour into pie shell. Bake at 350 degrees for 1 hour or until set. Yield: 6 servings.

Approx Per Serving: Cal 443; Prot 9 g; Carbo 66 g; Fiber 2 g; T Fat 17 g; Chol 90 mg; Sod 277 mg.

Wilma Burleson, Independence

PUMPKIN AND CHEESE PIE

8 ounces cream cheese
1 cup canned pumpkin
¾ cup packed brown sugar
1½ teaspoons flour
1½ teaspoons pumpkin pie spice
1 tablespoon vanilla extract
3 eggs
1 9-inch graham cracker pie shell

Place cream cheese in microwave-safe bowl. Microwave on High until cream cheese melts. Add pumpkin, brown sugar, flour, pumpkin pie spice, vanilla and eggs; beat until well blended. Microwave for 2 to 3 minutes, stirring once. Repeat until mixture is thickened. Pour into pie shell in microwave-safe pie plate. Microwave on High until firm to the touch. Yield: 6 servings.

Approx Per Serving: Cal 570; Prot 9 g; Carbo 67 g; Fiber 2 g; T Fat 31 g; Chol 148 mg; Sod 479 mg.

Kaye O'Neil, Hornets Nest

CREAMY PUMPKIN PIE

8 ounces cream cheese, softened
3/4 cup packed brown sugar
2 tablespoons flour
1 teaspoon ginger
1/4 teaspoon nutmeg
1 teaspoon cinnamon
1/2 teaspoon salt
1 16-ounce can pumpkin
1 5-ounce can evaporated milk
3 eggs
1 unbaked 9-inch pie shell

Combine cream cheese, brown sugar, flour, ginger, nutmeg, cinnamon and salt in mixer bowl. Beat at medium speed until well blended. Add pumpkin, evaporated milk and eggs; mix just until blended. Spoon into pie shell. Bake at 375 degrees for 30 minutes or until set. Yield: 6 servings.

Approx Per Serving: Cal 491; Prot 10 g; Carbo 51 g; Fiber 2 g; T Fat 28 g; Chol 155 mg; Sod 548 mg.

Lee Davis, Asheville

RITZ PIE

3 egg whites
1 cup sugar
1 teaspoon baking powder
1 teaspoon vanilla extract
20 Ritz crackers, crushed
1 cup chopped walnuts

Beat egg whites in mixer bowl until soft peaks form. Add sugar, baking powder and vanilla gradually, beating until stiff peaks form. Fold in crushed crackers and chopped walnuts. Spoon into 8-inch square baking dish. Bake at 325 degrees for 30 minutes. Cool. Garnish with whipped topping.
Yield: 9 servings.

Approx Per Serving: Cal 212; Prot 3 g; Carbo 30 g; Fiber 1 g; T Fat 10 g; Chol 0 mg; Sod 122 mg.

Teresa Manner, Coastal

SQUASH PIES

1¾ cups sugar
4 eggs
2½ cups shredded squash
1 tablespoon coconut extract
1 tablespoon lemon extract
¼ cup flour
½ cup melted butter
2 unbaked 9-inch pie shells

Combine sugar, eggs, squash, coconut extract and lemon extract in medium bowl; mix well. Stir in flour and butter. Spoon into pie shells. Bake at 350 degrees for 45 minutes or until set. Yield: 12 servings.

Approx Per Serving: Cal 371; Prot 5 g; Carbo 46 g; Fiber 1 g; T Fat 20 g; Chol 92 mg; Sod 272 mg.

Gladys Hinson, Independence

STRAWBERRY PIES

1 6-ounce package vanilla instant pudding mix
2 cups milk
8 ounces cream cheese, softened
8 ounces frozen whipped topping, thawed
1 pint strawberries, chopped
3 9-inch graham cracker pie shells

Beat pudding mix and milk at medium speed for 2 minutes in bowl. Add cream cheese; beat until smooth. Fold in whipped topping until smooth. Layer strawberries between 2 layers of pudding in pie shells. Chill in refrigerator. Yield: 18 servings.

Approx Per Serving: Cal 413; Prot 4 g; Carbo 49 g; Fiber 1 g; T Fat 23 g; Chol 17 mg; Sod 434 mg.

Shirley Carmichael, Hornets Nest

FRESH STRAWBERRY PIE

1 pint strawberries
1 baked 9-inch pie shell
1 cup sugar
6 tablespoons cornstarch
1 cup water
1/4 cup dry strawberry gelatin

Arrange strawberries in pie shell. Combine sugar, cornstarch and water in saucepan. Cook over medium heat until thickened, stirring constantly. Stir in dry gelatin. Pour over strawberries. Chill in refrigerator. Yield: 6 servings.

Approx Per Serving: Cal 346; Prot 3 g; Carbo 62 g; Fiber 2 g; T Fat 10 g; Chol 0 mg; Sod 205 mg.

Martha Berrier, Hornets Nest

STRAWBERRY CHIFFON PIE

1 12-ounce can evaporated milk
1 3-ounce package strawberry gelatin
1 cup sugar
1 egg
1 20-ounce can crushed pineapple
1 9-inch vanilla wafer pie shell

Chill evaporated milk in freezer until ice cold. Combine dry gelatin, sugar, egg and pineapple in saucepan; mix well. Bring to a boil. Cook for 1 minute, stirring constantly. Cool in refrigerator. Beat chilled evaporated milk in mixer bowl until soft peaks form. Fold into gelatin mixture. Spoon into pie shell. Chill in refrigerator until serving time. Yield: 6 servings.

Approx Per Serving: Cal 344; Prot 7 g; Carbo 71 g; Fiber 1 g; T Fat 5 g; Chol 52 mg; Sod 119 mg.
Nutritional information does not include vanilla wafer pie shell.

Rachel Day, Raleigh

DIETETIC STRAWBERRY PIE

1 cup unsweetened white grape juice
1 cup water
2 tablespoons cornstarch
1 small package sugar-free strawberry gelatin
1 pint strawberries
1 baked 9-inch pie shell

Combine grape juice, water and cornstarch in saucepan. Cook over medium heat until clear. Mixture will not thicken. Remove from heat. Stir in gelatin until dissolved. Chill in bowl in refrigerator until partially set. Stir in strawberries. Spoon into pie shell. Chill in refrigerator for 2 to 3 hours or until set.
Yield: 6 servings.

Approx Per Serving: Cal 203; Prot 3 g; Carbo 25 g; Fiber 2 g; T Fat 10 g; Chol 0 mg; Sod 218 mg.

Billie Mills, Independence

SWEET POTATO PIES

2 cups sugar
3/4 cup melted margarine
2 eggs, beaten
2 tablespoons milk
4 cups cooked, mashed sweet potatoes
2 tablespoons (heaping) flour
1 teaspoon cinnamon
1 teaspoon nutmeg
1/2 teaspoon allspice
2 unbaked 9-inch pie shells

Combine sugar, margarine, eggs and milk in medium bowl; mix well. Stir in sweet potatoes, flour, cinnamon, nutmeg and allspice. Spoon into pie shells. Bake at 350 degrees for 45 minutes. Yield: 12 servings.

Approx Per Serving: Cal 486; Prot 5 g; Carbo 67 g; Fiber 2 g; T Fat 23 g; Chol 36 mg; Sod 394 mg.

Virginia Bowie, Independence

SWEET POTATO CUSTARD PIES

4 medium sweet potatoes, cooked, peeled
2 cups sugar
2 eggs
1 cup melted butter
¼ cup milk
1 tablespoon flour
1 teaspoon vanilla extract
1 teaspoon lemon extract
2 unbaked 9-inch pie shells

Mash hot sweet potatoes in bowl. Add sugar, eggs, butter, milk, flour and flavorings; mix well. Spoon into pie shells. Bake at 350 degrees for 30 minutes or until set. Yield: 12 servings.

Approx Per Serving: Cal 487; Prot 4 g; Carbo 60 g; Fiber 2 g; T Fat 27 g; Chol 78 mg; Sod 333 mg.

Georgia Lee, Hornets Nest

LIGHT SWEET POTATO PIES

6 medium sweet potatoes, cooked, peeled
¼ cup margarine
1½ cups sugar
2 teaspoons apple pie spice
2 eggs
2 tablespoons milk
1 tablespoon self-rising flour
2 teaspoons vanilla extract
2 unbaked 9-inch pie shells

Mash hot sweet potatoes with margarine in bowl until butter melts and mixture is well blended. Add sugar and apple pie spice; mix well. Stir in beaten mixture of eggs and milk. Add flour and vanilla; mix well. Spoon into pie shells. Bake at 350 degrees for 30 minutes or until set. Yield: 12 servings.

Approx Per Serving: Cal 380; Prot 4 g; Carbo 58 g; Fiber 3 g; T Fat 15 g; Chol 36 mg; Sod 258 mg.

Cathy Douglas, Central

OLD-FASHIONED SWEET POTATO PIE

2 eggs, beaten
1 cup sugar
1 cup milk
1 teaspoon vanilla extract
1 teaspoon salt
1 1/2 cups mashed sweet potatoes
2 tablespoons melted margarine
1 unbaked 9-inch pie shell

Combine eggs, sugar, milk, vanilla and salt in bowl; mix well. Add sweet potatoes and margarine; mix well. Spoon into pie shell. Bake at 450 degrees for 10 minutes. Reduce temperature to 350 degrees. Bake for 30 to 40 minutes longer or until set. Yield: 6 servings.

Approx Per Serving: Cal 430; Prot 7 g; Carbo 64 g; Fiber 2 g; T Fat 17 g; Chol 77 mg; Sod 672 mg.

Daisy Dills, Central

SWEET POTATO PUDDING PIES

1/4 cup melted margarine
1 1/2 cups sugar
2 eggs
1 4-ounce package vanilla instant pudding mix
1 cup evaporated milk
2 cups mashed sweet potatoes
1 teaspoon vanilla extract
2 unbaked 9-inch pie shells

Combine margarine, sugar, eggs, pudding mix, evaporated milk, sweet potatoes and vanilla in medium bowl; mix well. Spoon into pie shells. Bake at 350 degrees for 40 to 45 minutes or until set. Yield: 12 servings.

Approx Per Serving: Cal 401; Prot 5 g; Carbo 59 g; Fiber 1 g; T Fat 17 g; Chol 42 mg; Sod 357 mg.

Lib Sandlin, Central

SOUTH'S FAVORITE SWEET POTATO PIE

2 cups puréed, cooked sweet potatoes
Juice and grated rind of 1/2 orange
3/4 cup sugar
2 eggs, beaten
1/2 cup evaporated milk, scalded
2 tablespoons butter
1/4 teaspoon mace
1/4 teaspoon nutmeg
1/4 teaspoon vanilla extract
1 teaspoon salt
1 unbaked 9-inch pie shell

Combine sweet potatoes, orange juice and rind in bowl; mix well. Add sugar and eggs; mix until well blended. Combine evaporated milk and butter in small bowl, stirring until butter melts. Add to sweet potato mixture; mix well. Stir in mace, nutmeg, vanilla and salt. Spoon into pie shell. Bake at 350 degrees for 30 minutes or until pie is set and crust is brown. Yield: 6 servings.

Approx Per Serving: Cal 425; Prot 7 g; Carbo 61 g; Fiber 3 g; T Fat 18 g; Chol 88 mg; Sod 680 mg.

Shirley Carmichael, Hornets Nest

TAR HEEL FRUIT PIE

12 ounces cream cheese, softened
1/2 cup sugar
1 cup whipping cream
1 1/2 bananas, sliced
1 baked 9-inch pie shell
1 16-ounce package frozen blueberries
1/3 cup sugar
1 tablespoon cornstarch

Combine cream cheese and 1/2 cup sugar in bowl; mix until smooth. Beat cream in small mixer bowl until stiff peaks form. Fold into cream cheese mixture gently. Place banana slices over bottom and around side of pie shell. Spoon cream cheese mixture over bananas. Chill in refrigerator until firm. Combine blueberries, remaining 1/3 cup sugar and cornstarch in saucepan. Cook over low heat until thickened, stirring constantly. Be careful not to break the berries. Cool. Spoon over cream cheese mixture. Chill in refrigerator for several hours to overnight.
Yield: 6 servings.

Approx Per Serving: Cal 683; Prot 7 g; Carbo 68 g; Fiber 3 g; T Fat 45 g; Chol 116 mg; Sod 368 mg.

Betty Owens, Hornets Nest

TAR HEEL CHOCOLATE PIE

½ cup melted butter
1 cup chocolate chips
½ cup sugar
½ cup packed brown
  sugar
2 eggs, beaten
½ cup flour
1 teaspoon vanilla extract
1 cup chopped pecans
1 unbaked 9-inch pie shell

Pour warm butter over chocolate chips in medium bowl, stirring until chocolate chips are melted. Add sugar, brown sugar, eggs, flour and vanilla; mix well. Stir in pecans. Pour into pie shell. Bake at 350 degrees for 30 to 40 minutes or until set. Yield: 6 servings.

Approx Per Serving: Cal 759; Prot 8 g; Carbo 76 g; Fiber 3 g;
  T Fat 51 g; Chol 112 mg; Sod 348 mg.

Joyce Pruitt, Independence

ANNE'S VANILLA PIE DESSERT

¾ cup butter
2 cups flour
¼ cup chopped pecans
8 ounces cream cheese,
  softened
2 cups confectioners'
  sugar
2 tablespoons warm water
1 6-ounce package
   instant vanilla pudding
   mix
3 cups cold milk
12 ounces frozen whipped
   topping, thawed

Melt butter in 9x13-inch baking dish. Sprinkle flour over butter evenly. Sprinkle with pecans. Bake at 350 degrees for 20 minutes or until lightly browned. Cool. Beat cream cheese, confectioners' sugar and water in mixer bowl until light and fluffy. Spread over prepared pastry. Combine pudding mix and milk in mixer bowl; beat until thickened. Spoon over cream cheese layer. Top with whipped topping. Garnish with coconut and maraschino cherries. Chill in refrigerator until serving time. Yield: 16 servings.

Approx Per Serving: Cal 388; Prot 5 g; Carbo 45 g; Fiber 1 g;
  T Fat 22 g; Chol 45 mg; Sod 211 mg.

Anne Chester, Foot Hills

☎ Tips for making perfect pie pastry:
- Sift the measured flour and salt into a bowl.
- Cut in shortening with pastry blender or knives until the mixture resembles coarse cornmeal.
- Sprinkle with cold water 1 tablespoon at a time; tossing lightly with a fork.
- Enough water has been added when the dough clings together and pulls away from the side of the bowl. It should not be moist or sticky.
- Shape dough into a ball, wrap tightly in plastic wrap and chill for several hours before rolling.
- Chilling the dough helps to insure tender pastry that doesn't shrink during baking.
- If possible, roll dough on a chilled surface such as marble.
- Sprinkle work surface *lightly* with flour, using as little flour as possible to prevent toughening the dough.
- Roll with rolling pin from center to outer edge never pressing down too hard or rolling toward the center.
- Do not reroll the dough. Patch tears with a touch of ice water and a bit of pastry pressed gently into torn place.
- Roll dough for bottom crust about 2 inches larger than diameter of pie plate and about 1/8 inch thick.
- Transfer dough from work surface to pie plate by rolling loosely around rolling pin or folding gently in half or quarters.
- Fit into pie plate carefully. Do not stretch.
- Repeat for top crust. Add filling and moisten edges with milk or water before adding top. Press to seal and crimp for a decorative edge. Don't forget to cut vents.
- Brush with milk and sprinkle with sugar for a golden crusty finish.

Desserts

ADOPT-A-HIGHWAY

DESSERTS

APPLE DELICIOUS

1 10-count can refrigerator biscuits
5 apples, peeled, cut into halves
2 cups sugar
1/2 cup margarine
2 cups water
Cinnamon to taste

Flatten biscuits with glass. Wrap 1 biscuit around each apple half. Place in baking dish. Bring sugar, margarine, water and cinnamon to a boil in saucepan. Cook for 3 minutes, stirring frequently. Pour around apples. Bake at 350 degrees for 25 minutes or until lightly browned. Yield: 10 servings.

Approx Per Serving: Cal 371; Prot 2 g; Carbo 60 g; Fiber 1 g; T Fat 15 g; Chol 0 mg; Sod 338 mg.

Dot Ottone, Foot Hills

APPLE DUMPLINGS

1 tablespoon sugar
2 tablespoons butter
6 apples, peeled, cored
Pastry (See page 505)
Cinnamon to taste
1 cup sugar
1/4 cup margarine
1/4 teaspoon cinnamon
2 cups water

Place 1/2 teaspoon sugar and 1 teaspoon butter inside each apple. Place 1 apple on each pastry square. Fold dough to enclose apple, sealing edges. Place in 9x13-inch baking dish. Sprinkle with cinnamon. Bring remaining 1 cup sugar, margarine, cinnamon and water to a boil in saucepan. Cook for 3 minutes, stirring frequently. Pour over dumplings. Bake at 350 degrees for 1 hour, basting with pan juices every 10 minutes.
Yield: 6 servings.

Pastry for Apple Dumplings

2 cups flour, sifted
1 teaspoon baking powder
1 teaspoon salt
1/2 cup shortening
3/4 cup milk

Combine flour, baking powder and salt in bowl; mix well. Cut in shortening until crumbly. Add milk; mix well. Roll 1/8 inch thick on lightly floured surface. Cut into 6 squares.

Approx Per Serving: Cal 620; Prot 5 g; Carbo 85 g; Fiber 4 g; T Fat 30 g; Chol 15 mg; Sod 546 mg.

Alice Oberndorf, Hornets Nest

CHEESE APPLES

8 apples, peeled, sliced
3/4 cup sugar
1/2 cup flour
1 cup shredded sharp Cheddar cheese
1/4 teaspoon salt
1/4 cup margarine
6 tablespoons water
2 tablespoons lemon juice

Place apples in 10-inch square baking dish. Combine sugar, flour, Cheddar cheese and salt in bowl. Cut in margarine until crumbly. Add to apples; mix well. Sprinkle with water and lemon juice. Bake at 350 degrees for 40 minutes. May prepare apples and cover in salted water. Drain apples and use as above omitting salt. May serve as side dish. Yield: 12 servings.

Approx Per Serving: Cal 188; Prot 3 g; Carbo 29 g; Fiber 2 g; T Fat 7 g; Chol 10 mg; Sod 148 mg.

Peggy W. Pearce, Raleigh

CRANBERRY-APPLE CRUNCH

1 cup sugar
1 cup water
2 cups cranberries
2 cups chopped tart apples
1 cup quick-cooking oats
1/2 cup packed brown sugar
1/3 cup flour
1/2 teaspoon salt
1/4 cup butter
1/2 cup chopped walnuts

Combine sugar and water in saucepan; mix well. Bring to a boil. Cook for 5 minutes, stirring frequently. Stir in cranberries. Cook over medium heat for 5 minutes or until cranberries pop, stirring occasionally. Add apples; mix well. Spread in greased 6x10-inch baking dish. Combine oats, brown sugar, flour and salt in bowl; mix well. Cut in butter until crumbly. Stir in walnuts. Sprinkle over fruit mixture. Bake at 350 degrees for 35 minutes. Serve warm with whipping cream or ice cream. Yield: 6 servings.

Approx Per Serving: Cal 442; Prot 5 g; Carbo 77 g; Fiber 5 g; T Fat 15 g; Chol 21 mg; Sod 253 mg.

Mr. and Mrs. William B. Heffner, Jr., Central

CRANBERRY-APPLE BAKE

3 cups sliced peeled apples
2 cups cranberries
1 1/4 cups sugar
1 1/2 cups oats
1/2 cup packed brown sugar
1/3 cup flour
1/3 cup chopped pecans
1/2 cup melted margarine

Combine apples, cranberries and sugar in bowl; mix well. Spoon into greased 2-quart baking dish. Combine oats, brown sugar, flour, pecans and melted margarine in bowl; mix well. Spoon over fruit mixture. Bake at 350 degrees for 1 hour. May freeze after baking. Reheat to serving temperature. Yield: 12 servings.

Approx Per Serving: Cal 279; Prot 2 g; Carbo 46 g; Fiber 3 g; T Fat 11 g; Chol 0 mg; Sod 94 mg.

Bernice Griffin, Hornets Nest

APPLE-CRANBERRY DESSERT CASSEROLE

2 cups cranberries
3 cups chopped unpeeled apples
1 cup sugar
1 1/2 cups oats
1/2 cup packed brown sugar
1/2 cup margarine, softened

Combine cranberries, apples and sugar in bowl; mix well. Spoon into greased 9x13-inch baking dish. Combine oats, brown sugar and margarine in bowl; mix well. Spoon over fruit mixture. Bake, covered, at 350 degrees for 30 minutes. Bake, uncovered, for 1 hour longer. May serve as side dish. Yield: 18 servings.

Approx Per Serving: Cal 153; Prot 1 g; Carbo 26 g; Fiber 2 g; T Fat 6 g; Chol 0 mg; Sod 63 mg.

Jo Anne Paulin, Coastal

APPLE DUMP DESSERT

1 20-ounce can sliced apples
1 20-ounce can sliced pineapple, drained
1 2-layer package yellow cake mix
1 cup chopped pecans
1/2 cup melted butter

Pour undrained apples into casserole. Layer pineapple, cake mix and pecans over apples. Drizzle with melted butter. Bake at 350 degrees for 1 hour. Do not use pie filling in this recipe. Yield: 12 servings.

Approx Per Serving: Cal 373; Prot 3 g; Carbo 52 g; Fiber 2 g; T Fat 18 g; Chol 21 mg; Sod 329 mg.

Eddie Haskin, Hornets Nest

☎ Create a quick dessert with fresh fruit slices, a dollop of sour cream or yogurt and a sprinkle of brown sugar or coconut.

BANANA SPLIT DESSERT CASSEROLE

- 1 20-ounce can crushed pineapple
- 3 large bananas, sliced
- 1/2 cup melted margarine
- 2 cups graham cracker crumbs
- 2 cups confectioners' sugar
- 1 cup margarine, softened
- 2 eggs
- 16 ounces whipped topping
- 1/2 cup chopped pecans
- 1/2 cup chopped maraschino cherries

Drain pineapple, reserving juice. Pour pineapple juice over banana slices in small bowl; set aside. Spread mixture of melted margarine and graham cracker crumbs in 9x13-inch baking dish. Cream confectioners' sugar, softened margarine and eggs in mixer bowl for 15 minutes or until light and fluffy. Spread into prepared dish. Layer banana slices, pineapple and whipped topping over creamed mixture. Sprinkle with pecans and cherries. Chill until serving time. Yield: 15 servings.

Approx Per Serving: Cal 486; Prot 3 g; Carbo 51 g; Fiber 2 g; T Fat 31 g; Chol 28 mg; Sod 330 mg.

Jo Ann Goins, Hornets Nest

CHOCOLATE-TOPPED BANANA SPLIT DESSERT

- 2 cups graham cracker crumbs
- 1/2 cup melted margarine
- 1 6-ounce package vanilla instant pudding mix
- 1 20-ounce can crushed pineapple, drained
- 4 bananas, sliced
- 16 ounces whipped topping
- 1 cup chopped pecans
- 1 4-ounce jar maraschino cherries, drained
- 1/2 cup chocolate syrup

Spread graham cracker crumbs in 9x13-inch baking dish. Pour melted margarine over crumbs. Prepare pudding mix using package directions. Layer pudding, pineapple, banana slices and whipped topping in prepared dish. Sprinkle with pecans. Arrange cherries on top. Drizzle with chocolate syrup. Chill until serving time. Yield: 10 servings.

Approx Per Serving: Cal 590; Prot 5 g; Carbo 78 g; Fiber 3 g; T Fat 32 g; Chol 0 mg; Sod 393 mg.

Wanda Williams, Independence

BLUEBERRY-GRAPE COMPOTE

¼ cup sugar
¼ cup water
½ teaspoon grated lime rind
¼ cup lime juice

2 cups blueberries
2 cups seedless white grape halves
2 kiwifruit, peeled, sliced

   Combine sugar, water and lime rind in saucepan; mix well. Cook over medium heat until sugar dissolves, stirring frequently. Stir in lime juice. Cool. Combine blueberries, grapes and lime mixture in bowl; mix well. Chill, tightly covered, until serving time, stirring occasionally. Top with kiwifruit just before serving. Yield: 4 servings.

Approx Per Serving: Cal 173; Prot 1 g; Carbo 44 g; Fiber 4 g; T Fat 1 g; Chol 0 mg; Sod 8 mg.

John E. Miles, Independence

BROWN SUGAR SURPRISES

½ cup margarine, softened
2 cups packed brown sugar
2 eggs

1 cup flour, sifted
1 teaspoon baking powder
1 teaspoon vanilla extract
1 cup chopped pecans

   Cream margarine and brown sugar in mixer bowl until light and fluffy. Beat in eggs. Stir in mixture of flour and baking powder. Add vanilla and pecans; mix well. Spread in 9-inch square baking dish. Bake at 300 degrees for 45 minutes or until lightly browned. Cool. Cut into squares. Yield: 20 servings.

Approx Per Serving: Cal 193; Prot 2 g; Carbo 27 g; Fiber 1 g; T Fat 9 g; Chol 21 mg; Sod 120 mg.

Betty Sigmon, Foot Hills

☎ Flavor whipped cream with cocoa or tint with food coloring for garnishes.

CHOCOLATE DREAM

1 cup flour
1/2 cup margarine, softened
1 cup chopped pecans
8 ounces cream cheese, softened
1 cup confectioners' sugar
1 cup whipped topping
1 4-ounce package vanilla instant pudding mix
1 4-ounce package chocolate instant pudding mix
3 cups milk
3 cups whipped topping

Combine flour, margarine and pecans in bowl; mix well. Spread evenly in ungreased 9x13-inch baking dish. Bake at 350 degrees for 20 to 25 minutes or until golden brown. Cool. Blend cream cheese, confectioners' sugar and 1 cup whipped topping in bowl. Spread in prepared dish. Prepare vanilla and chocolate pudding mixes individually using package directions reducing milk to 1 1/2 cups each. Layer puddings over cream cheese mixture. Cover with remaining 3 cups whipped topping. Chill, covered, until serving time. Yield: 15 servings.

Approx Per Serving: Cal 361; Prot 6 g; Carbo 37 g; Fiber 1 g; T Fat 23 g; Chol 23 mg; Sod 240 mg.

Donna T. McGee, Central

DIRT DESSERT

1/2 cup butter, softened
8 ounces cream cheese, softened
1/3 cup confectioners' sugar
4 cups milk
2 4-ounce packages French vanilla instant pudding mix
12 ounces whipped topping
2 16-ounce packages Oreo cookies

Cream butter, cream cheese and confectioners' sugar in mixer bowl until light and fluffy. Set aside. Combine milk and pudding mix in large bowl; mix well. Let stand until partially set. Fold in whipped topping and cream cheese mixture. Place cookies in food processor container. Process until crumbled. Layer cookie crumbs and pudding mixture alternately in 2 plastic flowerpots, ending with cookie crumbs. Yield: 12 servings.

Approx Per Serving: Cal 725; Prot 8 g; Carbo 87 g; Fiber 1 g; T Fat 39 g; Chol 52 mg; Sod 645 mg.

Synthia Albertson, Piedmont

PARTY DIRT PIE DESSERT

2 4-ounce packages vanilla instant pudding mix
3 1/2 cups milk
8 ounces whipped topping
1/4 cup margarine, softened
8 ounces cream cheese, softened
1/3 cup confectioners' sugar
1 20-ounce package Oreo cookies, crushed

Prepare pudding mix using package directions reducing milk to 3 1/2 cups. Fold in whipped topping. Cream margarine, cream cheese and confectioners' sugar in mixer bowl until light and fluffy. Fold into pudding mixture. Layer cookie crumbs and pudding mixture alternately in new waxed paper-lined flowerpot, ending with cookie crumbs. Garnish with long-stemmed silk flower. May be prepared 24 hours ahead. Chill until serving time. Yield: 8 servings.

Approx Per Serving: Cal 775; Prot 10 g; Carbo 95 g; Fiber 1 g; T Fat 41 g; Chol 45 mg; Sod 727 mg.

Donna Hord, Hornets Nest

ÉCLAIR

2 small packages vanilla instant pudding mix
3 cups milk
8 ounces whipped topping
1 16-ounce package graham crackers
3 tablespoons milk
6 tablespoons butter
1 ounce semisweet chocolate
1 cup confectioners' sugar

Combine pudding mix and 3 cups milk in bowl; mix well. Fold in whipped topping. Layer graham crackers and pudding 1/2 at a time in 9x13-inch dish. Combine 3 tablespoons milk, butter and chocolate in saucepan. Heat until butter and chocolate are melted, stirring to mix well. Add confectioners' sugar; mix well. Spoon evenly over top. Chill until serving time. Yield: 15 servings.

Approx Per Serving: Cal 333; Prot 4 g; Carbo 49 g; Fiber 1 g; T Fat 14 g; Chol 19 mg; Sod 326 mg.

Diane Grace, Raleigh

CHOCOLATE ÉCLAIR DESSERT

- 2 4-ounce packages French vanilla instant pudding mix
- 3 cups milk
- 8 ounces whipped topping
- 1 16-ounce package graham crackers
- 1 ounce unsweetened chocolate
- 2 teaspoons light corn syrup
- 3 tablespoons margarine, softened
- 1 1/2 cups confectioners' sugar
- 3 tablespoons milk

Prepare pudding mix using package directions reducing milk to 3 cups milk. Fold in whipped topping. Layer graham crackers and pudding mixture alternately in 9x13-inch baking dish, ending with graham crackers. Melt chocolate in saucepan over low heat, stirring occasionally. Stir in remaining ingredients. Cool slightly. Pour over graham crackers. Chill, covered, until serving time. Yield: 15 servings.

Approx Per Serving: Cal 344; Prot 4 g; Carbo 57 g; Fiber 1 g; T Fat 12 g; Chol 7 mg; Sod 340 mg.

Becky Adams, Coastal

EASY ÉCLAIR DESSERT

- 2 4-ounce packages French vanilla instant pudding mix
- 3 cups milk
- 12 ounces whipped topping
- 1 16-ounce package graham crackers
- 1 16-ounce can milk chocolate frosting

Prepare pudding mix using package directions reducing milk to 3 cups. Fold in whipped topping. Layer graham crackers and pudding mixture alternately in 9x13-inch baking dish, ending with graham crackers. Spread frosting over crackers. Chill, covered, for 8 hours or longer. Yield: 24 servings.

Approx Per Serving: Cal 257; Prot 3 g; Carbo 40 g; Fiber 1 g; T Fat 7 g; Chol 4 mg; Sod 236 mg.

Judy B. Richardson, Independence
Agnes Williams, Independence

CHOCOLATE TORTE

1 cup self-rising flour
1/2 cup margarine, softened
1 cup chopped pecans
1 cup sugar
8 ounces cream cheese, softened
8 ounces whipped topping
1 4-ounce package vanilla instant pudding mix
1 4-ounce package chocolate instant pudding mix
4 cups milk
1/2 cup chopped pecans

Combine flour, margarine and 1 cup pecans in bowl; mix well. Press into 9x13-inch baking dish. Bake at 325 degrees for 20 minutes. Cream sugar, cream cheese and half the whipped topping in mixer bowl until light and fluffy. Spread over cooled crust. Blend pudding mixes and milk in bowl. Pour over cream cheese mixture. Chill, covered, until set. Top with remaining whipped topping. Sprinkle with remaining pecans.
Yield: 15 servings.

Approx Per Serving: Cal 411; Prot 5 g; Carbo 43 g; Fiber 1 g; T Fat 26 g; Chol 25 mg; Sod 339 mg.

Dolores S. Howell, Hornets Nest

CHERRY YUM-YUM

2 cups graham cracker crumbs
1 1/2 cups margarine, softened
1 cup sugar
8 ounces cream cheese, softened
1 envelope whipped topping mix
1 cup milk
2 21-ounce cans cherry pie filling

Combine graham cracker crumbs and margarine in bowl; mix well. Cream sugar and cream cheese in small mixer bowl until light and fluffy. Stir in mixture of topping mix and milk. Spread half the cracker crumb mixture in 9x13-inch baking dish. Layer cream cheese mixture, pie filling and remaining cracker crumb mixture in prepared dish. Chill, covered, until serving time.
Yield: 15 servings.

Approx Per Serving: Cal 464; Prot 4 g; Carbo 51 g; Fiber 1 g; T Fat 29 g; Chol 19 mg; Sod 397 mg.

Virginia Bowie, Independence

DUMP CAKE DESSERT

1 20-ounce can pineapple chunks
1 21-ounce can cherry pie filling
1 2-layer package yellow cake mix
1/2 cup margarine
1 cup pecan halves
8 ounces whipped topping

Combine pineapple and pie filling in 9x13-inch baking dish; mix well. Sprinkle cake mix over fruit mixture. Dot with margarine. Top with pecans. Bake at 350 degrees for 45 minutes. Spread whipped topping over cooled cake. Chill, tightly covered, until serving time. Yield: 8 servings.

Approx Per Serving: Cal 691; Prot 5 g; Carbo 96 g; Fiber 3 g; T Fat 34 g; Chol 0 mg; Sod 557 mg.

Gladys S. Middleton, Hornets Nest

APPLE COBBLER

1/4 cup margarine
1/2 cup flour
1/2 cup sugar
1 teaspoon baking powder
1/2 cup milk
1 20-ounce can sliced apples, drained

Melt margarine in 8x12-inch baking dish. Combine flour, sugar and baking powder in bowl; mix well. Stir in milk. Spread in prepared dish. Spoon apples onto batter. Bake at 350 degrees until lightly browned. Batter will rise to top. May substitute favorite canned or fresh fruit for apples. Yield: 6 servings.

Approx Per Serving: Cal 247; Prot 2 g; Carbo 42 g; Fiber 2 g; T Fat 9 g; Chol 3 mg; Sod 156 mg.

Esther Sossamon, Independence

NO-FOOL COBBLER

6 tablespoons margarine
1 cup self-rising flour
3/4 cup sugar
3/4 cup milk
1 20-ounce can blackberries, drained

Melt margarine in 9x13-inch baking dish. Combine flour, sugar and milk in bowl; mix well. Spread in prepared dish. Spoon blackberries onto batter. Bake at 350 degrees for 30 to 40 minutes or until lightly browned and center springs back when touched. May substitute favorite canned or fresh fruit for blackberries. Yield: 8 servings.

Approx Per Serving: Cal 283; Prot 3 g; Carbo 48 g; Fiber 4 g; T Fat 10 g; Chol 3 mg; Sod 281 mg.

Aileen Munden, Independence

PEACH COBBLER

1 cup self-rising flour
1 cup sugar
1 cup milk
1/2 cup melted butter
1 16-ounce can peaches
Cinnamon to taste

Combine flour, sugar, milk and melted butter in bowl; mix well. Pour into casserole. Spoon undrained peaches over batter. Bake at 350 degrees for 35 to 45 minutes or until lightly browned. May substitute nutmeg for cinnamon. Yield: 6 servings.

Approx Per Serving: Cal 418; Prot 4 g; Carbo 66 g; Fiber 1 g; T Fat 17 g; Chol 47 mg; Sod 376 mg.

Linda Armstrong, Central

☎ Prepared whipped topping has 20 fewer calories per tablespoon than sweetened whipped cream.

COCONUT SUPREME

1 cup flour
1/2 cup butter, softened
1/2 cup chopped pecans
1 cup confectioners' sugar
8 ounces cream cheese, softened
1/2 teaspoon vanilla extract
12 ounces whipped topping
3 1/2 ounces coconut
2 4-ounce packages coconut pudding and pie filling mix
3 cups milk
3 1/2 ounces toasted coconut

Combine flour, butter and pecans in small bowl; mix well. Spread in 8-inch square baking dish. Bake at 350 degrees for 15 minutes. Cool. Cream confectioners' sugar, cream cheese and vanilla in bowl until light and fluffy. Fold in half the whipped topping. Spread over crust. Sprinkle 3 1/2 ounces coconut over cream cheese mixture. Prepare pudding mix using package directions reducing milk to 3 cups. Cool slightly. Spread over coconut. Chill, covered, until serving time. Top with remaining whipped topping. Sprinkle with remaining 3 1/2 ounces toasted coconut. Yield: 8 servings.

Approx Per Serving: Cal 794; Prot 9 g; Carbo 81 g; Fiber 5 g; T Fat 50 g; Chol 74 mg; Sod 456 mg.

Mildred Deese, Hornets Nest

CHOCOLATE CHEESECAKE

1 3/4 cups graham cracker crumbs
1/2 cup melted butter
1/2 teaspoon cinnamon
1 cup sour cream
24 ounces cream cheese, softened
1/4 cup baking cocoa
1 cup sugar
4 eggs

Combine first 3 ingredients in bowl; mix well. Pack firmly in springform pan. Combine sour cream, cream cheese, baking cocoa and eggs in mixer bowl; mix well. Pour into prepared pan. Bake at 325 degrees for 1 1/4 hours or until set. Cool in pan. Chill until serving time. Yield: 12 servings.

Approx Per Serving: Cal 488; Prot 9 g; Carbo 33 g; Fiber 2 g; T Fat 37 g; Chol 160 mg; Sod 370 mg.

Sue Rivenbark, Coastal

CREAM CHEESECAKE

1 3/4 cups finely crushed graham cracker crumbs
2 tablespoons dark brown sugar
3 tablespoons melted butter
1 teaspoon cinnamon
4 eggs
24 ounces cream cheese, softened
1 cup sugar
2 tablespoons milk
1 teaspoon vanilla extract
1/2 cup confectioners' sugar
2 cups sour cream

Combine first 4 ingredients in bowl; mix well. Pat over bottom and sides of 8x12-inch baking dish. Combine eggs, cream cheese, sugar and milk in mixer bowl. Beat at low speed for 30 minutes or until very smooth. Stir in vanilla. Pour into prepared dish. Bake at 350 degrees for 35 to 40 minutes or until firm. Top with mixture of confectioners' sugar and sour cream. Bake for 5 minutes longer. Yield: 12 servings.

Approx Per Serving: Cal 504; Prot 9 g; Carbo 41 g; Fiber <1 g; T Fat 35 g; Chol 159 mg; Sod 347 mg.

Mrs. George F. Cloninger, Foot Hills

DELUXE CHEESECAKE

1 recipe for graham cracker pie shell
16 ounces cream cheese, softened
1 teaspoon vanilla extract
1/2 cup sugar
3 eggs
2 cups sour cream
1/4 cup sugar
1 teaspoon vanilla extract
2 tablespoons graham cracker crumbs

Prepare graham cracker mixture. Press into lightly greased 9-inch springform pan. Beat cream cheese in mixer bowl for 2 to 3 minutes or until smooth. Stir in 1 teaspoon vanilla. Beat in 1/2 cup sugar and eggs gradually. Pour into prepared pan. Bake at 375 degrees for 20 minutes. Let stand for 15 minutes. Mix sour cream, remaining 1/4 cup sugar and vanilla in bowl. Spread over cheesecake. Sprinkle with graham cracker crumbs. Bake at 475 degrees for 10 minutes. Cool in pan. Chill until firm. Topping will be soft when warm and firm when chilled. Yield: 12 servings.

Approx Per Serving: Cal 428; Prot 7 g; Carbo 34 g; Fiber <1 g; T Fat 30 g; Chol 112 mg; Sod 318 mg.

Daphine Scarborough, Independence

NEW YORK CHEESECAKE

1¼ cups graham cracker crumbs
2 tablespoons melted butter
2 tablespoons sugar
¼ teaspoon cinnamon
32 ounces cream cheese, softened
2 cups sugar
6 eggs
2 teaspoons vanilla extract
2 cups sour cream

Combine graham cracker crumbs, melted butter, 2 tablespoons sugar and cinnamon in bowl; mix well. Pat into lightly greased 9-inch springform pan. Beat cream cheese in mixer bowl. Add remaining 2 cups sugar and eggs 1 at a time, beating well after each addition. Stir in vanilla. Fold in sour cream. Pour into prepared pan. Bake at 375 degrees for 45 minutes. Turn off oven. Let stand in cold oven for 1 hour. Cool to room temperature. Remove side of pan. Chill, covered, in refrigerator for 24 hours before serving. Yield: 16 servings.

Approx Per Serving: Cal 446; Prot 8 g; Carbo 37 g; Fiber <1 g; T Fat 30 g; Chol 158 mg; Sod 279 mg.

Martha Hood, Independence

GLAZED CHEESECAKE PUFFS

24 vanilla wafers
¾ cup sugar
16 ounces cream cheese, softened
2 eggs
1 teaspoon vanilla extract
1 21-ounce can cherry pie filling

Place vanilla wafers in paper-lined muffin cups. Cream sugar, cream cheese, eggs and vanilla in mixer bowl until light and fluffy. Fill prepared muffin cups ¾ full. Bake at 375 degrees for 10 to 15 minutes or until set. Cool. Spread pie filling on cooled cheesecakes. Chill until serving time. Yield: 24 servings.

Approx Per Serving: Cal 139; Prot 2 g; Carbo 16 g; Fiber <1 g; T Fat 8 g; Chol 41 mg; Sod 84 mg.

Becky Adams, Coastal

PETITE CHERRY CHEESECAKES

42 vanilla wafers, finely crushed
3/4 cup sugar
16 ounces cream cheese, softened
2 eggs
1 tablespoon lemon juice
1 teaspoon vanilla extract
1 21-ounce can cherry pie filling

Place crushed vanilla wafers in paper-lined miniature muffin cups. Cream sugar, cream cheese, eggs, lemon juice and vanilla in mixer bowl until light and fluffy. Pour into prepared muffin cups. Bake at 375 degrees for 15 to 20 minutes or until set. Do not brown. Top each warm cheesecake with 1 tablespoonful pie filling. Yield: 42 servings.

Approx Per Serving: Cal 88; Prot 1 g; Carbo 10 g; Fiber <1 g; T Fat 5 g; Chol 24 mg; Sod 55 mg.

Agnes Williams, Independence

TINY CHEESECAKES

1 cup graham cracker crumbs
3/4 cup sugar
16 ounces cream cheese, softened
3 egg yolks, beaten
3 egg whites, stiffly beaten
1 cup sour cream
2 tablespoons sugar
1/2 teaspoon vanilla extract

Place graham cracker crumbs in lightly greased miniature muffin cups. Shake to remove excess. Cream 3/4 cup sugar and cream cheese in mixer bowl until light and fluffy. Beat in egg yolks. Fold in stiffly beaten egg whites. Pour into prepared muffin cups. Fill 3/4 full. Bake at 375 degrees for 15 to 20 minutes or until set. Top cooled cakes with mixture of sour cream, remaining 2 tablespoons sugar and vanilla. Bake for 5 minutes longer. Garnish with red or green cherries. Yield: 24 servings.

Approx Per Serving: Cal 146; Prot 3 g; Carbo 12 g; Fiber <1 g; T Fat 10 g; Chol 52 mg; Sod 101 mg.

Margaret L. Fenner, Hornets Nest

CREAM CHEESE DELIGHT

1 cup flour
1/4 cup packed brown sugar
1/2 cup margarine, softened
1 cup chopped pecans
8 ounces cream cheese, softened
3/4 cup sugar
1 teaspoon vanilla extract
1 envelope whipped topping mix
1 21-ounce can blueberry pie filling

Combine flour, brown sugar, margarine and pecans in bowl; mix well. Press into 9-inch square baking dish. Bake at 325 degrees for 10 minutes. Chill in refrigerator. Beat cream cheese, sugar and vanilla in mixer bowl until light and fluffy. Prepare whipped topping using package directions. Fold into cream cheese mixture. Spread in chilled crust. Chill until serving time. Spread with pie filling. Garnish with additional whipped topping. May substitute cherry or strawberry pie filling for blueberry. Yield: 12 servings.

Approx Per Serving: Cal 405; Prot 4 g; Carbo 45 g; Fiber 2 g; T Fat 25 g; Chol 21 mg; Sod 174 mg.

Freda Barrett, Foot Hills

CREAM CHEESE DESSERT WITH PIE FILLING

20 graham crackers, crushed
1/4 cup melted butter
1/4 cup sugar
8 ounces cream cheese, softened
1 cup confectioners' sugar
1 cup sour cream
1 21-ounce can apple pie filling
8 ounces whipped topping

Combine crushed graham crackers, melted butter and sugar in bowl; mix well. Press into baking dish. Bake at 375 degrees for 8 minutes. Blend cream cheese, confectioners' sugar and sour cream in bowl. Spread over crust. Cover with pie filling. Serve with whipped topping. May substitute cherry or blueberry pie filling for apple. Yield: 10 servings.

Approx Per Serving: Cal 423; Prot 4 g; Carbo 49 g; Fiber 1 g; T Fat 25 g; Chol 47 mg; Sod 228 mg.

Kim Parker, Central

FOUR-LAYER DELIGHT

1 cup flour
1/2 cup margarine, softened
1/2 cup chopped pecans
1 cup confectioners' sugar
8 ounces cream cheese, softened
1 cup whipped topping
2 4-ounce packages chocolate instant pudding mix
3 cups milk
1 cup whipped topping
1/2 cup chopped pecans

Combine flour, softened margarine and 1/2 cup pecans in bowl; mix well. Spread in 9x13-inch baking dish. Chill in refrigerator. Cream confectioners' sugar, cream cheese and 1 cup whipped topping in mixer bowl until light and fluffy. Spread over chilled layer. Chill for 15 minutes. Prepare pudding mix using package directions reducing milk to 3 cups. Spread over creamed layer. Chill for 5 minutes. Spread with mixture of remaining 1 cup whipped topping and 1/2 cup pecans. Yield: 15 servings.

Approx Per Serving: Cal 339; Prot 4 g; Carbo 35 g; Fiber 1 g; T Fat 21 g; Chol 23 mg; Sod 240 mg.

Mae C. Gulley, Raleigh

GOOEY BUTTER DESSERT

1 2-layer package yellow pudding-recipe cake mix
1/2 cup melted margarine
1 egg, lightly beaten
1 cup chopped pecans
1 1-pound package confectioners' sugar
1/2 cup melted butter
2 eggs
8 ounces cream cheese, softened

Combine first 3 ingredients in bowl; mix well. Spread in greased 9x13-inch baking dish. Sprinkle with pecans. Blend confectioners' sugar, melted butter, remaining eggs and cream cheese in bowl. Spread over pecans. Bake at 350 degrees for 45 minutes or until golden brown. Garnish with pecan halves, maraschino cherries or pineapple tidbits. Yield: 15 servings.

Approx Per Serving: Cal 516; Prot 5 g; Carbo 67 g; Fiber 1 g; T Fat 27 g; Chol 76 mg; Sod 391 mg.

Aileen Munden, Independence

DOT'S GOOEY BUTTER DESSERT

1 2-layer package yellow pudding-recipe cake mix
1/2 cup melted margarine
1 egg
1 cup chopped pecans
2 eggs
8 ounces cream cheese, softened
1/2 cup margarine, softened
1 1 pound package confectioners' sugar

Combine cake mix, 1/2 cup margarine and 1 egg in bowl; mix well. Stir in pecans. Press into 9x13-inch baking dish. Combine 2 eggs, cream cheese, remaining 1/2 cup margarine and confectioners' sugar in bowl; mix until smooth. Spoon evenly into prepared dish. Bake at 350 degrees for 45 minutes or until golden brown. Yield: 15 servings.

Approx Per Serving: Cal 516; Prot 5 g; Carbo 67 g; Fiber 1 g; T Fat 27 g; Chol 59 mg; Sod 411 mg.

Dot Ottone, Foot Hills

HEAVENLY HASH

1 5-ounce can evaporated milk, chilled
1 16-ounce package marshmallows
1 16-ounce can fruit cocktail
1 8-ounce can crushed pineapple
1/2 cup sugar
1/2 cup maraschino cherries
1/2 cup chopped pecans

Whip evaporated milk in bowl. Combine marshmallows, fruit cocktail, pineapple, sugar, cherries and pecans in bowl; mix well. Fold in whipped evaporated milk. Chill, tightly covered, in refrigerator. Serve over pound cake. Yield: 12 servings.

Approx Per Serving: Cal 254; Prot 2 g; Carbo 55 g; Fiber 1 g; T Fat 4 g; Chol 3 mg; Sod 49 mg.

Virginia Bowie, Independence

HOMEMADE PEACH ICE CREAM

4 eggs, beaten
2 cups sugar
1 12-ounce can evaporated milk
2 cups half and half
2 cups chopped peaches
2 teaspoons vanilla extract
1/2 teaspoon salt
1 quart (about) milk

Combine eggs and sugar in bowl; mix well. Stir in evaporated milk, half and half, peaches, vanilla and salt. Pour into 1-gallon ice cream freezer container. Add milk to fill line. Freeze using manufacturer's instructions. May substitute favorite fruit for peaches. Yield: 32 servings.

Approx Per Serving: Cal 117; Prot 3 g; Carbo 20 g; Fiber <1 g; T Fat 4 g; Chol 40 mg; Sod 75 mg.

Linda S. Griffin, Independence

HOMEMADE BLACK WALNUT ICE CREAM

4 eggs
1 1/2 cups sugar
1 5-ounce can evaporated milk
1 14-ounce can sweetened condensed milk
8 cups milk
1 4-ounce can black walnuts, chopped
2 tablespoons black walnut extract

Combine eggs, sugar, evaporated milk and condensed milk in large bowl; mix well. Stir in milk, walnuts and flavoring. Pour into ice cream freezer container. Freeze using manufacturer's instructions. Yield: 32 servings.

Approx Per Serving: Cal 151; Prot 5 g; Carbo 20 g; Fiber <1 g; T Fat 6 g; Chol 40 mg; Sod 55 mg.

Mary Reeves, Independence

LEMON-LAYERED DESSERT

1½ cups flour
½ cup butter, softened
½ cup chopped pecans
8 ounces cream cheese, softened
1 cup confectioners' sugar
12 ounces whipped topping
3 4-ounce packages lemon instant pudding mix
4 cups milk

Combine flour, butter and pecans in bowl; mix well. Spread in 9x13-inch baking dish. Bake at 350 degrees for 20 to 30 minutes or until lightly browned. Beat cream cheese, confectioners' sugar and half the whipped topping in bowl until smooth. Spread over cooled crust. Combine pudding mix and milk in bowl. Beat until slightly thickened. Pour over cream cheese mixture. Top with remaining whipped topping. Chill, covered, for 2 hours. Yield: 12 servings.

Approx Per Serving: Cal 507; Prot 7 g; Carbo 60 g; Fiber 1 g; T Fat 28 g; Chol 52 mg; Sod 352 mg.

Ruby Brown, Raleigh

PEACH CRISP

8 ripe peaches, peeled, sliced
¼ cup sugar
½ teaspoon cinnamon
¼ teaspoon nutmeg
¾ cup sugar
¾ cup flour
1 teaspoon baking powder
1 egg
3 tablespoons melted margarine
½ teaspoon cinnamon

Place peaches in 8x11-inch baking dish. Sprinkle with mixture of ¼ cup sugar, ½ teaspoon cinnamon and nutmeg. Combine remaining ¾ cup sugar, flour, baking powder, egg and melted margarine in bowl until crumbly. Spread over peaches. Bake at 375 degrees for 30 minutes. Sprinkle with remaining ½ teaspoon cinnamon. May substitute apples for fresh peaches. Bake apple crisp at 350 degrees for 1 hour. Yield: 6 servings.

Approx Per Serving: Cal 299; Prot 4 g; Carbo 58 g; Fiber 2 g; T Fat 7 g; Chol 36 mg; Sod 134 mg.

Doris G. Miller, Central

MICROWAVE PEACH CRISP

6 cups sliced peeled peaches
1/4 cup sugar
1 teaspoon cinnamon
1/2 cup flour
1/2 cup quick-cooking oats
3/4 cup packed brown sugar
1 teaspoon cinnamon
1/4 cup butter

Place peaches in greased 2-quart glass baking dish. Sprinkle with mixture of sugar and 1 teaspoon cinnamon. Combine flour, oats, brown sugar and remaining 1 teaspoon cinnamon in bowl. Cut in butter until crumbly. Spread over peaches. Microwave on High for 8 minutes, turning once. Serve warm or cold with ice cream or whipped topping. Yield: 6 servings.

Approx Per Serving: Cal 339; Prot 3 g; Carbo 66 g; Fiber 4 g; T Fat 8 g; Chol 21 mg; Sod 78 mg.

Gail Blevins, Blue Ridge

PEACH PUSHOVER

1 16-ounce can peach halves
1/4 teaspoon orange extract
1 tablespoon melted butter
1 1-layer package white cake mix
1 tablespoon butter

Pour undrained peaches into 1 1/2 quart casserole. Stir in orange extract and 1 tablespoon butter. Sprinkle with cake mix. Dot with remaining 1 tablespoon butter. Bake at 350 degrees for 30 minutes. Yield: 6 servings.

Approx Per Serving: Cal 455; Prot 4 g; Carbo 87 g; Fiber 1 g; T Fat 11 g; Chol 10 mg; Sod 561 mg.

Pat Pope, Hornets Nest

☎ For a delicious topping for cobblers and puddings, mix 1 cup sour cream and 1/2 cup packed brown sugar. Chill in refrigerator for 1 hour or longer and mix well before serving.

PEACH STUFF

1 cup vanilla wafer crumbs
1 1/2 cups confectioners' sugar
1/2 cup butter, softened
1 egg
1 teaspoon vanilla extract
4 cups sliced peeled peaches
1/2 cup sugar
2 cups whipped topping
1/2 cup vanilla wafer crumbs

Sprinkle 1 cup crumbs in 8-inch square baking dish. Cream confectioners' sugar, butter, egg and vanilla in mixer bowl for 3 minutes or until light and fluffy. Spread in prepared dish. Combine peaches and sugar in bowl. Pour over creamed mixture. Spread with whipped topping. Sprinkle with remaining 1/2 cup crumbs. Chill, covered, for 2 hours or longer. Yield: 8 servings.

Approx Per Serving: Cal 391; Prot 2 g; Carbo 59 g; Fiber 2 g; T Fat 18 g; Chol 68 mg; Sod 171 mg.

Rose Ann McLelland, Piedmont

HIDDEN PINEAPPLE TREAT

1 16-ounce package graham crackers
1 6-ounce package vanilla pudding and pie filling mix
3 cups milk
1 8-ounce can pineapple chunks

Line 1-quart casserole with 1 layer graham crackers. Combine pudding mix and milk in saucepan; mix well. Cook over medium heat until thickened, stirring frequently. Crumble remaining graham crackers in bowl. Layer pineapple chunks, crumbled graham crackers and pudding alternately in prepared dish, ending with pudding. Serve warm or cool. Yield: 6 servings.

Approx Per Serving: Cal 533; Prot 10 g; Carbo 98 g; Fiber 3 g; T Fat 12 g; Chol 17 mg; Sod 706 mg.

Linda Armstrong, Central

☎ Make a quick dessert by pouring 1 to 2 tablespoons crème de menthe on vanilla ice cream.

FRUIT PIZZA

2¼ cups flour
¾ cup confectioners' sugar
1¼ cup butter, softened
½ teaspoon vanilla extract
½ teaspoon lemon extract
8 ounces cream cheese, softened
½ cup confectioners' sugar
½ teaspoon lemon extract

Combine flour, ¾ cup confectioners' sugar, butter, vanilla and ½ teaspoon lemon extract in bowl; mix well. Press onto pizza pan. Bake at 325 degrees for 12 to 15 minutes or until lightly browned. Blend cream cheese, remaining ½ cup confectioners' sugar and remaining ½ teaspoon lemon extract in bowl. Spread over crust. Top with your choice of fresh fruit such as banana slices, strawberries, blueberries, kiwifruit or crushed pineapple. Yield: 12 servings.

Approx Per Serving: Cal 372; Prot 4 g; Carbo 32 g; Fiber 1 g; T Fat 26 g; Chol 73 mg; Sod 218 mg.
Nutritional information does not include fruit.

Swannie Brown, Piedmont

GLAZED FRUIT PIZZA

1 15-ounce package sugar cookie mix
4 ounces whipped topping
8 ounces cream cheese, softened
1 cup fresh strawberries
½ cup sugar
1 tablespoon cornstarch
¼ cup water
⅛ teaspoon salt
2 tablespoons lemon juice

Prepare cookie mix using package directions. Press into 12-inch pizza pan. Bake at 350 degrees until lightly browned. Blend whipped topping and cream cheese in bowl. Spread over crust. Arrange strawberries in decorative pattern. Bring sugar, cornstarch, water, salt and lemon juice to a boil in saucepan. Cook for 1 minute, stirring constantly. Pour over strawberries. Chill until serving time. May substitute favorite fruit for strawberries. May keep for several days in refrigerator. Yield: 8 servings.

Approx Per Serving: Cal 436; Prot 5 g; Carbo 52 g; Fiber 1 g; T Fat 25 g; Chol 64 mg; Sod 413 mg.

Betty S. Bryant, Hornets Nest

QUICK FRUIT PIZZA

- 1 20-ounce package refrigerator sugar cookie dough
- 1/2 cup sugar
- 16 ounces cream cheese, softened
- 1 teaspoon vanilla extract
- 1 11-ounce can mandarin oranges, drained
- 1 8-ounce can crushed pineapple, drained
- 1 4-ounce jar maraschino cherries, drained

Spread cookie dough on lightly greased pizza pan. Bake using package directions. Cream sugar, cream cheese and vanilla in bowl until light and fluffy. Spread over cooled crust. Arrange fruit on filling just before serving. May add any other favorite fruit such as strawberries, kiwifruit or bananas.
Yield: 8 servings.

Approx Per Serving: Cal 635; Prot 8 g; Carbo 76 g; Fiber 2 g; T Fat 36 g; Chol 94 mg; Sod 426 mg.

Carolyn Helms, Independence

POPCORN DESSERT

- 16 cups popped popcorn
- 1 16-ounce package gumdrops
- 2 cups salted peanuts
- 1/2 cup margarine
- 1/4 cup oil
- 1 16-ounce package marshmallows

Combine popped popcorn, gumdrops and peanuts in large bowl; mix well. Combine margarine and oil in saucepan. Cook over low heat until margarine is melted, stirring frequently. Add marshmallows. Cook until marshmallows are melted, stirring frequently. Press into greased tube pan. Let stand until cool. Invert onto serving platter. Yield: 10 servings.

Approx Per Serving: Cal 843; Prot 13 g; Carbo 111 g; Fiber 8 g; T Fat 42 g; Chol 0 mg; Sod 638 mg.

Ruby M. Smith, Hornets Nest

APPLESAUCE PUDDING

2 cups applesauce
1/3 cup packed brown sugar
1/4 cup raisins
1/2 teaspoon cinnamon
1 cup baking mix
1/3 cup sugar
1/4 cup chopped pecans
1/4 cup margarine

Combine applesauce, brown sugar, raisins and cinnamon in bowl; mix well. Pour into lightly greased and floured 8-inch baking pan. Combine baking mix, sugar and pecans in bowl. Cut in margarine until crumbly. Spoon over applesauce mixture. Bake at 375 degrees for 30 to 35 minutes or until lightly browned. Yield: 6 servings.

Approx Per Serving: Cal 365; Prot 2 g; Carbo 60 g; Fiber 2 g; T Fat 14 g; Chol 0 mg; Sod 363 mg.

Kim Parker, Central

BANANA PUDDING

3 4-ounce packages vanilla instant pudding mix
5 cups milk
1 cup sour cream
6 ounces whipped topping
6 ripe bananas, sliced
1 16-ounce package vanilla wafers
6 ounces whipped topping

Combine pudding mix, milk and sour cream in bowl; mix well. Fold in 6 ounces whipped topping. Layer vanilla wafers, banana slices and pudding mixture alternately in large bowl. Top with remaining 6 ounces whipped topping. Chill until serving time. Yield: 24 servings.

Approx Per Serving: Cal 263; Prot 3 g; Carbo 40 g; Fiber 1 g; T Fat 11 g; Chol 13 mg; Sod 196 mg.

Madelon Haskin, Hornets Nest

BEST-EVER BANANA PUDDING

1/4 cup melted margarine
1 1/2 cups packed light brown sugar
2 tablespoons flour
1/8 teaspoon salt
1 12-ounce can evaporated milk
3/4 cup water
3 eggs
1 teaspoon vanilla extract
1 16-ounce package vanilla wafers
4 bananas, sliced
2 cups whipped topping

Combine melted margarine, brown sugar, flour, salt, evaporated milk, water, eggs and vanilla in double boiler; mix well. Cook until thickened, stirring frequently. Reserve 2 to 3 vanilla wafers. Layer banana slices, pudding and vanilla wafers alternately in large bowl. Crumble reserved wafers over top. Cover with whipped topping. Chill, covered, overnight. Yield: 8 servings.

Approx Per Serving: Cal 645; Prot 9 g; Carbo 103 g; Fiber 1 g; T Fat 24 g; Chol 128 mg; Sod 405 mg.

Mary Wilkins, Independence

CREAMY BANANA PUDDING

1 14-ounce can sweetened condensed milk
1 1/2 cups water
1 4-ounce package vanilla instant pudding mix
2 cups whipping cream, whipped
3 bananas, sliced
3 tablespoons lemon juice
36 vanilla wafers

Combine condensed milk and water in mixer bowl; mix well. Beat in pudding mix. Chill for 5 minutes. Fold in whipped cream. Dip banana slices into lemon juice. Layer pudding, vanilla wafers and banana slices in 2 1/2-quart casserole. Chill thoroughly. Yield: 8 servings.

Approx Per Serving: Cal 541; Prot 7 g; Carbo 66 g; Fiber 1 g; T Fat 30 g; Chol 110 mg; Sod 248 mg.

Robbie Huffstetller, Foot Hills

MICROWAVE BANANA PUDDING

3/4 cup sugar
3 tablespoons cornstarch
1/8 teaspoon salt
2 cups milk
3 egg yolks, lightly beaten
2 tablespoons butter
1 teaspoon vanilla extract
1 16-ounce package vanilla wafers
3 bananas, sliced

Combine sugar, cornstarch, salt and milk in microwave-safe bowl; mix well. Microwave on Medium-High for 7 minutes or until thickened, stirring twice. Stir a small amount of hot mixture into beaten egg yolks; stir egg yolks into hot mixture. Microwave on Medium-High until custard coats metal spoon, stirring once. Beat in butter and vanilla until butter is melted. Layer vanilla wafers, banana slices and custard alternately in bowl.
Yield: 8 servings.

Approx Per Serving: Cal 473; Prot 6 g; Carbo 75 g; Fiber 1 g; T Fat 17 g; Chol 131 mg; Sod 299 mg.

Roe Ann Hill, Independence

SOUR CREAM BANANA PUDDING

2 4-ounce packages vanilla instant pudding mix
3 1/2 cups milk
16 ounces whipped topping
1 cup sour cream
1 1/2 12-ounce packages vanilla wafers
8 bananas, sliced

Prepare pudding mix with 3 1/2 cups milk using package directions. Stir in 2 tablespoons whipped topping and sour cream. Layer vanilla wafers, banana slices and pudding mixture alternately in 9x13-inch dish, ending with vanilla wafers. Top with remaining whipped topping. Chill, covered, for 24 hours.
Yield: 15 servings.

Approx Per Serving: Cal 416; Prot 5 g; Carbo 61 g; Fiber 2 g; T Fat 19 g; Chol 33 mg; Sod 255 mg.

Wilma Sain, Foot Hills

EGG CUSTARD

1 cup sugar
3 tablespoons self-rising flour
3 eggs
1 12-ounce can evaporated milk
3 tablespoons melted butter
1 teaspoon vanilla extract
Nutmeg to taste

Combine sugar and flour in bowl; mix well. Stir in eggs, evaporated milk, melted butter and vanilla. Pour into lightly greased and floured 8-inch square baking dish. Sprinkle with nutmeg. Bake at 350 degrees for 25 to 35 minutes or until knife inserted near center comes out clean. May double recipe and bake in 9x13-inch baking dish. Yield: 6 servings.

Approx Per Serving: Cal 311; Prot 7 g; Carbo 42 g; Fiber <1 g; T Fat 13 g; Chol 139 mg; Sod 186 mg.

Ila Crabtree, Piedmont

CRUSTLESS EGG CUSTARD

6 tablespoons butter
1¼ cups sugar
3 tablespoons flour
3 eggs
1 12-ounce can evaporated milk
1 teaspoon vanilla extract

Melt butter in 9-inch pie plate. Combine melted butter, sugar and flour in bowl; mix well. Add eggs 1 at a time, mixing well after each addition. Stir in evaporated milk and vanilla. Pour into buttered pie plate. Bake at 350 degrees for 30 to 45 minutes or until knife inserted near center comes out clean.
Yield: 6 servings.

Approx Per Serving: Cal 395; Prot 7 g; Carbo 51 g; Fiber <1 g; T Fat 19 g; Chol 154 mg; Sod 192 mg.

Gladys Hinson, Independence

☎ Cook standard 3-egg custard recipe in individual mugs in pressure cooker for 3½ minutes. Sprinkle with nutmeg.

AUNT MAUDE'S RAISIN PUDDING

1 1/3 cups packed brown sugar
2 tablespoons butter
2 cups hot water
1 cup packed brown sugar
1 cup flour
3 tablespoons baking powder
1/2 teaspoon salt
1/2 cup milk
1 cup raisins
1/2 cup chopped pecans

Bring 1 1/3 cups brown sugar, butter and water to a boil in saucepan, stirring frequently. Cook until thickened, stirring constantly. Pour into deep baking dish. Combine remaining 1 cup brown sugar, flour, baking powder, salt and milk in bowl; mix well. Fold in raisins and pecans. Drop by tablespoonfuls into baking dish. Bake at 350 degrees for 30 minutes. Yield: 8 servings.

Approx Per Serving: Cal 447; Prot 3 g; Carbo 93 g; Fiber 2 g; T Fat 9 g; Chol 10 mg; Sod 565 mg.

Shirley Carmichael, Hornets Nest

PUDDING SPECTACULAR

1 1/2 cups flour
2 cups margarine, softened
3 tablespoons sugar
1/2 cup chopped walnuts
1 1/2 cups confectioners' sugar
8 ounces cream cheese, softened
1 1/2 cups whipped topping
2 4-ounce packages vanilla instant pudding mix
2 3/4 cups milk
2 1/2 cups whipped topping
1/2 cup chopped walnuts

Combine flour, margarine, sugar and 1/2 cup walnuts in bowl; mix well. Spread in 9x13-inch baking dish. Bake at 375 degrees for 15 minutes. Cream confectioners' sugar and cream cheese in mixer bowl until light and fluffy. Fold in 1 1/2 cups whipped topping. Spread over cooled crust. Prepare pudding mix with 2 3/4 cups milk using package directions. Spread over cream cheese mixture. Cover with remaining 2 1/2 cups whipped topping. Sprinkle with remaining 1/2 cup walnuts. Chill until serving time. Yield: 15 servings.

Approx Per Serving: Cal 528; Prot 5 g; Carbo 44 g; Fiber 1 g; T Fat 38 g; Chol 20 mg; Sod 447 mg.

Kim Parker, Central

BAKED SUNSHINE PUDDING

1/2 cup shortening
1 1/4 cups sugar
2 egg yolks
1 teaspoon lemon extract
1/2 teaspoon vanilla extract
1 1/2 cups shredded carrots
1 1/2 cups flour
3 tablespoons baking powder
3/4 teaspoon salt
1/4 cup milk
2 egg whites
Sunshine Sauce

Cream shortening and sugar in mixer bowl until light and fluffy. Beat in egg yolks, flavorings and carrots. Mix flour, baking powder and salt in bowl. Add to carrot mixture alternately with milk, mixing well after each addition. Beat egg whites in bowl until stiff. Fold into batter gently. Pour into greased 9-inch square baking dish. Bake at 350 degrees for 50 to 55 minutes or until lightly browned. Top warm pudding with Sunshine Sauce.
Yield: 12 servings.

Sunshine Sauce

2 cups water
2 tablespoons margarine
3/4 cup sugar
2 tablespoons cornstarch
1/8 teaspoon salt
1 teaspoon vanilla extract
2 tablespoons vinegar
1/3 cup shredded carrots
2 tablespoons lemon juice
1/8 teaspoon nutmeg

Bring water and margarine to a boil in saucepan. Mix sugar, cornstarch and salt in bowl. Add to boiling water all at once. Cook for 2 to 3 minutes or until mixture is clear and slightly thickened, stirring vigorously. Stir in vanilla, vinegar, carrots, lemon juice and nutmeg.

Approx Per Serving: Cal 313; Prot 3 g; Carbo 50 g; Fiber 1 g; T Fat 12 g; Chol 36 mg; Sod 445 mg.

Louise M. Stahl, Salem

☎ Make a quick elegant sauce for ice cream or baked pears by melting chocolate-covered mint patties in the microwave.

SWEET POTATO PUDDING WITH WHISKEY

2 cups half and half
3 sweet potatoes, peeled
3 eggs, beaten
2/3 cup packed brown sugar
2 teaspoons cinnamon
1/2 cup slivered blanched almonds
1/4 cup melted butter
1/2 cup whiskey

Pour half and half into shallow casserole. Shred sweet potatoes. Stir into half and half. Stir mixture of beaten eggs, brown sugar and cinnamon into sweet potato mixture. Sprinkle with almonds. Drizzle melted butter over top. Bake at 300 degrees until firm and lightly browned. Pour whiskey over warm pudding. May substitute rum for whiskey. Yield: 6 servings.

Approx Per Serving: Cal 491; Prot 9 g; Carbo 48 g; Fiber 4 g; T Fat 26 g; Chol 157 mg; Sod 154 mg.

Ila Mae Moses, Hornets Nest

PUMPKIN CRISP

1 16-ounce can pumpkin
1 14-ounce can sweetened condensed milk
1/2 cup sugar
3 eggs
1/2 teaspoon cinnamon
1/2 teaspoon nutmeg
1 2-layer package yellow cake mix
1 cup chopped pecans
1 cup melted butter
8 ounces cream cheese, softened
3/4 cup whipped topping
1/2 cup confectioners' sugar

Combine pumpkin, condensed milk, sugar, eggs, cinnamon and nutmeg in bowl; mix well. Pour into waxed paper-lined 9x13-inch baking dish. Cover with dry cake mix. Pat pecans into dry cake mix. Drizzle melted butter over pecans. Bake at 350 degrees for 50 to 60 minutes or until lightly browned. Invert onto serving tray; remove waxed paper. Blend cream cheese, whipped topping and confectioners' sugar in bowl. Spread over cooled cake. Chill until serving time. Yield: 24 servings.

Approx Per Serving: Cal 328; Prot 5 g; Carbo 37 g; Fiber 1 g; T Fat 19 g; Chol 63 mg; Sod 255 mg.

Linda S. Griffin, Independence

PUNCH BOWL DESSERT

- 1 2-layer package yellow cake mix
- 1 6-ounce package vanilla instant pudding mix
- 3 cups milk
- 1 21-ounce can cherry pie filling
- 1 20-ounce can crushed pineapple, drained
- 1 12-ounce package frozen coconut, thawed
- 16 ounces whipped topping

Prepare and bake cake mix using package directions for 10x15-inch cake. Prepare pudding mix with 3 cups milk using package directions. Layer crumbled cake, pudding, pie filling, pineapple, coconut and whipped topping 1/2 at a time in punch bowl. Garnish with maraschino cherries. Chill until serving time. May keep for several days in refrigerator. Yield: 16 servings.

Approx Per Serving: Cal 502; Prot 6 g; Carbo 77 g; Fiber 3 g; T Fat 19 g; Chol 7 mg; Sod 270 mg.

Jessie M. Godwin, Raleigh

FROZEN RASPBERRY DESSERT

- 1 cup flour
- 1/2 cup packed light brown sugar
- 1/2 cup chopped walnuts
- 1/2 cup butter, softened
- 2 egg whites
- 1/2 cup sugar
- 1 10-ounce package frozen raspberries
- 2 teaspoons lemon juice
- 3 cups whipped topping

Combine flour, brown sugar, walnuts and butter in bowl; mix well. Roll 1/4 inch thick on ungreased baking sheet. Bake at 350 degrees for 20 minutes or until crumbly, stirring every 5 minutes. Cool and crumble. Sprinkle half the crumbs into 9x13-inch baking dish. Beat egg whites in bowl. Add sugar gradually, beating constantly until stiff peaks form. Stir in raspberries and lemon juice. Fold in whipped topping. Spread in prepared pan. Cover with remaining crumbs. Freeze until serving time. Yield: 16 servings.

Approx Per Serving: Cal 196; Prot 2 g; Carbo 26 g; Fiber 1 g; T Fat 10 g; Chol 16 mg; Sod 60 mg.

Nelle Laetsch, Asheville

STRAWBERRY DELIGHT

16 ounces whipped topping
2 cups sour cream
1 cup confectioners' sugar
1 5-ounce can evaporated milk
1 12-ounce angel food cake
4 cups fresh strawberries
1 package strawberry glaze

Blend whipped topping, sour cream, confectioners' sugar and evaporated milk in bowl; do not use electric mixer. Tear cake into small pieces. Stir into sour cream mixture. Spread in 9x12-inch baking dish. Mix strawberries and glaze in bowl. Spread over cake layer. Chill unto serving time. Yield: 15 servings.

Approx Per Serving: Cal 207; Prot 3 g; Carbo 28 g; Fiber 1 g; T Fat 10 g; Chol 16 mg; Sod 145 mg.
Nutritional information does not include glaze.

Wilma Burleson, Independence

CONGEALED STRAWBERRY SHORTCAKE

1 12-ounce angel food cake
1 6-ounce package strawberry gelatin
2 10-ounce packages frozen strawberries, thawed
16 ounces whipped topping

Shred cake. Place in 9x13-inch dish. Prepare gelatin using package directions. Mix with thawed strawberries in bowl. Spread over cake. Chill, covered, until set. Cover with whipped topping. Yield: 15 servings.

Approx Per Serving: Cal 141; Prot 3 g; Carbo 28 g; Fiber 1 g; T Fat 3 g; Chol 0 mg; Sod 154 mg.

Gladys Smith, Hornets Nest

☎ To unmold desserts, run a thin hot knife around the edge and wrap mold with a kitchen towel dipped in hot water and squeezed dry.

FROZEN STRAWBERRY DESSERT

- 1 6-ounce package wild strawberry gelatin
- 1 cup boiling water
- 2 10-ounce packages frozen strawberries, partially thawed
- 1 20-ounce can crushed pineapple, drained
- 3 bananas, mashed
- 1/2 cup chopped pecans
- 1 12-ounce package no-bake cheesecake mix

Dissolve gelatin in boiling water in bowl. Stir in strawberries, pineapple, bananas and pecans. Pour half the gelatin mixture in 9x13-inch dish. Chill, covered, for 30 to 50 minutes or until set. Prepare cheesecake using package directions. Spread over congealed gelatin. Cover with remaining gelatin mixture. Chill until set. Yield: 15 servings.

Approx Per Serving: Cal 345; Prot 6 g; Carbo 46 g; Fiber 3 g; T Fat 17 g; Chol 136 mg; Sod 201 mg.

Ila Mae Moses, Hornets Nest

SWEET POTATO CRUNCH

- 3 cups mashed cooked sweet potatoes
- 1 cup sugar
- 1/2 teaspoon salt
- 1/3 stick butter, melted
- 1/2 cup milk
- 1 teaspoon butter extract
- 2 eggs, beaten
- 1 cup packed brown sugar
- 1 cup chopped pecans
- 1/3 cup flour
- 1/3 stick butter, melted

Combine sweet potatoes, sugar, salt, melted butter, milk, butter extract and eggs in bowl; mix well. Spread in casserole. Mix brown sugar, pecans, flour and remaining melted butter in bowl. Sprinkle over sweet potato mixture. Bake at 350 degrees for 35 minutes. Yield: 8 servings.

Approx Per Serving: Cal 510; Prot 6 g; Carbo 81 g; Fiber 3 g; T Fat 20 g; Chol 76 mg; Sod 305 mg.

Linda S. Griffin, Independence

HOMEMADE VANILLA EXTRACT

10 vanilla beans   **1 fifth of vodka**

Fill airtight glass container with vanilla beans and vodka. Store in dark place for 8 weeks. Use vanilla extract as needed. Add enough vodka to fill container as vanilla extract is used. Store in dark place.

Nutritional information for this recipe is not available.

Martha Crumpler, Independence

☎ Try these suggestions for easy desserts:

- Be very continental and serve a plate of assorted fruits and cheeses with individual knives for paring and slicing.
- Serve fancy or flavored coffees as the dessert. Provide some add-in selections such as whipped cream, shaved coconut, grated orange rind, cinnamon sticks or grated nutmeg.
- Let guests make their own sundaes. Arrange scoops of different flavors of ice cream in a large bowl. Provide toppings such as crushed pineapple, chocolate syrup, mandarin oranges, marshmallow creme, preserves, crushed peppermint or toffee, chopped nuts, chocolate chips and whipped cream.

EQUIVALENT CHART

	When the recipe calls for:	Use:
Baking	½ cup butter 2 cups butter 4 cups all-purpose flour 2½ to 5 cups sifted cake flour 1 square chocolate 1 cup semisweet chocolate pieces 4 cups marshmallows 2¼ cups packed brown sugar 4 cups confectioners' sugar 2 cups granulated sugar	4 ounces 1 pound 1 pound 1 pound 1 ounce 6 ounces 1 pound 1 pound 1 pound 1 pound
Cereal–Bread	1 cup fine dry bread crumbs 1 cup soft bread crumbs 1 cup small bread cubes 1 cup fine cracker crumbs 1 cup fine graham cracker crumbs 1 cup vanilla wafer crumbs 1 cup crushed corn flakes 4 cups cooked macaroni 3½ cups cooked rice	4 to 5 slices 2 slices 2 slices 28 saltines 15 crackers 22 wafers 3 cups uncrushed 8 ounces uncooked 1 cup uncooked
Dairy	1 cup shredded cheese 1 cup cottage cheese 1 cup sour cream 1 cup whipped cream ⅔ cup evaporated milk 1⅔ cups evaporated milk	4 ounces 8 ounces 8 ounces ½ cup heavy cream 1 small can 1 13-ounce can
Fruit	4 cups sliced or chopped apples 1 cup mashed banana 2 cups pitted cherries 3 cups shredded coconut 4 cups cranberries 1 cup pitted dates 1 cup candied fruit 3 to 4 tablespoons lemon juice plus 1 tablespoon grated lemon rind ⅓ cup orange juice plus 2 teaspoons grated orange rind 4 cups sliced peaches 2 cups pitted prunes 3 cups raisins	4 medium 3 medium 4 cups unpitted ½ pound 1 pound 1 8-ounce package 1 8-ounce package 1 lemon 1 orange 8 medium 1 12-ounce package 1 15-ounce package

When the recipe calls for:	Use:
Meat 4 cups chopped cooked chicken 3 cups chopped cooked meat 2 cups cooked ground meat	1 5-pound chicken 1 pound, cooked 1 pound, cooked
Nuts 1 cup chopped nuts	4 ounces shelled 1 pound unshelled
Vegetables 2 cups cooked green beans 2½ cups lima beans or red beans 4 cups shredded cabbage 1 cup grated carrot 8 ounces fresh mushrooms 1 cup chopped onion 4 cups sliced or chopped potatoes 2 cups canned tomatoes	½ pound fresh or 1 16-ounce can 1 cup dried, cooked 1 pound 1 large 1 4-ounce can 1 large 4 medium 1 16-ounce can

Measurement Equivalents

1 tablespoon = 3 teaspoons 2 tablespoons = 1 ounce 4 tablespoons = ¼ cup 5⅓ teaspoons = ⅓ cup 8 tablespoons = ½ cup 12 tablespoons = ¾ cup 16 tablespoons = 1 cup 1 cup = 8 ounces or ½ pint 4 cups = 1 quart 4 quarts = 1 gallon	1 6½ to 8-ounce can = 1 cup 1 10½ to 12-ounce can = 1¼ cups 1 14 to 16-ounce can = 1¾ cups 1 16 to 17-ounce can = 2 cups 1 18 to 20-ounce can = 2½ cups 1 20-ounce can = 3½ cups 1 46 to 51-ounce can = 5¼ cups 1 6½ to 7½-pound can or Number 10 = 12 or 13 cups

Metric Equivalents

The metric measures are approximate benchmarks for purposes of home food preparation.

Liquid	Dry
1 teaspoon = 5 milliliters 1 tablespoon = 15 milliliters 1 fluid ounce = 30 milliliters 1 cup = 250 milliliters 1 pint = 500 milliliters	1 quart = 1 liter 1 ounce = 30 grams 1 pound = 450 grams 2.2 pounds = 1 kilogram

SUBSTITUTION CHART

	Instead of:	Use:
Baking	1 teaspoon baking powder	¼ teaspoon soda plus ½ teaspoon cream of tartar
	1 tablespoon cornstarch (for thickening)	2 tablespoons flour or 1 tablespoon tapioca
	1 cup sifted all-purpose flour	1 cup plus 2 tablespoons sifted cake flour
	1 cup sifted cake flour	1 cup minus 2 tablespoons sifted all-purpose flour
	1 cup fine dry bread crumbs	¾ cup fine cracker crumbs
Dairy	1 cup buttermilk	1 cup sour milk or 1 cup yogurt
	1 cup heavy cream	¾ cup skim milk plus ⅓ cup butter
	1 cup light cream	⅞ cup skim milk plus 3 tablespoons butter
	1 cup sour cream	⅞ cup sour milk plus 3 tablespoons butter
	1 cup sour milk	1 cup milk plus 1 tablespoon vinegar or lemon juice or 1 cup buttermilk
Seasoning	1 teaspoon allspice	½ teaspoon cinnamon plus ⅛ teaspoon cloves
	1 cup catsup	1 cup tomato sauce plus ½ cup sugar plus 2 tablespoons vinegar
	1 clove of garlic	⅛ teaspoon garlic powder or ⅛ teaspoon instant minced garlic or ¾ teaspoon garlic salt
	1 teaspoon Italian spice	¼ teaspoon each oregano, basil, thyme, rosemary plus dash of cayenne
	1 teaspoon lemon juice	½ teaspoon vinegar
	1 tablespoon mustard	1 teaspoon dry mustard
	1 medium onion	1 tablespoon dried minced onion or 1 teaspoon onion powder
Sweet	1 1-ounce square chocolate	¼ cup cocoa plus 1 teaspoon shortening
	1⅔ ounces semisweet chocolate	1 ounce unsweetened chocolate plus 4 teaspoons granulated sugar
	1 cup honey	1 to 1¼ cups sugar plus ¼ cup liquid or 1 cup corn syrup or molasses
	1 cup granulated sugar	1 cup packed brown sugar or 1 cup corn syrup, molasses or honey minus ¼ cup liquid

REFRIGERATION STORAGE

Food	Refrigerate	Freeze
Beef steaks	1-2 days	6-12 months
Beef roasts	1-2 days	6-12 months
Corned beef	7 days	2 weeks
Pork chops	1-2 days	3-4 months
Pork roasts	1-2 days	4-8 months
Fresh sausage	1-2 days	1-2 months
Smoked sausage	7 days	Not recommended
Cured ham	5-7 days	1-2 months
Canned ham	1 year	Not recommended
Ham slice	3 days	1-2 months
Bacon	7 days	2-4 months
Veal cutlets	1-2 days	6-9 months
Stew meat	1-2 days	3-4 months
Ground meat	1-2 days	3-4 months
Luncheon meats	3-5 days	Not recommended
Frankfurters	7 days	1 month
Whole chicken	1-2 days	12 months
Chicken pieces	1-2 days	9 months
Whole turkeys	1-2 days	6 months

Freezing Tips

- Date all items when you put them in the freezer.
- Frozen canned hams become watery and soft when thawed. Processed meats have a high salt content which speeds rancidity when thawed.
- Do not freeze stuffed chickens or turkeys. The stuffing may suffer bacterial contamination during the lengthy thawing process.
- Partially thawed food which still has ice crystals in the package can be safely refrozen. A safer test is to determine if the surface temperature is 40° F. or lower.

Herbs And Spices

Allspice	Pungent aromatic spice, whole or in powdered form. It is excellent in marinades, particularly in game marinade, or in curries.
Basil	Can be chopped and added to cold poultry salads. If the recipe calls for tomatoes or tomato sauce, add a touch of basil to bring out a rich flavor.
Bay leaf	The basis of many French seasonings. It is added to soups, stews, marinades and stuffings.
Bouquet garni	A must in many Creole cuisine recipes. It is a bundle of herbs, spices and bay leaf tied together and added to soups, stews or sauces.
Celery seed	From wild celery rather than domestic celery. It adds pleasant flavor to bouillon or a stock base.
Chervil	One of the traditional *fines herbes* used in French-derived cooking. (The others are tarragon, parsley and chives.) It is good in omelets or soups.
Chives	Available fresh, dried or frozen, it can be substituted for onion or shallot in any poultry recipe.
Cinnamon	Ground from the bark of the cinnamon tree, it is important in desserts as well as savory dishes.
Coriander	Adds an unusual flavor to soups, stews, chili dishes, curries and some desserts.
Cumin	A staple spice in Mexican cooking. To use, rub seeds together and let them fall into the dish just before serving. Cumin is also available in powdered form.
Garlic	One of the oldest herbs in the world, it must be carefully handled. For best results, press or crush garlic clove.
Marjoram	An aromatic herb of the mint family, it is good in soups, sauces, stuffings and stews.
Mustard (dry)	Brings a sharp bite to sauces. Sprinkle just a touch over roast chicken for a delightful flavor treat.
Oregano	A staple herb in Italian, Spanish and Mexican cuisines. It is very good in dishes with a tomato foundation; it adds an excellent savory taste.

Paprika	A mild pepper that adds color to many dishes. The very best paprika is imported from Hungary.
Rosemary	A tasty herb important in seasoning stuffing for duck, partridge, capon and other poultry.
Sage	A perennial favorite with all kinds of poultry and stuffings. It is particularly good with goose.
Tarragon	One of the *fines herbes*. Tarragon goes well with all poultry dishes.
Thyme	Used in combination with the bay leaf in soups and in stews.

ALLSPICE	BASIL	BAY LEAF	CELERY SEED	CHERVIL	CHIVES
CINNAMON	CORIANDER	CUMIN	GARLIC	MARJORAM	MUSTARD
OREGANO	PAPRIKA	ROSEMARY	SAGE	TARRAGON	THYME

No-Salt Seasoning

Salt is an acquired taste and can be significantly reduced in the diet by learning to use herbs and spices instead. When using fresh herbs, use 3 times the amount of dried herbs. Begin with small amounts to determine your favorite tastes. A dash of fresh lemon or lime juice can also wake up your taste buds.

Herb Blends to Replace Salt

Combine all ingredients in small airtight container. Add several grains of rice to prevent caking.

No-Salt Surprise Seasoning — 2 teaspoons garlic powder and 1 teaspoon each of dried basil, oregano and dehydrated lemon juice.

Pungent Salt Substitute — 3 teaspoons dried basil, 2 teaspoons each of summer savory, celery seed, cumin seed, sage and marjoram, and 1 teaspoon lemon thyme; crush with mortar and pestle.

Spicy No-Salt Seasoning — 1 teaspoon each cloves, pepper and coriander, 2 teaspoons paprika and 1 tablespoon dried rosemary; crush with mortar and pestle.

Herb Complements

Beef — bay leaf, chives, cumin, garlic, hot pepper, marjoram, rosemary

Pork — coriander, cumin, garlic, ginger, hot pepper, savory, thyme

Poultry — garlic, oregano, rosemary, savory, sage

Cheese — basil, chives, curry, dill, marjoram, oregano, parsley, sage, thyme

Fish — chives, coriander, dill, garlic, tarragon, thyme

Fruit — cinnamon, coriander, cloves, ginger, mint

Bread — caraway, marjoram, oregano, poppy seed, rosemary, thyme

Salads — basil, chives, tarragon, parsley, sorrel

Vegetables — basil, chives, dill, tarragon, marjoram, mint, parsley, pepper

Basic Herb Butter

Combine 1 stick unsalted butter, 1 to 3 tablespoons dried herbs or twice that amount of minced fresh herbs of choice, 1/2 teaspoon lemon juice and white pepper to taste. Let stand for 1 hour or longer before using.

Basic Herb Vinegar

Heat vinegar of choice in saucepan; do not boil. Pour into bottle; add 1 or more herbs of choice and seal bottle. Let stand for 2 weeks before using.

Bread Baking Guide

The pleasure of baking homemade bread is matched only by eating it, except when something goes wrong. Most problems can be determined and easily avoided the next time.

Problem...	Cause...
Bread or biscuits are dry	Too much flour; too slow baking; over-handling
Bread has too open texture or uneven texture	Too much liquid; over-handling in kneading
Strong yeast smell from baked bread	Too much yeast; over-rising
Tiny white spots on crust	Too rapid rising; dough not covered properly while rising
Crust has bad color	Too much flour used in shaping
Small flat loaves	Old yeast; not enough rising or rising much too long; oven temperature too hot
Heavy compact texture	Too much flour worked into bread when kneading; insufficient rising time; oven temperature too hot
Coarse texture	Too little kneading
Crumbly texture	Too much flour; undermixing; oven temperature too cool
Yeasty sour flavor	Too little yeast; rising time too long
Fallen center	Rising time too long
Irregular shape	Poor technique in shaping
Surface browns too quickly	Oven temperature too hot
Bread rises too long during baking and is porous in center and upper portion of loaf	Oven temperature too cool

Cake Baking Guide

Problem...	Cause...	
	Butter-Type Cakes	**Sponge-Type Cakes**
Cake falls	Too much sugar, liquid, leavening or shortening; too little flour; temperature too low; insufficient baking	Too much sugar; overbeaten egg whites; egg yolks underbeaten; use of greased pans; insufficient baking
Cake cracks or humps	Too much flour or too little liquid; overmixing; batter not spread evenly in pan; temperature of oven too high	Too much flour or sugar; temperature too high
Cake has one side higher	Batter spread unevenly; uneven pan; pan too close to side of oven; oven rack or range not even; uneven oven heat	Uneven pan; oven rack or range not level
Cake has hard top crust	Temperature too high; overbaking	Temperature too high; overbaking
Cake has sticky top crust	Too much sugar or shortening; insufficient baking	Too much sugar; insufficient baking
Cake has soggy layer at bottom	Too much liquid; eggs underbeaten; undermixing; insufficient baking	Too many eggs or egg yolks; underbeaten egg yolks; undermixing
Cake crumbles or falls apart	Too much sugar, leavening or shortening; batter undermixed; improper pan treatment; improper cooling	
Cake has heavy, compact quality	Too much liquid or shortening; too many eggs; too little leavening or flour; overmixing; oven temperature too high	Overbeaten egg whites; underbeaten egg yolks; overmixing
Cake falls out of pan before completely cooled		Too much sugar; use of greased pans; insufficient baking

Glossary Of Cooking Techniques

Bake: To cook by dry heat in an oven or under hot coals.

Bard: To cover lean meats with bacon or pork fat before cooking to prevent dryness.

Baste: To moisten, especially meats, with melted butter, pan drippings, sauce, etc. during cooking time.

Beat: To mix ingredients by vigorous stirring or with electric mixer.

Blanch: To immerse, usually vegetables or fruit, briefly into boiling water to inactivate enzymes, loosen the skin, or soak away the excess salt.

Blend: To combine two or more ingredients, at least 1 of which is liquid or soft, to produce a mixture that has a smooth uniform consistency quickly.

Boil: To heat any liquid until bubbly; the boiling point for water is 212 degrees, depending on altitude and atmospheric pressure.

Braise: To cook, especially meats, covered, in a small amount of liquid.

Brew: To prepare a beverage by allowing boiling water to extract flavor and/or color from certain substances such as coffee, tea, herbs or spices.

Broil: To cook by direct exposure to intense heat such as a flame or an electric heating unit.

Caramelize: To melt sugar in heavy pan over low heat until golden or light brown, stirring constantly.

Chill: To cool in refrigerator or in cracked ice.

Clarify: To remove impurities from melted margarine or butter by allowing the sediment to settle, then pouring off the clear yellow liquid. Other fats may be clarified by straining.

Cream: To blend butter, margarine, shortening, usually softened, or sometimes oil, with a granulated or crushed ingredient until the mixture is soft and creamy. It is usually described in the method as light and fluffy.

Curdle: To congeal milk with rennet or heat until solid lumps or curds are formed.

Cut in: To disperse solid shortening into dry ingredients with a knife or pastry blender. Texture of the mixture should resemble coarse cracker meal. Described in method as crumbly.

Decant: To pour a liquid such as wine or melted butter or margarine carefully from 1 container into another leaving the sediment in the original container.

Deep-fry: To cook in a deep pan or skillet containing hot cooking oil. Deep-fried foods are generally completely immersed in the hot oil and will rise to the surface when almost cooked through.

Deglaze: To heat stock, wine or other liquid in the pan in which meat has been cooked, mixing liquid with pan juices, sediment and browned bits to form a gravy or sauce base.

Degorger: To remove strong flavors or impurities before cooking, i.e. soaking ham in cold water or sprinkling vegetables with salt, then letting stand for a period of time and pressing out the excess fluid.

Degrease: To remove accumulated fat from surface of hot liquids.

Dice: To cut into small cubes about 1/4-inch in size. Do not use dice unless ingredient can truly be cut into cubes.

Dissolve: To create a solution by thoroughly mixing a solid or granular substance with a liquid until no sediment remains.

Dredge: To coat completely with flour, bread crumbs, etc, usually before frying.

Filet: To remove bones from meat or fish. (Pieces of meat, fish, or poultry from which bones have been removed are called filets.)

Flambé: To pour warmed Brandy or other spirits over food in a pan, then ignite and continue cooking briefly to allow alcoholic content to burn off.

Fold in: To blend a delicate frothy mixture into a heavier one so that none of the lightness or volume is lost. Using a rubber spatula, turn under and bring up and over, rotating bowl 1/4 turn after each folding motion.

Fry: To cook in a pan or skillet containing hot cooking oil. The oil should not totally cover the food.

Garnish: To decorate food before serving.

Glaze: To cover or coat with sauce, syrup, egg white, or a jellied substance. After applying, it becomes firm, adding color and flavor.

Grate: To rub food against a rough, perforated utensil to produce slivers, crumbs, curls, etc.

Gratiné: To top a sauced dish with crumbs, cheese or butter and broil until brown.

Grill: To broil, usually over hot coals or charcoal.

Grind: To cut, crush, or force through a chopper to produce small bits.

Infuse: To steep herbs or other flavorings in a liquid until liquid absorbs flavor.

Julienne: To cut vegetables or meat into long thin strips.

Knead: To press, fold, and stretch dough until smooth and elastic. Method usually notes time frame or result.

Lard: To insert strips of fat or bacon into lean meat to keep the meat moist and juicy during cooking. Larding is an internal basting technique.

Leaven: To cause batters and doughs to rise, usually by means of a chemical leavening agent. This process may occur before or during baking.

Marinate: To soak, usually in a highly seasoned oil-acid solution, to flavor and/or tenderize food.

Melt: To liquify solid foods by the action of heat.

Mince: To cut or chop into very small pieces.

Mix: To combine ingredients to distribute uniformly.

Mold: To shape into a particular form.

Panbroil: To cook in a skillet or pan using a very small amount of fat to prevent sticking.

Panfry: To cook in a skillet or pan containing only a small amount of fat.

Parboil: To partially cook in boiling water. Most parboiled foods require additional cooking with or without other ingredients.

Parch: To dry or roast slightly through exposure to intense heat.

Pit: To remove the hard inedible seed from peaches, plums, etc.

Plank: To broil and serve on a board or wooden platter.

Plump: To soak fruits, usually dried, in liquid until puffy and softened.

Poach: To cook in a small amount of gently simmering liquid.

Preserve: To prevent food spoilage by pickling, salting, dehydrating, smoking, boiling in syrup, etc. Preserved foods have excellent keeping qualities when properly prepared and then properly stored.

Purée: To reduce the pulp of cooked fruit and vegetables to a smooth and thick liquid by straining or blending.

Reduce: To boil stock, gravy or other liquid until volume is reduced, liquid is thickened and flavor is intensified.

Refresh: To place blanched drained vegetables or other food in cold water to halt cooking process.

Render: To cook meat or meat trimmings at low temperature until fat melts and can be drained and strained.

Roast: (1) To cook by dry heat either in an oven or over hot coals. (2) To dry or parch by intense heat.

Sauté: To cook in a skillet containing a small amount of hot cooking oil. Sautéed foods should never be immersed in the oil and should be stirred frequently.

Scald: (1) To heat a liquid almost to the boiling point. (2) To soak, usually vegetables or fruit, in boiling water until the skins are loosened; see blanch, which is our preferred term.

Scallop: To bake with a sauce in a casserole. The food may either be mixed or layered with the sauce.

Score: To make shallow cuts diagonally in parallel lines, especially meat.

Scramble: To cook and stir simultaneously, usually eggs.

Shirr: To crack eggs into individual buttered baking dishes, then bake or broil until whites are set. Chopped meats or vegetables, cheese, cream, or bread crumbs may also be added.

Shred: To cut or shave food into slivers.

Shuck: To remove the husk from corn or the shell from oysters, clams, etc.

Sieve: To press a mixture through a closely meshed metal utensil to make it homogeneous.

Sift: To pass, usually dry ingredients such as flour, through a fine wire mesh in order to produce a uniform consistency.

Simmer: To cook in or with a liquid at or just below the boiling point.

Skewer: (1) To thread, usually meat and vegetables, onto a sharpened rod (as in shish kabob). (2) To fasten the opening of stuffed fowl closed with small pins.

Skim: To ladle or spoon off excess fat or scum from the surface of a liquid.

Smoke: To preserve or cook through continuous exposure to wood smoke.

Steam: To cook with water vapor in a closed container, usually in a steamer.

Stew: To simmer, usually meats and vegetables, for a long period of time. Also used to tenderize meats.

Stir-fry: To cook small pieces of vegetables and/or meat in a small amount of oil in a wok or skillet over high heat, stirring constantly, until tender-crisp.

Strain: To pass through a strainer, cheesecloth or sieve in order to break down or remove the solids or impurities.

Stuff: To fill or pack cavities especially those of meats, vegetables and poultry.

Toast: To brown and crisp, usually by means of direct heat or to bake until brown.

Toss: To mix lightly with lifting motion using 2 forks or spoons.

Truss: To bind poultry legs and wings close to the body before cooking.

Whip: To beat a mixture until air has been thoroughly incorporated and the mixture is light and fluffy, the volume of mixture is greatly increased, and the mixture holds its shape.

Wilt: To apply heat causing dehydration, color change and a limp appearance.

INDEX

ACCOMPANIMENTS
Apple-Orange Marmalade, 285
Canned Sweet Peppers, 291
Cranberry Relish, 286
Frozen Strawberry
 Preserves, 287
Jalapeño Jelly, 286
Paula's Apple Butter, 285
Pepper Relish by Mrs. Glenn, 291
Spiced Peaches, 287
Squash Relish, 292

APPETIZERS. *See also* Cheese
 Balls; Cheese Spreads; Dips
Best Hors d'Oeuvres in Texas, 27
Cheese Pennies, 38
Chili Quiche Appetizers, 28
Clam Quiche, 29
Cocktail Meatballs, 31
Crab Spread, 25
Fresh Mushroom Pâté, 27
Gourmet Meatballs, 32
Jalapeño Cheese Squares, 28
Kabob Appetizers, 30
Mexican Pinwheels, 33
Miniature Ham and Cheese
 Rolls, 35
Molded Shrimp Spread, 26
Owens' Vegetable Munch, 33
Party Strawberries, 34
Pickled Hot Dogs, 30
Sausage Meatballs, 31
Spinach Balls, 34
Sunny-Side Grapefruit, 29

APPLE
Apple Bread, 306
Apple Cobbler, 514
Apple Delicious, 504
Apple Dump Dessert, 507
Apple Dumplings, 504
Apple Pie, 465
Apple-Cranberry Casserole, 507
Apple-Orange Marmalade, 285
Applesauce Pudding, 529
Applesauce Salad, 54

Banana-Apple Oat Muffins, 311
Cheese Apples, 505
Cheesy Apple Slaw, 82
Coleslaw with Apple, 82
Cranberry-Apple Bake, 506
Cranberry-Apple Crunch, 506
Frozen Waldorf Salad, 66
Paula's Apple Butter, 285
Sour Cream Apple Pie, 465
Spiced Applesauce Bread, 306

APRICOT
Apricot Delight, 54
Apricot Gelatin Salad, 55

ASPARAGUS
Asparagus Casserole, 224
Asparagus Casserole au
 Gratin, 224
Asparagus Casserole
 Supreme, 225

BACON
Bacon and Egg Casserole, 147
Brunch Casserole, 148
Quiche, 148

BANANA
Banana and Pecan Pound
 Cake, 385
Banana Bran Loaf, 307
Banana Bread, 307
Banana Granola Crunch, 37
Banana Pudding, 529
Banana Punch, 48
Banana Split Dessert
 Casserole, 508
Banana Stack Pancakes, 315
Banana-Apple Oat Muffins, 311
Banana-Nut Muffins, 312
Best-Ever Banana Pudding, 530
Chocolate-Topped Banana
 Split Dessert, 508
Creamy Banana Pudding, 530
Microwave Banana Pudding, 531
Sour Cream Banana Pudding, 531

BARBECUE SAUCES
Barbecue Sauce, 293
Barbecue Sauce for
  Hamburgers, 132
Barbecue Sauce for Pork, 292
Homemade Barbecue Sauce, 294
Mayberry's Barbecue Sauce, 293
Quick Barbecue Sauce, 293

BEANS
Baked Beans, 225
Baked Beans Casserole, 226
Baked Beans with Molasses, 228
Baked Lima Beans, 226
Chuck Wagon Beans, 229
Dr. Anderson's Nine-Bean
  Soup, 272
Gran's Baked Lima Beans, 227
Green Bean Salad, 74
Ground Beef and Green Bean
  Casserole, 112
Joyce's Baked Beans, 229
Lima Bean Casserole, 227
Poor Man's Lunch
  Sandwiches, 36
Southern Bean and Ham
  Soup, 151
Texas Caviar, 94
Three-Bean Bake, 228
Three-Bean Salad, 75

BEEF. *See also* Ground Beef
Barbecued Brisket, 98
Beef and Broccoli Stir-Fry, 101
Beef Bourguignon, 102
Beef Brisket, 98
Beef Burgundy, 102
Beef Stew, 106
Beef Stroganoff, 103
Brunswick Stew, 108
Chinese Beef, 104
Crock•Pot Roast Beef, 99
Crock•Pot Roast, 99
Eye-of-Round Roast with
  Vegetables, 100
Five-Hour Stew, 107
Hearty Beef Stew, 106
Make-A-Meal Soup, 105
Marinated Shish Kabobs, 104
Peking Roast Beef, 100
Simply Elegant Steak and
  Rice, 103
Stewed Beef in Wine Sauce, 107
Veal Piccata, 108

BEVERAGES, COLD. *See also* Punches
Vegetable Juice Cocktail, 50
Wassail Bowl Punch, 52

BEVERAGES, HOT
Christmas Wassail, 52
Hot Cranberry Punch, 51
Hot Mulled Punch, 52
Hot Spiced Cranberry Tea, 51

BISCUITS
Cheese Biscuits, 296
Easy Biscuits, 296
Homemade Biscuits, 297
Quick Low-Cholesterol
  Biscuits, 297
Sour Cream Biscuits, 298
V-8 Biscuits, 298

BLUEBERRY
Blueberry-Grape Compote, 509
Grape-Blueberry Congealed
  Salad, 60

BREAD, LOAVES. *See also* Pumpkin Bread
Apple Bread, 306
Banana Bran Loaf, 307
Banana Bread, 307
Cheese Bread, 299
Cheese-Wine Bread, 316
Italian Sausage Bread, 305
Spiced Applesauce Bread, 306
Spicy Pineapple Zucchini
  Bread, 311
Zucchini Bread, 310

BREADS. *See also* Biscuits; Bread, Loaves; Coffee Cakes; Corn Bread; Muffins; Rolls
Banana Stack Pancakes, 315
Crêpes, 304
Funnel Cakes, 305
Onion Biscuit Dough, 162

Pizza Dough, 316

BROCCOLI. *See also* Salads, Broccoli
Beef and Broccoli Stir-Fry, 101
Broccoli and Cheese Casserole, 231
Broccoli and Chicken Casserole, 174
Broccoli and Corn Bake, 236
Broccoli and Pecan Casserole, 234
Broccoli and Rice Casserole, 235
Broccoli and Stuffing Casserole, 234
Broccoli Bake, 230
Broccoli Casserole, 237
Broccoli Casserole Deluxe, 237
Broccoli Cheese Soup, 273
Broccoli Medley Casserole, 236
Broccoli Puff, 235
Broccoli-Rice Chicken Casserole, 175
Cheesy Broccoli and Chicken Bake, 174
Cheesy Broccoli Casserole, 231
Chicken and Broccoli Casserole, 173
Chicken and Broccoli Roll, 177
Chicken Divan, 175, 176
Chicken-Broccoli Casserole, 173
Company Broccoli Casserole, 232
Creamy Broccoli Casserole, 232
Dottie's Broccoli and Ground Beef Casserole, 109
Easy Broccoli Casserole, 233
Favorite Broccoli Casserole, 233
Julia's Broccoli Casserole, 230
Squash and Broccoli Casserole, 259

BROWNIES
Blonde Brownies, 443
Chocolate Brownies, 444
Easy Brownies, 443
Graham-Chocolate Brownies, 444

CABBAGE. *See also* Slaws
Beefy Cabbage Wedge Meal, 110
Cabbage au Gratin, 238
Cabbage Casserole, 238
Ground Beef and Cabbage Casserole, 109

CAKES. *See also* Cakes, Name of Flavor or Type; Fruitcakes
Applesauce Cake, 327
California Cake, 376
Caramel Nut Cake, 329
Coca-Cola Cake, 344
Do-Nothing Cake, 376
Friendship Cake, 358
Grandma's Hot Milk Cake, 363
Honey Bun Cake, 364
Honey Graham Cracker Cake, 364
Hummingbird Cake, 373
Hummingbird Cake Deluxe, 374
Italian Crème Cake, 365
Lazy Daisy Oatmeal Cake, 368
Mary Carter's Ten-Layer Cake, 420
Neva's Hummingbird Cake, 375
Nut Cake, 367
Pepsi Cake, 345
Pineapple Fluff Cake, 377
Potato and Caramel Cake, 328
Rocky Mountain Cake, 412
Rum Cake, 413
Sauerkraut Cake, 414
Sour Cream and Cinnamon Cake, 351
Sundrop Cake, 417
Vanilla Wafer Cake, 421
White Layer Cake, 421

CAKES, APPLE
Apple and Butterscotch Chip Cake, 326
Apple Cake, 322
Apple Cake with Walnuts, 325
Applesauce Cake, 327
Dutch Apple Cake, 323
Fresh Apple Cake, 326
Fresh Apple Nut Cake, 323
Glazed Fresh Apple Cake, 324
Saucy Apple Swirl Cake, 322

CAKES, CARROT
  Carrot and Pecan Cake, 331
  Carrot Cake, 330
  Easy Carrot Cake, 333
  Fruited Carrot Cake, 329
  Supreme Carrot Cake, 332

CAKES, CHERRY
  Cherry and Chocolate
    Cake, 349
  Cherry and Pecan Pound
    Cake, 387
  Chocolate and Cherry Bundt
    Cake, 350

CAKES, CHOCOLATE. *See also*
  Cakes, German Chocolate
  Basic Chocolate Pound
    Cake, 389
  Basic Red Velvet Pound
    Cake, 393
  Bertie's Red Velvet Pound
    Cake, 394
  Black Walnut and Chocolate
    Pound Cake, 388
  Cherry and Chocolate Cake, 349
  Chocolate and Cherry Bundt
    Cake, 350
  Chocolate Cake, 334
  Chocolate Fudge Sheet
    Cake, 339
  Chocolate Pound Cake, 388
  Chocolate Sheath Cake, 338
  Chocolate Sour Cream
    Cake, 340
  Coca-Cola Cake, 344
  Coconut Devil's Food Cake, 346
  Double Chocolate Cake, 340
  Double Chocolate Pound
    Cake, 391
  Favorite Chocolate Pound
    Cake, 390
  Flourless Chocolate Cake, 334
  Hot Fudge Pudding Cake, 343
  Jo Ann's Red Velvet Pound
    Cake, 395
  Kerr Scott's $10,000.00
    Chocolate Cake, 337
  Low-Cholesterol Chocolate
    Pound Cake, 392
  Mound Cake, 347
  Old-Fashioned Chocolate
    Cake, 335
  Old-Fashioned Chocolate
    Pound Cake, 390
  Pepsi Cake, 345
  Quick Chocolate Fudge
    Cake, 336
  Red Velvet Cake, 348
  Red Velvet Cocoa Pound
    Cake, 396
  Red Velvet Pound Cake, 392
  Sour Cream and Chocolate
    Pound Cake, 396
  Super Delight Cake, 347
  Velvet Almond Fudge Cake, 349

CAKES, COCONUT
  Coconut Cake, 351
  Coconut Devil's Food Cake, 346
  Coconut Pound Cake, 397
  Mound Cake, 347
  Prize-Winning Coconut Pound
    Cake, 397
  Rich Coconut Pound Cake, 398
  Sour Cream and Coconut
    Cake, 352
  Three-Day Coconut Cake, 352

CAKES, CREAM CHEESE
  Basic Cream Cheese Pound
    Cake, 400
  Cream Cheese and Pecan
    Pound Cake, 401
  Cream Cheese Pound Cake, 399
  Crusty Cream Cheese Pound
    Cake, 400

CAKES, FRUIT COCKTAIL
  Bonnie's Fruit Cocktail Cake, 361
  Favorite Fruit Cocktail Cake, 360
  Fruit Cocktail Cake, 359
  Mrs. Gibson's Fruit Cocktail
    Cake, 360

CAKES, GERMAN CHOCOLATE
  Chocolate Delight Cake, 341
  German Chocolate Cake, 342
  German Chocolate Upside-
    Down Cake, 343

CAKES, LEMON
Cholesterol-Free Lemon Chiffon Cake, 366
Easy Lemon Delight Cake, 366
Heart-Healthy Lemon Pound Cake, 401
Lemon Buttermilk Pound Cake, 402
Lemon Gem Miniature Cakes, 367
Lemon Pound Cake, 402

CAKES, ORANGE
Irene's Mandarin Orange Cake, 370
Mandarin Orange Cake, 369
Mandarin Orange Cake Deluxe, 370
Orange Fruitcake, 372
Orange Sherbet Cake, 372
Tiny Orange Cupcakes, 371

CAKES, POUND
Almond Pound Cake, 384
Anna Rena Blake's Pound Cake, 379
Banana and Pecan Pound Cake, 385
Basic Chocolate Pound Cake, 389
Basic Cream Cheese Pound Cake, 400
Basic Pound Cake, 378
Basic Red Velvet Pound Cake, 393
Bertie's Red Velvet Pound Cake, 394
Black Walnut and Chocolate Pound Cake, 388
Black Walnut Pound Cake, 386
Brown Sugar Pound Cake, 386
Butter Pound Cake, 380
Cherry and Pecan Pound Cake, 387
Chocolate Pound Cake, 388
Coconut Pound Cake, 397
Cold Oven Pound Cake, 399
Company Pound Cake, 380
Cream Cheese and Pecan Pound Cake, 401
Cream Cheese Pound Cake, 399
Crusty Cream Cheese Pound Cake, 400
Crusty Pound Cake, 381
Double Chocolate Pound Cake, 391
Easy Moist Pound Cake, 382
Easy Pound Cake, 381
Favorite Chocolate Pound Cake, 390
Favorite Pound Cake, 382
Five-Flavor Pound Cake, 383
Heart-Healthy Lemon Pound Cake, 401
Heavenly Pound Cake, 383
Jean's Pound Cake, 378
Jewel's Pound Cake, 379
Jo Ann's Red Velvet Pound Cake, 395
Lemon Buttermilk Pound Cake, 402
Lemon Pound Cake, 402
Low-Cholesterol Chocolate Pound Cake, 392
Low-Cholesterol Pound Cake, 402
Old-Fashioned Chocolate Pound Cake, 390
Perfect Pound Cake, 384
Pineapple Pound Cake, 403
Prize-Winning Coconut Pound Cake, 397
Red Velvet Cocoa Pound Cake, 396
Red Velvet Pound Cake, 392
Rich Coconut Pound Cake, 398
Seven-Up Pound Cake, 404
Sour Cream and Chocolate Pound Cake, 396
Sour Cream Pound Cake, 406
Special Seven-Up Pound Cake, 405
Unfrosted Seven-Up Pound Cake, 405
Whipping Cream Pound Cake, 407

CAKES, PRUNE
Easy Prune Cake, 410
Prune Cake, 408

Saucy Prune Cake, 409

CAKES, PUMPKIN
Pumpkin and Raisin Cake, 411
Pumpkin Cake, 410

CAKES, SEVEN-UP
Seven-Up Pound Cake, 404
Special Seven-Up Pound Cake, 405
Unfrosted Seven-Up Pound Cake, 405

CAKES, SOUR CREAM
Chocolate Sour Cream Cake, 340
Sour Cream and Chocolate Pound Cake, 396
Sour Cream and Cinnamon Cake, 351
Sour Cream and Coconut Cake, 352
Sour Cream Pound Cake, 406

CAKES, STRAWBERRY
Strawberry and Pecan Cake, 416
Strawberry Cake, 415

CAKES, SWEET POTATO
Frosted Sweet Potato Cake, 419
Glazed Sweet Potato Cake, 418

CANDY. *See also* Candy, Chocolate
Christmas Divinity, 425
Cinnamon Graham Confections, 424
Cookie Confections, 425
Microwave Peanut Brittle, 429
Party Strawberries, 34
Peanut Brittle, 428
Pecan Divinity, 426
Praline Confections, 440
Tommy's No-Cook Peanut Butter Candy, 440

CANDY, CHOCOLATE. *See also* Fudge
Chocolate Peanut Clusters, 424
Peanut Butter Balls, 429

Reece's Cup Squares, 430
Rocky Road Squares, 430

CARROTS. *See also* Cakes, Carrot
Carrots Delight, 240
Copper Pennies, 239
Gingered Carrots, 240
Marinated Carrots, 239

CHEESE BALLS
Bleu Cheese Ball, 22
Cheese Ring, 22
Chipped Beef Cheese Ball, 23
Deviled Ham Cheese Log, 23
Pineapple Cheese Balls, 25
Salmon Party Ball, 26

CHEESE SPREADS
Creamy Pimento Cheese Spread, 24
Pimento Cheese Spread, 24

CHEESECAKES
Chocolate Cheesecake, 516
Cream Cheesecake, 517
Deluxe Cheesecake, 517
Glazed Cheesecake Puffs, 518
New York Cheesecake, 518
Petite Cherry Cheesecakes, 519
Tiny Cheesecakes, 519

CHERRY. *See also* Cakes, Cherry
Cherry Salad, 56
Cherry Winks, 446
Cherry Yum-Yum, 513
Chocolate Cherry Bars, 447
Good Cherry Salad, 55
Impossible Cherry Pie, 467
Petite Cherry Cheesecakes, 519

CHICKEN. *See also* Chicken Pies; Chicken Salads, Hot; Salads, Chicken
Baked Chicken and Rice, 186
Baked Chicken in Wine Gravy, 163
Beefy Chicken Breasts, 172
Broccoli and Chicken Casserole, 174

559

Broccoli-Rice Chicken
  Casserole, 175
Brunswick Stew, 108
Cheddar Chicken Salad
  Sandwiches, 35
Cheesy Broccoli and Chicken
  Bake, 174
Chicken and Beef Casserole, 171
Chicken and Broccoli
  Casserole, 173
Chicken and Broccoli Roll, 177
Chicken and Dressing
  Casserole, 189
Chicken and Rice, 185
Chicken and Rice Casserole, 185
Chicken and Rice Dinner, 186
Chicken and Rice Soup, 206
Chicken and Rice Supreme, 187
Chicken and Sausage
  Casserole, 187
Chicken and Stuffing
  Casserole, 189
Chicken and Vegetable
  Casserole, 190
Chicken and Water Chestnut
  Soufflé, 166
Chicken Breast Bake, 188
Chicken Breast Strips, 164
Chicken Casserole, 181
Chicken Casserole with Rice, 183
Chicken Continental, 183
Chicken Deluxe, 167
Chicken Desirée, 188
Chicken Dijon, 178
Chicken Divan, 175
Chicken Divine, 168
Chicken Enchiladas, 178
Chicken Parmigiana, 191
Chicken Royal, 191
Chicken Stew, 207
Chicken Supreme, 172
Chicken Tetrazzini, 208
Chicken with Cauliflower and
  Peas, 177
Chicken-Broccoli Casserole, 173
Chicken-in-a-Garden, 165
Chicken-in-the-Limelight, 169
Company Chicken, 180
Company Chicken Casserole, 182
Company Chicken Divan, 176
Confetti Chicken Casserole, 181
Country Chicken with Onion
  Biscuits, 162
Crusty Brown Whole Baked
  Chicken, 163
Curried Chicken, 166
Easy Chicken and Dressing
  Casserole, 190
Easy Chicken Casserole, 184
Easy Chicken Tetrazzini, 207
Favorite Chicken Divan, 176
Four-Can Chicken Casserole, 179
Glenn's Birthday Chicken, 171
Golden Chicken Cheddar
  Bake, 179
Hawaiian Chicken, 168
Hot Chicken and Rice
  Casserole, 184
I Can Do It, 180
Lemon Parmesan Chicken, 182
Light and Tasty Baked
  Chicken, 164
Marinated Chicken Breasts, 169
Microwave Elegant Chicken, 203
Oven-Fried Chicken, 170
Rolled Chicken Breasts, 170
Rolled Chicken Washington, 209
Stir-Fry Vegetables and
  Chicken, 208
Wine and Cheese Chicken, 210

CHICKEN PIES
  Busy-Day Chicken Pie, 192
  Chicken and Biscuits
    Potpie, 196
  Chicken and Vegetables
    Potpie, 195
  Chicken Breast Potpie, 194
  Chicken Pie, 193
  Chicken Pie Casserole, 203
  Chicken Potpie Like
    Grandma's, 199
  Easy Chicken Pie, 192
  Easy Chicken Potpie, 196
  Joanne's Chicken Pie, 200
  Linda's Chicken Potpie, 198
  Melt-in-your-Mouth Chicken
    Potpie, 199
  Old-Fashioned Chicken Pie, 200
  Quick Chicken Pie, 193

Quick Chicken Potpie, 197
Sunday Chicken Pie, 198
Sunday Chicken Potpie, 201
Two-Crust Chicken Pie, 194
Veg-All Chicken Potpie, 201
Vegetable Chicken Potpie, 202

CHICKEN SALADS, HOT
Baked Chicken Salad, 204
Chicken Salad Bake, 205
Chicken Salad Casserole, 205
Hot Chicken Salad, 206

CHILI
Alarm Chili, 121
Chasen's Famous Chili, 122
Easy Chili, 120
Favorite Chili, 123
Quick Beefy Chili Beans, 124
Ring of Fire Chili, 122
Turkey Chili, 211
Venison Chili, 160

CHOCOLATE. *See* Cakes, Chocolate; Candy, Chocolate; Desserts, Chocolate; Frostings, Chocolate; Pies, Chocolate

CHOWDERS
Beefy Nacho Cheese Chowder, 142
Clam Chowder, 219
Fish Chowder, 220
Salmon Chowder, 220
Seafood Chowder, 221
Shrimp Chowder, 221

COBBLERS
Apple Cobbler, 514
No-Fool Cobbler, 515
Peach Cobbler, 515

COCONUT. *See also* Cakes, Coconut; Pies, Coconut
Coconut Supreme, 516

COFFEE CAKES
Butterquick Coffee Cake, 300
Fresh Berry Coffee Cake, 299

CONFECTIONS. *See also* Cookies, No-Bake
Cinnamon Graham Confections, 424
Cookie Confections, 425
Praline Confections, 440
Tommy's No-Cook Peanut Butter Candy, 440

COOKIE BARS. *See also* Brownies
Apricot-Walnut Bars, 442
Brown Sugar Surprises, 509
Chocolate Cherry Bars, 447
Fruit Bars, 450
Fruitcake Bars, 450
Lemon Squares, 452
Lemon-Cream Cheese Brownies, 452
Neiman Marcus Squares, 453

COOKIES. *See also* Cookies, No-Bake
Ambrosia Cookies, 441
Angel Drops, 441
Biscochitos, 442
Butter Cookies, 445
Butterhorns, 446
Cherry Winks, 446
Christmas Balls, 449
Christmas Peanut Butter Cookies, 458
Cinnamon Graham Confections, 424
Cookie Confections, 425
Cowboy Cookies, 449
Cream-Filled Oatmeal Cookies, 455
Crunchy Peanut Butter Cookies, 459
Easy Peanut Butter Cookies, 458
Grandma's Tea Cookies, 464
Greek Butter Cookies, 445
Ice Cream Cookies, 451
Icebox Sugar Cookies, 463
Ladyfingers, 451
Molasses Oatmeal Cookies, 454
Nutty Fingers, 456, 461
Oat Bran Cookies, 454
Old-Time Tea Cakes, 463

Orange Slice Cookies, 457
Peanut Butter Cookies, 457
Pecan Chews, 459
Pecan Crispies, 460
Pecan Fingers, 460
Ranger Cookies, 461
Seven-Layer Cookies, 462
Sour Cream Oatmeal
    Cookies, 456
Sugar Cookies, 462
Thumbprint Cookies, 464

COOKIES, CHOCOLATE. *See also* Brownies
Chocolate Cherry Bars, 447
Chocolate Chip Cookies, 447
Easy Chocolate Chip
    Cookies, 448
St. Louis Chocolate Chip
    Cookies, 448

COOKIES, NO-BAKE
Baby Ruth Bars, 431
Boiled Peanut Butter
    Cookies, 439
Chocolate and Peanut Butter
    Oatmeal Cookies, 433
Chocolate Bourbon Balls, 431
Chocolate Oatmeal
    Cookies, 432
Chocolate Oatmeal No-Bake
    Cookies, 432
Date and Coconut Balls, 434
Date Balls, 433
Date Nut Balls, 435
Golf Balls, 435
Goof Balls, 436
Graham Cracker Bars, 436
Holiday Date Balls, 434
Humdingers, 437
Incredibles, 437
Nutty Clusters, 438
Nutty Graham Squares, 438
Peanut Butter Coconut
    Balls, 439

CORN
Broccoli and Corn Bake, 236
Corn Pudding, 242
Fresh Corn Pudding, 242

CORN BREAD
Beefy Mexican Corn Bread
    Casserole, 111
Broccoli Corn Bread, 300
Hush Puppies, 304
Jerry's Favorite Corn Bread, 301
Mississippi Corn Bread, 301
Never-Fail Corn Bread, 302
Old Southern Corn Bread, 302
Skillet Corn Bread, 303
Spoon Bread, 303
Topping for Corn Bread Pie, 138
Topping for Corn Pone
    Casserole, 110

CRAB MEAT
Broiled Crab Sandwiches, 36
Crab Meat Dip, 44
Crab Spread, 25
Curried Crab Meat Rice Salad, 73
Hot Crab Dip, 44
Seafood Casserole, 215

CRANBERRY
Apple-Cranberry Dessert
    Casserole, 507
Cranberry and Orange Salad, 58
Cranberry Relish, 286
Cranberry Salad, 56
Cranberry-Apple Bake, 506
Cranberry-Apple Crunch, 506
Easy Cranberry Salad, 57
Holiday Cranberry Salad, 57
Hot Cranberry Punch, 51
Hot Spiced Cranberry Tea, 51
Thanksgiving Cranberry Relish
    Mold, 58

CROCK•POT RECIPES
Beef Stew, 106
Chili con Queso, 43
Christmas Wassail, 52
Crock•Pot Roast, 99
Crock•Pot Roast Beef, 99
Taco Salad, 72
Taco Salad Stack-Ups, 71

CUCUMBER
Cucumber Salad, 85
Minnesota Cucumbers, 288

Molded Cucumber Salad, 86
Refrigerator Sweet Pickles, 289

DESSERTS. *See also* Fruit Pizzas
Apple Delicious, 504
Apple Dump Dessert, 507
Apple Dumplings, 504
Apple-Cranberry Dessert
    Casserole, 507
Banana Split Dessert
    Casserole, 508
Blueberry-Grape Compote, 509
Brown Sugar Surprises, 509
Cherry Yum-Yum, 513
Coconut Supreme, 516
Congealed Strawberry
    Shortcake, 537
Cranberry-Apple Bake, 506
Cranberry-Apple Crunch, 506
Cream Cheese Delight
    Desserts, 520
Cream Cheese Dessert with Pie
    Filling, 520
Dot's Gooey Butter Dessert, 522
Dump Cake Dessert, 514
Easy Éclair Dessert, 512
Éclair, 511
Frozen Raspberry Dessert, 536
Frozen Strawberry Dessert, 538
Gooey Butter Dessert, 521
Heavenly Hash, 522
Hidden Pineapple Treat, 526
Lemon-Layered Dessert, 524
Microwave Peach Crisp, 525
Peach Crisp, 524
Peach Pushover, 525
Peach Stuff, 526
Popcorn Dessert, 528
Pumpkin Crisp, 535
Punch Bowl Dessert, 536
Strawberry Delight, 537
Sweet Potato Crunch, 538

DESSERTS, CHOCOLATE
Chocolate Cheesecake, 516
Chocolate Dream, 510
Chocolate Éclair Dessert, 512
Chocolate Torte, 513
Chocolate-Topped Banana Split
    Dessert, 508

Dirt Dessert, 510
Four-Layer Delight, 521
Party Dirt Pie Dessert, 511

DIPS
Artichoke Dip, 41
Bell Pepper Dip, 42
Chili con Queso, 43
Chili Dip, 43
Crab Meat Dip, 44
Curry Dip for Vegetables, 44
Dill Dip, 45
Easy Shrimp Dip, 47
Easy Taco Dip, 48
Hot Artichoke Dip, 42
Hot Cheese Dip, 42
Hot Crab Dip, 44
Mock Sour Cream, 48
Nacho Dip, 45
Pepperoni Pizza Dip, 46
Shrimp Dip, 46
Taco Dip, 47

EGG DISHES
Bacon and Egg Casserole, 147
Best Hors d'Oeuvres in Texas, 27
Breakfast Casserole, 154
Breakfast Sausage and Cheese
    Bake, 155
Breakfast Sausage and Egg
    Soufflé, 152
Brunch Casserole, 148
Carolyn's Breakfast Soufflé, 154
Cheese and Sausage
    Quiche, 156
Chili Quiche Appetizers, 28
Chris' Sausage Casserole, 157
Huevos, 149
Jalapeño Cheese Squares, 28
Pickled Eggs, 289
Quiche, 148
Quick and Easy Quiche, 149
Sausage and Cheddar
    Quiche, 157
Sausage and Egg Bake, 156
Sausage and Egg Breakfast
    Casserole, 153
Sausage and Egg
    Casserole, 153
Sausage Casserole, 155

FILLINGS
  Cheddar Filling, 209
  For Oatmeal Cookies, 455

FISH. *See also* Salmon
  Baked Flounder, 213
  Beer-Battered Bass, 213
  Broiled Mackerel, 214
  Fish Chowder, 220
  Quick and Easy Barbecued
    Tuna, 214
  Red Salmon Loaf, 215

FROSTINGS. *See also* Frostings
  For; Frostings, Boiled;
  Frostings, Chocolate;
  Frostings, Cream Cheese;
  Frostings, Pudding; Glazes;
  Glazes For
  Caramel Icing, 422
  Frostings for Many Cakes, 423
  Nutty Cream Cheese Frosting, 411

FROSTINGS FOR
  $10,000.00 Chocolate Cake, 337
  Apple Cake with Walnuts, 325
  Applesauce Cake, 327
  Banana and Pecan Pound
    Cake, 385
  Bertie's Red Velvet Pound
    Cake, 394
  Bonnie's Fruit Cocktail Cake, 361
  Carrot and Pecan Cake, 331
  Carrot Cake, 330
  Chocolate Fudge Sheet
    Cake, 339
  Chocolate Pound Cake, 389
  Chocolate Sheath Cake, 338
  Coca-Cola Cake, 344
  Coconut Devil's Food Cake, 346
  Do-Nothing Cake, 376
  Double Chocolate Cake, 341
  Double Chocolate Pound
    Cake, 391
  Easy Carrot Cake, 333
  Fruit Cocktail Cake, 359
  German Chocolate Cake, 342
  Hummingbird Cake Deluxe, 374
  Irene's Mandarin Orange
    Cake, 370

  Italian Crème Cake, 365
  Jo Ann's Red Velvet Pound
    Cake, 395
  Lazy Daisy Oatmeal Cake, 368
  Mandarin Orange Cake, 369
  Mandarin Orange Cake
    Deluxe, 371
  Neva's Hummingbird Cake, 375
  Old-Fashioned Chocolate
    Cake, 335
  Pepsi Cake, 345
  Pineapple Fluff Cake, 377
  Potato and Caramel Cake, 328
  Prune Cake, 408
  Quick Chocolate Fudge Cake, 336
  Red Velvet Cake, 348
  Red Velvet Pound Cake, 393
  Rocky Mountain Cake, 412
  Sauerkraut Cake, 414
  Seven-Up Pound Cake, 404
  Sour Cream Pound Cake, 406
  Special Seven-Up Pound
    Cake, 405
  Strawberry and Pecan Cake, 416
  Strawberry Cake, 415
  Sundrop Cake, 417
  Supreme Carrot Cake, 332
  Sweet Potato Cake, 419
  Ten-Layer Cake, 420
  Whipping Cream Pound
    Cake, 407

FROSTINGS, BOILED
  Caramel Icing, 422
  Frosting for Applesauce
    Cake, 327
  Frosting for Bonnie's Fruit
    Cocktail Cake, 361
  Frosting for Chocolate Fudge
    Sheet Cake, 339
  Frosting for Chocolate Sheath
    Cake, 338
  Frosting for Coca-Cola Cake, 344
  Frosting for Coconut Devil's Food
    Cake, 346
  Frosting for Do-Nothing Cake, 376
  Frosting for Fruit Cocktail
    Cake, 359
  Frosting for German Chocolate
    Cake, 342

Frosting for Many Cakes, 423
Frosting for Old-Fashioned
    Chocolate Cake, 335
Frosting for Potato and Caramel
    Cake, 328
Frosting for Prune Cake, 408
Frosting for Quick Chocolate
    Fudge Cake, 336
Frosting for Rocky Mountain
    Cake, 412
Frosting for Sweet Potato
    Cake, 419
Pineapple Frosting, 365
Topping for Favorite Fruit Cocktail
    Cake, 361

FROSTINGS, CHOCOLATE
Chocolate Icing, 422
Frosting for $10,000.00 Chocolate
    Cake, 337
Frosting for Chocolate Fudge
    Sheet Cake, 339
Frosting for Chocolate Pound
    Cake, 389
Frosting for Chocolate Sheath
    Cake, 338
Frosting for Coca-Cola Cake, 344
Frosting for Double Chocolate
    Cake, 341
Frosting for Double Chocolate
    Pound Cake, 391
Frosting for German Chocolate
    Cake, 342
Frosting for Old-Fashioned
    Chocolate Cake, 335
Frosting for Pepsi Cake, 345
Frosting for Quick Chocolate
    Fudge Cake, 336
Frosting for Sauerkraut Cake, 414
Frosting for Ten-Layer Cake, 420

FROSTINGS, CREAM CHEESE
Chocolate Icing, 422
Cream Cheese Frosting, 325
Frosting for Banana and Pecan
    Pound Cake, 385
Frosting for Bertie's Red Velvet
    Pound Cake, 394
Frosting for Carrot and Pecan
    Cake, 331

Frosting for Carrot Cake, 330
Frosting for Easy Carrot
    Cake, 333
Frosting for Hummingbird Cake
    Deluxe, 374
Frosting for Italian Crème
    Cake, 365
Frosting for Jo Ann's Red Velvet
    Pound Cake, 395
Frosting for Red Velvet Pound
    Cake, 393
Frosting for Seven-Up Pound
    Cake, 404
Frosting for Sour Cream Pound
    Cake, 406
Frosting for Special Seven-Up
    Pound Cake, 405
Frosting for Supreme Carrot
    Cake, 332
Frosting for Whipping Cream
    Pound Cake, 407
Nutty Cream Cheese Frosting, 411

FROSTINGS, PUDDING
Frosting for Irene's Mandarin
    Orange Cake, 370
Frosting for Mandarin Orange
    Cake Deluxe, 371
Frosting for Pineapple Fluff
    Cake, 377

FRUIT PIZZAS
Fruit Pizza, 527
Glazed Fruit Pizza, 527
Quick Fruit Pizza, 528

FRUITCAKES
Candied Fruitcake, 354
Fruited Pecan Cake, 356
Icebox Fruitcake, 356
Lemon Extract Fruitcake, 355
Light Fruitcake, 354
Miniature Bourbon
    Fruitcakes, 353
Orange Fruitcake, 372
Pecan Fruitcake, 357
Refrigerator Fruitcake, 353

FUDGE
Fudge, 427

Margaret Tucker's Chocolate Fudge, 426
Peanut Butter Fudge, 428
Peanut Fudge, 427

GAME
Sautéed Dove, 210
Venison Chili, 160

GINGERBREAD
Jim Adams' Great-Grandmother's Gingerbread, 363
Light-as-a-Feather Gingerbread, 362

GLAZES
Orange and Lemon Glaze, 423

GLAZES FOR
Brown Sugar Pound Cake, 387
Chocolate and Cherry Bundt Cake, 350
Fresh Apple Cake, 324
Rich Coconut Pound Cake, 398
Rum Cake, 413

GRAPE
Grape and Almond Chicken Salad, 68
Grape-Blueberry Congealed Salad, 60

GRAPEFRUIT
Grapefruit Punch, 49
Sunny-Side Grapefruit, 29

GROUND BEEF. *See also* Chili; Ground Beef Pies; Lasagna; Meat Loaves; Meatballs
Aunt Martha's Chinese Dish, 124
Beefy Cabbage Wedge Meal, 110
Beefy Mexican Corn Bread Casserole, 111
Beefy Nacho Cheese Chowder, 142
Cabbage and Beef Soup, 142
Chili Macaroni and Cheese, 112
Chinese Ground Beef Casserole, 125
Chow Mein Casserole, 126
Chuck Wagon Surprise, 113
Corn Pone Casserole, 110
Dottie's Broccoli and Ground Beef Casserole, 109
Easy Spaghetti, 117
Ground Beef and Cabbage Casserole, 109
Ground Beef and Green Bean Casserole, 112
Ground Beef and Potato Casserole, 117
Ground Beef and Rice Casserole, 120
Ground Beef and Vegetable Chow Mein, 125
Ground Beef Casserole, 114
Jean's Ground Beef Skillet, 126
Macaroni Pizza Casserole, 113
Mexican Ground Beef Delight, 115
Pizza Casserole, 114
Potato and Ground Beef Moussaka, 118
Quick Beefy Chili Beans, 124
Quick Pepperoni Spaghetti, 116
Roman Holiday, 116
Scalloped Ground Beef and Potatoes, 119
Skillet Macaroni and Ground Beef, 115
Stuffed Peppers, 118
Taco Salad, 72
Taco Salad Stack-Ups, 71
Tater Tot and Ground Beef Casserole, 119
Texas Hash, 127
Vegetable Beef Soup, 143

GROUND BEEF PATTIES
Barbecued Hamburgers, 132
Burger Bundles, 133
Creole Burgers, 132
Easy Patties, 133
Salisbury Steaks, 134

GROUND BEEF PIES
Corn Bread Pie, 138
Ground Beef and Corn Pie, 139
Hamburger Pie, 139

Lasagna Pie, 137
Potato Burger Pie, 141
Railroad Pie, 141
Tamale Pie 140

HAM
Cheesy Ham Loaf, 150
Hamroni, 150
Kabob Appetizers, 30
Miniature Ham and Cheese Rolls, 35
Quick and Easy Quiche, 149
Southern Bean and Ham Soup, 151

HOT DOGS
Fun in the Bun, 158
Hot Dog Casserole, 158
Pickled Hot Dogs, 30

ICE CREAM
Homemade Black Walnut Ice Cream, 523
Homemade Peach Ice Cream, 523

LASAGNA
Easy Company Lasagna, 134
Easy Lasagna, 136
Lasagna, 136
Lasagna Deluxe, 135
Lasagna Pie, 137

MACARONI
Busy-Day Macaroni and Cheese Casserole, 282
Chili Macaroni and Cheese, 112
Chuck Wagon Surprise, 113
Ground Beef Casserole, 114
Hacienda Dinner, 152
Hamroni, 150
Macaroni and Cheese, 281
Macaroni Pizza Casserole, 113
Macaroni Salad, 73
Macaroni-Cheese Casserole, 281
Pizza Casserole, 114
Skillet Macaroni and Ground Beef, 115

MARINADES FOR
Chicken Breasts, 169

Chicken-in-a-Garden, 165

MEAT LOAVES
Cheesy Ham Loaf, 150
Mini Meat Loaves, 131
Oriental Meat Loaf, 131
Saucy Meat Loaf, 130

MEATBALLS
Cocktail Meatballs, 31
Gourmet Meatballs, 32
Ground Beef Porcupines, 129
Italian Meatball Spaghetti Sauce, 128
Meatballs for Italian Meatball Spaghetti Sauce, 128
Meatballs in Sweet and Sour Sauce, 130
Meatballs with Sauce, 127
Porcupine Meatballs with Sauce, 129
Sausage Meatballs, 31

MEATS. *See also* Names of Meats
Elephant Stew, 160
Leg of Lamb with Artichokes, 159
Venison Chili, 160

MICROWAVE
Banana Granola Crunch, 37
Banana Pudding, 531
Chicken Deluxe, 167
Chicken Dijon, 178
Chicken with Cauliflower and Peas 177
Easy Taco Dip, 48
Elegant Chicken, 203
Hot Cheese Dip, 42
Onion Soup Potatoes, 252
Peach Crisp, 525
Peanut Brittle, 429

MUFFINS
Banana-Apple Oat Muffins, 311
Banana-Nut Muffins, 312
Bran Muffins, 312
Cheddar-Pimento Muffins, 313
Lemon-Raspberry Muffins, 314
Oat Bran and Raisin Muffins, 314
Six-Week Bran Muffins, 313

Sweet Potato Muffins, 315

MUSHROOM
Fresh Mushroom Pâté, 27
Mushroom Business, 243

NUTS
Roasted Pecans, 40
Special Toasted Pecans, 41
Sugar-Coated Peanuts, 39
Vonda's Spiced Pecans, 40

ONION
Crunchy Onion Casserole, 244
Hearty French Onion Soup, 245
Onion Casserole, 244
Swiss Onion Casserole 244

ORANGE
Apple-Orange Marmalade, 285
Cheesy Orange Salad, 63
Cranberry and Orange
   Salad, 58
Orange and Lemon Glaze, 423
Orange Fluff Salad, 62
Orange Fruitcake, 372
Orange Gelatin Salad, 62
Orange-Pineapple Salad, 63
Orange Slice Cookies, 457

PASTA. *See also* Lasagna;
   Macaroni; Salads, Pasta;
   Spaghetti
Chicken Tetrazzini, 208
Easy Chicken Tetrazzini, 207
Fettucini Alfredo, 280
Italian Pork Pasta Sauce, 144
Pasta and Fresh
   Vegetables, 282
Pasta in Shrimp and Wine
   Sauce, 218

PEACH
Homemade Peach Ice
   Cream, 523
Microwave Peach Crisp, 525
Peach Crisp, 524
Peach Pushover, 525
Peach Stuff, 526
Spiced Peaches, 287

PICKLES
Ed's Pickled Okra, 290
Minnesota Cucumbers, 288
Pickled Eggs, 289
Pickled Okra, 290
Refrigerator Sweet Pickles, 289
Sweet Dill Pickles, 288

PIES. *See also* Pies, Name of
   Flavor
Anne's Vanilla Pie Dessert, 501
Apple Pie, 465
Buttermilk Pie, 466
Chess Pie, 467
Cream Cheese Pies, 475
Creamy Pumpkin Pie, 494
Dietetic Strawberry Pies, 497
Egg Custard Meringue Pie, 481
Egg Custard Pie, 480
Eggnog Pie, 482
Fresh Strawberry Pie, 496
Fruit Pie, 482
Hawaiian Pies, 484
Heavenly Pies, 484
Helen's Japanese Fruit Pie, 483
Ice Cream Pies, 485
Impossible Cherry Pie, 467
Japanese Fruit Pie, 483
Mama's Butterscotch Pie, 466
Nutty Buddy Pies, 485
Oatmeal Pie, 486
Peanut Butter Pies, 486
Peppermint Candy Ice Cream
   Pie, 492
Pineapple Cool Whip Pies, 492
Pumpkin and Cheese Pie, 493
Pumpkin Pie, 493
Quick Peanut Butter Pie, 487
Ritz Pie, 494
Sour Cream Apple Pie, 465
Squash Pies, 495
Strawberry Chiffon Pie, 496
Strawberry Pies, 495
Sugarless Pear and Date Pie, 487
Tar Heel Fruit Pie, 500
Texas Custard Pie, 481

PIES, CHOCOLATE
Chocolate Brownie Pie, 470
Chocolate Fudge Nut Pies, 473

Chocolate Meringue Pie, 469
Chocolate Nut Pie, 471
Chocolate Pie, 468
Chocolate Swirl Cheese Pie, 474
Favorite Chocolate Pie, 468
Favorite German Chocolate
  Pies, 472
Fudge Pie, 474
German Chocolate Coconut
  Pie, 472
German Chocolate Pies, 471
Mother's German Chocolate
  Pie, 473
Old-Fashioned Chocolate
  Pie, 470
Rich Chocolate Meringue
  Pie, 469
Tar Heel Chocolate Pie, 501

PIES, COCONUT
Amanda' Coconut-Pineapple
  Pies, 479
Aunt Lula's Coconut Pies, 477
Coconut and Pineapple Pies, 479
Coconut Cream Pies, 478
Coconut Custard Pie, 476
Coconut Meringue Pie, 476
Coconut Pies, 475
Creamy Coconut Pies, 477
Impossible Coconut Pies, 478
No-Crust Toasted Coconut
  Pie, 480

PIES, MAIN DISH. *See* Chicken
  Pies; Ground Beef Pies

PIES, PECAN
Best Pecan Pie, 488
Deep-Dish Pecan Pie, 489
Mystery Pecan Pie, 489
Old-Fashioned Pecan Pies, 490
Pecan Pies, 488
Pecan Tarts, 491
Quick Pecan Pies, 490
Southern Pecan Pie, 491

PIES, SWEET POTATO
Light Sweet Potato Pies, 498
Old-Fashioned Sweet Potato
  Pie, 499
South's Favorite Sweet Potato
  Pie, 500
Sweet Potato Custard Pies, 498
Sweet Potato Pies, 497
Sweet Potato Pudding Pies, 499

PINEAPPLE
Chicken and Pineapple Salad, 69
Orange-Pineapple Salad, 63
Strawberry and Pineapple
  Salad, 65

PORK
Brunswick Stew, 108
Chasen's Famous Chili, 122
Hopping John Pork Chops, 145
Italian Pork Pasta Sauce, 144
Mexican Pork Stew, 147
Pork Chop Casserole, 144
Pork Chops and Potato
  Dinner, 145
Pork Tenderloin in Wine
  Sauce, 146
Quick Pork Supper Dish, 146
Roast Pork Barbecue, 143

POTATOES
Easy Hashed Brown
  Casserole, 248
Favorite Potato Casserole, 250
German Potato Salad, 254
Ground Beef and Potato
  Casserole, 117
Gruyère Potatoes, 253
Hashed Brown Casserole, 248
Hot German Potato Salad, 254
Onion Soup Potatoes, 252
Party Potatoes, 253
Peggy's Potato Salad, 89
Pop's Potato Potluck, 249
Pork Chops and Potato
  Dinner, 145
Portuguese Potatoes, 252
Potato and Cheese Casserole, 251
Potato and Ground Beef
  Moussaka, 118
Potato Delight, 251
Potato Salad, 89
Potato Wedges, 255
Red's Potato Casserole, 247

Scalloped Ground Beef and
    Potatoes, 119
Shirley's Potato Casserole, 249
Special Potato Casserole, 250
Supreme Potato Casserole, 252
Tater Tot and Ground Beef
    Casserole, 119
Twice-Baked Potatoes, 247

PUDDINGS. *See also* Frostings,
    Pudding
Applesauce Pudding, 529
Aunt Maude's Raisin
    Pudding, 533
Baked Sunshine Pudding, 534
Banana Pudding, 529
Best-Ever Banana Pudding, 530
Creamy Banana Pudding, 530
Crustless Egg Custard, 532
Egg Custard, 532
Microwave Banana Pudding, 531
Pudding Spectacular, 533
Sour Cream Banana
    Pudding, 531
Sweet Potato Pudding with
    Whiskey, 535

PUMPKIN. *See also* Cakes,
    Pumpkin; Pumpkin Bread
Creamy Pumpkin Pie, 494
Pumpkin and Cheese Pie, 493
Pumpkin Crisp, 535
Pumpkin Pie, 493

PUMPKIN BREAD
Harvest Pumpkin Bread, 310
Moravian Pumpkin Bread, 308
Pumpkin and Date Bread, 309
Pumpkin Bread, 308
Walnut Pumpkin Bread, 309

PUNCHES
Banana Punch, 48
Fruit Punch, 49
Grapefruit Punch, 49
Holiday Punch, 50
Hot Cranberry Punch, 51
Hot Mulled Punch, 52
Request Punch, 50
Wassail Bowl Punch, 52

RELISHES
Cranberry Relish, 286
Pepper Relish by Mrs. Glenn, 291
Squash Relish, 292
Thanksgiving Cranberry Relish
    Mold, 58

ROLLS
Betty's Homemade Rolls, 318
Cinnamon Rolls, 317
Feather Rolls, 318
Prize Rolls, 317
Sour Cream Dinner Rolls, 319
Sour Cream Yeast Rolls, 319

SALAD DRESSINGS FOR
Bacon and Broccoli Salad, 76
Cheesy Broccoli Salad, 77
Cold Vegetable Salad, 75
Confetti Sauerkraut Salad, 90
Fruited Curried Chicken Salad, 68
Grape and Almond Chicken
    Salad, 69
Green Bean Salad, 74
Marinated Mixed Vegetables, 95
Peggy's Potato Salad, 89
Sauerkraut Salad, 91
Shrimp and Pasta Salad, 71
Spinach Salad, 96
Three-Bean Salad, 75

SALADS, BROCCOLI
Bacon and Broccoli Salad, 76
Cheesy Broccoli Salad, 76
Cindy's Broccoli Salad, 77
Easy Broccoli Salad, 78
Favorite Broccoli Salad, 79
Gwen's Broccoli Salad, 78
Overnight Broccoli Salad, 79

SALADS, CHICKEN
Chicken and Pineapple Salad, 69
Chicken Pasta Salad Oriental, 70
Fruited Curried Chicken Salad, 68
Grape and Almond Chicken
    Salad, 69

SALADS, CONGEALED
Applesauce Salad, 54
Apricot Delight, 54

Apricot Gelatin Salad, 55
Cherry Salad, 56
Congealed Vegetable Salad, 85
Cooling Summer Salad, 61
Cranberry and Orange Salad, 58
Cranberry Salad, 56
Cucumber Salad, 85
Easy Cranberry Salad, 57
Grape-Blueberry Congealed Salad, 60
Holiday Cranberry Salad, 57
Molded Cucumber Salad, 86
Orange Fluff Salad, 62
Orange Gelatin Salad, 62
Orange-Pineapple Salad, 63
Pretzel Salad, 64
Pretzel Strawberry Salad, 64
Russian Salad, 61
Strawberry and Cream Cheese Salad, 65
Strawberry and Pineapple Salad, 65
Sunset Salad, 66
Thanksgiving Cranberry Relish Mold, 58
Tomato Ring, 94
Vegetable Health Salad, 86

SALADS, FROZEN
Frozen Fruit Salad, 59
Frozen Waldorf Salad, 66

SALADS, FRUIT
Applesauce Salad, 54
Apricot Delight, 54
Apricot Gelatin Salad, 55
Cheesy Orange Salad, 63
Cherry Salad, 56
Cooling Summer Salad, 61
Cranberry and Orange Salad, 58
Cranberry Salad, 56
Easy Cranberry Salad, 57
Five-Cup Fruit Salad, 60
Frozen Fruit Salad, 59
Frozen Waldorf Salad, 66
Good Cherry Salad, 55
Grape-Blueberry Congealed Salad, 60
Holiday Cranberry Salad, 57
Mixed Fruit Salad, 59

Orange Fluff Salad, 62
Orange Gelatin Salad, 62
Orange-Pineapple Salad, 63
Pretzel Salad, 64
Pretzel Strawberry Salad, 64
Russian Salad, 61
Sara's Watergate Salad, 67
Strawberry and Cream Cheese Salad, 65
Strawberry and Pineapple Salad, 65
Sunset Salad, 66
Thanksgiving Cranberry Relish Mold, 58
Watergate Salad, 67

SALADS, MAIN DISH
Curried Crab Meat Rice Salad, 73
Shrimp and Pasta Salad, 70
Taco Salad, 72
Taco Salad Stack-Ups, 71

SALADS, PASTA
Chicken Pasta Salad Oriental, 70
Linguine Salad, 72
Macaroni Salad, 73
Shrimp and Pasta Salad, 70

SALADS, VEGETABLE. *See also* Salads, Broccoli
Cauliflower and Green Pea Salad, 84
Cold Vegetable Salad, 74
Confetti Sauerkraut Salad, 90
Congealed Vegetable Salad, 85
Cucumber Salad, 85
Green Bean Salad, 74
Layered Salad, 87
Mandarin Salad, 92
Marinated Mixed Vegetables, 95
Marinated Scandinavian Salad, 93
Martha's Lettuce Salad, 88
Marvelous Make-Ahead Salad, 87
Molded Cucumber Salad, 86
Owens' Vegetable Munch, 33
Peggy's Potato Salad, 89
Potato Salad, 89
Sauerkraut Salad, 91
Scandinavian Salad, 92
Seven-Layer Salad, 88

Sweet Pea Salad, 90
Tangy Kraut Salad, 91
Texas Caviar, 94
Three-Bean Salad, 75
Tomato Ring, 94
Vegetable Health Salad, 86

SALMON
Red Salmon Loaf, 215
Salmon Chowder, 220
Salmon Party Ball, 26

SANDWICHES
Broiled Crab Sandwiches, 36
Cheddar Chicken Salad
  Sandwiches, 35
Miniature Ham and Cheese
  Rolls, 35
Poor Man's Lunch
  Sandwiches, 36
Vegetable Sandwich Spread, 37

SAUCES. *See also* Barbecue
  Sauces; Sauces For
Italian Pork Pasta Sauce, 144
Lemon Sauce, 362
Red Wine Sauce, 32
Sauce for Saucy Prune Cake, 409
Sunshine Sauce, 534
Sweet and Sour Sauce for
  Meatballs, 130

SAUCES FOR
Hamburgers, 132
Meatballs, 127, 130
Porcupine Meatballs, 129
Pork, 292
Saucy Prune Cake, 409

SAUSAGE
Breakfast Casserole, 154
Breakfast Sausage and Cheese
  Bake, 155
Breakfast Sausage and Egg
  Soufflé, 152
Carolyn's Breakfast Soufflé, 154
Cheese and Sausage
  Quiche, 156
Chicken and Sausage
  Casserole, 187

Chris' Sausage Casserole, 157
Grilled Kielbasa Hawaiian, 151
Hacienda Dinner, 152
Quick Pepperoni Spaghetti, 116
Sausage and Cheddar
  Quiche, 157
Sausage and Egg Bake, 156
Sausage and Egg Breakfast
  Casserole, 153
Sausage and Egg Casserole, 153
Sausage Casserole, 155
Sausage Meatballs, 31

SEAFOOD. *See also* Crab Meat;
  Fish; Salmon; Shrimp
Clam Chowder, 219
Scallops à la Dorothy, 216
Seafood Chowder, 221

SHRIMP
Barbecued Shrimp, 216
Curried Shrimp, 217
Easy Shrimp Dip, 47
Molded Shrimp Spread, 26
Pasta in Shrimp and Wine
  Sauce, 218
Seafood Casserole, 215
Shrimp and Pasta Salad, 70
Shrimp Capri, 217
Shrimp Casserole, 218
Shrimp Chowder, 221
Shrimp Dip, 46

SIDE DISHES. *See also* Side
  Dishes, Fruit; Side Dishes,
  Rice
Barley Casserole, 280
Fettucini Alfredo, 280
Gravy, 294
Mom's Corn Bread Stuffing, 279
Old-Fashioned Corn Bread
  Dressing, 279

SIDE DISHES, FRUIT
Baked Pineapple Casserole, 276
Cheesy Pineapple Casserole, 277
Easy Pineapple and Cheese
  Casserole, 277
Fruit Casserole, 274
Pineapple Casserole, 275

Pineapple Strata, 278
Pineapple-Cheese Bake, 275
Ritzy Pineapple Casserole, 276
Special Fruit Casserole, 274
Spiced Peaches, 287
Wine Fruit, 278

SIDE DISHES, RICE
Brown Rice, 283
Christmas Rice, 283
Dirty Rice, 283
French Rice, 284
Wild Rice Pilaf, 284

SLAWS
Cheesy Cabbage and Apple Slaw, 82
Coleslaw with Apple, 82
Confetti Slaw, 84
Marinated Coleslaw, 83
Marinated Slaw, 81
Marty's Coleslaw, 83
Refrigerator Slaw, 81
Shredded Refrigerator Slaw, 80
Sweet Marinated Slaw, 80

SNACKS
Banana Granola Crunch, 37
Cheese Pennies, 38
Oyster Cracker Snacks, 38
Roasted Pecans, 40
Snack Crackers, 39
Special Toasted Pecans, 41
Sugar-Coated Peanuts, 39
Vonda's Spiced Pecans, 40

SOUPS. *See also* Chowders
Broccoli Cheese Soup, 273
Cabbage and Beef Soup, 142
Chicken and Rice Soup, 206
Dr. Anderson's Nine-Bean Soup, 272
Hearty French Onion Soup, 245
Make-A-Meal Soup, 105
Southern Bean and Ham Soup, 151
Thick Tomato-Vegetable-Beef Soup, 273
Vegetable Beef Soup, 143

SPAGHETTI
Easy Spaghetti, 117
Italian Meatball Spaghetti Sauce, 128
Quick Pepperoni Spaghetti, 116

SPINACH
Mandarin Salad, 92
Spinach and Tomato Salad, 96
Spinach Balls, 34
Spinach Casserole, 255
Super Spinach Casserole, 256

SQUASH
Cheesy Squash Casserole, 257
Easy Squash Casserole, 257
Glazed Squash with Onions, 260
Special Squash Casserole, 258
Squash and Broccoli Casserole, 259
Squash and Stuffing Casserole, 259
Squash Casserole, 256
Squash Croquettes, 261
Squash Fritters, 261
Squash Garden Casserole, 258
Squash Pies, 495
Squash Relish, 292
Summer Squash Casserole, 260

STEWS
Beef Stew, 106
Brunswick Stew, 108
Chicken Stew, 207
Elephant Stew, 160
Five-Hour Stew, 107
Hearty Beef Stew, 106
Mexican Pork Stew, 147
Stewed Beef in Wine Sauce, 107

STRAWBERRY. *See also* Cakes, Strawberry
Congealed Strawberry Shortcake, 537
Dietetic Strawberry Pie, 497
Fresh Strawberry Pie, 496
Frozen Strawberry Dessert, 538
Frozen Strawberry Preserves, 287
Pretzel Strawberry Salad, 64

Strawberry and Cream Cheese
 Salad, 65
Strawberry and Pineapple
 Salad, 65
Strawberry Chiffon Pie, 496
Strawberry Delight, 537
Strawberry Pies, 495

SWEET POTATO. *See also* Cakes,
 Sweet Potato; Pies, Sweet
 Potato
Bourbon Sweet Potatoes, 262
Busy-Day Sweet Potato
 Casserole, 262
Coconut-Topped Sweet Potato
 Casserole, 267
Company Sweet Potato
 Casserole, 267
Crunchy Top Sweet Potato
 Casserole, 265
Favorite Sweet Potato
 Soufflé, 265
Holiday Sweet Potato
 Casserole, 266
Orange-Candied Sweet
 Potatoes, 264
Orange-Glazed Sweet
 Potatoes, 264
Souffléed Sweet Potatoes, 266
Sweet Potato Casserole, 263
Sweet Potato Crunch, 538
Sweet Potato Muffins, 315
Sweet Potato Pudding with
 Whiskey, 535
Sweet Potato Soufflé, 263

TOMATO
Spinach and Tomato Salad, 96
Tomato Casserole, 269
Tomato Delight, 269
Tomato Ring, 94

TOPPINGS FOR
Baked Chicken Salad, 204
Chicken and Biscuits Potpie, 196
Chicken and Vegetables
 Potpie, 195
Chicken Breast Potpie, 195
Corn Bread Pie, 138
Corn Pone Casserole, 110
Easy Chicken Potpie, 197
Favorite Fruit Cocktail Cake, 361
Lasagna Pie, 137
Mrs. Gibson's Fruit Cocktail
 Cake, 360
Quick Chicken Potpie, 197
Tamale Pie, 140

TURKEY
Kabob Appetizers, 30
Marinated Turkey, 212
Roast Turkey Breast, 211
Turkey and Hominy
 Scramble, 212
Turkey Chili, 211

Vanilla Extract, Homemade, 539

VEGETABLES. *See also* Names of
 Vegetables
Artichoke Dip, 41
Bell Pepper Dip, 42
Calico Casserole, 270
Cheesy Vegetable Casserole, 271
Country Collards, 241
Curry Dip for Vegetables, 44
Eggplant Soufflé, 242
Garden Pea Casserole, 246
Hot Artichoke Dip, 42
Stuffed Peppers, 246
Swiss Vegetable Medley, 270
Tangy Mustard Cauliflower, 241
Thick Tomato-Vegetable-Beef-
 Soup, 273
Veg-All Casserole, 272
Vegetable Casserole, 271
Vegetable Juice Cocktail, 50
Vegetable Sandwich Spread, 37

YAMS
Candied Yams, 268
New Perry Hotel's Shredded
 Yams, 268

THIS COOKBOOK IS A PERFECT GIFT FOR HOLIDAYS, WEDDINGS, ANNIVERSARIES AND BIRTHDAYS

You may order as many cookbooks as you wish for the price of:

$8.00 each plus postage of
within N. C. $4.00
outside N. C. $5.00
per book ordered

We will even giftwrap for an additional $1.00

Mail your order to:
**North Carolina Chapter No. 35
Telephone Pioneers of America
606 Southern National Center
P.O. Box 30188
Charlotte, North Carolina 28230**

You may save postage by picking up your books at the above address or from the Council Budget & Fund Raisers.

Make checks payable to:
N.C. Chapter 35 Telephone Pioneers

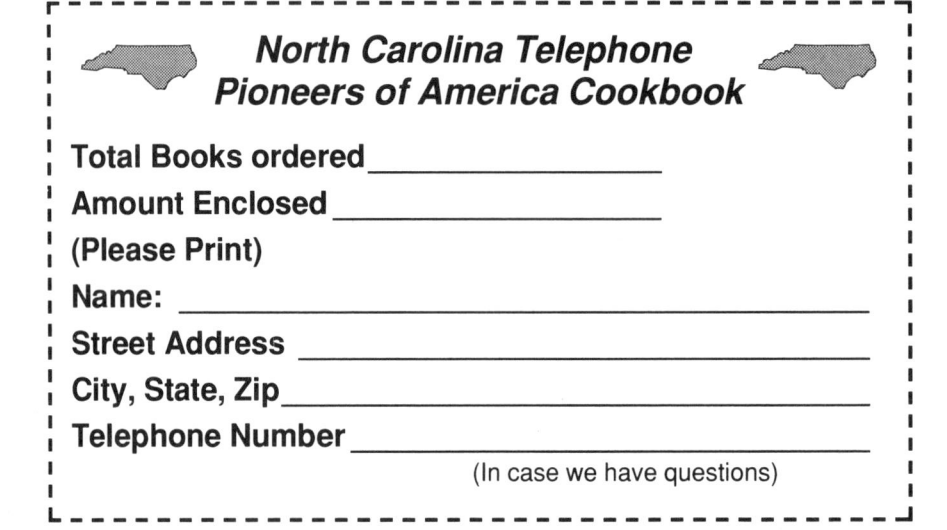

North Carolina Telephone Pioneers of America Cookbook

Total Books ordered _____

Amount Enclosed _____

(Please Print)

Name: _____

Street Address _____

City, State, Zip _____

Telephone Number _____
(In case we have questions)